# PICTURING THE APOCALYPSE

## THE BOOK OF REVELATION IN THE ARTS OVER TWO MILLENNIA

NATASHA O'HEAR

AND

ANTHONY O'HEAR

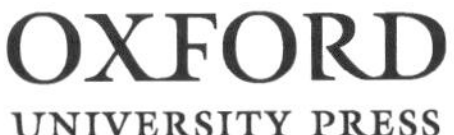

OXFORD

UNIVERSITY PRESS

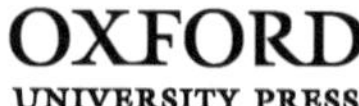

# OXFORD
**UNIVERSITY PRESS**

Great Clarendon Street, Oxford, OX2 6DP,
United Kingdom

Oxford University Press is a department of the University of Oxford.
It furthers the University's objective of excellence in research, scholarship,
and education by publishing worldwide. Oxford is a registered trade mark of
Oxford University Press in the UK and in certain other countries



Published in the United States of America by Oxford University Press
198 Madison Avenue, New York, NY 10016, United States of America

British Library Cataloguing in Publication Data
Data available

Library of Congress Cataloging in Publication Data
Data available

ISBN 978–0–19–968901–9 (Hbk.)
ISBN 978–0–19–877927–8 (Pbk.)

For Zac and Freddie, the next generation

'Natasha and Anthony O'Hear are to be congratulated for their book on Revelation, which takes as its starting point its central theme—its visionary claim. It offers a very necessary reminder that the visual character of this remarkable text can often be best communicated through art, music, and poetry, which they illustrate so well. Not only does it introduce us to the ways in which this apocalyptic text has stimulated some of the most dramatic and inspired paintings down the centuries, but it also helps us get some sense of why this book has grasped the imagination of readers past and present. It is based on the best modern scholarship and presents Revelation to the general reader, primarily through the riches of the art it has inspired. Readers will find much here to treasure which will encourage further reflection.'

**Professor Christopher Rowland**

'Natasha O'Hear and Anthony O'Hear tackle [the Book of Revelation] with vigour, taking us on an almost breathless *tour d'horizon*.'

**Andrew Hammond, *Times Literary Supplement***

'Extraordinary book.'

**Jane O'Grady, *Times Higher Education***

'[A] stimulating treatment of a complex subject, it is to be thoroughly recommended.'

**C. M. Kauffmann, *Burlington Magazine***

'[C]learly organized, and beautifully written, . . . impeccable, yet always access-ible scholarship and effortless interdisciplinarity combining New Testament biblical study, art-historical method, and what is now known as reception history.'

**Micah D Kiel, *Theology***

'This study of the Book of Revelation in the Arts over two millennia is a true blast to the modern mind and imagination.'

**Steve Craggs, *Northern Echo***

'To tackle so large and potentially difficult a topic is a significant challenge and the O'Hears have chosen an accessible and uncluttered format . . . Despite the complexity of the primary material (both literary and visual) the authors avoid convoluted ramblings and the text is highly readable.'

**Chloë Reddaway, *Art and Christianity***

'Natasha and Anthony O'Hear have produced a fascinating book on how the Apocalypse or the Book of Revelation has figured in the Arts for 2,000 years.'

***The Church of England Newspaper***

# PICTURING THE APOCALYPSE

The book of Revelation has been a source of continual fascination for nearly two thousand years. Concepts such as the Lamb of God, the Four Horsemen, the Seventh Seal, the Beasts and Antichrist, the Whore of Babylon, Armageddon, the Millennium, the Last Judgement, the New Jerusalem, and the ubiquitous Angel of the Apocalypse have captured the popular imagination. One can hardly open a newspaper or click on a news website without reading about impending financial or climate change Armageddon, while the concept of the Four Horsemen pervades popular music, gaming, and satire. Yet few people know much about either the basic meaning or original context of these concepts or the multiplicity of different ways in which they have been interpreted by visual artists in particular. The visual history of this most widely illustrated of all the biblical books deserves greater attention.

This book fills these gaps in a striking and original way by means of ten concise thematic chapters which explain the origins of these concepts from the book of Revelation in an accessible way. These explanations are augmented and developed via a carefully selected sample of the ways in which the concepts have been treated by artists through the centuries. The 120 visual examples are drawn from a wide range of time periods and media including the ninth-century Trier Apocalypse, thirteenth-century Anglo-Norman Apocalypse Manuscripts such as the Lambeth and Trinity Apocalypses, the fourteenth-century Angers Apocalypse Tapestry, fifteenth-century Apocalypse altarpieces by Van Eyck and Memling, Dürer and Cranach's sixteenth-century Apocalypse woodcuts, and more recently a range of works by William Blake, J. M. W. Turner, Max Beckmann, as well as film posters and stills, cartoons, and children's book illustrations. The final chapter demonstrates the continuing resonance of all the themes in contemporary religious, political, and popular thinking, while throughout the book a contrast will be drawn between those readers of Revelation who have seen it in terms of earthly revolutions in the here and now, and those who have adopted a more spiritual, other-worldly approach.

**Natasha O'Hear** is Honorary Lecturer in Theology, Imagination and the Arts at the University of St Andrews and also teaches at Ark Burlington Danes Academy in West London.

**Anthony O'Hear** is Professor of Philosophy at Buckingham University and Director of the Royal Institute of Philosophy.

# *Acknowledgements*

*Picturing the Apocalypse* has as its starting point the work done by one of us in *Contrasting Images of the Book of Revelation in Late Medieval and Early Modern Art* (Oxford University Press, 2011). To that extent the debts of thanks and gratitude offered there spill over into this book too.

However this is a completely new book, different in scope and approach, and written by two authors rather than one, both of whom have played a full part in the writing of the whole. So for *Picturing the Apocalypse*, we would like to thank David Reynolds for his help with presenting and developing the original idea. Then, apart from the many authorities on Revelation we have drawn on (and some of whom one of us has been taught by), we would like to single out Ian Boxall for his responses to particular questions of interpretation we have had at various points. Particular thanks are also due to Chris Rowland and Sue Gillingham who both read and commented on earlier drafts of the book and remained supportive throughout. Three anonymous readers for the Oxford University Press also gave us invaluable help on matters of content, style and approach. Lizzie Robottom at Oxford University Press commissioned the book and was our original editor, after which she was ably succeeded by Karen Raith, Aimee Wright, and Caroline Hawley.

Daria Pezzoli-Olgiati gave us some very helpful advice on contemporary apocalyptic culture, particularly films. Bryan Appleyard and Alex Pumfrey also helped us with references to contemporary culture, while Ian McEwan and Roger Scruton greatly helped us in refining our attitude to Revelation by getting us to face up to, and in part to respond to, its dark side. Ruth Padel's interest and quiet encouragement during this time of struggle, so to speak, was invaluable, as was David Matthews, who also introduced us to Vaughan Williams' *Sancta Civitas*. Phillida Gili alerted us to the breadth of the Spanish *Beatus* Apocalypse tradition. At a very late stage we were fortunate enough to speak to James MacMillan about his musical journeys in Revelation. Working with the artist Michael Takeo-Magruder on his exhibition De/ Coding the Apocalypse brought a new dimension to our thinking.

There are 120 illustrations in the text, and we have received help from many individuals and institutions in sourcing these and obtaining permissions. To all who have helped here, we would like to record our gratitude. We cannot list everyone here, but for particular help we would like to mention first the artists Gordon Cheung, Kip Gresham, and Siku, who were all most generous in allowing us to reproduce their work. Marie-Jose Friedlander was most helpful in discussing Revelation images from Ethiopia, and in allowing us to reproduce one of her lovely photographs. Nomi Rowe helped us in tracking down the image of Cecil Collins' *Angel of the Apocalypse*, and Clive Hicks, the photographer, sought out his photograph for us. Jonathan Robe helped us with the James Chadderton image, and we would like to thank them both. Cheryl Sukut from Tyndale House Publishers went to a great amount of trouble to supply us with the *Left Behind* image, while Barbara Bernard from the marvellous National Gallery of Art in Washington went way beyond any call of duty in finding for us a photograph of Max Beckmann's lithograph '*And God shall wipe away all tears...*'. It was extremely difficult to track down the image we wanted from Frans Masereel's Apocalypse series, but, following help from Pauline Bonnard of DACS, Peter Riede, President of the Frans Masereel Stiftung in Saarbrucken came to the rescue just in time. Michael Stone from the Chicano Studies Research Center, UCLA, put us in touch with Yolanda Lopez, while Patrick Rogers from the Rosenbach of the Free Library in Philadelphia was most helpful with Blake's *The Number of the Beast is 666*, as was Martin Townsend, editor of the Sunday Express, over the Bunbury cartoon. We are also grateful to Michèle Brezel of the Musée Virtuel de Protestantisme and to the Chapter of York and York Glaziers Trust for freely supplying images. The Master and Fellows of Trinity College Cambridge were very generous and we would also like to thank John Moelwyn-Hughes for helping us navigate the Bridgeman Art Library.

Finally, we would like to thank our constant readers, critics, and supporters Philippe Bonavero, Patricia O'Hear, Jacob O'Hear, and Thea O'Hear (who also helped with the Index).

# Contents


List of Illustrations     xiii
List of Plates     xix
List of Tables     xxiii

Introduction: Revelation: Meanings and Interpretations     I

1. The Angel of the Apocalypse: John's Journey and his
   Angelic Guides     38

2. The Lamb     52

3. The Four Horsemen     70

4. The Seven Seals: Angelic Destruction     93

5. The Woman Clothed with the Sun     III

6. The Satanic Trinity     131

7. The Whore of Babylon     155

8. Armageddon, the Millennium, and the Last Judgement     176

9. The New Jerusalem     212

10. The Apocalypse in the Twentieth and Twenty-First Centuries:
    A Survey of Different Approaches to Revelation in the
    Arts and Popular Culture     235

Revelation: Artistic Reception and Relevance     284

Notes     295
Glossary     309
Suggestions for Further Reading     313
Bibliography     315
Index     323

# List of Illustrations


0.1. Topology of Revelation   9

0.2. The *Angers Apocalypse Tapestry*, *c.*1373–80, The Seven Churches of Asia (Rev. 2–3), Maine et Loire: Chateau d'Angers. © Bridgeman Art Library   10

1.1. The *Flemish Apocalypse*, *c.*1400, The Angel of the Throne Room Calling John (Rev. 4), Paris: Bibliothèque Nationale. © BnF   42

1.2. Albrecht Dürer, *Apocalypse* Series, *c.*1498, John and the Mighty Angel (Rev. 10), London: British Museum. © The Trustees of the British Museum   45

1.3. Albrecht Dürer, *Apocalypse* Series, *c.*1498, St Michael and the Dragon (Rev. 12), London: British Museum. © The Trustees of the British Museum   48

1.4. The *Angers Apocalypse Tapestry*, *c.*1373–80, John Kneeling before the Angel (Rev. 22), Maine et Loire: Chateau d'Angers. © Centre Des Monuments Nationaux   50

2.1. Albrecht Dürer, *Apocalypse* Series, *c.*1498, The Heavenly Throne Room (Rev. 4–5), London: British Museum. © The Trustees of the British Museum   54

2.2. The *Trinity Apocalypse*, *c.*1260, The Twenty-four Elders in the Heavenly Throne Room (Rev. 4), Cambridge: Trinity College. © The Master and Fellows of Trinity College, Cambridge   55

2.3. The Van Eycks, central panel from the *Ghent Altarpiece*, 1432, Ghent: St Bavo's Cathedral. © Bridgeman Art Library   59

2.4. The *Trinity Apocalypse*, *c.*1260, The Lamb with the Flagpole (Rev. 5), Cambridge: Trinity College. © The Master and Fellows of Trinity College, Cambridge   63

2.5. The *Angers Apocalypse Tapestry*, *c.*1373–80, The Lamb Bleeding from the Neck and Feet (Rev. 5), Maine et Loire: Chateau d'Angers. © Bridgeman Art Library   64

3.1. Four Horsemen cartoon. © www.cartoonstock.com   71

3.2. The *Trier Apocalypse*, ninth century, The Four Horsemen (Rev. 6.2–8), Trier: Stadtbibliothek. With permission, Stadtbibliothek, Trier   72

3.3.   The *Lambeth Apocalypse*, *c.*1260, The Second Horseman (Rev. 6.3–4),
       London: Lambeth Palace Library. © Bridgeman Art Library                    77

3.4.   The *Angers Apocalypse Tapestry*, *c.*1373–80, The Fourth Horseman
       (Rev. 6.7–8), Maine et Loire: Chateau d'Angers. © Bridgeman
       Art Library                                                                77

3.5.   Albrecht Dürer, *Apocalypse* Series *c.*1498, The Four Horsemen
       (Rev. 6.2–8), London: British Museum. © The Trustees of the British
       Museum                                                                     80

3.6.   Lucas Cranach the Elder, Apocalypse Illustrations for Luther's New
       Testament, 1522, The Four Horsemen (Rev. 6.2–8), London:
       The British Library. © The British Library Board, C.36.g.7                  82

3.7.   J. Haynes after John Hamilton Mortimer, *Death on a Pale Horse*,
       1784, London: British Museum. © The Trustees of the British
       Museum                                                                     84

3.8.   James Gillray, *Presages of the Millenium—With the Destruction of the
       Faithful, as Revealed to R. Brothers, the Prophet, and Attested by MB
       Hallhead Esq*, 1795, London: British Museum. © The Trustees of the
       British Museum                                                             85

3.9.   William Blake, *Death on a Pale Horse*, *c.*1800, Cambridge: Fitzwilliam
       Museum. © Bridgeman Art Library                                            86

3.10.  *Sunday Express* Bunbury cartoon, August 1943. © Sunday Express            88

3.11.  Peter Brookes cartoon, The *Sunday Times*, 1977. © News Syndication        89

4.1.   The *Trinity Apocalypse*, *c.*1260, The Fifth Seal: The Martyrs Sheltering
       under the Altar (Rev. 6.9–11), Cambridge: Trinity College. © The
       Master and Fellows of Trinity College, Cambridge                           97

4.2.   The *Trinity Apocalypse*, *c.*1260, The Sixth Seal: The Great Earthquake
       (Rev. 6.12–17), Cambridge: Trinity College. © The Master and
       Fellows of Trinity College, Cambridge                                      98

4.3.   The *Gulbenkian Apocalypse*, *c.*1270, Elijah Separating the Good and
       Bad Jews, Lisbon: Museo Calouste Gulbenkian. © Museo Calouste
       Gulbenkian                                                                 99

4.4.   Francis Danby, *The Opening of the Sixth Seal*, 1828, London: British
       Museum. © Bridgeman Art Library                                            101

4.5.   Albrecht Dürer, *Apocalypse* Series, *c.*1498, The Six Trumpets (Rev. 8–9),
       London: British Museum. © The Trustees of the British Museum               105

4.6.   Albrecht Dürer, *Apocalypse* Series, *c.*1498, The Four Avenging Angels
       (Rev. 9.13–15), London: British Museum. © The Trustees of the British
       Museum                                                                     107

5.1.   The *Bamberg Apocalypse*, *c.*1000, The Woman Clothed with the Sun:
       Woman, Dragon, and Child, Bamberg: Bamberg State Library.
       © Bridgeman Art Library                                                    117

5.2.  The *Bamberg Apocalypse*, *c.*1000, The Woman Clothed with the Sun:
The Flight of the Woman, Bamberg: Bamberg State Library.
© Bridgeman Art Library    118

5.3.  The *Trinity Apocalypse*, *c.*1260, The Woman and the Dragon
(Rev. 12.3–5), Cambridge: Trinity College. © The Master and
Fellows of Trinity College, Cambridge    120

5.4.  The *Trinity Apocalypse*, *c.*1260, The Woman Enters the Wilderness
(Rev. 12.6–17), Cambridge: Trinity College. © The Master and
Fellows of Trinity College, Cambridge    121

5.5.  Albrecht Dürer, *Apocalypse* Series, *c.*1498, The Woman Clothed with
the Sun (Rev. 12), London: British Museum. © The Trustees of the
British Museum    123

5.6.  Albrecht Dürer, *Apocalypse* Series, 1511, Frontispiece, London: British
Museum. © The Trustees of the British Museum    124

5.7.  William Blake, *The Great Red Dragon and the Woman Clothed with
the Sun*, *c.*1805, New York: The Brooklyn Museum of Art.
© Bridgeman Art Library    126

5.8.  Odillon Redon, *A Woman Clothed with the Sun* (Rev. 12.1), 1899,
London: British Museum. © The Trustees of the British Museum    128

6.1.  Albrecht Dürer, *Apocalypse* Series, *c.*1498, The Two Beasts (Rev. 13),
London: British Museum. © The Trustees of the British Museum    135

6.2.  The *Gulbenkian Apocalypse*, *c.*1270, The Earth Beast Rising from the
Abyss, Lisbon: Museo Calouste Gulbenkian. © Museo Calouste
Gulbenkian    142

6.3.  The *Angers Apocalypse Tapestry*, *c.*1373–80, Worship of the Sea Beast
(Rev. 13), Maine et Loire: Chateau d'Angers. © Bridgeman
Art Library    143

6.4.  The *Angers Apocalypse Tapestry*, *c.*1373–80, The Three Beasts Vomiting
Frogs (Rev. 16.13–14), Maine et Loire: Chateau d'Angers.
© Bridgeman Art Library    143

6.5.  Detail from the *Master Bertram Apocalypse Altarpiece*, *c.*1400, London:
Victoria and Albert Museum. © Victoria and Albert Museum,
London    144

6.6.  Lucas Cranach the Elder, Apocalypse Illustrations for Luther's New
Testament, 1522, The Beast from the Abyss (Rev. 11), London: The
British Library. © The British Library Board, C.36.g.7    149

6.7.  William Blake, *The Great Red Dragon and the Beast from the Sea*, *c.*1805,
Washington: National Gallery of Art. Courtesy National Gallery of
Art, Washington, Rosenwald Collection    151

7.1.  The *Lambeth Apocalypse*, *c.*1260, The Whore of Babylon (Rev. 17),
London: Lambeth Palace Library. © Bridgeman Art Library    161

7.2.  The *Angers Apocalypse Tapestry*, *c.*1373–80, The Whore of Babylon
      (Rev. 17), Maine et Loire: Chateau d'Angers. © Bridgeman
      Art Library                                                          162

7.3.  The *Flemish Apocalypse*, *c.*1400, The Whore of Babylon Offers the
      Cup of Abominations to John (Rev. 17), Paris: Bibliothèque Nationale.
      © BnF                                                                163

7.4.  Albrecht Dürer, *Apocalypse* Series, *c.*1498, The Whore of Babylon
      (Rev. 17–19), London: British Museum. © The Trustees of the British
      Museum                                                              167

7.5.  Lucas Cranach the Elder, Apocalypse Illustrations for Luther's New
      Testament, 1522, The Whore of Babylon (Rev. 17), London:
      The British Library. © The British Library Board, C.36.g.7          169

7.6.  Otto Dix, *Visit to Madame Germaine at Méricourt,* 1924, London:
      British Museum. © The Trustees of the British Museum                172

7.7.  Kip Gresham, *The Whore of Babylon*, 1993. © Kip Gresham, by kind
      permission of the artist                                            174

8.1.  *Last Judgement*, detail from the West Portal, Amiens Cathedral,
      13th century. © Bridgeman Art Library                               177

8.2.  The *Lambeth Apocalypse*, *c.*1260, Christ and his Army versus the
      Army of the Beast (Rev. 19.11–21), London: Lambeth Palace Library.
      © Trustees of Lambeth Palace Library                                184

8.3.  The *Gulbenkian Apocalypse*, *c.*1270, The Saints Attacked by the Armies
      of Gog and Magog (Rev. 20.8), Lisbon: Museo Calouste Gulbenkian.
      © Museo Calouste Gulbenkian                                         186

8.4.  The *Flemish Apocalypse*, *c.*1400, The Marriage of the Lamb,
      Armageddon, and the Last Judgement (Rev. 19–20), Paris: Bibliothèque
      Nationale. © BnF                                                    187

8.5.  Frans Masereel, *Aeroplanes over Mankind* (*Flügzeuge über Menschheit*),
      1944. © DACS 2014, Die Apokalyptische Reiter (1954), plate no. 5,
      Flügzeuge über die Menschheit                                       189

8.6.  The *Trinity Apocalypse*, *c.*1260, Satan Bound and Led to the Pit
      (Rev. 20.1–3), Cambridge: Trinity College. © The Master and
      Fellows of Trinity College, Cambridge                               194

8.7.  The *Trinity Apocalypse*, *c.*1260, The Millennium (Rev. 20.4–6),
      Cambridge: Trinity College. © The Master and Fellows of Trinity
      College, Cambridge                                                  195

8.8.  Albrecht Dürer, *Apocalypse* Series, *c.*1498, The Binding of Satan
      (Rev. 20), London: British Museum. © The Trustees of the
      British Museum                                                      196

8.9.  Last Judgement ivory relief, ninth century, London: Victoria and
      Albert Museum. © Victoria and Albert Museum, London                 201

8.10.  John Martin, *The Last Judgement* (engraving by Charles Mottram),
       1853, London, Tate. © Bridgeman Art Library                    205

8.11.  William Blake, *The Vision of the Last Judgment*, 1808, Sussex:
       Petworth House. © Bridgeman Art Library                        207

8.12.  Max Beckmann, *Resurrection*, 1918, London: British Museum.
       © The Trustees of the British Museum                           209

9.1.   The *Flemish Apocalypse*, *c.*1400, John is shown the New Jerusalem
       (Rev. 21), Paris: Bibliothèque Nationale. © BnF                226

9.2.   Max Beckmann, 'And God shall wipe away all tears' (Rev. 21. 4),
       1943, from *The Apocalypse*, Washington, DC, National Gallery of Art.
       © Washington, National Gallery of Art, Bequest of Mrs Mathilde
       Q. Beckmann                                                    232

10.1.  Max Beckmann, *The Grenade*, 1915, London: The British Museum.
       © The Trustees of the British Museum                           246

10.2.  Otto Dix, *Dance of Death*, 1917, London: British Museum.
       © The Trustees of the British Museum                           248

10.3.  Albrecht Dürer, *Apocalypse* Series, *c.*1498, The Martyrdom of
       St John, London: British Museum. © The Trustees of the
       British Museum                                                 255

10.4.  Detail from the Manga Bible, 2007. Reproduced by kind
       permission of Siku                                             278

# List of Plates


1. The Van Eycks, *The Ghent Altarpiece*, 1432, Ghent: St Bavo's Cathedral. © Bridgeman Art Library

2. The *Gulbenkian Apocalypse*, *c.*1270, The Last Judgement (Rev. 20.11–15), Lisbon: Museo Calouste Gulbenkian. © Museo Calouste Gulbenkian

3. Hans Memling, *The Apocalypse Panel*, detail from the *St John Altarpiece*, 1474–9, Bruges: The Memling Museum. © Bridgeman Art Library

4. The *Lambeth Apocalypse*, *c.*1260, John Receiving his Vision on Patmos (Rev. 1), London: Lambeth Palace Library. © Bridgeman Art Library

5. The *Lambeth Apocalypse, c.*1260, John Kneeling before Christ (Rev. 22), London: Lambeth Palace Library. © Bridgeman Art Library

6. Hieronymous Bosch, *St John the Evangelist on Patmos, c.*1489 or later, Berlin: Gemäldegallerie. © Bridgeman Art Library

7. The *Angers Apocalypse Tapestry, c.*1373–80, The Tears of St John (Rev. 5), Maine et Loire: Chateau d'Angers. © Bridgeman Art Library

8. The *Angers Apocalypse Tapestry, c.*1373–80, John Taking and Eating the Scroll (Rev. 10), Maine et Loire: Chateau d'Angers. © Bridgeman Art Library

9. Cecil Collins, *The Angel of the Apocalypse* (Rev. 10), 1969. Photograph courtesy of Clive Hicks © Tate, London 2014

10. J. M. W. Turner, *The Angel Standing in the Sun*, 1846 (Rev. 19.17/Rev. 12), London: Tate. © Tate, London 2014

11. *The Lamb of God* (Rev. 5), *c.*sixth century, Ravenna, San Vitale, chancel vault mosaic. © Bridgeman Art Library

12. William Blake, *The Four and Twenty Elders*, *c.*1805, London: Tate. © Tate, London 2014

13. Jean-Pierre Bretegnier, *c.*1950, *The Lamb*, stained glass, Héricourt. © Bretegnier, by kind permission of the Musée Virtuel du Protestantisme

14. Gordon Cheung, *The Four Horsemen of the Apocalypse*, 2009, London. © Gordon Cheung

15. El Greco, *The Opening of the Fifth Seal, c.*1608–14, New York: Metropolitan Museum. © 2014. Image Copyright the Metropolitan Museum of Art/ Art Resource/Scala. Florence

16. The *Angers Apocalypse Tapestry*, *c.*1373–80, The Silence in Heaven (Rev. 8.1), Maine et Loire: Chateau d'Angers. © Bridgeman Art Library

17. The *Trinity Apocalypse*, *c.*1260, The First and Second Trumpets (Rev. 8.7–9), Cambridge: Trinity College. © The Master and Fellows of Trinity College, Cambridge

18. The *Trinity Apocalypse*, *c.*1260, The Third and Fourth Trumpets (Rev. 8.10–12), Cambridge: Trinity College. © The Master and Fellows of Trinity College, Cambridge

19. The *Trinity Apocalypse*, *c.*1260, The Fifth Trumpet (Rev. 9.1–11), Cambridge: Trinity College. © The Master and Fellows of Trinity College, Cambridge

20. The *Trinity Apocalypse*, *c.*1260, The Sixth Trumpet (Rev. 9.13–20), Cambridge: Trinity College. © The Master and Fellows of Trinity College, Cambridge

21. *Apocalypse Now* promotional poster, 1979. © Bridgeman Art Library

22. The *Flemish Apocalypse*, *c.*1400, The Seven Angels with the Seven Bowls (Rev. 16), Paris: Bibliothèque Nationale. © BnF

23. *The Silos Apocalypse*, twelfth century, The Woman and the Dragon (Rev. 12), London: British Library. © Bridgeman Art Library

24. Diego Velázquez, *St John the Evangelist on the Island of Patmos*, *c.*1618, London: National Gallery. © Bridgeman Art Library

25. Diego Velázquez, *The Immaculate Conception*, *c.*1618, London: National Gallery. © Bridgeman Art Library

26. The *Trinity Apocalypse*, *c.*1260, The Dragon and the Sea Beast (Rev. 13. 1–3), Cambridge: Trinity College. © The Master and Fellows of Trinity College, Cambridge

27. The *Trinity Apocalypse*, *c.*1260, The Earth Beast and the Statue of the Sea Beast (Rev. 13.14–15), Cambridge: Trinity College. © The Master and Fellows of Trinity College, Cambridge

28. The *Master Bertram Apocalypse Altarpiece*, *c.*1400, London: Victoria and Albert Museum. © Victoria and Albert Museum, London

29. The *Flemish Apocalypse*, *c.*1400, The Dragon and the Two Beasts (Rev. 13), Paris: Bibliothèque Nationale. © BnF

30. Luca Signorelli, *The Sermon and Deeds of Antichrist*, from the Last Judgement fresco cycle, 1499-1504, Orvieto Cathedral. © Bridgeman Art Library

31. William Blake, *The Number of the Beast is 666*, *c.*1810, Philadelphia: Free Library of Philadelphia. © The Rosenbach of the Free Library of Philadelphia

32. Nicolae Carpathia, image from the *Left Behind* graphic novel series
    © Tyndale House Publishers

33. The *Hortus Deliciarum*, 12th century, The Whore of Babylon Cast to
    her Death, Paris: Bibliothèque Nationale. © BnF

34. York Minster Great East Window, *c.*1400, detail of the Whore of
    Babylon Astride the Beast (Rev. 17). Photo the York Glaziers Trust,
    reproduced courtesy of the Chapter of York.

35. La Sainte Chapelle, Western Rose Window, *c.*1500, detail of the
    Whore of Babylon with Red Feet (Rev. 17). © Bridgeman Art Library

36. William Blake, *The Whore of Babylon*, *c.*1809, London: British
    Museum. © The Trustees of the British Museum

37. Robert Roberg, *Babylon the Great is Fallen*, 1990, Washington:
    Smithsonian Museum. Smithsonian American Art Museum,
    Gift of Chuck and Jan Rosenak and museum purchase through
    the Luisita L. and Franz H. Denghausen Endowment. © 1990
    Robert Roberg

38. Contemporary photograph of Tell Megiddo. © Hanay

39. *St Sever Beatus Manuscript*, *c.*1076, Armageddon (Rev. 19–20), Paris:
    Bibliothèque Nationale. © BnF

40. The *Lambeth Apocalypse*, *c.*1260, Satan Cast into the Hellmouth
    (Rev. 20.10), London: Lambeth Palace Library. © Bridgeman
    Art Library

41. Illustration by Pauline Baynes from *The Last Battle* by C. S. Lewis.
    © C. S. Lewis Pte. Ltd. 1956. Extract reprinted by permission

42. Sandro Botticelli, *The Mystic Nativity*, *c.*1500, London: National
    Gallery. © Bridgeman Art Library

43. The *Trinity Apocalypse*, *c.*1260, The Last Judgement (Rev. 20.11–15),
    Cambridge: Trinity College. © The Master and Fellows of Trinity
    College, Cambridge

44. William Blake, *The River of Life*, *c.*1805, London: Tate. © Tate,
    London 2014

45. The *Trinity Apocalypse*, *c.*1260, The New Jerusalem (Rev. 21–2),
    Cambridge: Trinity College. © The Master and Fellows of
    Trinity College, Cambridge

46. The *Angers Apocalypse Tapestry*, *c.*1373–80, John sees the New Jerusalem
    Descending (Rev. 21.2), Maine et Loire: Chateau d'Angers.
    © Bridgeman Art Library

47. The *Angers Apocalypse Tapestry*, *c.*1373–80, John and the River of the
    Water of Life (Rev. 22.1–5), Maine et Loire: Chateau d'Angers.
    © Bridgeman Art Library

48. John Martin, *The Plains of Heaven*, 1851–3, London: Tate.
© Tate, London 2014

49. Gordon Cheung, 2007, *Rivers of Bliss.* London. © Gordon Cheung

50. James Chadderton, *Apocalypse V2,* 2014. © James Chadderton

51. *The Seventh Seal*, promotional film poster, 1957. © Bridgeman
Art Library

52. Twenty-four Elders in the dome, Koraro Church, Ethiopia.
© Courtesy of Maria-Jose Friedlander, Bob Friedlander and
Richard Pankhurst from *Hidden Treasures of Ethiopia: A Guide
to the Remote Churches of an Ancient Land*, Tauris Edition 2014

53. Yolanda Lopez, *Margaret F. Stewart: Our Lady of Guadalupe*, 1978.
© All rights reserved. Used by permission of the artist. Image
courtesy of The Chicano Studies Research Centre, UCLA

# List of Tables


0.1. Outline of the three sequences of seven woes/disasters     12

0.2. Chapter themes     31

3.1. Individual characteristics ascribed to each Horseman     73

# Introduction
## Revelation: Meanings and Interpretations

Around 400 CE, when he was translating the Bible into Latin, St Jerome, the Christian saint and scholar, exclaimed, 'The Apocalypse of St John has as many mysteries as words. All praise is insufficient. In each of St John's words there are many meanings.'[1] Even more emphatic in his praise of this mysterious last book of the Bible was the late John Tavener, the composer, as recently as 1999: 'When St John saw, he saw everything. Out of his burning, thunderous love, he saw the vision of the end, the wholesale destruction of humanity, the New Jerusalem beyond all comprehension, imagination and thought.' This certainly gives a sense of the book's tone.[2]

But it is not a tone which has appealed to all its readers. 'Beware of the Apocalypse, which, when studied, almost always finds a man mad or makes him so' thundered the editor of *Rainbow: A Magazine of Christian Literature* in 1866.[3] More succinct and more cheeky was Buffy, the Vampire Slayer, in who in a 1997 episode of the series deadpanned, 'If the Apocalypse comes, beep me,' showing that the apocalyptic ideas and themes encapsulated in Revelation remain pervasive in the pop culture of our day. This is also the case with journalism. As recently as August 2014, Matt Ridley wrote in *The Times2* that 'From Gaza to Liberia, from Donetsk to Sinjar, the four horsemen of the Apocalypse—conquest, war, famine and death—are thundering across the planet, leaving havoc in their wake.'[4] In both the Buffy quote and in Ridley's article 'the apocalypse' has only negative connotations.

D. H. Lawrence, in what turned out to be his last substantial work, was more measured, but also more damning of the work itself, when he wrote that 'we can understand that the Fathers of the Church in the East wanted the Apocalypse left out of the New Testament. But like Judas among the disciples, it was inevitable that it should be included. The Apocalypse is the feet of clay to the grand Christian image. And down crashes the image, on the weakness of those very feet.'[5] That was written in the winter of 1929–30. Rather more literalistic, and actually following a long tradition of altogether more positive interpretations of the text, was Allan Boesak, the anti-apartheid campaigner. In 1987 he enlisted the apocalypse as a political weapon against the then rulers of South Africa: 'What was true in the time of John is proven to be true over and over again in the history of the church … Your fate shall be the fate of Babylon, which is called Egypt, which is called Rome, which is called Pretoria' (Pretoria being the capital of South Africa).[6]

The references somewhat randomly assembled in these opening paragraphs range from the serious and moving through the critical to the flippant. But they are linked by a common theme. They are all a response to the last book of the Bible, Revelation. The fact that there are numerous international websites in existence replete with thousands of such quotations and images is evidence in itself that this text continues to exert a powerful and colourful influence on all our lives, whether we are Christian or not, whether we know about the book or not.

This book aims to introduce the reader to Revelation via a carefully compiled survey of some of the many literary, artistic, musical, and, more recently, popular responses, provoked over the last two millennia by this complex work, which is in itself inspired and maddening in almost equal measure. At the very least, our book will demonstrate the truth of St Jerome's claim that there are many readings of this enigmatic text, and not only readings of a literary kind. Indeed, part of the point of this book is to show how and how differently Revelation has been interpreted through the ages. In doing this we will look not so much at commentators and theologians, but much more at artists of various sorts, who, in our view, have made many significant and innovative contributions to Revelation's interpretation—to what has come to be known in academic circles as its reception history.[7]

Many, like Tavener, have been fascinated by the gripping content of Revelation, which does indeed describe the destruction and human tragedy that John, the visionary who wrote it, foresaw would take place on earth in its last days. This 'John of Patmos', as he describes himself, has often been identified with the John who wrote the fourth Gospel, and even with John, the beloved disciple of John's Gospel, and these identifications, particularly the first, have often been made by the artists whose work we will look at. But scholars are now universally agreed that the author of Revelation was neither the beloved disciple nor John the Evangelist (which needn't detract from the power or relevance of the artistic images which make the identification).[8] There is also considerable consensus that the visionary who wrote Revelation did so around 90 CE (though a minority of scholars would date it to around 70 CE, the time of the destruction of the Temple of Jerusalem by the Romans).[9]

It is also important to realize that Revelation did not receive immediate, unqualified acceptance by the early Christian church. In particular its vivid descriptions of what we now have to call apocalyptic catastrophes did not sit well with those Christians who, when Christ did not reappear as many had believed in the early days, began to want some sort of accommodation with Rome. As we will see, this in turn encouraged a predominance of what might be called 'spiritual' interpretations of Revelation, where its message came to be seen primarily in terms of things going on within the souls of believers and in another realm altogether, rather than in terms of worldly events, such as a new reign of Christ about to happen on earth. In this 'spiritual' view, most influentially developed by St Augustine in the fifth century CE, we are indeed living in a new era (since Christ's resurrection) and awaiting an end to what we know, to culminate in a last judgement. But this new era is playing itself out in the world as it is, in the activity of the Christian church, and it would be futile to try to calculate when exactly the final events foretold in Revelation will actually happen, though of course the thought of these things will be ever present in the mind of the believer.

Whoever he was, though, whenever exactly he wrote, and what exactly he meant, John of Patmos thought and wrote in vivid, sometimes terrifying symbols, which is no doubt one of the reasons why visual artists have been so attracted to the work. He describes how the Four Horsemen will come riding down from Heaven bringing with them war, famine, and death (Rev. 6.8). Other figures such as the Whore of Babylon and Satan, he says, will be sent to test and divide humanity prior to the final battle between good and evil at Armageddon, and their own ultimate and final destruction (Rev. 12 and 17). These names—the Four Horsemen, the Whore of Babylon, Satan, and Armageddon—will no doubt be familiar to you, even if you have never read Revelation. It is the fact that symbols from Revelation endure to this day in most people's cultural vocabulary that has inspired this book. We write for those who seek to understand these exciting and often obscure terms in more depth, and even to see their continuing relevance for us today. It is our contention that looking at these symbols through the art they have inspired can bring deeper illumination and engagement than grappling with their theological meaning in a more academic way.[10]

Intuitively this may seem obvious. Listening to a church cantata by Bach, evoking at once a sense of humanity's sinfulness and the healing sense of God's redeeming power, may give us more of a sense of what it would be to be a pious Lutheran in eighteenth-century Germany than reading the great reformer Luther himself, or even the words which Bach set on their own; likewise Michelangelo's figures of the dead Christ in the arms of his mother, by showing us the bodily expression of the mother's emotion and the divine son's lifeless helplessness, are more poignant than a written account could be.[11] This intuitive sense of the power of art to transcend the rationally literal was given a formal articulation by the Neoplatonist thinkers and artists of fifteenth-century Italy.[12] From their point of view, discursive reasoning was a more reliable route to knowledge than mere sense experience; but higher than both was the intuitive grasp of the truth afforded by artistic and poetic experience. This superiority arises both from the immediacy of a work of art and from the way that the whole person responding to a work of art is involved—sense, reason, and heart altogether, so to speak. Taking this Neoplatonic line, it is our contention that the true significance of a visionary text such as Revelation may be brought out more fully in works of art, visual and otherwise, than in theological treatises on the significance of its symbols.

More generally, and outside a purely Neoplatonic context, the eighteenth-century philosopher Gotthold Ephraim Lessing drew an important distinction between the discursive, sequential nature of written narratives, where one event follows another in time, even where they are in fact simultaneous, and the spatially inclusive nature of paintings and other visual representations of the world, in which it is possible to embody and perceive many events, laid out before us, in one moment or pictorial space.[13] The simultaneous or synchronic possibilities of visual representations will, as we will see, become particularly helpful when dealing with a visionary text such as Revelation, where time sequences may be muddled, and where, even if this were not so, it is crucial that we see the various themes in relation to each other and perhaps even as recapitulations of each other. In visual representations this possibility is literally realizable—we can, on occasion, actually see different events or moments in one moment, which can help us to appreciate their interrelationships with an immediacy that a verbal narrative is bound to lack.

The meaning of Revelation has been progressively developed and explored in the centuries since 90 CE, as already suggested, and these explorations have been conducted in significant part by the different ways artists through the ages have interpreted the text and focused on different parts and themes of the text. The notion that a biblical text (or any text for that matter) does not have one set meaning but, on the contrary, that its meaning continues to develop as it is interpreted and reinterpreted over the centuries finds support in the work of reception theologian Ulrich Luz, who argues that biblical texts are not like reservoirs containing fixed amounts of water that can be measured exactly. Rather, they are like a natural water source from which new water constantly emerges.[14] In what follows we will show both the power of the artistic explorations of Revelation's meaning and the way they have contributed, over the years, to the new water flowing from the original source that is Revelation.

Our book is thus thoroughly interdisciplinary. It combines New Testament biblical study, art history, and what is known as reception history, the ways in which texts have been received and interpreted through the ages. And in showing the overlaps and connections between these different strands, we hope it will throw light back onto Revelation itself.

## Revelation: relevant for today?

It is Revelation's fleeting signifiers of ultimate destruction, now commonly referred to by the noun, *the apocalypse*, that have remained uppermost in the public consciousness, even as large parts of the developed world have become resolutely less Christian and less religious.[15] Thus, when Buffy refers to the apocalypse, she does so in a way that is largely divorced from its tethering in Revelation. We will be looking in more detail at some of the recent popular uses and interpretations of Revelation in Chapter 10. This final chapter will encompass both more abstract and less scriptural uses, as in the case of Buffy, as well as more engaged examples, such as Ingmar Bergman's famous film *The Seventh Seal* and Johnny Cash's song 'When the Man Comes Around'.

As both D. H. Lawrence and the *Rainbow* magazine suggest, Revelation is a book that elicits strong opinions, driving its devotees to insanity, and its critics to despair, both at the violence of some of the imagery and at the way the book has inspired violent, even crazy, political fantasies. Some, like Lawrence, have found it to be unconvincing as a Christian text; he saw it rather as a melange of different material, mixing ancient apocalyptic religious mythology with a Christian message uneasily superimposed at a later date. Lawrence himself saw the earlier material, predominantly pagan in his view, as testifying to the power, fecundity, and destructiveness of life itself in its most elemental forms, in contrast to what he took to be the milk and water Christian additions.[16] Lawrence is not alone in this general view. Martin Luther was, if anything, more suspicious of the book's Christian credentials. In 1522 he mused on whether it should be left out of the New Testament altogether on the grounds that 'Christ is neither known nor taught in it [the Book of Revelation]'.[17] (Later on, though, he revised his view somewhat, enlisting the apocalyptic notion of Antichrist in his campaign against the Roman papacy.)

Others, in contrast to Luther, have viewed Revelation as the very embodiment of the Christian message of humility, endurance, and ultimate reward (just what Lawrence objected to). Thus, as we have seen, for the politically engaged South African pastor Allan Boesak, writing under the domination of the apartheid regime in 1987, Revelation functions as a metaphorical text that describes the situation of the oppressed majority blacks in South Africa, and offers them hope. The apartheid regime, supported by the Dutch Reformed Church, and identified by Boesak with the Beasts, Antichrist, and the Whore of Babylon, will eventually be crushed and the righteous will be liberated, as foretold by John of Patmos; though in John's case the evil figures of Revelation represented the Roman empire rather than the empire Boesak was opposing.[18]

For someone like Tavener, however, Revelation is not solely, or even mainly, about destruction. It is, as he says, about God's burning, thunderous love, and about how, out of destruction, God will bring about the New Jerusalem, something beyond comprehension, imagination, and thought. We misconstrue Revelation if, as people in recent times have tended to do, we see it solely in terms of Armageddon and destruction. For orthodox Christians for the last two thousand years the destruction foretold in Revelation is always balanced by hope in the New Jerusalem, but this can easily be forgotten by a modern audience.

Mention of an 'orthodox Christian' interpretation of Revelation, in contrast to contemporary secular views of apocalypse, raises a more general and more pressing question: has Revelation really got anything to say to contemporary non- or post-Christians? If the answer is no, as might seem obvious at first sight, then the interest our book has will be somewhat theoretical, rendering it an antiquarian mixture of somewhat obscure religion and art history, engaging up to a point, but not really of vital or existential importance to people today. We think, though, that this would be too quick a judgement.

The symbols and themes of Revelation have a power and significance which transcend their embedding in straightforward Christian doctrine—to that extent we agree with Lawrence. Its vivid portrayals of destruction and of the evils which beset humankind, in the images of the Four Horsemen and the scourges they unleash on us, present to us realities we all have to come to terms with, if anything more urgently in the absence of religion.

The idea that there is or could be a better form of life than the one presently engaging us on earth, a Millennium or a New Jerusalem, has lost none of its power since John envisioned it—though, as we will see, its power is not always benign. The images of the feminine presented in the passages describing the Woman Clothed with the Sun and the Whore of Babylon are, by turns, inspiring and troubling even today. The mockery of virtue and justice personified by the Beasts and Antichrist is no less real today than it was in Roman times, and, conversely, the critique of imperial power that they embody remains extremely potent, as the work of Boesak and other liberation theologians attests to. The notion of and hope for a just judgement is no less important than it ever was, if no less elusive; but it is one which haunts the mind, from the despairing hope of the oppressed that the wrongs afflicting them will be redressed, somehow, sometime, to our universal fascination with tales of wrongs being righted and the guilty brought to justice. There is also the question as to whether the justice is to be tempered with mercy, a theme taken up in many medieval representations of the Last Judgement, as well as in depictions of Revelation more generally.

And the transformational nature of a morality based on the self-sacrificial Lamb of God, rather than on worldly power, remains as challenging now as it was then—even as many of us abandon the religious basis on which that morality originally rested. Similarly the angelic messengers, which play a key role in Revelation, may be seen as symbolizing the persisting belief that we humans are bound by a morality and a sense of value which we do not construct for ourselves.

In the chapters which follow we will be examining all these themes as they are presented in the imagery of Revelation, and in doing so we will show that Revelation continues to have a vital relevance even in the twenty-first century—if anything even more pressing in the light of the secular assumptions of our time.

# Outline of Revelation

(Terms shown in this section for the first time in bold are key terms. They are further defined in the Glossary, along with some other key theological and art historical terms.)

There may be some readers of this book who are already familiar with Revelation, and of those who are not, some may wish only to dip in and out of discrete chapters. However, given the complexity and at time confusing nature of what we are told in Revelation, without more ado we will now give an outline of the book, so as to guide the reader through it, and also to highlight its main themes and place them in their context. For readers both of this book and of Revelation itself, this outline will provide a route map, which may itself be read in conjunction with the schematic topology of Revelation that we provide in Figure 0.1.[19]

Seeing in a more visual way how we envisage that the various chapters of Revelation fit together and complement each other will, we trust, be a helpful way of getting to grips with the book. And the fact that we have turned to the visual for this purpose underlines the way in which what the book describes is itself a vision or series of interconnected visions, maybe with something of the fluidity of a dream, which the visionary is attempting to convey in words.

Indeed, the most helpful way to approach Revelation is to see it as a series of interconnected visions granted to its author, 'John of Patmos', who is then told to communicate these visions to various communities and to the wider world. We are introduced to this John in Rev. 1.1, where he is described as Jesus' servant and the recipient of the visions that follow, and it is John's voice that ends the book in Rev. 22, where he states, with prophetic grandeur, that not only should those reading or hearing the book obey its messages, but they should also leave it as it is and not try to add anything to it, on pain of being refused entry to the **New Jerusalem** (Heaven).

In Rev. 1.9 John affirms that he is sharing his visions with **seven Asian churches,** as he has been told to do by Jesus in the first vision. He then recounts this first vision, a strange evocation of Jesus as the 'Son of Man' with a sword protruding from his mouth and fiery eyes, in Rev. 1.12–20. John's prophetic mission is repeated and strengthened in Rev. 10, where he is given a prophetic scroll to eat by an angel from Heaven (in what is a clear echo of the Old Testament account in Ezekiel 2–3). This is an indication to

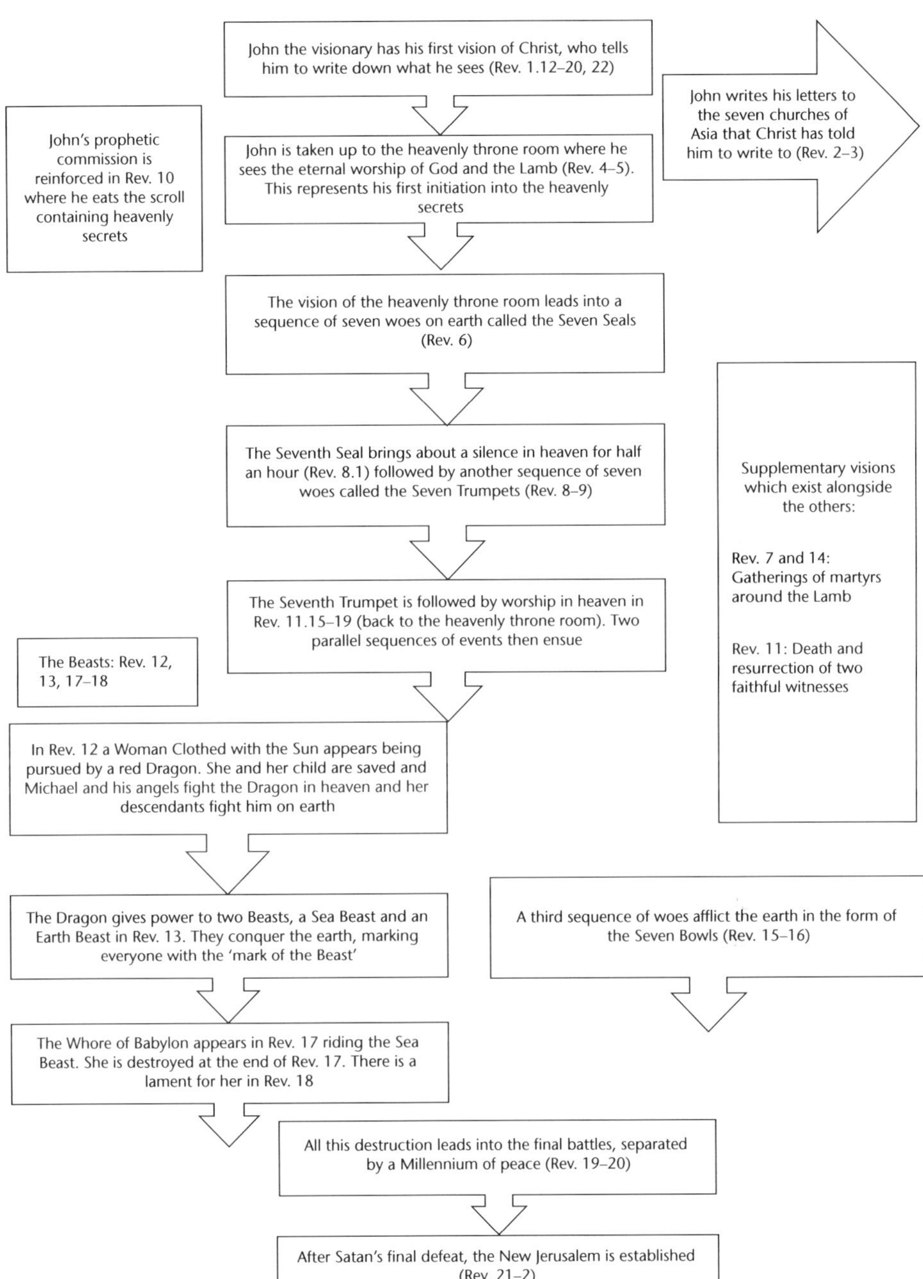


**Figure 0.1.** Topology of Revelation. Revelation is difficult to follow if you read it as a straightforward narrative. Here we attempt to disentangle the main visionary strands in a diagrammatic format

the reader or hearer of the depth and authority of his knowledge of the heavenly mysteries of which he speaks.

In Rev. 2–3 John delivers personalized messages, which are made up of admonitions and encouragement, from Jesus to the seven Asian (i.e. what would now be Turkish) churches (see Figure 0.2 for an image of the Laodicean church from the fourteenth-century *Angers Apocalypse Tapestry*).[20] In a sense, although we should bear in mind that some of the messages recounted here are repeated in other ways in the body of the text (such as the aforementioned admonition in Rev. 3.15–22 to the Laodiceans not to be so 'lukewarm' and apathetic in their conduct), these chapters can be left on one side. They are comparatively rarely illustrated, although they have sometimes been evoked by composers and writers (as well as theologians, of course).

This takes us to the next vision, in Rev. 4–5, in which John is taken up to the **heavenly throne room**, a scene which marks the beginning of his initiation into the divine plan for the world. In this crucial scene John glimpses the eternal Heaven. God is naturally portrayed as being at the centre of this vision, seated on a fiery throne encased in a rainbow, which itself is surrounded by

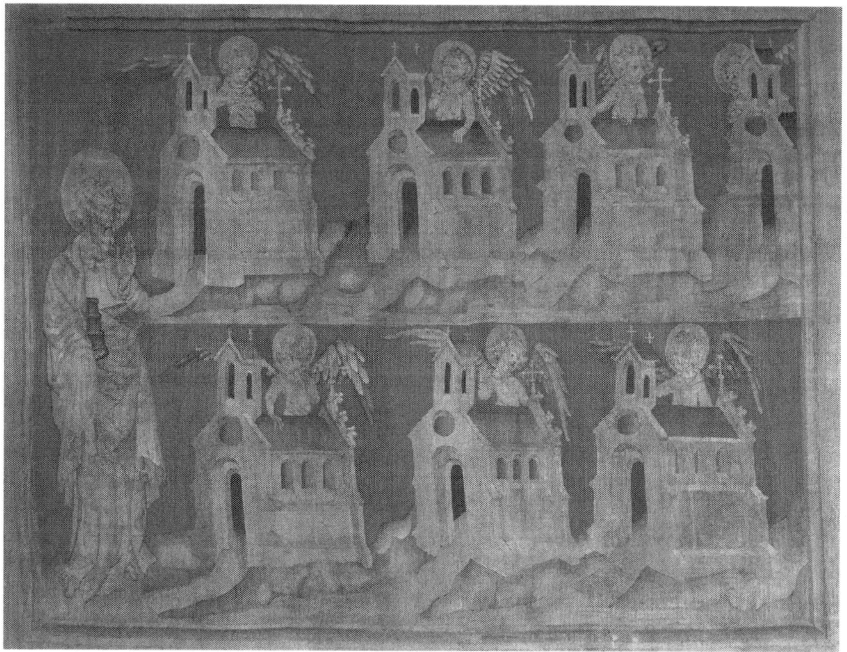

**Figure 0.2.** The *Angers Apocalypse Tapestry*, c.1373–80, The Seven Churches of Asia (Rev. 2–3), Maine et Loire: Chateau d'Angers. © Bridgeman Art Library

**Twenty-four Elders** all worshipping God, as well as four mysterious animals covered in eyes. God is presented as the object of unceasing worship from all that surround him, with thunder and lightning proceeding from the throne, and a sea of glass, like crystal, before it. Into this scene, in Rev. 5, comes the **Lamb** (who is Christ in his manifestation as sacrificial victim), the only being deemed worthy to receive and open the scroll with **Seven Seals**. This scroll is shown to John, and, as we later find out, contains the heavenly mysteries and the future of the world. All this is a metaphor for Christ's historical appearance on earth, the scroll symbolizing the task of mission, crucifixion, and resurrection that only he could perform.

This second vision passes seamlessly into the next. At the beginning of Rev. 6, John sees the Lamb open the first of the seals on the scroll. This sets in motion a series of cosmic disasters which enact God's judgement on an ungrateful and disobedient world, whose inhabitants we are meant to understand have had many chances to amend their ways. First there are the famous **Four Horsemen of the Apocalypse**, who bring war, famine, pestilence, and wild beasts to the earth (Rev. 6.1–8); they are followed by a great earthquake and an eclipse (Rev. 6.12–17). Similar sequences are also presented in Rev. 8–9 and 15–16, where once again John has visions of world-encompassing disasters being heralded first by the blowing of trumpets and then by the emptying of seven bowls on the earth. As in the first sequence, these later disasters also centre on war, pestilence, and famine. While the details are slightly different in each case, as in a dream, their purpose is the same: to emphasize the extent of the upheaval required in order for this world to end and to be replaced by the New Jerusalem. The world and most of its inhabitants have strayed so far from God's intended path that divine justice of this magnitude is required to counteract it.

This catalogue of recapitulated but also progressively escalating woes, sent down from Heaven, presents us with a frightening vision of God indeed. He seems capricious and seemingly indiscriminate as to the extent of the destruction he is prepared to unleash upon the world. To understand this, we need to consider the context that Revelation was written in. As already mentioned, the text was written in the late first century for a set of Asian churches. At that time, these churches, having been established only some twenty to thirty-five years earlier, were probably not yet subject to systematic persecution from the Roman empire. The problem with these Asian churches, from John's point of view, was that they were torn between two worlds or cultures, the Christian world and that of the Roman empire

**Table 0.1.** Outline of the three sequences of seven woes/disasters

| Seven Seals (Rev. 6.2–17; 8.1) | Seven Trumpets (Rev. 8.2–9.20; 11.15–19) | Seven Bowls (Rev. 15–16) |
|---|---|---|
| 1 The First Horseman (War) | 1 One third of the earth burnt up with fire | 1 Plague |
| 2 The Second Horseman (Famine) | 2 One third of the seas poisoned | 2 All the seas poisoned |
| 3 The Third Horseman (Plague) | 3 One third of all fresh water poisoned by a falling star called Wormwood | 3 All fresh water on earth poisoned |
| 4 The Fourth Horseman (Death) | 4 An eclipse of the sun, moon, and stars | 4 The earth scorched with fire |
| 5 A vision of Christian martyrs killed on account of their faith | 5 The attack of the locust army on earth for five months | 5 Pestilence and sores |
| 6 The Great Earthquake | 6 The attack of the demonic cavalry of the Avenging Angels | 6 The Euphrates dried up and demonic spirits unleashed |
| 7 Silence in Heaven for half an hour | 7 Worship in Heaven | 7 A huge earthquake and hailstones destroy all the great cities of the earth |

and the cult of Rome, which included the worship of emperors like Nero and Domitian.

Whilst convinced enough of the Christian message to have become part of a church, the members of these churches seem also to have been seduced by the authority and power, as well as the cultural aspects, of the Roman empire. And how much more appealing and powerful must the Roman empire have seemed at times. Thus we have a rationale for both the severity and the certainty of the punishments in the cycles of divinely ordained disasters that appear in the text in Rev. 6, 8–9, and 15–16 (three sequences of sevens—seals, trumpets, and bowls). They were intended to assure the first hearers of the text that those who capitulated to the temptations of the 'world' would be swept away in the punishments that would occur before the end times. At the same time they would come to understand that, for all its power and cruelty (as shown in the destruction of the Temple), Rome itself would fall, and the order of might would be overturned.

If Revelation simply consisted of these three sequences of disasters, it would be fairly easy to follow. Interspersed within and around these frightening cycles of 'woes', however, are different sections of material. These other chapters or visions can be seen to represent in a more metaphorical sense the battle between the two worlds or ideologies that the Christians in the seven Asian churches had seemingly found themselves at the heart of.

The visions of Rev. 12, 13, 17, and 18 have been labelled 'The Beasts' in Figure 0.1. They have more of a political feel and, like the sequences of seven disasters, can be seen in broad terms to be repetitions of each other. They all feature a terrifying, interconnected but different beastly figure that represents a threat to a more vulnerable figure or group of people. Thus most commentators have seen these beastly figures, who all in one way or another represent **Satan** or his power, as manifestations of the Roman empire, which posed a great threat to both the existence and the moral integrity of the early Christian churches at the time that John was writing, as we have already seen.

In Rev. 12, a woman who is described as being 'clothed with the sun' (the **Woman Clothed with the Sun**) and who has a male child, and who may be identified with Mary as the mother of Christ, is being pursued by a beast in the form of a **Dragon**, who is traditionally identified with Satan himself. The woman is helped by an angel and manages to escape the Dragon, who goes on to fight St Michael and his angels in Heaven. In Rev. 17, another beastly figure, the **Whore of Babylon**, is also eventually destroyed, as is Babylon (= Rome) itself. Thus in Rev. 12 and 17, two beasts are decisively beaten. In Rev. 13, however, a further two beasts, an **Earth Beast** and a **Sea Beast**, who receive their power from the Dragon (or Satan) in Rev. 13.1, are shown to be deceiving and persecuting the 'inhabitants of the earth' and remain undefeated, unthreatened even, by the end of the chapter, thus clearing the way for a final battle or battles between good and evil at the end of Revelation (Rev. 16–20). There are actually two of these battles, and the name **Armageddon** is, strictly speaking, associated with the first, though sometimes it is loosely used (though not in Revelation) to cover both.

It is worth mentioning here that in the Middle Ages the Beasts of Rev. 13, and the Sea Beast in particular, became closely associated with the figure of **Antichrist**.[21] The idea of Antichrist, a diabolical figure that most in the Middle Ages believed would appear prior to the end of the world, has no one biblical source but was formed from several sources in the New Testament, including Revelation, 1 and 2 John, and 1 and 2 Thessalonians. The Antichrist figure borrows aspects of both the demonic and absolute power of the Sea Beast and the deceptive nature of the Earth Beast of Rev. 13.[22] For the Earth Beast prophesies and performs miracles, such as making fire appear from the sky, which might be interpreted by the unwary as signs of Christlike powers and divinity. But he also leads the inhabitants of the earth to worship the Sea Beast, who, as worshipped, is Antichrist, and the Earth Beast his prophet—which is how the legend was more commonly interpreted in the Middle Ages.

Rev. 7, 11, and 14 are different again; they have been labelled in Figure 0.1 as 'supplementary visions' as they do not follow a traceable narrative as the material pertaining to the Beasts does. They do however represent an attempt to reassure the faithful in metaphorical terms, and in this sense provide an important counterbalance to the visions depicting the various beasts. Thus, the visions of Rev. 7 and 14, with their gatherings of saintly multitudes, depict the promise of salvation for the persecuted, a reminder to the text's hearers and readers to remain strong against the coercion and seduction of the Roman way of life. Rev. 11 tells of the triumphant deliverance of the mysterious **two Witnesses**, who remain true to their prophetic mission in the face of derision and ridicule from their earthly audience. Those who rejected and killed them, and many more besides, are duly punished when God sends a great earthquake which kills over seven thousand people.

Thus by the time the narrative returns to a more linear trajectory in Rev. 19, having passed through the third sequence of seven woes in Rev. 15–16, we, the readers, may be confident that evil will be definitively defeated, privy as we have been to the many different explorations of this idea that make up Rev. 11–18. However, in light of the fact that the Beasts of Rev. 13 were left undefeated and unchallenged, it is important that this final battle be played out in more expansive terms via a final vision that spans Rev. 19–21. These final chapters feature an extended version of the decisive encounter between the forces loyal to Christ and those loyal to the two Beasts of Rev. 13. The defeat of these Beasts and therefore of Satan himself is explored and recapitulated in remarkably similar terms in both Rev. 19 and 20. Confusingly Satan, of whom the Beasts are a manifestation, is defeated not once but twice. After the first defeat, there is a thousand years of peace under Christ's rule (called the **Millennium**), after which Satan is released for one more battle and a definitive defeat (Rev. 20.7–10). The name Armageddon occurs in Revelation in connection with these final battles, but contrary to what one might expect, it is mentioned only once, at Rev. 16.16. In Revelation there are actually two 'final' battles against Satan and his forces and the term Armageddon seems to refer more to the first battle against the two Beasts. After the second 'final battle' Rev. 20 culminates in the **Last Judgement**. This in turn paves the way in Rev. 21 for the destruction of the first Heaven and the first earth, and the establishment of the New Jerusalem, into which all those who have remained faithful to Christian values in the face of temptation and coercion will be admitted.

It is this ending which in many ways helps us to understand the rest of the text, as an attempt to establish two fundamental points: first that God's power, both his benevolence and his vengeance, is infinitely *more* powerful than any earthly authority; and that consequently and secondly, according to Revelation, the need to remain steadfast to God's wishes, as mediated through Jesus, in order to avoid the ultimate fate of the Beasts, is of the utmost importance. That these two, seemingly simple, points are made via a series of highly metaphorical, at times overlapping, and confusing visions is testament not only to the dangerous times in which John of Patmos lived (hence the need for obfuscation), but also to the extent of his extraordinary imagination, what some may call his divine inspiration.

## One narrative or many? Finding a way into Revelation

Now that the reader has an overview of the chronology and content of Revelation in place, we will look at some of the key theological and literary issues raised by this complex text. The first is that on opening Revelation at any point, rather than finding oneself in the midst of a straightforward linear narrative, one is plunged into a kaleidoscope of fantastic images and themes, as we have just seen. The images of Revelation have the vividness and potency of dreams—but also, at times, the elusiveness of dreams. While in Revelation it is always very clear that good will and does triumph over evil, and that in the end the righteous will be saved, as in a dream, events come and go without being fully resolved and are repeated in apparently illogical fashion. The seeming illogicality can perhaps be resolved if we see Revelation not as a straightforward narrative, but as a series of vivid images, all centring around the battle or battles between good and evil, casting different perspectives on the basic drama. The vividness of the vision—for that is what Revelation is—has a poetic coherence, a logic and a force of its own, but it is not the logic of a straightforward narrative. For this reason those who attempt to read Revelation as if it were a piece of journalistic reportage may find it initially impenetrable, which is why, as we hope to show in this book, visual and even musical interpretations of Revelation may help us to understand it in a way literary and textual treatments cannot.

In addition to its visionary core, as a text Revelation is a veritable jumble of genres and styles: letters to churches, fantastical apocalyptic visions, and dire warnings, all delivered to a visionary called John who was residing in exile on the Greek island of Patmos at the time. Nor is it in any clear sense a summation of the other books of the New Testament, the Gospels and Paul's letters, despite the fact that it appears right at the end of the twenty-seven books that make up this work.

And neither is it just about the cataclysmic end of the world, as one might imagine from modern usage of the term 'apocalypse', but which just a cursory overview of the text has shown to be false. To look at Revelation as if it were just about the desolation following some sort of post-nuclear cataclysm, as if John of Patmos were a first-century Cormac McCarthy spinning his version of *The Road* (powerful as that book is), would be completely to miss its point. Revelation was actually intended to reassure, console, and above all to inspire its first audience, who would have been Christians (the seven Asian churches) living around 90 CE in western Anatolia, within the Roman empire. While the persecution of Christians had not yet become institutional practice for the Romans, the empire still provided a largely hostile, and also seductive, environment for those early followers of the Christian faith.

In Revelation John fulminates against those pallid, half-hearted believers in the Asian churches who were prone to such seduction, who were over-impressed by Roman might (as well, in worldly terms, they might be), and who were prepared to compromise. These believers were, as he says, 'lukewarm', neither hot nor cold (Rev. 3. 15–16), or in other words not explicitly immoral but not strictly living by the Christian commandments either. Roman might in 90 CE was, of course, overwhelming, not just in general terms, but particularly to Jews and to the Christianized Jews of the early church, who would have been only too well aware of the vicious and wholesale destruction by the Romans of the great and symbolic Jewish Temple in Jerusalem and of Jerusalem itself in 70 CE. Even today the brutality shocks: 60,000 Roman legionaries slaughtered and enslaved up to half a million Jews in Jerusalem, as well as destroying the Temple (for ever) and wrecking the city. Rome's enemies, it must have seemed at the time, were inevitably doomed—hence the fear and the temptation to find a way of accommodating oneself to the empire. Wrong, says Revelation, not just because compromise was wrong in itself, but rather more because in the great struggle between good and evil, evil (in this case the Roman empire) will be thoroughly and eternally defeated. Revelation provides a vision of the total wasting of the evil empire, of all evil empires, and of all who belong to them. In Revelation there is and can be no compromise between good and evil; for the unrighteous the lake of fire, for the righteous the New Jerusalem of Rev. 21–2.

There is no doubt, however, that this pastoral and essentially anti-worldly, anti-Roman message was not delivered to its hearers in the straightforward manner of, say, a Pauline epistle. That could, by 90 CE, have resulted in execution for John, who was already in exile on Patmos. But one also senses that John himself was a more esoteric, more imaginative character than Paul anyway, a visionary whose mind was teeming with barely controlled or controllable inspiration and imagery. And thus we are left with this fantastical, superficially impenetrable work.

In the circumstances it is not surprising that different New Testament scholars have had different ways of trying to explain the material found in Revelation, material that draws on many different sources ( Jewish, Christian, Roman, and mythological) and on many genres (apocalyptic, visionary, prophetic, epistolary). Few of them agree with each other and many of the interpretations produced verge towards the idiosyncratic.[23] However, if one is reminded that Revelation is purportedly an account of the visions received by John on Patmos when he was 'in the spirit' (Rev. 1.10), it perhaps becomes a little easier to comprehend.

Although it may be difficult for a sceptical modern reader to accept that John was the recipient of visions from Heaven, all one has to accept in reading Revelation is that the man responsible for writing the text *felt* himself to be experiencing visions.[24] In that sense he did have visions from some source or other—maybe from God, maybe not—but whichever way, visions which he then felt an overwhelming urge to record and to communicate. Far from distinguishing him as a madman, this capacity for visionary experience actually places John of Patmos within a long and distinguished visionary tradition which included the Jewish prophets Daniel and Ezekiel.

John's own time (in the first century CE) was in fact full of visionaries, and indeed of apocalypses. They or their works are known to us under such exotic titles as 4 Ezra, 2 Baruch, 2 Enoch, the Ascension of Isaiah, and the Apocalypse of Abraham. Nor did visionary experience and writing die out with John of Patmos and his contemporaries in the first century CE. Within the Christian world there are the twelfth-century Hildegard of Bingen, the fourteenth-century Bridget of Sweden, and the sixteenth-century Ignatius of Loyola, Teresa of Avila, and John of the Cross. In the eighteenth and nineteenth centuries there were many others, including Emanuel Swedenborg, William Blake, and Mary Ann Girling. Present-day mystics from all sorts of traditions inside and outside our own, such as shamans in the Inuit culture, continue to report their experiences. Indeed, the biblical scholar Ian Boxall makes the interesting point that readers from other cultures more in touch with the concept of a spirit world are much more open to what we might call the 'visionary structure/logic' of Revelation than post-Enlightenment Western readers who, rightly or wrongly, find themselves at odds with this way of approaching the world.[25] If Boxall is right, John of Patmos may then represent the norm rather than the exception, with the majority of humanity likely to find less intrinsic difficulty in his Revelation than the contemporary Western reader, brought up in a secular, empirical, and predominantly sceptical environment.

To reinforce the visionary nature of Revelation we should note that John's narrative is peppered with over sixty references to 'seeing' (e.g. Rev. 1.12–13: 'and I *saw* seven golden lampstands and in the middle of the lampstands I *saw* one like the Son of Man'). He also uses metaphorical language to capture the magnitude and complexity of what he saw (e.g. Rev. 13.2: 'And the Beast that I saw was *like* a leopard and its feet were *like* a bear's'). John has been accused of creating confusion with his literary imagery and of overusing similes (e.g. Rev. 9.7–10 and its confusing description of the 'locust army' or the nonsensical description of the New Jerusalem as having tiny outer walls in comparison to its 1,500 mile high inner walls, Rev. 21.15–18) to the extent that some feel that Revelation cannot be easily or coherently used as a source for visualization. But this did not prevent artists in large numbers from the late medieval and early modern period from engaging with the text, usually at the behest of their patron.[26] Even when some of these images are physically impossible or sometimes faintly comical, their visual immediacy vividly brings home the essential nature of Revelation itself, arising out of visionary experience.

## Revelation and the end times

John of Patmos was almost certainly a Jew, albeit a follower of Christ. Like the Jewish writers of apocalypses from his time which we have just mentioned,

John was drawing on a well-established Jewish tradition of prophecy and of messianic writing more generally. And like them, John was responding to recent and contemporary events such as the destruction of the Temple in 70 CE and possibly even the eruption of Vesuvius in 69 CE (which may have left its traces in some of the natural disasters depicted in Revelation). As with John, the visions of his more orthodox Jewish contemporaries all in one way or another saw the contemporary (Roman) world order being overturned, and understandably so, given the way the Romans had treated Jerusalem and the Temple (cf. Daniel 7–12 and 4 Ezra).[27]

So Revelation's general theme of an imminent reversal of the world order is by no means peculiar to John. Many Jewish writers and groups of his time were expecting in the most vivid terms the appearance of a Messiah who would liberate Israel from the Roman oppressors, restoring her to her lost glory, bringing about a final and lasting triumph.[28] Early Christians, adapting this Jewish belief, often believed that Christ would return in the near future, and, as Revelation gradually gained acceptance among them as part of their scripture, despite a degree of initial suspicion, it was co-opted by some to support this view, and, though not invariably, sometimes in a crudely literal way. Thus, for example, Lactantius and other Christian writers of the early fourth century interpreted the Millennium—Christ's thousand-year rule of peace—in a material way, as something that would actually come about on earth, after the fall of the Roman empire and the disastrous violence which would follow that, out of which an Antichrist figure would emerge, who would then be defeated by Christ himself.[29]

Nor indeed is belief in an imminent cataclysm or end of the world confined to explicitly religious thinking of the first century CE. As Frank Kermode argued in his book *The Sense of An Ending*, humans have a seemingly irresistible urge to impose systems and narratives on time, thinking in terms of the world having one definite history, one goal, *the* history as it were, rather than consisting of a succession of unconnected and directionless histories in the plural.[30] And we, or those who speak or think on our behalf, like, somewhat self-importantly, to see ourselves at a uniquely cataclysmic stage in the world's development, often at the point of the final crisis before the end. We may laugh at what we see as the naivety of earlier apocalyptic visions, but in the 1960s when Kermode was writing it was the Bomb, and later, in the 1970s, the new ice age or nuclear winter, while in the early twenty-first century it is climate change and Islamic terrorism leading to an apocalyptic 'clash of civilizations'. (Have we already forgotten that the Cold War, which seemed at the time to presage the end of civilization, ended not so much with a bang as with a whimper, as the apparently invincible Eastern bloc proved to be no more than a house of cards?) And we should also note the way that these visions of annihilation tend to be purveyed by seers possessed of a secret knowledge not initially available to common sense.

There are certainly elements of all this sort of thinking in Revelation. But there are also important differences too, differences which some, and sometimes those most influenced by Revelation, have overlooked. The key figure in John's Revelation is the Lamb, symbol of Christ. First and foremost a suffering, sacrificial victim, the Lamb stands in contrast to Christ's other representation in Revelation (Rev. 19)—the triumphant Rider on the White Horse who defeats Satan's armies towards the end of the book. It is true that this Rider, 'faithful and true', and his battles are described in Revelation in terms reminiscent of the holy war tradition of Israel—so the aggressive, exclusionary aspects of Revelation, which some admirers and critics have focused on, are there, as we will show in Chapter 2.[31] Certainly there is a degree of ambivalence in this regard at the heart of the text of Revelation, which is not, after all, a theological treatise but a vision to inspire, encourage, and uplift. But even granting a degree of ambivalence or tension between the Lamb who wins through suffering and the holy warrior who destroys his (and our) oppressors, what is made explicit in Rev. 21–2 is that the New Jerusalem of Revelation is no standard earthly city; indeed, if we take it literally, it is not an earthly city at all, but one descending from Heaven after this earth has passed away.

On earth, it seems, the struggles and the woes will never cease, something which is made explicit via the three sets of seven woes interspersed with occasional triumphs, and even in the curious way that what is described as the final battle between good and evil happens more than once, suggesting that there will be no final resolution in the present order of things. As a result the New Jerusalem of Revelation, far from being built up on earthly foundations, is a city which descends from Heaven itself and seems to gather this earth into Heaven, thus bringing about a new Heaven and a new earth. That it *descends* from Heaven (Rev. 21.2) is (or should be) crucial to understanding its meaning: it descends, in contrast to the idolatrous attempt to build the tower of Babel, by which human beings would *ascend* to Heaven by their efforts (see Genesis 11.1–9). For all that it has been misinterpreted, Revelation is about God's grace coming to us at the end of time, rather than we humans constructing a new world in this time.

Revelation's vision is transformative rather than restorative, and in stressing the redemptive suffering of the Lamb, it is ethically transformative as well. Attempting to read Revelation solely as a key to current or future events can therefore be construed as a somewhat futile, even impious, misreading of the text, again for all the attempts there have been to interpret it in this way. Particularly scathing in his rejection of Lactantius and others who attempted to read Revelation in a material way, as predicting real events to be literally interpreted, was the aforementioned St Jerome: 'To take it [Revelation] according to the letter is to "Judaize". If we treat it in a spiritual way (as it was written), we go against the views of many older authorities', among whom he mentions Lactantius by name; further, 'the saints will in no wise have an earthly kingdom, but only a celestial one; thus must cease the fable of one thousand years'.[32] Jerome's view became the orthodox view in the Christian church, and what he referred to as the fable of a thousand years did indeed cease—at least until the thirteenth century or so.

Jerome's view of Revelation was given solid theological backing by his near contemporary St Augustine (particularly in *The City of God*, Book 20, sections 6–10). Following in the footsteps of an earlier commentator, Tyconius, Augustine reads Revelation in a symbolic or so-called typological way, taking many of its prophecies to refer to things that are already present—at least to those who could see. Thus he interpreted the Millennium (Rev. 20.3–10, when Satan is said to be bound, leading to one thousand years of peace on earth) metaphorically, as referring to the positive strand in the currently existing Christian church, that part which was redeemed following Christ's crucifixion. In this Augustinian sense the Millennium is already around us, in the activity of the church (or at least in some of it), and although the world would eventually come to an end, as Revelation says, Augustine insists that, in line with Matthew 24.26, it is not for us to know the time or the day, and otiose for us to speculate on it. This sense of the need for patient waiting is also to be found in Rev. 6.9–11 (the Fifth Seal), in which the martyrs sheltering under the altar ask, 'Sovereign Lord, holy and true, how long will it be before you judge and avenge our blood on the inhabitants of the earth?' Although, within the context of the rest of the text, it is certain that they will be 'avenged', there is no answer to the question of when this will be.

By the time of the Middle Ages the more orthodox Christian interpretations of Revelation, as we will see, did not envisage the Millennium and the New Jerusalem in terrestrial or temporal terms at all. They saw this and the last days in terms of spiritual transformations of the believers, and the New Jerusalem in terms of eternal, heavenly life. In many medieval and late medieval representations, from the *Gulbenkian Apocalypse*, one of a number of beautiful Anglo-Norman illuminated manuscripts of the thirteenth century, to the Van Eycks' great *Ghent Altarpiece*, from around 1432 (see Plate 1), the church, as represented by bishops, clergy, and the pope himself, far from being vilified, is seen as the vehicle by which redeemed Christians make their way from this earthly city to the celestial New Jerusalem. In this interpretation, the church on earth (the church militant) is seen as the third term between Heaven (the church triumphant) and the 'fallen' earth, a kind of bridge or staircase by which humankind might ascend from this fallen earth to its true home, which is not of this world.

Despite all this, through the centuries many in the spirit of Lactantius *have* understood Revelation as offering a precise chronology or way of decoding historical and contemporary events. In our own time, evangelical and particularly Dispensationalist Christians have interpreted phenomena such as nuclear proliferation, the Israel–Palestine conflict, or the recent financial crisis within its framework.[33] And this use of Revelation as a key to current events, and even as a call to arms, so to speak, has a long and sometimes unpalatable history. This history goes some way to explaining the visceral dislike the book evokes in some of its readers, who see it in terms of the divisiveness and cruelty it appears to have unleashed on the world. Thus, throughout the Middle Ages, beginning with the Crusades, leaders of populist movements have used Revelation to inspire fantasies of actually realizing the Millennium and the New Jerusalem foretold in the text (Rev. 20–2). From their point of view this meant an earth free from sin, often egalitarian in structure and sometimes admitting of free love, but, always and most important, brought about through the bloody purging of enemies, variously identified as the Jews, Saracens (or Muslims more generally), the rich, the higher clergy, and often the papacy.

Highly influential among those who wanted to see Revelation in terms of a history unfolding here and now were the so-called Joachite doctrines of a 'third age'. Joachim of Fiore was a twelfth-century monk and mystic (d. 1202), who believed that there were three ages in Salvation History, the age of the Father (corresponding to the Old Testament), the age of Son (from the time of Christ until 1260 CE, in Joachim's estimation), and then the age of the Holy Spirit, a 'third' age, calculated to begin in 1260, in which the universal love and freedom of the Gospel would reign, and humankind would enter into direct contact with God without the need for the existing hierarchies and laws.[34] Following Revelation, which, as we have seen, includes many series of seven, he split the age of the Son/era of the church into seven *tempora*. Joachim fixed on the year 1260 as the end of the second age based on his reading of Rev. 11.3 and 12.6, in which 1,260 days are mentioned. He believed himself to be living right at the end of the sixth *tempora* of the second age, in other words right on the cusp of the opening of the Sixth Seal and the transition to the third age that that would engender. Joachim's interpretation of the Millennium is fraught with difficulty, in terms of whether he actually envisaged it in literal terms as the ushering in of an age of a new and purified church. Most Joachite scholars argue that Joachim's Millennium should not be seen in terms of a completely new beginning, as he himself stresses its continuity with a process that began with Adam.[35] However, Joachim's complicated doctrines gained appeal and (perhaps not surprisingly) were misinterpreted both among those who sought spiritual renewal and among those increasingly strident followers inspired by dreams or fantasies of an imminent new secular order. By 1300 followers of Joachim such as Peter Olivi, Ubertino of Casale, and Arnold of Villanova, who were offering increasingly radical anti-Augustinian readings of Revelation, inevitably came into conflict with the official church (who condemned the idea of a literal Millennium). Interestingly, they all interpreted the thousand years of the Millennium as referring to different and shorter lengths of time. It was left to John of Rupescissa, in the mid-fourteenth century, to go back to the Lactantian reading of it as literally one thousand years, and in the later Middle Ages, after a millennium underground, so to speak, Lactantius himself became more read and cited in unorthodox and revolutionary circles.[36]

Throughout the Middle Ages, millenarian apocalyptic movements tended to arise among the dispossesed, often following famines, plagues, and other disasters. As Norman Cohn documented in his seminal book *The Pursuit of the Millennium*, they were thoroughly terrestrial in ambition, expecting a total and miraculous transformation of life on earth, following a bloody triumph of the elect over their enemies, and few regrets over the massacres involved. Naturally, whether they were the pastoreaux and flagellants of the fourteenth century, the Taborites of the fifteenth, or the Anabaptists of the sixteenth, these millenarian movements were bitterly opposed by the official churches (including in this last case by Luther and the Lutherans), and as Cohn points out their 'apocalyptic lore' would typically be constructed not just out of Revelation itself.[37] Pagan sources were often added to Joachite embellishments of Revelation, as well as other biblical prophecies. These sources included the Sybylline oracles and classical golden age doctrines, which were in various ways elaborated, reinterpreted, and vulgarized. In a later reimagining of this time, we see a graphic portrayal of a group of wild-eyed apocalyptic flagellants racing through the plague- and famine-ridden medieval Swedish countryside in hopeless pursuit of a new earth in Ingmar Bergman's film *The Seventh Seal* (see Chapter 10).

A further noteworthy interpretation of elements from the Revelation is to be found in the Islamic tradition. Like the New Testament, the Quran itself talks urgently of a Day of Judgement or resurrection, and this apocalypticism was later developed into a full-blown eschatology, significantly for our time, indeed, much of it focused on Jerusalem. The Dome of the Rock, built by the early Islamic rulers in Jerusalem at the end of the seventh century CE, on the site of the old Jewish Temple, was to be the site of the Last Judgement. In the last days, according to much Islamic belief, when evil and corruption had increased to an extreme degree, prior to the Day of Judgement, a Mahdi or redeemer of Islam will appear. In his struggles against the evildoers the Mahdi will be joined by Christ, who in Islamic tradition did not actually die, but was raised by God into Heaven while still alive. The Mahdi and Christ will fight against an Antichrist figure and his forces, and defeat him, after which there will be a period of peace and general unity, until Christ actually dies. There will then be a final onslaught of Satanic forces and universal chaos, until the trumpet will sound for the Day of Judgement itself, and the final division of the peoples of the earth into the just and the unjust. The parallels with and differences from the Revelation are clear enough, and need no further elaboration here; suffice it to say that these or cognate beliefs are influential even now among those Muslims who see themselves as engaged in last days struggles.[38]

From the point of view of the official church, the medieval apocalyptic visionaries described by Cohn, including those inspired by Joachite expectations of a forthcoming third age on earth, were regarded as dangerous heretics and dangerously subversive. This is not, however, to say that Christian or pseudo-Christian applications to one's own time of the prophecies of Revelation dried up after the sixteenth and seventeenth centuries. Around the time of the French Revolution, two English prophets emerged, Joanna Southcott who claimed to be the Woman Clothed with the Sun and about to give birth to the Messiah, and Richard Brothers who claimed to be the nephew of the Almighty and preached the imminence of the Second Coming. Napoleon was often identified (in England) as Antichrist, and William Blake had his visions of a New Jerusalem in England. In the USA in 1844 the so-called Millerites suffered their 'Disappointments' when the end of the world they predicted on the basis of their reading of Revelation and other biblical texts failed more than once to materialize. From these Disappointments Seventh Day Adventism emerged. The unfortunate adherents of the Branch Davidian cult, burnt to death after a gun battle with state and federal agents in Waco, Texas in 1993, were themselves an offshoot of Seventh Day Adventism, and their leader, David Koresh, was much given to interpreting and quoting from Revelation, and saw himself in terms drawn from it.[39]

In the latter half of the nineteenth century so-called Dispensationalism began to get a hold in the evangelical Christian communities in the USA, the belief that the history of the world is divided into 'dispensations'.[40] The present Christian dispensation (or sixth age, known as the Great Parenthesis or age of the church following the crucifixion) will, according to Dispensationalists, soon be replaced by the seventh age or Millennial dispensation. In between these two ages, however, Dispensationalists have, based mainly on 1 Thessalonians 4.16–17, inserted another sequence of events beginning with the Rapture. The Rapture ensures that good evangelical Christians (and possibly young children, although this varies from interpretation to interpretation) will be taken up into Heaven at a predetermined moment, thus avoiding the ensuing Tribulation period in which non-evangelical Christians, non-Christians, and non-believers will be subject to a series of trials, woes, and natural disasters (usually associated with the sequences of seven woes found in Rev. 6, 8–9, and 15–16), which provide the circumstances for a final opportunity to convert to evangelical Christianity. The Tribulation period ends with the second coming (Parousia) of Rev. 19.11ff. and the battle of Armageddon, after which the Beasts are destroyed (Rev. 19.20) and Satan is cast into his pit for one thousand years (Rev. 20.1–3). There follows a thousand years of peace (the Millennial dispensation), itself to be ended by a final battle with Satan, who, as Revelation has it, is unleashed for the last time, and the definitive Last Judgement. Often associated with beliefs of this sort is a conflation of Old Testament prophecies of the return of the Jews to the Holy Land (e.g Jeremiah 30.3; Isaiah 11.12; Ezekiel 37.12) and of other Old Testament apocalyptic scenarios more generally (e.g. Daniel 11–12) with Revelation, to the effect that the return of the Jews to the Holy Land was a precondition of Christ's second coming. Oliver Cromwell (who readmitted Jews to England after three or more centuries of banishment) believed something of the sort, and Christians working for a Jewish homeland in Palestine became more prominent and influential among certain Protestant sects, particularly in the nineteenth and twentieth centuries, continuing right to this day.

With the rise of evangelical fundamentalism in the second half of the twentieth century in the USA and beyond, prophecy 'scholarship', drawing on Dispensationalist themes and largely consisting in applications of Revelation to the contemporary world by individual interpreters, has become highly influential. As we will see in Chapter 10, first Hal Lindsey in the 1970s and then the creators of the *Left Behind* Series in the 1990s have capitalized on the fact that 44 per cent of Americans profess to belief in the Rapture and its associated ideas to produce best-selling books and films.[41] There is of course an uneasy conflict at the heart of prophecy scholarship and so called Rapture-fiction and films, in that while the Great Tribulation is feared, it is also welcomed as both a necessary step on the way to redemption/the New Jerusalem and also as a vindication of the evangelical belief system.[42] Indeed Dispensationalists typically actually welcome what they see as signs of Antichrist and the Great Tribulation, because they read them as signs that the final redemption is close, though maybe the belief that most of them will be raptured before the Great Tribulation helps to preserve their equanimity in face of what is going to befall most of the human race!

Fundamentalist prophecy 'scholars' are also typically preoccupied with the fate of Israel, with some foreseeing an eventual 'day of calamity' for the Jews brought about by the defeat of Israel in a war with the Arabs and/or Russia (or Iran, or whoever)—the people of the north from Daniel 11—with a remnant (the 144,000 who are 'sealed', according to Rev. 7.4) converting to Christianity, as presaging the second coming of Christ. According to research conducted by the well-regarded Pew Research Center in 2006, 35 per cent of American citizens believe that events subsequent to the restoration of Israel will play a crucial role in fulfilling prophecies of Christ's second coming, which helps to explain their largely pro-Israeli stance, and also the peculiar but influential phenomenon known as Christian Zionism. (Despite the fact that the conversion of at least some of the Jews and the eventual defeat of Israel appears to be part of the Dispensationalist creed, Israeli politicians have welcomed the work of Christian Zionists, at least for the time being.)[43]

Whatever bizarre and dogmatic uses have been and are being made of Revelation's necessarily imprecise visions, which were almost certainly intended as more metaphorical, symbolic, and recapitulative than Dispensationalist scholars give them credit for, it would be quite wrong to follow Luther and say that Revelation is devoid of 'Christian' content and theology, as we will show in Chapter 2 on the Lamb (the title by which Christ is referred to in Revelation). Rev. 5 in which the Lamb and his anti-Messianic nature and selfless sacrifice are revealed is seen by many interpreters as the key to understanding the whole text.

We will also suggest in subsequent chapters that a more compassionate and non- or anti-violent reading should be elicited from it. As we will see, even in the Middle Ages there are visual representations of Revelation which have the elect opposing the forces of worldly might not with weapons and armoury but, as in the *Gulbenkian Apocalypse*, armed with prayers, mitres, and croziers (see Figure 8.3). And in many medieval representations of the Last Judgement, Christ's implacable justice is tempered by showing the wounds of his Passion and also by his mother and John the beloved disciple interceding before him. To continue this counterbalancing qualification of Cohn's picture of apocalyptic anti-clericalism and subversiveness, in *Gulbenkian* we can also see identifiable bishops, priests, Franciscans, Benedictines, and Dominicans all trooping into Heaven (or the New Jerusalem), which in other images is itself often represented as a Gothic church, complete with intricate gables, pinnacles, and tracery (see Plate 2). Further, as Tavener emphasizes, there is also an often neglected 'hopeful' theme running through Revelation, which ought to inspire those Christians overwhelmed by the oppression and suffering in the world without necessarily turning them into revengeful mirror images of the very oppressive and humanly divisive regimes they are opposing.

Nor, in considering the violently revolutionary messages some have derived from Revelation, should we overlook the fact that far more vicious and bloody movements seeking to bring about earthly millennia have arisen outside Christianity and outside religion altogether. Hitler, Stalin, Mao, Pol Pot, and many others have preached the necessity of cleansing bloodshed in pursuit of their apocalyptic millennial goals. The ruthless and murderous Pursuit of the Millennium, to use Cohn's phrase, is not confined to Revelation or to Christianity. We will attempt to show that it could and should be seen as an aberration of both. But whether or not this is so, it is certainly a perennial temptation of humankind, which seems to arise in all kinds of contexts, religious and non-religious.

# Revelation as an inspiration to art

As will be clear already, through the centuries Revelation has been appropriated by many religious and non-religious movements and counter-movements, and these appropriations have been reflected in the art that springs from Revelation. For large numbers of artists, composers, writers, and, more recently, film-makers and journalists have found the text of Revelation to be an endlessly rich and fascinating source of imagery on which to draw for artistic inspiration and for polemical force. Not surprisingly, given its colourful and provocative imagery and content, it is one of the most widely read and referred to books in the Bible. It is also the most widely illustrated, even including the Gospels, and the richness of this work is what we hope to convey in this book.

Arising from this rich tradition are many different forms of artistic interpretation. Some of the visual interpretations that we have selected are more illustrative and literal in both their intent and execution. They follow either the text or perhaps a contemporary commentary on Revelation very faithfully. Other images are more metaphorical in their interpretation of the same text, perhaps focusing on one episode from Revelation, or bringing together several important episodes into one pictorial space, thus utilizing what Lessing referred to as the 'strange power' of the image.[44] Images such as these have been particularly powerful at capturing the visionary aspect of Revelation.

Although known to us today as a text and arranged as such in a chronological, narrative fashion, Revelation purports to be a visionary experience and it is images in their immediacy and synchronicity that can put us in touch with what that visionary experience, in all its vividness and disorder, may have been like. Yet other images have been chosen for their polemical interpretations of Revelation, again a reminder of the power of the image in this regard. Thus in the chapters that follow, we aim to reveal not only the diversity and richness of the visual tradition associated with Revelation but also the power of the image as an interpretative or exegetical tool, something that is not always recognized by biblical theologians. Visual and textual interpretations can and should be used alongside each other to illuminate different facets of the biblical text in question, rather than images being relegated to a sort of second-tier of interpretation, if indeed they are viewed as having interpretative potential at all.

One image in particular serves as an encapsulation of the above argument. Between 1474 and 1479 Hans Memling painted his *St John Altarpiece*, a triptych commissioned to hang in the chapel of the St John Hospital in Bruges. While fascinating in its own right, it is the right-hand panel of the triptych that interests us. For this right-hand panel, hereafter the *Apocalypse Panel*, Memling has visualized the first thirteen chapters of Revelation as happening simultaneously (see Plate 3).[45] In short, he has tried to capture the moment of John's visionary experience, when, as Tavener says, he 'saw everything'. Although the visual 'narrative' ends at Rev. 13 (with the Dragon handing over his power to the Sea Beast, which can just be seen in a tiny scene on the horizon), the implication is very much that the events continue to unfold out of eyesight. It has even been suggested that the central panel of the altarpiece (which depicts the so-called 'mystic marriage' of St Catherine to Jesus) may in some way evoke the New Jerusalem of Rev. 21–2, whose arrival is initiated by the marriage of the Lamb to Israel in Rev. 19.7ff.[46] Returning to the *Apocalypse Panel* and what we can undoubtedly see, we are presented in the foreground with John, as author of Revelation, pen poised above a blank page with all his technicolour visions passing before his eyes at the same time. In the top left-hand corner of the image is Heaven, as described by John in Revelation as a great throne room on top of a sea of glass and enclosed in a rainbow. There are fiery images of the destruction taking place on 'earth' (depicted here in the middle and top right-hand corner of the image; see, for instance, the Four Horsemen, the fourth of whom is depicted as a skeleton, cantering across the centre of the image). Nevertheless some comfort is afforded the Christian viewer by the fact that God and Christ (depicted here as the human figure on the throne and the white Lamb resting on God's knee) are present throughout. While this may be typical of Memling's serene style (even his images of the grisly beheading of John the Baptist have a tranquil air to them), it also perfectly captures one of the great theological paradoxes of Revelation and of Christianity itself: that the apocalyptic drama so vividly described in this text seems to be not just accepted by God, but in some places actively brought about by him.

Therein lies the power of a masterly image such as this. Not only does it attempt to visualize for the viewer what it might be like to have a religious vision in all its confusion and exhilaration, it also illuminates some of the theological or ethical nuances of the text in an accessible and arresting way. Much more so, one might argue, than a theological commentary which very few people will read and/or really understand. Apart from anything else, Memling's image shows the connections between the visionary, his vision, and the divine source of both, and although it shows only the first half of the vision—no mean feat—there is also a sense of calm endurance pervading the whole, something missing in more lurid visualizations before and after, but which, if we read the whole book, is part of what faithful Christians would be expected to take from Revelation.

We hope that what has been said already of the enduring fascination of Revelation, its particular suitability for visualization, as well as the wide array of contrasting responses it has inspired, has already fired the imagination. For our book has been designed as a breathtaking, if not dizzying, tour of some of the highlights of the many thousands of artistic, literary, musical, and cultural responses to this vivid and highly visual text. We have taken nine of the most famous themes from Revelation, all of which will strike some sort of a chord with most readers, even those unacquainted with the New Testament, but which may, in their original context, be little known or understood. It is our aim to explain each of these familiar yet unfamiliar terms, chapter by chapter, showing how it appears in Revelation and how it has been interpreted in different ways by different artists since the text was written. Thus each chapter will include around a dozen contrasting images ranging from the sixth to the twenty-first centuries CE. Although we hope to provide a coherent account of the whole of Revelation and its themes, it will be possible to read individual chapters in isolation.

After the nine chapters looking at key themes from Revelation in their own terms, we conclude with a longer chapter, which will offer an impressionistic cross-section of ways in which the Revelation as a whole has featured in twentieth- and twenty-first-century culture, both high and popular. Much of this material will probably be familiar in some way or other to many readers, but we hope to illuminate it further and more successfully by putting it in the context of the book from which its symbols have been drawn. At the same time, some of the less familiar material in this chapter will testify to the endless imaginative fertility of Revelation, even in a secular age, and even to minds who may know little of its original sense.

This is, therefore, a book about the wealth of cultural responses that Revelation has inspired over nearly two millennia, and continues to inspire even now. We will demystify this endlessly fascinating text for the modern reader by illustrating its reception history. In doing this we will demonstrate the ways in which each age adds to the lenses through which the book is

**Table 0.2.** Chapter themes

| | |
|---|---|
| 1 | The Angel of the Apocalypse: John's journey and his angelic guides (Rev. 1, 4–5, 10, 17, 21–2) |
| 2 | The Lamb of God (Rev. 5, 7, 14, 19, 21–2) |
| 3 | The Four Horsemen of the Apocalypse (Rev. 6.2–8) |
| 4 | The Seven Seals: angelic destruction (Rev. 6) |
| 5 | The Woman Clothed with the Sun (Rev. 12) |
| 6 | The Satanic Trinity (the Dragon and the Beasts/Antichrist) (Rev. 12–13, 16, 17, 19–20) |
| 7 | The Whore of Babylon (Rev. 17–18) |
| 8 | Armageddon (the final battle, Rev. 16.14), the Millennium (Rev. 20.1–6), and the Last Judgement (Rev. 20.11–15) |
| 9 | The New Jerusalem (Rev. 21–2) |
| 10 | The Apocalypse in the twentieth and twenty-first centuries: a survey of different approaches to Revelation in art, media, music, and popular culture |

refracted, each according to its own style. As well as illustrating facets of the book which had hitherto remained neglected, misunderstood, and unloved, engaging with this reception history of Revelation can also provide insights into the interpretive bias of the creators. Do their interpretations sometimes tell us as much about the interpreters as about Revelation itself? We hope in what follows to throw some light on this question.

But, in examining the themes and images of Revelation, and the ways they have been developed over the ages, we will also indicate their continuing significance in a world very different from that in which they were originally presented. As already suggested, part of the power and longevity of Revelation's images is that they symbolize fundamental aspects of our existence and experience, which transcend both the time and the religious-cum-mythological context in which they were originated. We will indicate how this might be so as we look at Revelation's themes and the ways they have been visualized through the ages.

## Key works of art referred to in this book

During the course of this book we refer to a number of key works of art and artists, chosen partly to illustrate contrasting approaches to Revelation. In order to guide the reader, and also to avoid repetitiousness, we will now list some of the most important of these in chronological order, giving essential background information on each. Information on other important works of art, which are discussed only in one or two places in the book, will be found in the text at the appropriate place.

## The *Trier Apocalypse*

In the Middle Ages manuscript books giving the text of Revelation, and often a commentary as well, became common. These were produced for devotional use in monasteries and convents, or for private patrons, and richly illustrated the events of Revelation, often in sumptuous style. The so-called *Trier Apocalypse*, one of the earliest surviving examples, was produced in northern France in the early ninth century. It contains seventy-five illustrations, which are thought to draw on earlier Christian manuscripts dating from the fifth and sixth centuries.[47]

## The *Beatus* Apocalypses

The *Beatus* Apocalypse manuscripts are a collection of twenty-six illustrated manuscripts produced mainly in Spain, from monasteries in Catalonia, Aragon, Navarre, and elsewhere, from around the ninth to the twelfth centuries, all based around the Apocalypse commentary of the eight-century Abbot Beatus of Liebana (hence their name) and all of which follow a fairly similar iconography.[48] The *Beatus* images are typically vivid, rather simple drawings illuminated with bright colours, and often have considerable dramatic power. Relatively numerous in the Spain of their time, their influence did not extend much beyond the Pyrenees, although one of the most important surviving examples is the *Saint-Sever Beatus Manuscript* from an abbey in south-west France (the manuscript is now in Paris).

## The Anglo-Norman Apocalypses

By the thirteenth century Apocalypse manuscript cycles had become a major cultural phenomenon. Some of the most spectacular of these were produced in England from 1250 onwards (the Anglo-Norman Apocalypses). Around twenty Anglo-Norman Apocalypses survive from this time. In this book we will look particularly at the *Lambeth, Trinity,* and *Gulbenkian* Apocalypses (so called because that is where they are currently located, Lambeth Palace, London, Trinity College, Cambridge, and the Gulbenkian Museum in Lisbon, respectively). In each of them the text is broken up into small sections and an accompanying image appears at the top of each page, giving rise to an overall impression of being guided step by step through Revelation through some eighty or more discrete images, often in the company of John who is himself represented in many of them. These images are far more detailed than those in the *Beatus* manuscripts, and are even cluttered at times, in an effort to render all the detail of the text, which can make them arguably less dramatic. It may be that the patrons who commissioned these works would not have been able to read the Latin or Anglo-Norman text (which includes commentaries as well as Revelation itself, usually the somewhat earlier Berengaudus commentary, with its tendency to interpret Revelation in Christological and indeed anti-semitic terms) and therefore needed the images in order to understand and internalize the narrative. The images thus play a crucial role. *Lambeth* and *Trinity* both date from around 1260, *Gulbenkian* probably a bit later. *Lambeth* and *Trinity* (both produced for or owned by aristocratic female patrons) add illustrated lives of St John to the texts of Revelation and the commentary, and *Lambeth* shows some of the miracles attributed to the Virgin as well. *Gulbenkian*, unusually for the genre, illustrates the commentary as well as the text of Revelation, and, like *Lambeth*, it adds images of the activities of Antichrist and a strong anti-semitic gloss.[49] In contrast to the *Beatus* Apocalypses, these Anglo-Norman manuscripts had a wide influence throughout the Middle Ages, their approach inspiring painters, sculptors, and glass and tapestry makers, as well as manuscript illustrators.

## The *Angers Apocalypse Tapestry*

The *Angers Apocalypse Tapestry* is a monumental-scale French tapestry version of Revelation, measuring 130 m in length, 4.5 m in height, and comprising over eighty-four individual scenes of the text. It was produced for Louis 1st of Anjou (and brother of the French king) between 1377 and 1382 by the workshop of Jean de Bondol of Bruges. Like medieval Apocalypse manuscripts, the large number of images available to the designer meant that many textual details could be pictorialized in a leisurely and detailed way, but here, of course, on a much grander scale. Walking through the galleries in Angers, in which the tapestry is now housed, is like walking through Revelation itself, in the presence of John himself, whose reactions and emotions are forcefully represented in every panel and who himself seems to be participating in a journey from incomprehension and fear to enlightenment.[50]

## The *Flemish Apocalypse*

The *Flemish Apocalypse* is an illustrated Apocalypse produced around 1400. As the first extant illustrated Apocalypse book or manuscript from the Low Countries (the Netherlands, Belgium, and Luxembourg), it differs from the Anglo-Norman Apocalypse manuscripts in an important way. Rather than inserting the images into the text, the creator of this manuscript made the decision to devote an entire page to each of the twenty-two images (one for each chapter of Revelation). The text was set opposite the images in a format and a stylistic approach which foreshadows Dürer's printed Apocalypse books of 1498. Like many of its medieval predecessors, the Berengaudus commentary is also added, but there are only twenty-two illustrations in total. In comparison with earlier manuscripts, much more is included in each image, and the narrative of Revelation has necessarily had to be condensed and edited, giving a very 'busy' impression. It is now in the Bibliothèque Nationale in Paris.[51]

## The *Ghent Altarpiece*

Painted by Hubert and Jan van Eyck, and finished in 1432, the *Ghent Altarpiece* (also known as *The Lamb of God*) consists of twenty-four interior and exterior panels, made for a side chapel in St Bavo's Cathedral in Ghent. Taken as a whole, it is a visual unfolding of the entire history of salvation, from Adam and Eve in Genesis, through the Incarnation and Passion of Christ, and on to the promise of the New Jerusalem in Revelation. It is presided over by God in Heaven (flanked by the Virgin and John the Baptist), and includes Old Testament patriarchs, Christian martyrs, and saints, John the Baptist, the donors of the panels and the people and buildings of Ghent, and even pagan prophets. The Lamb, as both sacrifice and as the source of the Eucharist, is the central figure not just of the central panel, but of the whole altarpiece; geometrically and interpretatively everything in the altarpiece moves to or stems from Him.[52]

## Memling's *St John Altarpiece*

As already mentioned, Hans Memling's *St John Altarpiece* was commissioned for St John's Hospital (a hospice for the dying) in Bruges, where it may be seen to this day. Painted in 1474–9, it is a triptych, the central panel of which represents the mystic marriage of St Catherine and the left-hand panel the life and death of John the Baptist. Although there are interconnections between the panels, it is the right-hand one, the *Apocalypse Panel*, representing John of Patmos, which is of most relevance to us. As John sits on a rock, with book and pen in hand, to the left above him he sees God in the heavenly throne room, enclosed in an elliptical rainbow, while across the sea before him visions of the events from the first thirteen chapters of Revelation pass by simultaneously. Interestingly some of these, such as the handing over of power from the Dragon to the Sea Beast (Rev. 13.1–2) are so small that none of the inhabitants of the hospice could actually have seen them when in the chapel (nor indeed can casual visitors today), but Memling still painted them with exquisite skill. As far as is known, this depiction of Revelation is the earliest-known attempt to visualize the events of John's vision, or at least a good part of it, in one image. Over and above this, Memling's painting captures as well as any other work the visionary, even dreamlike, nature of Revelation.

## The *Apocalypse* series of Albrecht Dürer
## and Lucas Cranach

Dürer produced the German version of his *Die heimliche Offenbarung Johannis* in 1498 and the Latin *Apocalypsis cum Figuris* in 1511, two of the earliest and most successful examples of the new medium of woodcut prints.[53] Dürer was influenced by the eight Apocalypse images in the Koberger Bible woodcut series (from 1483, produced by his godfather Anton Koberger), but his own fifteen Apocalypse woodcuts are of an unparalleled force and majesty, and for many even today his Four Horsemen image is definitive. Dürer's possible depiction of the figure of John as himself and of an idealized Nuremberg as the New Jerusalem are notable, as is the contemporaneous sense of apocalyptic doom he conveys, with references to the 'threat from the East' also included. Although the fact that Dürer rendered the entirety of Revelation in just fifteen images (as opposed to the eighty or so preferred by the earlier manuscript artists of Revelation) may first and foremost have been an economic decision, Dürer's condensed narrative has both a synchronicity and an immediacy that earlier book versions of Revelation had lacked, often depicting the juxtaposition of heavenly and earthly realms in one image. He also issued a later series without a text, as if to insist that images could do the work on their own. In order to make it an economically viable proposition, Dürer's images have, in one way or another, influenced many or most subsequent illustrators of Revelation, right down to the present day, where some artists are consciously trying to escape his artistic legacy in order to see Revelation afresh.

Dürer was, broadly speaking, an orthodox Catholic. Rather different is the series of twenty-one Apocalypse woodcuts produced by Lucas Cranach in 1522 (heavily influenced by Dürer's series), which appeared in Luther's German translation of the New Testament. Cranach's series of twenty-one images expands upon the dramatic condensation of incidents and levels we find in Dürer's fifteen, in part because he was responding to Luther's insistence on adherence to the literal text of the Bible. Wary of Revelation as a text and the 'imaginative' and potentially non-Lutheran readings that it might give rise to, Luther thought that accompanying the text with a set of very literalistic interpretations would help to guide his readers towards a 'correct' interpretation of the text. No other New Testament text was illustrated in this way: Revelation was seen as a very special case. This concern with the literal did not, however, stretch to a ban on Cranach producing polemical images to accompany Revelation, as we shall see. For it was at this very time that Luther was engaged in the bitter dispute with Rome that would eventually lead to a schism within the church and the demarcation of the two main branches of Christianity, Catholicism and Protestantism. Thus, in other images in this series, the bestial characters of Revelation are depicted using symbols of the 'Catholic' church, such as the papal triple tiara (see especially Chapter 7 on the Whore of Babylon for more on this).[54]

## William Blake's Apocalypse images

William Blake (1757–1827), the English poet, artist, and visionary, was no orthodox Christian; indeed, he may not have been a Christian at all. However, he was clearly affected by the power of Revelation and its images. In watercolours and engravings produced from the 1790s until 1809, especially in the watercolours done for Thomas Butts between 1800 and 1805, we find the slaughtered Lamb (beneath rather than on the throne of God), the Dragon and Beasts, the Woman Clothed with the Sun, the Whore of Babylon, the binding of Satan, the fire of judgement as a necessary cleansing, the River of Crystal (for him the River of Life), and, of course, Jerusalem as the antithesis of Babylon (which for Blake equals London) and as the locus of a new birth. All these images and Blake's representations of them testified to his sense that with the subversion of the values and laws of the material world, the divine could be realized, both here on earth (partially) and in eternity (or was it that we could attain the eternal now?).[55]

## Max Beckmann

Max Beckmann (1884–1950) was a German artist, who served as a medical orderly in the First World War. He turned to apocalyptic themes and images, first to convey the dislocation and horror of war, and, after a breakdown in 1915, the sense that the world was about to end, for which he cursed God. After Hitler had denounced 'degenerate' (i.e. modern) art in 1937, Beckmann moved to Holland, where he lived until 1947. While there he turned to the mystical and consolatory aspects of religion in general and Revelation in particular, to paint, among other things, a memorable image of God wiping away all tears from the eyes of humankind, as part of a final series of lithographs of Revelation (see Figure 9.2).[56]

# 1

# The Angel of the Apocalypse

## John's Journey and his Angelic Guides

In the Introduction we stressed that John of Patmos is the medium through which Revelation is primarily transmitted and interpreted. John is given a greater degree of interpretative freedom than the recipients of apocalyptic visions in the Jewish tradition. Nevertheless, in line with that tradition, in Revelation angelic guides and actors are still prominent, a key feature even. And while, as will emerge in Chapter 4, some of these angels are cosmically destructive forces, others are an integral part of John's own prophetic and visionary journey, urging and guiding him on his way. Indeed, Revelation opens and closes with an angelic messenger being sent to John. In Rev. 1.1–2 we are told that Christ sends his angel 'to his servant John' so that John might testify about 'all that he saw', i.e. his vision, to the world. Prior to the coda in Rev. 22 where Christ himself addresses John directly, John attempts to worship the angel who has shown him the New Jerusalem and is sharply rebuked: 'You must not do that! I am a fellow servant with you … Worship God!'[1] The angels of Revelation could therefore be said to represent a frame for the narrative that takes place within.

Within this 'angelic frame' angels also appear at strategic points *throughout* John's visionary journey, either as guides to John, particularly in the later chapters (Rev. 17–22), as guardians of the prophetic message (see Rev. 10), or even, as in Rev. 5, as interrogators. While angelic guides were a key feature of apocalyptic literature, they tended to have more of a privileged interpretative role, such as in Daniel 7–12 where the angel Gabriel interprets all of Daniel's visions for him.[2] In Revelation, while the angels appear at key points throughout the text, the emphasis is on John seeing and understanding for himself (there is one exception in Rev. 17 where an angel interprets the vision of the Whore of Babylon for John). The angels produce the conditions in which John can respond to the call to personal transformation represented by the sequences of Seven Seals, Trumpets, Bowls and other visions. After the destruction unleashed by the sequence of Seven Trumpets in Rev. 8–9, in what is generally regarded as a significant point in the narrative, a mighty angel with a face like the sun and shrouded in clouds and a rainbow appears to John and gives him a prophetic scroll, symbolic of profound understanding, to eat. This marks the midway point between John's prophetic commission in Rev. 1, when he is told to write down everything that he sees but does not necessarily understand what he is seeing, and the end of his prophetic journey Rev. 22, which represents the high point of his visionary comprehension.[3]

Not surprisingly, both the destructive and the transformative angels of Revelation have captured the imagination of both medieval and Renaissance artists, as well as later artists such as Blake, Turner, and Cecil Collins. The mighty angel of Rev. 10 also forms the cornerstone of Messiaen's *Quartet for the End of Time*, as we will see in Chapter 10. This chapter will therefore explore a range of images inspired by the angelic guides of Revelation, focusing on their role in John's journey from fearful incomprehension to enlightenment.

What the visual examples selected for this chapter help to emphasize primarily is something we are inclined to overlook in a purely verbal or literary reading of Revelation. It is the way that John's vision is continually brought to him by angelic messengers; he does not just see: he sees what he is shown. These are visions and messages given to him from without, terrifying or consoling as the case may be. In a purely literary reading of the text we will be inclined to forget the messenger and the fact that it is a message, in favour of what is shown in the message. We are not allowed to overlook the element of something being given to someone from without, either in the Anglo-Norman manuscripts and subsequent medieval representations of Revelation or even, in different ways, in the later visions of Blake, Turner, and Cecil Collins, a point which perhaps reaches its apogee when in his woodcuts Dürer represents himself as the seer to whom the vision is entrusted. We, the viewers, are thus in the hands of the artist visionary!

## John's prophetic commission

We have chosen two contrasting representations of the defining moment in which John receives his prophetic commission. One is the very first of the seventy-eight images that the thirteenth-century *Lambeth Apocalypse* (here-after *Lambeth*) devotes to the text of Revelation. Our second image is the Flemish painter Hieronymous Bosch's *St John the Evangelist on Patmos* (c. 1500).

The first image in the *Lambeth* series (Plate 4), which takes up around one third of the page space, depicts John asleep on Patmos. Next to him flies the angel of Rev. 1.1 with a banner, which reads (in Latin), 'What thou *seest* write in a book and send to the seven churches who are in Asia.' While John's large size (particularly in relation to the angel) surely symbolizes his importance to the narrative, the symbolic importance of his closed eyes becomes clear only when contrasted with his alert expression in the final miniature of the series (Plate 5), in which he has an unmediated vision of Christ, a climactic moment which marks both the end of his journey and the high point of his prophetic understanding. Thus he moves from incom-prehension (closed eyes) to comprehension (open eyes) via his visionary journey, depicted for us, the viewer, via the seventy-eight miniatures. John's closed eyes in the main image can also be contrasted with the smaller image embedded in the left-hand column of text, where he is depicted sitting at a writing desk, receiving instruction from another angel. This acts as a visual reminder that, whilst baffled at the beginning of his vision, he did in fact obey the instruction to write down all that he had seen.[4]

Two centuries or more later, the Flemish artist Hieronymus Bosch's *St John the Evangelist on Patmos* from around 1500 is not part of a compre-hensive representation of Revelation in the way that *Lambeth* is (Plate 6). It is an evocation of the visionary experience itself rather than an attempt to depict the entire narrative of Revelation. Like the first *Lambeth* image, how-ever, it is striking for its strong focus on the seer. In a pose that is reminiscent of Memling's John in his *Apocalypse Panel* of 1474–9 (see Plate 3), Bosch's visionary sits on a rocky outcrop, pen poised, staring eagerly up at the sun inside which is seated the Woman Clothed with the Sun of Rev. 12. She is here being interpreted by Bosch as symbolic of the visionary experience itself, or as John's muse, just as Velázquez was to imagine her later, as we will see in Chapter 5.

It is as if we, the viewers, have caught John in the midst of his visionary experience. In between John and the Woman Clothed with the Sun stands an angel, presumably the angel of Rev. 1.1, painted using the grisaille tech-nique so that it resembles a Gothic statue. The placement of the angel in the middle of the image evokes its intermediary role in the narrative of Revelation. It has been sent down from Heaven to deliver this important vision to John. The rendering of the angel in grisaille next to a very lifelike John creates a curious visual effect, although those who are familiar with Bosch will have come to expect all manner of curiosities in his works (and even in this—for Bosch—unusually calm little painting, there is a malicious little imp in the right-hand corner and some hardly visible ships burning in the sea behind John). In interpretative terms, the grisaille angel seems to shift responsibility for the vision onto the very human, naturalistically conceived figure of John. Its statue-like, almost generic, presence suggests that its role is limited, whereas John in all his imperfect humanity has been tasked both with comprehending and interpreting, and then successfully delivering the messages of Revelation to the seven churches of Asia.[5]

## The vision of the heavenly throne room

Having been commissioned by the angel in Rev. 1.1, John receives a vision of Christ ('one like the Son of Man') in Rev. 1.9–20. The report of the vision is then interrupted by the addition of John's letters to the seven churches in Asia in Rev. 2–3. It is not until Rev. 4 that we encounter the angel of the throne room calling John up through an open door in Heaven, saying, 'Come up here, and I will show you what must happen after this' (Rev. 4.1). This dramatic moment has been visualized in many ways. One of the most interesting is an image found in the *Flemish Apocalypse* (Figure 1.1). Although most of the images in this manuscript are quite 'busy' and visualize a large amount of text, this is not the case in this depiction of the heavenly throne room of Rev. 4. Here a large angel dominates the central foreground of the image, arms upstretched towards the throne room, inside which sits God on the throne surrounded by his 'four living creatures' of Rev. 4.6–8. Around the throne room, against a deep blue background, are arranged the Twenty-four Elders, identifiable only by their gold crowns and instruments.

As we are told in the text, the divine throne has before it a sea of glass like crystal, which was taken by medieval preachers to refer to baptism, for, as they believed, just as crystal is hardened water, so baptism transmutes unstable men into firm Christians.[6] No doubt here, as elsewhere, what the preachers told their largely illiterate congregations the people would see in the images set before them, something we should bear in mind when looking at medieval representations of biblical themes. To the left of this central

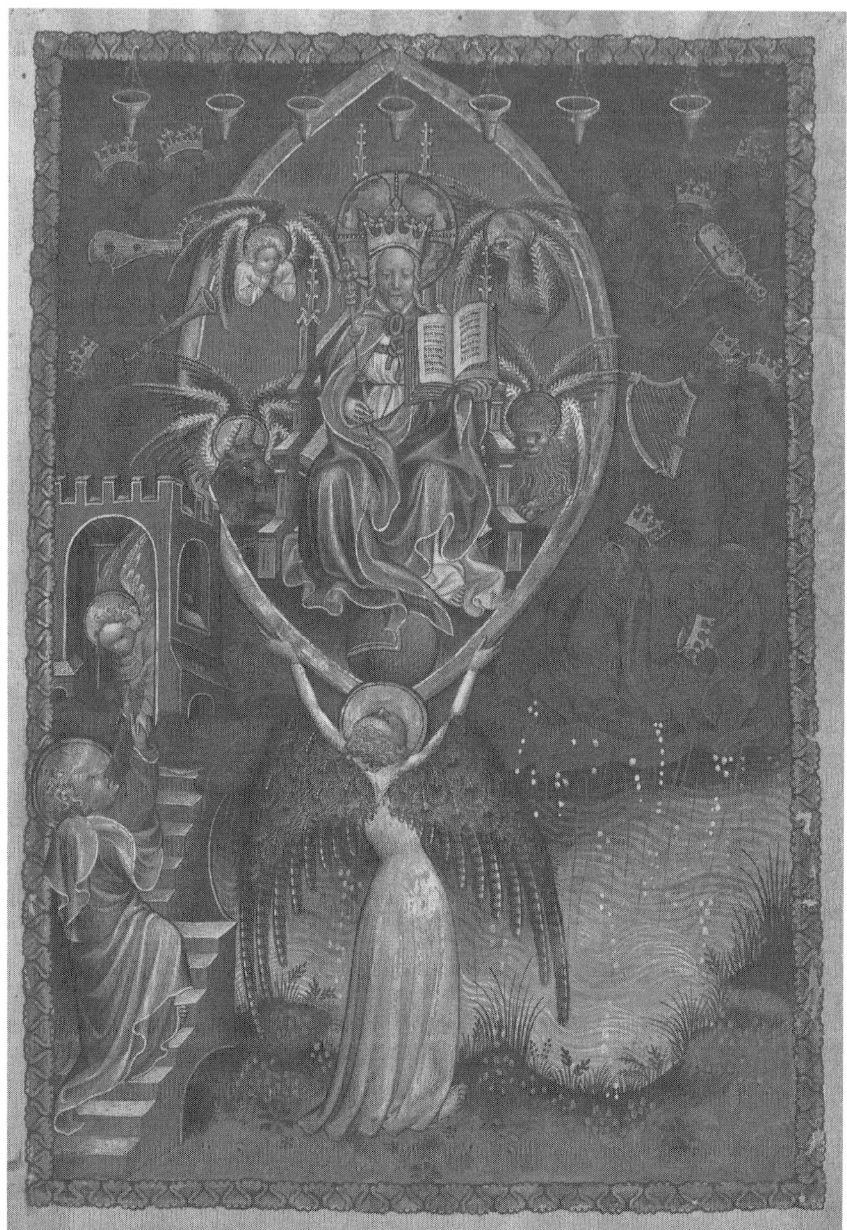

**Figure 1.1.** The *Flemish Apocalypse*, *c.*1400, The Angel of the Throne Room
Calling John (Rev. 4), Paris: Bibliothèque Nationale. © BnF

scene, John is being helped/pulled up some stairs by another, smaller angel into the 'door in Heaven'. The central angel physically and symbolically dominates the image, in part due to its bright white robe and impressive wingspan but mostly because its expressive stance creates the impression that it has just conjured the throne room out of thin air amidst a quite ordinary earthly setting, suggested here by the grass and vegetation at the foreground of the image. In contrast to Bosch's static angel, this angel has been given a privileged and powerful position by the Flemish artist, who has relegated John to the periphery.[7]

Once John has viewed the heavenly throne room and seen the eternal worship of God, he is asked a searching question by a 'mighty angel' (who could be the same 'mighty angel' of Rev. 10 (see section 'The mighty angel (Rev. 10)'). Referring to a scroll in God's right hand, the angel says, 'Who is worthy to break the seals and open the scroll?' (Rev. 5.2). Having seen the throne room in all its eternal glory, John realizes that there is no one worthy (equal to God) to open the scroll and starts to 'weep bitterly'. At that moment, one of the Elders announces the conquering 'Lion of Judah' as the one worthy to open the scroll, but it is in fact a Lamb and not a lion that appears in the centre of the divine throne and performs the office. This theological paradox and its related visualizations are discussed in Chapter 2. What is fascinating in terms of the visualization of Revelation's angels (and indeed John himself), however, are depictions of John's tears in front of the angel of the throne room of Rev. 5. A particularly striking example of this is found in The *Angers Apocalypse Tapestry* (*c.*1373–80, Plate 7) (hereafter to be referred to as *Angers*). Here we see the angel with the scroll on the left-hand side of the image, almost thrusting the scroll at John, the central figure, who cradles his head in his right arm, whilst being led away by one of the Twenty-four Elders. It is both an artistically attractive composition, in its visual balance and sense of movement, and one of the few times that John's emotions are so openly pictorialized. The psychological burden of the visionary's mission is never more apparent than in this image.


## The mighty angel (Rev. 10)

After the drama of the two sequences of Seven Seals and Trumpets, which follow the throne room scene of Rev. 4–5, the narrative is paused by the appearance of 'another mighty angel' coming down from Heaven to give

John further instruction. In an echo of Ezekiel 2–3, John is instructed by a voice from the sky to take and eat a little scroll from this strange-looking angel (with a face like the sun, legs like pillars of fire, and a rainbow around his head). The scroll is initially as 'sweet as honey' but then turns sour in John's stomach. After this John is ordered to proclaim God's message 'about many nations, races, languages and kings'. Theologically this chapter is very significant as it marks John's transition from passive observer to active participant in the visions as well as commissioned prophet.[8] The mighty angel is clearly a key part of this transitional chapter and accordingly has been much illustrated.

*Angers* devotes two images to this sequence. In the first image the angel appears to John, who is writing (his visions, we presume) into a book. The angel holds the prophetic scroll (depicted here as a book) in his left hand. The second image (Plate 8) depicts two different stages in the participatory process, both the taking of the scroll by John and the eating of it, communicated to the viewer by the presence of two books, one in John's hand and the other being held to his mouth. Another angel supports John as he eats the book, a powerful visual reminder of both the urgency of the activity and the anticipated bitterness of the scroll. The repeated presence of the book/scroll also provides a visual link with the scroll of Rev. 5, which only the Lamb was able to open. In this way John's privileged position as seer and prophet is visually emphasized by the *Angers* artist.

As with the *Flemish Apocalypse*, Dürer's abbreviated representation of the text, in his case into a mere fifteen images, meant that sections had to be condensed, depicted synchronically, or got rid of altogether. What has been included or left out gives us important clues as to Dürer's interpretative emphases. The fact that he chose to devote a whole image to the 'mighty angel' sequence (of Rev. 10) is significant (Figure 1.2). Dürer's predilection for depicting religious figures in his own likeness is well documented and there is persuasive evidence to suggest that he has also done so in this series.[9] Thus the John/Dürer figure is depicted in the right-hand corner of the image, writing materials strewn around him, devouring the book or scroll, leaving the viewer in no doubt of the theological significance of this prophetic turning point. While this part of the image is full of naturalistic movement and urgency, the mighty angel himself has been rather literalistically and awkwardly depicted, exposing the difficulties involved with depicting some parts of Revelation. For how can one feasibly depict a figure who is described as having legs like pillars of fire, straddling the land and the sea, and with a face like the sun? It will

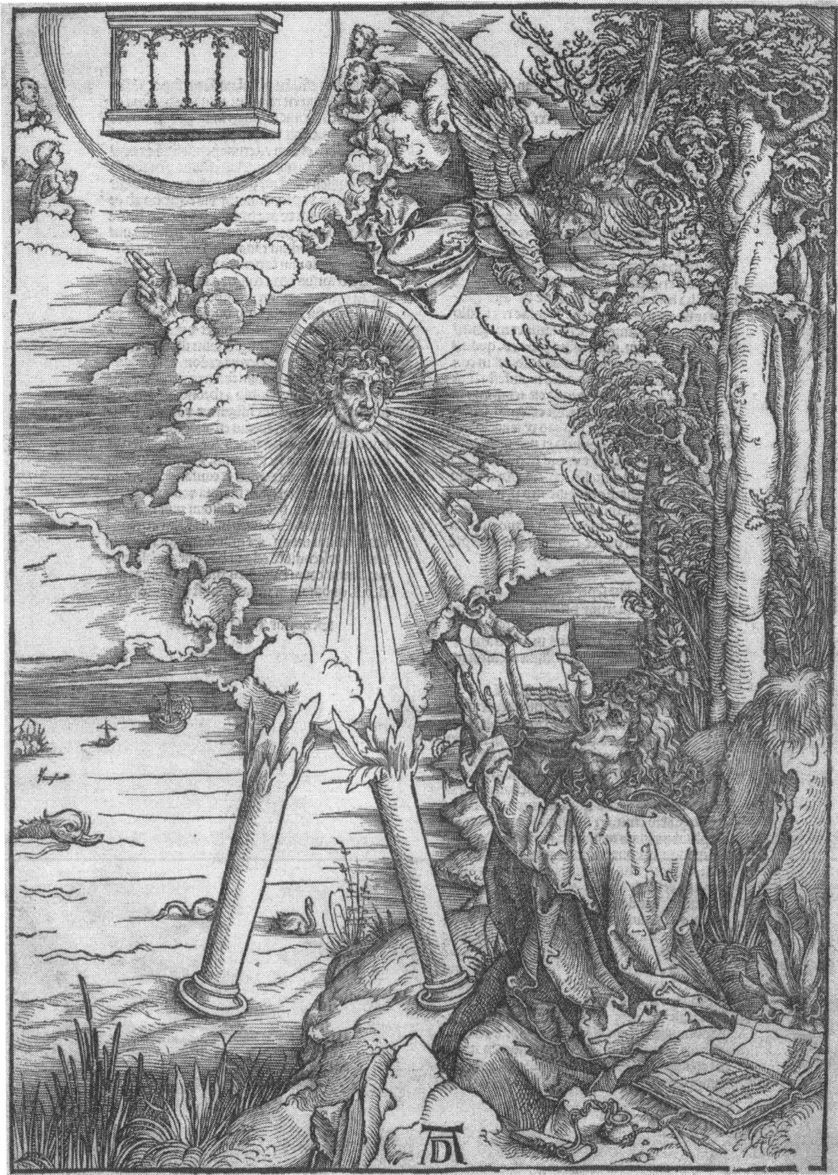

**Figure 1.2.** Albrecht Dürer, *Apocalypse* Series, *c.*1498, John and the Mighty Angel (Rev. 10), London: British Museum. © The Trustees of the British Museum

always look faintly ridiculous, even in the hands of an artistic genius such as Dürer. This raises a wider question regarding the limitations of using language to describe a vision and then of using that same text to revisualize the vision in a literalistic way.[10]

There are some theologians, however, who go further than this and argue that Revelation should not be visualized at all on account of the fact that it is a 'literary vision' rather than an actual vision report. Thus Schüssler-Fiorenza argues that 'it is impossible to picture or draw this vision, for its images and symbols function more like words and sentences in a composition'.[11] While we have argued above, and against Schüssler-Fiorenza, in favour of the hypothesis that Revelation is in its most important aspects a vision report (whether that vision was divinely inspired or not), this Dürer image is perhaps an example of how images of Revelation that are more metaphorical in tone are more successful than those which stick rigidly to the letter of the text.

The twentieth-century visionary artist Cecil Collins was also inspired by the mighty angel from Revelation 10. His *Angel of the Apocalypse* (1969, Plate 9) intimates a sense of stability against a background of chaos. Unusually for this most lyrical and gentle of artists, there is a feeling of force and of implacable determination here. The angel appears to be to be striding through a darkly livid firescape—maybe a memory of the horrific bombing raids on Plymouth in 1941, which Collins had witnessed. Unlike most of Collins' visionary angels, who are infused with a calmly sublime peace and purity, this one's fiery demeanour, jagged wings, and discordant colour remind us of the struggle the apocalyptic angel had or has to announce the start of God's rule on a fallen world.[12]

The mighty angel of Rev. 10 is also the occasion of another significant theme arising from Revelation. At Rev. 10.6 he says to John, before he is told to eat the book, 'there will be no more delay' in the things which are about to be prophesied (God's mysterious plan), which creates an urgency regarding the need for immediate repentance (especially in light of the following chapter, Rev. 11, which is focused entirely on the need to obey the two Witnesses' command to repent). At least, that is what many translations have the mighty angel say. However, in the authorized version of the Bible and elsewhere, what he says is 'there should be time no longer', and this has been taken by some early commentators to indicate that time itself is coming to an end. This no doubt has profound implications, suggesting that what is about to come is a transition to a state beyond time, which would, of course, count strongly against interpretations seeing the Last Judgement and the New Jerusalem in this-worldly terms, as things which might be realizable in time, in the world as it is. As we will see in Chapter 10 it is in this mystical, atemporal sense that Olivier Messiaen interprets Rev. 10.6 in his *Quartet for the End of Time*, but, profound as such an interpretation no doubt is, it may not be justified by the text.

# Warrior angels

Following the dramatic appearance of the mighty angel in Rev. 10, the only named angel in the text appears shortly afterwards, in Rev.12. This is of course the angel Michael, who defeats the Dragon (Satan) and his angels in order to protect the Woman Clothed with the Sun and her child. Although Chapter 5 is devoted to this mysterious female figure, it seems pertinent to include the Dürer image of this episode between Michael and the Dragon here (Figure 1.3). What is striking about this image, apart from its artistic majesty, is that it is the only image in the whole Dürer series in which there is any conflict depicted in Heaven. In the other fourteen images, the turmoil takes place on earth, beneath the heavenly realm, which is protected by billowing clouds and stern-looking angels. Here however, the earthly realm, reminiscent of fifteenth-century Nuremberg, is calm, light and oblivious to the dark and stormy battle raging above, which is focused on large figures of Michael and the Dragon/Satan. This image, in contrast to most of the other images in the Dürer series, seems to raise complex questions about God's omnipotence and his ability successfully to control the malign forces that exist on Heaven and earth. It is impossible to know if this was Dürer's intent and it is unlikely that the first viewers of his Apocalypse woodcuts would have interpreted the image in this more philosophical way. Unlike us, they are unlikely to have seen a theological problem in the idea of a battle between good and evil within a theological system that holds God to be omnipotent. Indeed, at this time, Satan himself was believed to be a fallen angel.

While there are many other angels who appear in the following chapters, they are largely associated with the opening of the Seven Bowls (Rev. 16) and with bringing further messages and guidance to John (see especially Rev. 14 and 17). This moment in Rev. 12 with Michael and his angels prepares the way, therefore, for what we might call the 'warrior angels' of Rev. 18–19 who are involved in the final battle between Satan and his armies. One of these angels is what has come to be known as the 'angel in the sun' of Rev. 19.17. He appears in the middle of the battle between the Rider on

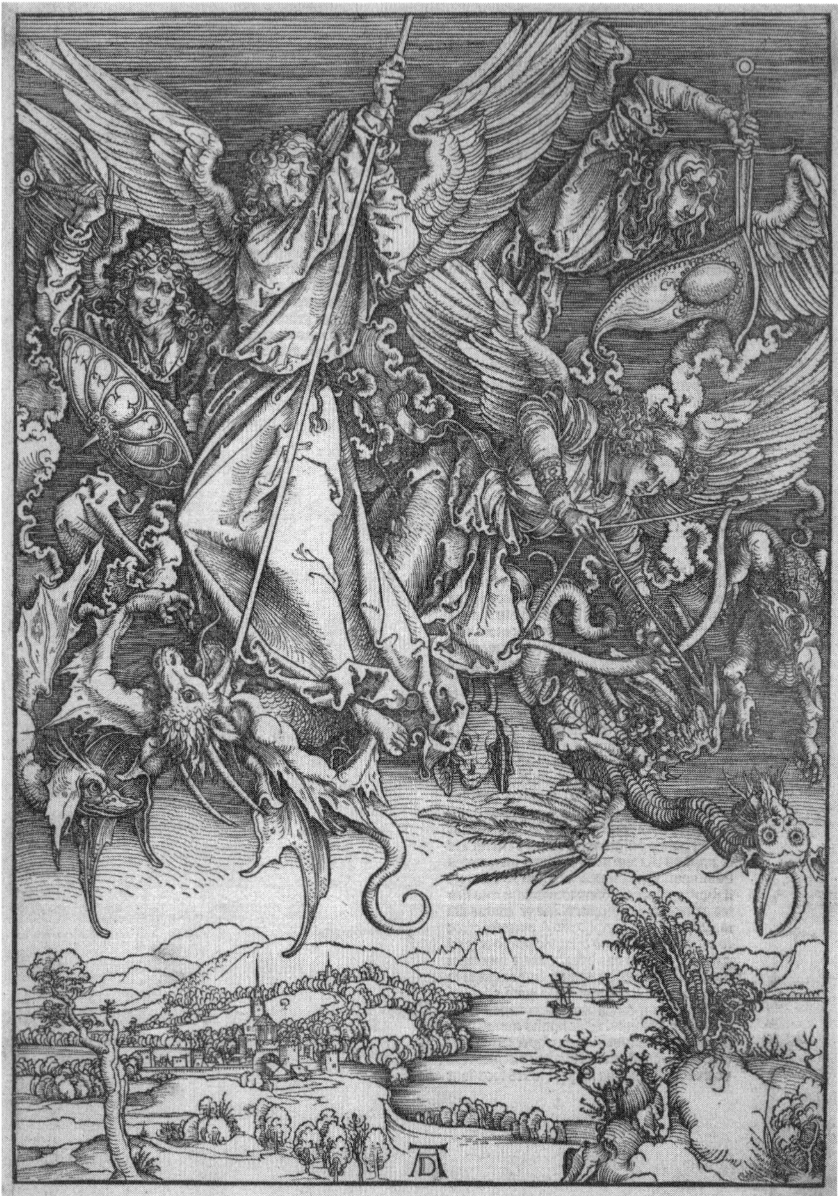

**Figure 1.3.** Albrecht Dürer, *Apocalypse* Series, c.1498, St Michael and the Dragon (Rev. 12), London: British Museum. © The Trustees of the British Museum

the White Horse (Christ) and Satan's armies, calling upon the 'birds that fly in mid- Heaven' to come and feast on the carcasses of the defeated armies of Satan (which includes human kings, generals, and soldiers). Significantly, like the Woman Clothed *with* the Sun and the mighty angel of Rev. 10, who has a face '*like* the sun', this angel stands *in* the sun. This scene was memorably evoked by Turner in his *Angel Standing in the Sun* of 1846 (Plate 10). Here Turner seems to have conflated the angel of Rev. 19.17 with the angel Michael from Rev. 12, as the angelic figure is here depicted with Michael's sword of judgement. Above him circle the birds he has summoned, ready to feast. Below him are scenes from the Old Testament featuring murder and betrayal. On the left Adam and Eve weep over the body of Abel, while on the right Judith stands over the headless body of Holofernes.[13]

The overall impression is one of despair at the state of humanity. While in Revelation itself this moment can either be viewed as the moment at which the faithful are vindicated and the unfaithful punished, or as a necessary but grim precursor to the establishment of the New Jerusalem, the Turner image stands alone, a snapshot of one of the bleakest moments in Revelation.

## Angels in the New Jerusalem

The New Jerusalem and its attendant visual interpretations will be explored in Chapter 9. However, in terms of the angelic presence at the end of John's journey, it is interesting to note how, in the medieval interpretations in particular, they fade away as John reaches the paradisal apex of his vision. While there is a striking angel in the penultimate image from *Angers* at whose feet John kneels (Figure 1.4), by the final images in all these series John is depicted as being alone in the presence of Christ. Thus in the final image from *Lambeth*, John kneels at the foot of Christ's throne, hands outstretched towards him, against a gold background, another signifier of the great theological importance of this closing scene, as gold plating was very expensive (Plate 5). Having reached enlightenment via his visionary experience and been commissioned as a prophet, it is as if John no longer needs the support, guidance, and explanation of the angels who have been the mainstays of his extraordinary visions, but, as we have already mentioned above, can now see Christ face to face, with open eyes. Angels and closed eyes are therefore absent from the final image.

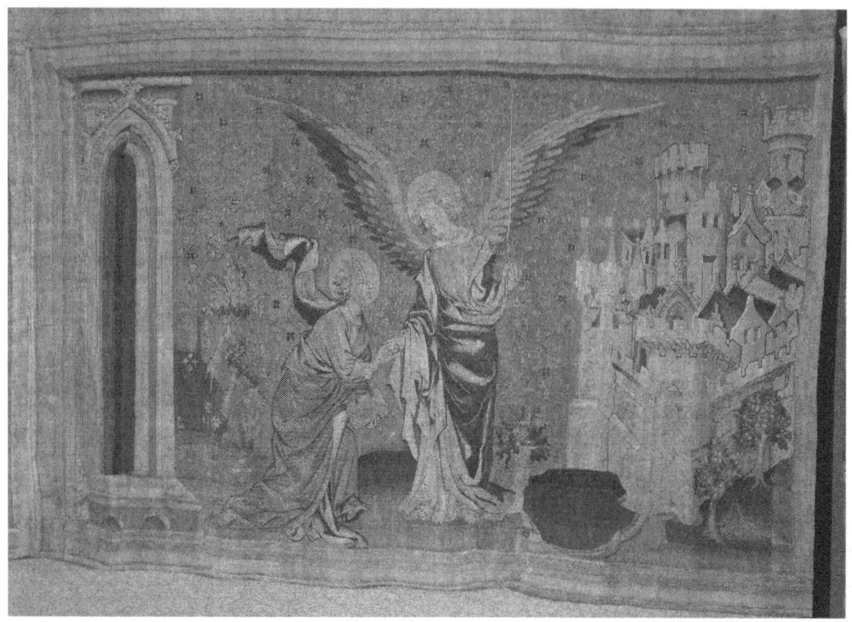

**Figure 1.4.** The *Angers Apocalypse Tapestry*, *c.*1373–80, John Kneeling before the Angel (Rev. 22), Maine et Loire: Chateau d'Angers. © Centre Des Monuments Nationaux

# Conclusion

In interpretative terms, the angels of Revelation serve many functions: bearers of divine messages and commissions, guides, bringers of woes, agents in the cosmic war between good and evil. It is, however, quite easy to overlook the extent and significance of their role. One tends to almost pass over them in one's reading or viewing in favour of exploration of the more colourful characters such as the Four Horsemen or the Whore of Babylon, not to mention the changing faces of Christ himself (Lamb, 'one like a son of man', Rider on the White Horse etc.). Visually, however, even if one is predominantly focusing on other 'characters' in the pictorial narrative, one cannot ignore the presence of the many angels that grace nearly all visualizations of the text (at least up until around the seventeenth century). Their celestial presence serves as a visual reminder both of John's dependence on his guides and, perhaps more interestingly in theological terms, of the role that God's messengers play in the cosmic drama, in both positive and negative ways.

It is these recurrent angelic presences, above all, which, in contrast to the purely verbal, our visual interpretations underline.

It may be thought that for the non-believer the angelic presences and epiphanies are the most alien aspect of Revelation. On a purely literal level this is no doubt true: we can, for example, appreciate the weight and dread of Turner's apocalyptic vision without reading his angel as real. However, simply to dismiss Revelation's angelic presence would be too quick a response. What the angels point to is the sense that we human beings are in a world neither controlled by us nor, more fundamentally, constructed by us, even in terms of the values we recognize. Many, if not most of us, find it hard to accept that our values, our sense of right and wrong, our feelings of obligation and conscience, are simply willed by us, either individually or collectively. We have a strong intuition that these things are there, and binding on us, whether we accept them or not, and in a way what the angels are doing is most forcibly reminding us of where our (or John's) duties lie. Many too have a sense—like Turner, perhaps, and like the atheist philosopher Heidegger—that there are situations in which it is the case that (in Heidegger's words) 'only a God can save us', setting the scene for an angelic vision, or at least clearing the way for one. We could thus see the angels of Revelation not so much as simply throwbacks to ancient Jewish mythology (though they are that), but rather as dramatic manifestations of deep human yearnings which transcend their mythological representations. Whether these yearnings are well founded or not, we need to recognize their power and their persistence, and in that sense the angels of Revelation still have something to say to us.

2

# The Lamb

Then one of the elders said to me, 'Do not weep. See the Lion of the tribe of Judah, the Root of David, has conquered, so that he can open the scroll and its seven seals.' Then I saw between the throne and the four living creatures and among the elders a Lamb standing as if it had been slaughtered, having seven horns and seven eyes, which are the seven spirits of God sent out into all the earth. (Rev. 5.5–6)

After John's account of his prophetic mission and his letters to the churches, his visions proper begin, as we have seen, with God presiding over the heavenly throne room, surrounded by worshippers. Into this scene of divine majesty Christ is introduced, as Lamb. Some recent commentators, due to the fact that there is little direct overlap with the Gospels or Paul's letters, have argued that Revelation should be seen as consisting of visions derived from Jewish messianism, which had been appropriated by Christians for their own purposes. However, this is completely to overlook the pivotal role of the Lamb in Revelation, who embodies the humility, suffering, and self-sacrifice of Christ, whilst at the same time being inextricably linked with God the Father. Christ as Lamb is in many ways, therefore, the doctrinal centre of Revelation, as we will now attempt to show. Of necessity this chapter will be a little weightier theologically than those that follow, which will rely on the scaffolding we erect here.

## The Lamb in Revelation

Many people will initially link the Lamb not with Revelation but with John's Gospel. The first time Jesus enters John's Gospel (setting the Prologue aside) is in verse 1.29 when John the Baptist sees Jesus and proclaims, 'Here is the

Lamb of God, who takes away the sin of the world.' This verse has given rise to countless images of John bearing witness to Jesus as the Lamb. Indeed, the Lamb became John the Baptist's 'symbol' or signifier in images from the medieval period onwards, a male figure with a Lamb being instantly recognizable as John the Baptist.[1] However, the epithet 'Lamb', referring to Christ, also appears twenty-eight times in Revelation and is therefore the most common way of referring to Jesus in this text (as opposed to the Gospels and Paul, where Jesus is normally referred to by a variety of different titles including, Christ, Son of God, Son of Man, Son of David, etc.). Accordingly, there have been many visual and cultural depictions of this Lamb; but what is the significance of this term, what are its connotations, and why is this title used for Jesus, instead of the other, better known titles?

Revelation has a very 'theocentric' theology.[2] Everything begins and ends with God. Accordingly, in marked contrast to the Synoptic Gospels, John's concept of God seems to include not just God the Father but also Christ, God the Son. Thus they both use the same phrases to describe themselves. In Rev. 21.6 God (the Father) says, 'I am the Alpha and the Omega, the beginning and the end.' A little later, in Rev. 22.13, Christ says, 'I am the Alpha and the Omega, the first and the last, the beginning and the end.' Additionally, this is very similar language to that used to describe God at the beginning of Revelation (Rev. 1.8). This very 'high' theology is emphasized in the throne room scene of Rev. 4–5, where John is let through a door into Heaven (beautifully conceptualized by Albrecht Dürer; see Figure 2.1) by an angel and as a result is able to witness what the contemporary theologian Richard Bauckham refers to as 'the sphere of ultimate reality'.[3] As this scene unfolds throughout Rev. 4–5, unusually for this early point in Christianity, God the Father and God the Son are presented as equals in terms of power. The ways in which they manifest this power in the world is, however, very different, and this is what makes them distinct, with the Father being the source of ultimate power, while the Son is He who is the suffering redeemer, sacrificed on behalf of us all.

Visits to the heavenly throne room were an important part of Jewish and Christian apocalyptic literature in the first century CE, in such texts as 1 Enoch and the Apocalypse of Abraham. In Rev. 4 John sees God the Father (described not anthropomorphically, but as a collection of rare jewels spewing forth thunder and lightning) seated on a throne that is itself enclosed in a rainbow (a reminder of God's renewed covenant with the Jewish people after the great Flood of Genesis 9, which is sealed with a rainbow). Arranged

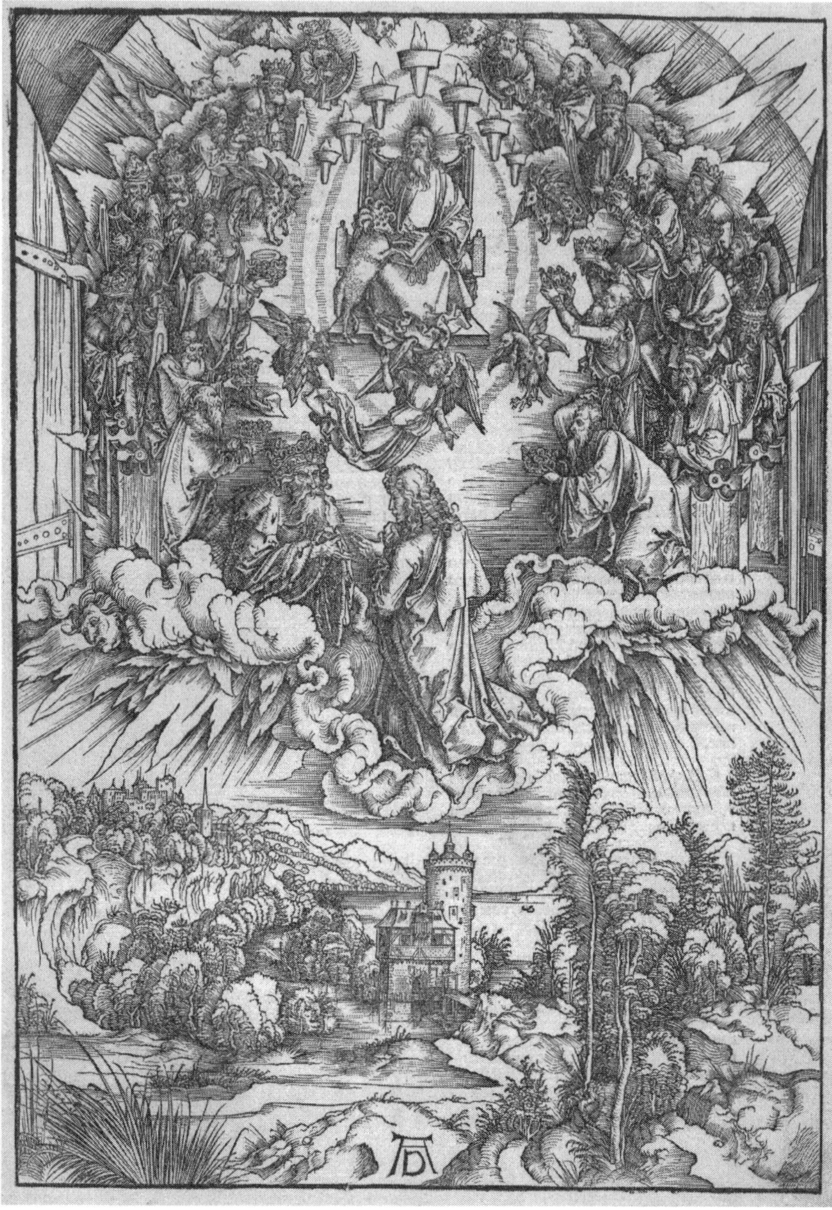

**Figure 2.1.** Albrecht Dürer, *Apocalypse* Series, *c.*1498, The Heavenly Throne Room (Rev. 4–5), London: British Museum. © The Trustees of the British Museum

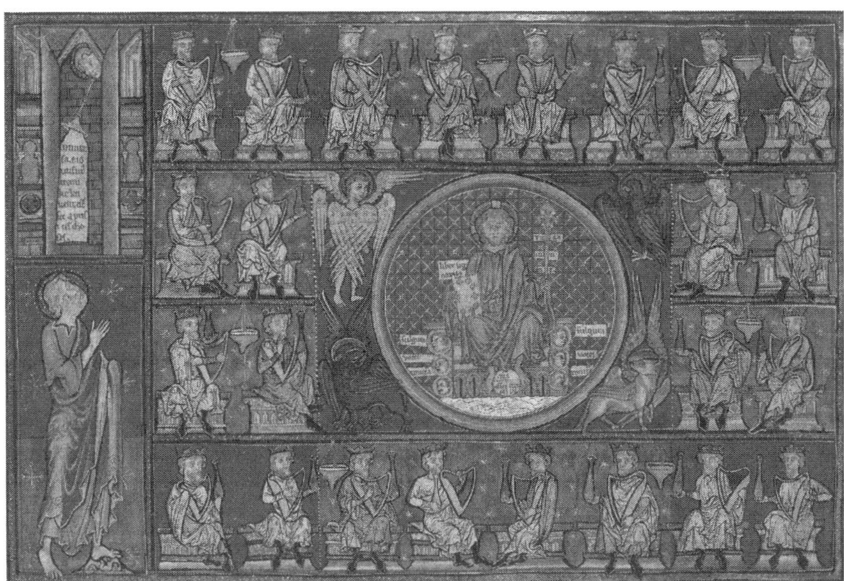

**Figure 2.2.** The *Trinity Apocalypse*, *c.* 1260, The Twenty-four Elders in the Heavenly Throne Room (Rev. 4), Cambridge: Trinity College. © The Master and Fellows of Trinity College, Cambridge

around God are the Twenty-four Elders and Four Living Creatures, who resemble a lion, ox, man, and eagle respectively, who are engaged in constant worship and glorification of him, the creator and sustainer of the world. The implication is that this is how 'things *should* be'. (See Figure 2.2 for an example of this scene from the *Trinity Apocalypse.*) But how does this 'ultimate', seemingly immutable picture of the heavenly throne room relate to the unpredictable, sometimes disappointing, very human world described in Rev. 2–3 in the letters of advice to the seven churches of Asia? The answer is of course through the Lamb, the mediator between God and man, who appears to John in Rev. 5.

In Rev. 5.4 John becomes worried and upset because there is seemingly no one on Heaven or earth who is worthy of opening the scroll held by God, which seems to carry a great significance (see Plate 7). One of the Elders tells him not to weep but rather to expect the 'Lion of the tribe of Judah, the Root of David', who is coming and will be able to open the scroll because he has 'conquered', though what he has conquered is not made clear. The twenty-first-century reader may, quite understandably, require some clarification at this point. The angel is referring to the hope that the first-century Jewish population in Israel and in the diaspora had in the coming of a triumphant Messiah figure, in the mould of the great Jewish king, King David, who would free them from the tyranny of Roman oppression. The Jewish texts that are available to us from this time (such as 1 Enoch and 4 Ezra) suggest that this figure would be a warrior or a king who would physically conquer the Romans, who at this time were occupying Israel, and restore Israel to former glories. In the Psalms, too, we get continual visions of God and Israel overcoming their enemies, very much on this earth. Thus Psalm 110, for example, looks forward to Zion reigning in the midst of foes, to heads being shattered over the earth and God making Israel's enemies his footstool. However, in contrast to what this so-called holy war tradition might have predicted, what the Jews actually received, according to the authors of the New Testament, was Jesus, a humble preacher who allowed the Romans to crucify him for a crime that he didn't commit (claiming to be the King of the Jews and thus inciting insurrection). This 'Christ story', as we might refer to it, which challenged traditional Jewish ideas of what a Messiah figure might be or might look like, is presented in Revelation's typically symbolic terms in Rev. 5.

Instead of seeing the mighty Lion that the angel has told him to expect, John sees instead a slain Lamb (Rev. 5.6). This Lamb, despite his humble, sacrificial appearance, is able to take and open the important scroll held by God. We are given an intimation of his special power through the description of him having seven horns and seven eyes, seven being a perfect number in Jewish thinking.[4] But more than that, he also becomes the recipient of the same worship that God had received in Rev. 4 from the Elders and the Four Living Creatures (Rev. 5.8: 'When he had taken the scroll, the four living creatures and the twenty-four elders fell before the Lamb'). In this way, the idea of the 'traditional' Jewish Messiah figure is overturned and replaced with a symbol of humility and sacrifice, for the fact that the Lamb has been slain refers to the crucifixion. Through the image of the slaughtered Lamb, who is to be worshipped for all eternity in this incarnation as an injured sacrificial animal, Revelation overturns the first-century world's own self-image, in which Roman might and power and Babylonian luxury predominate. Henceforth it will be the Lamb who 'inherits'—though, as we have already suggested, there may, for some at least, be some ambiguity as to whether the Lamb's inheritance is on this earth (as an earthly Messiah) or, as Revelation actually seems to suggest, in a new Heaven and a new earth, after the end of time (Rev. 21).

But how does this amount to the 'conquest' ascribed to the one worthy of opening the scroll? Quite simply, this Lamb (Christ) has conquered through suffering and by suffering. By placing this scene at the heart of the heavenly throne room of Rev. 4–5, John, the author of Revelation, makes it clear that this sanctification of suffering is very much part of the overall divine plan for the world, and perhaps even the way in which 'God the Father' relates to his people. This is not to suggest that the 'paradox' of Christianity, the idea of salvation through sacrifice, is a simple concept.

We are so used to the notion of the Lamb, the *Agnus Dei* of the Catholic liturgy and musical masses, as sacrificial victim that we forget to ask ourselves just what might be meant by sacrifice. How can it be that by killing a person or an animal a community achieves some form of expiation or exoneration? Are we talking here about a scapegoat, either an outsider or one who becomes an outsider by being pushed out, whose suffering somehow carries away the sins of the community and in so doing reunites the community? Is it, as the contemporary French thinker René Girard and his followers have suggested, that human communities were originally formed and sustained by rituals of this sort, and that communities actually depend for their existence on identifying themselves in distinction to the 'others' they cast out?[5]

In Revelation the Lamb is certainly a scapegoat, in whose death the Christian community is united (see the letters to the Christian communities in Rev. 2–3), and who takes on his own back the sins of the world. But far from being an outsider, unwillingly led to slaughter, he is the Creator of the community, intimately identified with the 'one who sits on the throne', or God. Moreover this divine victim, unlike traditional scapegoats, voluntarily undergoes sacrifice in order to heal the rift which has opened up between God and man by virtue of Adam's sin (and by the sinfulness of all humanity more generally). In doing this, he also reveals to us God's own participation in the suffering of the world.

But, as is implicit throughout Revelation, in creating Adam and free human beings, it is God himself who has opened up the possibility of all the ensuing sin and suffering. His love for humanity could only be proven if He himself—as Lamb—were to enter into the suffering of the world, deflecting the sin on to His shoulders by undergoing a voluntary death on humanity's behalf. So, in this sacrifice, the executioner is also the victim. God is both the redeemer and the one to whom redemption is offered; and the rift which is healed is one which God, as Alpha and Omega, has allowed to come about—for the good of humanity, and which He, as Lamb, heals—also on behalf of humanity.

Nor should we underestimate the revolutionary nature of the notion of the divine Lamb undergoing sacrifice voluntarily. If the Girardian speculation about scapegoating has any substance to it, then all the human communities of which we are aware originated in violence and depend on violence for their preservation. Historically this primeval violence inherent in the marking off of human communities and territories one from another seems undeniable; and it remains the case that all the human communities of which we are aware continue to define themselves by reference to those who are outside them, and also use state violence internally to maintain peace and order. Yet here is a religious vision where the outsider not only willingly accepts the violence wreaked upon him, but is revealed as divine, as Alpha and Omega. And his message is one which aims to rub out and transcend the divisions and violence on which human community as we know it depends. It is hard to imagine a more thorough subversion of worldly wisdom, or a more thorough rejection of the sort of traditional messianism in which God's people, defined in distinction to the rest of humankind, will be led to an earthly success and earthly conquest by defeating their enemies in battle.

In the view of some theologians the very close relationship between God ('the one who is seated on the throne') and the Lamb actually evolves into an identity between the two.[6] Whether this is so or not, this relationship and the willing and salvific sacrifice made by the Lamb should be kept in mind as the backdrop to the events that unfold in the rest of the text, which will certainly help to temper some of the surprising triumphalism of the rest of Revelation. For the ultimate purpose of the Lamb (or Christ) is to overturn the kingdoms of the world (exemplified for John in the Roman empire, with its brutality and power worship) and to establish God's kingdom, otherwise known as the New Jerusalem (Rev. 11.15 and 21.2). This is to be achieved not through combat but through humility, passive resistance, and through bearing witness to the truth and universality of the Christian message. As we have already suggested, it is not to be achieved on the earth as we currently know it, as some sort of earthly utopia. The members of the seven churches addressed by John are being enjoined to prepare themselves and their communities for an altogether new form of existence, for a form of existence which will be realized only after the current earth and Heaven have passed away.

Thus in Rev. 6.9 (the opening of the Fifth Seal, which happens after the heavenly throne room scene) we are given a glimpse of the 'souls of those who have been slaughtered for the Word of God' sheltering under an altar until the Last Judgement and establishment of the New Jerusalem. This is further echoed in Rev. 7 and 14, where those who have remained faithful to the Gospel and who have been martyred in its name are celebrated as they assemble to worship the Lamb. These scenes are brilliantly captured by the Van Eycks in the central panel of the *Ghent Altarpiece* (Figure 2.3).[7]

But it is not just that the faithful members of the church *worship* the Lamb. After the destruction of the Whore of Babylon, and by contrast with her impurity and licentiousness, the Lamb himself comes to marry Israel (Rev. 19.7–9). Israel would be understood by John's early readers to refer here to the church, now joined in chaste spiritual union with Lamb. Further, the wedding banquet to which they are invited in Rev. 19 is, of course, the Eucharist, in which the Christ's sacrifice is commemorated and re-enacted. This link is made explicit in some medieval art, for example in a carving in the north porch of Chartres cathedral, where the figure of Faith is receiving a Eucharistic chalice shown being filled with the blood of a bleeding Lamb, slain on an altar. As the Eucharist is re-enacted daily and throughout the Christian world, this is a way of pointing to the timelessness

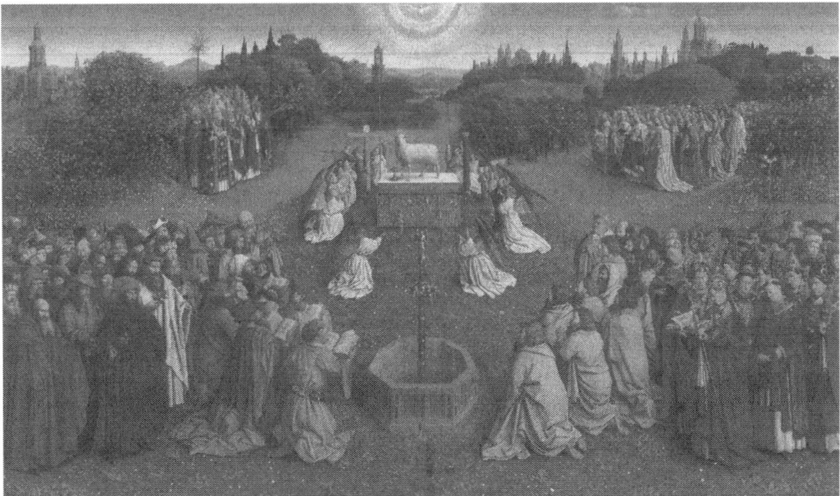

**Figure 2.3.** The Van Eycks, central panel from the *Ghent Altarpiece*, 1432, Ghent: St Bavo's Cathedral. © Bridgeman Art Library

of the Lamb's sacrifice. It also illustrates the way in which the medievals tended to see beyond appearance to eternal truths.

However, it could not be denied that alongside passive resistance and reconciling sacrifice, judgement is also very much present as a theme in Revelation. It is interesting to note that most of this judgement issues directly and unashamedly from Heaven. Yes, followers of Christ are expected to join in the last great battle (Rev. 19–20), but on the whole the destruction that pervades the book is Heaven sent, which is a fact that, although very much in keeping with the apocalyptic world view, raises complex questions about the goodness of God. Neither is Christ-as-Lamb portrayed directly as the perpetrator of this judgement. That is left to Christ's other representation as the Rider on the White Horse of Rev. 19, various angels, and other forces. These could all be seen as manifestations of a different side of Christ. The Lamb emphasizes his salvific, suffering, reconciling side, while the Rider on the White Horse emphasizes his judgemental, combative one. It could be that at the heart of Revelation there are actually two contrasting visions, somewhat in tension with each other, the Lamb, with it subversion of worldly order and wisdom, and the Rider on the White Horse, a much more well-known type of militaristic saviour.

Before leaving the subject of the Lamb, we must finally mention Rev. 13.8, which has prompted much speculation as to whether the sacrifice of the Lamb (the crucifixion) is an event which occurs (merely) within history, as is usually assumed, or whether, on the basis of this verse, it is to be seen as an eternal event or truth. In most modern versions Rev. 13.8 tells us that there exists a book written at the foundation of the world that belongs to the slain Lamb. In some readings of the original Greek, however, and in some translations (including the Authorized Version), this book is the book of the Lamb, who is himself 'slain from the foundation of the world'. This would suggest that Christ's sacrifice is pre-existent, with, in the words of one medieval theologian, Thomas Bradwardine, his grace preceding the world 'both in time and in nature'.[8] If one accepts this, it has serious implications regarding grace and salvation, because it allows for the possibility of those who lived before Christ to have been saved *before* his historical crucifixion, under Pontius Pilate, around 33 CE. We do not aspire to unravel these complexities here, on which theologians have pondered for two millennia, save to suggest not only the extent to which Revelation has been the source of the profoundest religious speculation, but also the centrality of the Lamb to that speculation.

# The Lamb in visual imagery

We turn now to a selection of images inspired by the Lamb of Revelation. The challenge for the artist has been, in short, how to visualize an injured (slain) Lamb in a suitably Christ-like way and perhaps also to encapsulate the notion of its sacrifice alongside his characteristics of strength and judgement. Earlier images tend to emphasize the more triumphant aspect of the Lamb (if indeed a Lamb can ever truly be said to look triumphant), while later ones, such as Blake's memorable image, emphasize his frailty and meekness. Unlike some of the other themes in Revelation, the Lamb has remained mostly a religious or devotional symbol and has not fired the popular or secular imagination in the same way as, say, the Four Horsemen or the Whore of Babylon have done.

Nevertheless, there are some significant developments even within the devotional iconography. In the Anglo-Norman manuscripts and the *Angers Tapestry*, the Lamb is represented with flags and nationalistic coats of arms, English in the case of *Trinity*, French at *Angers* (in which the army of the Beast are recognizably English soldiers). Obviously these deeply contextualized readings of Revelation are contrary to the spirit of the text, but they serve to underline the way in which Revelation has so often been used to serve ulterior and polemical ends. Dürer, by contrast, makes an interesting theological point by having his Lamb open the First Seal with his foot, thus emphasizing the intimate connection between the Lamb and the judgements wreaked on a recalcitrant humanity—for all his meekness and compassion, the Lamb should not be thought of as lacking in a necessary steel and firmness (which would perhaps appeal to more recent politicized interpreters of Revelation, who emphasize its judgemental aspects). Dürer's image reinforces this point in a way that verbal descriptions will struggle to recapture. In music, while in his B Minor Mass Bach is able to bring out with equal force both the suffering and the glorious sides of the Lamb, in *The Messiah*, Handel, for all his undoubted brilliance, attempts a glorified Lamb. When we come to Blake, though, we get a Lamb wholly fragile and meek, which shows once again the extent to which this image in particular responds so sensitively to the preconceptions of its interpreters.

## Medieval visualizations of the Lamb

No doubt due to the fact that the Lamb is in many ways the most potent symbol of the paradox of Christianity, images of the Lamb, particularly in church art, began to appear, albeit in a largely decontextualized way, from the fifth and sixth centuries onwards. Mosaics such as the triumphal arch mosaic at the Basilica of SS Cosma e Damiano in Rome (sixth century) are typical. This mosaic, which depicts at its centre the Adoration of the Lamb, draws upon the ceremonial homage given to the Roman emperor, which is surely something of a paradox, one might think, given the savage critique of that office in Revelation (has Christianity already forgotten its origins?). Unusually in terms of later iconography of this figure, the Lamb is depicted as seated on a throne, above the scroll with the Seven Seals, and surrounded by the Seven Lampstands of Rev. 1.12–20 and a group of angels.[9] (The Twenty-four Elders of Rev. 4 were not yet part of the iconography of this scene.)

Even more impressive is the apse mosaic in the Basilica of San Vitale in Ravenna, again dating from the sixth century (Plate 11). The Lamb is depicted standing at the centre of the apse being worshipped by a multitude of angels and animals, including peacocks, symbols of eternal life and of the 'all-seeing' church. The liberal use of gold leaf and bright colours serves to underline the celebratory aspect of the worship of the Lamb, which is undoubtedly a feature of Rev. 5.

Our next example is from the *Trier Apocalypse*. Though this Carolingian work draws on earlier iconography, its depiction of the Lamb shows some development. The fact that this is a manuscript illustration rather than an example of church art also contributes to that the greater detail of this image. Here the Lamb appears standing and clutching the book of the Seven Seals with his left front leg. This serves to emphasize the importance of his role in opening the book that will unleash the first cycle of judgement on the earth, initiated by the Four Horsemen (Seals 1–4). Around the Lamb are the Four Living Creatures, clearly identifiable as the lion, ox, man, and eagle. They are depicted with prominent eyes on their wings, in strict accordance with the description in Rev. 4.8. Beneath the Lamb and the living creatures are firstly the Twenty-four Elders (although it is possible to count only nineteen) and then underneath them a representation of the 'myriads of worshippers' (Rev. 5.11) all holding golden cups. Another clever characteristic of this image is that all the worshippers (Living Creatures included) are depicted with their eyes slightly turned up towards the Lamb, serving to emphasize his centrality as well as his divinity.

Later Revelation manuscripts such as the English *Trinity Apocalypse* (*c.*1260) also depict the Lamb standing upright and proud, even if he is small in scale next to the God the Father figure who occupies the central position on the throne (Figure 2.4). By this point, the Lamb also holds in his front leg a flagpole topped with a cross. This is reminiscent of the heraldry used when armies went into battle, and in this way the Lamb begins to be associated not just with the 'war in Heaven' but also with earthly wars, which almost certainly goes against the original spirit of the text. In English manuscripts the Lamb bears the arms of the English patrons of whichever manuscript it appears in, whereas in the fourteenth-century monumental

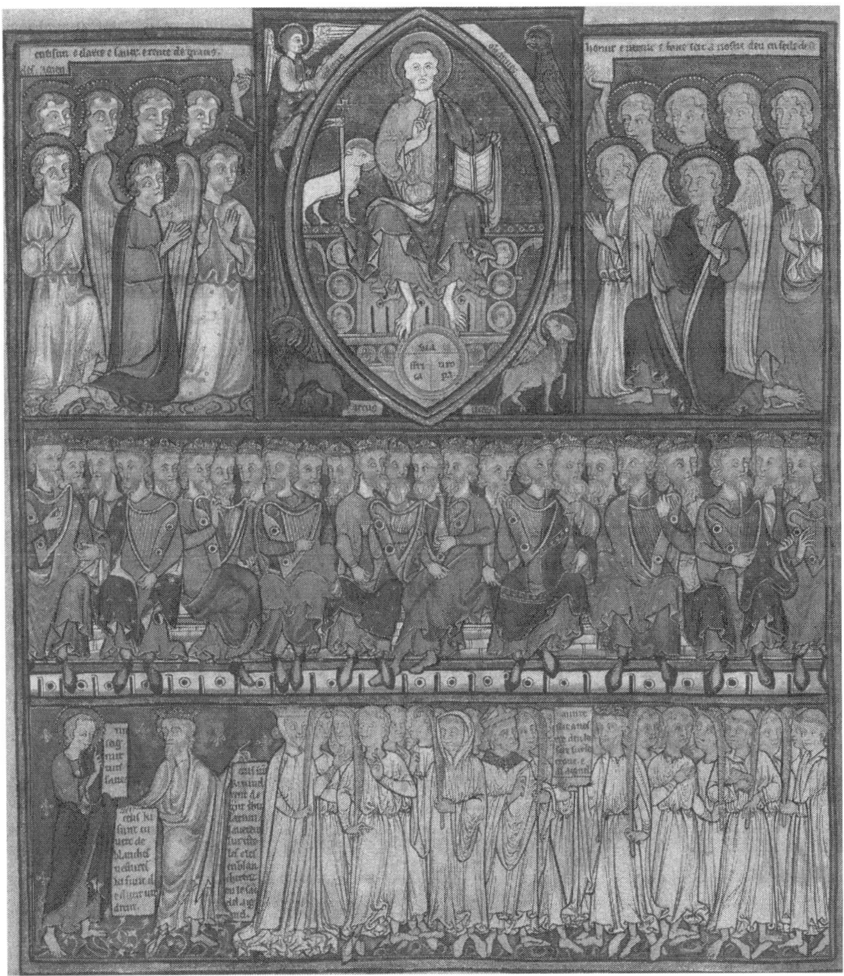

**Figure 2.4.** The *Trinity Apocalypse*, *c.*1260, The Lamb with the Flagpole (Rev. 5), Cambridge: Trinity College. © The Master and Fellows of Trinity College, Cambridge

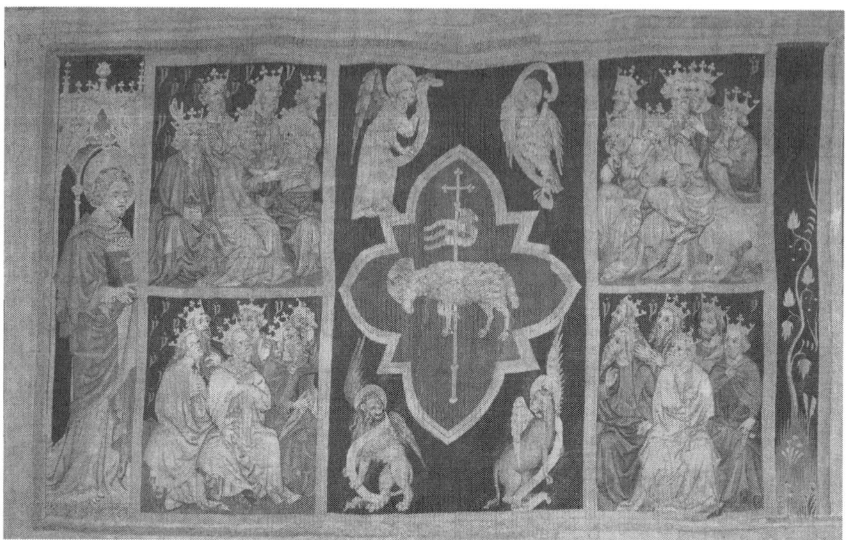

**Figure 2.5.** The *Angers Apocalypse Tapestry*, *c.*1373–80, The Lamb Bleeding from the Neck and Feet (Rev. 5), Maine et Loire: Chateau d'Angers. © Bridgeman Art Library

French *Angers Tapestry*, for example, commissioned by Louis, Duke of Anjou, the Lamb bears the arms of the house of Anjou (Figure 2.5). The depiction of the Lamb in the *Angers Tapestry* is also noteworthy on account of the fact that the Lamb is clearly bleeding from its neck and feet. Thus his sacrificial nature is clearly juxtaposed with his triumphal one in a neat depiction of the paradox of Christianity which we have been discussing in this chapter.

While physically huge, the *Angers* image of the Lamb cannot hope to compete with the symbolic scope of the early fifteenth-century *Ghent Altarpiece*, at the centre of which is the famous *Adoration of the Lamb* (Figure 2.3). In short, this twenty-four-panel altarpiece, painted by the Van Eyck brothers, is a visualization of biblical history from Genesis to Revelation. The Annunciation is shown on the outside of the altarpiece, which, once opened, uses a riot of colour and gold leaf to depict a sort of eternal Eucharist in the central panel of the lower level, presided over by God the Father and the heavenly host (as well as the fallen Adam and Eve) on the upper level. The Lamb appears at the centre of this eternal Eucharist in the central panel, standing on an altar as his redemptive blood pours into the Eucharistic cup, as in the Chartres carving already mentioned, and with similar implications regarding the timelessness of the Lamb's sacrifice. In

Ghent the Lamb is in a lush Edenic landscape, in which literally hundreds of plants and flowers are individually painted, while behind him a group of imposing Flemish buildings represents the New Jerusalem. At the same time key figures from the Old and New Testament and from Revelation in particular process towards him. It is thought that there was originally a predella, or lower section of the altarpiece, probably representing the Last Judgement or Hell, and thus embracing all three cosmic levels, as well as the whole of Salvation History, in the scene before us.

As already mentioned, Revelation's Lamb had become a symbol for the essential paradox of Christianity and also of the Eucharist itself, the act which commemorates Christ's salvific death and resurrection, and so was the obvious choice for an altarpiece on this theme. Other motifs from Revelation abound in this central panel, in addition to those already mentioned. In front of the altar is the fountain of life from the New Jerusalem (Rev. 21), while in the top left- and right-hand corners of the panel the martyrs and virgins from Rev. 7 and Rev. 14 process towards the Lamb. Although the New Jerusalem is clearly evoked via the fountain of life and the idealized Flemish buildings in the background of the central panel, the arguably top-heavy upper panel can also be interpreted as the metaphorical descent of the New Jerusalem. God the Father, Mary, and John the Baptist can therefore be seen as the New Jerusalem descending to the earth below on which the Lamb stands (Rev. 21.2). But whilst symbolically, theologically, and even geometrically absolutely central, representing the eternal nature and efficacy of Christ's sacrificial act and the way all else flows to and from that act, it is worth noting that although standing erect and proud, the Lamb is a strangely small, fluffy, white figure at the apex of this momentous panel, a visual encapsulation of the paradox of Christianity.

## Later visualizations of the Lamb

The Renaissance and Reformation artists who tackled Revelation largely followed Albrecht Dürer's fifteen woodcut prints of the text from around 1498. His depiction of the Lamb focuses on the act of the Lamb opening the scroll with the Seven Seals in Rev. 5. Thus in his image (Figure 2.1) the Lamb is depicted next to God the Father, with his feet resting on the scroll, which itself has been placed on God's lap. The seven eyes are clearly visible, which represent his divine perfection. The emphasis here is therefore not so much on the Lamb as a suffering symbol of Christianity but rather on his pivotal role in cosmic events. For in pulling open the First Seal, the Lamb sets in motion all the events that follow, from the unleashing of the Four Horsemen to, ultimately, the establishment of the New Jerusalem. Thus for Dürer and his successors the Lamb, whilst physically small and unprepossessing, plays an active and vital role in the drama.

Moving forward in time to the nineteenth century, we come to an image by William Blake entitled *The Four and Twenty Elders Casting Their Crowns before the Divine Throne* from *c.*1805 (Plate 12). This image, with its swirling figures, eyes, and rainbows encircling the central figure of God, emphasizes the visionary aspect of Rev. 4–5, which Blake saw as a recasting of Ezekiel's *Merkabah* or throne vision from the Old Testament (Ezekiel 1).[10] In this way Revelation's place in the long tradition of apocalyptic literature and experiences is brought to the fore and we are reminded of John's role as an important visionary in the Christian tradition. Throughout our discussion of images of the Lamb, some images have stressed his triumphal aspect and others his passivity. The tradition of 'passive' interpretations surely culminates with Blake's image, where the Lamb could be said to be remarkable by virtue of the sheer unremarkable nature of its appearance. Indeed, one could be forgiven for not noticing the Lamb in this image at all, tucked as it is beneath the feet of the imposing, bearded figure of God the Father who resides at the centre of the image. Blake's Lamb is lying down, lifeless, dead even, a visual crystallization of Blake's conviction that the wisdom of the Bible lies not in the material emphasized by the established church, but in its neglected verses and paradoxes. The viewer is drawn to the splendour of Heaven and God the Father but it is through the barely visible, lifeless Lamb that salvation is offered. It would be hard to find a bigger contrast between this and the triumphal Lamb at the centre of the San Vitale mosaic, whereas in Blake there is a disjunct between what you see and what is crucial.

The twentieth century sees a return to an emphasis on the Lamb in church art. Like the sixth-century mosaics of the Lamb that we discussed above, the Lamb often appears in contemporary stained-glass windows in a largely decontextualized fashion. This example from a Protestant church in Héricourt in northern France, is typical (Plate 13). Here the Lamb is depicted in a lifeless fashion, suspended alone amidst the Seven Seals and Trumpets of Revelation. The throne room, God the Father, the Twenty-four Elders and other features are nowhere to be seen, thus placing the emphasis solely on the Lamb and its symbolic centrality to the notion of Christian salvation, with the intricacy and complexity of the original narrative all but lost.

# The Lamb in music

The Agnus Dei (Lamb of God) is an integral part of the Catholic Mass, and as such has frequently been set to music by many of the greatest composers. It is not always easy to see the liturgical Agnus Dei ('Lamb of God, who takest away the sins of the world, have mercy on us…give us peace') as the Lamb of Revelation, partly because the liturgical emphasis is often on the worshipper's own plea for mercy. But, as might be expected, Bach's setting in the B Minor Mass has both a directness and an objectivity not always present in other settings, and at the same time seems to encapsulate the strongest features of most of the rest.

Bach's Agnus Dei is actually in two halves, halves which correspond to the dual nature of the Lamb as slaughtered and as triumphant. The Miserere section is a plangent solo for alto voice, emphasizing *peccata* (sins) and *miserere* (the prayer for mercy) over an achingly beautiful melody for strings and continuo pulse. It is simple and gentle, as appropriate to the Lamb, but at the same time beseeching and with a desolation reminiscent of arias from Bach's *Passions*. By contrast the Dona nobis pacem ('give us peace') movement is for full chorus and in complicated counterpoint, with sopranos above the lower voices. Austere at first, it gradually broadens into a solemnly triumphant hymn of praise, coloured with blazing trumpets and thunderous drums, the music recalling the Gratias agimus ('let us give thanks to the lord for his great glory') section from the Gloria earlier in the Mass. As so often with Bach, profound, subtle, and complex theology shines forth in the music, in this case a mere eight minutes long.

Although we will be looking at it in more detail in the final chapter, it is worth mentioning here the central role the Lamb plays in Franz Schmidt's oratorio *Das Buch mit Sieben Siegeln* (The Book with Seven Seals), for it is, of course, the Lamb who opens the seals. The music associated with the Lamb is by turns lyrical and pastoral, and then solemn, reverential, and hieratic. When the Lamb is first introduced into the throne room, 'as if it had been slaughtered', it is all trilling flutes and oboes, heart-rendingly beautiful, but as the Lamb becomes the object of worship, we hear the solemn chords and blazing trumpets of the Lord as Alpha and Omega, together with an ecstatic chorus of praise for the Lamb, something Schmidt has in common with Handel's *Messiah*, which contains what is surely the most famous musical evocation both of the Lamb and of Revelation itself.

For the second part of *Messiah* (that devoted to Christ's Passion and resurrection) opens with John the Baptist's evocation to Christ as baptismal Lamb, and ends with the Hallelujah Chorus, which is inspired by Rev. 11 and 19. After verses from Psalm 2, which foretell of God dashing his enemies into pieces like a potter's vessel, the famous chorus, in music of blazing power and fugal grandeur, glorifies the everlasting reign of God and 'his' Christ, who at that point in Revelation is represented as the Rider on the White Horse, leading the armies of Heaven to smite the enemies, as prophesied. Even more striking for the purposes of this chapter is the final chorus of Handel's whole work, which is based on Rev. 5. A vast double fugue, in Handel's grandest and most imperious manner, proclaims the worthiness of the slain Lamb to share with 'him who sits on the throne' everlasting power and glory and blessing and honour and wisdom. There is not much in the prelude preceding the first fugue about slaying; it is more a solemn, reverent acclamation of the Lamb before the glorification. While Handel is somewhat unusual in focusing so much on the triumph of the Lamb, for all his dramatic prowess, consummate artistry, ease of writing, and undeniable splendour, *Messiah* is somewhat one-dimensional in its emphasis on the glorious aspects of Revelation and indeed of Salvation History more generally, and so it is theologically less interesting, compared to Bach, or even to Schmidt.

Schmidt, like Handel, certainly emphasizes the proximity of the Lamb to the Lord (and indeed tries to out-Handel Handel with his own Hallelujah Chorus). In the section from *Das Buch mit Sieben Siegeln* evoking the Woman Clothed with the Sun from Rev. 12 (who, in Christian practice, becomes traditionally identified with both the Virgin Mary and the church itself), we hear music close to the Lamb's own original soft music, before we are eventually returned to the joint triumph of Lamb and Lord. In connecting these key figures—Lamb and Woman, Lamb and Lord—musically, Schmidt gives a powerful sense of the unity and coherence of Revelation itself, something which can be lost in its descriptive and theological detail. In their different ways both Bach and Schmidt demonstrate the power music has to bring out theological meanings which are not so clear on the page.[11]

## Conclusion

The complexity that Bach and Schmidt bring to the figure of the Lamb of God is slightly lost in some of the images that we have looked at. One of the great advantages of the image, in general terms, is that it can bring together different themes and moments in one visual space. However, as we have seen, it is very difficult to visualize the sacrifice and the triumph of the Lamb simultaneously. As with the Bach piece, perhaps this concept is one that has to unfold over time, or at least over a series of images. Thus in the images discussed above, the Lamb either appears to look passive and defeated or proud and strong (or as proud and strong as a lamb can look) but not both. And images of the Marriage of the Lamb to Israel can even seem bizarre, as in the *Trinity Apocalypse* image of this scene, where the Lamb stands awkwardly on the table perched under Israel's arm, who is depicted as a contemporary woman. The viewer must then 'fill in' the other qualities of the Lamb for themselves. The 'passive tradition' culminates in the Blake image, in which one might miss the Lamb altogether (and so miss the whole point, theologically speaking), while the 'victorious' or triumphalist tradition, which began as early as the sixth century, perhaps found its zenith in the Van Eycks' *Adoration of the Lamb* (although even here the Lamb provides a surprisingly small focal point). In both incarnations, the Lamb is impressive in its universality: people of all sexes, races, and times can relate to this enduring and powerful symbol of passive resistance, even in the decontextualized form we see in the Héricourt window. The Lamb thus retains even now something of its core meaning, a symbol for the paradox of Christianity itself.

# 3

# The Four Horsemen

'I got bored with the pale horse, so I swapped it for a white van' (Figure 3.1). Thus speaks the fourth Horseman of the Apocalypse to his rather bemused-looking colleagues in this turn of the century cartoon in a joke that is not only sending up the Four Horsemen but also the 'white van man'. Usually silent and menacing and cast as the bringers of the worst scourges imaginable to earth, the Four Horsemen are so well known as a symbol of doom that by the twentieth-first century (and even before this) they could be used for comic effect in a completely secular setting. From the ninth-century *Trier Apocalypse* (Figure 3.2) to a surprising number of twentieth-first-century computer games, many thousands of artists, designers, authors, and commentators have appropriated the Four Horsemen for their own ends. Even the most secular among us will, on hearing the term, be overtaken by a mental image of four dark, ferocious horses, foaming at the mouth and trailing destruction in their wake. To some the image will be comic, to others terrifying. But we all know that once those horses start galloping, the jig is up and the end is upon us. They have, in recent times, therefore become a byword for the end times, the so-called eschaton itself. But it has not always been thus. This chapter will trace the journey that these first-century creations have been on, from terrifying harbingers of doom in the Middle Ages to agents of popular humour in our time.

## The Four Horsemen in Revelation

In order to gain a more rounded understanding of these fascinating characters or creations, we must return to the text of Revelation itself. It may surprise some to learn that the wealth of cultural interpretations of the Four Horsemen springs from just seven verses of text: Rev. 6.2–8. In terms of the

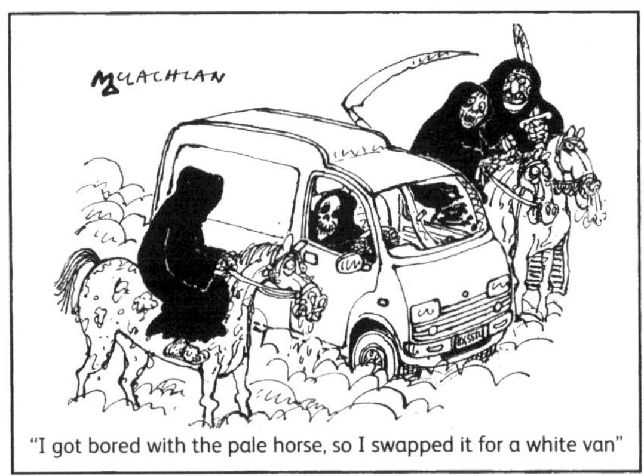



**Figure 3.1.** Four Horsemen cartoon. © www.cartoonstock.com

'macro-narrative' of Revelation, this section follows on directly from the heavenly throne room scene of Rev. 4–5, which we looked at in the last chapter, in which John (and through him the reader or hearer of the text) has come face to face with both God and Christ (in the form of the slaughtered Lamb). Only the Lamb is deemed 'worthy' to open the scroll held by God, and at the beginning of Rev. 6 the Lamb does just that, opening the First Seal on the scroll. The significance of this action, of which we, as readers or hearers, have hitherto been unaware, soon becomes clear: the opening of the First Seal sets in motion the release of the Four Horsemen and their 'woes' upon an unrepentant and sinful world. Each Horseman is 'introduced' by one of the Four Living Creatures that surround God's throne (the lion, the ox, the one 'like' a man, and the eagle), and John tells us what colour the horse is, what the Horseman is carrying and which woe they each bring to earth. Thus the formula used for the first Horseman is repeated for all the others, but with different information to refer to the colour of the horse and the attributes of the rider: 'Then I saw the Lamb open one of the Seven Seals, and I heard one of the four living creatures call out, as with a voice of thunder, 'Come!' I looked and there was a white horse! Its rider had a bow; a crown was given to him, and he went out conquering and to conquer.' (Rev. 6.1–2. The 'giving of the crown' is an interesting detail in this case, which is often picked up on by artists, who depict an angel hovering above the first Horseman and placing a crown upon his head.)

After the other Horsemen have all been described using the same formula, their joint mission is then summarized for us by John in Rev. 6.8b.

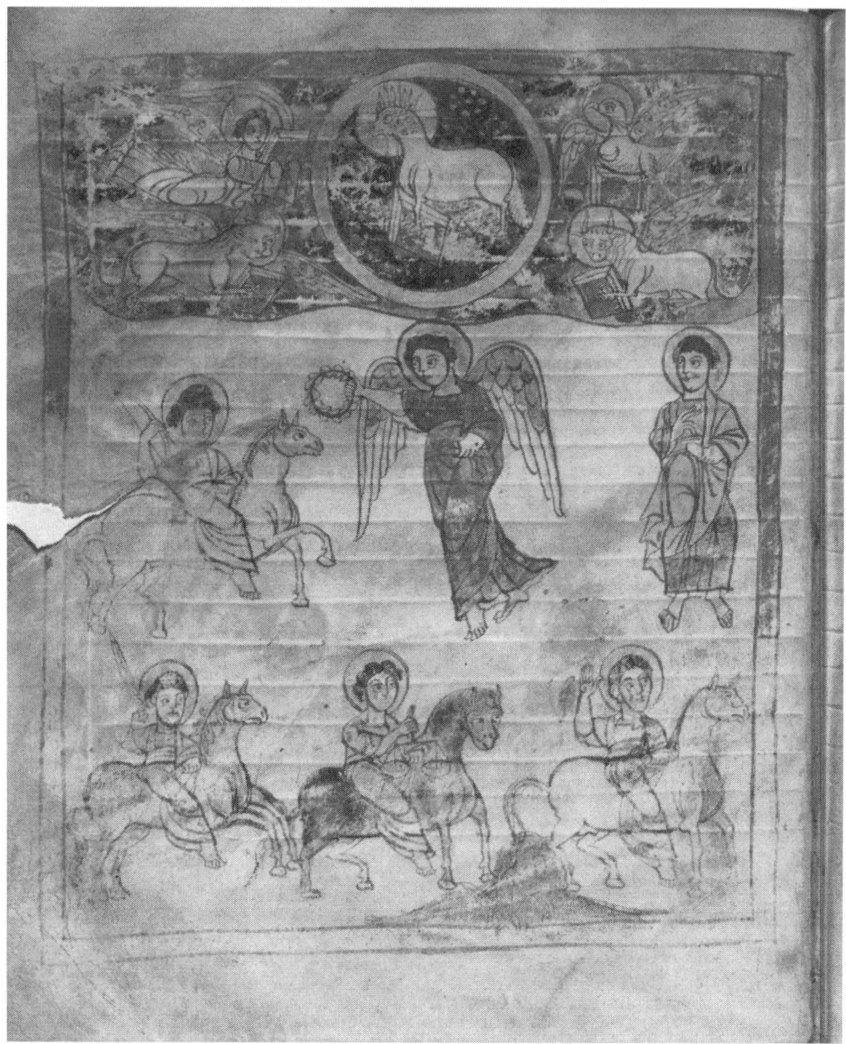

**Figure 3.2.** The *Trier Apocalypse*, ninth century, The Four Horsemen (Rev. 6.2–8), Trier: Stadtbibliothek. With permission, Stadtbibliothek, Trier

Slightly confusingly, we are told in this verse that the Horsemen are 'given authority over a fourth of the earth, to kill with sword, famine and pestilence and by the wild animals of the earth'. These woes do not match up with the woes ascribed to the Four Horsemen in the individual descriptions. However, it is the woes from Rev. 6.8b that have traditionally been associated with the Four Horsemen, particularly in artistic interpretations

Table 3.1. Individual characteristics ascribed to each Horseman

| Horseman | Living Creature | Colour of horse | Attribute | Woe | Woe ascribed in Rev. 6.8 |
|---|---|---|---|---|---|
| First Horseman (Rev. 6.2) | Lion | White | Bow and crown | Conquest | Sword (war) |
| Second Horseman (Rev. 6.3–4) | Ox | Bright red | Sword | War | Famine |
| Third Horseman (Rev. 6.5–6) | One like a man | Black | Scales | Famine? | Pestilence |
| Fourth Horseman (Death) (Rev. 6.7–8) | Eagle | Sickly green (rendered by the unusual Greek χλωρός) | Followed by Hades | Death | Wild beasts |

and, more recently, in popular interpretation. Thus the first Horseman is associated with war (the sword), the second with famine, the third with pestilence, and the fourth with wild animals (and with Hades, the underworld). And so it is courtesy of Rev. 6.8 that we end up with the traditional quartet of war, famine, pestilence, and death (see Table 3.1).

Before moving on to look at some exciting, and often contrasting, cultural interpretations of the Four Horsemen, we will pause momentarily to consider the two main questions that these eight verses have prompted interpreters to ask.[1]

First, do the Four Horsemen, who bring death, destruction, and plague to the world, raise questions about God's goodness? For these Horsemen are not presented as Satanic powers, attempting to pervert God's plans. In fact their very existence is brought about by the Lamb himself, who opens the First Seal of the sacred scroll. The Horsemen are given their powers by the Four Living Creatures. Thus it would seem that they are actually an integral part of the divine plan for the world. Given that they bring great suffering and destruction, how are we to square this with an all-loving God?

While there is no easy answer to this question, it is important to recognize that Revelation is part of the tradition of Jewish and Christian apocalyptic literature in which God's judgement and vengeance is often harsh and sometimes unfathomable. This may be seen in part as a reaction to the difficult political and social situations experienced by the

Jewish and Christian communities that most of the apocalyptic texts arose from, nor are harsh passages absent from the writings of St Paul or from the Gospels themselves. Additionally, it might be argued that the global punishments initiated by the Four Horsemen are very much the end of the road, as it were. Although this is not made explicit in Revelation, from the divine perspective the world has had plenty of opportunity to acknowledge Christ and repent, so their judgement is not coming out of the blue. While the modern reader may not be satisfied by these explanations, they do go some way towards explaining why an ancient reader might have accepted these seemingly conflicting concepts without much questioning. We will, though, see in Chapter 10 that even today liberation theologians reading Revelation 'from below', as they would put it, have little problem with the harshness of the judgements, nor apparently do born again 'prophecy scholars'.

Secondly, does the first Horseman have any connection to Christ? Many early interpreters of Rev. 6.1–2, from the fourth century onwards, noticed that there are similarities between how this Horseman is described and how Christ is described elsewhere in Revelation. For instance, the first Horseman rides a white horse and wears a crown. In Rev. 19.11ff. Christ in his guise as 'the Rider on the White Horse' rides down from Heaven to commence the last battle with the forces of evil, riding a white horse and wearing a crown of many diadems. Similarly, the first Horseman is given the power to 'conquer' in Rev. 6.2. This same verb ($\nu\iota\kappa\acute{a}\omega$ in Greek) is used explicitly of Christ in Rev. 3.21, 5.5, and 17.14, thus indicating some further link. But how can this be? The first Horseman is part of a destructive quartet who bring suffering to one quarter of the earth. Some recent interpreters have come up with a clever and rather attractive solution to this problem. They have argued that far from being connected with Christ, this first Horseman is intended rather as a parody of Christ, an Antichrist, if you like, just as later on the Beasts from Rev. 13 are presented as parodies of Christ.[2] So, for instance, the first Horseman's horse is white because elsewhere in Revelation (e.g. Rev. 7.13) the colour white is associated with the victory and purity of Christ's followers. The white horse is thus to be seen as a deliberately deceptive inversion of these positive qualities. Many artists, however, have stuck with the traditional interpretation, that the first Horseman is indeed Christ, and for this reason he is often set apart from the other Horsemen in images. A good example of this sort of interpretation is to be found in the *Trier Apocalypse*, *c.*800, which we will consider shortly.

# The Four Horsemen in visual imagery

In general in medieval treatments of the Four Horsemen there is an emphasis on making visual their connection with Heaven; they are represented as being sent from Heaven, and consequently we see (literally see, in the case of the images) their scourges as being Heaven-sent, and their actions as being willed by a transcendent God. This identification of the Horsemen's mission with divine providence is underlined by the insertion, common in medieval manuscripts, of one of the Four Living Creatures into pictures of the individual Horsemen, as indeed Rev. 6 requires. More modern visualizations, by contrast, depict the Horsemen as terrifying forces acting independently.

A further significant development, common from the time of Dürer onwards (and probably influenced by him), is the tendency to depict the Horsemen as a group rather than as individuals; and as this collective depiction develops, there is a greater preoccupation with the fourth Horseman as Death or Hades, and also an absence of the fairly common medieval identification of the first Horseman with Christ. Indeed by the time we come to the Haynes–Mortimer image (around the end of the eighteenth century; see Figure 3.7 below), the fourth Horseman (or Death) on his own seems to encapsulate the woes associated earlier with all four.

It would be stretching the point somewhat to suggest that great theological insight is (intentionally) offered by some of our later examples of the Four Horsemen. Nevertheless, in the transition from the detailed individual depictions, presented in sequence in the Anglo-Norman manuscript Apocalypses to Dürer's and subsequent presentations of the four as working simultaneously and collectively in a group, we would not be wrong to see the woes as all part of one universal devastation, occurring all at the same time, rather than as separate moments in a linear history. We will see the same point of interpretation when, in the next chapter, we come to look at the three sequences of seven woes: are they to be seen as three separate sequences of separate disasters, or are they different ways of referring to a universal calamity, or even to the continual recapitulation of ever-present ills besetting us?

## Medieval images

The *Trier Apocalypse* image of the Four Horsemen is a very interesting example of how visual interpretations can often be the most powerful, and certainly have more impact than a textual or oral interpretation (Figure 3.2). Here we see the Lamb and the Four Living Creatures at the top of the image, a visual reminder that everything that takes place below has been sanctioned by God and Christ. 'Heaven' or the heavenly throne room is cut off from earth by a decisive black line. Under this the Four Horsemen gather as John watches from the right-hand side. The first Horseman is clearly differentiated from the others by virtue of the fact that he is being handed his crown by an angel, in accordance with Rev. 6.2. The *Trier* image is also interesting because the first Horseman and its rider bear a striking visual resemblance to the other depiction of Christ on his white horse in Rev. 19, in line with the popular identification of the first Horseman either with Christ himself or, at the very least, with a sort of parody of Christ or Antichrist.

We move from the ninth century to some visualizations of Revelation from the thirteenth and fourteenth centuries. While the *Trier* image grouped the Four Horsemen together, ensuring that the first Horseman was clearly demarcated, standard medieval iconography of the Four Horsemen is altogether more stilted. It had become fashionable, in manuscripts since the twelfth century, to depict them separately and this is what we see in images from *Lambeth* and *Angers*. The *Lambeth* image (fig. 3.3) depicts the second Horseman, who rides a red horse and brandishes a sword. Although latterly more commonly associated with famine, the medieval iconographers tended to focus on the militaristic connotations of this horseman. While the horse itself is rather fine and passive-looking, the fully armoured rider has his right hand raised as if about to strike someone with his sword. Also clearly visible is the ox which introduces the horseman in Rev. 6.3.

The panel depicting the third Horseman in *Angers* is a rather quaint example of how, even in as magisterial a project as this, commissioned by the French prince, Louis of Anjou no less, human error can creep in. For although we can identify the rider quite clearly as the third Horseman, due to the fact he is carrying a pair of scales (cf. Rev. 6. 5–6), his horse is not black but red (the colour of the second Horseman's horse). It is just possible that this error crept in in the nineteenth century when the tapestry was restored in a very inadequate fashion, but we shall never know.

Finally, *Angers* depicts the fourth Horseman as a skeleton riding a paler horse (Figure 3.4). The artist who conceived the designs for the tapestry (probably Jean de Bondol of Bruges) was clearly interpreting the detail given in Rev. 6.8, that this rider was 'death', literally: for he has depicted him

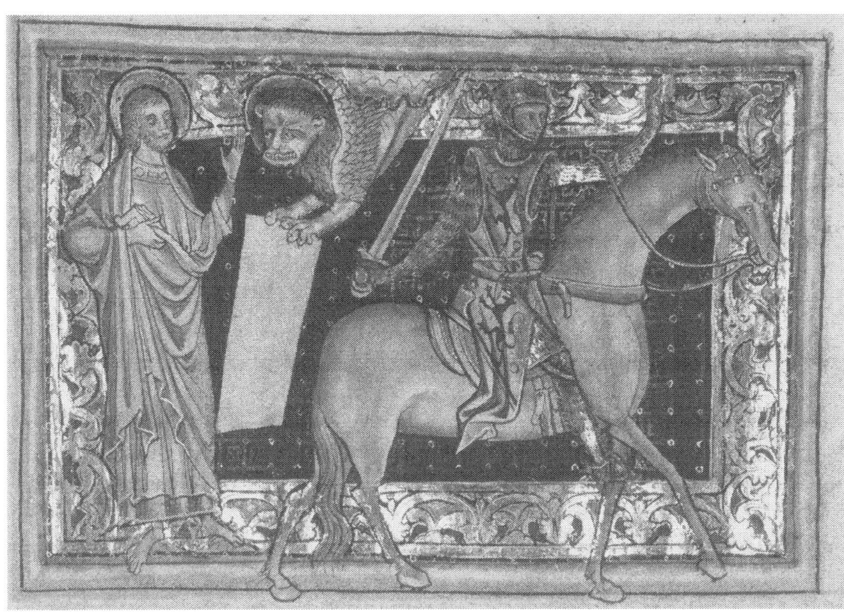

**Figure 3.3.** The *Lambeth Apocalypse*, *c.*1260, The Second Horseman (Rev. 6.3–4), London: Lambeth Palace Library. © Bridgeman Art Library

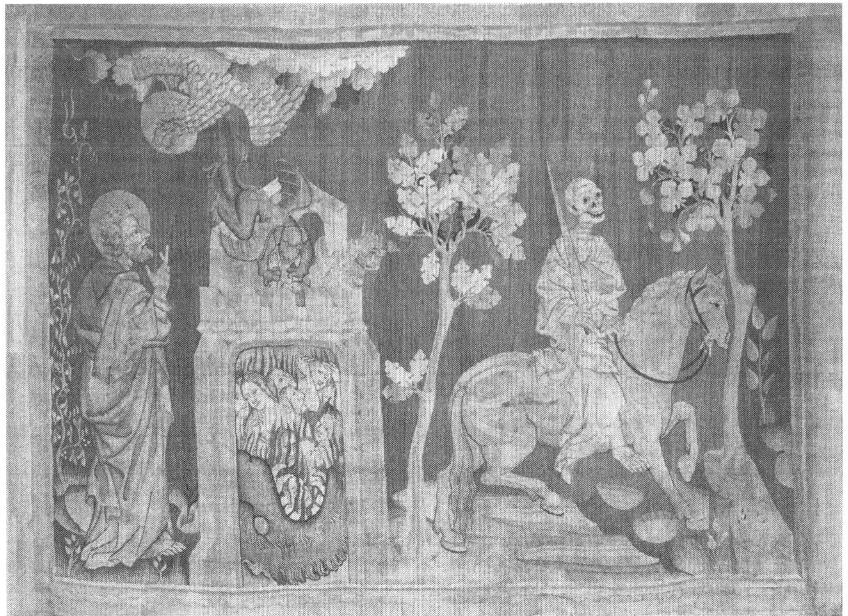

**Figure 3.4.** The *Angers Apocalypse Tapestry*, *c.*1373–80, The Fourth Horseman (Rev. 6.7–8), Maine et Loire: Chateau d'Angers. © Bridgeman Art Library

as a skeleton. This skeletal envisioning of this figure became very popular and is repeated in most images of the fourth Horseman from this time onwards. The artist also took literally the detail that the fourth Horseman was being followed by Hades. Here Hades is depicted not as the god of the underworld but as a Hellmouth into which some unfortunate souls are being coerced by a little devil on top of the stone shrine-like structure in which the Hellmouth is enclosed. It is typical of *Angers'* aversion to anything too visually shocking that Hades is enclosed in this stone structure, as if this somehow minimizes the horror which it symbolizes.

Dating from around one century later, Memling's 'synchronic' visualization of Revelation presents a completely different picture of the four Horsemen assembling as a whole rather than as separate episodes in the narrative (Plate 3). The top left-hand corner of the panel represents the heavenly throne room. The apocalyptic 'action' (if one may call it that) begins with the depiction of the Four Horsemen galloping across the middle of the panel. The events of Revelation continue to unfold, snaking back towards the sea's horizon, becoming smaller and smaller in size until they are no longer visible with the naked eye. Memling's rendering of the Four Horsemen is striking, both by virtue of the fact that they have been given such a central position in the panel, as well as the fact that he has placed them on separate islands and rendered them in very striking colours. They have not been kept completely separate as in the *Angers* images but neither do they enjoy the cohesion of the *Trier* image where they are grouped together. The first Horseman stands out by virtue of the fact that his horse is facing in the opposite direction from the others. This may indicate his separation from the others in a possible endorsement of the idea that there is something Christlike about him. The second Horseman also stands out on account of the brilliant red colour used for his horse. This may indicate a possible association with the Dragon of Rev. 12, which is depicted at the top centre of the panel attacking the Woman Clothed with the Sun and is the same vivid red. This suggests that three of the Horsemen at least are in league with the other evil characters of Revelation such as the Dragon and the Beasts. As had now become traditional, the fourth Horseman is depicted as a skeleton, his dun-coloured horse being pursued by a fiery, giant dog's head, which evokes images of Cerberus, the three-headed dog who guarded Hades.

Memling's image thus rounds off our exploration of medieval images of the Four Horsemen. We have encountered three different ways of depicting them: all together, completely separately, and as a sort of disparate group. In all three, the fact that their actions have been sanctioned by those in the heavenly throne room has been emphasized by the artists, reminding the modern viewer of the ethical challenge flagged earlier in this chapter. How can a good God sanction the destruction caused by the Four Horsemen?

## Dürer and Cranach and the Four Horsemen

This question, about the implications for God's goodness, given his connection with the Four Horsemen, remains in our minds as we turn to two examples from a different artistic era and genre, that of the Renaissance and Reformation print or woodcut. Albrecht Dürer's image of the Four Horsemen is perhaps the most iconic of all (Figure 3.5). As already mentioned, his series of fifteen woodcuts of Revelation, published in 1498, has had a huge influence on subsequent artistic representation of this text. By compressing the text into fifteen images, he was able to inject his series with pace and urgency whilst simultaneously remaining faithful to the narrative.

In Dürer's black-and-white image (the fourth in his series), we see the first three Horsemen thundering along together in perfect synchronicity, as if in a whirlwind. The fourth, very different in appearance, is set slightly apart. Are the first three horsemen three individuals or three manifestations of the same woe? We hardly know any more, in contrast to the earlier images we have looked at where the four riders were clearly demarcated. They are attired in fine clothes and all ride fine horses, befitting of knights or kings (indeed, they resemble some of Dürer's other woodcuts of knights' horses) and we can easily identify them.[3]

The first Horseman (now not distinguished in any way from the others) rides with his bow poised, the second with his sword raised, and the third with his scales (of justice?) swinging out behind him. For the first time, in contrast to the almost serene earlier images of the Four Horsemen, here we see their human victims being trampled underfoot. One man crouches with his arm up in a futile gesture of resistance to the thundering steeds, while the others have already fallen to the ground, powerless. The unexpected nature of the apocalypse (i.e. it could happen at any time) is perhaps underlined here via the fact that the woman at the front of the image has seemingly just come from her sewing, her sewing tools (scissors and knitting needles) still tied to her waist. The egalitarian nature of the apocalypse is also being emphasized here by Dürer, for it is not just commoners who are

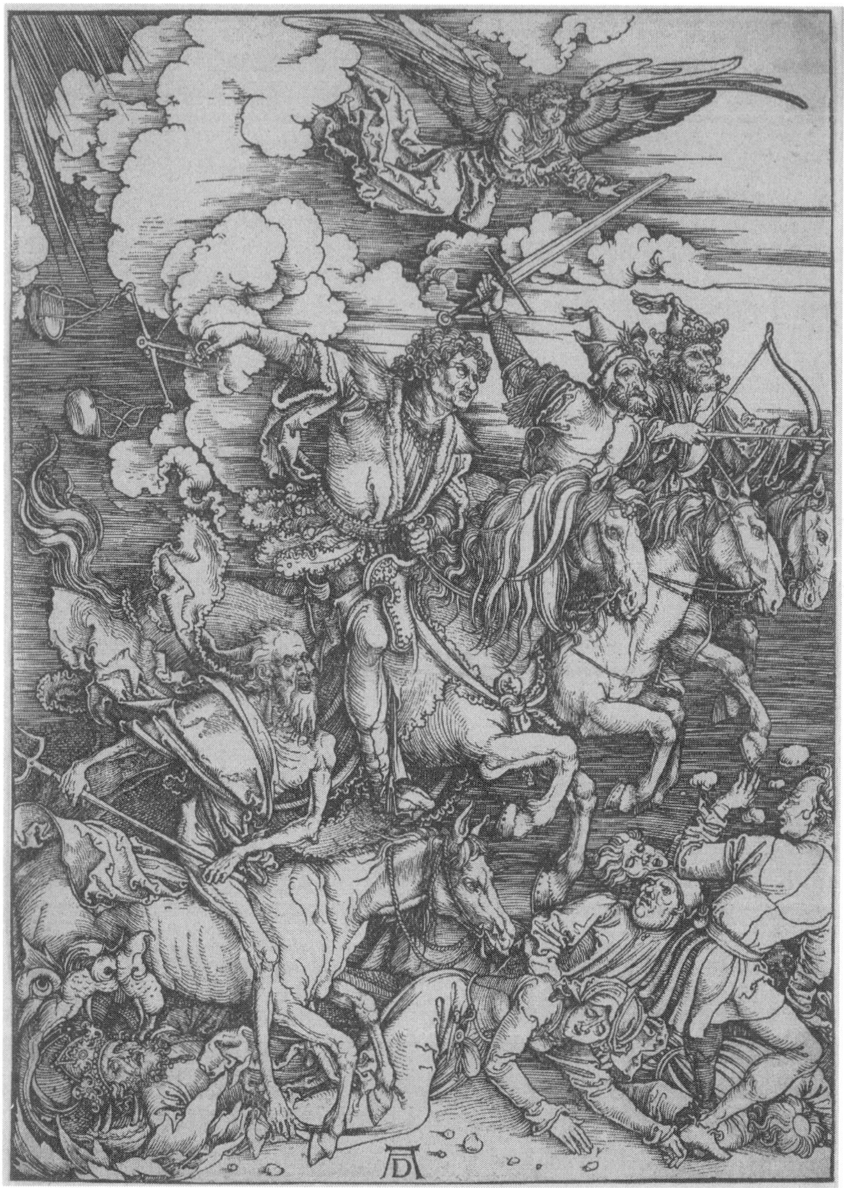

**Figure 3.5.** Albrecht Dürer, *Apocalypse* Series *c.*1498, The Four Horsemen (Rev. 6.2–8), London: British Museum. © The Trustees of the British Museum

trampled by the Horsemen but a bishop too. He is clearly visible in the bottom left-hand corner of the image, thanks to his bejewelled bishop's mitre, as he is devoured by Hades, here once again depicted as a monstrous head following in the wake of the fourth Horseman—maybe a hint on Dürer's part of some early Reforming sympathy.

Discussion of Dürer's fourth Horseman has purposefully been left until last as it seems to us that he has depicted him (rather than the first Horseman, as in earlier images) in a rather distinctive manner. Although he is symmetrically in line with the other three riders, the fourth Horseman stands out due to the fact that he is emaciated, is dressed in rags, is carrying a pitchfork, and rides upon a small, scrawny nag rather than a fine steed. Dürer's imaginative take on the figure of Death can be seen to usher in a new age of artistic interest in this character, which was to continue (as we shall see) well into the twentieth century. Finally, the angel at the top of the image, seemingly pointing the riders onwards, his right hand raised in benediction, reminds us that the actions of the Four Horsemen are sanctioned by the powers in Heaven as part of the overall divine plan that John is being allowed to glimpse. While more politically provocative than the earlier images, especially in his portrayal of the victims, Dürer, as an orthodox believer, is content to let the theological paradox stand.

After Dürer's vivid image, Cranach's pastiche of the same scene (undoubtedly crafted in the knowledge of Dürer's images) seems rather tame by comparison and is certainly less arresting (Figure 3.6).[4] In this image, the third in the Cranach series, all four Horsemen seem altogether less menacing than in Dürer's image. Rather than being physically trampled, the human victims of the riders have been politely moved back from under the horses' hooves into the right-hand corner of the image, perhaps in order to spare the feelings of the viewer. Interestingly, given the deeply polemical nature of some of Cranach's other images in this series, he has removed the bishop that sat in the mouth of Hades in the Dürer image. Although one must be wary of reading too much into images, this may have been for a serious reason. For Luther's attack was not on the clergy per se but rather on the papacy itself. All the polemical touches in this series of images of Revelation are aimed directly at the papacy and not at the clergy in general. Thus by removing the bishop from this scene of destruction by the Four Horsemen and rendering their victims as a far more generic group, Cranach could shield Luther from the charge that the clergy (of which he of course was one) were being singled out for particular apocalyptic judgement.[5]

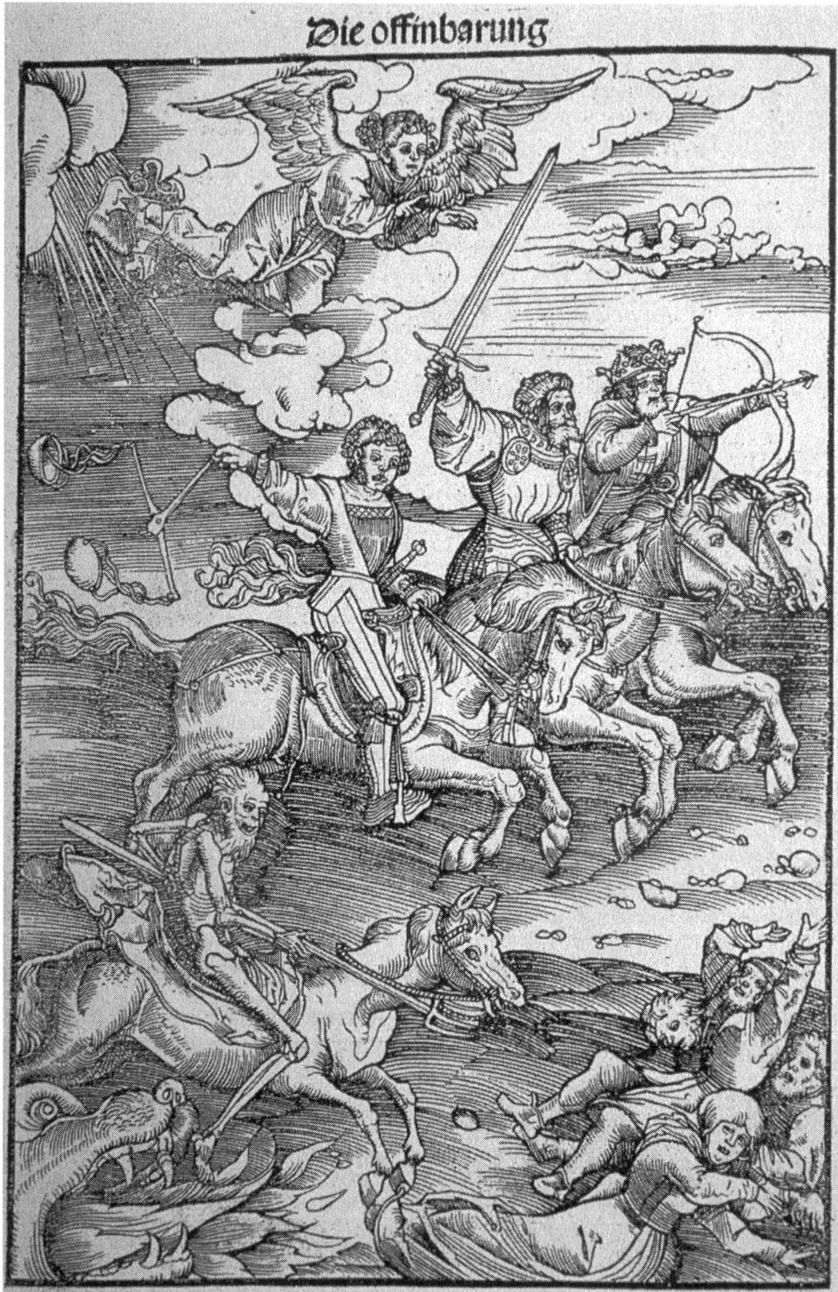



**Figure 3.6.** Lucas Cranach the Elder, Apocalypse Illustrations for Luther's New Testament, 1522, The Four Horsemen (Rev. 6.2–8), London: The British Library. © The British Library Board, C.36.g.7

# The Four Horsemen in the eighteenth
# and nineteenth centuries

Dürer's image of the Four Horsemen gave rise to a thousand imitations over the next couple of centuries. Like Cranach, many of these imitators used the concept as a peg on which to hang polemical material, usually of a Protestant nature. The turbulent political context of the late eighteenth and nineteenth centuries (the French Revolution of 1789; American Independence, 1776) brought with it an altogether different take on these iconic figures.[6] The image by J. Haynes, after John Hamilton Mortimer's drawing, is typical (Figure 3.7). Not conceived as part of a series of pictures of Revelation, this image of the Fourth Horseman only stands alone. Depicted as a ghoulish, emaciated figure with a skull-like head, this Horseman rides a striking white horse which tramples some unfortunate human victims underfoot. Around the Horseman's head circle demonic, prehistoric-looking birds and ominous black clouds. Neither God, nor Christ, nor even any angels are anywhere to be seen. This is a glimpse of a terrifying, godless world in which the Fourth Horseman seems to encapsulate all the woes of Revelation with none of the redemption.

This fascination with the Fourth Horseman is even in evidence in an example of political satire from 1795 known as *Presages of the Millennium* (Figure 3.8). In this image James Gillray depicts the prime minister of the day, William Pitt, as the Fourth Horseman. While he is skeletal with straggly, flowing hair, he rides a powerful white horse. This horse has a dual association in that while the Fourth Horseman's horse is said to be 'pale' (Rev. 6.8) a white horse was also the symbol of the house of Hanover. The monkey seated behind Pitt is the Prince of Wales. Pitt had formerly supported his accession to the throne during George III's period of mental illness, an act which linked them in a sort of alliance. Pitt's political followers trail behind him, represented here as little devils. Pitt himself holds a dragon by the neck in a possible allusion to the Dragon of Rev. 12. Meanwhile, Pitt's opponents, including Charles James Fox, have been trampled and thrown into Hell (Hades) in the right-hand corner of the image. The pigs on which Pitt's horse is also trampling are thought to be a reference to the common people, whom Pitt apparently referred to as the 'Swinish Multitude'. As in many of these apocalyptic images, therefore, it is the common man who bears the brunt of the apocalyptic woes represented by the Four Horsemen. As well as being a satire on Pitt, this etching is also a satire on the visionary

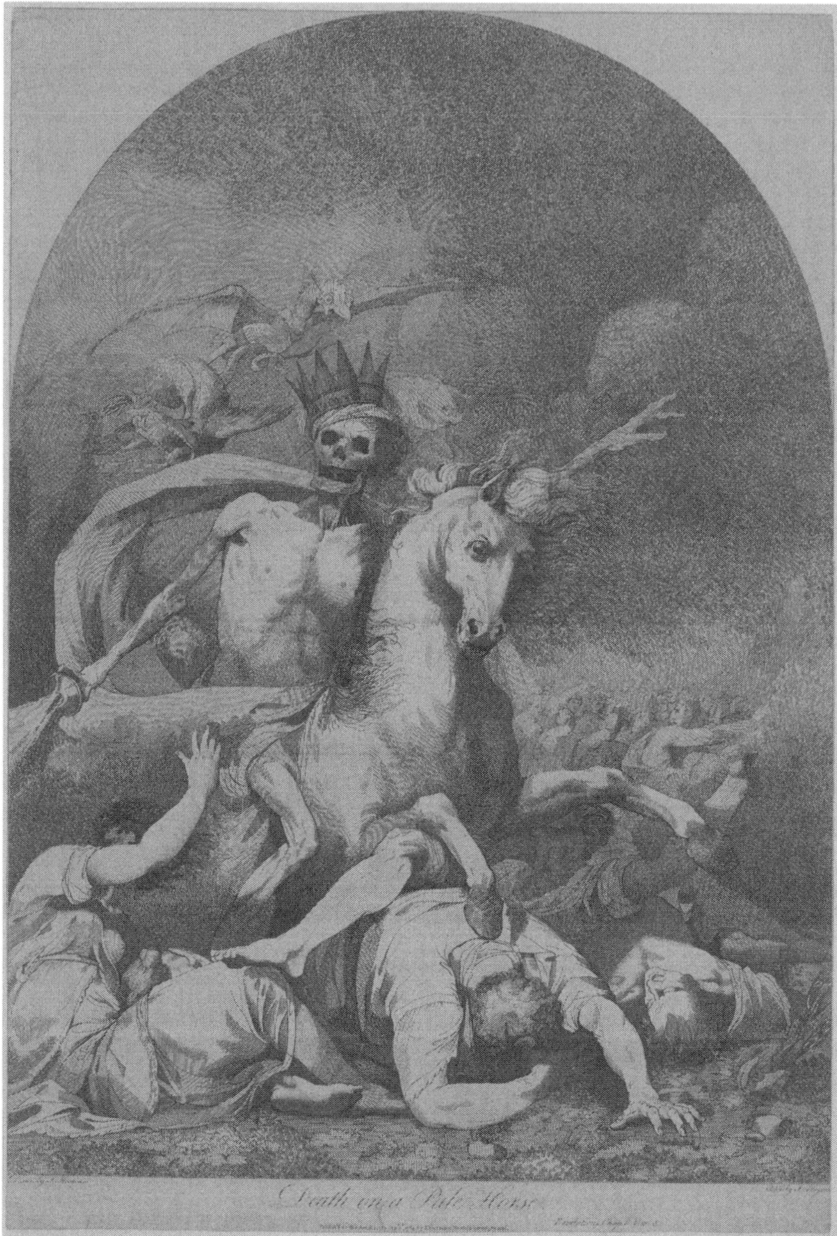


**Figure 3.7.** J. Haynes after John Hamilton Mortimer, *Death on a Pale Horse*, 1784, London: British Museum. © The Trustees of the British Museum

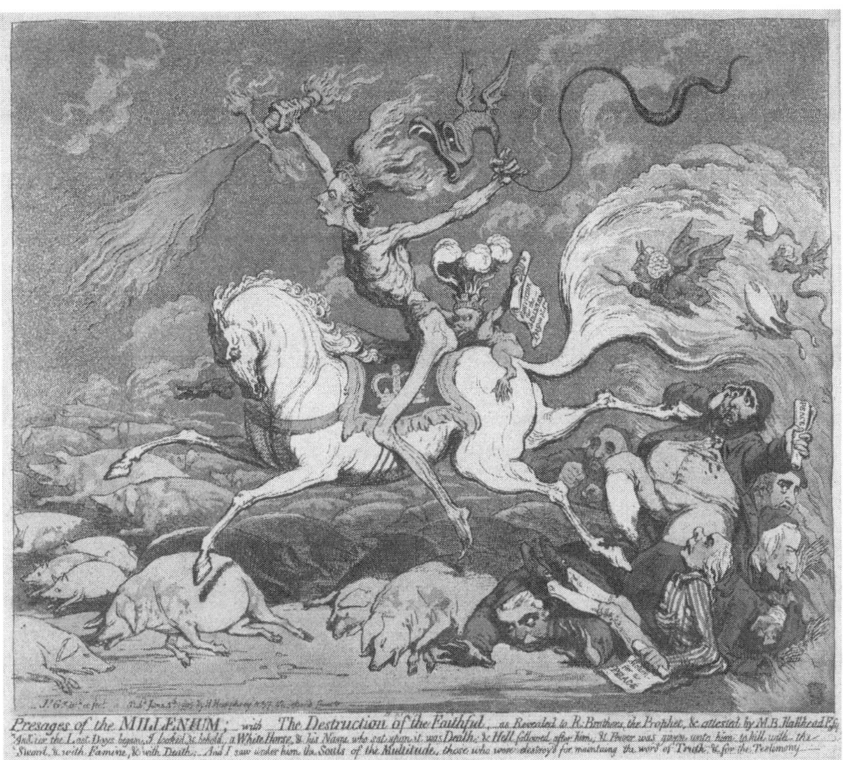



**Figure 3.8.** James Gillray, *Presages of the Millenium—With the Destruction of the Faithful, as Revealed to R. Brothers, the Prophet, and Attested by MB Hallhead Esq*, 1795, London: British Museum. © The Trustees of the British Museum

art which had become popular at this time.[7] This rather irreverent attitude to Revelation is taken up by a number of twentieth-century cartoonists who also found mileage in the subject matter of the Four Horsemen and to whom we shall shortly turn.

The last image that we shall look at from this period is Blake's *Death on a Pale Horse* (*c.*1800, ink and watercolour, Figure 3.9). This image, probably the first of the long series of watercolour illustrations of Revelation and the Bible that Blake created for his patron Butts, is interesting for the simple reason that Blake appears to have conflated the Four Horsemen into two, and in doing so makes an interesting interpretative point. While the image is entitled *Death on a Pale Horse*, the central Horseman, with his crown and magnificent white charger, looks altogether more like the first Horseman. He is, however, also holding a sword, symbol of the second Horseman.

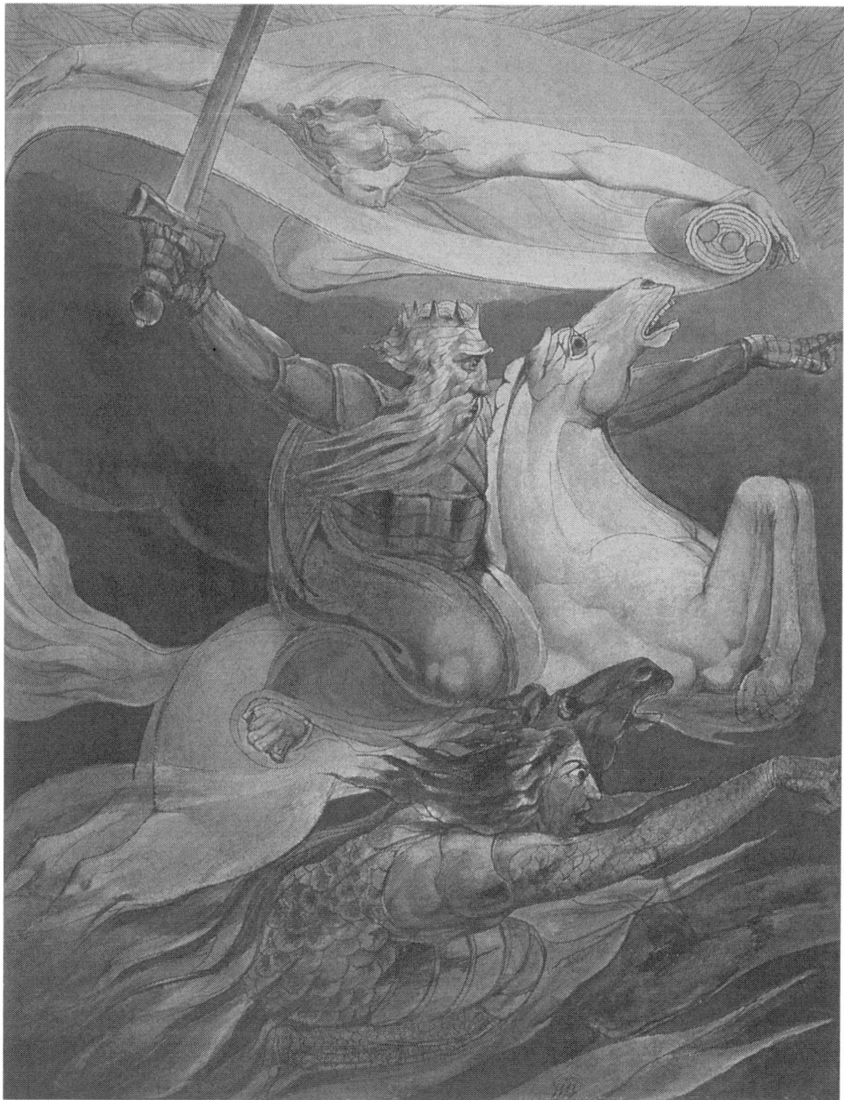

**Figure 3.9.** William Blake, *Death on a Pale Horse*, c.1800, Cambridge: Fitzwilliam Museum. © Bridgeman Art Library

Below, a shadowy figure with reptilian skin and seemingly tinged with fire rides a black horse, the colour of the third Horseman's steed. But perhaps the reptilian skin and flames are supposed to evoke Hades, which follows the fourth Horseman around? Above a Blakean angel holds an unfurled scroll with three seals left unopened. This, then, must in some way represent the opening of the Fourth Seal, that which unleashes the fourth Horseman. What then are we to make of this image? It has been suggested that while the central rider is almost certainly meant to evoke the fourth Horseman, its altogether more healthy, vibrant appearance than in other contemporary images of the same figure is due to the fact that Blake is not only conflating the Four Horsemen (and thus suggesting that they all represent manifestations of the same divine judgement) but is also intimating that the Horsemen may share some of the transformative power of the Rider on the White Horse (Christ) from Rev. 19. Thus, in line with Blake's idiosyncratic, possibly pantheistic, theology, even Death (the fourth Horseman) is here being presented in a more positive light.

## The Four Horsemen in twentieth-century satire

As was clearly the case with Gillray, the Four Horsemen continued to appeal to twentieth-century satirists as well. The two satirists featured below have both used the Four Horsemen as a lens through which to view their own realities. They are not 'decoding' or explaining the original concept of the Four Horsemen as it is found in Revelation but are attempting to give it new meaning.

In a striking cartoon from the *Sunday Express* in August 1943, Heinrich Himmler, Reichsführer and unofficial head of the SS, is depicted entering the 'Reich Home Office' tailed by none other than the Four Horsemen (Figure 3.10). They are without their horses but this is part of the joke which seals their identification. For the caption has Himmler saying to some Reichstag functionaries, 'I assume it's all right for temporary civil servants to leave their horses in the hall?' The Horsemen are also recognizable from their appearance, although they are not arranged in order. The first figure on the left is covered in sores and so presumably represents pestilence (the third Horseman). The second figure is attired as a Roman gladiator and so must be war (the first Horseman). The third is simply a skeleton and so represents famine (the second Horseman) and the fourth carries the scythe of the grim reaper in what has become the characteristic representation of Death, the fourth Horseman. Heavy storm clouds follow the Horsemen up the stairs and the sky is an inky black. This cartoon is clearly suggesting that such is the evil of the Nazi regime that it should come as no surprise that the Four Horsemen of the Apocalypse, symbols of eschatological and universal destruction, are actually working for it. Given their associations

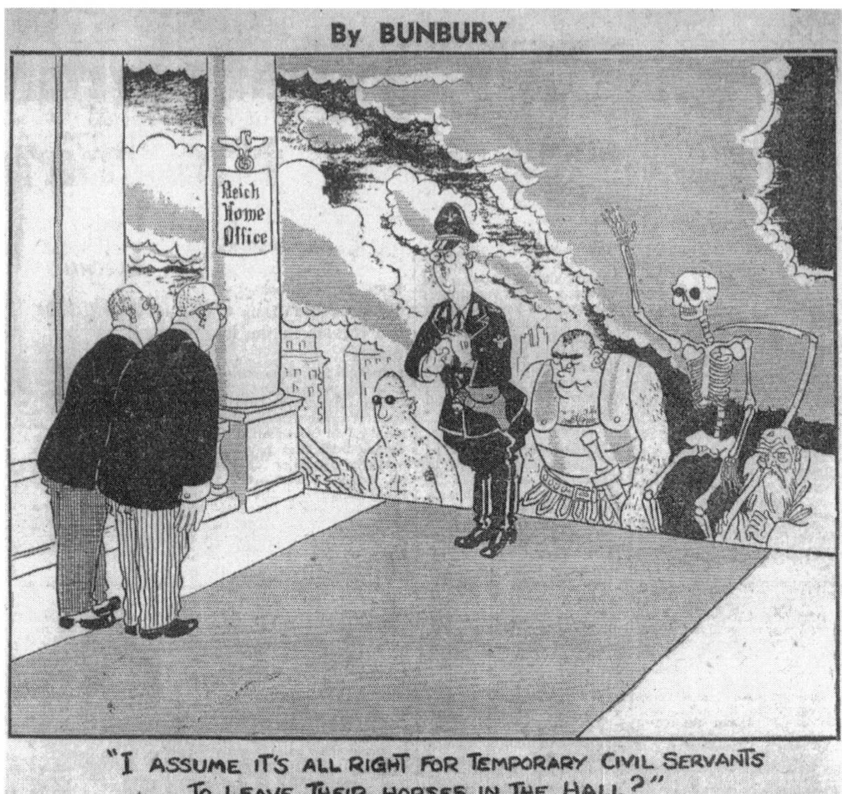


**Figure 3.10.** *Sunday Express* Bunbury cartoon, August 1943. © Sunday Express

with the end of the world, it may also offer some hope that the Nazi regime, despite appearances, is nevertheless a finite entity, which will end. Finally, there is also a propagandist slant to the cartoon: despite their hubris Nazi Germany is shown as having picked the wrong side, and will have to submit to the divine judgement of Rev. 19–20 when the time comes.

Another political cartoon from the *Sunday Times* on 1 May 1977 utilizes the Four Horsemen in a less momentous but nevertheless powerful way (Figure 3.11). The cartoon was published in advance of the meeting of the G7 in London on 7–8 May 1977. The meeting (of seven of the worlds' richest industrialized nations) was an unofficial summit designed to help the leaders of those nations resolve their differences in the midst of a world recession not dissimilar in scale to the one we have faced since 2008. Thus on the right-hand side of the image the meeting is imagined. World lead-

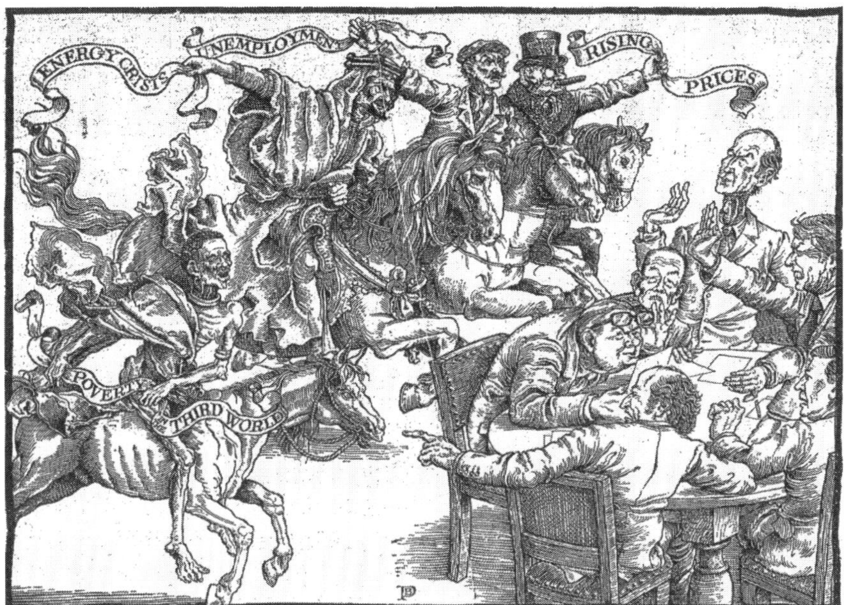


**Figure 3.11.** Peter Brookes cartoon, *The Sunday Times*, 1977. © News Syndication

ers James Callaghan (UK), Jimmy Carter (USA), Takeo Fukada (Japan), Giscard D'Estaing (France), Helmut Schmidt (Germany), and Pierre Trudeau (Canada) debate the issues at hand while behind them, in a representation that is heavily influenced by Dürer (indeed the horses themselves have been lifted directly from Dürer's image), the Four Horsemen thunder towards them. They bear not bows and arrows and swords but rather banners depicting the crises facing the world leaders: Rising Prices, Unemployment, the Energy Crisis, and Poverty in the Third World. Peter Brookes, the cartoonist, is clearly intimating that in the face of these momentous problems the meeting of the G7 is merely a piecemeal gesture. The fact that D'Estaing and Carter are mirroring the futile hand gesture of the man in the Dürer image who vainly tries to stop the charge of the Horsemen emphasizes the point.

## Conclusion

This playful image with a serious point brings to an end this selective survey of the Four Horsemen in artistic representation. We have seen how, in line with orthodox interpretation, it was initially the first Horseman who was singled out by artists for special treatment. Viewed either as Christ himself, or perhaps as a parody of Christ, he was often represented either completely separately (*Trier* and *Angers*) or facing in a different direction in order to signify his 'special' position (Memling). This tradition was swept away by Dürer's seminal image of the Four Horsemen (part of his *Apocalypse* series of 1498), who in the interests of artistic economy depicted the Four Horsemen riding out together. Copied by Cranach and many others besides, Dürer's image also introduced an element of realism into the destruction brought about by the Four Horsemen. His human victims have both a physical and a psychological realism that his predecessors' victims lacked.

This prompts us, the viewers, to ask again where a good God fits into this picture. While we might be able to understand that the Four Horsemen and the suffering that they cause are part of an overall divine plan, we might still feel uncomfortable with this notion when confronted with an image such as this, full of anguish and real suffering. These feelings of discomfort continued when faced with the three images from the eighteenth and nineteenth centuries by Haynes, Gilray, and Blake. In theological terms this is problematic. With God removed from the picture (and from the pictures), all the focus is on the demonic aspects of the Horsemen. These images depict a world out of control, with the fourth Horseman especially prominent (indeed, he alone appears in both Haynes' and Gilray's images), and there is no hint of the redemption offered at the end of Revelation.

This is a trend that continued into the twentieth and twenty-first centuries with added vigour. As we will see in the final chapter of this book, which takes a deeper look at how Revelation has been interpreted in more recent art, music, literature, and popular culture, the Four Horsemen became a potent and all-encompassing visual symbol of all things apocalyptic, a lens through which all sorts of disastrous events can be pictured. Included in the survey of cultural output associated with these figures are images and literary references to be sure, but there are also many references found in the moving image, computer games, popular music, and album covers, as well as an abundance of references in the modern media generally, as we see, for example, in the painting by Gordon Cheung of *The Four Horsemen of the Apocalypse* from 2009 (Plate 14). Although their faces are obscured, the Horsemen are clearly recognizable from the colours and shapes of their horses. The first is white, the second red, the third black, and the fourth a blue/green colour and decidedly more scrawny. They ride, as if suspended, above a skyline of mountains and skyscrapers which have themselves been daubed with huge ghostlike figures. As with much of Cheung's apocalyptic work, the scene is devoid of human life and seems to evoke a post-apocalyptic mood, perhaps prefiguring the destruction wrought by the Four Horsemen. Indeed, the skyscrapers (which may represent the Beast of our time, capitalist greed and economic inequality?) seem to be sinking before our eyes (into the lake of fire of Rev. 19.20 perhaps). It is significant that this painting was part of a larger show that Cheung devoted to the theme of the apocalypse, which included bulls' skulls, bucking broncos on lonely beaches with mountains on the horizon, new versions of Dürer's woodcuts, pictures of financiers and celebrities, and pages from the then crashing financial markets. The general sense of a world in rapid decline was clear and, indeed, somewhat mesmeric, but it is clear that he has used some themes from Revelation as a springboard for visual comment in other areas. A critique of the financial markets is also evoked in Hans Haacke's skeletal *Gift Horse*, displayed on the Fourth Plinth in London's Trafalgar Square in 2015. An LED device fashioned around its foreleg into a bow-shape constantly displays updates from the London Stock Exchange. Whether intentional or not, thoughts of the death-bringing fourth Horseman are inevitable.

So, while the Four Horsemen loom large in the popular imagination, they do so in a largely decontextualized way. Clint Eastwood's *Pale Rider*, a film from 1985, serves as a good example of this sort of decontextualized usage. The film, which clearly takes its name from Rev. 6.8 ('I looked and there was a pale (green) horse'), is set in a mining village in California in the 1880s. A mysterious pale rider known as the Preacher appears from the desert while another character, Megan, reads aloud from Rev. 6. He has arrived in answer to her prayers to protect the villagers from 'enforcers' sent by a big mining company. Preacher's main enemy is a man named Sheriff Stockburn, a name which has connotations of a fiery Hell and who works for the mining company. Stockburn has already tried to kill Preacher, or perhaps has killed him and the figure in the film is to be seen as a ghost. By the end of the film Preacher has defeated Stockburn and rides back off into the distance. Eastwood has appropriated the name and the idea of the pale rider from Revelation in a somewhat perverse way, completely overlooking the fact that in the biblical text the pale rider and Hell (Hades), far from being enemies, are bound together as companions ('its rider's name was Death and Hades followed him'). Conversely, Eastwood's Preacher/pale rider is a mysterious but heroic figure.[8]

Finally, and most decontextualized of all, we could mention the self-dramatizing attempt of the well-known atheists Dawkins, Harris, Dennett, and Hitchens to style their 2007 DVD of a cosy discussion they had on the (supposed) iniquities of religion as 'The Four Horsemen' in conversation.[9] Intended no doubt to be humorous, their appropriation of the term also leads us to expect a fierce tirade against religion, which is deeply ironic, given that in Revelation the Four Horsemen are sent to punish those who do not repent and submit to the Lamb.

Dawkins and Dennett are famous not just for their strident (new) atheism, but also for their deployment of the notion of a meme. Memes are images, concepts, and even world views which somehow capture people's minds or brains, much as, in Dawkins' view, 'selfish' genes capture and direct the bodies of the creatures in which they exist. On this view, rather than the larger animal or organism using the genes of which it is composed, genes use the creatures in which they exist. They direct the behaviour of those creatures so that those creatures reproduce—and so propagate the genes which are driving them, so, contrary to appearance, manipulating these larger creatures so as to get themselves reproduced.

Memes similarly live on in the brains and behaviour of the people whose minds they capture, regardless of what people actually want or think, and possibly even contrary to their conscious beliefs. In this way, as with genes in the biological kingdom, memes in the human world will live on in other brains, be passed on from one to another as we talk to each other and educate our children, and mutate in unexpected ways and contexts.[10] The Four Horsemen theme would itself be a good example of a meme.

However, thinking of the Four Horsemen meme in a decontextualized way obscures the deeper questions and meanings originally associated with it. In particular these questions relate to the ways we confront the scourges brought to us by the Horsemen, scourges whose urgency and import show no sign of declining: war, famine, plague, and death itself. These remain with us, whatever our religious preoccupations, and whether we have any or none. For those who strive to retain a religious sense, the question of their relation to a benign providence was always there, as the medieval images of the Horsemen actually being sent from Heaven demonstrate, even if in the twenty-first century these theological mysteries have been trampled into the dust beneath the horses' thundering hooves, pondered only by a handful of theologians.

# 4

# The Seven Seals

## Angelic Destruction

While Revelation's Four Horsemen have found global fame in a number of different incarnations, the Seven Seals were made famous, in recent times at least, by the Ingmar Bergman film *The Seventh Seal*. The film itself is something of a misnomer in that the viewer is left to make for themselves the links between the Seventh Seal of Revelation and Bergman's cinematic narrative (see Chapter 10 for more on Bergman's *The Seventh Seal*). Despite the fact that the film opens and closes with quotations from Rev. 8 describing the Seventh Seal, the first of which announces half an hour of silence in Heaven, viewers of the film will be left none the wiser as to the content and meaning of Revelation's Seven Seals. Many people may not be aware, for example, that the Seven Seals are both intimately connected with the Four Horsemen and the two other sequences of seven that occur within Revelation, the Seven Trumpets and Seven Bowls or Vials.[1]

## Revelation's sequences of seven

These sequences, placed at strategic points throughout the text, warn of specific disasters that will be sent down to earth from Heaven to symbolize apocalyptic upheaval and provoke repentance. When Revelation was written, the sequences of seven were no doubt intended to assure and/or reassure first-century hearers and readers that the Roman empire, although seemingly eternal and impregnable, could be swept away in an instant by God and his angelic army. Thus the wavering and lukewarm churches addressed in Rev. 2–3 should resist the superficially attractive Roman empire at all costs.

While initially the woes unleashed by the Seven Seals may have been viewed as typical messianic woes, such as those found in both contemporary Jewish literature, such as 4 Ezra, and the so-called Synoptic Apocalypse (Mark 13), as the sequences progress it becomes clear that both the woes contained therein and the structure are unique in the context of contemporary Judeo-Christian literature. It is for this reason that they have, since the time of Victorinus, one of the earliest commentators on Revelation, provoked much discussion. Some commentators have seen the sequences of Seven Seals, Trumpets, and Bowls as recapitulations of the same event, while others have argued that they build in a sequential way.[2] In support of the latter position it is true that the first sequence (the Seals) affects only a quarter of the earth, the second (the Trumpets) a third of the earth, and the final sequence (the Bowls) the whole earth. Thus the sequences of seven clearly escalate in scope and scale. There is also some evidence to suggest that the first sequence, the Seven Seals, with its different pattern of woes, which begin with the unleashing of the Four Horsemen, should be seen as distinct.

There are, however, clear similarities between the sequences. They all consist of seven woes, similar to the Exodus plagues on Egypt, such as plagues, hail attacks, locust attacks, and eclipses, and each new woe is introduced by an angel (See Exodus 8–11). In a sense it is this intimate connection with Heaven that makes the three sequences of seven woes so interesting, rather than debates over whether they are recapitulative or sequential. The destruction that is unleashed by the Seals, Trumpets, and Bowls is a divine and angelic destruction and not one linked to the demonic beasts of Rev. 11, 13, or 17.

## Depictions of the sequences of seven

Just as was the case with the depictions of the Four Horsemen (Chapter 3), the artists who have illustrated the sequences of seven, of which there have been many, have not shied away from representing the theological conundrum of *angelic* destruction. In most of the images that we shall look at, angels are clearly present amidst the destruction, and in some cases actually orchestrating the destruction, hence the subtitle of this chapter. However, there is no sense in which these are bad or rogue angels, as all the events which take place up to the final battle and defeat of Satan in Rev. 19–20 can be seen as a form of necessary and radical purgation prior to the establishment of the New Jerusalem in Rev. 21–2. Indeed, in many representations God or Christ himself is seen as presiding over the angelic punishments of a sinful people.

Since the Four Horsemen make up the first four seals in the sequence of Seven Seals (Rev. 6.2–17), we shall focus in this chapter mainly on artistic interpretations of the remaining three seals and the sequence of Seven Trumpets. Perhaps due to the repetitive, recapitulative dimension of the sequences of seven, the final sequence, of the Seven Bowls (Rev. 15–16), has not been depicted with such regularity or originality by artists, something that is also reflected in our treatment. In the interests of clarity, we will therefore first discuss a selection of images of the Seven Seals followed by a selection of images of the Seven Trumpets and, finally, just one image of the Seven Bowls. These images will appear in order of composition in the three separate sections but, unlike in previous chapters, there will not be a chronological progression throughout the chapter, starting with the earliest and finishing with the latest image. It may therefore be useful to hold in mind the following, general chronological trends.

The medieval illuminated manuscripts, such as the *Trinity Apocalypse*, which is featured in this chapter, tended to illustrate Revelation almost on a verse by verse basis and so could include around eighty images. Each of the seven woes in the three sequences has therefore generally been allocated one, or in some cases two or even three, images. *Trinity*'s Sixth Trumpet, for example, due to its vivid textual description (involving angels from the River Euphrates and an army of 200 million horsemen) is visualized across not one, but three images.

With the advent of the printing press and the commercialization of the publishing industry, such lavish, expansive productions were no longer commercially viable. Artists such as Dürer and Cranach radically condensed the way Revelation was pictorialized, allowing roughly one image per chapter. In these images, the sequences of seven tend to be depicted more synchronically, as if they are all happening at the same time. Indeed, Dürer, consciously or unconsciously following the lead given to him by Memling a few decades earlier, and also by the Koberger Bible, which condenses the entire narrative of Revelation into eight images, has the disasters appearing to the visionary all at once, in a way that would not be possible in a linear text, which raises interesting interpretative questions. Are we to think of the vision itself as developing sequentially, or rather of the vision and what it portrays as happening synchronically, within a single time frame? Considering the world as a whole, we might think that most, if not all, of the types of events described in the sequences are all happening at the same time, indeed somewhere in the world at all times. If that is how the seer saw them, mightn't that be a more powerful and realistic way of experiencing them than the way they are depicted in, say, *Trinity*, where sometimes one woe alone occupies three images?

Subsequent artists of Revelation, such as El Greco, Turner, and Danby, who are also featured in this chapter, took a more decontextualized approach to the text, producing single, discrete images focusing dramatically on a single section or theme, so as to stand for the whole lot. One possible consequence of this sort of extremely attenuated depiction of the woes—as we find particularly in artists such as Danby and Martin—may have been to encourage a reading of Revelation as a text concerned simply with destruction, forgetting altogether that in the text itself the woes are part of a larger process which ends in heavenly redemption. But this is not, on the whole, how Revelation's sequences of seven are viewed today. While the Four Horsemen have taken centre stage in the twentieth and twenty-first centuries as the predominant apocalyptic symbol, who can forget the group of helicopters flying over the dawn sky in *Apocalypse Now*, a menacing evocation of Revelation's locust army (Rev. 9) for our own times?

## The Seven Seals

### *The* Trinity Apocalypse

*Trinity*, in accordance with Anglo-Norman apocalyptic iconography, depicts the sequences of seven one by one, in a very clear, if somewhat repetitive way. After the appearance at Rev. 6.8 of the fourth Horseman (Death), pursued by Hades, there is a pause in the narrative. Instead of more destruction there is a description of some Christian martyrs sheltering under an altar and then receiving clothes from angels (Rev. 6.9–11). In New Testament scholarship these figures have been compared to the sacrificial animals whose blood was poured onto the base of the altar in Jewish ritual.[3] More generally they have been identified with the souls of the righteous (not necessarily exclusively Christian) waiting for their reward in Heaven. As mentioned in the last chapter, they can also be seen to represent God's more 'caring' side amid the seemingly indiscriminate destruction and suffering caused by the opening of the Seven Seals.

The scene is illustrated in a characteristically straightforward manner in *Trinity* (Figure 4.1). In the middle of the image is a large altar (which the commentary accompanying the images in the manuscript tells us symbolizes Christ) under which shelter four small, naked martyrs who stand in a crypt. To the right two winged angels clothe two additional martyrs. The angels are approximately twice the size of the martyrs, giving the martyrs a very childlike, defenceless aura. This image is followed on the next page by a depiction of the opening of the Sixth Seal, which sees a return to the drama of the first four (Figure 4.2). Rev. 6.12–17 describes, among other things, in one of the most poetic passages in the New Testament, a great earthquake, a solar and lunar eclipse, and stars falling from the sky. Kings, rich men, merchants, and ordinary people shelter from this unnatural destruction in mountainous caves and pray that the mountains will cave in on top of them rather than face 'the wrath of the Lamb'.[4]

This is once again depicted rather literally in *Trinity*. In the middle of the image crumbling towers teeter dangerously, thus evoking the earthquake. On the right-hand side of the image a group of men (some crowned) scramble into holes in some rocks, while on the left, observed by the ever-present John, the blackened sun and reddened crescent moon are suspended in a cosmic semicircle. In typically anti-Semitic style, the commentary accompanying this image explains that the 'earth' is a metaphor for 'the Jews'. There was an increase of anti-Semitism in the Apocalypse manuscripts of

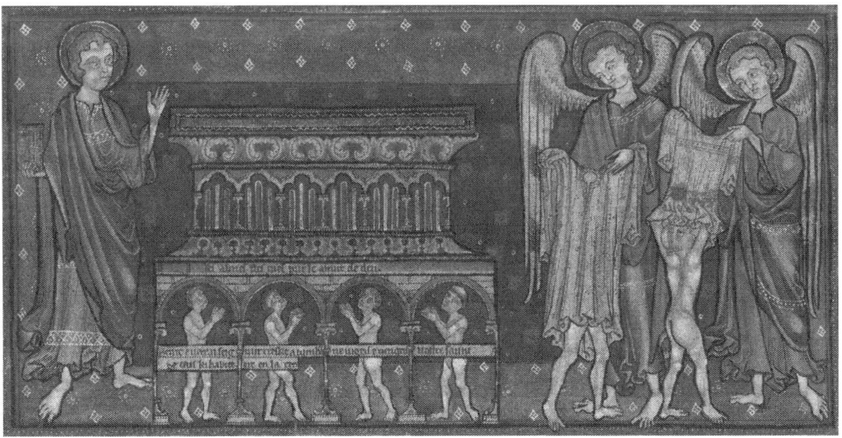

**Figure 4.1.** The *Trinity Apocalypse*, *c.*1260, The Fifth Seal: The Martyrs Sheltering under the Altar (Rev. 6.9–11), Cambridge: Trinity College. © The Master and Fellows of Trinity College, Cambridge

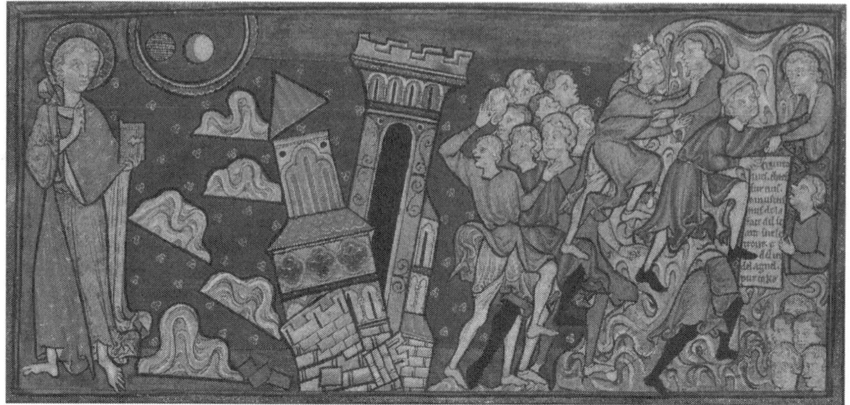

**Figure 4.2.** The *Trinity Apocalypse*, *c.*1260, The Sixth Seal: The Great Earthquake
(Rev. 6.12–17), Cambridge: Trinity College. © The Master and Fellows of Trinity
College, Cambridge

the mid- to late thirteenth century. This trend was itself a reflection of
increased discrimination against the English Jews, which culminated in
their expulsion from England in 1290.[5] Thus the blackening of the sun in
this image represents the punishment given to the Jews on account of
their having failed to recognize Christ. Similarly the falling stars represent,
according to the accompanying Berengaudus commentary, the demise of
the Jewish chief priests, scribes, and Pharisees, and so on. In the *Gulbenkian
Apocalypse*, also reliant for its interpretations of Revelation on the Berengaudus
commentary, there are a number of polemical images of Jews, with the
opening of the Sixth Seal being taken to involve their destruction, and
there is a striking image (38v) of the prophet Elijah separating the Jewish
people into those who convert to Christianity and those who don't
(Figure 4.3).

While it is a fascinating experience to piece together the text, image, and
commentary sections of *Trinity*, and indeed of the other beautiful and intricate Anglo-Norman Apocalypses, like *Lambeth*, *Gulbenkian*, and *Abingdon*, it
is slow and painstaking work. One loses the sense that one is experiencing
a vision, although cerebrally you remain aware of this via the presence of
John the seer in every image.

### El Greco

El Greco's rendering of the Fifth Seal (*c.*1608–14; Plate 15) takes the same
subject matter and reinvigorates it with both a visionary fluidity and an

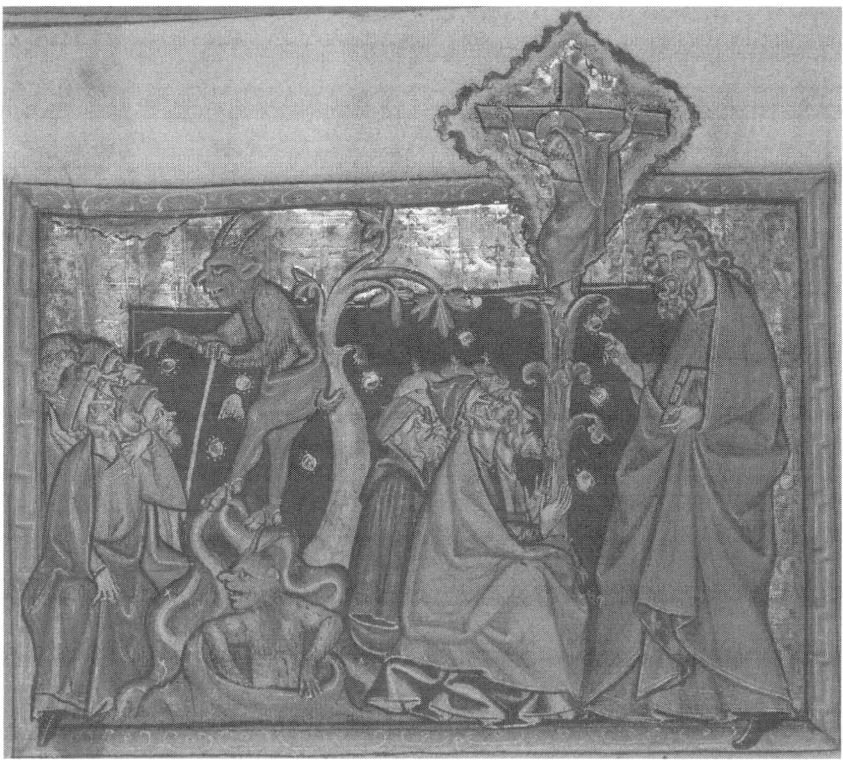

**Figure 4.3.** The *Gulbenkian Apocalypse*, c.1270, Elijah Separating the Good and Bad Jews, Lisbon: Museo Calouste Gulbenkian. © Museo Calouste Gulbenkian

immediacy that most late medieval and even post-Reformation illustrations had lacked. As has become clear in preceding chapters, it was rare for artists to take just one verse or section of Revelation in order to make an individual painting or altarpiece. Illustrated manuscript or illustrated book versions of the text were far more common. For reasons that are not entirely clear, El Greco decided to incorporate the martyrs from Rev. 6.9–11 into a three-altarpiece project that he had begun for the church at the Hospital of Saint John the Baptist in Toledo, Spain in 1608. The other sections of the altarpiece depict an Annunciation and a Baptism.[6] The painting is one of the best extant examples of El Greco's later, more mystical, hallucinatory even, style. In this period his paintings lack any natural light source and appear to be lit from within. While many of the by now long-established iconographic elements of Rev. 6.9–11 are present, such as the naked martyrs (here both male and female), and the angels handing out the white robes, the altar is missing. This fact, taken in combination with John's extremely large, elongated size and ecstatic pose, has led some art historians to question whether El Greco was in fact evoking John's vision more generally rather than Rev. 6.9–11 specifically. As with many paintings and images from the premodern period, El Greco did not himself ascribe a title to the work but it was listed in his studio inventory on his death in 1614 as *Saint John the Evangelist Witnessing the Mysteries of the Apocalypse*. It was first associated with the Fifth Seal in particular in 1908 by El Greco scholar Manuel Cossio.[7] Whatever the initial intention, this painting can either be viewed as a haunting evocation of the Fifth Seal or as an attempt, perhaps in homage to Memling and Dürer, to reimagine John's visionary experience from his perspective. In either case, the swirling movements of the martyrs and angels as evoked here by El Greco certainly help to capture the fluidity and even the confusion of John's visionary experiences.

### *Danby's* The Opening of the Sixth Seal

Irish painter Francis Danby's *The Opening of the Sixth Seal* (1828) focuses not on the contemplative moment represented by the Fifth Seal, but instead attempts to convey the cataclysmic destruction of the Sixth Seal (Figure 4.4). Danby was heavily influenced by his contemporary John Martin's apocalyptic paintings, of which more in Chapters 8 and 9. Unlike the static, naïve depiction of *Trinity's* Sixth Seal (see section 'The *Trinity Apocalypse*'), Danby gives expression to the global drama envisaged in the text of Rev. 6.12–17. The clouds really do look like they have been rolled up to let through a destructive force from above. Rocks fall in every direction like meteorites from outer space raining down on a cowering humanity dwarfed by the cosmic events that rage around them. *Trinity's* handful of victims are here replaced by as many classically attired sufferers as the eye can see (and as many as Danby's brush could fit in). No doubt in its time this would have been seen as an evocation of the sublime.[8] Some in our own more sceptical age might find it as humorous as it is terrifying, but Danby's evocation of a tiny humanity crushed by overpowering natural forces (with no angels in sight) certainly anticipates so many of today's disaster films (such as *Independence Day*, *The Day after Tomorrow*, and *2012*) and apocalyptic-inspired games that enjoy such popularity today.[9]

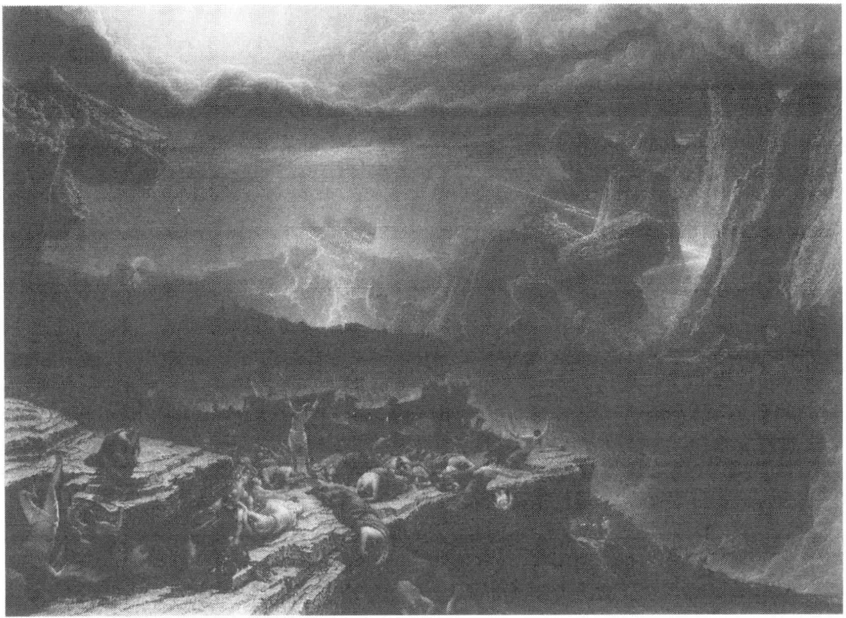

**Figure 4.4.** Francis Danby, *The Opening of the Sixth Seal*, 1828, London: British Museum. © Bridgeman Art Library

## The Seventh Seal

After all the tumult of the six earlier seals, the silence of the Seventh Seal is powerful: 'And when he (that is, the Lamb) had opened the Seventh Seal, there was silence in Heaven for about half an hour' (Rev. 8.1). On the most literal interpretation the sound of the angelic worshippers and the divine voice, which we have been told in Rev. 4 are perpetual, are stilled, itself striking enough. But what does it actually signify? Over the centuries there have been a host of interpretations, not all mutually contradictory. These include a passage of silent worship, which is the creaturely response to the divine; a moment in which the prayers of the martyrs, mentioned in the Fifth Seal, can be heard; a lull in the cosmos prior to the storm, both terrifying and splendid, of the new creation, which is about to occur in the form of the New Jerusalem; a moment in which all creation can ponder the salvific mystery; the peace and everlasting rest which follows all the earlier disasters and destructions, which are interpreted by some as being tantamount to the reign of Antichrist; and finally, in an interpretation specifically related to the Gospel story, the silence of holy Saturday after the crucifixion and before the resurrection.[10]

Paradoxically silence and stillness are difficult to depict even in a medium which is itself silent and still. The medieval artists typically depicted the silence as the angels of the heavenly throne room laying down their trumpets or instruments, as in an image from the *Angers Tapestry* (Plate 16). Here John looks on from the right, from behind the safety of his shelter, as the seven cherubic-looking angels stand or kneel before God and the Lamb, holding their trumpets away from their mouths. They are thus ready to commence the next sequence of seven (the Seven Trumpets) but are clearly pausing before doing so. The effect is remarkably contemplative, a rare visual moment of calm in the midst of these vivid, sometimes seemingly never-ending tableaux. With the printing revolution, space was now at a premium, leading to more condensed representations of Revelation, as in Dürer's *Apocalypse* of 1498. Thus the silence in Heaven (the Seventh Seal) fell out of favour with visual artists, although, as if to compound the paradox, twentieth-century musicians, like Messiaen and Franz Schmidt, made it a central focus of their aural treatments of Revelation; and, as we will see, Bergman makes a lot of the silence and its aftermath in his film *The Seventh Seal*, though in a somewhat ambiguous manner. (See Chapter 10 for a treatment of Schmidt, Messiaen, and Bergman.)


## The Seven Trumpets

### *The* Trinity Apocalypse

In order to recreate the experience of engaging with a sequential representation of one of the series of seven, we have here reproduced six of the Seven Trumpets from *Trinity*.[11] As discussed above, the *Trinity Apocalypse* is known for its legible style and richly elaborate colours. In contrast to some of the other thirteenth-century Apocalypse manuscripts, it allows one image for each trumpet blast. In the first page of this series (*Trinity* folio 8v; Plate 17), the upper image depicts the blowing of the First Trumpet and the rain of fire upon the earth, here depicted by some small trees (Rev. 8.7). With John looking on from the left, the other angels with trumpets queue up behind the first angel, their own trumpets at the ready. The lower image on this page depicts the blowing of the Second Trumpet, which turns a third of the seas into blood, destroying sea life and causing shipwrecks (Rev. 8.8–9). The poisoning of the sea is represented by upturned fish. The extremely large scale of the actual trumpets in these images, as compared to the other figures and objects, is effective at conveying their destructive scope.

The unusual design feature of *Trinity*, of sometimes having two or even three images per page (rather than one image at the top of the page followed by text, as is usual in Anglo-Norman manuscripts), works well as a depiction of the sequences of seven. While the images themselves are naïve in terms of style and perspective, the presence of several images on each page adds a grim inevitability to the unfolding of the sequences of seven, with each trumpet pointing forwards to the next. The Third Trumpet depicts the appearance on earth of a curious star named Wormwood (Rev. 8.10–11; Plate 18). Wormwood poisons a third of the fresh water on earth, killing 'many people'. In the *Trinity* image Wormwood's victims lie in a heap on the right-hand side. One man clutches his head or tears at his hair while the others try desperately to drink from the poisoned river. The star itself, near the bottom of the image, is labelled '[A]bscinthium', which refers to the *Artemisia absinthium* plant, which has a very bitter taste. As before, this image is much more specific in its visual detail than other images of Revelation from the same period.

After this crowded and fairly dramatic composition, the image accompanying the Fourth Trumpet (another solar and lunar eclipse, Rev. 8.12) appears almost like a void, the space to the right of John and the angel filled only by a darkened sun and moon (both fairly small in scale), across which flies the eagle which brings woe to the inhabitants of the earth. The blank space renders this image a bleak accompaniment to the text and commentary and forms a useful compositional contrast to the following image at the top of the next page. This depicts the Fifth Trumpet, which brings with it an army of locusts, which have been ordered to kill anyone who has been unfaithful to God (Plate 19). The King of the Locusts, Abaddon, described in the text as the 'angel of the bottomless pit' (Rev. 9.11), is normally represented as a human being but *Trinity* depicts him as a devil, labelled in French as 'Devastator'. He rides amongst his locust army as they surge up from under the ground towards a cowering heap of humanity, who are seen to be physically reacting to the stings of the locusts.[12]

The depiction of the Sixth Trumpet in *Trinity* (Plate 20) comprises three separate images of some complexity. The first image itself comprises three distinct sections, the angel blowing the trumpet on the left and a representation of God in the middle, under whom a head emerges uttering the words, 'Release the Four Angels who are bound at the great River Euphrates'

(Rev. 9.14). On the right we see the angel with the trumpet untying the hands of the unhappy looking angels. This image is important for reminding us of the centrality of God's dominion under which all the events of Revelation are taking place. Then we have a striking representation of the four, now unbound, angels about to undertake their task to destroy a 'third of humankind'. John is unusually and noticeably absent from this image. The artistic composition of this second image shows the angels dancing gracefully on the river against a background of stars and reveals an artistry that goes beyond the bounds of the theological task that the creators of this illuminated manuscript had been given. Finally, at the bottom of the page, we see John and the sixth angel looking at the 'myriad' horsemen (said to number 200 million in Rev. 9.16), here depicted as demonic riders aboard monstrous horses with heads of lions and tails of serpents, as described in Rev. 9.17–19. A pile of dead bodies represents the third of humankind that are destroyed by their fiery breath. Simultaneously, another group look on from the top right of the image, representing the section of society that Revelation tells us remained unrepentant of their murders, fornications, sorceries, and thefts, despite the destruction that they see all around them. The sequence of Seven Trumpets is brought to a close later on in Rev. 11 and so the Seventh Trumpet is not depicted in this sequence from *Trinity*.

Whilst on some levels an extremely literal and at times simplified rendering of Revelation, *Trinity*, because of its sharpness and clarity, constitutes a highly legible visualization of the text that also captures something of its visionary aspect, if not in the same way as the El Greco. With *Trinity* the visionary aspect evoked is more to do with a sense of being immersed in a continuously unfolding vision. This is partly due to the presence of John in so many of the images, as well as the striking visual references to the presence of God presiding over all that is happening. We, as the viewers, are not supposed to forget that Revelation in both its good and bad aspects is part of God's plan for humankind.

### *Dürer and the Seven Trumpets*

Dürer's condensed approach to his artistic representation of Revelation led him to depict six of the Seven Trumpet blasts across just two images. As was the case with the *Trinity* images, the first five trumpets are represented almost as a warm up to the visual grandeur of the Sixth Trumpet, which is both more detailed and more violent in content. Dürer's first image juxtaposes the handing out of the trumpets by God in the top half of the image

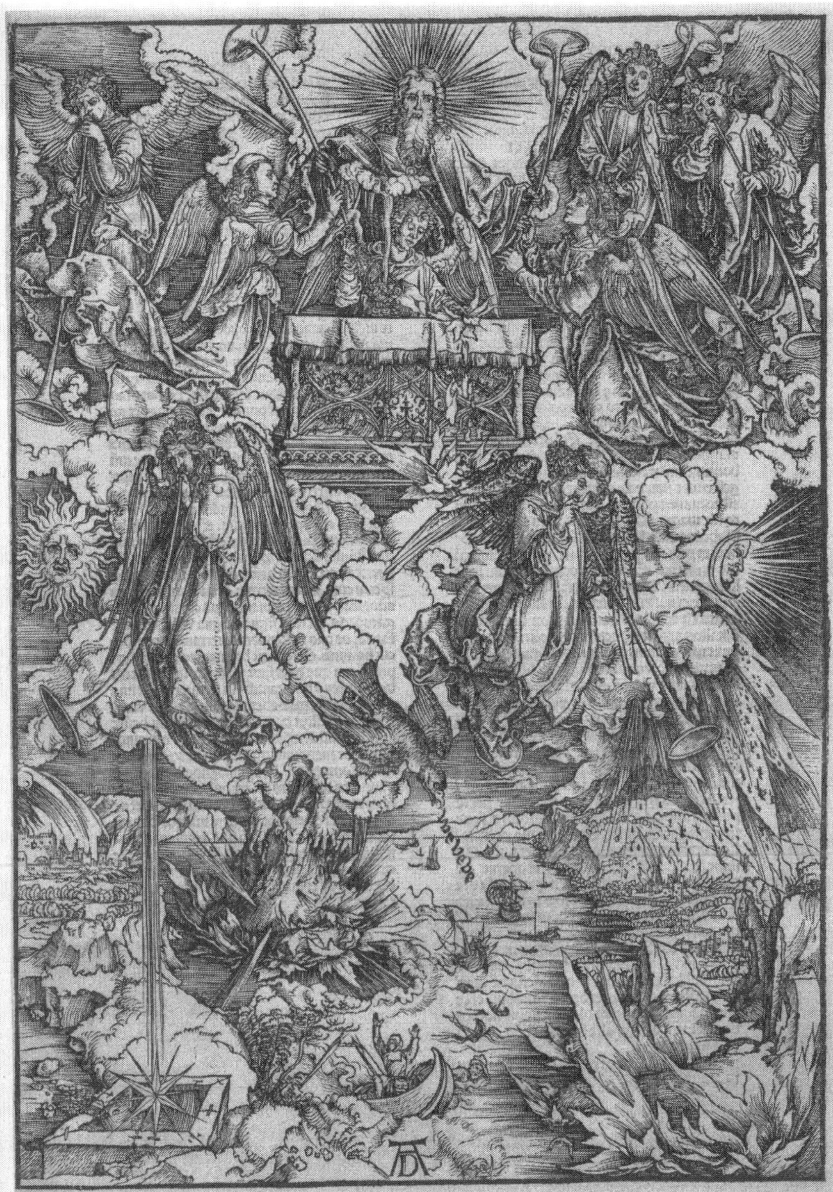

**Figure 4.5.** Albrecht Dürer, *Apocalypse* Series, *c.*1498, The Six Trumpets (Rev. 8–9), London: British Museum. © The Trustees of the British Museum

with the destructive events that they set in motion in the bottom half (Figure 4.5). An impressive synchronicity is therefore created, which raises questions not only about the temporal relationship between events in Heaven and on earth, but also about the chronology of the sequences of seven in the text itself. Are we to imagine them, as is suggested by the *Trinity* images, as unfolding one after the other, or, as is suggested by the Dürer image, as attacking one third of humankind at the same time? For here we see the First Trumpet's blood falling from the sky, the shipwrecks of the second, the distinctive Wormwood star of the third, and the darkened sun and moon and woeful eagle of the fourth all occurring simultaneously.

In a very literalistic touch by Dürer, we also see the great mountain of Rev. 8.8 (Second Trumpet) that is 'thrown into the sea' being thrust down from Heaven by a pair of huge hands into the midst of the other chaos. This image is also suggestive, as so many of Dürer's apocalypse images are, of John's purported visionary experience. For is it not more likely that John too experienced the sequences of seven as a terrifying jumble of events, as evoked here, rather than as an orderly, sequentially occurring series? It was, then, after the vision and when he, or some other early Christian, came to commit the vision to paper, that the events had to be categorized in a numerical fashion. Speculative though this may be, this image raises some fundamental questions about the useful and revealing role that images have to play in the interpretation of biblical text, and in particular texts that claim to be based on visions. Images such as this one by Dürer can take us behind the text itself to the very nature of the experiences, real or imagined, which have inspired it.

Dürer omits to represent the Fifth Trumpet and, like the anonymous artists of *Trinity*, chooses to capitalize on the artistic potential of the Four Avenging Angels of the Euphrates (Figure 4.6). In a vertical reimagining of the *Trinity* scenes, we see God handing out trumpets at the top of the image as he hovers in the clouds above an altar and flanked by angels. Below him, in the middle section of the image, the myriad horsemen thunder down from the sky, whilst on earth the grim-faced avenging angels scythe their way indiscriminately through piles of victims, amongst whom are popes, bishops, kings, knights and women, as we also saw with the victims of the Four Horsemen. Once again the chronology of the passage from Revelation has been deliberately distorted so that the angels appear in the foreground of the image, whereas in the text they materialize before the myriad horsemen. Whether Dürer wanted to prioritize the angels over the myriad horsemen for artistic or theological reasons cannot be known, but the effect is striking

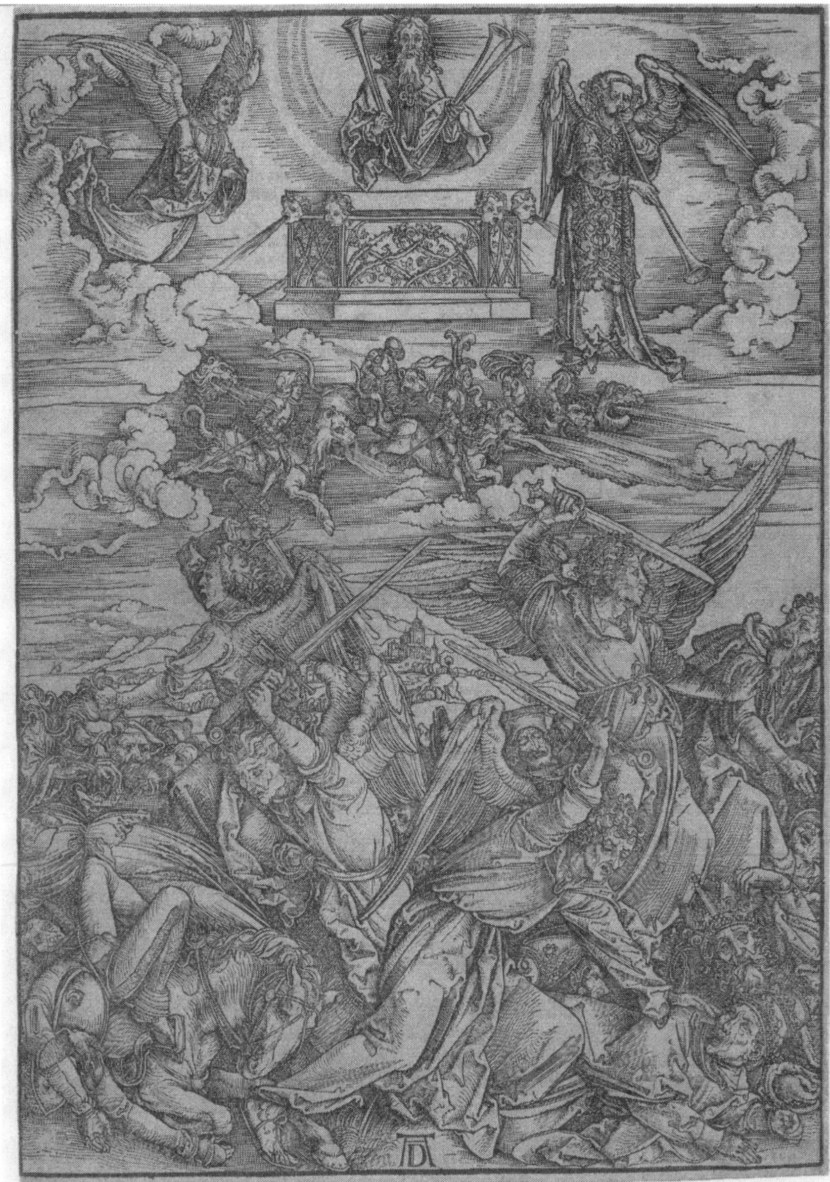

**Figure 4.6.** Albrecht Dürer, *Apocalypse* Series, *c.*1498, The Four Avenging Angels (Rev. 9.13–15), London: British Museum. © The Trustees of the British Museum

and serves to remind the viewer of that other frightening group of four in the earlier Dürer image of the Four Horsemen.

### *Coppola's* Apocalypse Now

Whilst it is actually quite difficult to make specific links between *Apocalypse Now* and Revelation (see Chapter 9), when one looks at the famous poster image of that film one cannot help but think of the locust army heralded by the Fifth Trumpet or the myriad horsemen announced by the sixth (Plate 21). While marauding armies of horsemen from Rome or Persia were the most frightening enemies that John could conceptualize, to us, in our mechanized, computerized age, the horse—even a monstrous, hybrid version— has lost some of its power as a symbol of terror. What would John 'see' if he experienced his visions today? Is it not quite likely that he would see swarms of Apache helicopters or even Drone aeroplanes? The *Apocalypse Now* poster, with its helicopters silhouetted against a burning sky, gives potent visual form to such ideas. The sleek, metallic, and anonymous appearance of these helicopters serve as a menacing symbol not only of the destruction that was perpetrated in Vietnam but also of other recent conflicts involving advanced weaponry. To their victims, they must appear as terrifying, robotic, and as lacking in compassion or remorse as the locust army or avenging angels would have seemed to John's hearers in 90 CE.

## The Seven Bowls

### *The* Flemish Apocalypse

As mentioned above, after the medieval illuminated manuscripts, which pictured the entirety of Revelation, the artistic attention paid to the Seven Bowls (or vials, as they are sometimes known) tends to be minimal. This perhaps adds weight to the suggestion made at the beginning of this chapter that the sequences of seven are intended to be viewed as recapitulations of the same events. Thus there is no need to represent the Seven Bowls as well as the Seven Seals and Trumpets. One exception to this is the *Flemish Apocalypse*, which devotes two images to the Seven Bowls (one to their distribution amongst the angels and one to their effects on earth). In an artistically inferior version of the Dürer image of the Seven Trumpets (Figure 4.5), the *Flemish Apocalypse*'s second image of the bowls depicts them synchronically (Plate 22). The bowls are poured out directly from Heaven by angels and the red liquid that pours from them is seen falling onto the unsuspecting earthly victims, symbolizing God's wrath (Rev. 16.1). The different punishments described in Rev. 16 are all visible here. For example, we see a small group towards the top right of the image being scorched with fire (Rev. 16.8–9, the Fourth Bowl) and, directly in front of them, another group of four 'gnawed their tongues in agony' (Rev. 16.10–11, the Fifth Bowl).

Most striking is the appearance of the Dragon from Rev. 12 and the Two Beasts from Rev. 13 at the right-hand side of the image. This clearly differentiates the sequence of Seven Bowls from the other two sequences of seven, which are not linked explicitly with the other Beasts of Revelation. However, in Rev. 16.13 these three figures are reintroduced with 'foul spirits like frogs' emanating from their mouths and this is what we see here. Whilst visually striking, mainly due to its stunning colours, this image is quite cluttered and difficult to read. It also fails to capture the lack of human repentance that is repeatedly stressed in Rev. 16, although this is very difficult to do in visual form. In spite of the terrible events that are befalling the victims of the woes, humanity simply will not repent. It is into this crescendo of unrepentance and defiance that the Whore of Babylon of Rev. 17 enters, which marks the climax of the chaos into which the world has fallen as it stands on the precipice of the final battle of Rev. 19–20.

## Conclusion

One might be forgiven for finding a certain repetitiousness in these sequences of disasters. On the other hand, it could not be said two thousand years after John of Patmos' vision that the world is free of any of them, whether caused by nature or inflicted by human beings upon themselves. At the time of writing the Philippines have been devastated by typhoon Haiyan, while in Syria, Iraq, the Ukraine, Israel and Palestine, the Central African Republic, Sudan, and doubtless in other places too, bloody conflicts still rage. But in considering the role of the disasters in Revelation, it is important not to minimize the countervailing redemption to which these disasters—which are, after all, unleashed on us by angels operating under divine command—are only a step on the way. This is perhaps best conveyed in a visual sense in the medieval manuscript or book versions of Revelation that we have looked at in this chapter, which take the reader or viewer on a visual journey towards the New Jerusalem via the sequences of seven woes.

More decontextualized images, rather like many of us in this more secular age, tend to be fixated on the negative aspects of the text and of existence itself. There is nothing wrong with this *per se*; indeed, it may even be a more realistic way of viewing existence. But in the interpretative context of Revelation, this 'negative' reading, which foregrounds the sequences of seven and their related disasters at the expense of other material in the text, may end up missing the point. It is the juxtaposition of terrible disasters with glimpses of salvation that make Revelation such a rich text. In the midst of the sequences of seven of Rev. 6, 8–9, and 16, for example, appears the Woman Clothed with the Sun of Rev. 12, herself a symbol of maternal protectiveness and of better things to come, and to this we will now turn.

# 5

# The Woman Clothed
# with the Sun

The Woman Clothed with the Sun (Rev. 12) is one of the most strikingly beautiful images in Revelation. The narrative associated with her is strangely self-contained, and the Woman does not reappear later, although the Dragon who pursues her does.

## The Woman Clothed with the
## Sun in Revelation

Perhaps more than any other chapter in Revelation, Rev. 12 weaves together elements from several sources, not all of them biblical. There are echoes of Genesis 3 (the story of Eve and the Serpent), of Exodus 14 and 19 (Israel pursued into the wilderness by Pharaoh), and, as will become evident, of the Gospel traditions connected with Mary and Jesus himself. However, there are also echoes of the Babylonian combat myth (the Enuma Elish) in which the warrior god Marduk fights the female mother god Tiamat,[1] as well as the Egyptian goddess Isis and the Greek myth of the birth of Apollo.[2] In this his mother Leto, pregnant with Zeus' twins, Apollo and Artemis, is pursued by the dragon Python. She is rescued by Zeus and Poseidon and gives birth safely. Apollo later kills Python (and, as if to underline the charmed mystery attaching to the whole saga, sets up the oracle at Delphi, the most sacred shrine of the classical world). Boxall argues that John's readers and hearers (from Roman Asia Minor) would probably have been familiar with both the biblical material and the Near Eastern and Greek myths alluded to in this chapter and that they would have been surprised at John's self-conscious transformation of them.[3]

The Woman in Rev. 12 appears as a great and mysterious sign in Heaven, following the blowing of the Seventh Trumpet in Rev. 11, which heralds a new phase of divine judgement in the textual narrative. She is described (Rev. 12.1–2) as being 'clothed with the sun', which denotes her heavenly status, with the moon under her feet, twelve stars on her head (possibly a reference to the twelve tribes of Israel), and pregnant. As she is about to give birth, she is pursued by the red Dragon (part of the Satanic trinity of Beasts, which appear and reappear throughout Revelation). This Dragon, who is shortly to be identified with Satan himself, has seven heads and ten horns (seven heads being normally a symbol of perfection, as we saw with the Lamb in Chapter 5, but here symbolic of the Dragon's deceptive nature, rather like the first Horseman who imitates Christ). He sweeps stars down from Heaven in his wake, which symbolizes the threat he poses to the heavenly order of things.[4] We are also told that the Woman's child will rule over all the nations of the earth with an iron rod. When he is born, the Dragon is not able to harm him and the child is snatched away (literally 'raptured') and taken up to God and to his throne, an allusion to Christ's resurrection and ascension. The Woman, meanwhile, flees into the desert (Rev. 12.5–6), here represented as a place of safety rather than the place of threat it often is in the Old Testament (e.g. Numbers 14).

In the tradition of Judeo-Christian apocalyptic literature, this chapter is what is known as a two-level drama ranging across both the heavenly and earthly realms, with the action in Heaven often prefiguring the action on earth.[5] At Rev. 12.7, therefore, the narrative switches abruptly from earth to Heaven, where a battle takes place between the angel Michael and his angels and the Dragon and his. The latter are defeated and thrown down to earth. God's victory is announced, and the Dragon, who is now explicitly identified with Satan, that 'ancient serpent' (Rev. 12.9), is cast down to earth. There follows a canticle or hymn of praise about the defeat of Satan, assuring John's hearers that even though Satan's presence may still be felt on earth and even in the sea (cf. Rev. 13), he has been definitively defeated in Heaven and that 'his time is short'.

Once back on earth, the frame narrative resumes and the Dragon/Satan begins to pursue the Woman for a second time. She is given eagles' wings, allowing her to escape. A flood pours from the mouth of the Dragon, to engulf the Woman, but the earth (Mother Earth or perhaps the Ge, or Gaia, the goddess of earth of Greek mythology) swallows the waters. The Dragon remains on the sea shore, vowing to fight on against the Woman and her descendants, who are further defined as 'those who keep the commandments of God and hold the testimony of Jesus', in other words Christians. This suggests that there are still struggles ahead for the church, with whom the Woman is often identified. This leads directly into Rev. 13, where the Dragon hands over his power to the Sea Beast, the second member of Revelation's Satanic trinity, to be discussed in more detail in the next chapter. After Rev. 12 the power of evil is principally personified by the two Beasts of Rev. 13 and the Whore of Babylon (Rev. 17), who rides on the Sea Beast of Rev. 13. In Rev. 20, however, with the Beasts defeated, the Dragon, once again identified as Satan, reappears. He is first chained for a thousand years (in what has come to be known as the Millennium, see Chapter 8), before being let loose again on the earth, and finally and definitively cast into the lake of fire and sulphur for all time (Rev. 20.10).

In some of its aspects Rev. 12 (the Woman Clothed with the Sun and the Dragon) resembles the sequences of seven, which can also be viewed as overlapping and repetitive accounts of what is essentially the same cosmic struggle between the forces of good and evil. However, unlike the themes and characters in the sequences of seven, as already mentioned, the Woman Clothed with the Sun does not appear again in the narrative. She has her own individuality and drama, and that is reflected in the artistic representations of this figure.

The intervening story of Michael and the initial defeat of the Dragon in the heavenly realm (Rev. 12.7–17) has perhaps received the greatest amount of literary and artistic attention overall. It has, of course, been interpreted as an explanation of the initial fall of the angel Satan, most notably perhaps by Milton in *Paradise Lost*. There Satan's anger is seen as arising from his jealousy of God's Son as being proclaimed equal to God: 'fraught/ With envy against the Son of God, that day/ Honored by his great Father, and proclaimed/ Messiah, King anointed, could not bear/ Through pride that sight, and thought himself impaired./ Deep malice then conceiving …'[6] But in *Paradise Lost* God's Son is not yet incarnated, nor at the time of the battle with Satan had human beings been created. However, the Dragon's resentful ire against Adam and Eve and their descendants, precisely because of God's love for them, is a very strong theme in Milton, and something which in the biblical context is earlier than Revelation.

The identification of the Woman Clothed with the Sun with the Virgin Mary, and her child with the Christ child, has seemed natural to many. Milton, though, as a strict Protestant, would have had no desire to give any support to what many Protestants regarded as the essentially Catholic devotion to Mary. This devotion, intensely felt throughout the Middle Ages, had in fact been reinforced as late as 1476 by the establishment of the feast of the Immaculate Conception of the Blessed Virgin Mary (meaning that she was born without original sin). But for Protestants like Milton this tendency to raise Mary so high, and to treat her as the mediator between men and God, was perilously close to idolatry. Accordingly, Milton does not refer at all to the Woman Clothed with the Sun, nor, in contrast to the more Catholic interpretations of the defeat of Satan, does he portray Mary, the second Eve, as the one who finally crushes the Dragon/Serpent.[7] This interpretation—of the ultimately triumphant Woman as Mary, the second Eve—does have a nice symmetry, if, as some have done, we see the chasing of the Woman by the Dragon as a figure of the first Eve being tempted by the serpent.

In fact, surprising at it might seem today, the Woman was not seen as the Virgin Mary by the early commentators on Revelation either. They interpreted her as the Holy Spirit (who was often seen as female) or as Israel (or even as Jerusalem, a point to which we will return). As her child is interpreted as either Christ, or the church, or both, she herself was often identified with the church. She came to be viewed as the heavenly counterpart of the earthly community of the faithful, the Church Triumphant in Heaven as opposed to the Church Militant on earth, an interpretation which once again draws upon the apocalyptic perception of the world as functioning on two levels, the divine and the earthly.

The fourth-century exegete Tyconius actually saw the Woman as a metaphor for his own Donatist church, which was embroiled in a schism with the rest of the early Christian church, and her severe labour pains are a symbol of the dawning of the messianic age, which brings great upheaval with it.[8] The Dragon meanwhile was often identified in early interpretations as the emperor Nero.[9] Actually the failure to see the Woman as Mary at least until the time of Bishop Quodvultdeus in the fifth century should not surprise us too much; it should rather remind us that doctrine has always developed in the church, and that Mary only began to feature doctrinally in a major way after several centuries of Christian practice. Of course, by the medieval period, when the earliest of our images was created, Mary had become a central figure in the Christian pantheon and devotion to her a central element of Christian practice, but even so not all the medieval images we have chosen here explicitly link Mary with the Woman Clothed with the Sun. Indeed, as late as the fifteenth century, in the commentary attached to the *Master Bertram Apocalypse Altarpiece* (which we will consider in Chapter 6), the Woman is identified with the church, the twelve stars with the Apostles, and the Sun (rather than the Child) with Christ.

## Imagery of the Woman Clothed with the Sun

What begins to emerge around the thirteenth century in images of the Woman Clothed with the Sun are interpretations of the Woman as Mary. Thus in *Trinity* she is represented as wearing the blue Marian gown and in a convent-like setting, though against any wholesale Marian identification it is worth noting that as late as Dürer the image is ambiguous on that score. Further, as we have seen with other themes, the earlier sequences tend to depict the incidents in the Woman's history in painstaking detail, whereas later images, from Dürer onwards, tend to sum up the main elements of the story in just one or two images. In the interesting case of Velázquez's pair of images of the Woman Clothed with the Sun, we see one image of John of Patmos having his vision, in which what he sees in the top left corner of the painting *is* the Woman and the Dragon, and a second of the woman herself, standing on the moon and crowned with stars. It has often been remarked that the Woman herself has a calm and beautiful presence, but she is actually an ordinary human girl rather than a classic ethereal beauty or an unrealistically unblemished saint. This may tell us something about the devotion of Velázquez's time, which focused on presenting the mysteries of salvation as events we were to imagine happening before us, and ourselves as participating in. With Blake, as so often, a further twist is given to the story: he depicts the moment the Woman is attacked by the Dragon, but the Dragon is not wholly malign-looking, nor the Woman wholly averse, a suggestion of some sort of cooperation between the two in a deeper mystery.

Nevertheless, for all the complexity which can be found in some of the artistic representations of the Woman, recent feminist criticism has a point in that—in distinction to Velázquez—the norm is for the Woman to be presented as an idealized virgin/mother type, even where the text may imply something more spirited on the part of the Woman, and where the Woman also has, as we have seen, many positive features, such as bringing and bearing light and grace. The feminist criticism is raising a point which, *mutatis mutandis*, will arise again when we come to consider the artistic representations of the Whore of Babylon. Sometimes it seems to the contemporary mind at least that religious art, in picturing women, is eternally caught between the classic virgin/whore dichotomy.

## Medieval visualizations

The first image that we have chosen of this episode is from the eleventh-century *Bamberg Apocalypse*. Made around 1000 ce for the emperor Henry II, this early Apocalypse manuscript contains fifty illuminated images of the narrative (painted by several different artists), not as many as the later thirteenth-century manuscripts such as *Lambeth*, *Gulbenkian*, and *Trinity* but still enough to create a real sense of unfolding drama. The images themselves are relatively uncluttered, usually taking just one or two figures as the visual focus. The result is a series of visually arresting, sometimes haunting images. The art historian Van der Meer draws our attention particularly to the eyes of the figures, which he says are never centrally focused but rather dart to the left or the right and as a result often seem 'silently filled with horror'.[10]

*Bamberg*'s representation of the Woman Clothed with the Sun, the Child, and the Dragon is a case in point (Figure 5.1). Here we see a huge Woman with a sun wheel around her head standing on the moon and holding a male child with enlarged genitals, thus shown in order to underline the fact that the child is male, and so is the expected messianic king. Below them the multicoloured serpentine Dragon hisses menacingly. As Van der Meer suggests, the Woman's eyes look up towards the top left-hand corner of the image, giving her an unsettled expression. Interestingly, she has no clear iconographic links to Mary. If she had been meant to represent Mary, she might well have been smaller, less hieratic, and certainly more human, more like other contemporary Marian images. It is far more likely that here she is the church, presiding over Salvation History. The second image of the Woman in the *Bamberg* series, a representation of the flight of the Woman into the wilderness (Rev. 12.13–17), suggests the Woman as a contending cosmic force rather than as the figure who shrunk from the angel Gabriel at the Annunciation or wept at the foot of the Cross (Figure 5.2). Leaving aside the precise interpretation of the Woman in these images, what is striking in them is their expressiveness. Their artist, by eliminating all extraneous detail, captures so well the essence of this complex chapter, and in the flight image

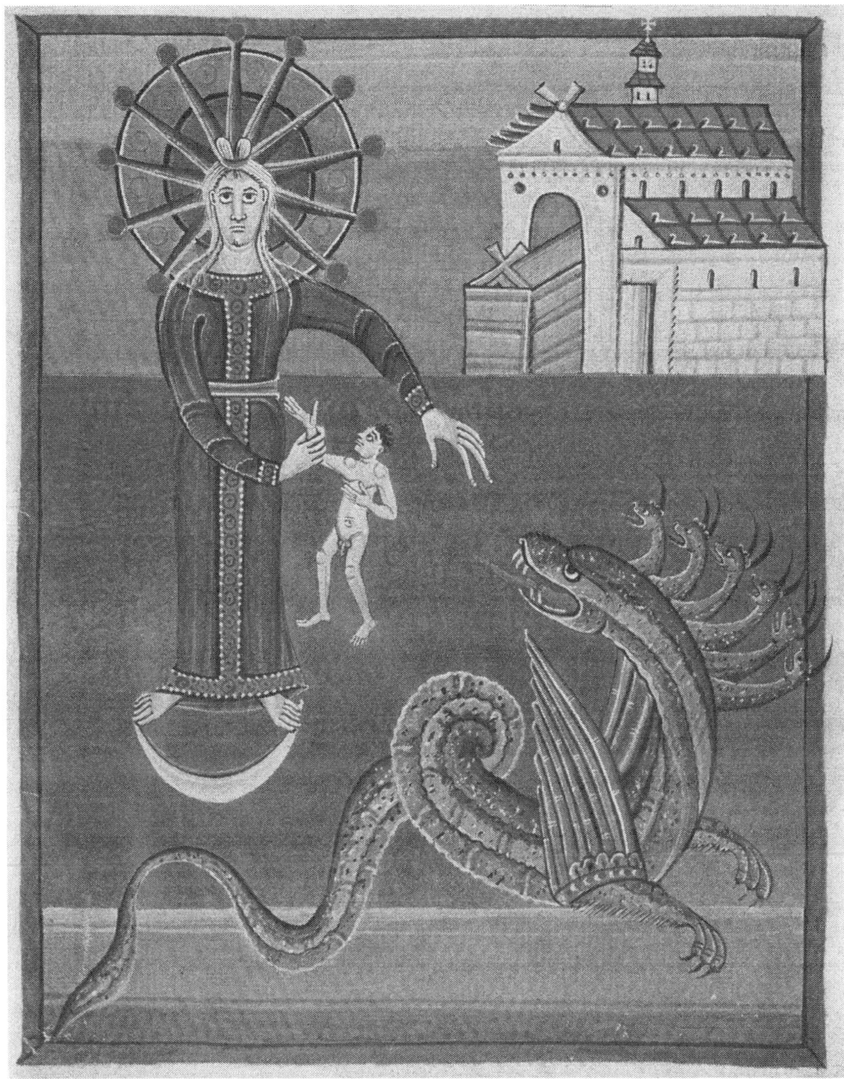

**Figure 5.1.** The *Bamberg Apocalypse*, *c.*1000, The Woman Clothed with the Sun: Woman, Dragon, and Child, Bamberg: Bamberg State Library. © Bridgeman Art Library

in particular, contrasts the determined calm of the Woman with the coiled and spitting venom of the Dragon.

A century later than *Bamberg* is a striking image from one of the *Beatus Apocalypses*, this one from the Silos Manuscript of 1109 (Plate 23). The *Beatus* commentary itself is characterized by an interest in conflicts within

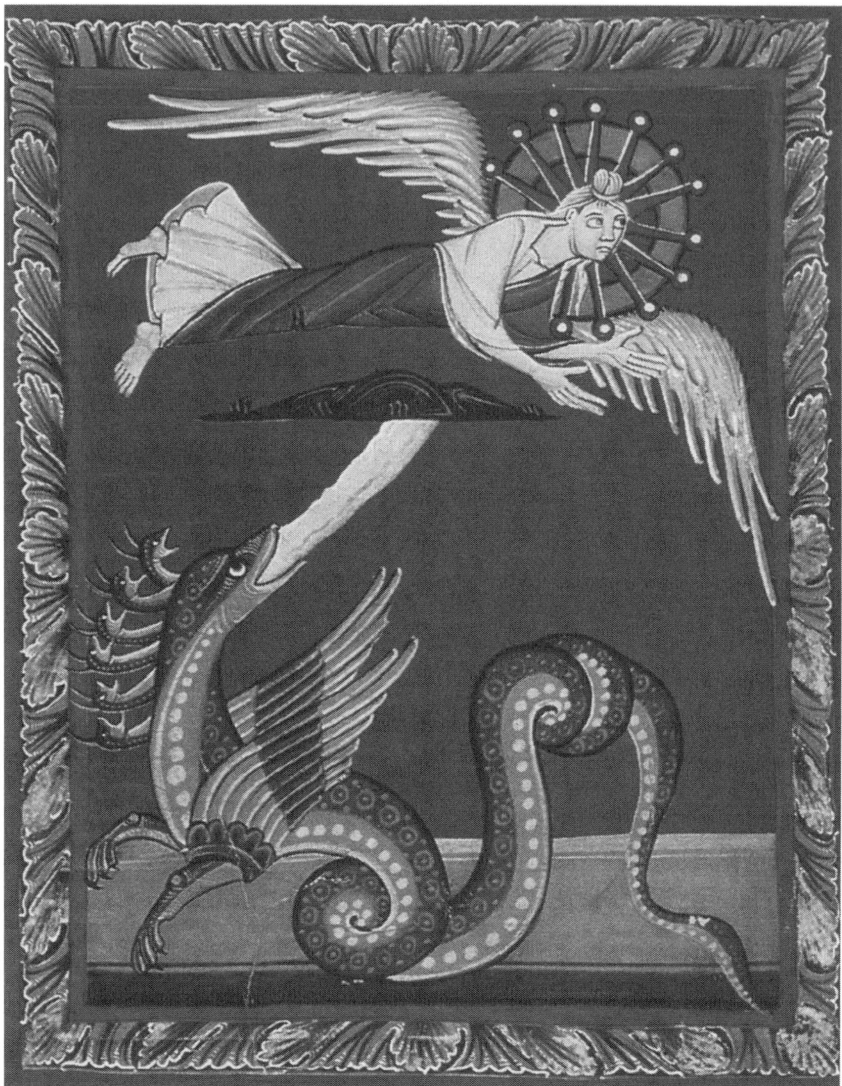

**Figure 5.2.** The *Bamberg Apocalypse, c.*1000, The Woman Clothed with the Sun: The Flight of the Woman, Bamberg: Bamberg State Library. © Bridgeman Art Library

the church as well as by an association with the Beasts of Revelation not with Rome, as had been traditional up until this point, but with Islam, which posed a serious threat to Spanish Christianity by the eighth century. This image follows a pattern established in many of the *Beatus* manuscripts. It manages to show us nearly all the main incidents of Rev. 12

within one pictorial space as well as Satan inside the pool of fire in the bottom right corner (Rev. 20) and Christ being presented to God in the top right (Rev. 5 or 22). In artistic terms it is rare and very striking to see the first and second battles between the Woman and the Dragon as well as the battle between the Dragon and Michael and his angels all taking place simultaneously. Nevertheless the idea of a two-level drama is respected, with the second battle, in which the earth rescues the Woman from the flood emanating from one of the Dragon's mouths, clearly taking place on earth and the others in the heavens, and, of course, the devil's pit at the very bottom. The fact that, textually, the Dragon is said to have seven heads was perhaps one of the motivating factors for such an ambitious composition, as this meant that different heads could be depicted as being engaged in different acts of the drama. In interpretative terms, such an image gives weight to the idea that Rev. 12, like the sequences of seven, is a multi-faceted evocation of what is essentially the same battle between good and evil.

The Dragon, silhouetted against the vivid orange and blue background, dominates the whole of the double-page spread, not just by his size, but also by his very sinuosity, his tentacles reaching into every available niche. Note for instance his tail sweeping down the stars from Heaven (Rev. 12.4) in the far right of the image. This is so striking an evocation of the insidious power of evil that one might be forgiven for wondering, in contrast to the *Bamberg* Woman, whether the comparatively small and rather static *Beatus* Woman, seemingly confined in a narrow section on the far left of the image, could ever prevail against him.

In contrast to both *Bamberg* and *Beatus* images are the depictions from *Trinity*, from the Anglo-Norman Apocalypse family. Here the Woman and Dragon are far more equally matched. As is in keeping with the Anglo-Norman manuscripts, which tended to utilize up to one hundred images to depict the narrative of Revelation, *Trinity* spreads this episode across five images (across two folios). The first folio depicts the first part of Rev. 12, the menacing of the Woman by the Dragon as she gives birth and the saving of the male child (Figure 5.3). The image on the upper register actually depicts the Woman reclining, as if she has just given birth. She is tastefully draped in a Marian-blue stole, which had come to be an integral part of Marian iconography by the thirteenth century. She hands the baby to the angel on the right while the muscular red Dragon flies in from the left, once again trailing a clutch of stars. The lower register of the first folio depicts the Woman

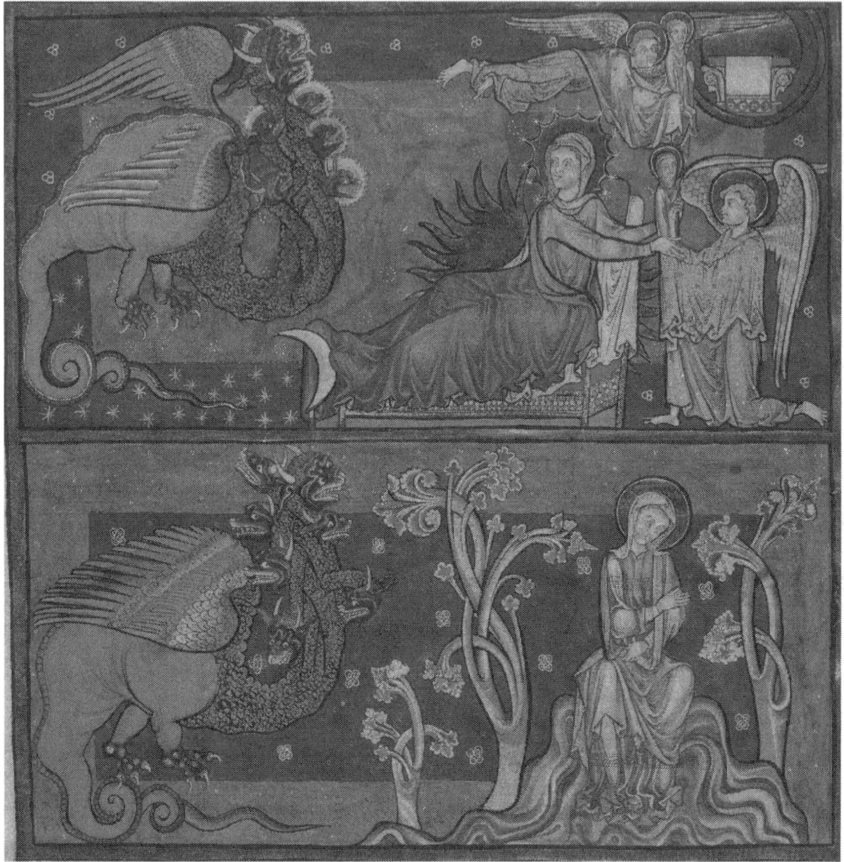

**Figure 5.3.** The *Trinity Apocalypse*, *c.*1260, The Woman and the Dragon (Rev. 12.3–5), Cambridge: Trinity College. © The Master and Fellows of Trinity College, Cambridge

in the wilderness, rather poignantly cradling her arms as if in remembrance of the absent child.

Figure 5.4, the second *Trinity* image, shows the second attack on the Woman by the Dragon and also the giving of the eagle wings by the angel, enabling her once again to fly to the wilderness. Here the wilderness is protected by an enclosed garden of rainbow–coloured plants, a natural *hortus conclusus*, so to speak. The convent-like setting of this Woman, and the way she is depicted with a gentle demeanour and cloak of blue and gold, would, in this case, certainly suggest an identification with the Virgin. And even when she is being threatened by the Dragon, her calmness and inner repose

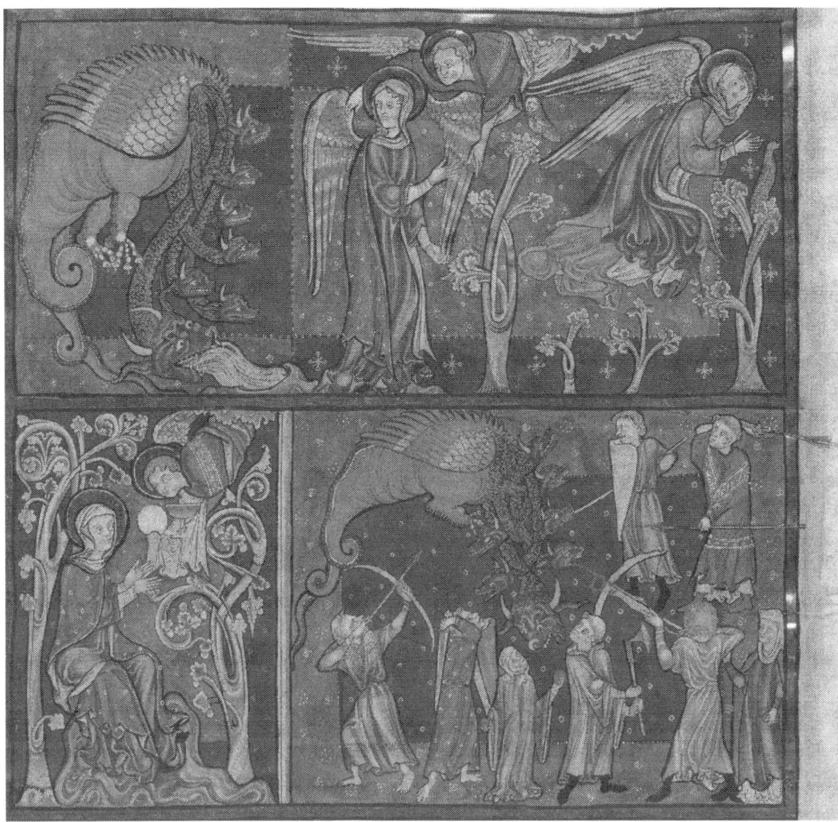

**Figure 5.4.** The *Trinity Apocalypse*, *c.*1260, The Woman Enters the Wilderness (Rev. 12.6–17), Cambridge: Trinity College. © The Master and Fellows of Trinity College, Cambridge

are very typical of contemporary representations of the Virgin Mary, intimating that in this case, at least, Marian devotion is being interwoven with apocalyptic struggle. In the bottom right-hand corner of the lower register we see the descendants of the Woman being attacked by the Dragon as described in Rev. 12.17.

## The fourteenth and fifteenth centuries

In Memling's *St John Altarpiece* of 1474–9, too, Mary is suggested by the deep blue cloak of the Woman Clothed with the Sun, as well as by her golden crown (see Plate 3). Here the Woman appears twice in the apocalyptic drama, at both the heavenly and earthly levels. She appears in her heavenly incarnation standing in a bright yellow, oval-shaped sun just to the right of the heavenly throne room. The Dragon attempts to enter the sun from the right as the Woman hands her baby up to an angel. Almost directly beneath this scene, she also appears on the rocky island behind the mighty angel, being menaced by the Dragon (Rev. 12.13–17). Although very few, if any, of the original viewers of this altarpiece would have been able to see these tiny scenes of the Woman, their textual fidelity is remarkable, right down to the detail of the Dragon waiting on the horizon to hand his 'power' over to the Sea Beast (Rev. 13.1). This helps to imbue the visual narrative with a sense of purpose.

Strangely, perhaps, when we come to Dürer's image of Rev. 12 from his *Apocalypse* series of 1498, the Woman, though very naturalistically portrayed, is not immediately identifiable as Mary (Figure 5.5). While it is true that she has been depicted with the long flowing hair of the young Virgin, and with the iconographical features of the Woman Clothed with the Sun (a crown of stars and standing on the crescent moon) and with the angelic wings given to the Woman at Rev. 12.14, she closely resembles the young women Dürer might have met any day in the markets of Nuremberg. In this sense we wonder if she is intended to be neither Mary nor the church but rather perhaps a sort of every-woman figure.

Dürer's Woman Clothed with the Sun is therefore very much in keeping with his revolutionarily naturalistic approach to the text, though in his frontispiece to the Latin version of the book, in which John is depicted envisaging the Woman and Child, she is far more traditionally Marian (Figure 5.6). Here she is depicted as an older, more regal Mary/Woman Clothed with the Sun, holding the Christ child and wearing a large crown. As we will see in the next section, this identification of Mary with the Woman Clothed with the Sun was taken up again a few decades later by Federico Barocci, and then in the seventeenth century by Velázquez. Finally, although it has already been referred to in Chapter 1, mention must be made of Dürer's depiction of the heavenly battle between St Michael and his archangels and Satan (Figure 1.3). This dramatic subject matter was often subsequently depicted in isolation from Revelation, such as in Raphael's *Michael and the Dragon* in the Louvre. Since this chapter is focusing on the Woman, who is absent from Raphael's battle, we will now move to Velázquez's re-envisaging of the Woman, which places her firmly centre stage.

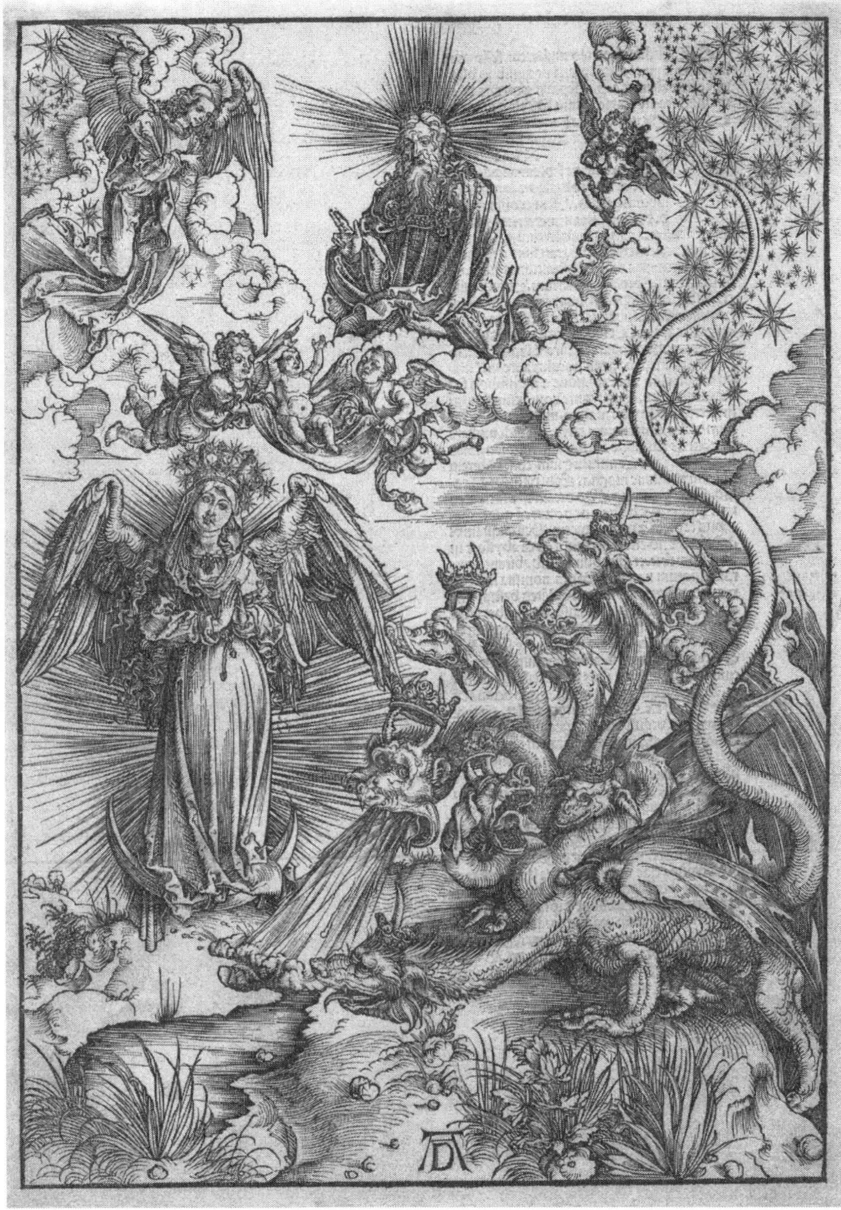

Figure 5.5. Albrecht Dürer, *Apocalypse* Series, c.1498, The Woman Clothed with the Sun (Rev. 12), London: British Museum. © The Trustees of the British Museum

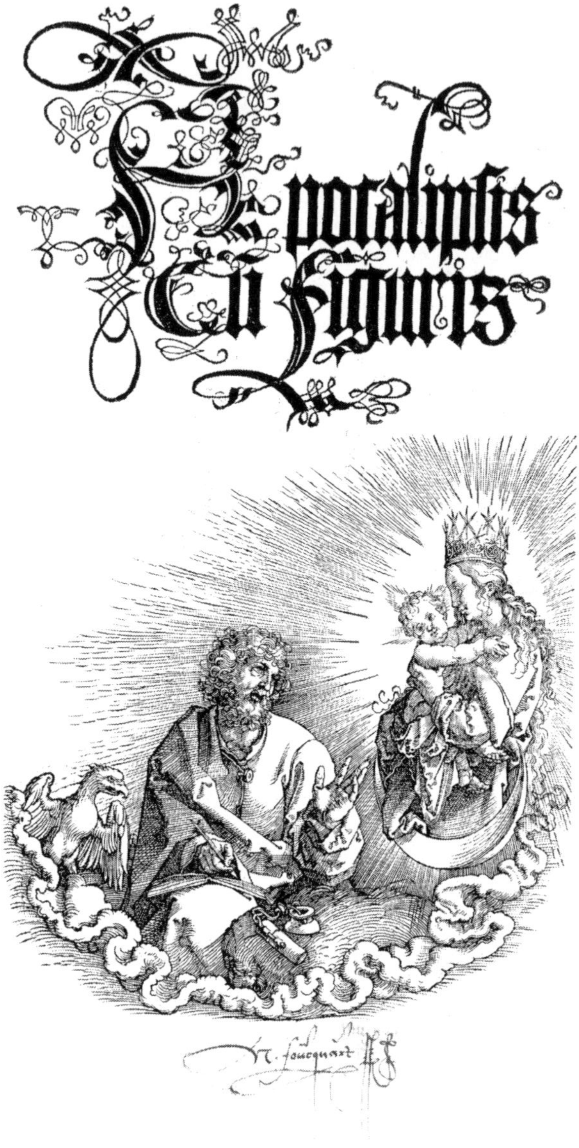

**Figure 5.6.** Albrecht Dürer, *Apocalypse* Series, 1511, Frontispiece, London: British Museum. © The Trustees of the British Museum

# Velázquez, Blake, Redon

Velázquez's pair of paintings *St John the Evangelist on the Island of Patmos* and *The Immaculate Conception* were executed in Seville *c.*1618 in the wake of celebrations there in 1617 to mark a papal decree defending the doctrine of the Immaculate Conception and prohibiting public criticism of it (Plates 24, 25).[11] Both of the young Velázquez's paintings feature the Woman Clothed with the Sun. In the first image we see John (described as the Evangelist, but obviously the author of Revelation) in a dark wood ecstatically transfixed by his vision in true Baroque style, his pencil poised over the empty page on which he will write, as instructed. The John who dominates the painting is no old greybeard (like Jean Duvet's famous John of Patmos), but an earnest and beardless young man, seen by some commentators to be a self-portrait of the artist.[12] In the top left-hand corner of the painting we see what it is he is transfixed by, an evocation of the Woman being pursued by the Dragon. This is tantamount to claiming that this scene from Rev. 12, with its sharp visual focus on the battle between the forces of good and evil, here symbolized by the Woman and the Dragon, somehow embodies the essence of Revelation itself. The Woman is also the main subject of the second painting, *The Immaculate Conception*.

In this second painting Velázquez is following in the footsteps of the Italian artist Federico Barocci, whose own softly beautiful *Immaculate Conception* altarpiece of 1575 anticipates much of the iconography we find in Velázquez, although without Velázquez's drama and colour contrasts.[13] In Velázquez what stands out is the deep blue colouring of the atmosphere, the translucent moon on which the Woman stands, the corona of stars above her head, and the mysterious and symbolic forms below her feet, where Barocci has the heads of the real-life patrons who commissioned his painting. These objects, including a fountain and an enclosed garden, are derived from the Old Testament text The Song of Songs and are intended to symbolize the Virgin's purity.[14] Most striking of all in the Velázquez is the Woman herself. Like Dürer's woman, this is a young, local girl (some say she was Velázquez's fiancée), and, as already mentioned, there is no attempt to idealize her or her features, or to disguise her youth. But in her rapt devotion the ordinary girl is transfigured, a Madonna one can believe actually existed. It would be difficult to see her as the church or the Holy Spirit, but we can see her as a true *virgine bella*, one of flesh and blood, who might have walked the streets of Nazareth (or Seville), but who is *also* clothed with the sun *and* is the bridge, the mediatrix between the divine and the human.

Nearly two hundred years after Velázquez, William Blake produced a far more mythological Woman attacked by the Dragon, under the title *The Great Red Dragon and the Woman Clothed with the Sun: the Devil is Come Down* (Figure 5.7). The image is indeed striking, but like so much of Blake

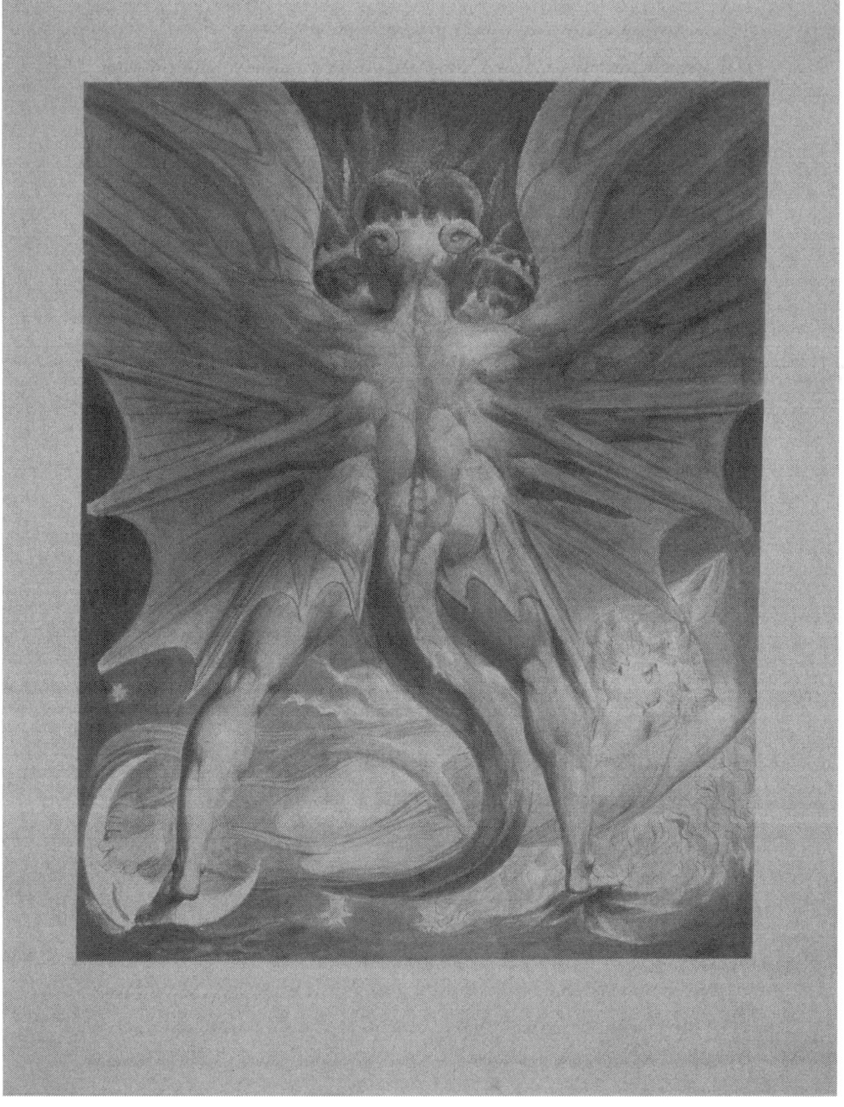

**Figure 5.7.** William Blake, *The Great Red Dragon and the Woman Clothed with the Sun*, c.1805, New York: The Brooklyn Museum of Art. © Bridgeman Art Library

fantastical and enclosed in what looks like his own private constructions and interpretations, hard to place within the linear tradition of Christian interpretation. It is hard even to see the Dragon, menacing as he is, as wholly evil. He is, after all, flying with angel-like wings, and there is some suggestion that he may be a chrysalis on the road to a more perfect nature. And is the Woman's expression and gesture one of terror or of something else? It is interesting also to note, as in the Barocci, the presence of human figures at the bottom of the image, appearing as the flood of Rev. 12.16 (created by the Dragon to engulf the Woman) subsides after the intervention of (Mother) earth. What role do they play in this drama, and whose side are they on? As so often, Blake leaves us with more questions than answers.

If Blake's image is hard to interpret, the same could not be said of Odilon Redon's *fin de siècle* lithographs; In them, the Dragon is depicted as a serpent, chained down (so here perhaps intended to symbolize the chained Dragon of Rev. 20) but writhing and coiling with lubricious menace; while, in the image we show, the Woman is a Loïe Fuller-type dancer, rising suggestively out of a dark background into the sun, in a style that is redolent of Redon's visions of sensuously seductive, half-mythical women (Figure 5.8). Revelation was by this point (1899) on the cusp of becoming a secularized text, a compendium of images for uses quite different from the original intention, hinting at transgression and suggestions of *fin-de-siècle* evil. In Redon's series, commissioned by Ambroise Vollard, art is complicit in a worldliness which somehow jars with the underlying thesis of the text itself, which functions as a counter-cultural critique of the worldly materialism of its own time.[15]

## Twentieth-century visualizations

Perhaps closer to the spirit of Revelation is a photo collage from 1993 by the Chicana artist Alma Lopez of a very young Mexican girl as Woman Clothed with the Sun. A kitsch yet arresting image, the girl stands on a crescent moon and has fancy dress butterfly wings instead of the eagle's wings of Rev. 12.14. In the background is a montage of images from the border between Mexico and the USA, including a patrol car and an old map, symbols of enforcement and of the erosion of boundaries. There is a prominent piece of graffiti of the Virgin Mary on a section of the border fence, providing an iconographic nod to the long-standing link between the girl/Woman

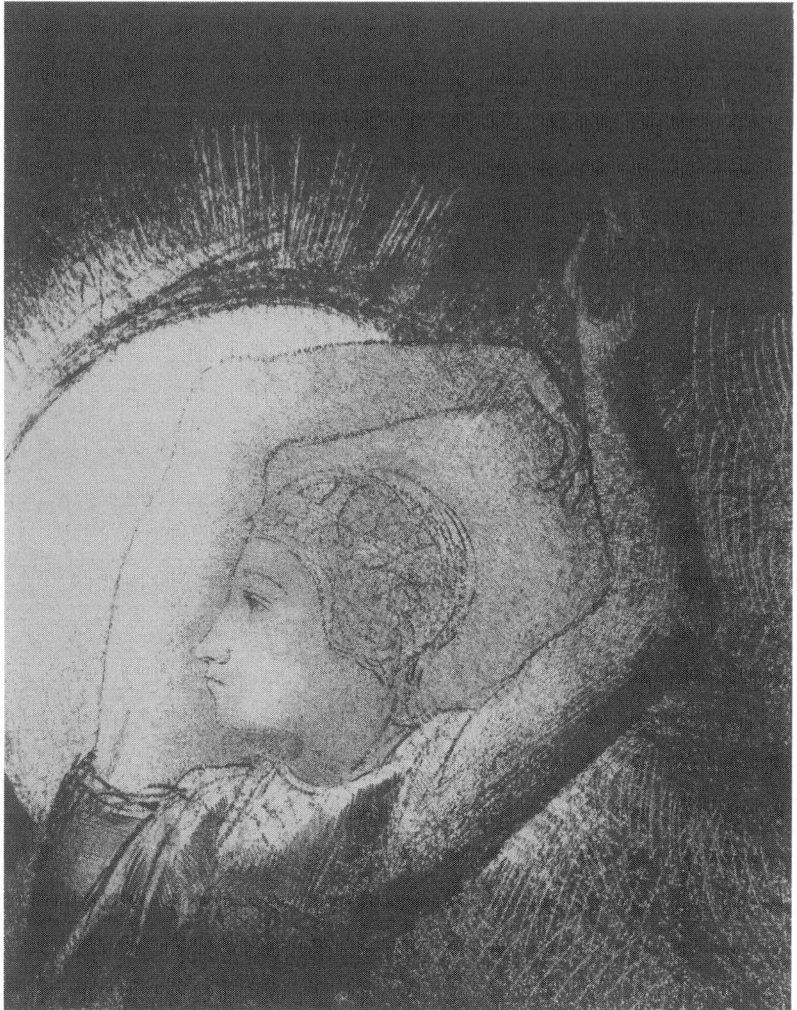

**Figure 5.8.** Odillon Redon, *A Woman Clothed with the Sun* (Rev. 12.1), 1899, London: British Museum. © The Trustees of the British Museum

Clothed with the Sun and the Virgin herself. As we will see in the final chapter, there is also a link within the South/Latin American tradition between the Woman Clothed with the Sun and the appearance of the Virgin of Guadeloupe in the sixteenth century, a link which has been frequently documented in visual form. In this image, however, the young girl/Woman Clothed with the Sun/Virgin of Guadeloupe stands at the border crossing between Mexico and the United States, menaced not by the red Dragon but by the more pervasive forces of poverty, suspicion, and violence that are all connected with the migrant experience.

# Conclusion

As noted at the beginning of this chapter, the Woman Clothed with the Sun is a somewhat anomalous figure in Revelation. She appears and disappears, standing on her own, at a slight tangent to the rest of the book. She has, as we have seen, been interpreted in two rather different ways, first as a symbol of the church and later as an evocation of Mary herself. The earlier images that we selected tend to identify the Woman with the church, the Renaissance images with Mary, and the more modern evocations are ambiguous and diverse in their interpretations.

There is strong poetry in the textual image, in the linking of woman and sun, of femininity and light, as sources of life and goodness, as life-giving inspirations in a world given over to darkness, aggression, and negativity. If in Revelation the Lamb represents the ultimate triumph of the victim and the innocent, the Woman Clothed with the Sun is a strong affirmation from within Christianity's most confrontational book of the power and necessity of the anima, of the female principle. This poetry is surely reflected in an image such as Velázquez's *Immaculate Conception*. However, it is no coincidence that although the Woman is present in all her femininity in the images we have selected, there are only a few in which she is presented as a strong and compelling figure in her own right. In most of the images it is the fiery red, muscular Dragon with seven heads that draws the eye. Or, as we shall see in the next chapter, it is the Dragon's fight with Michael that has captured the male artistic imagination. The Woman herself can seem somewhat meek and passive in these images, the Dürer image being a case in point.

This visual tradition largely reflects feminist criticism of Revelation, which in recent times has argued that the women included therein are stereotypical and two-dimensional to say the least.[16] They are either obedient mothers of male children (such as the Woman Clothed with the Sun) or brides (see Rev. 19), or they are whores (Rev. 17; see Chapter 7) and Jezebels (Rev. 2.20–3). There is little or no middle ground. In 1898 the controversial proto-feminist Elizabeth Cady Stanton praised Revelation 12, saying 'here is a little well-intended respect for woman as representing the church'.[17] However, most feminist critics since then have found it hard to look beyond

Revelation's presentation of the Woman Clothed with the Sun as an archetypical passive and dependent mother figure.[18] And while others have argued that much of the 'female' language used in Revelation is intended metaphorically, this nuance is often lost in the imagery associated with those figures, which seems to these critics simply to reinforce the stereotypes.[19] In this context the Velázquez image is surely a refreshing exception, an evocation of a femininity at once fully human and serenely engaging, neither degraded nor idealized. But, rather than concluding this survey of work inspired by the Woman Clothed with the Sun with a work of genius from the seventeenth century, it is worth coming right up to date and mentioning a remarkable piece of music, the *Woman of the Apocalypse*, written in 2012 by the composer James MacMillan. In a three movement work, composed for the Cabrillo Festival in Santa Cruz, California, MacMillan has, as he says, attempted to transform ideas from Scripture into orchestral sound; but not just ideas from Scripture. In his thinking about his composition, he has also, as we have done, reflected on relevant works of art, including those from medieval manuscripts, Dürer, Rubens and Blake and others, and, appropriately for the setting for which the work was composed, representations of Our Lady of Guadalupe, similar to those which inspired Alma Lopez.

In this way MacMillan is retracing, in musical terms, much of the journey we have travelled in this chapter. The work consists of three movements, the Woman clothed by the Sun, the Woman being taken up into Heaven and her Coronation (in which MacMillan makes explicit her now widely accepted identification with the Virgin Mary). During the piece the great battle in Heaven and the Woman being given the wings of an eagle are also evoked. In his inimitable and very individual way, by turns dramatic and poetic, MacMillan thus demonstrates how, even in our own time, music, itself inspired by visual representations of an ancient visionary text, can add yet another layer of depth and significance to that same text.

6

# The Satanic Trinity

The Four Horsemen of Revelation 4 aside, the most colourful reception history of all the characters in Revelation is that of the two Beasts who emerge from the sea (itself a primeval source of creation but also of destruction) and the earth respectively in Rev. 13. The ground for their appearance has been prepared by two other creatures which arise from the infernal pit—Abaddon (in Rev. 9.11), the king of the locusts, and the monster from the abyss in Rev. 11.7, which kills the mysterious two Witnesses (who are probably supposed to represent the church)—as well as the Dragon of Rev. 12. In Rev. 13 the Sea Beast emerges first, a monstrous hybrid, composed of leopard, bear, and lion with seven heads and ten crowned horns, who is given his power by the Dragon and 'allowed' to rampage over the earth, demanding worship from all. This first beast is then followed by the mysterious Earth Beast, which looks like a lamb but speaks like a dragon and which performs various 'anti-miracles' and deceptions. Between them the two Beasts embody power, oppression, showmanship, and deception and continue to appear at strategic points throughout the narrative before being definitively destroyed by Christ's army in Rev. 20.

## Interpreting the Beasts

Not surprisingly, therefore, interpreters have from the very outset made links between these seemingly irrepressible Beasts and the oppressive powers of their day. The association between the Beasts and the Roman empire of John's day seems undeniable, with many seeing the number 666, which is ascribed to the Sea Beast in Rev. 13.18, as code for Nero Caesar (based on the Hebrew practice of *gematria*, or numerology; see below).[1] In a sense making an exact link is less interesting and less important than examining how different Christian communities have interpreted the Beasts of Rev. 13 for their own times. Interestingly, as Kovacs and Rowland have argued, interpretations have tended to view the Beasts either as representing two separate entities or more synchronically as representing two types of opposition to the church, one political and one religious.[2]

In terms of more precise identifications, since John's day in the late first century the Beasts have continued to be interpreted frequently as being a symbol for Rome and, later, of the Roman Catholic Church and various specific popes (Pope Innocent IV and Pope Benedict XI to name but two). However, they have also been interpreted as symbolic of Mohammed and Islam (particularly in Spanish Catholicism), of Antichrist, a figure that became popularized in the eleventh century, and more recently of figures as diverse as Napoleon Bonaparte, Adolf Hitler, the apartheid regime, Ronald Reagan, Bill Gates, Saddam Hussein, and Barack Obama. Other more recent interpreters (mostly evangelical American Christians) have also made links between the Beasts and corporate organizations such as the EU, barcoding systems, and modern technology (although this is starting to change as the evangelizing potential of social media has become clearer).[3] Thus in both textual and visual interpretation, the Beasts have served as a particularly potent distillation of the major contemporary fears of the communities that have produced them.

In tracing the significance of the Beasts for so many interpreters, it is important to understand their connection with the Dragon of Rev. 12, the key protagonist in the heavenly battle between the Woman Clothed with the Sun and her descendants and the angel Michael. The Dragon is, in the words of Rev. 12.9, 'that ancient serpent, who is called the Devil and Satan, the deceiver of the whole world'. The Devil and Satan are familiar enough, but what are we to make of his role as the great deceiver? After all, there is no deception in his pursuit of the Woman, frightening as that is. She, as the manifestation of purity, grace, and goodness, and as the mother of those who keep the commandments of God, is transparently his enemy, and he hers. It is when the personal struggle of Rev. 12 broadens out into a struggle played out over the whole earth in Rev. 13 that the Devil is presented as deploying deception as a technique of enslavement, as indeed his main technique. Here and subsequently we are presented with a powerful critique of worldly power. Evil is presented as appearing good and desirable, as part of the natural order of things, as something to be worshipped. The 'inhabitants of the earth' of Rev. 13.8 are seduced by the Beasts' powerfulness, by their institutional strength, and by their hypocritical semblance of benignity.

The polyvalence of the bestial imagery used to create this earthly critique has meant that those who might have struggled to apply the celestial fight between the Woman and the Dragon to their own situation find much that is relevant and provocative here. Indeed, even those who are not Christian can find much to apply to their own context in Rev. 13. For the Western reader the symbolic critique of institutional practices may resonate with the glossy but empty political landscape and celebrity culture of the twenty-first century. And readers from less economically developed countries may be prompted to question the corruption of their own leaders.[4]

It is when the Dragon loses the Woman (in Rev. 12.17) and begins to extend his campaign of malice against her children (surely a metaphor for the Christian community) that we encounter the first Beast. As mentioned above, this is a regal creature (part lion, bear, and leopard) with ten horns and seven heads, which rises out of the sea, his seven heads being a diabolical parody of the Lamb's seven horns in Rev. 5.1. His horns are covered with diadems (crowns) and his heads with blasphemous names, a startling image of power and of pretension to divinity, and to this Beast the Dragon gives power and authority (Rev. 13.2). Contemporary readers would have been aware of the links not only with Job's invincible sea creature, Leviathan (see Job 41), but also with Daniel's vision of Daniel 7.1–8 in which three creatures resembling a lion, a bear, and a leopard emerge from the sea followed by a fourth monster with ten horns. In typical apocalyptic fashion Daniel is informed by an angel that the monsters represent a succession of four empires, typically thought by interpreters to be the Babylonians, the Medes, the Persians, and the Greeks (who had all colonized and oppressed the Israelites).[5] Thus John was reinterpreting an extant vision for his own times, casting the Roman empire as a sort of climactic hybrid culmination of all the evil empires that had preceded it. In a sense this can be said to legitimize attempts by other interpreters to do the same with John's own text.

Importantly, and unlike the Beasts in Daniel, as with the Hydra of classical myth, in Rev. 13.3 one of the Sea Beast's heads is struck dead, and is then is healed and grows again (a detail understood by some early commentators to refer to the belief that the dead emperor Nero would return to life). It is as a consequence of this miraculous act that the 'whole earth' begins to worship the Sea Beast, just as the Roman empire held in its iron grip all the world known to John of Patmos and the early Christians. Notoriously, the Sea Beast's name translates somewhat obscurely into the number 666, which has been the subject of much numerological speculation. In the ancient world, in languages such as Hebrew and Greek, each individual letter had a numerical value. In the Greek alphabet $\alpha = 1$, $\kappa = 20$, and $\omega = 800$, for example.[6] Thus peoples' 'numbers' could be calculated by adding together the numerical equivalent of each letter of their name. In the Hebraicized version of Nero's name (Nero Caesar) the values of the letters do indeed add up to 666. Even then, most commentators caution an absolute identification, as other names could of course add up to the same total and some readings of Rev. 13.18 give the Sea Beast's number as 616, which rather undermines the fixation on 666 and its interpretations.[7]

Interestingly, perhaps shockingly even, we are also told that the Sea Beast's campaign of coerced worship, which becomes increasingly violent and totalitarian as the chapter progresses, was permitted by God, who 'allows' the Sea Beast to exercise authority for forty-two months (Rev. 13.5). What might seem to us a paradoxical state of affairs was largely accepted without question by most interpreters and artists. Dürer's *Two Beasts*, in which an ecclesiastically attired God sits in judgement over the reign of the Beasts, but stays entirely separate, as if allowing it to take place, is a good example of this (Figure 6.1). Perhaps these earlier interpreters were not being as theologically unquestioning as it might first appear. Even within an apocalyptic framework which sees God as ordaining the final outcomes of history, his 'allowing' of the reign of the Beasts, just like his use of the Four Horsemen and the punishing sequences of seven, opens the door to a more relaxed or libertarian view of his role. While God does foresee the ultimate outcome of things, he allows the evil empire of Rome, and human beings generally, a degree of latitude and freedom in their individual actions. In this freedom, there is scope for human activity, both faithful and faithless, good and bad. Those who are marked with the sign of the Beast by the second Beast (the Earth Beast, who works for the Sea Beast, Rev. 13.16) and those who manage to resist the Beasts are not simply pawns in a preordained system; everyone is seen as having his or her our own contributions to make in a world which God is allowing to develop in its own way. And while God's judgements may be ultimately inexplicable, he does show compassion for the righteous, and the punishments and dominion of the Beasts are reserved for those who fail to repent. Once again this may be indicated in the Dürer image via the fact that God is depicted as holding a sickle, which had (and still has) powerful connotations of judgement.

Whether this 'free will' reading of Rev. 13 holds up is complicated slightly by a deeply mysterious passage in Rev. 13.8, which we have already looked

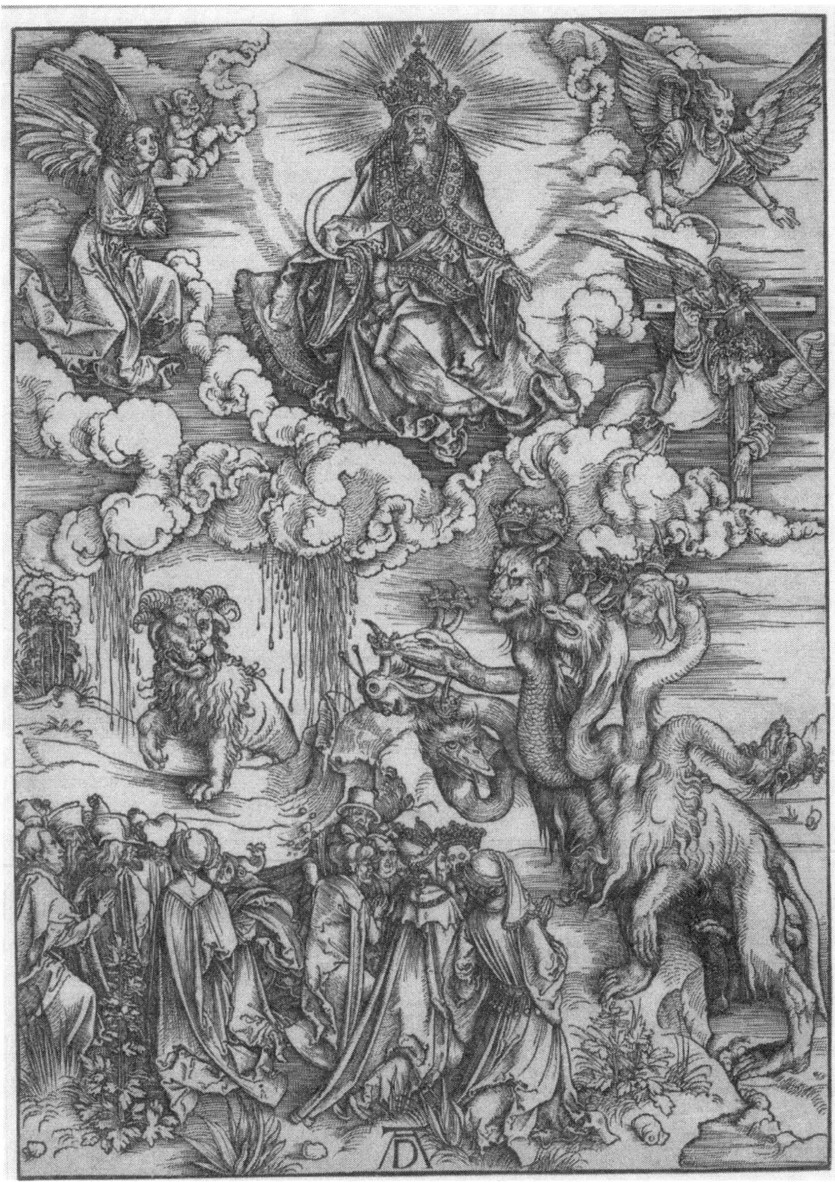

**Figure 6.1.** Albrecht Dürer, *Apocalypse* Series, *c.*1498, The Two Beasts (Rev. 13), London: British Museum. © The Trustees of the British Museum

at in Chapter 2, where we are also told that those whose names were written 'from the foundation of the world' in the 'book of life' belonging to the slaughtered Lamb would not worship the Beast.[8] This apparently implies that it was preordained that when these Christians were taken captive, they would endure in faith and not succumb to the Beasts—a thought which has inspired many through all the ages of tyranny and oppression from John's time to ours, not least the theologian Dietrich Bonhoeffer, who in the 1930s urged the German churches to listen to Revelation in order to resist the evil of Nazism.[9] And were their names really written from the foundation of the world? For many Christians, including John Calvin, this enigmatic phrase has underwritten a belief in predestination, the idea that we are powerless in ourselves and that all we are and do depends on God's will and decision.[10]

We simply do not know what exactly John meant by these words, beyond an insistence that, unlike the Roman (or any other) empire, God's law and reign and providence are eternal and rooted in the depths of creation, and this may or may not leave room for individuals to act freely and unpredictably within God's overall watchful providence. And, raising our heads from these tricky questions of interpretation, even for non-believers, the idea that some values are absolute, and that compromising them in the face of power is to be resisted through endurance and faith, is a source of inspiration, and indeed of much inspiring action; so at least this aspect of this apocalyptic message, as well as the idea that one's institutional and political context should be subject to reflection, can be shared more widely.

The call for endurance and faith in the face of the Sea Beast is followed by the appearance of another beast, this one rising out of the earth, which would perhaps have reminded early readers or hearers of the Earth Beast or Behemoth of Job 40, who can only be tamed by God himself. As mentioned above, the Earth Beast, which is given his authority by the Sea Beast (in a mirroring of the handover of power from the Dragon), has two horns, which give him the appearance of a Lamb, but it speaks like a dragon (note the overlap again). The Earth Beast performs ambiguous prophetic signs, like bringing fire down from Heaven (Rev. 13.13). It also persuades the inhabitants of the earth to make an image of the Sea Beast, and to worship this statue after he has breathed life into it. Those who refuse are killed (Rev. 13.15). The Earth Beast also marks human beings on the forehead in order that they should be allowed to buy and sell (the mark of the Beast).

The Earth Beast or False Prophet (as he is also referred to) also plays a significant role in the narrative of Revelation, in his deceptive attempts to mirror the language and actions of Christ. There are clearly resemblances between the Earth Beast and the true Lamb, in his Lamb-like horns, in his prophetic powers (referred to as signs; cf. John's Gospel, where Jesus' miracles are also referred to as 'signs'), and in his preaching of worship, idolatrous though it is. These specifically 'religious' acts have led many to view the Earth Beast in terms of the emperor cult of Rome, to which most of the early Christians would have been under pressure to conform.

The term 'Antichrist' itself does not appear in Revelation, as already mentioned, but in the Middle Ages commentators began to see the one worshipped at the behest of the Earth Beast (i.e. the Sea Beast) as Antichrist, although, confusingly, sometimes it seems that the Earth Beast itself is identified as Antichrist. This could reflect a general muddle in the development of what is, after all, a somewhat colourful legend of comparatively recent origin, or perhaps it also reflects a general sense that the diabolical forces—Dragon, Beast, Antichrist—are at root emanations of the same evil force.

In the medieval legend or legends Antichrist was a diabolical figure (literally the anti-Christ), the son of the Devil and a prostitute, and it was widely believed that he would appear prior to the end of the world. His life is a mirror image of Christ's. Born into the tribe of Dan rather than of Judah, like Christ, Antichrist is a Jew. At around the age of thirty he will begin his ministry, which unlike Christ's true miracles, will consist merely of tricks. Once again, unlike Christ, who is shunned by the Jews, he will be hailed as a king by the Jews upon his entry into 'Jerusalem' and then preside over a period of persecution of Christians (three and a half years), before finally being destroyed by Christ. The Last Judgement will follow shortly afterwards.[11]

The Antichrist figure has no one biblical source but was formed from several sources in the New Testament, including 2 Thessalonians, 1 and 2 John, and Revelation. Even Antichrist readings of Revelation are not entirely consistent: not only is there some ambiguity in them over which of the two Beasts is Antichrist, but, as discussed in Chapter 3, some readings have the first Horseman, the white one, as Antichrist, being a parody of Christ and of the Rider on the White Horse who eventually comes in Rev. 19.11 to rescue the world.

The Antichrist idea first gained popularity in the tenth century following the publication of Bishop Adso's *Life and Times of Antichrist* and was still current in the sixteenth century when Lucas Cranach the Elder produced an illustrated book entitled *Passional Christi und Antichristi* (with a preface by

Luther and a commentary by Melanchthon) in which the lives of Christ and Antichrist were contrasted, with Antichrist now portrayed as the pope.[12] In Revelation too the Sea Beast is contrasted with Christ. In the very next section after the worship of the Sea Beast and the marking of mankind with his number we are shown the true Lamb (Rev. 14). He is standing on Mount Zion and worshipped—not by those marked with the sign of the beast (Rev. 13.17), but by the 144,000 with the name of the Father on their foreheads. And then, anticipating what is to come, angels announce the eventual fall of Babylon and the divine anger to be wrought on those marked with the sign of the Beast, before commending endurance and faith once more to the faithful.

After Rev. 13 the two Beasts (and the Dragon) make further intermittent appearances in the text. In preparation for the final battle, Armageddon, unclean spirits appear from the mouths of the Dragon, the Sea Beast, and the Earth Beast in Rev. 16.13 (in a demonic parallel of the cleansing sword in the mouth of the Son of Man at the beginning of John's vision in Revelation). When the Whore of Babylon appears in Rev. 17, she is riding on the Sea Beast, a malignant pairing, bringing together pride, power, luxury, and sexual enslavement, four causes of so much suffering, cruelty, and evil. In the end, as the forces of evil turn on each other, the Whore is devoured by the Sea Beast (how many times does one see that?), and eventually the two Beasts are thrown into the lake of fire (Rev. 20). Endurance then endures, despite the beastly might, wiles, and deception, something hard for the early Christians to see even in faith, and maybe no easier for Christians, or indeed others, today. The message of the description of the Beasts is very much that of the difficulty of seeing through their intimidating and cajoling magnificence, a theme picked up in many of the visual representations they have inspired over the centuries.

## The Beasts in visual imagery

Visual imagery can embody two important aspects of the Beast narratives. On the one hand there is the sheer power of the Beasts, their size, dominance, and overwhelming might. On the other there is their deceptiveness, the way that they can simulate virtue and the appearance of virtue, seducing not so much by might, as by insinuation, persuasion, and pretence. We find both these tendencies in the works we will look at, and there are also many examples of identifications of Beasts and their followers with figures of contemporaneous relevance, be they Saracens, enemy armies, medieval prelates, popes, or politicians of the day.

As always, in the medieval representations there are separate images devoted to the different incidents relating to the Beasts. In *Angers*, for example, there are seven separate images. However, it is interesting that whereas in *Trinity* the Beasts are always two clearly separate entities, in *Angers* the second Beast has the seven horns of the first, suggesting (what is surely the case) that the two Beasts are both manifestations of the same malign force. Part of the deception worked by the Beasts is to sow confusion, for example by making things which are fundamentally the same look many and different. This deceptive multiplicity of malignity and its tendency to reproduce itself is shown vividly in images of the Earth Beast getting human beings to worship the image of the Sea Beast into which it breathes life (and killing those who refuse).

As far as presentist visualizations of the Beasts go, it is worth noting that the *Master Bertram Apocalypse Altarpiece* has the Earth Beast as Mohammed. In Dante's *Purgatorio* (Canto 32), meanwhile, the Chariot of the unfaithful Church sprouts the seven heads of the Sea Beast, a theme taken up by Cranach in his depiction of the Whore of Babylon wearing the papal triple tiara and riding the seven-headed Sea Beast. In our own day President Obama has been represented as both Beasts and Antichrist by elements of his fundamentalist opposition, which perhaps says more about their visceral dislike of a mere politician than about their exegetical skill, or even their sanity.

Picking up on that point, it is interesting that seeing the Beasts as having a human form with which to deceive is a comparatively late development. The *Flemish Apocalypse* (1400; Plate 29) has the Earth Beast depicted as a lamb in a Franciscan habit, which is a telling interpretive development, warning us in strong visual terms against seduction by the most gentle and Christian of appearances (although in counterbalance a Cistercian monk is confronting him, while other 'good' religious figures are trampled down by the forces of evil). Luca Signorelli's Antichrist is surely the classic image of the false shepherd, whose rottenness within is revealed only by the context, and never more powerfully conveyed (Plate 30). Blake's Beasts have significantly human characteristics (Plate 31), while, in our own day the *Left Behind* series' Antichrist is one Nicolae Carpathia, a good-looking politician who appears as if he has been constructed by focus groups.

One interesting aspect of the vast majority of the Beast images over the years is that, with the notable exception of Dürer's image, God is notably absent from them. We might speculate that, for the observer, the Beasts will often take the place of God, simulating the power and even the appearance of the divine. If such was in the mind of the illustrators of Revelation 13, then this would be another example of where visual images can powerfully convey messages beyond the purely verbal.

## Medieval Beasts

As would be expected, the treatment of the Beasts in the early medieval manuscripts, such as the *Trinity Apocalypse*, is both detailed and literal. Thus one initially sees a red Dragon standing next to a sleek-looking Sea Beast, which has just risen from a murky green sea, and handing him a sceptre (Plate 26). Save for the seven heads, *Trinity*'s Sea Beast mostly resembles a grey leopard, as is recorded in Rev. 13.2. There has been some attempt to render his feet as bear's feet and the heads become leonine in the image below. The Sea Beast and the Dragon dominate the centre of the image, watched by John on the left, with finely dressed potential worshippers on the right. One of the worshippers holds a scroll, which reads (in Anglo-Norman French), 'Who is like the Beast and who can fight against it?' This is a direct quotation from Rev. 13.4 but in many ways could be said to sum up the whole chapter: how can any human resist this mysterious force?

In the image below, potentiality becomes actuality, as the Sea Beast slays anyone who attempts to fight against it. Among the victims are women and three tonsured monks. On the right, the Beast's worshippers bend their knees and stretch out their hands in supplication. One of them wears a feathered cap, which in medieval iconography denoted an evil person, thus making it even easier for the medieval viewer to understand the image at a glance. In the second pair of *Trinity* images of the Beasts, a distinctly simian Earth Beast, referred to in the accompanying commentary as the False Prophet (in antici-pation of Rev. 16.13), sets up the statue of the Sea Beast on an altar, before which refuseniks are slain and worshippers grovel (Plate 27). Once again the brutality of the system that the two Beasts preside over, rather than its super-ficial allure, is emphasized by the *Trinity* artists. In the final image, the Beasts themselves are nowhere to be seen (save for the image of the Sea Beast) but the brutal system that they have inculcated continues regardless.

In the *Gulbenkian Apocalypse* we find many references, both visual and in the commentary, to Antichrist. Indeed the traditional Berengaudus commentary is supplemented in *Gulbenkian* with a copy of the medieval 'Life of Antichrist' we have just mentioned, and in the text of *Gulbenkian* references are made to Antichrist's deeds. So, in the *Gulbenkian Apocalypse* it is Antichrist who kills the two Witnesses (identified here with Enoch and Elijah from the Old Testament). In other *Gulbenkian* images we see Antichrist with swords, soldiers, and weaponry, with a scroll saying 'I am the Son of God' (35v), while in an adjoining image (36v), on the left the beast is proclaiming that Christ is not God—though on the right we see Christ himself, surrounded by Dominicans and Franciscans praying at an altar and preaching. We also see Antichrist enjoining his followers to indulge in sinfulness and blasphemy. Perhaps most emphatic of all, in 34v there is an image of the Earth Beast actually rising from the abyss, below which is the caption 'haec bestia AntiXrm significat': 'this beast signifies the Antichrist' (Figure 6.2). The identification is explicit, even if it is of the Earth Beast rather than the more usual Sea Beast, and Antichrist is firmly established at the heart of Revelation.

The *Angers Apocalypse Tapestry*, which devotes a full seven images to Rev. 13, focuses quite strongly on the transfer of power between the three Beasts (the Dragon, the Sea Beast, and the Earth Beast). In one image, for example, the Earth Beast is seen holding a gold sceptre with a distinctive fleur-de-lis tip whilst presiding over the worship of the image of the Beast (Rev. 13.14–15; Figure 6.3) . Previously the sceptre is handed from the Dragon to the Sea Beast, who himself holds it in three images. In terms of the context of *Angers*, this sceptre, a symbol of supreme authority, had special resonance. It had been adopted as the French royal coat of arms in 1376 (during the seven-year-long production of the tapestry). Thus the idea of a Beast coming from the sea to take the sceptre would have been deeply disturbing for contemporary viewers, who would have automatically associated the Beast with the threat from the English, with whom the French had been engaged in war—the Hundred Years War—since 1337. Those seen obediently worshipping the statue of the Sea Beast under the sceptre of the Earth Beast may therefore be intended as symbolic of those who had collaborated with the English after the Battle of Poitiers in 1356. It is also worth noting that in the *Angers* images the Earth Beast is portrayed not with the 'lamb's horns' of Rev. 13.11 but with seven horns, implying that he is to be identified not as an associate of the Sea Beast but as another manifestation of him. This is in line with the more synchronic interpretation of the Beasts suggested by

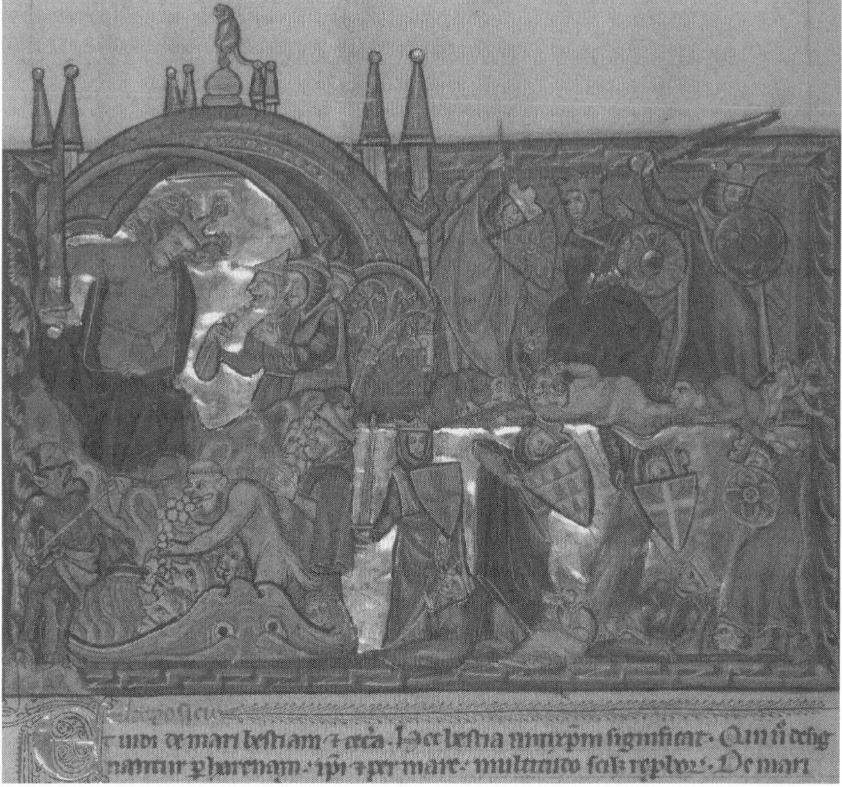

**Figure 6.2.** The *Gulbenkian Apocalypse*, c.1270, The Earth Beast Rising from the Abyss, Lisbon: Museo Calouste Gulbenkian. © Museo Calouste Gulbenkian

Kovacs and Rowland (see section 'Interpreting the Beasts'). They represent different manifestations of the same evil consortium.

As was common in medieval visual interpretations *Angers* also identifies the Earth Beast with the False Prophet of Rev. 16.13, and in a particularly dramatic image it is depicted with both Dragon and Sea Beast all vomiting frogs from their many mouths (Figure 6.4). Here the Dragon stands on the back of the Sea Beast, creating an impression of a super-Beast, for which the Earth Beast/False Prophet acts as a sort of forerunner. Seeing the three Beasts brought together in one visual space is perhaps a demonic parody of the Trinitarian understanding of God ('the one who sits on the throne', the seven spirits, and Jesus Christ) given in Rev. 1.4–5.[13] In an era of hydra-headed internet and social media, this image also acts as a vivid reminder of the way malicious rumours and incitement can spread uncontrollably, like multiplying

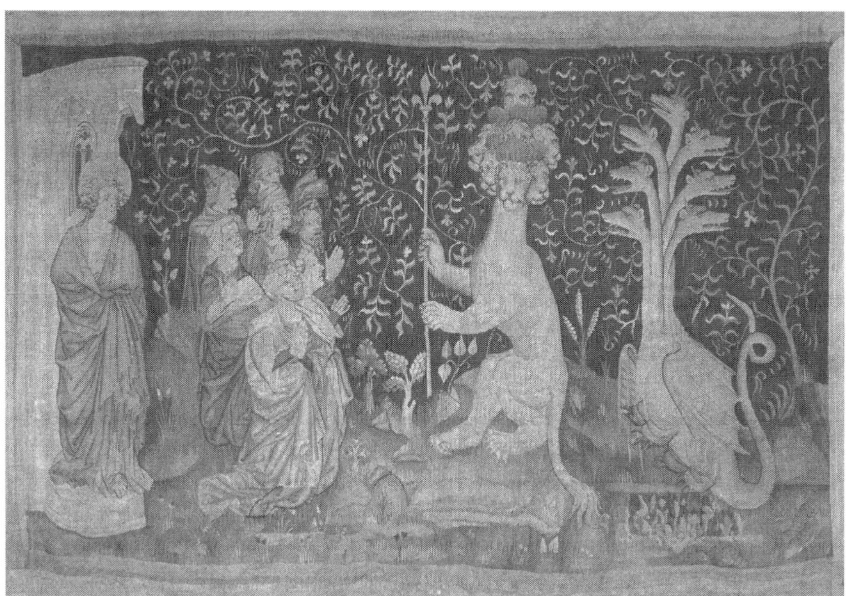

**Figure 6.3.** The *Angers Apocalypse Tapestry*, *c*.1373–80, Worship of the Sea Beast (Rev. 13), Maine et Loire: Chateau d'Angers. © Bridgeman Art Library

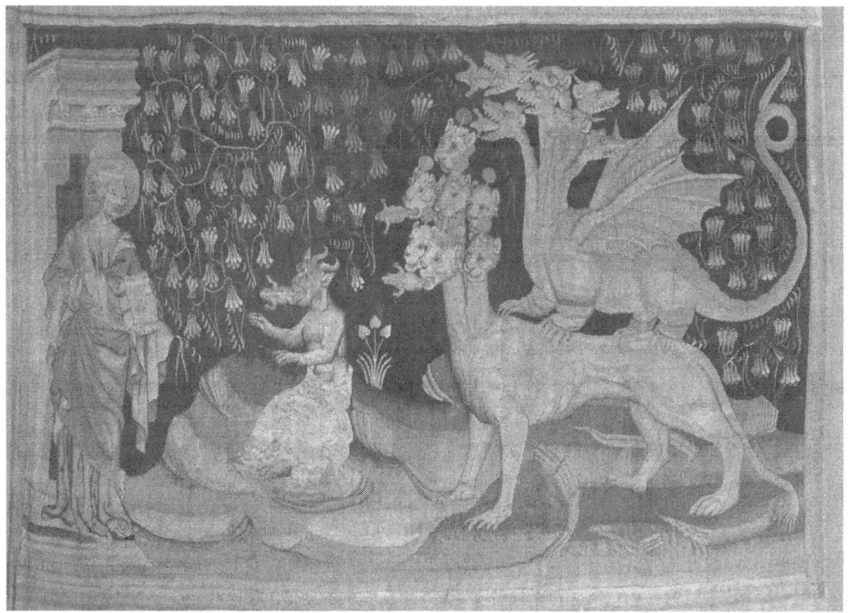

**Figure 6.4.** The *Angers Apocalypse Tapestry*, *c*.1373–80, The Three Beasts Vomiting Frogs (Rev. 16.13–14), Maine et Loire: Chateau d'Angers. © Bridgeman Art Library

frogs, just as they no doubt did in the supposedly more credulous Middle Ages. One is also reminded of the film *Magnolia,* which ends with a deluge of frogs from the sky, although there may be a reference to Exodus here as well.[14]

Time-specific in a different way from *Angers* is the slightly later *Master Bertram* or *Victoria and Albert Apocalypse Altarpiece, c.*1400. Apart from the Van Eycks' *Ghent Altarpiece* and Memling's later *Apocalypse Altarpiece (c.*1479), this is the only surviving Apocalypse altarpiece from this time period, which makes it a rare, almost unique piece.[15] *Bertram* visualizes the narrative of Revelation from chapters 1–16 on the front (forty-five scenes; Plate 28), and the lives of John the Evangelist, the Virgin, Mary Magdalene, and St Giles on the reverse. It is episodic and intended to be read from left to right, and line by line, like a manuscript version of Revelation, as opposed to Memling's *Apocalypse Altarpiece* where the events of Revelation 1–13 are pictorialized in one visual space. Rather than identifying either of the Beasts with the threat from the English (as in *Angers*), here the Earth Beast or False Prophet, who is portrayed as a double bear, is identified via the

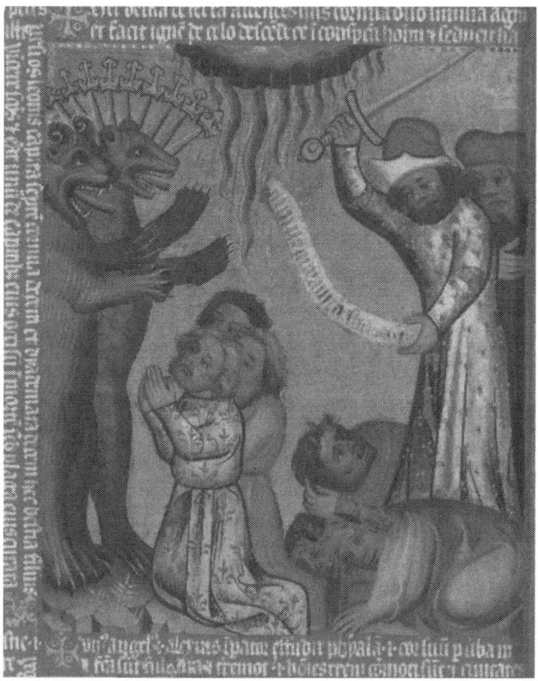

**Figure 6.5.** Detail from the *Master Bertram Apocalypse Altarpiece, c.*1400, London: Victoria and Albert Museum. © Victoria and Albert Museum, London

commentary extracts surrounding the images with Mahomet (Mohammed) (Figure 6.5). His two horns are said to represent his claim to wisdom and holiness, respectively, and the fire descending from Heaven is the Holy Scripture, from which elements of the Quran were derived. Those killing the people who are refusing to worship the Sea Beast (also a bear-like creature) are clearly represented as Saracens (Muslim soldiers), so as to leave no doubt in the minds of medieval observers of the intended interpretation of this aspect of Revelation.[16] This image serves to remind us today of the threat Islam was perceived as representing to medieval Christianity, and in this way it played the role that the Roman empire had played for earlier interpreters of John's visionary text. Master Bertram himself was German and the Alexander commentary on which it was based was a thirteenth-century German work, with Spanish influences. Thus it seems that in the medieval era the Earth Beast had a number of associations and connections, from English soldiers to Mohammed to, on occasion, Antichrist himself.

## The Beasts in the Renaissance:
## Antichrist and the church

As already mentioned, in the early medieval Apocalypses there is not yet a clear identification of the Beasts with Antichrist. An exception was to be found in the *Gulbenkian Apocalypse* (*c.*1270), where in the commentary accompanying the illustrations Antichrist (AntiXt in the text) is explicitly referred to on a number of occasions. A further step in this direction is taken in the *Flemish Apocalypse* of around 1400. In this beautiful multi-layered image of the Beasts, we see what is now the familiar picture of the Dragon handing the Sea Beast his sceptre at the top of the image (Plate 29). Below this a group including a bishop and a king worship the Sea Beast, while others are slaughtered on the right. Despite this, a procession of Cistercian monks continue to defy him. But in the bottom tier of the picture the Earth Beast, still to be sure a beast with two horns (who is seen on the far left rising up from an abyss, cf. Rev. 9.2, 11.7, 17.8, and 20.1) but now a lamb in a Franciscan's habit, having set up the statue of the Sea Beast in a chapel, is marking a bishop, a king, and a friar with the sign of the Beast. The Earth Beast is not only deeply implicated in the corrupt empire; he is now disguised as a man of the church, like Antichrist himself. This subtle critique of the church prefigures not only Dürer's image of the two Beasts from 1498,

but also of course the Reformation itself, in which the papal office was to
be identified with both Antichrist and the Beasts of Revelation, now viewed
as one and the same.

Dürer's image (Figure 6.1) is altogether more frightening that that of the
*Flemish Apocalypse*. The Sea Beast is a seething mass of seven crowned ser-
pentine/leonine heads, one of which, true to the text, has clearly been
injured. Below him a gaggle of worshippers, amongst them kings, bishops,
and laymen, appear to talk excitedly amongst themselves, which serves to
emphasize the 'amazement' that the whole world feels upon seeing the
Beast (Rev. 13.3). If some of the Sea Beast's heads are potentially comic in
their hybridity, the Earth Beast is truly terrifying. Visualized as a lion with
lamb's horns (a reference to the Lion of Judah of Rev. 5.5?), the Earth Beast
surges up from the 'abyss' surrounded by clouds which rain down blood on
either side of him (in a slight alteration to Rev. 13.13, which speaks of fire
coming down). Most striking of all is the presence of God at the head of this
image, which represents a clear departure from the medieval images, where
God is markedly absent. Does his presence, which can at first appear jarring,
signify 'permission' or future judgement or both? He holds a sickle, an
iconographic symbol of judgement, which prefigures Rev. 14.7–15, which
talks of the punishment that will be handed out to any who have worshipped the Beast on Judgement Day (the Harvest of the Earth). Thus his
presence perhaps serves as a reminder of the ultimate judgement that will
befall the Beasts, even though they look so powerful at this moment.
However, on a more philosophical level, as intimated above, God's prominent presence in this image could be a reminder that it is human folly, a
consequence of the freedom that God 'allows' us, that has facilitated the
success of the Beasts. He acts, at this stage, therefore not so much as divine
judge but as ultimate observer. The fact that God, in this image, is attired in
a bishop's cope and mitre can be interpreted in one of two ways, either as
an attack on the church or as a reminder of God's status as the true head of
the church. The latter is more plausible, given Dürer's orthodox faith.[17]

No doubt picking up on the popular medieval sermons and prophecies
regarding Antichrist (themselves inspired by Bishop Adso's *Life*), five years
after Dürer's woodcuts came Luca Signorelli's *The Sermon and Deeds of Antichrist*, a fresco in Orvieto Cathedral dating from 1501 (Plate 30).[18] Known
to many as the definitive image of Antichrist, it exudes psychological power
and plausibility. The fresco is dominated by a large square with a strange
classical building in the background, around which dark figures, some

armed, are moving. In the foreground are a number of apparently disconnected groups of people, who include some who seem to be arranging executions, a sickbed miracle, a Jew handing out money to a crowd around him, including a prostitute, a tightly knit group of religious folk (including Franciscans, Benedictines, and Augustinians, being led by a Dominican) perhaps discussing the Bible, and in the centre a Christlike figure apparently being manipulated by a bald figure with two horns and surrounded by a listening crowd.

What we have here is clearly a transformation of Rev. 13.11–12, with the man with two horns (the Earth Beast) getting the people to worship Antichrist (the Sea Beast) who here has the traditional appearance of Christ. The whole effect is decidedly unsettling, even more so when we realize that those surrounding this faux-Christ are hardly pious, but include dandies and rich and haughty figures, as well as the prostitute and the Jew (in the Antichrist legend, Antichrist was said to have assembled his followers primarily from the Jewish population). 'Christ' and his minder are on a dais, and at their feet are offerings they seem to have collected. There is clearly a symbiotic relationship between the Christ figure and the horned man behind him, so much so that it is unclear whose hand is protruding from 'Christ's' cloak. Maybe Signorelli is hinting that the two Beasts of Revelation are really manifestations of the same, single diabolical force, but however we read it, this image remains sinister and troubling after more than half a millennium, maybe in part precisely because of its ambiguity.

Given the whole atmosphere, it is clear that this fresco is Signorelli's evocation not only of the medieval Antichrist but also of the Sea Beast of Revelation, as set up by the Earth Beast for mankind to worship (Rev. 13.14–15).[19] This impression is reinforced when we see that at the extreme left of the fresco Signorelli himself, like John of Patmos, and another man, both dressed in black and sometimes also identified as the two Witnesses of Rev. 11.3, are looking on as a group of men murder another man on the ground. Meanwhile in the sky, also on the left, fire is raining down from Heaven, and Antichrist and another figure are being cast down on to the earth. So Signorelli represents not just Antichrist's preaching and its temporary effect, but also its final result (an impression compounded when we see that the Antichrist fresco is accompanied by further frescos depicting the Last Judgement and the woes of Revelation). It is possible that amid all the corruption, deception, and violence the group of clerics is

meant to represent the true faith, and that we are meant to see the whole
ensemble in terms of the end time, but what is undeniable is the sense of
sickly insinuation and evil complicity emanating from 'Christ' and Satan,
the absolute antithesis of the New Testament temptation of Christ in
which Christ and Satan are polar opposites, rather than, as in this case, all
but joined at the hip.

## The papal Beast: the Beasts and the Reformation

If Dürer and Signorelli provide us with provocative yet subtle images of
Revelation's Beasts, the images that accompanied the major biblical translations and polemical pamphlets of the Protestant Reformation provide
something else altogether. Here we have visual polemic on a startling yet
highly effective scale. The thirteenth image in Cranach's series illustrating
Luther's New Testament, itself an inferior pastiche of the Dürer image
discussed above (see Figure 6.1), sees the Earth Beast clothed in a monk's
cowl, a surprisingly subtle criticism of the church within the context of
this particular series. For in the eleventh image the Beast from the Abyss
who comes to kill the Witnesses in Rev. 11.7, and who Luther sees as
another manifestation of the Beasts of the Satanic trinity of Rev. 13, is
actually depicted wearing the famous papal triple tiara, that unmistakable
symbol of the papacy (Figure 6.6). The boldness of this visual detail cannot be underestimated. The two Witnesses, one of the symbols of the
church within Revelation, are depicted as being menaced by Satan incarnate, who also turns out to be the pope. In case the point had not been
underlined firmly enough, in the image accompanying Rev. 17 the Whore
of Babylon appears riding on the Sea Beast, who once again wears the
papal triple tiara (to be discussed further in Chapter 7). This particular
strand of anti-Catholic visual polemic was to continue for the rest of the
sixteenth century and beyond. This is captured particularly strikingly,
almost comically, in Dutch artist Hendrick Hondius' *Papist Pyramid* of
1599. Here a pyramid of snakes, each wearing some form of Catholic
headdress, culminates in a larger, more threatening-looking snake wearing
the papal triple tiara. Around the image are quotations from 2 Thessalonians
2.4, Daniel 7.25, and Rev. 17–18, all of which were thought to refer in
some way to Antichrist, and therefore, in the eyes of the sixteenth-century
Reformers, to the pope also. It is interesting to note that, like Cranach the

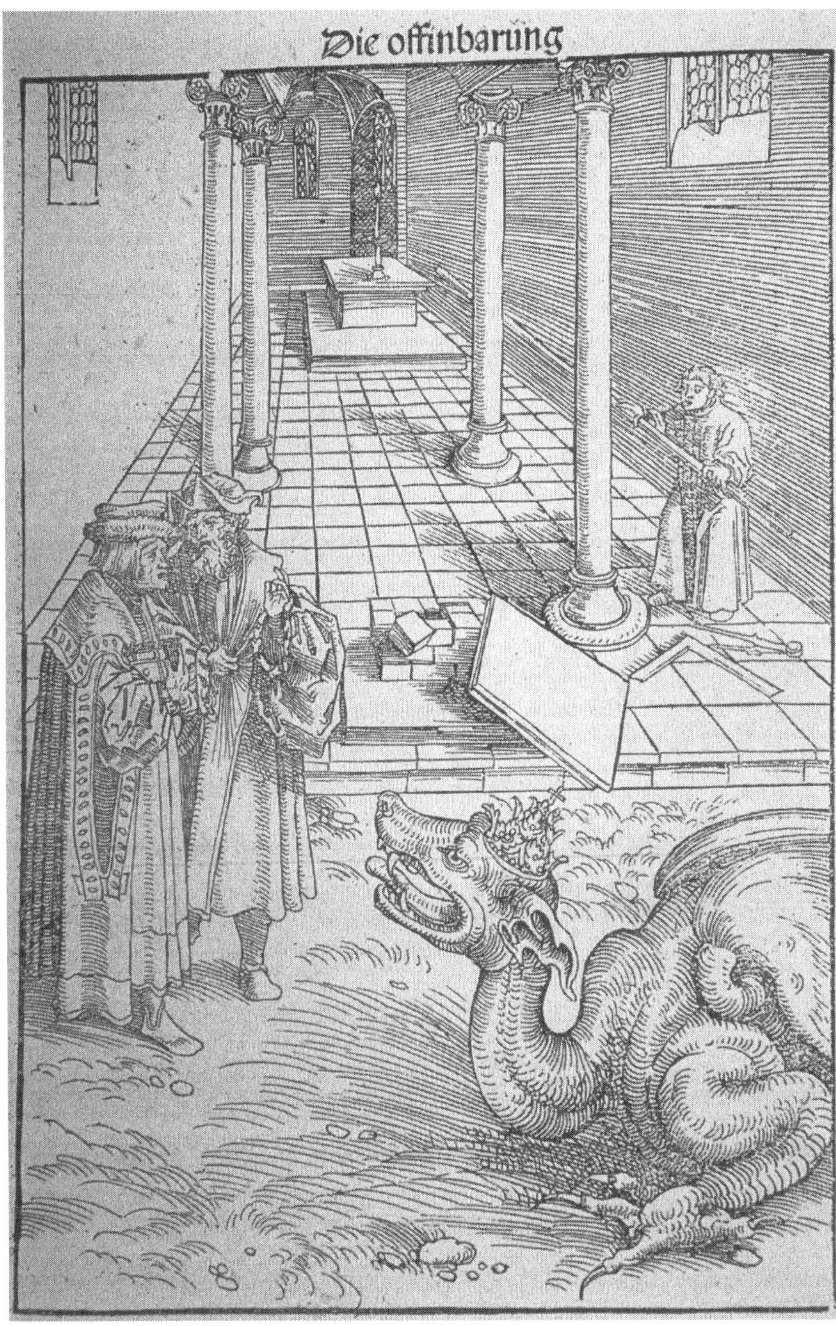


**Figure 6.6.** Lucas Cranach the Elder, Apocalypse Illustrations for Luther's New Testament, 1522, The Beast from the Abyss (Rev. 11), London: The British Library. © The British Library Board, C.36.g.7

Elder, Hondius continued to work for Catholic as well as Protestant patrons, even while designing and producing such virulent anti-Catholic polemic. It seems that for the successful sixteenth-century printmaker, business was indeed just business.[20]

## William Blake and the Beasts of Revelation

Blake's images of the Beasts of Rev. 13 are part of a series of four water-colours painted in the first decade of the nineteenth century on the theme of the Woman Clothed with the Sun and the Dragon. Blake's Revelation watercolours have been interpreted as a veiled critique of Benjamin West's Revelation paintings (exhibited in 1798). West's paintings depict the Beasts in a naturalistic way, rendering them on the same scale as their human victims. Blake's Beasts on the other hand are immense in scale and alto-gether more complex. As pointed out by David Bindman, the Dragon, whom we encountered in the Blake images in the previous chapter (see Figure 5.7), is not a wholly demonic figure.[21] In fact he has a classically ideal physique, which is recognizable as the Dragon of Rev. 12 only through the addition of wings, a serpentine tail, and six extra heads. In the *Great Red Dragon and the Beast from the Sea* we see the 'Dragon' seemingly giving birth to (or alternatively defecating out) the Sea Beast in a fascinat-ing interpretation of the transfer of power between the Dragon and the Sea Beast of Rev. 13.1 (Figure 6.7). The Sea Beast himself, although very far from the hybrid, leopard-like creatures of the medieval manuscripts, is less recognizably human than Blake's Dragon. Interestingly, in this image, the predominant heads of both the Dragon and the Sea Beast have ram's horns. This represents an interesting interpolation of the main feature of the Earth Beast (his deceptive, Christlike horns) into the iconography of the other two Beasts. In the second image in this series of four which visualizes the Dragon, *The Number of the Beast is 666*, the Sea Beast of the former image sits with his back to us presiding over a massed sea of wor-shippers, who cower before him as far as the eye can see (Plate 31). In front of him is the Earth Beast, here visualized quite simply as a lamb with human arms. In typical Blakeian fashion, it is difficult to tell whether it is the Sea Beast or the Earth Beast who has been cast as the statue referred to in Rev. 13.14–15. The Sea Beast (with his back to us) certainly seems very animated for a statue, although we are told in Rev. 13.15 that the

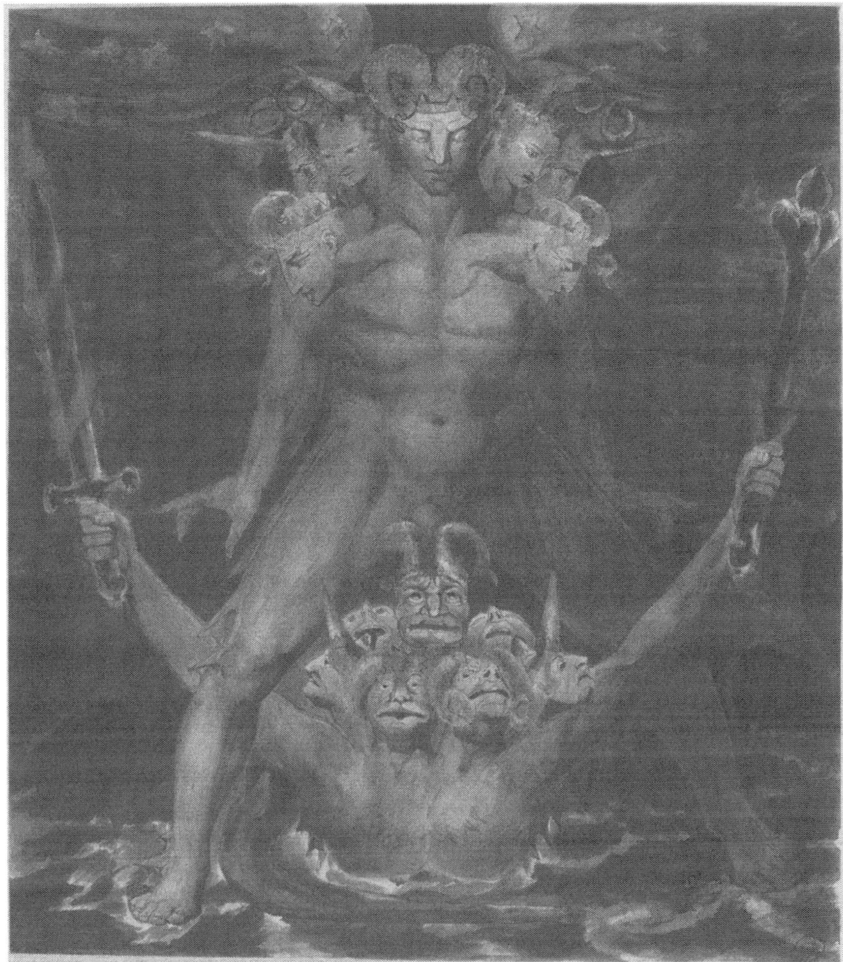

Figure 6.7. William Blake, *The Great Red Dragon and the Beast from the Sea*, c. 1805, Washington: National Gallery of Art. Courtesy National Gallery of Art, Washington, Rosenwald Collection

statue can talk. The Lamb/Earth Beast meanwhile appears very static and passive, but that may be part of its deception. The appearance of the Dragon at the top of the image compete the Satanic trinity, although it is true that he appears startled, which has been interpreted as him hearing of his own doom via the 'voice from heaven' in Rev. 14.[22] Perhaps his more human appearance is an outward indication that he possesses a certain sensitivity or humanity that the other two Beasts, in their mechanical quest for world domination, manifestly lack.

## The Beasts and modernity

In more recent times the Beasts of Revelation have become an all-purpose image for conspiracy theorists and fanatics of all descriptions and orientations. At the very least one has to say that the Beasts have become radically decontextualized, with interpretations ranging from those who know nothing of the original context of the Beasts to fundamentalist Christians who know a great deal of the text and try to read detailed interpretations into its imagery. The polyvalency of the imagery used to describe the Beasts in Rev. 12–13 and elsewhere means that many different groups can find comfort in the imagery by identifying their oppressors and aligning themselves with the oppressed nations of Rev. 13. Conversely the polyvalency of the imagery means that others can hijack it for more sinister ends. The images generated range from the terrifying to the kitsch and are predominantly associated with the USA.

Thus (and in no particular order apart from chronological) in the early twentieth century Aleister Crowley, a prominent occultist, claimed that he was the Beast of Rev. 13 and referred to himself as the Great Beast 666.[23] Hal Lindsey, to be discussed at further length in Chapter 10, associates the Beasts of Rev. 13 with the EU. Other fundamentalist Christians, following his lead, also argue that the Beasts are housed in Europe in the form of a 'supercomputer' in Brussels. In Iran America is loosely associated with the Beasts, where it is a commonplace of fundamentalist Islamic rhetoric to refer to America and the West as the Great Satan. While the immediate source for this may not be Revelation itself, some of the associated imagery is clearly borrowed from Revelation.

In contrast to the rather fanciful Crowleyesque visions, Antichrist sometimes looks like a clean-cut all-American hero, as shown by Nicolae Carparthia from the popular *Left Behind* series, authored by evangelical preachers Tim LaHaye and Jerry Jenkins (to be discussed further in Chapter 10). Following the lead of Signorelli, this Antichrist is well dressed and blonde haired, a convincing deceiver indeed (Plate 32). And neither is Barack Obama immune to the charge that he too may be Antichrist. Some fundamentalist Christian bloggers who associate the Beast or Rev. 13 with the US government, produced doctored images of Obama's iconic 'Hope' and 'Change' campaign posters (designed by Shepard Fairey) in which he is directly identified with Antichrist/the Beasts of Rev. 13. In the doctored images, devil's

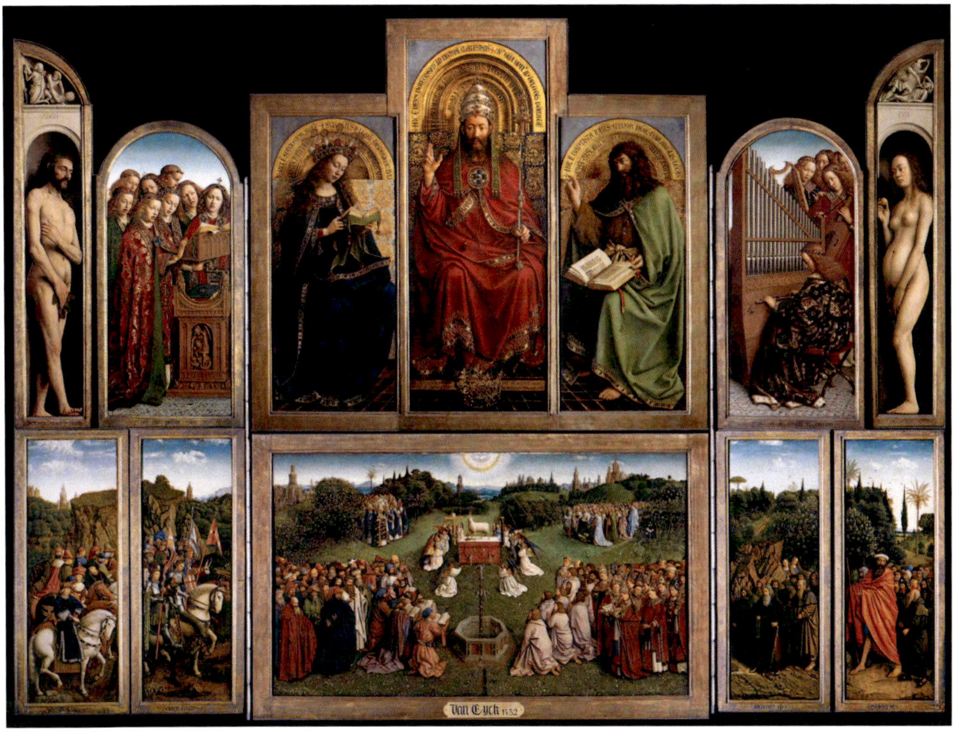

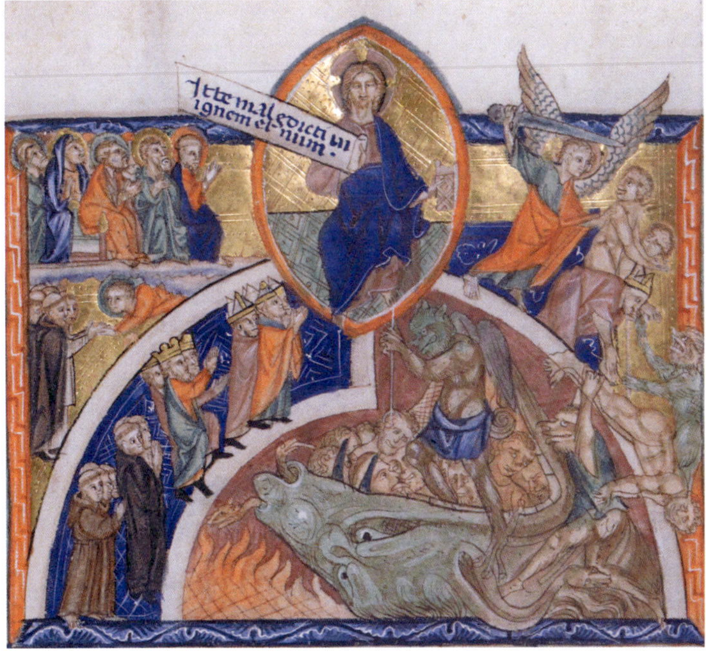



**PLATE 1.** The Van Eycks, The *Ghent Altarpiece*, 1432, Ghent: St Bavo's Cathedral. © Bridgeman Art Library

**PLATE 2.** The *Gulbenkian Apocalypse*, *c.*1270, The Last Judgement (Rev. 20.11–15), Lisbon: Museo Calouste Gulbenkian. © Museo Calouste Gulbenkian

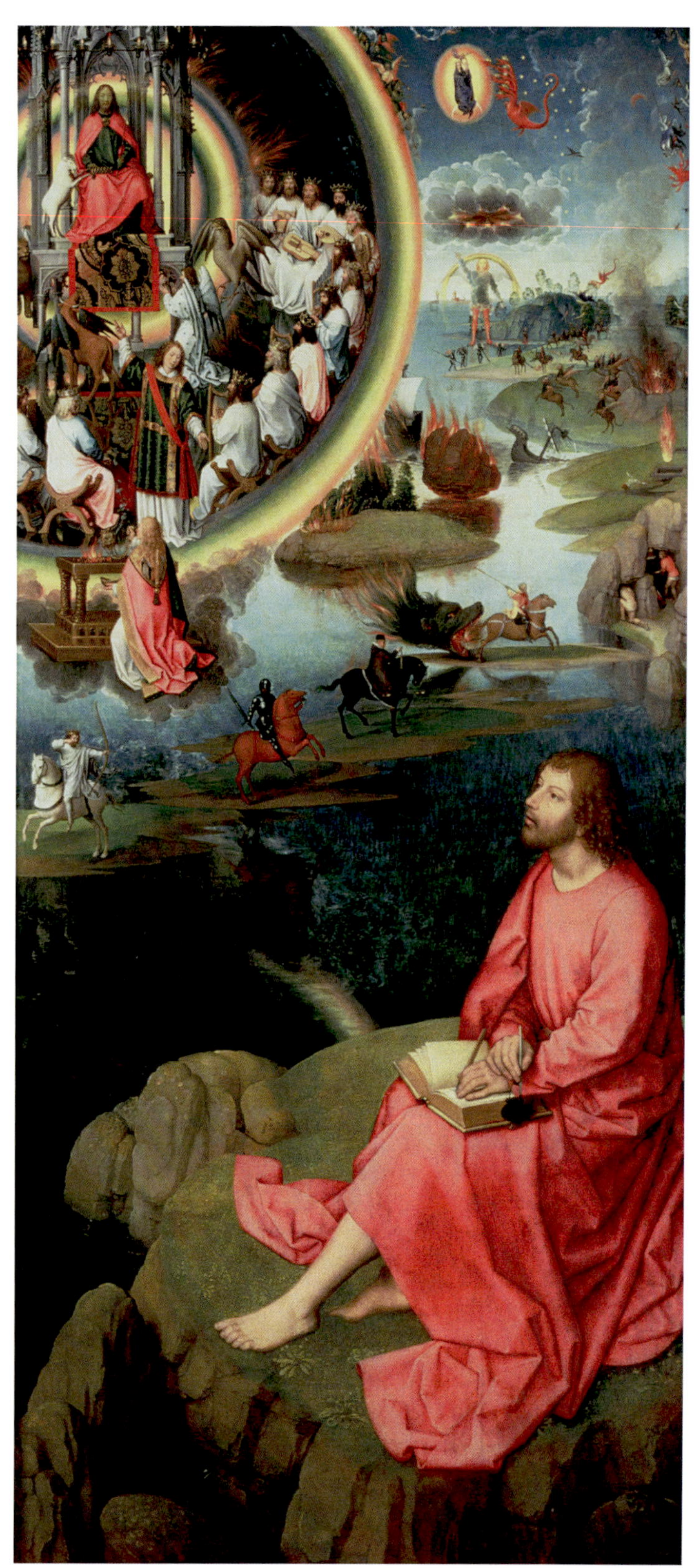

PLATE 3.  Hans Memling, *The Apocalypse Panel*, detail from the *St John Altarpiece*, 1474–9, Bruges: The Memling Museum. © Bridgeman Art Library

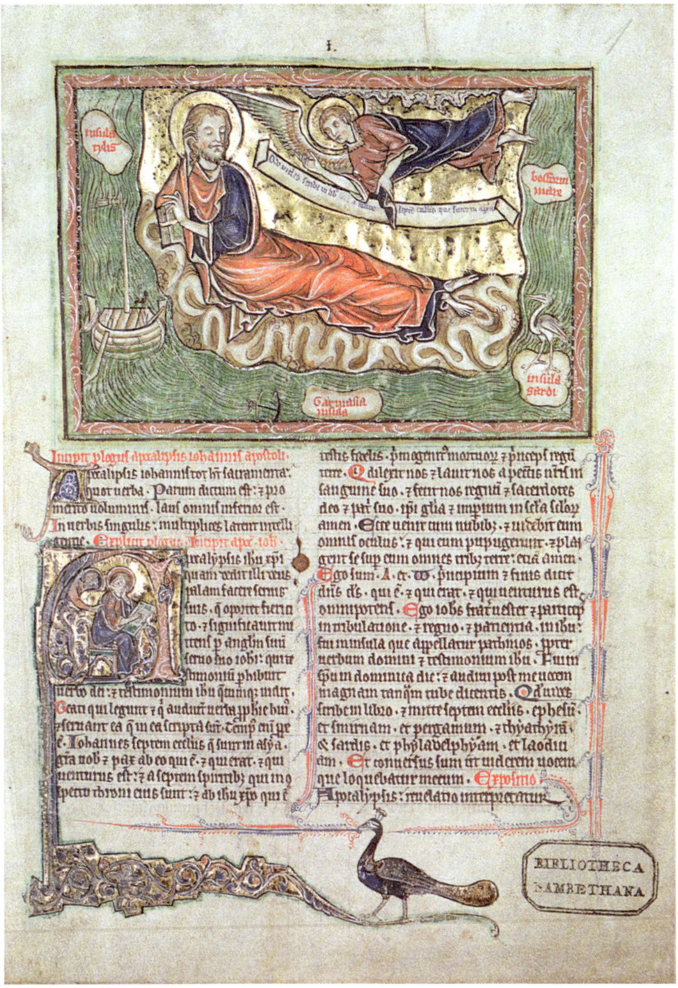

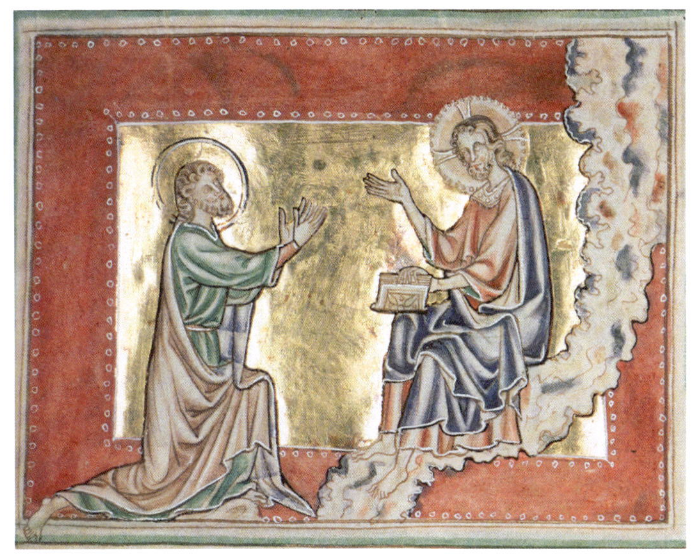

PLATE 4. The *Lambeth Apocalypse*, *c.*1260, John Receiving his Vision on Patmos (Rev. 1), London: Lambeth Palace Library. © Bridgeman Art Library

PLATE 5. The *Lambeth Apocalypse*, *c.*1260, John Kneeling before Christ (Rev. 22), London: Lambeth Palace Library. © Bridgeman Art Library

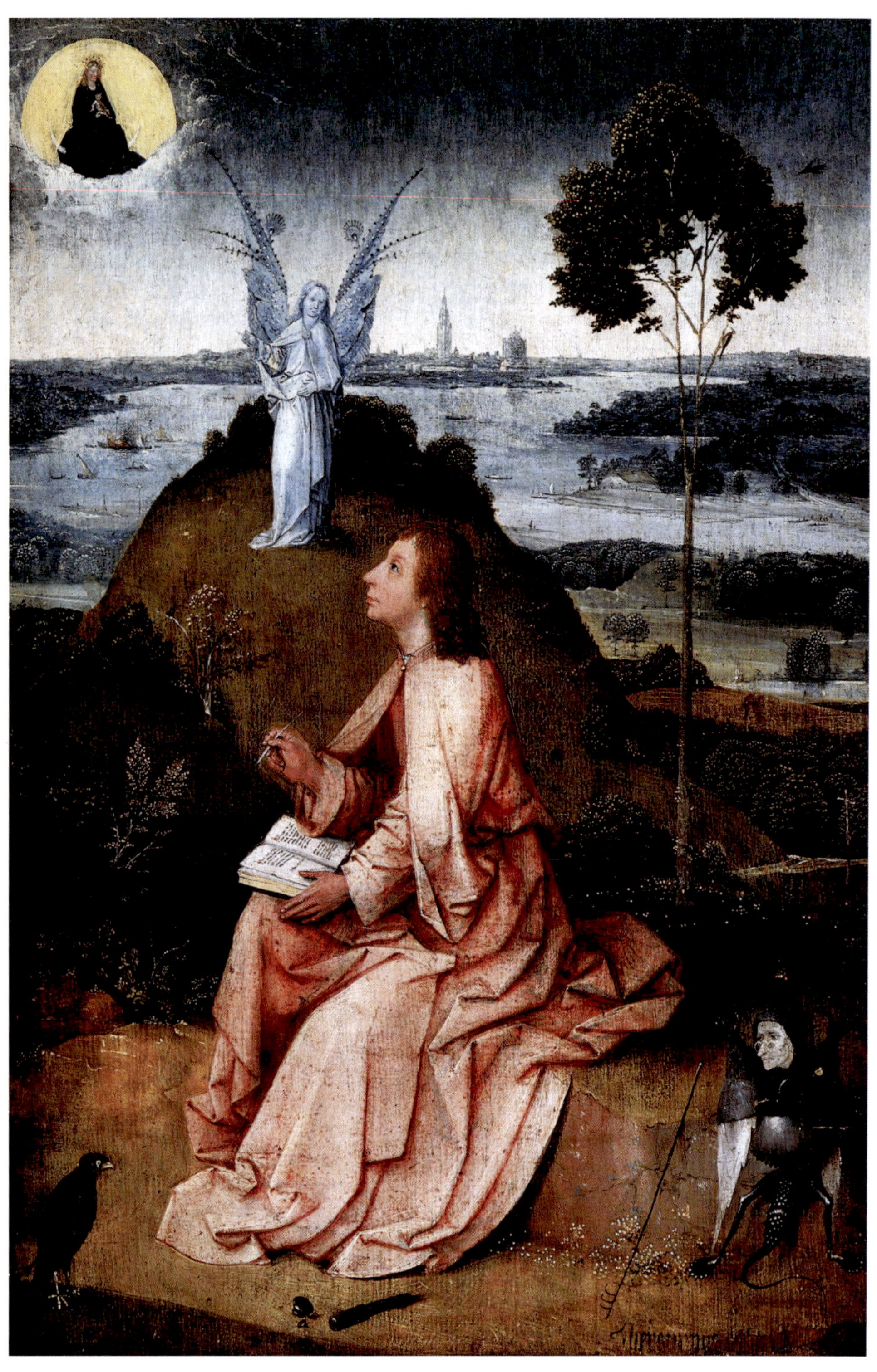

**PLATE 6.** Hieronymous Bosch, *St John the Evangelist on Patmos*, *c.*1489 or later, Berlin: Gemäldegallerie.
© Bridgeman Art Library

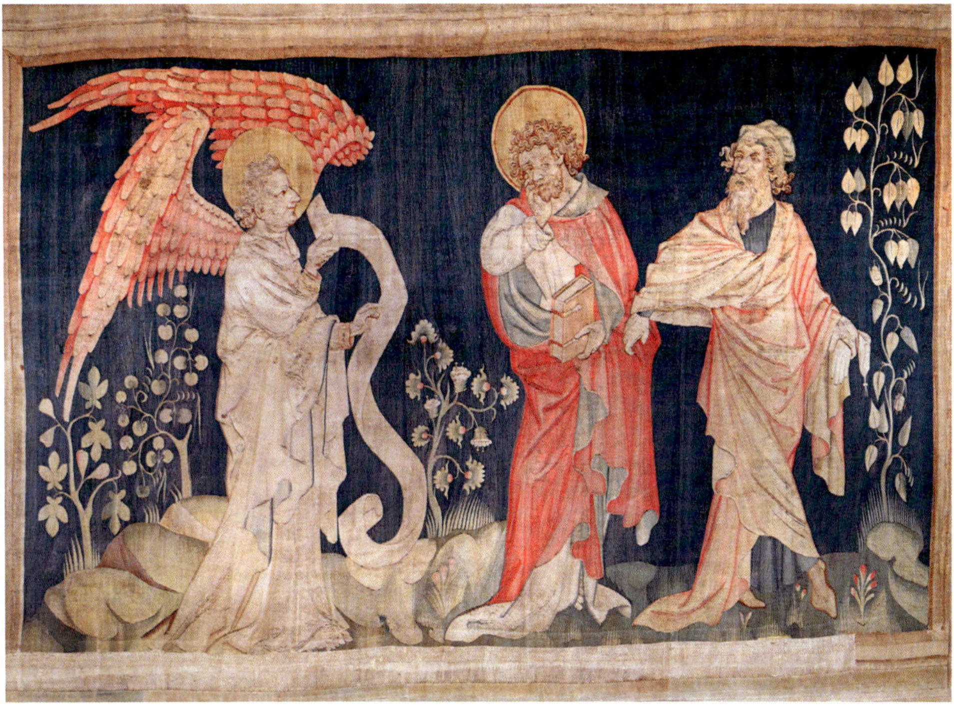

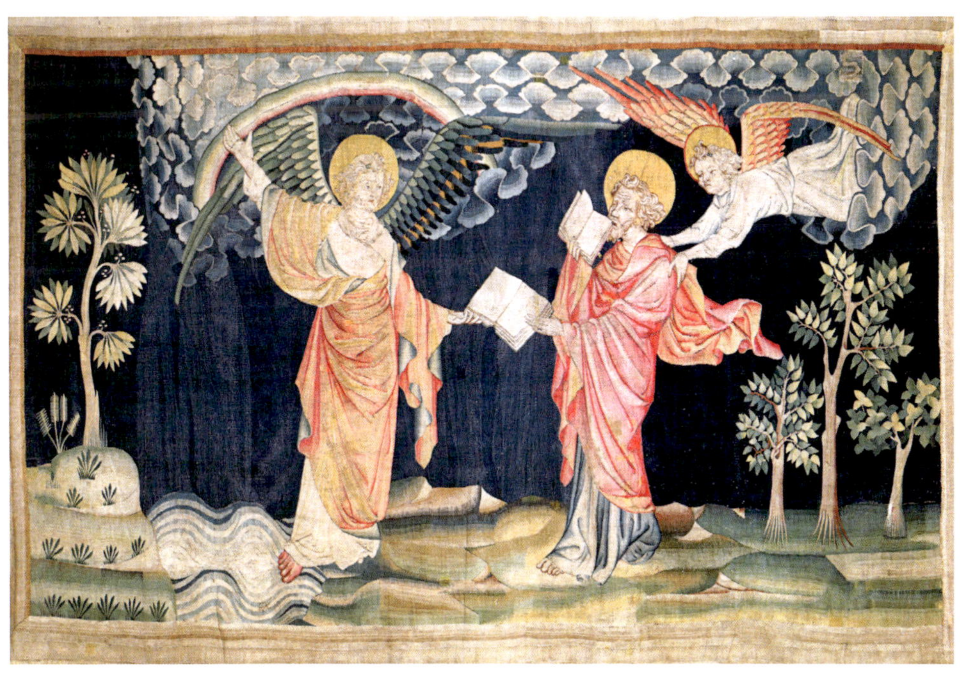

PLATE 7. The *Angers Apocalypse Tapestry, c.*1373–80, The Tears of St John (Rev. 5), Maine et Loire: Chateau d'Angers. © Bridgeman Art Library

PLATE 8. The *Angers Apocalypse Tapestry, c.*1373–80, John Taking and Eating the Scroll (Rev. 10), Maine et Loire: Chateau d'Angers. © Bridgeman Art Library

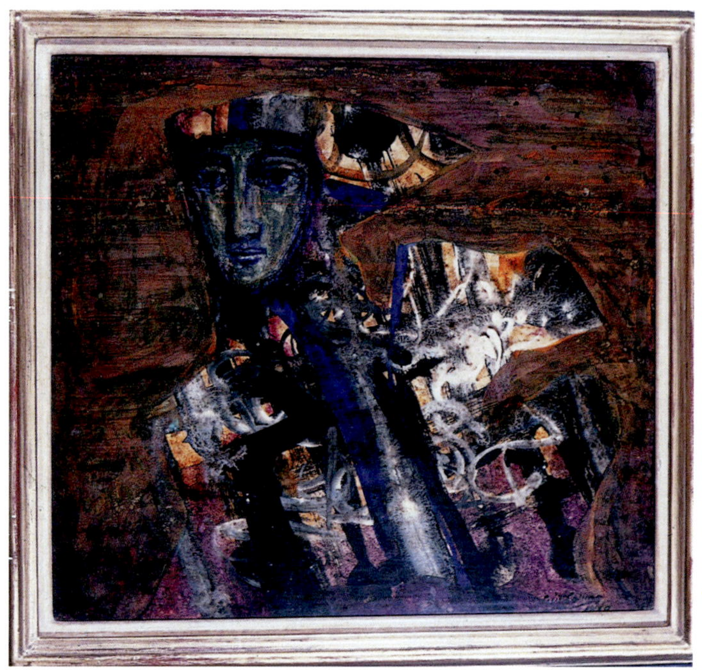

PLATE 9. Cecil Collins, *The Angel of the Apocalypse* (Rev. 10), 1969. Photograph courtesy of Clive Hicks © Tate, London 2014

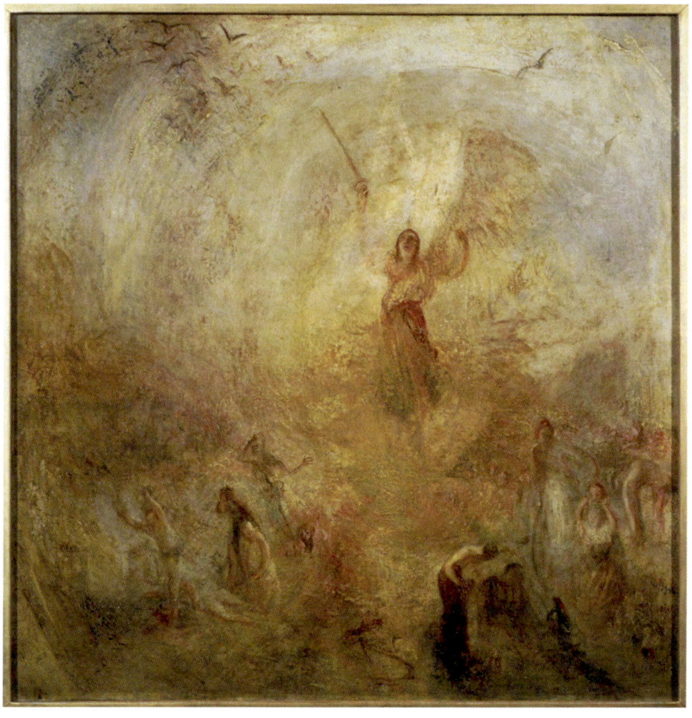

PLATE 10. J. M. W. Turner, *The Angel Standing in the Sun*, 1846 (Rev. 19.17/Rev. 12), London: Tate. © Tate, London 2014

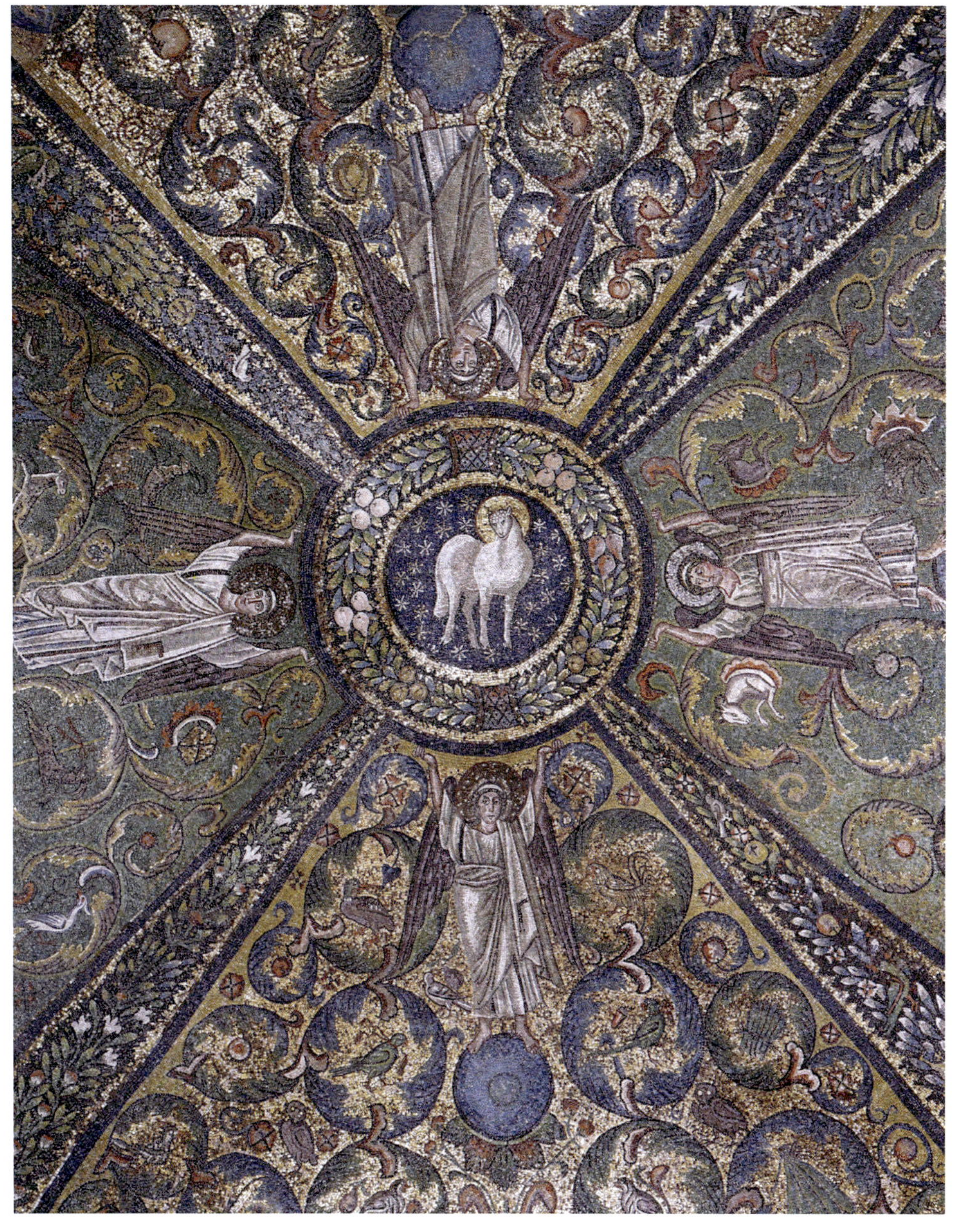

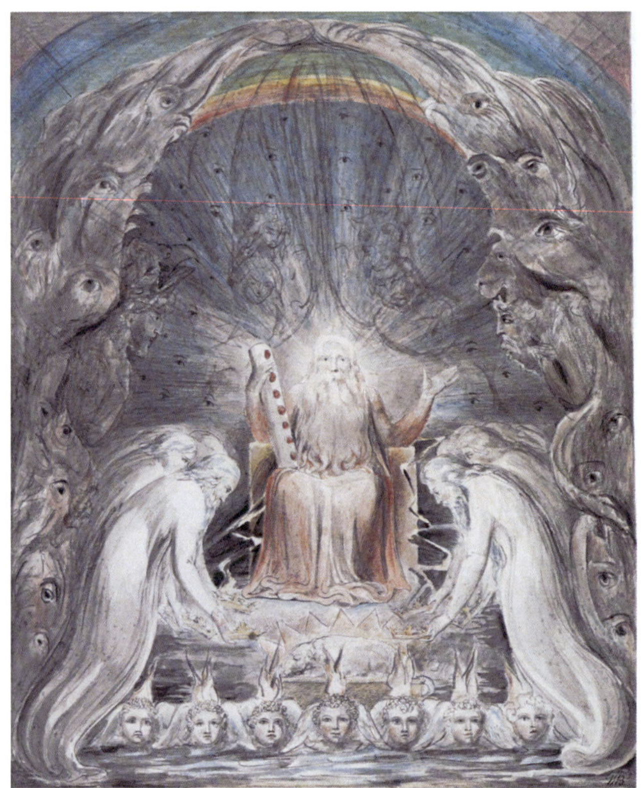

PLATE 12.  William Blake, *The Four and Twenty Elders*, *c.*1805, London: Tate. © Tate, London 2014

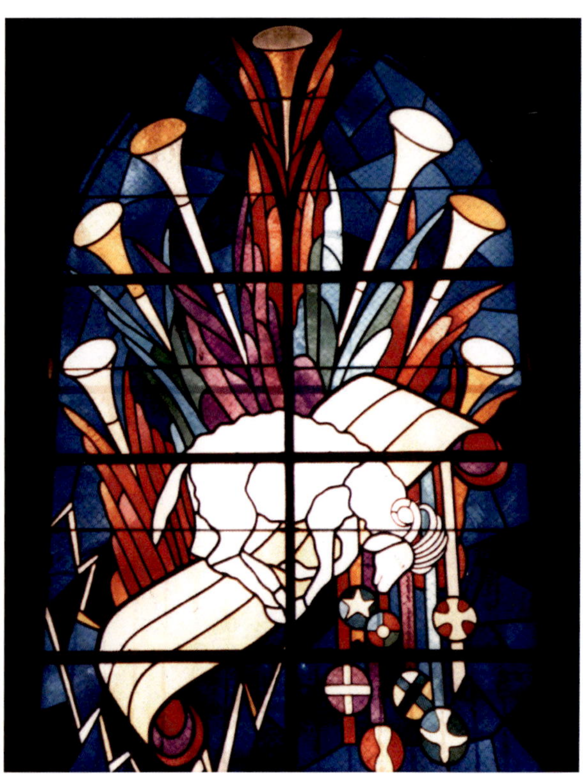

PLATE 13.  Jean-Pierre Bretegnier, *c.*1950, *The Lamb*, stained glass, Héricourt. © Bretegnier, by kind permission of the Musée Virtuel du Protestantisme

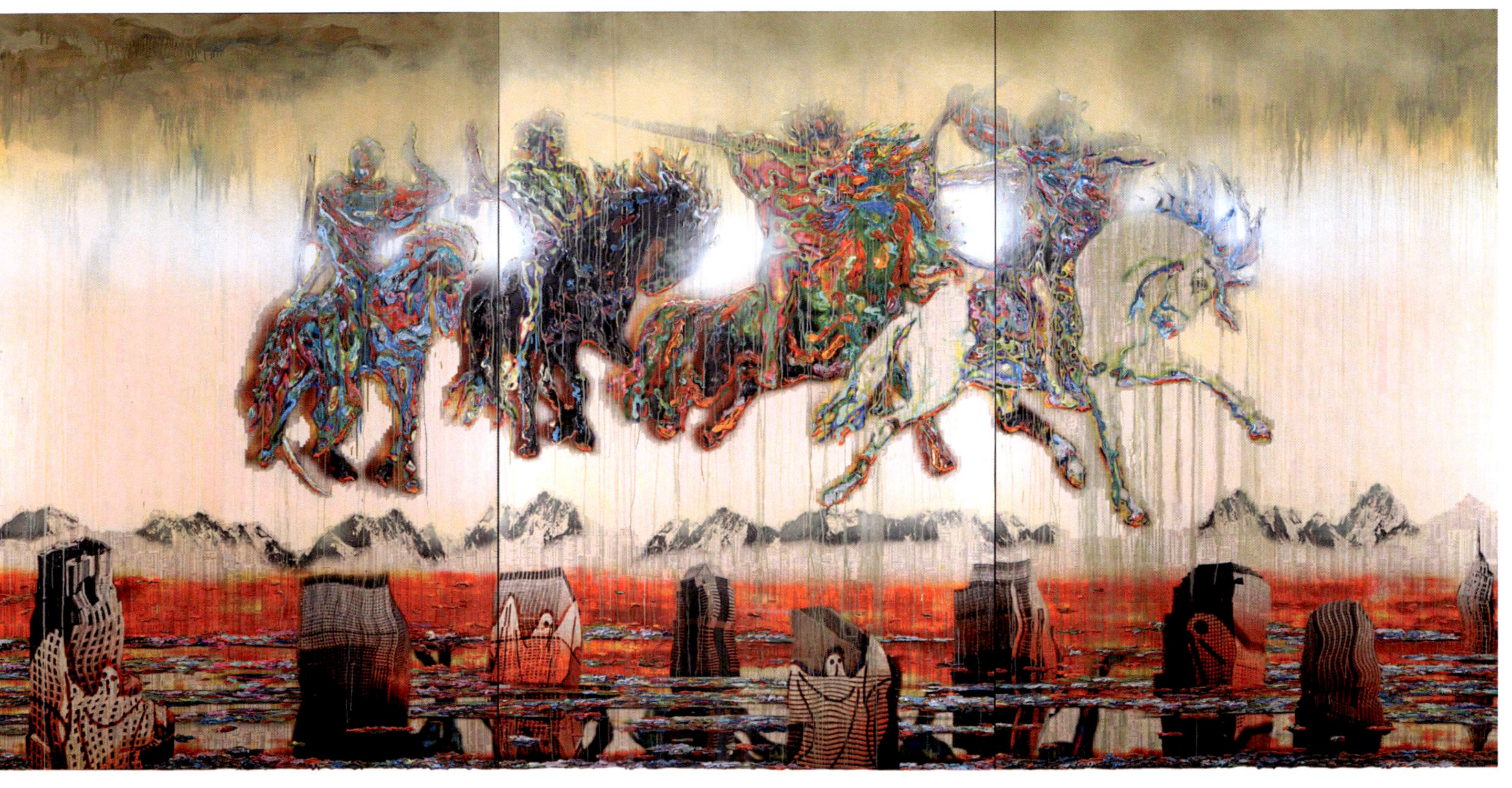

PLATE 14.  Gordon Cheung, *The Four Horsemen of the Apocalypse*, 2009, London. © Gordon Cheung

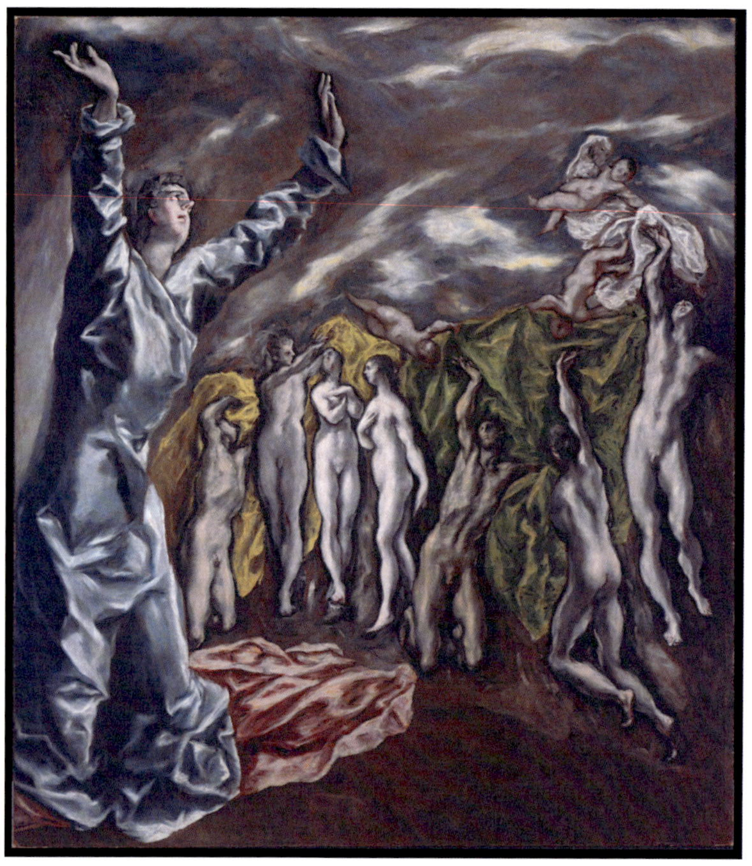

PLATE 15.    El Greco, *The Opening of the Fifth Seal*, *c*.1608–14, New York: Metropolitan Museum. © 2014. Image Copyright the Metropolitan Museum of Art/ Art Resource/Scala. Florence

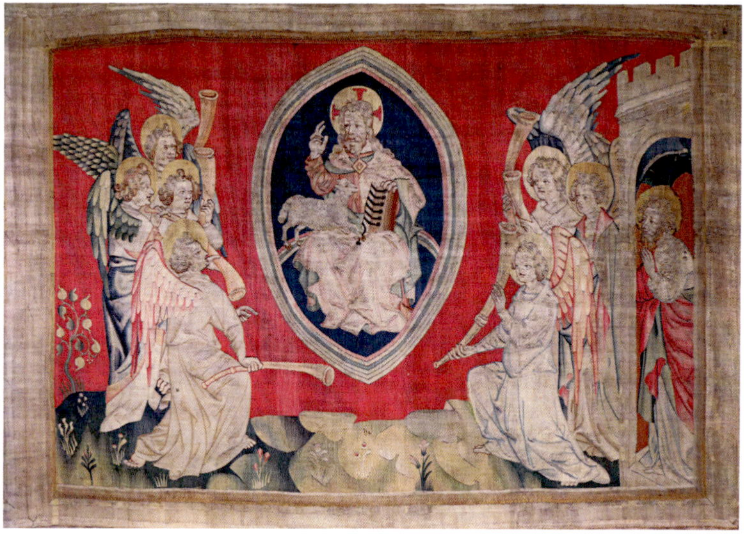

PLATE 16.    The *Angers Apocalypse Tapestry*, *c*.1373–80, The Silence in Heaven (Rev. 8.1), Maine et Loire: Chateau d'Angers. © Bridgeman Art Library

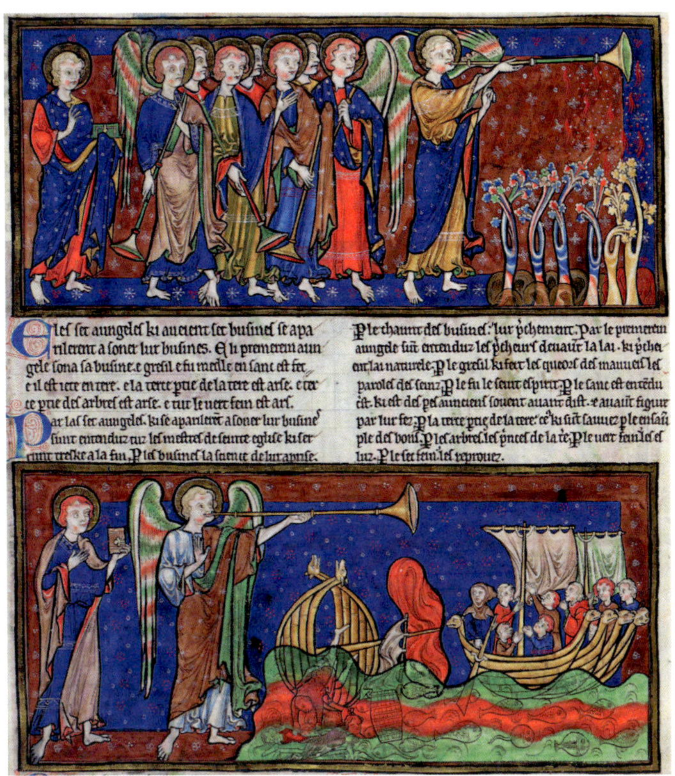

PLATE 17. The *Trinity Apocalypse*, *c.*1260, The First and Second Trumpets (Rev. 8.7–9), Cambridge: Trinity College. © The Master and Fellows of Trinity College, Cambridge

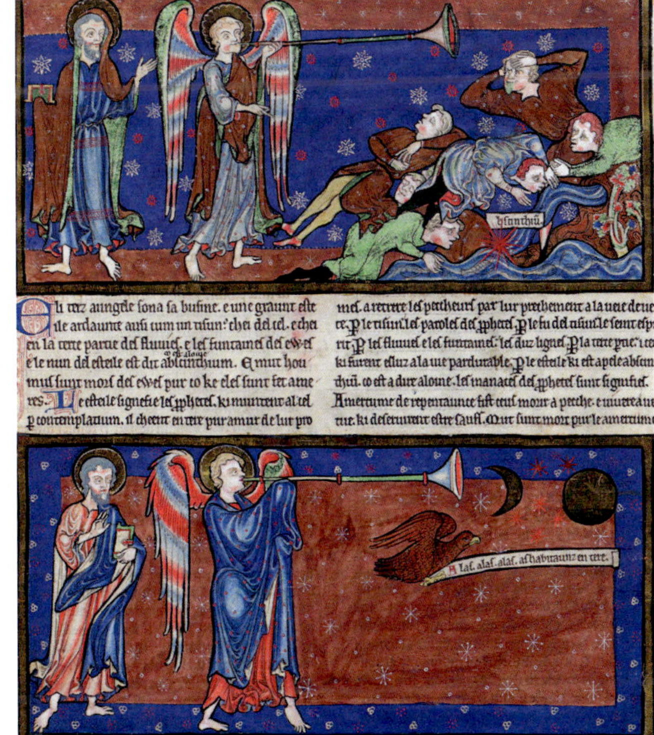

PLATE 18. The *Trinity Apocalypse*, *c.*1260, The Third and Fourth Trumpets (Rev. 8.10–12), Cambridge: Trinity College. © The Master and Fellows of Trinity College, Cambridge

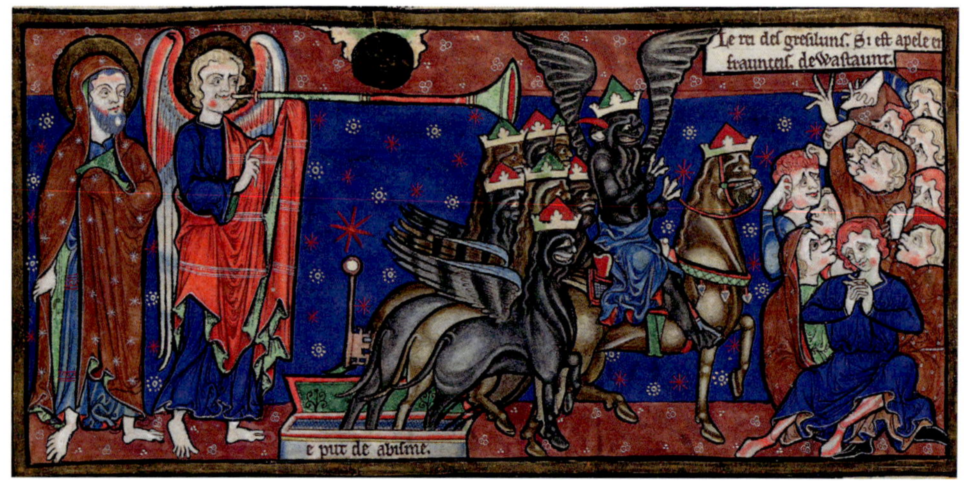

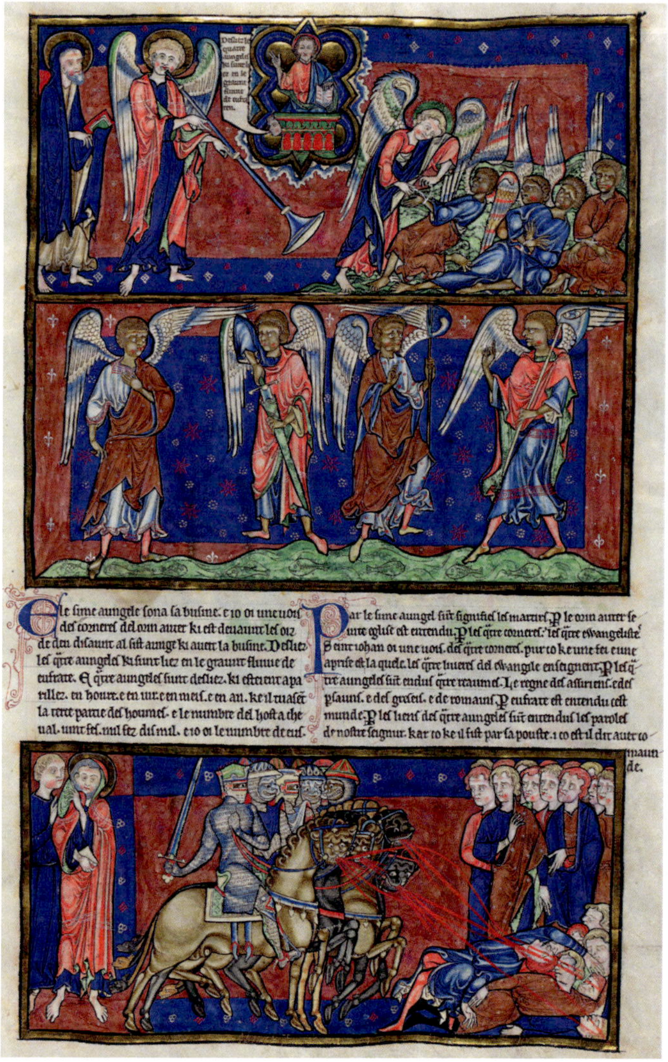

Le rei des gresiluns. Si est apele en frauntens. de Wastaunt.
e pur de abisme.

PLATE 21.  *Apocalypse Now* promotional poster, 1979. © Bridgeman Art Library

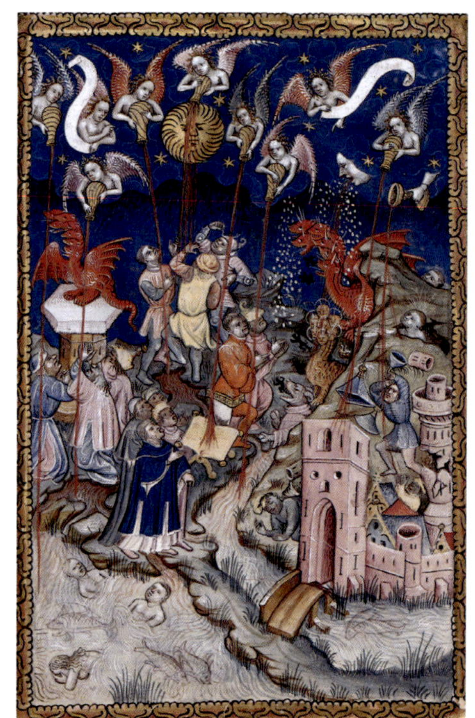

PLATE 22.   The *Flemish Apocalypse*, *c.*1400, The Seven Angels with the Seven Bowls (Rev. 16), Paris: Bibliothèque Nationale. © BnF

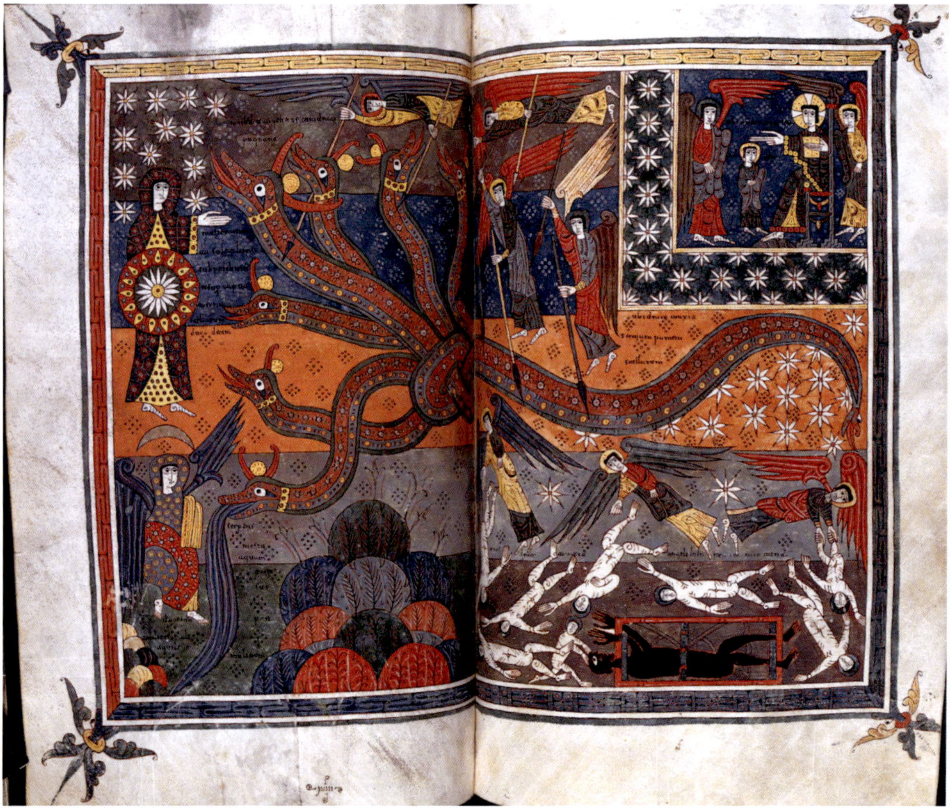

PLATE 23.   *The Silos Apocalypse*, twelfth century, The Woman and the Dragon (Rev. 12), London: British Library. © Bridgeman Art Library

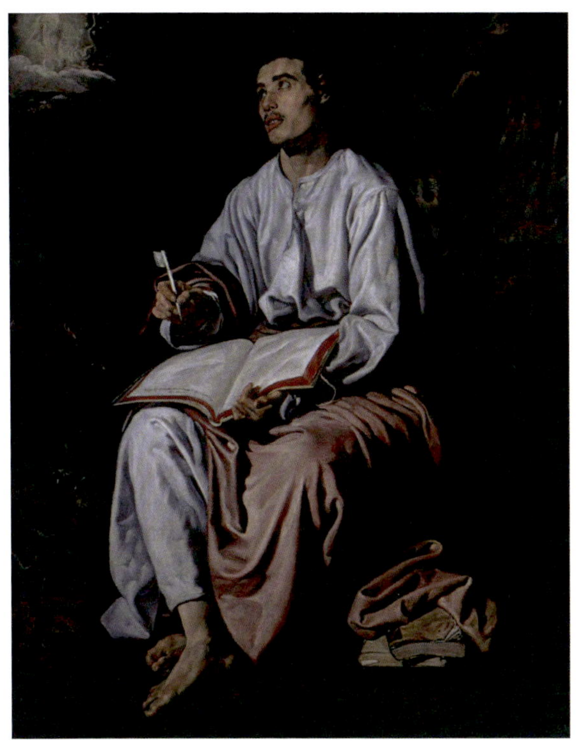

**PLATE 24.** Diego Velázquez, *St John the Evangelist on the Island of Patmos*, *c.*1618, London: National Gallery. © Bridgeman Art Library

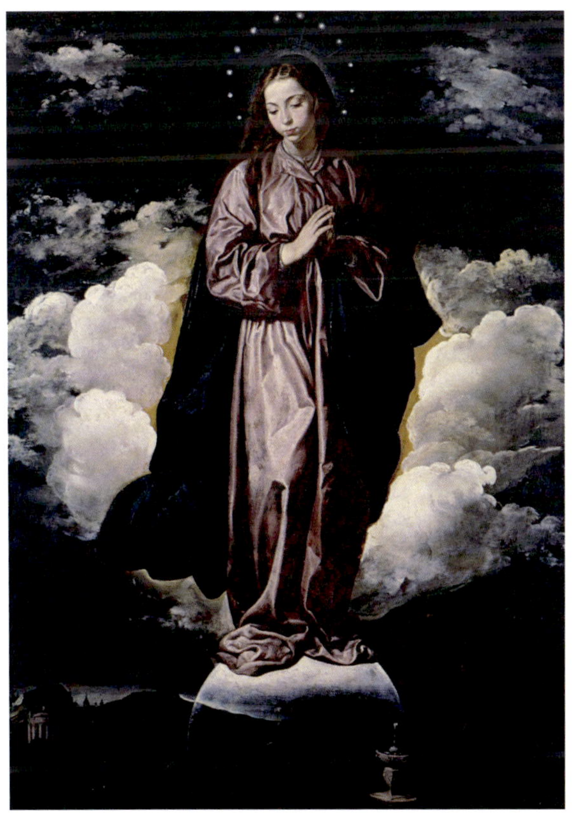

**PLATE 25.** Diego Velázquez, *The Immaculate Conception*, *c.*1618, London: National Gallery. © Bridgeman Art Library

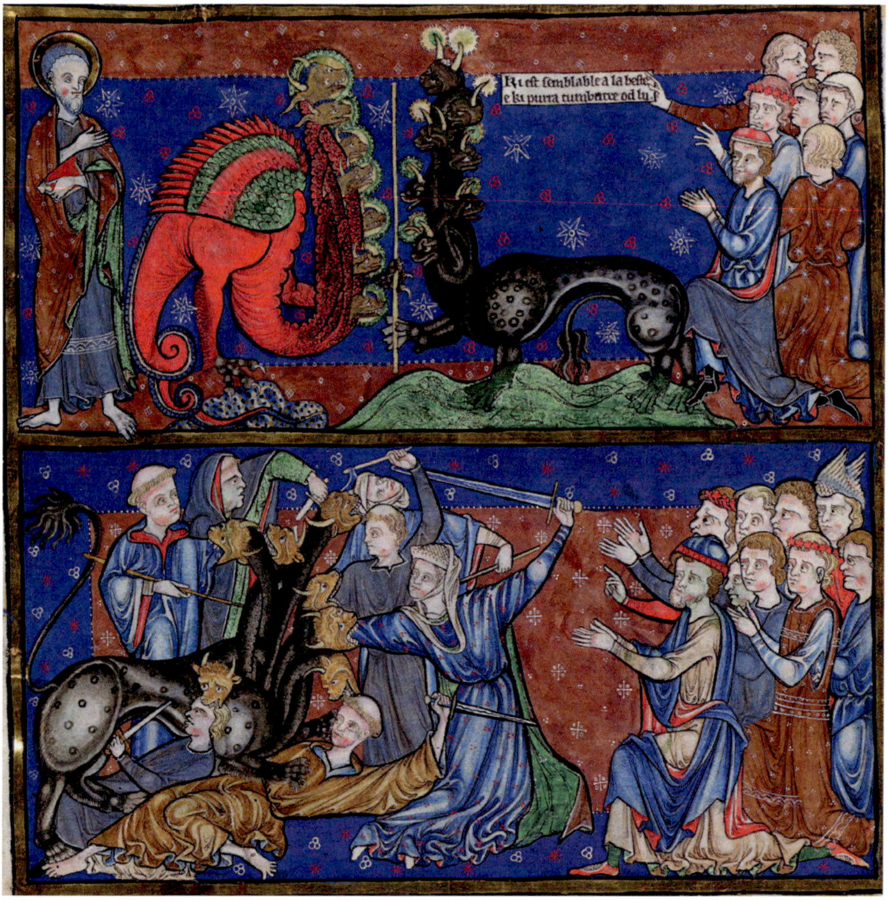

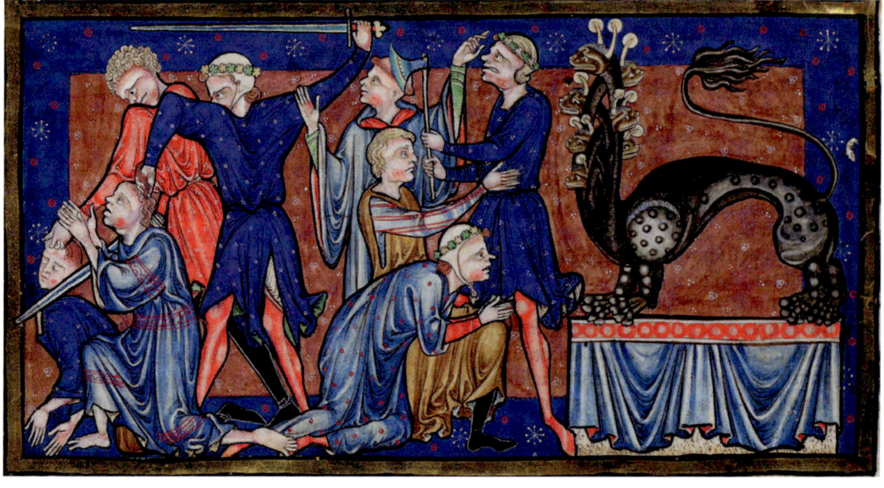

PLATE 26.   The *Trinity Apocalypse*, *c.*1260, The Dragon and the Sea Beast (Rev. 13. 1–3), Cambridge: Trinity College. © The Master and Fellows of Trinity College, Cambridge

PLATE 27.   The *Trinity Apocalypse*, *c.*1260, The Earth Beast and the Statue of the Sea Beast (Rev. 13.14–15), Cambridge: Trinity College. © The Master and Fellows of Trinity College, Cambridge

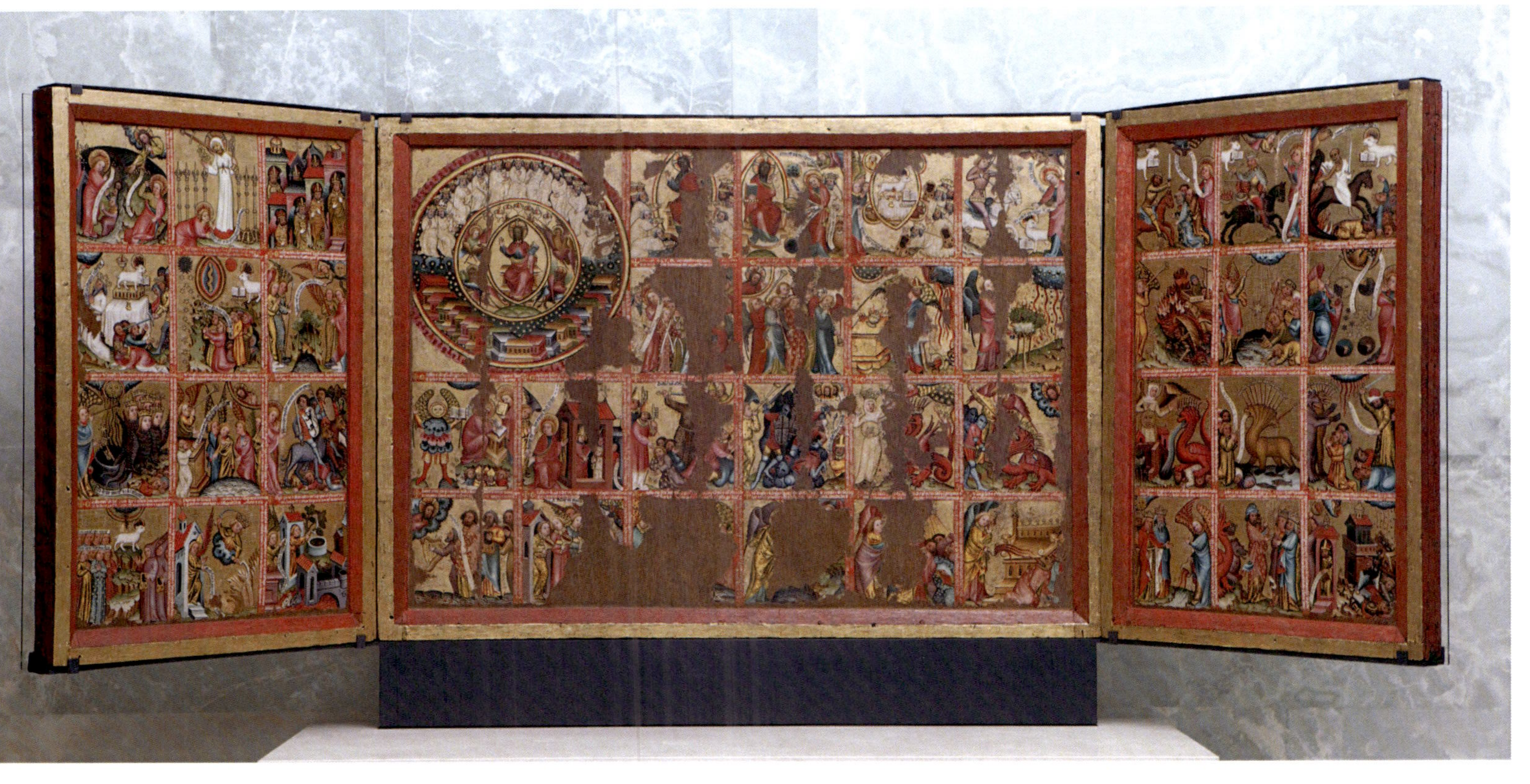

PLATE 28. The *Master Bertram Apocalypse Altarpiece*, c.1400, London: Victoria and Albert Museum. © Victoria and Albert Museum, London

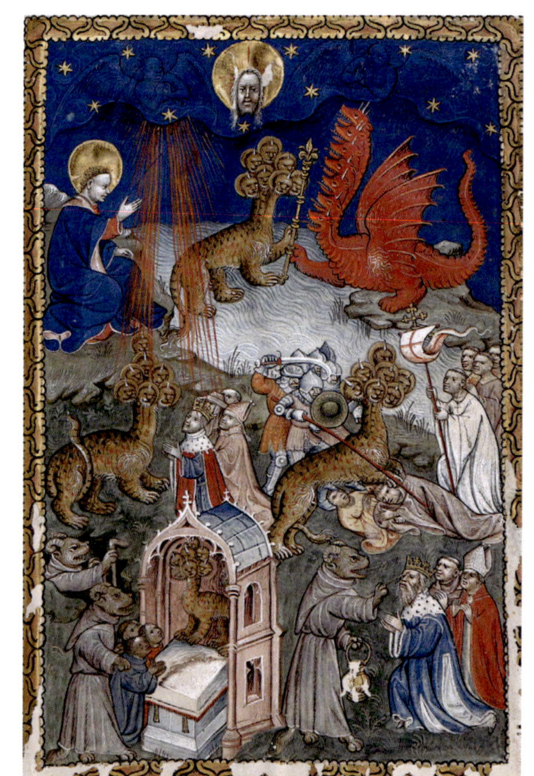

PLATE 29.   The *Flemish Apocalypse*, *c.*1400, The Dragon and the Two Beasts (Rev. 13), Paris: Bibliothèque Nationale. © BnF

PLATE 30.   Luca Signorelli, *The Sermon and Deeds of Antichrist*, from the Last Judgement fresco cycle, 1499–1504, Orvieto Cathedral. © Bridgeman Art Library

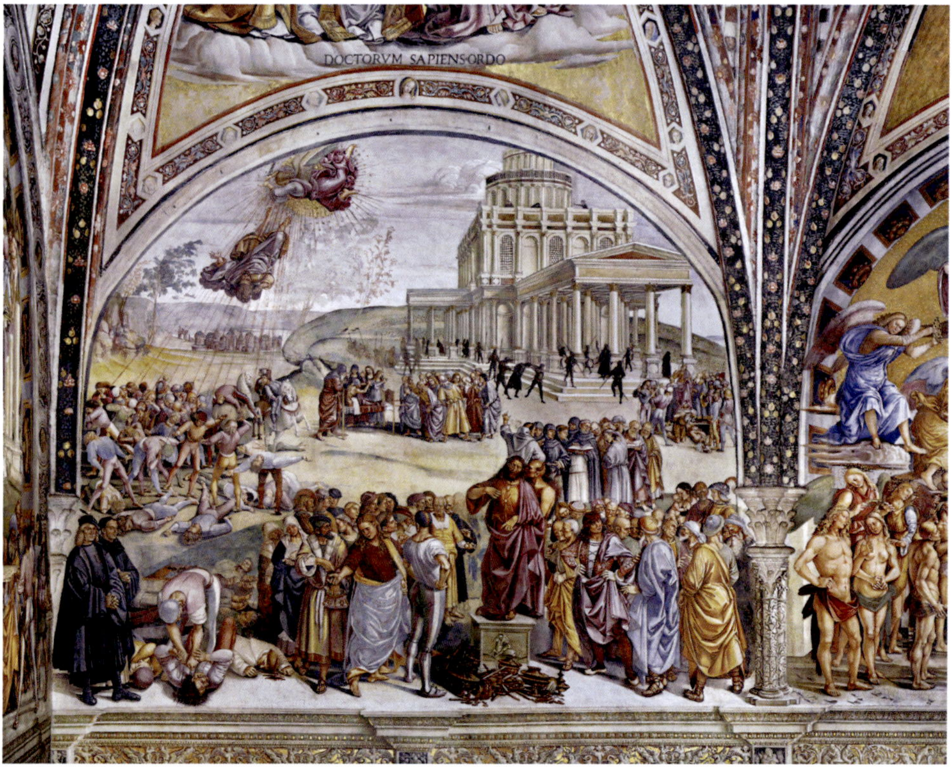

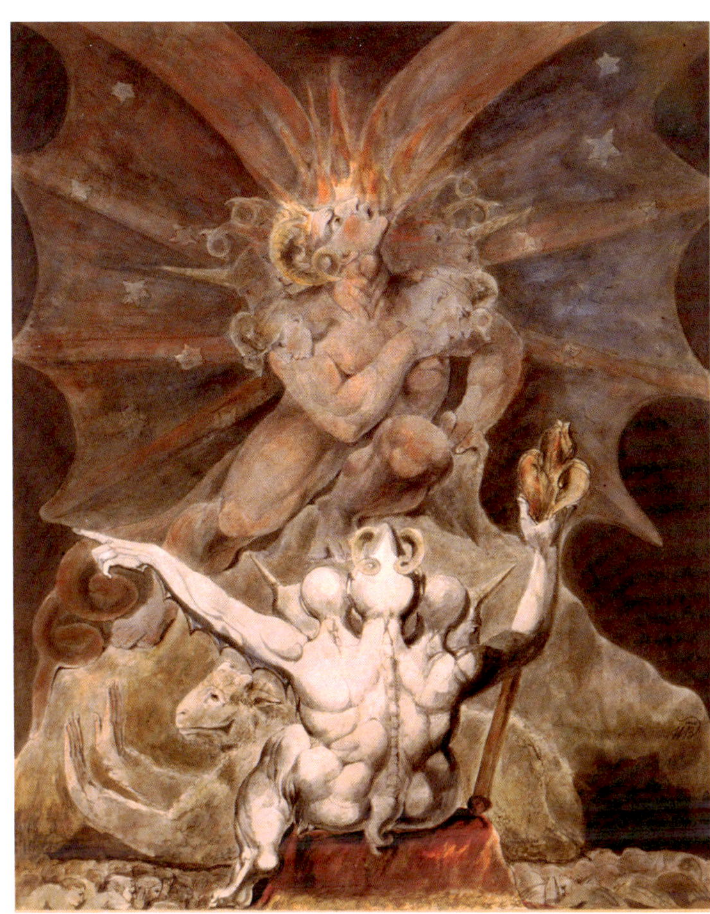



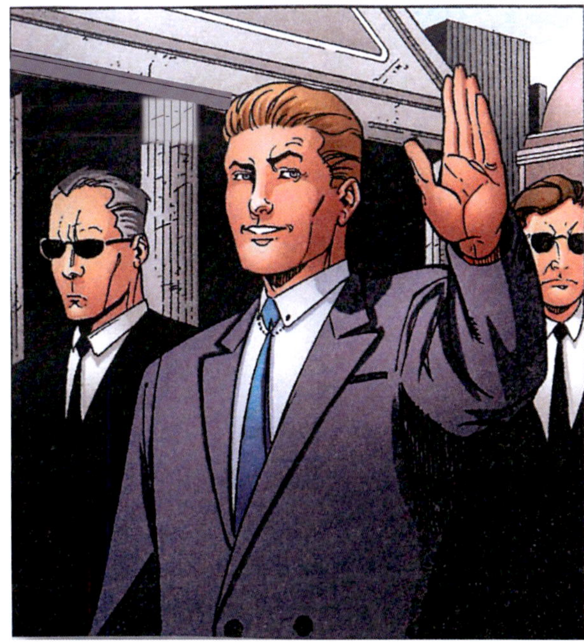

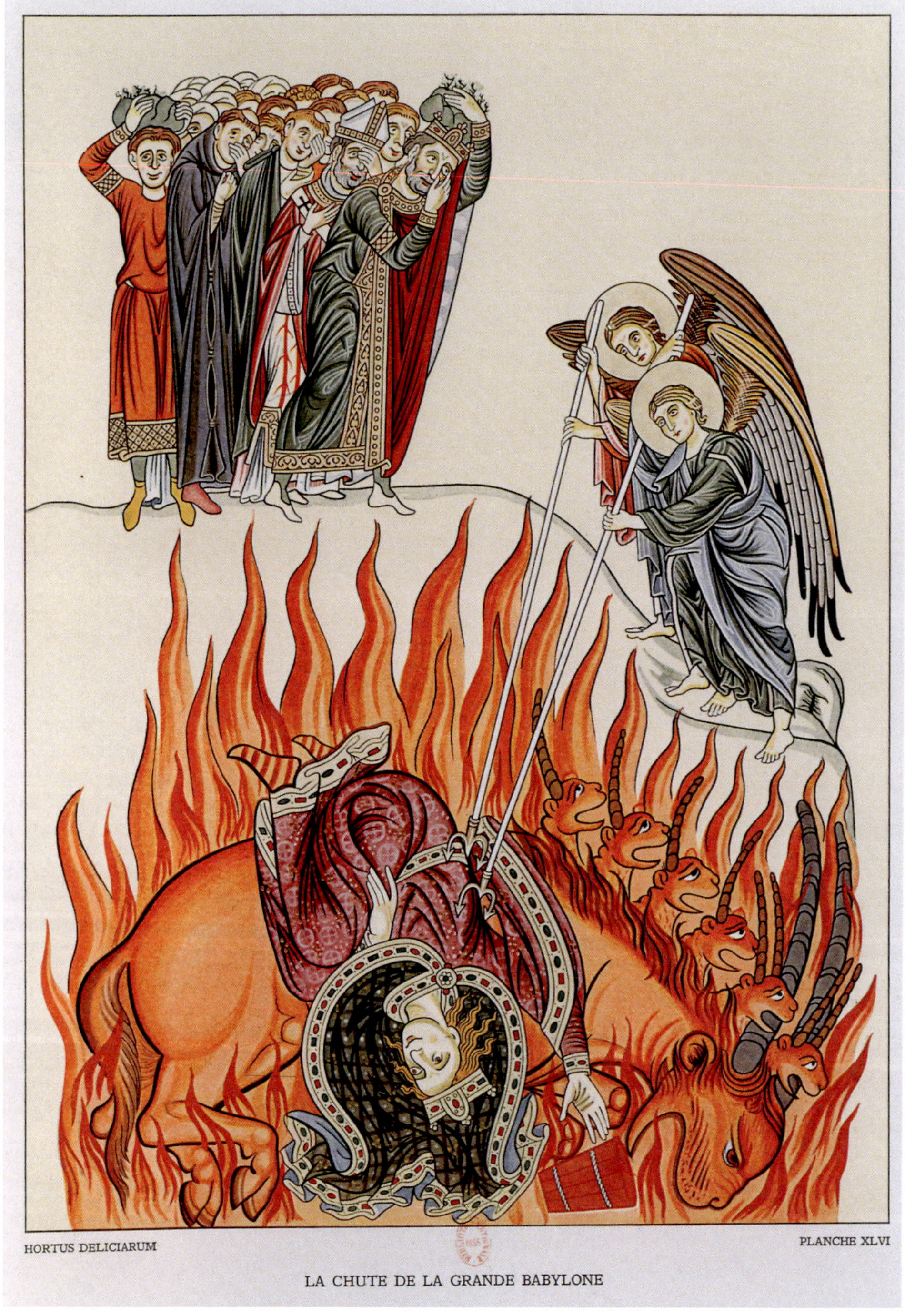



**plate 33.** The *Hortus Deliciarum*, 12th century, The Whore of Babylon Cast to her Death, Paris: Bibliothèque Nationale. © BnF

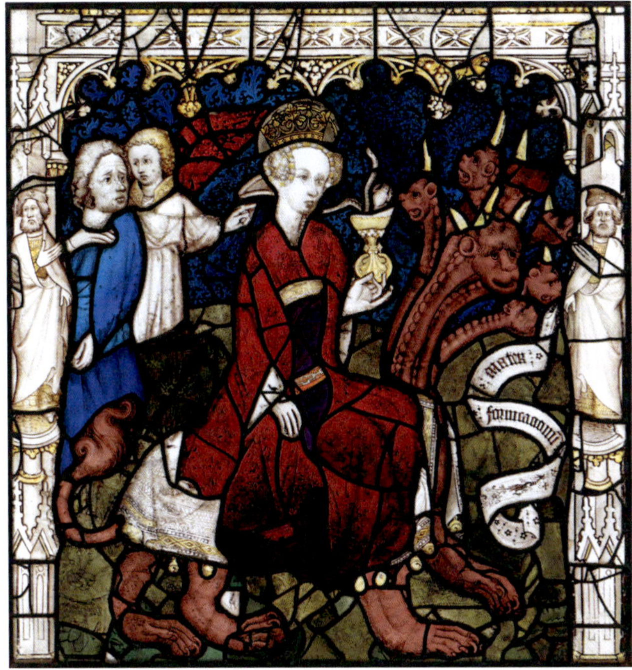



PLATE 34.    York Minster Great East Window, *c.* 1400, detail of the Whore of Babylon Astride the Beast (Rev. 17). Photo the York Glaziers Trust, reproduced courtesy of the Chapter of York.

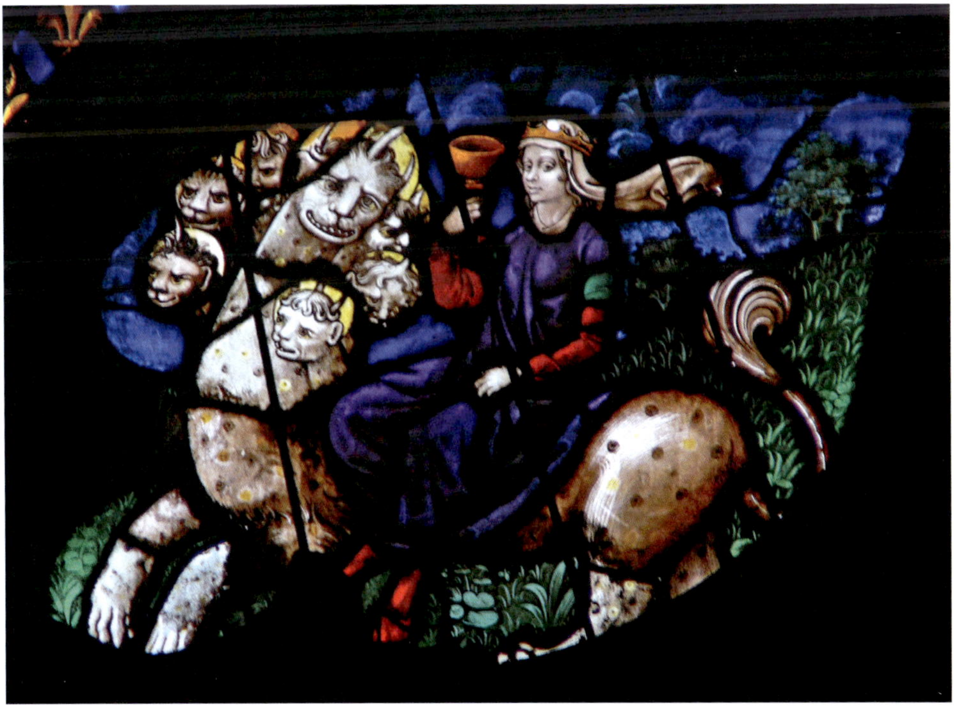

PLATE 35.    La Sainte Chapelle, Western Rose Window, *c.* 1500, detail of the Whore of Babylon with Red Feet (Rev. 17). © Bridgeman Art Library

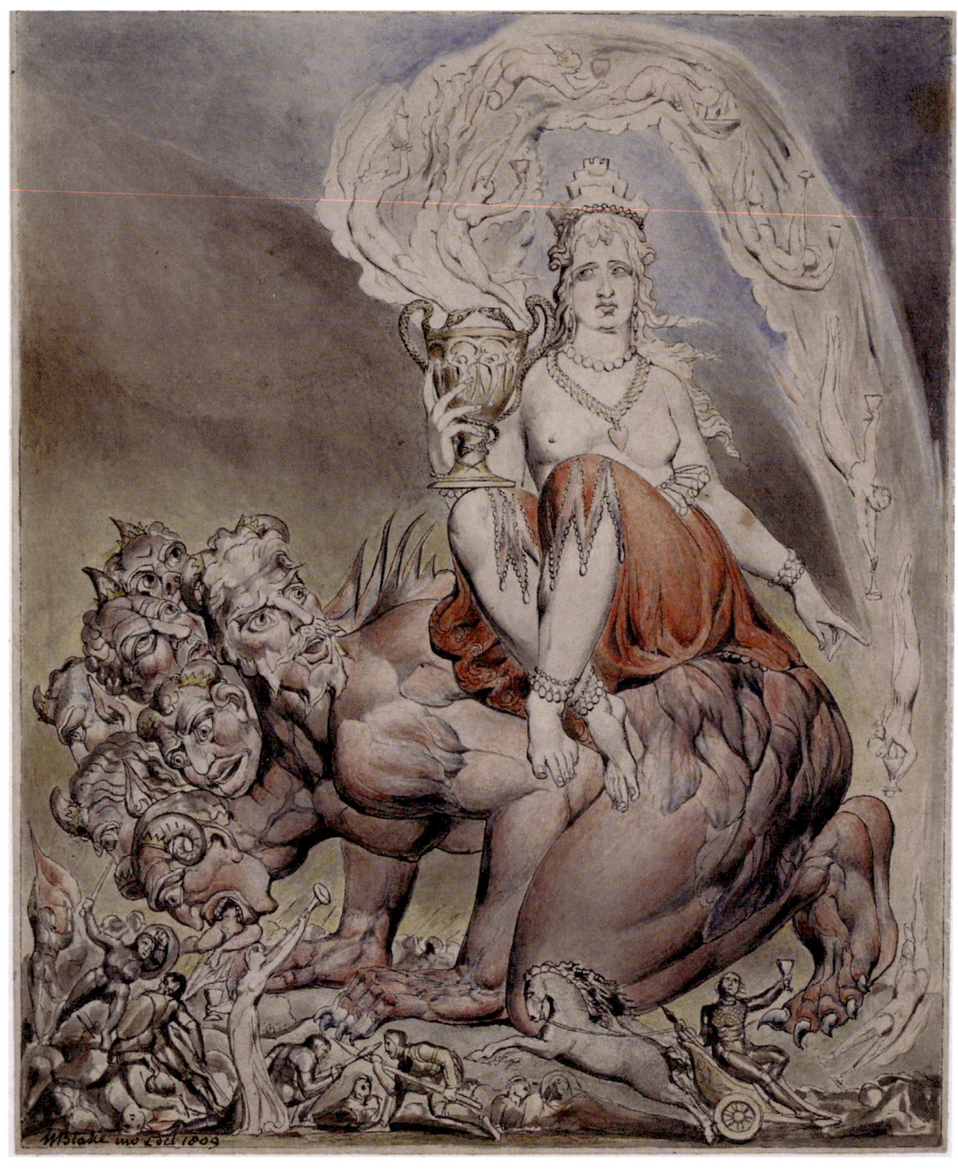

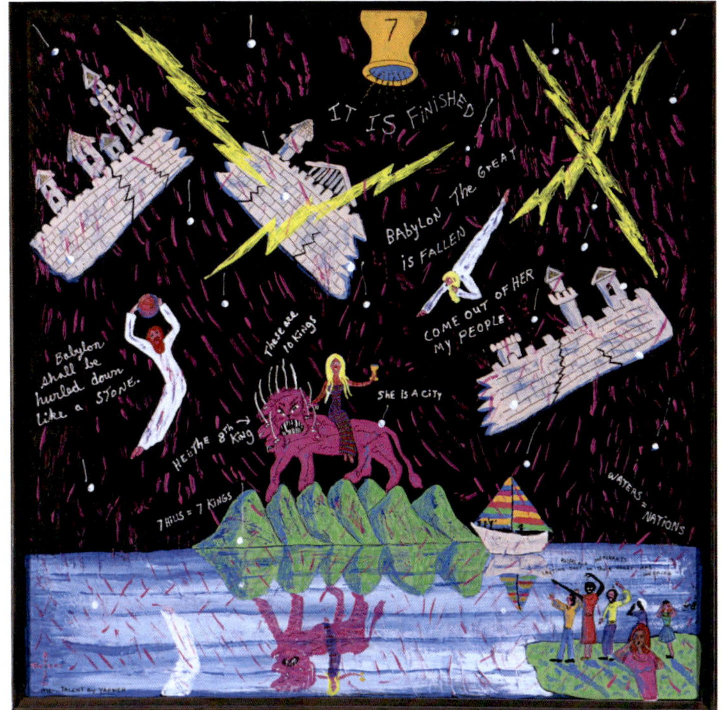


**PLATE 37.** Robert Roberg, *Babylon the Great is Fallen*, 1990, Washington: Smithsonian Museum. Smithsonian American Art Museum, Gift of Chuck and Jan Rosenak and museum purchase through the Luisita L. and Franz H. Denghausen Endowment. © 1990 Robert Roberg

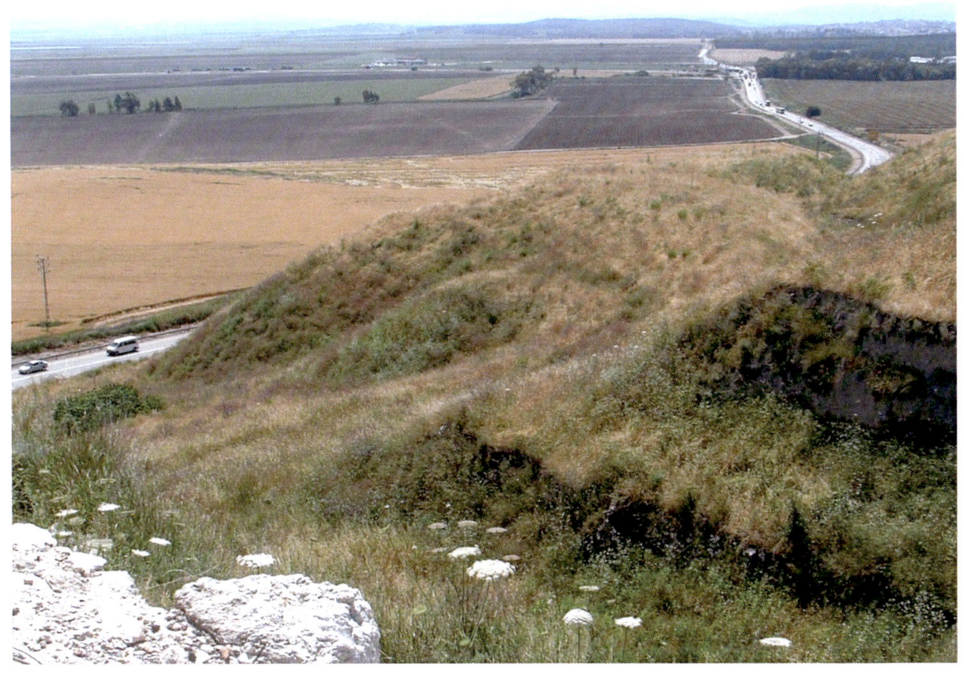

**PLATE 38.** Contemporary photograph of Tell Megiddo. © Hanay

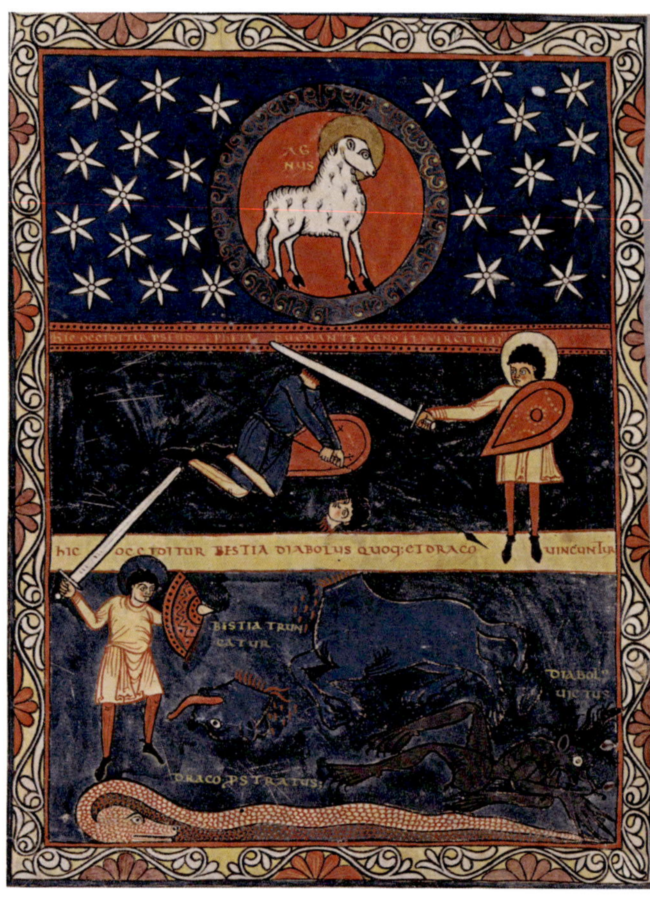

PLATE 39. *St Sever Beatus Manuscript*, c.1076, Armageddon (Rev. 19–20), Paris: Bibliothèque Nationale. © BnF

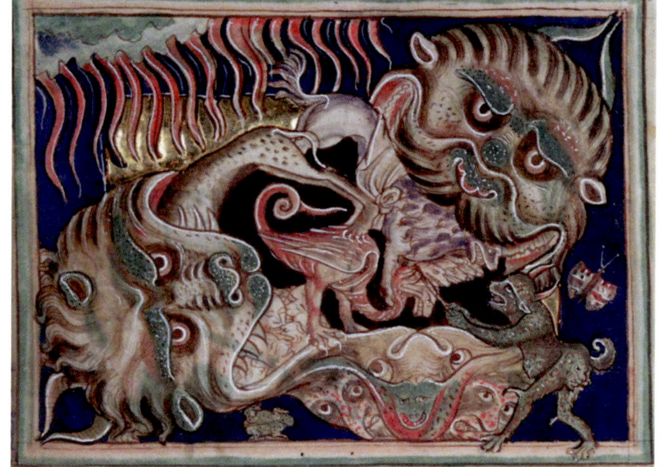

PLATE 40. The *Lambeth Apocalypse*, c.1260, Satan Cast into the Hellmouth (Rev. 20.10), London: Lambeth Palace Library. © Bridgeman Art Library

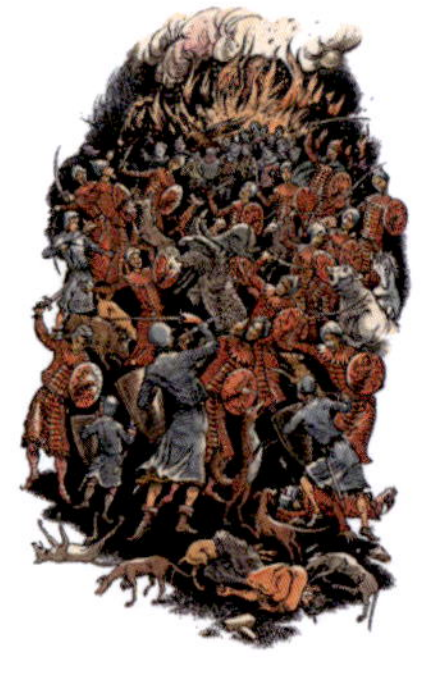

PLATE 41. *(left)* Illustration by Pauline Baynes from *The Last Battle* by C. S. Lewis. © C.S. Lewis Pte. Ltd. 1956. Extract reprinted by permission

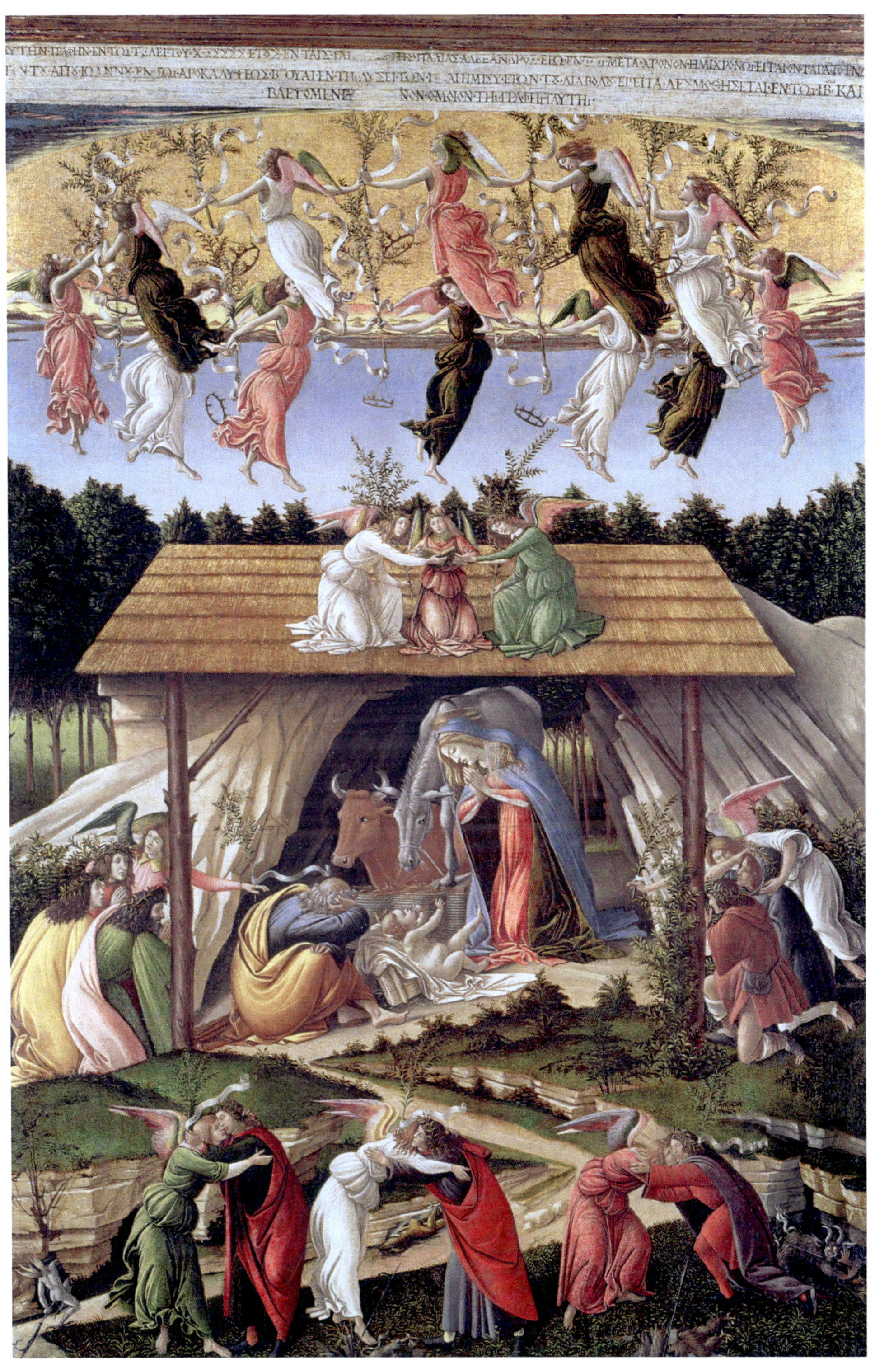



**PLATE 42.**    Sandro Botticelli, *The Mystic Nativity*, c. 1500, London: National Gallery. © Bridgeman Art Library

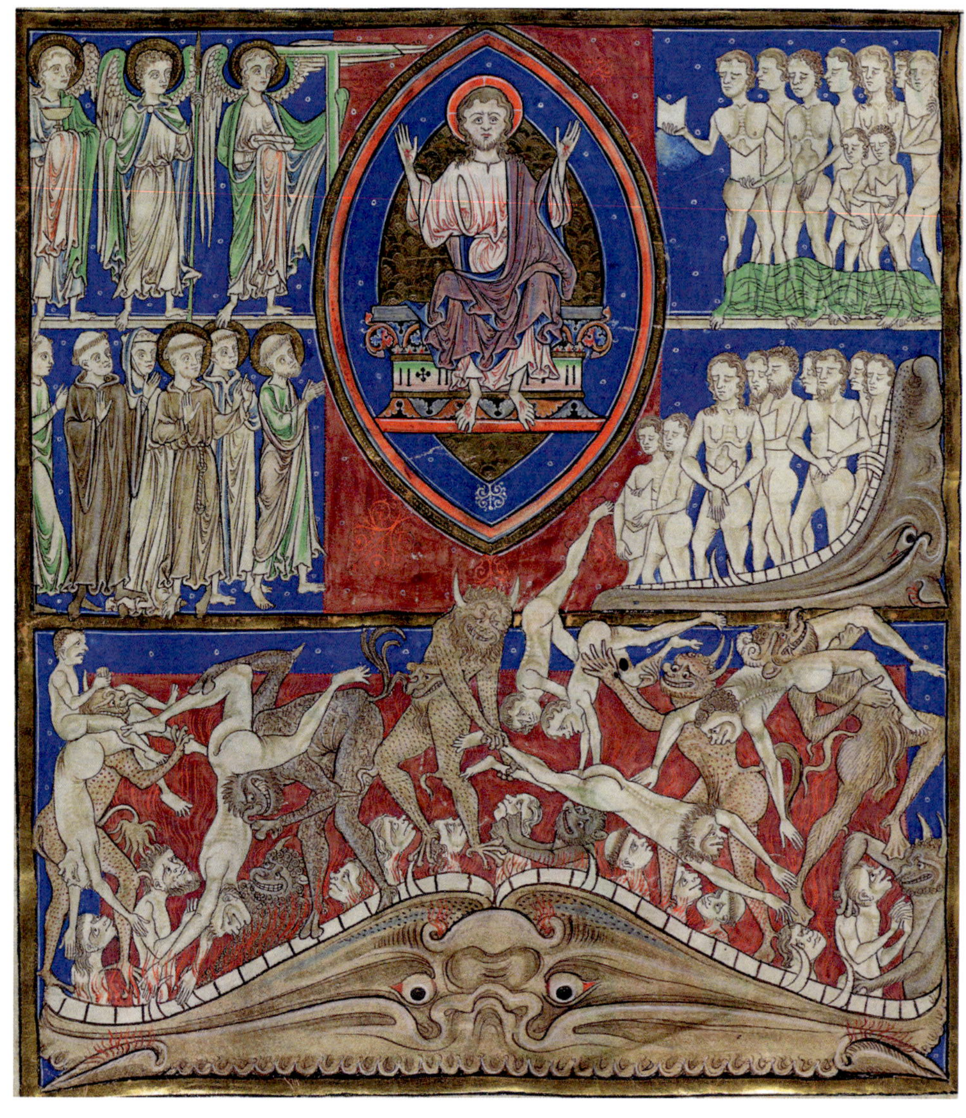

PLATE 43. The *Trinity Apocalypse*, c.1260, The Last Judgement (Rev. 20.11–15), Cambridge: Trinity College.© The Master and Fellows of Trinity College, Cambridge

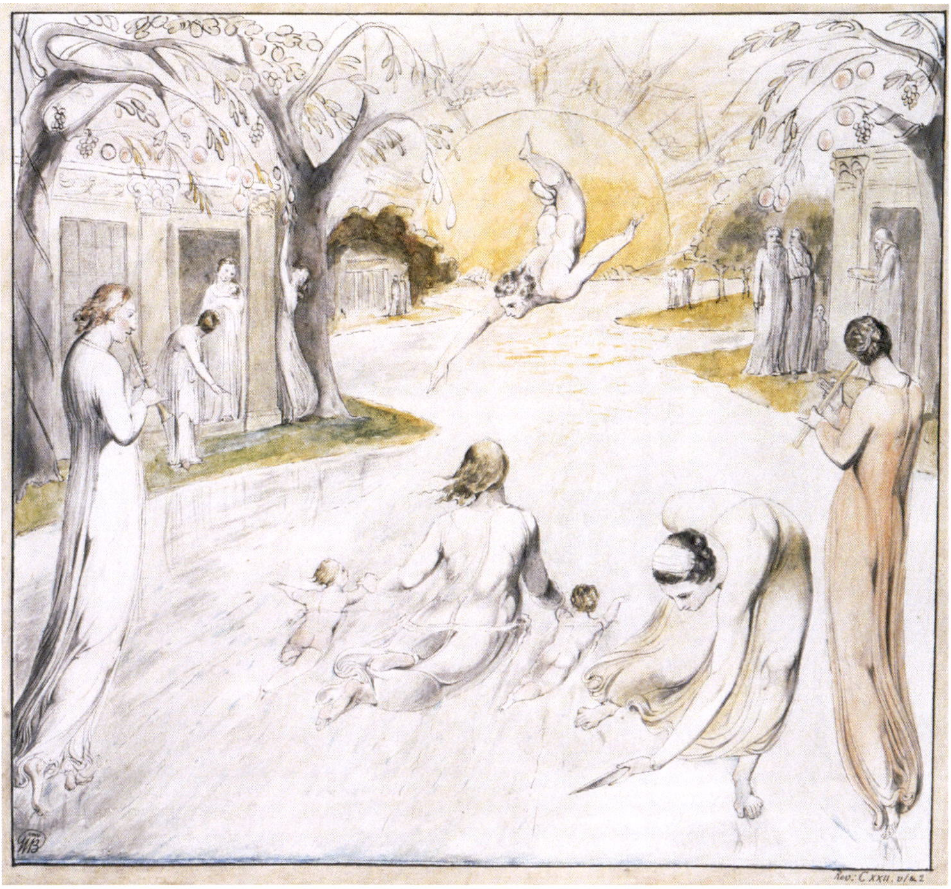

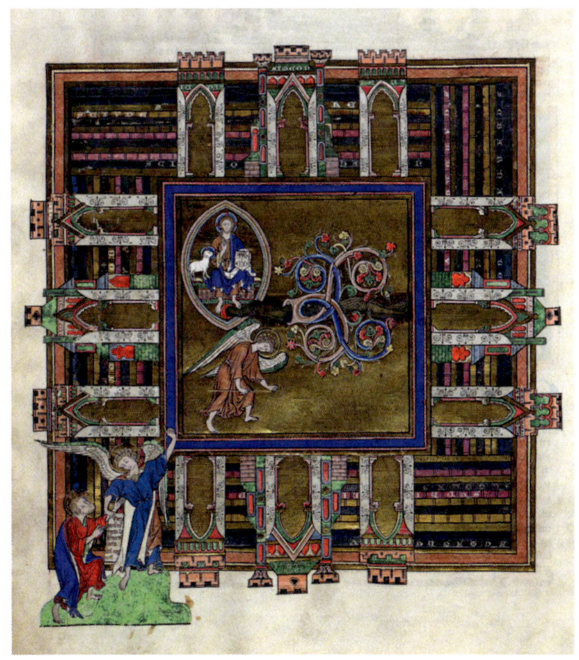

PLATE 44. William Blake, *The River of Life*, c.1805, London: Tate. © Tate, London 2014

PLATE 45. The *Trinity Apocalypse*, c.1260, The New Jerusalem (Rev. 21–2), Cambridge: Trinity College. © The Master and Fellows of Trinity College, Cambridge

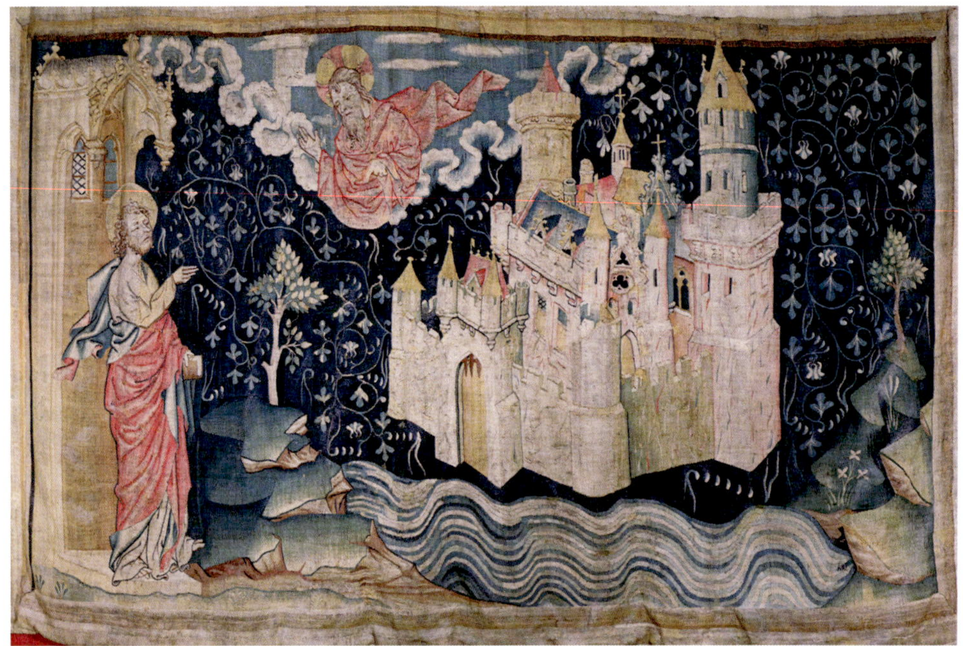

**PLATE 46.** The *Angers Apocalypse Tapestry*, *c.*1373–80, John sees the New Jerusalem Descending (Rev. 21.2), Maine et Loire: Chateau d'Angers. © Bridgeman Art Library

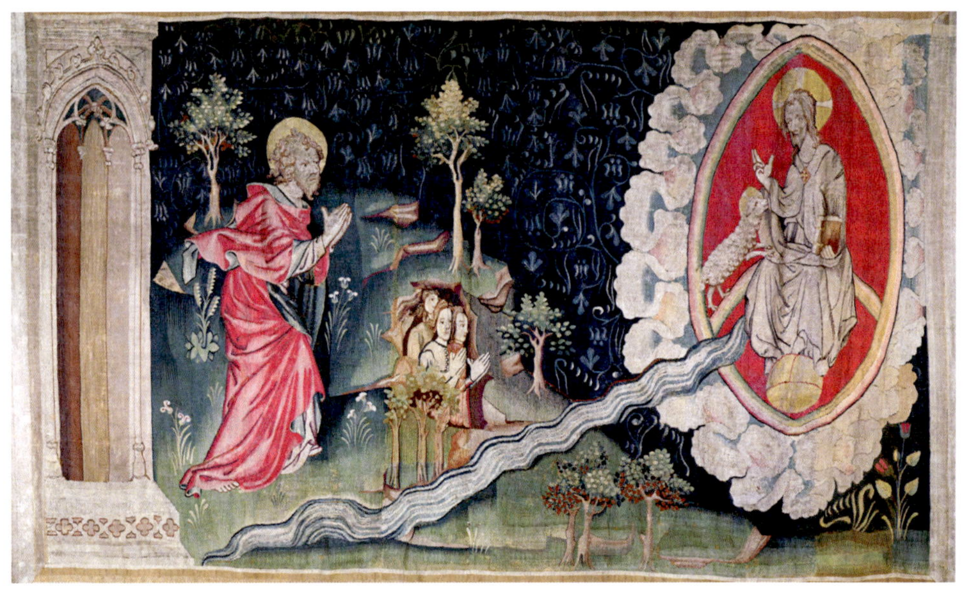

**PLATE 47.** The *Angers Apocalypse Tapestry*, *c.*1373–80, John and the River of the Water of Life (Rev. 22.1–5), Maine et Loire: Chateau d'Angers. © Bridgeman Art Library

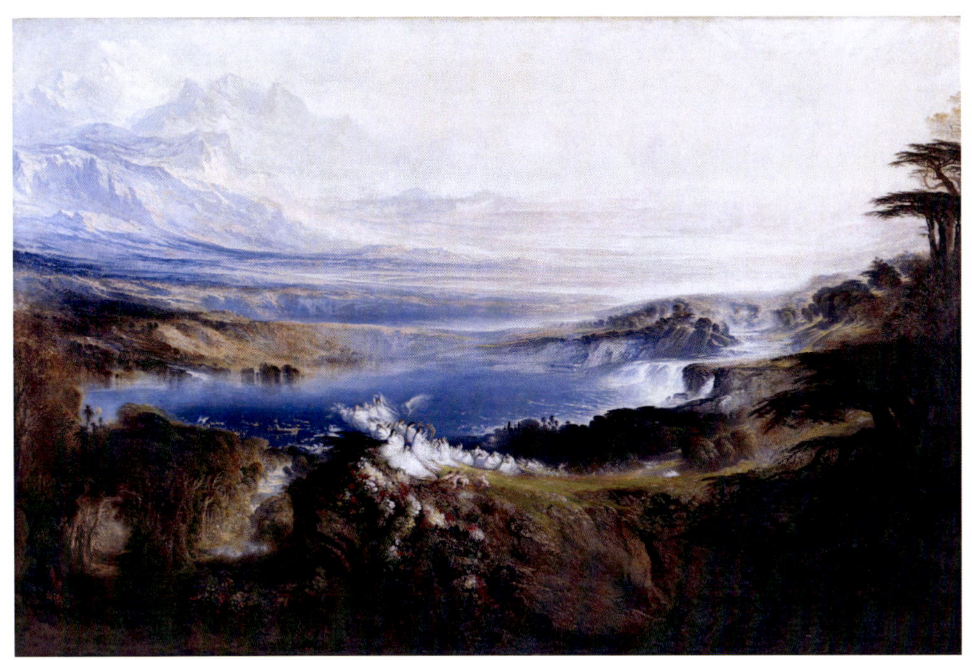

PLATE 48.    John Martin, *The Plains of Heaven*, 1851–3, London: Tate. © Tate, London 2014

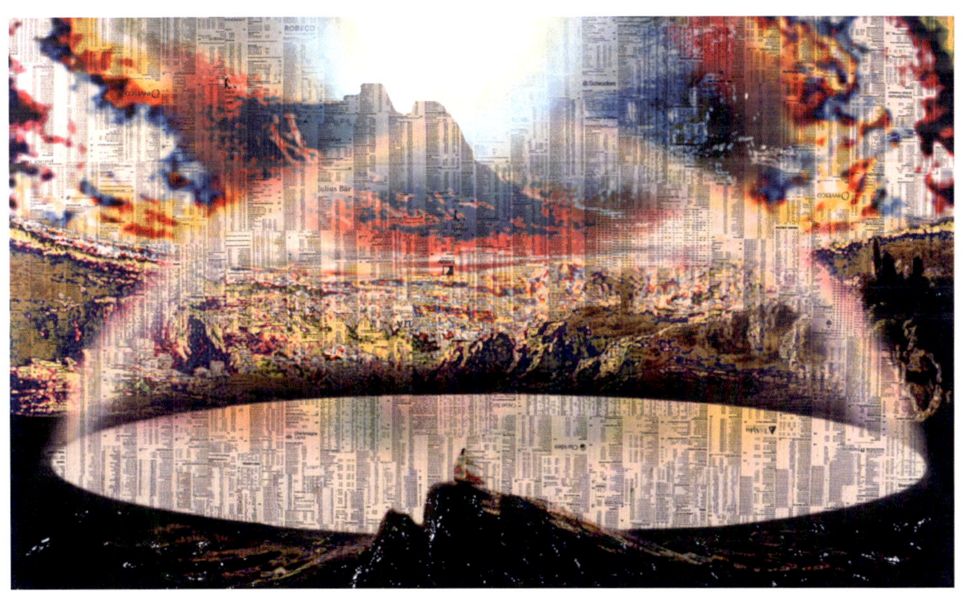

PLATE 49.    Gordon Cheung, 2007, *Rivers of Bliss.* London. © Gordon Cheung

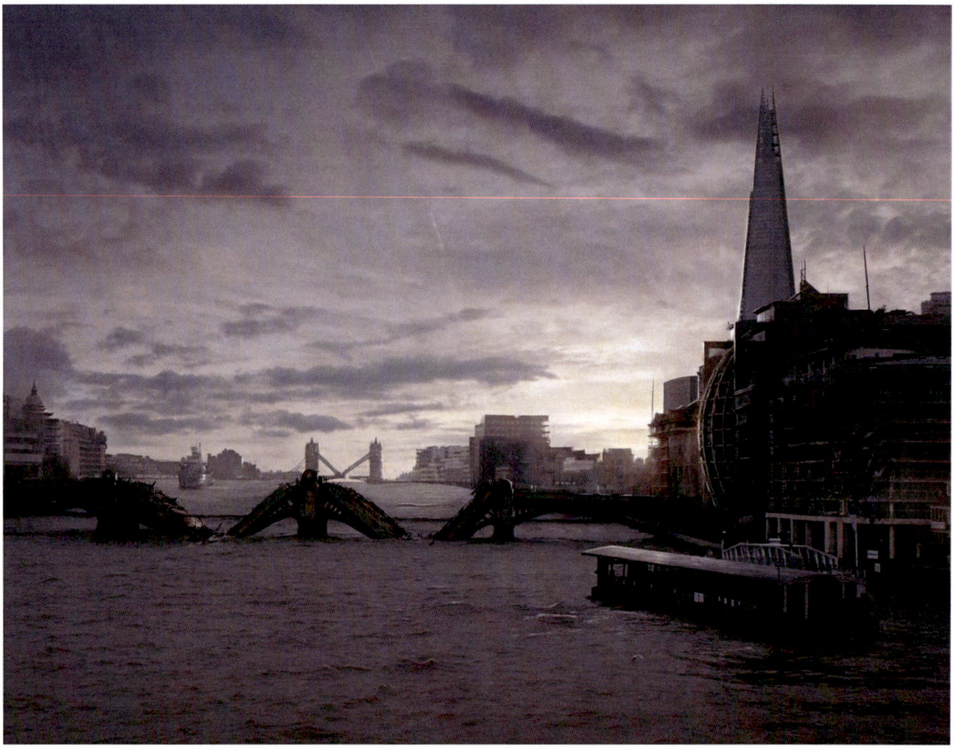

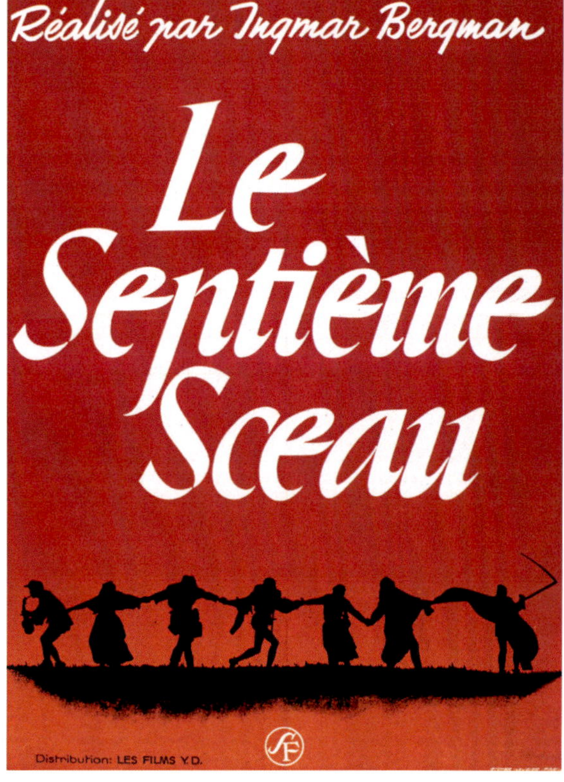



**PLATE 50.**   James Chadderton, *Apocalypse V2*, 2014. © James Chadderton

**PLATE 51.**   *The Seventh Seal*, promotional film poster, 1957. © Bridgeman Art Library

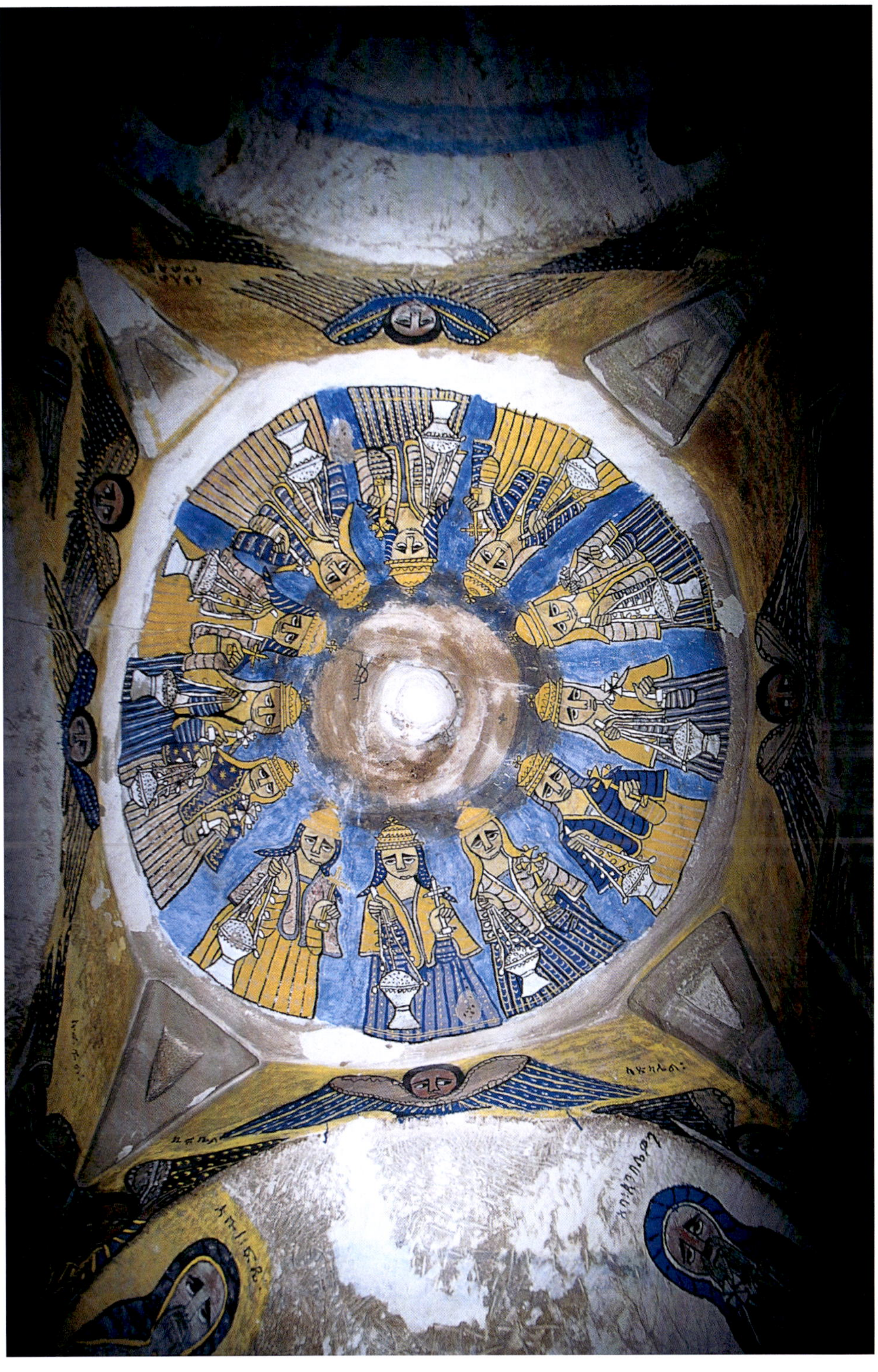

PLATE 52. Twenty-four Elders in the dome, Koraro Church, Ethiopia. © Courtesy of Maria-Jose Friedlander, Bob Friedlander and Richard Pankhurst from *Hidden Treasures of Ethiopia: A Guide to the Remote Churches of an Ancient Land*, Tauris Edition 2014

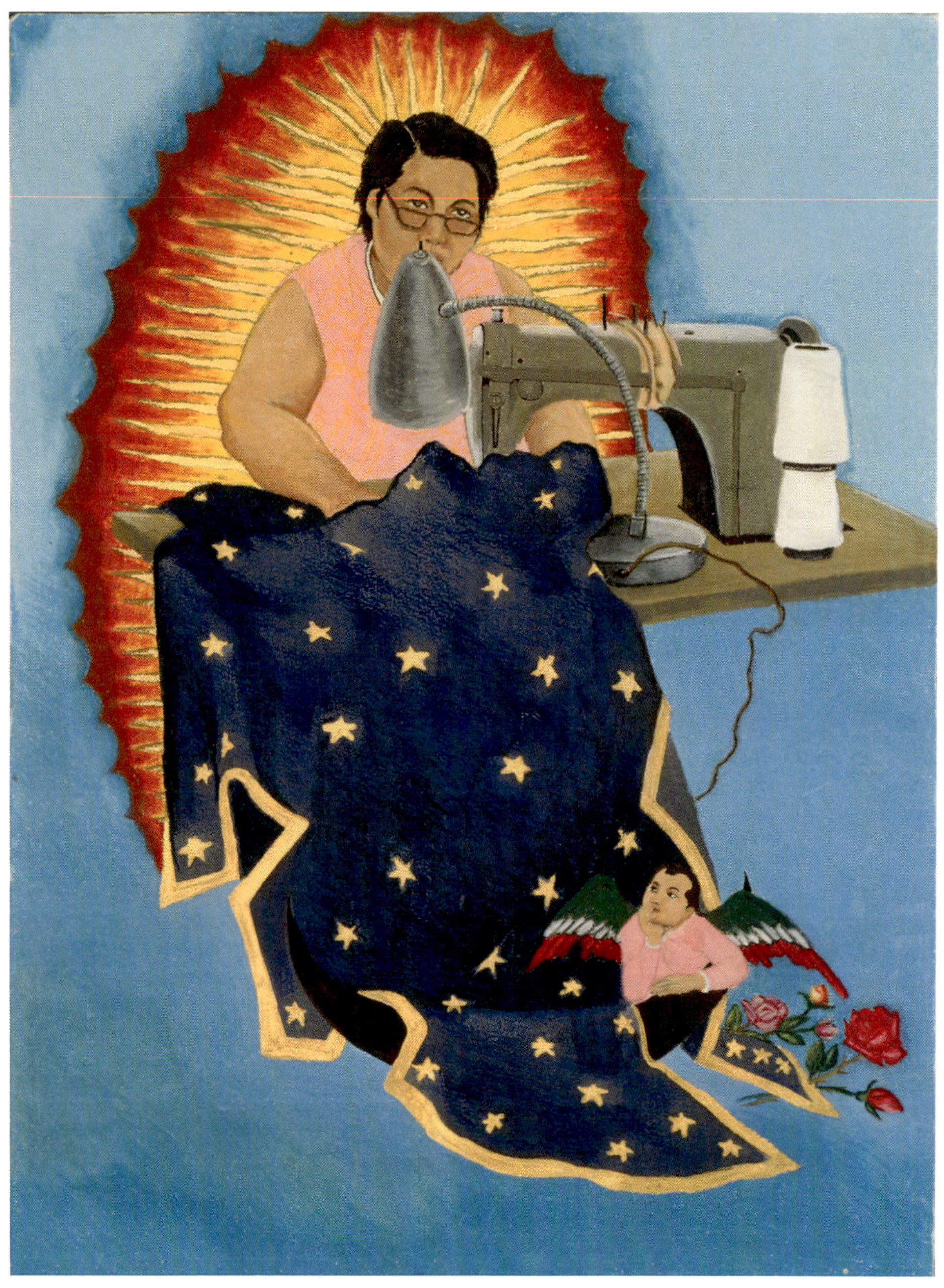

horns have been added to Obama's head and the word 'Antichrist' replaces the 'Hope' tagline at the bottom of the poster.[24]

# Conclusion

The three Satanic Beasts of Revelation have obviously provided rich stimulation for artists and interpreters throughout the ages. In the development of the imagery connected with them we see a very powerful example of the way the understanding of Revelation has changed and grown over time, particularly in the introduction of the Antichrist figure and its identification with one or other of the Beasts.

But the depiction of the Beasts clearly poses a question for the artist. Does one concentrate on their physical or bestial form, as described in Revelation itself, in which their sheer power and size are enough to quell and crush human opposition? Or does one emphasize their more psychological menace, in which they seduce by deception and subterfuge, superficially indistinguishable from the forces of good they seek to subvert? Perhaps not surprisingly the early medieval representations focus on the hybrid, obviously intimidating forms described in Revelation. Signorelli, by contrast, gives us what must be the perfect image of Antichrist as a Christlike figure or a figure with a Christlike mask and facade, all the more dangerous to those who fail to see that his beauty is counterfeit, and what lies behind. If this tendency reaches its apogee in the *Left Behind* series' Nicolae Carpathia, the square-jawed, blonde-haired (Romanian) statesman leading the United Nations, this does nothing to devalue the power of Signorelli's vision. But it might suggest that there are interpretive dangers in the temptation to depart too radically from Revelation's own overtly mythical representations of its monsters, and to remind us that in Revelation there is actually no Antichrist.

More generally the Beasts and their associated symbolism and mythology may seem to the modern mind to be the most unfortunately superstitious and outdated aspects of Revelation. Their very endurance is a scandal to our scientific age, where what happens is attributed to purely natural forces, and to the way we, who are ourselves products of nature, react to those forces. Can there be room in the modern world view for gigantic, supernatural forces conspiring against us and needing to be defeated in some final apocalyptic showdown?

Clearly as they are depicted in Revelation, the Beasts will have to be seen as at best symbolic; and there is certainly something distasteful in the posturings of figures like Aleister Crowley claiming contact with the Devil. Nevertheless, as fast as we moderns eliminate talk of evil or wickedness in our explanations of human behaviour, we seem with ever more depressing regularity to be confronted with the most appalling actions, on both personal and collective scales. Referring to 'the Beast' in this sort of context may be a crude personification of aspects of human behaviour we would prefer not to acknowledge, but averting our eyes from it would, from the perspective of Revelation, doubtless be an aspect of Beast worship, guided by the deceptions of Antichrist. Indeed one could argue that the Beasts in Revelation remain a powerful warning against the perennial human temptations both to worship power and also to be seduced by falsity posing as virtue. From the point of view of Revelation itself the modern tendency to deny the existence of the Beasts and to ignore what they represent would actually be their greatest triumph.

# 7

# The Whore of Babylon

'I [ John] saw a woman sitting on a scarlet beast which was full of blasphemous names and it had seven heads and ten horns. The woman was clothed in purple and scarlet, and adorned with gold and jewels and pearls, holding in her hand a golden cup full of abominations and the impurities of her fornication . . . and when I saw her I was greatly amazed . . .' (Revelation 17.3–6)

While the Beasts are a more pervasive presence in Revelation and beyond, the Whore of Babylon, who appears only in Rev. 17–18, has also had vibrant reception history and to this day seems to possess a curious power as a symbol. In contemporary language, the term Whore of Babylon may be used as a generic insult for a woman viewed as behaving in an inappropriate or immoral way. It may also be used as a metaphor for something evil or threatening or seductive, depending on your point of view. In 2003 the singer Madonna planned a Concert Tour, originally to be called the Whore of Babylon World Tour, presumably in an effort to exploit the powerful contemporary resonance of the term and to be provocative. The tour was in fact renamed the Re-Invention Tour, but it still opened with a recitation from Revelation. Within religious circles Jehovah's Witnesses view the Whore of Babylon as symbolic of all types of false religion, whereas some other Christians still identify the pope and the Catholic Church with the Whore of Babylon. The Ulster politician Rev. Ian Paisley, for example, is reputed to have referred to the Catholic Eucharist as 'pancakes for the Queen of Babylon'.[1] As we will see, this identification between the Whore of Babylon and the papacy has its origins in the Reformation, when Luther made the link between the excesses and hypocrisy of the Whore of Babylon as described in Revelation 17 and the popes of his day.

## Interpreting the Whore of Babylon

Within Revelation itself, the term Babylon functions as a potent but ambiguous symbol. To John's readers/hearers Babylon would have evoked mental images of a fabulous yet faded city, centre of a great and ancient Middle Eastern empire and a historic enemy of Israel. And in some sections, such as Rev. 14 and 18, Babylon indeed appears in the guise of a city. But the term is also used during Rev. 17 to refer to a woman, the harlot or Whore of Babylon. Generally speaking, in Revelation, whether Babylon is the city or the Whore, the term is used to signify luxury, sensuality, licentiousness, vice, and also exoticism, the allure of false values, and the seductiveness of pagan cults.[2]

On her first appearance in the visionary narrative (Rev. 17.3–6), the Whore of Babylon is described as a very well-dressed harlot astride a scarlet seven-headed beast (whom we have already met in Rev. 13). She is clothed in purple and scarlet (colours of royalty) and adorned with gold, pearls, and precious stones (note the overlap with the precious stones and pearls that the New Jerusalem is built with, Rev. 21.19–21). However, she also holds a gold cup, filled on the inside with 'abominations' which are the result of the 'impurities of her fornication'. This description of the Whore of Babylon, with its sting in the tail, is another reminder of one of the main themes of Revelation: that outward appearance, however magnificent, is not to be trusted and may even be highly deceptive. By way of emphasis, we are also told that, like a common Roman prostitute, she has her name written on her forehead ('Babylon the great, the mother of whores and earth's abominations').[3]

John is initially intrigued by this mysterious, glamorous woman but is promptly warned by the angel who accompanies him not to be deceived or taken in by her. Having an angelic interpreter is a classic feature of apocalyptic literature but this is one of the only times this occurs in Revelation.[4] In Rev. 17.9 this angel signals to John that this Babylon is actually a symbol for Rome (the seven heads of the beast on which she rides would naturally be identified with the seven hills of Rome) and the woman herself is interpreted by the angel as symbolizing the 'great city that rules over the kings of the earth' (Rev. 17.18). The angel also prophesies that the Whore of Babylon will eventually be destroyed in a most violent way by the Beast on which she rides, and in so doing will become a victim of the system which she has helped to maintain ('they will make her desolate and naked; they will devour her flesh and burn her up with fire'). In Rev. 18–19 John has a further vision of the destruction of Babylon, who has now been transmogrified into a city.

As both a city and an actual harlot, Babylon is seen by most commentators as being used by John covertly to criticize the Roman society in which he, a persecuted Christian, lived and worked. It is the sense of temptation that existed in Roman society that John lived and worked within that is embodied in his vision of the Whore of Babylon in Rev. 17. Babylon—woman or city or both—thus represents a warning to the early Christians (such as those addressed in Rev. 2–3) not to be seduced by Rome and the Roman way of life. If the Beast represents the military and political power of Rome then the Whore of Babylon can be seen more in terms of the goddess Roma, the figurehead of Roman religion. The meaning of the Whore has been modified in various ways over the centuries: the anti-Roman interpretation was explicitly denied by Augustine in the fourth-century Roman empire, but picked up again in a different incarnation by the Protestant reformers in the sixteenth, who identified the Whore with the Roman Catholic Church and with the papacy in particular. Like the goddess Roma, the outward sign of the cult of Rome, the papacy was the luxuriant public face of the Roman Catholic Church, yet, in the view of the Reformers, irremediably corrupt. As Kovacs and Rowland rightly point out, however, and as some of the pre-Reformation images to be surveyed below attest to, the link between the Whore of Babylon and the papacy had already been prefigured in the medieval period by both radical Franciscans and Wycliffites.[5]

In more recent times, the luxury and duplicitousness of the Whore has been taken by liberation theologians as symbolic of the corruption of authoritarian regimes in South America and South Africa, as well as of capitalism more generally.[6] In such readings the violent death of the Whore is welcomed unashamedly as the longed for destruction of the main oppressing forces. The South African liberation theologian Allan Boesak is typical: 'Again and again John hammers home the fact that the violence of the oppressor shall be turned against him.'[7] It is interesting that Boesak uses the masculine pronoun here, even though he is explicitly referring to the Whore of Babylon. Does that perhaps betray some slight squeamishness regarding the ugly manner in which this female figure is dispatched?

The way in which female characters are painted in Revelation has already been touched upon in Chapter 5 ('The Woman Clothed with the Sun'). Although undoubtedly intended to be read metaphorically, and despite the fact that the male characters are not always fully rounded characters either, it cannot be denied that the female characters are stereotyped either as brides or virtuous mothers or as whores (see also 'Jezebel' of Rev. 2.20, who is accused of setting herself up as a prophet and leading the church into fornication and idolatry). And the Whore of Babylon is not only a whore, but a whore with ambition. Indeed, the feminist critic Tina Pippin argues that the grisly destruction of the Whore of Babylon is in part a punishment for her egotism (see Rev. 18.7: 'She glorified herself and lived luxuriously…since in her heart she says, "I rule as a queen".'). In Pippin's view the communal carnival that constitutes her death is the 'ultimate misogynist fantasy', her erotic power and her independence having been framed as extremely threatening to men.[8] Pippin rejects Revelation from the Christian canon altogether on account of what she sees as its thoroughgoing sexism. Others, such as Boxall, are more circumspect, reclaiming the Whore of Babylon as a useful tool for ecclesial self-criticism rather than as an easy (yet potentially damaging) scapegoat for another group.[9] The visual interpretations which follow range from the tastefully respectful to the gratuitous, with one (from the twelfth-century *Hortus Deliciarum*) seemingly delighting in the Whore's grotesque fate.

## The Whore of Babylon in visual imagery

As should be clear, the Whore continues the theme of deception and false appearance which began with the Beasts in Rev. 13, and so also provides a rich seam for visual interpreters to mine.[10] Interestingly, over the centuries depictions of the figure have become less subtle. In the Anglo-Norman and medieval representations more generally she is portrayed as a straightforwardly beautiful woman, with the clues to her identity being given by her holding the cup of abominations of Rev. 17.4 (sometimes seen as a mock-Eucharistic chalice, to compound the deception), her looking at a mirror (as a symbol of vanity), or her being accompanied by a snake (Eve's serpent). Later representations tend to be bound up with ecclesiastical or political critiques, as with Cranach (where the Whore is equated unashamedly with the papacy) or Otto Dix (where she is equated with the profiteers of war), which leave us in no doubt as to her corrupt nature but, equally, such polemical representations do little to explain her allure.

There is a similar contrast in how her character is portrayed, though this does not follow a straightforward chronological pattern. Thus she is sometimes seen as passive, almost as a victim of forces beyond her, a tendency which reaches its climax in her destruction in Rev. 17.6. Here we could point to her representation in the *Hortus Deliciarum*, and to those by Dürer, Blake, and Robert Roberg, a contemporary American artist. By contrast *Lambeth*, *Angers*, the York East Window, and Cranach emphasize her regal status and her arrogance. What we can say about all the representations of the Whore is that they show how the same figure can be approached in very different ways, depending on the context and the bias of the interpreter. And, as would be expected, both the figure and her representations have inspired powerful feminist analyses, pointing to misogynistic tendencies explicit or implied which relate to the Whore, and, in the work of an contemporary artist such as Kip Gresham at least, a response to those tendencies.

## Medieval interpretations

Early interpreters of the Whore of Babylon viewed the figure in one of two ways. Some, like Tertullian (d. *c.*220) see her as a warning about the dangers of immorality and excessive wealth; others follow Victorinus (d. 304) in interpreting the Whore as a negative symbol for Rome, the city at the centre of the Roman empire. Although there are no surviving illustrations from this very early period, it is the former interpretation that was taken up by medieval illustrators. One of the earliest known images comes from the *Hortus Deliciarum*, a twelfth-century illuminated encyclopaedia intended as an educational tool for young nuns in a convent in Alsace. The work thus had a female readership and most probably a female commissioner. In spite of this, or perhaps because of it, there is, among the pages of the encyclopaedia, a very violent image of the Whore of Babylon being cast to her death in the fiery pit of Rev. 17.16 (Plate 33). This image would have served to highlight to the first readers of the encyclopaedia the dangers of vanity and pride, as embodied by the Whore of Babylon. Accordingly the Whore is here depicted as a young woman, attired in lavish garments and wearing a golden crown.

This image is noteworthy for several reasons other than the lavish appearance of the Whore of Babylon. First, it is striking to see two winged angels actually wielding the spears that are keeping her down in the bottomless pit with the Beast. It seems incongruous to see two agents of good spearing a young woman in this manner, until, that is, one remembers that the angels of Revelation are more than capable of all manner of destruction (see Chapter 1). Second, the seven-headed Beast (the Sea Beast) has been cast into the pit with the Whore of Babylon, presumably to be burnt with her. In Rev. 17.16, however, we are told that it is the Beast and his horns (which are an ancient symbol of power) which will destroy the Whore. This is quite a complex (although very potent) idea (evil turning on evil) and difficult to visualize.[11] The *Hortus Deliciarum* has therefore chosen a simpler depiction of the Whore and the Beast definitively being destroyed together by God's agents. Lastly, it is somewhat shocking to see that the death of the Whore is being mourned by a crowd of contemporary, well-dressed kings, noblemen, and bishops. Although this is merely following Rev. 18.9–19, this is surely also a veiled critique of the excesses of the day from the high moral ground of the Alsatian convent.

An interpretation of the Whore of Babylon as a warning to female readers and viewers is clear in many of the surviving images of the figure from the thirteenth and fourteenth centuries. For example, in *Lambeth* the Whore of Babylon is depicted across two separate miniatures. First she is shown as a vain, young, aristocratic woman looking at herself in a mirror, and secondly astride the seven-headed beast, holding her golden cup of abominations aloft, a clear warning of the spiritual dangers facing her (Figure 7.1). In the first image (not shown), the presence of the mirror (a non-textual addition) may signify a link with the well-known medieval figure of Luxuria or Vanity.[12] The Whore of Babylon's frontal pose may also be interpreted as sexually suggestive and confrontational. In the second image her purple gown is adorned with both a large necklace and a bejewelled belt from which hangs the Whore's name (Rev. 17.5). Thus, although outwardly respectable looking, she has literally been labelled as a whore or prostitute, although it must be pointed out that the label has here been hung around her waist and not written on her forehead, as specified in the text. Perhaps a branded Whore of Babylon would have been a step too far for the likely patron of the work, Eleanor de Quincy.

Nor does John himself escape visual censure here. He is depicted as a very small figure (smaller than in previous images) being carried by the angel

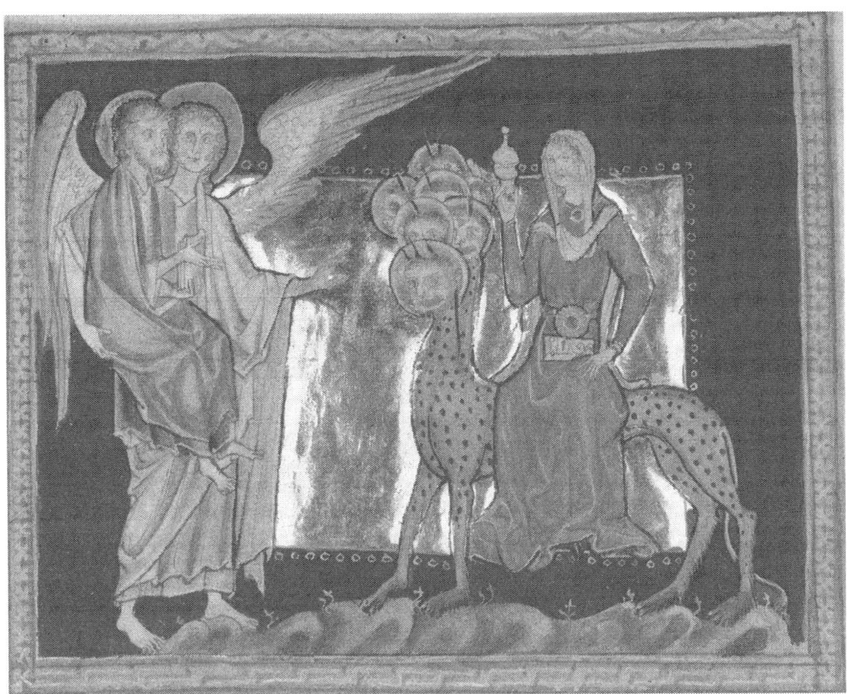

**Figure 7.1.** The *Lambeth Apocalypse*, *c.* 1260, The Whore of Babylon (Rev. 17), London: Lambeth Palace Library. © Bridgeman Art Library

(in line with Rev. 17.3) and staring directly at the Whore of Babylon figure, with what we may assume is the fascination invoked in Rev. 17.6 ('when I saw her I was greatly amazed'). Even John was not immune to the ever-present temptation offered by riches, empires, and competing religions. John's small size and childlike demeanour only serve to emphasize the aristocratic bearing of the Whore of Babylon herself. And thus is the viewer reminded of the aristocratic pretensions and the egotism that bring about her eventual downfall.

A similarly young and beautiful Whore of Babylon is to be found over a century later in the *Angers Apocalypse Tapestry* (Figure 7.2). She once more combs her hair as she holds a large mirror in which we can see her reflection. The 'many waters' on which she is described as sitting in Rev. 17.2 are here visualized as a grassy knoll with a stream running around it, thus playing down the chaotic connotations of the primeval waters from which she has emerged. As noted in other chapters, this tendency to play down or contain the horror of Revelation is typical of *Angers*. John is led tentatively

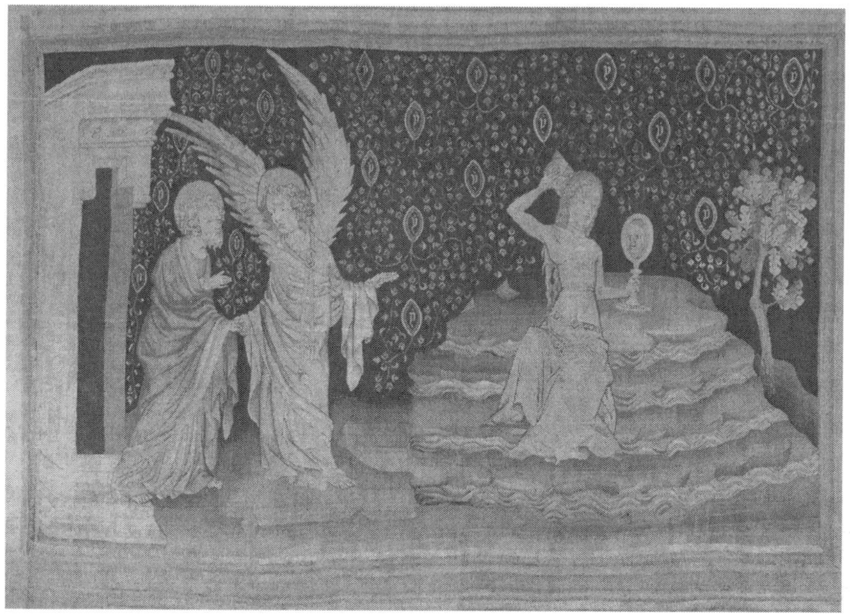

**Figure 7.2.** The *Angers Apocalypse Tapestry*, *c.*1373–80, The Whore of Babylon (Rev. 17), Maine et Loire: Chateau d'Angers. © Bridgeman Art Library

out of his shelter by his accompanying angel, who motions conspiratorially towards the Whore of Babylon. The background of the image is made up of small mandorlas bearing a 'y' motif against a dark blue backdrop. The 'y' motif is a medieval symbol for the divergent paths of virtue and vice and has previously been seen in the background of the earlier *Angers* image depicting the slaughtered Lamb (see Figure 2.5). In this image the Lamb is a victim but also the conqueror of vice and death and thus a source of life and virtue. In the *Angers* image of the Whore of Babylon the 'y' motif serves as a reminder of the fact that, in contrast to the Lamb, she has the appearance of something great but is in fact a purveyor of vice, the 'mother of whores', no less.[13] The juxtaposition of these symbols with a young and beautiful Whore of Babylon thus reminds the viewer that virtue and vice are properties which are all too easily confused.

Slightly later than *Angers* is the visualization in the *Flemish Apocalypse* of *c.*1400. In the nineteenth image we see the Whore of Babylon in all her splendour in the middle of the image (Figure 7.3). She is offering up her 'cup of abominations' to John and the angel in an action reminiscent of a priest presiding over the Eucharist, a reminder of her links with false religion

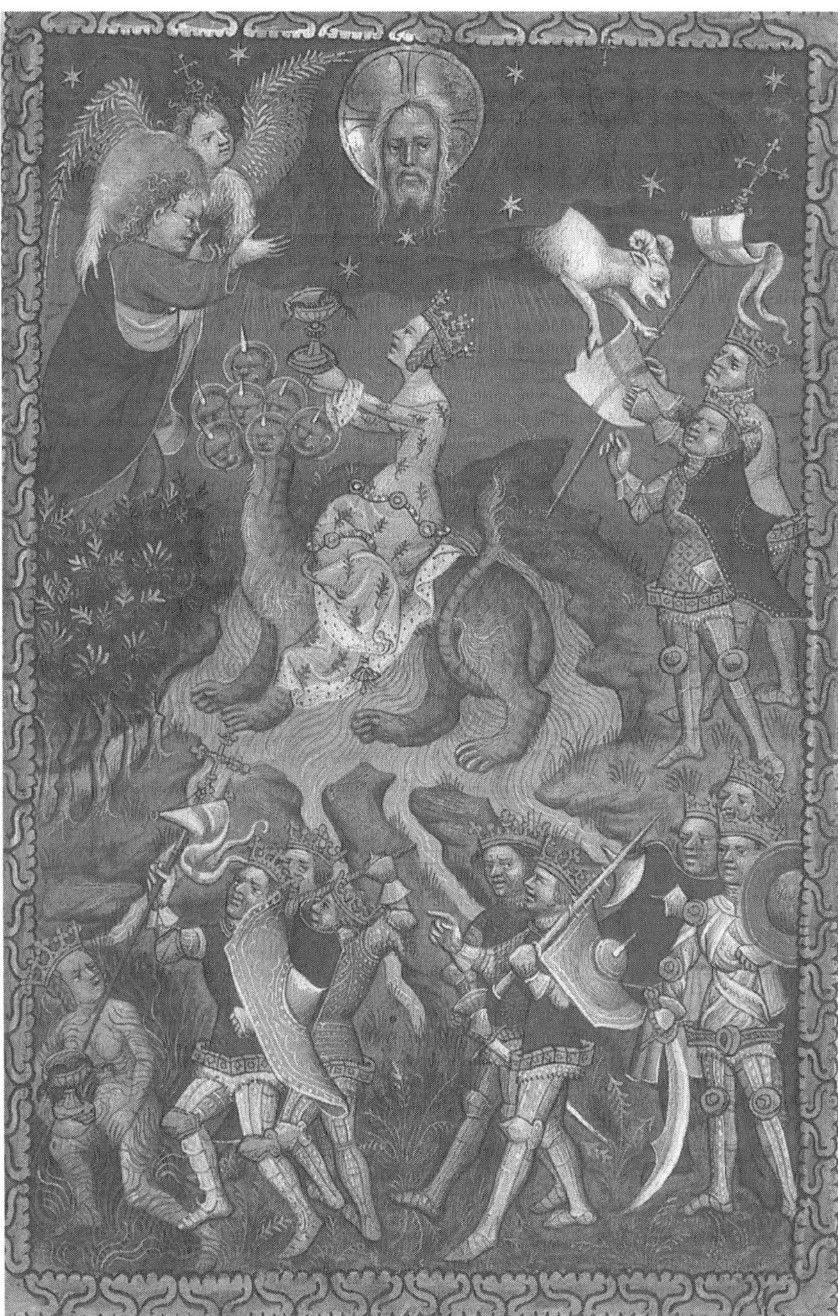



Figure 7.3. The *Flemish Apocalypse, c.*1400, The Whore of Babylon Offers the Cup of Abominations to John (Rev. 17), Paris: Bibliothèque Nationale. © BnF

and idolatry (cf. Rev. 2.20, Jezebel). In the foreground of the image, in the left-hand corner, we can see a later event, that of the violent destruction of the Whore of Babylon. The men who are attacking the Whore (as ordered by God in Rev. 17.16–17) are here dressed as Crusaders and the spear being driven into the Whore is tipped with the St George's flag. The Whore, who can clearly be seen burning up in a pit of flames, is here implicitly linked with the Eastern 'other', the enemy of the Crusaders, an identification which becomes explicit when first Albrecht Dürer and later William Blake came to depict the Whore—all, it might be thought, early examples of the hostile Western interpretation of the East (or Middle East) as alien, exotic, and licentious, an interpretation named Orientalism by Edward Said.[14]

Finally from the medieval era come two magnificent stained-glass visualizations of Revelation depicting the Whore of Babylon astride the Beast. One must remember in both cases that the images about to be discussed are small details from much larger stained-glass windows depicting the whole of Revelation. In the case of the York Minster Great East Window, even the narrative of Revelation is just one part of the overall tableau which, rather like the *Ghent Altarpiece*, ranges across the whole of biblical history from the Creation (Genesis) to Revelation. The narrative of Revelation has, however, been privileged and takes up almost the entire middle and lower registers of the window (the majority of the window).[15] Like *Angers*, the monumental rendering of Revelation in tapestry, both the York Great East Window and the Sainte Chapelle Apocalypse Rose Window owe a great deal to the Anglo-Norman Apocalypse manuscripts (such as *Lambeth*), although judicious editing was necessary in order to adapt the complex and sometimes repetitive narrative into this very different format.

The detail from the York Minster Great East Window (c.1400; Plate 34) depicts the Whore of Babylon riding side-saddle (it would have been unthinkably provocative to depict even the Whore of Babylon as riding astride the Beast at this time).[16] As usual she holds the golden cup. Here, however, there is a frog climbing out of the cup and a snake curling around her left shoulder. In contrast with earlier depictions, the Whore's true nature is being made more explicit to the viewer (although whether these details would have been viewable by the congregation is another matter). Within both the Old and the New Testament, and within Revelation itself, frogs are used as a symbol for evil (see Rev. 16.13, for example). This negative association endured into the medieval era, where frogs, although sometimes also viewed as a symbol of resurrection, were used to symbolize heresy, greed, evil, and sin.[17] The negative associations of the snake around her neck and its purported connection with Satan are obvious.

The Western Rose Window from La Sainte Chapelle in Paris dates from the end of the fifteenth century. It was constructed to replace an earlier, thirteenth-century rose window, also a depiction of Revelation. Although, as specified above, the window is indebted in some respects to the iconography of the Anglo-Norman manuscripts, the transposition of the imagery into a completely different format is striking.[18] The vision starts in the middle of the circular window with John's vision of the seven candlesticks and continues outwards in a spiralling shape. This pattern serves to capture the essence of John's vision which, as we suggested in the Introduction, may or may not have followed the chronology imposed upon it by a textual format.

Thus the Whore of Babylon image appears on the outer circle about three quarters of a turn away from the New Jerusalem (Plate 35). Good and evil are perilously close. The Sainte Chapelle Apocalypse Rose Window does not hint at the Whore's true nature except for the fact that her feet are red, the colour of danger and blood, doubtless an allusion to the fact that she is said in the text to be 'drunk with the blood of the saints' (Rev. 17.6). What is striking in the case of both the windows is the richness of the colours used to depict the Whore's clothing. Richness of colour is a particular characteristic of stained-glass windows, made possible by the interplay between the light and the glass. In both stained-glass windows the Whore is attired in rich blue or purple, royal colours alluding to the vanity which Rev. 18.7 cites as one of the reasons for her destruction. When the light streams through the windows the colours become richer and more luminous, the physical embodiment of the dilemma posed by this outwardly attractive yet intrinsically demonic character.

## Renaissance and Reformation visualizations

While the visualizations viewed hitherto have focused primarily on the immorality of the Whore of Babylon as well as the temptations she embodies, the images from the Renaissance period offer a more overtly political interpretation. This is not surprising, given Revelation's intensely political nature as a call to resistance against the Roman empire and all its temptations, economic, religious, and otherwise.[19] Two woodcuts by Dürer and

Cranach emphasize different aspects of the political. Cranach identifies the Whore of Babylon with specific historical figures, while Dürer's image links the figure with the very real threat from the East at the time. The images of Dürer and Cranach thus mirror contemporaneous historical developments and thinking about Revelation much more closely than the earlier images discussed in this chapter. This was in no small part due to the proliferation of print as a mass medium throughout Europe in the late fourteenth and early fifteenth century. Rather than being the property of one wealthy patron, texts and images could now be mass-produced and sold to a much wider audience. The printed image or woodcut had become an important tool for disseminating particular messages, such as those generated by the Reformation.

Dürer's image (from his aforementioned Revelation series) presents the Whore as a deceptive Venetian seductress (Figure 7.4). She is dressed in the clothes of a Venetian courtesan and is being presented to a crowd of rather wary-looking onlookers by an Eastern sultan with his back to us. The sultan has already appeared at the beginning of the series as a fifteenth-century reincarnation of the Roman emperor who exiled John to Patmos (see Figure 10.3). Thus we, the viewers, understand that the Whore is part of a wider conglomerate of evil and threat of Eastern provenance, Venice at the time being pervaded with Eastern influences and representing the gateway between Western Europe and the East. The threat from the East was a real one, with Constantinople having fallen to the Turks in 1453. In the Western European imagination it took on a particular resonance fuelled by the burgeoning apocalyptic expectation that surrounded the half-millennium year of 1500.[20]

Thus Dürer's Whore can be seen to represent the dangerous allure of the 'other', just as the Whore of Babylon of the original text represents the exotic allure of Rome to the early Christians. Lest the viewers of the image were themselves seduced by this attractive Whore of Babylon, Dürer depicts the destruction of Babylon (the city) in the top right-hand corner behind the Whore, a reminder that her reign is only a temporary one in contrast to the eternal church.

There are other signs that the Whore is not quite what she seems. Although superficially beautiful, Dürer has used tiny optical black lines to create wrinkling around her eyes and mouth and the suggestion that she is actually rather haggard. Furthermore, the reptilian hatching at the bottom of her dress mirrors the hatching on the body of the Beast itself, suggesting

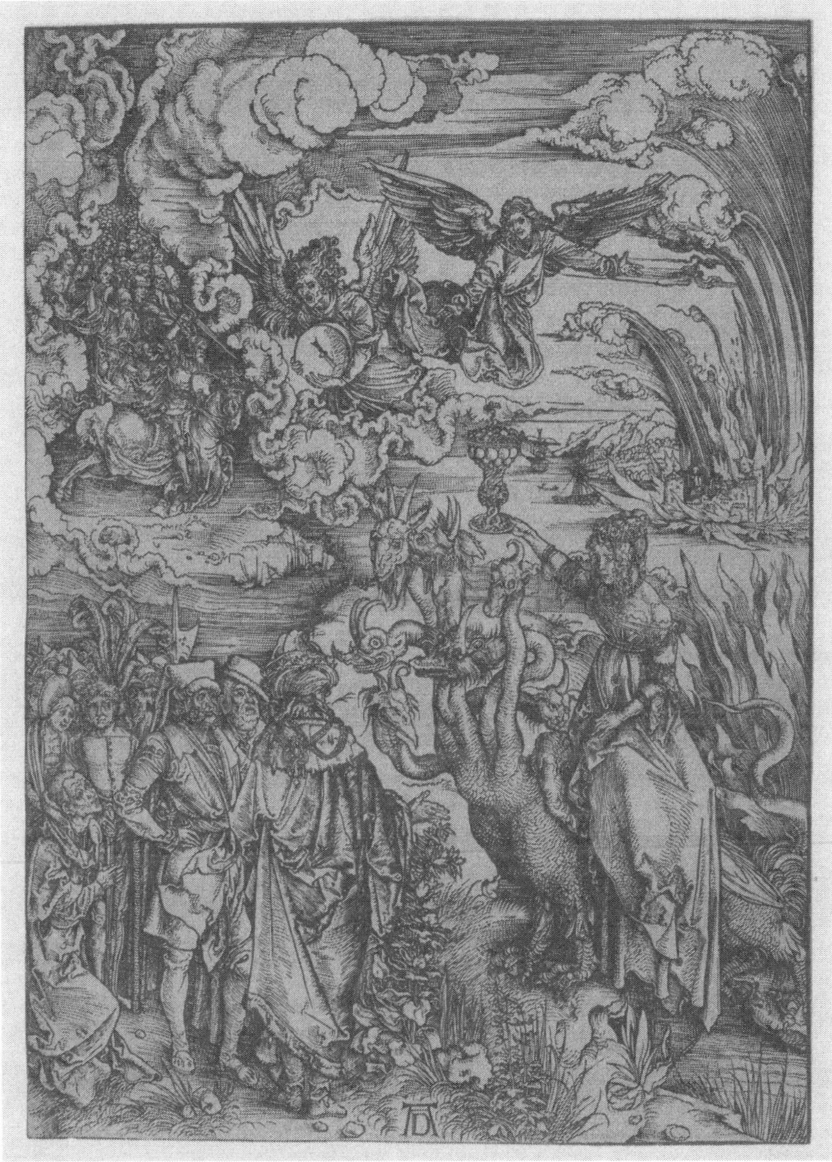

**Figure 7.4.** Albrecht Dürer, *Apocalypse* Series, *c.*1498, The Whore of Babylon (Rev. 17–19), London: British Museum. © The Trustees of the British Museum

perhaps that just as the Earth Beast/False Prophet is something of a puppet-eer (he sets up the statue of the Beast that all must worship in Rev. 13), so the Whore may derive her power from the Beast on which she rides. This fits well both with the rather passive demeanour of Dürer's Whore and also with Rev. 17.16, which asserts that it is the Beast which ultimately turns on the Whore, torturing her and then devouring her. Thus her reign, such as it is, is destined to be short-lived. This is also intimated by the presence of another rider at the top left-hand corner of the image thundering down from the crowds (the Rider on the White Horse of Rev. 19), representing, as is so common in Dürer's images of Revelation, a direct visual contrast to the Whore of Babylon on her demonic steed. Much has been made of whether Dürer's Whore of Babylon image represents a sort of proto-Reformation. This debate turns largely on whether one feels that the monk (in the bottom left-hand corner of the image) is worshipping the Whore and whether she is intended to represent papal Rome. However, none of the arguments in favour of this line, proposed most notably by the art historian Max Dvořák, ultimately convince.[21]

This notion of the Whore as the alluring embodiment of a generalized threat to the church was taken to an extreme in 1522 by Lucas Cranach the Elder's image of the Whore of Babylon as the pope (Figure 7.5). Produced as part of Cranach's series of woodcut images of Revelation designed to accompany the publication of Luther's first translation of the New Testament into German, the image was and is a highly controversial one, which set in motion centuries of anti-Catholic visual polemic. The success of the image as polemic is perhaps due to its powerful simplicity. On first viewing it seems to be a pale imitation of Dürer's image (which was certainly known to Cranach), but the eye is then caught by one inflammatory detail. The Whore of Babylon is wearing a papal triple tiara, thereby creating an unmistakable identification of the office of the papacy with a character from Revelation widely regarded as a symbol for evil (see also Figure 6.6 from the Cranach series, of the Beast from the Abyss of Rev. 11 wearing the papal triple tiara).

In fact, whether they knew it or not, Cranach and the Lutherans were not the first to identify the whore with the papacy. In Canto 31 of Dante's *Purgatorio* in his *Divine Comedy*, in the Chariot which is representing the church pride of place is occupied by Beatrice, Dante's ideal woman and herself a symbol of divine wisdom and grace. But in Canto 32 the church is attacked by various malignant forces, and Beatrice is replaced in the Chariot

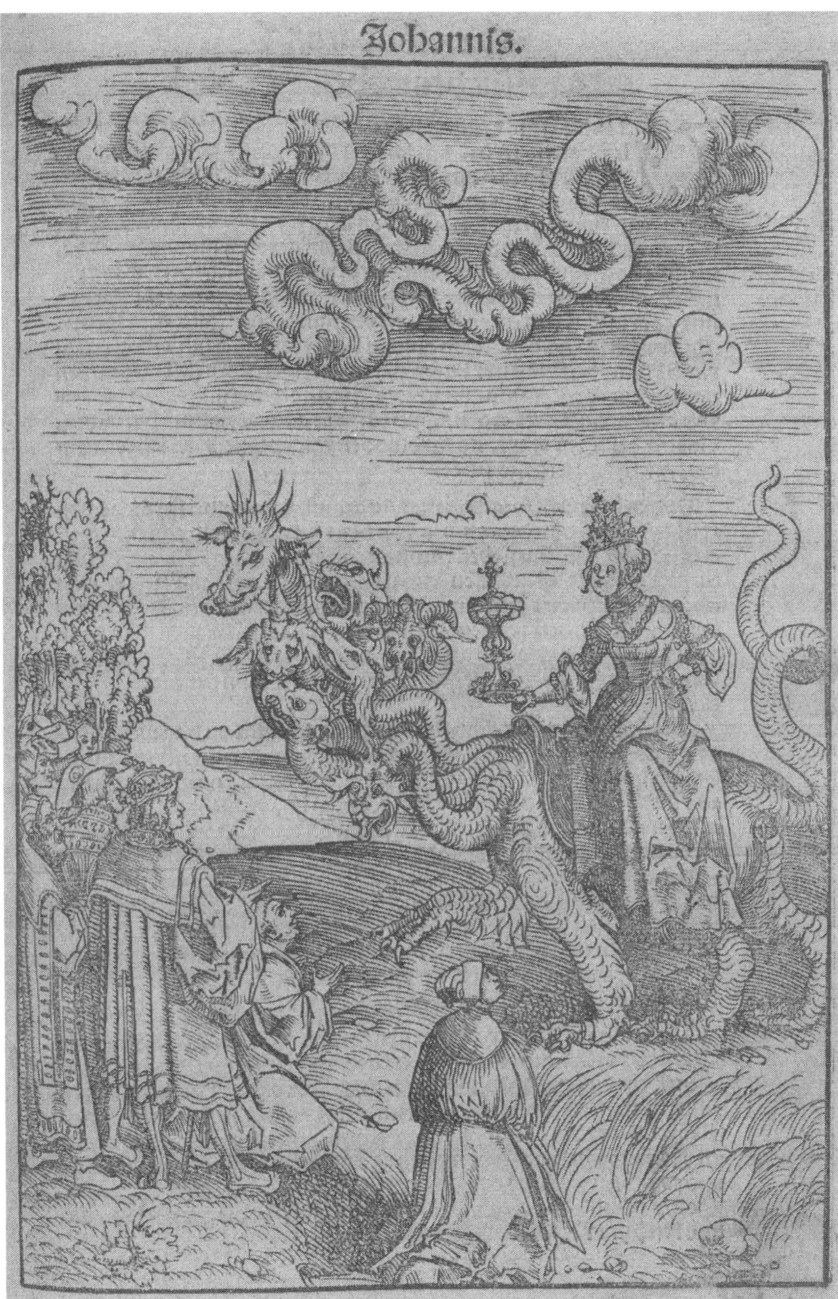


**Figure 7.5.** Lucas Cranach the Elder, Apocalypse Illustrations for Luther's New Testament, 1522, The Whore of Babylon (Rev. 17), London: The British Library. © The British Library Board, C.36.g.7

by a whore, who is making salacious love to a giant. The Chariot also grows seven heads, becoming the Sea Beast of Revelation 13, on which the Whore traditionally rides. In Dante's vision the church is being piloted by the Whore of Babylon and her giant paramour, who is identified with the king of France (Philip IV), and who had, in Dante's time, seized and imprisoned the pope, all of which is a striking and strikingly effective example of a pre-sentist reading of Revelation. One does not imagine that papal history following his own time would have lessened Dante's scorn for papal misrule, even if, unlike Luther, he would never have contemplated an actual schism with Rome.

In the wake of his break with Rome, however, Luther's New Testament became an immediate bestseller, which was banned in the remaining Catholic German provinces. Many imitations followed, and even today there are fundamentalist Protestants who identify the Catholic Church with the Whore of Babylon. In this rather negative sense, the image of the papacy as the Whore, particularly in Cranach's representation of it, is an iconic and extremely important one. There may have been a legitimate reason for interpreting Rev. 17 as a critique of a corrupt papacy in Dante's time (around 1300) and even more in 1522 when the Reformers were being persecuted by the Roman Catholic Church. However, continuing to use the same polemical imagery is more problematic once the formerly persecuted Protestants became the oppressors and Catholics victims.[22]

## Blake and modern interpretations

We turn finally to four altogether more diverse images dating from the nineteenth century onwards. William Blake created a stand-alone image of the *Whore of Babylon* in 1809 (Plate 36). He had painted another image of the Whore as part of his illustrations to *Edward Young's Night Thoughts* in 1795–7. In the later image he has cast the Whore of Babylon as a topless Eastern courtesan, echoing in Orientalist style, the fascination with the East which pervaded the artistic culture of his day. Blake himself did not fear sensuality or exoticism in themselves. He was, though, critical of the use of these attributes in support of ends of which he did not approve, such as shallow pleasure-seeking or the exploitation of the weak by the strong. In his image the Whore is worldly and sensuous, but also strangely passive. By contrast the Beast whom she rides symbolizes war and is actively participating in the battle that rages below (namely by actually eating those who dare to resist him). For Blake, war brings with it not only death and economic deprivation but also lust and temptation, a timely comment on the Napoleonic wars which were raging while Blake was creating this image.

The souls of those whom the Whore has intoxicated and ensnared (Rev. 17.2) flow out of the cup of abominations which she is holding. In the *Flemish Apocalypse* (Figure 7.3) and the York Minster Great East Window (Plate 34) the abominations are depicted as frogs and snakes (common symbols of evil) but Blake here envisages them in a more metaphorical way as the souls of those who have been deceived by a corrupt world. Interestingly one can also make out angels with bowls flowing from the cup, a strange intermingling of good and evil, which is something of a hallmark for Blake. Whilst the Whore of Babylon and the Beast are clearly huge in comparison to the human and even the angelic figures in the image (once again, as we have seen, Blake often utilizes size in his images of Revelation), the angel blowing the trumpet in the bottom left-hand corner of the image is still prominent. Rowland links this trumpet blast with the death and destruction caused by the sequence of Seven Trumpets of Rev. 8–9.[23] This allows the image to be viewed more synchronically. The Whore of Babylon is no longer confined only to Revelation 17, but can be seen as having more wide-reaching links with other instances of deception and suffering occurring throughout the text. As was the case with the Sainte Chapelle Apocalypse Window, Blake has cleverly captured the idea of a vision in this image.

War is also central to Otto Dix's take on the Whore of Babylon in an etching from his *Der Krieg* (War) series of 1924 (Figure 7.6). Here the Whore of Babylon is depicted as a large, unattractive prostitute in the brothel of Madame Germaine, with whom a German soldier is consorting. This is an allusion to the French brothels run by the German army as a way of controlling their troops during the First World War. Dix here underlines the notion that the Whore is a tool of war and oppression by adorning her outfit with flowers, which do nothing to conceal her underlying ugliness. Babylon as a symbol for Rome has in Dix's twentieth-century hands become a symbol for the German authorities. Dix himself made a personal journey from enthusiastic recruit to the German army in 1915 to a traumatized victim by the end of the war. Like the Whore's victims, he was initially taken in, only to realize the truth later on. Unsurprisingly in the 1930s Dix was condemned by the Nazis for his depictions of the traumas and deceptions of war. He lost his job as an art teacher and was conscripted into the

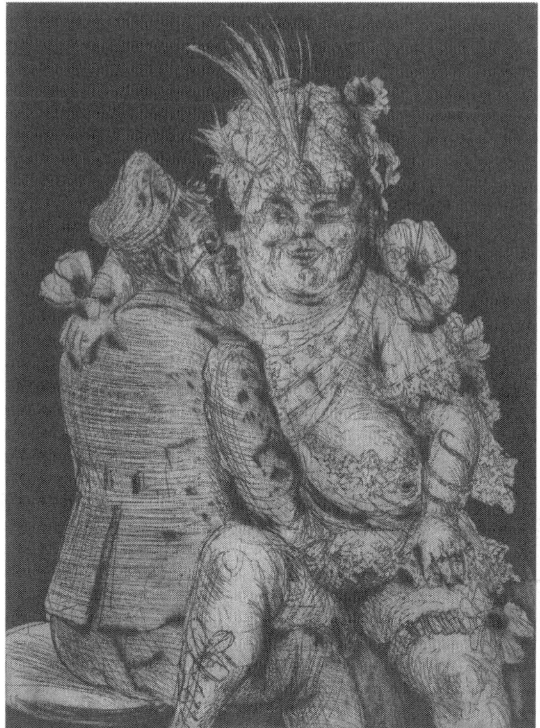

**Figure 7.6.** Otto Dix, *Visit to Madame Germaine at Mericourt*, 1924, London: British Museum. © The Trustees of the British Museum

German army once again. Here we find an appropriate parallel with John the author of the Book of Revelation, who was condemned and exiled by the Romans for his hostility to their political and religious regimes.[24]

Another take on the Whore and the Beast comes via *Babylon the Great is Fallen* (1992), one of a series by the twentieth-century folk artist Robert Roberg (whose work is now shown in the Smithsonian Institute in Washington, DC; Plate 37). In this image Roberg has used bright acrylics and even glitter to depict a relatively small Whore of Babylon astride a bright pink Sea Beast (who himself stands on the seven hills of Rome). Around her, buildings, which one assumes symbolizes the actual city of Babylon of Rev. 18, tumble from the dark sky, alongside quotations from Revelation predicting the fall of Babylon. In the bottom right-hand corner the mourners of Rev. 18.15–19 can be seen mourning the fate of Babylon. Further quotations (e.g. 'Waters = Nations') help to interpret the image for the viewer and to link it to the biblical text. In many ways, therefore, this is a strangely didactic visualization, seemingly afraid to let the images contained therein to speak for themselves without textual qualification.

Brash and even ironic at first sight, this image of the Whore is actually quite traditional, though she has been updated for our times as a sexy blonde in a slinky dress. In an earlier image on the same theme *The Whore of Babylon Riding on a Beast with Seven Heads*, by Roberg from 1991, which appeared on the front cover of the *New York Times* in May 2005, the Whore is depicted in similar attire, seemingly downing a glass of red wine from her golden 'cup of abominations'. Looked at on her own, in isolation from the rest of the image, these depictions of the Whore of Babylon could be seen as a playful attempt to satirize the materialism and sexual immorality that fundamentalist Christians find pervasive in contemporary American society. In the 1970s the Reverend Hal Lindsey, a fundamentalist author and preacher (of whom more in Chapter 10), interpreted the Whore as a prophecy of what he saw even then as an epidemic of drug addiction and social immorality overtaking the young; while some contemporary internet sites view Hillary Clinton with her liberal values as the modern-day American manifestation of the Whore of Babylon.[25] Despite these negative connotations, Roberg's Whore of Babylon seems apparently unaware of the destruction going on around her, and the judgement implied by the angelic figure of Rev. 18.21 about to hurl a boulder or thunderbolt in her direction. Maybe this is a comment on the blindness of contemporary society to its apocalyptic fate, but also an intimation that while Roberg's Whore is clearly a potentially dangerous temptress, there is also an air of victimhood about her, no doubt presaging her inescapable fate, as described in Rev. 17.16. Thus the image has a complexity and an interpretative tension that may not be immediately obvious but which is certainly worth pondering. The notion of depicting the Whore as victim has a long history, stretching back to the *Hortus Deliciarum*, and it may also be implied in the Dürer and Blake images, and this seems to be what Roberg is reminding of us here, alongside his critique of the society which has created and sustained her.

Kip Gresham's pictogram of Revelation 17 from 1993 is rather more subtle than Roberg's or Dix's, and different from anything preceding it (Figure 7.7). John is a haunting, androgynous white figure staring out into the sea (cf. Rev. 17.1). On the water another androgynous figure, the Whore of Babylon herself, pulls along a boat of unrecognizable cargo, maybe dead bodies. From the time of Dürer onwards, the Whore has been depicted as a prostitute or at least as an overtly sexual female. Kip Gresham's visualization

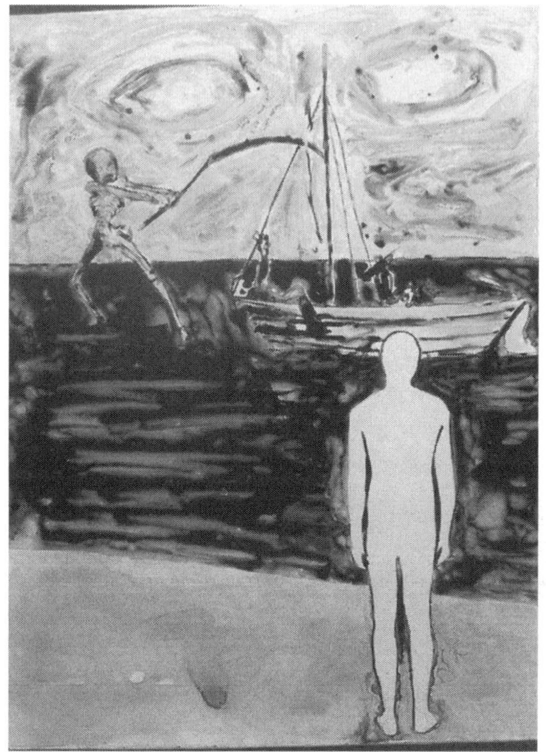

**Figure 7.7.** Kip Gresham, *The Whore of Babylon*, 1993. © Kip Gresham, by kind permission of the artist

of her as an androgynous skeleton therefore represents a conscious attempt to extricate himself from earlier, sometimes misogynistic, ways of representing the figure. Gresham's ultimate meaning is troublingly elusive, poetic even. But perhaps that is the point. In a sea of images in which the Whore is presented in bold, inescapable, and stereotypical ways, even by the great artists, Gresham presents us with a more ambiguous visualization of the Whore on which to ponder.

## Conclusion

Gresham's reworking may be powerful but the equally potent and less ambiguous images from earlier times cannot be so easily expunged from our collective memory. In Revelation itself the remarkably polyvalent

Whore of Babylon (whore, city, symbol of idolatry, symbol of empire) is balanced by the Woman Clothed with the Sun and the Bride Jerusalem (or do both these images in their own way represent unreal stereotypes of the feminine?). But there is no doubt that the Whore and the way she has been represented over the ages represents a decidedly negative image of woman. We say of woman or of women because—in contrast to the Beasts, say, whose masculinity is not the source or essence of their evil power—in the case of the Whore it is precisely her sexuality which is problematic and which, in its allure, gives her sway over men. Unlike the Beasts, the Whore neither fights nor speaks cleverly. She gazes at herself and is gazed at, even sneakily by John himself. And for this crime (of egoism), as is depicted very graphically in the *Hortus Deliciarum* image and certainly alluded to in other images such as the Dürer and the Roberg, she is herself destroyed. Nor should we think that in our supposedly more enlightened times this image of woman as a seductive temptress is any less potent than it might have been in earlier ages. The mass media are fuelled by just this conception, ever more slickly and glossily presented, and without the warnings to be found in Revelation. So let us concede that the Whore is inherently and frankly misogynist, but suggest that for that very reason she remains troublingly significant in ways other than those envisaged by John of Patmos in 90 CE.

# 8

# Armageddon, the Millennium, and the Last Judgement

Armageddon, the Millennium, and the Last Judgement: three huge concepts within Christian and Western thought more generally. Why then have we grouped them together? The short answer is that, surprisingly perhaps, there are not many images of huge interest of Armageddon and the Millennium, and given that this is primarily a book about visual interpretations of Revelation, this is necessarily a determining factor.[1] By contrast, as anyone with even a passing interest in church art will know, there are countless thousands of extant images of the Last Judgement, including Michelangelo's *Last Judgement* in the Sistine Chapel and the great Judgement doors at Amiens and many other medieval cathedrals and churches (see the West Portal of Amiens Cathedral; Figure 8.1). However, as we will show below, the iconography in these images is derived mainly from the Gospel of Matthew (chapters 3, 12, 13, and 25) and not from Revelation at all, which only devotes three verses to the issue of the Last Judgement, at Rev. 21.11–13. The Last Judgement is also mentioned in John 5, Daniel 7, and 1 Enoch. Thus it is something of a common mistake to assume that images of the Last Judgement have been inspired by Revelation, and it must be acknowledged that sometimes it is difficult to tell whether the image or relief in question has been inspired by Matthew, John, Revelation, or indeed by some general conflation of the various sources.[2] With the exception of one image, the Last Judgement images that will appear in this chapter can all be linked to Revelation at least in part.

Practical issues aside, it also makes sense in interpretative terms to take these concepts together: although they do not appear exactly consecutively within the text, they are part of a clear, unbreakable continuum. A supposedly

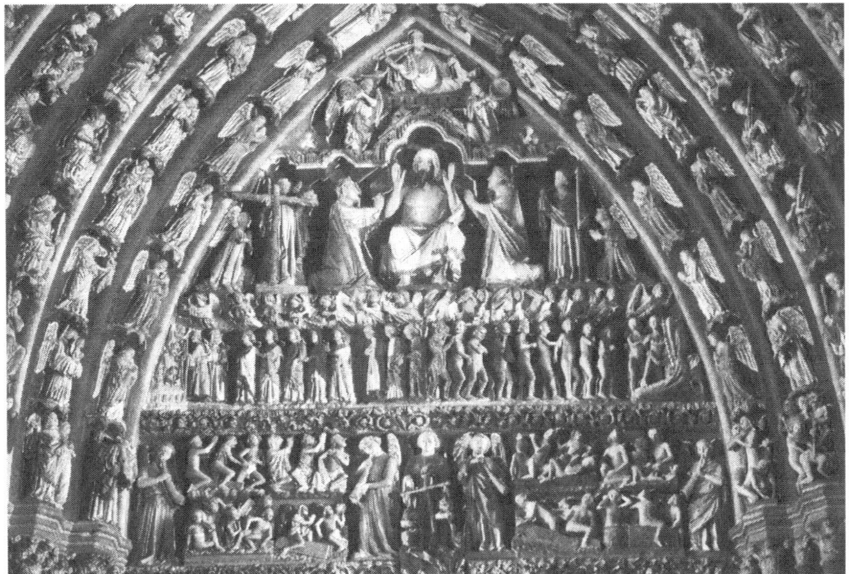

**Figure 8.1.** *Last Judgement*, detail from the West Portal, Amiens Cathedral, 13th century. © Bridgeman Art Library

final battle (Armageddon) prepares the way for the Millennium (one thousand years of peace), after which there is, somewhat confusingly, another final battle, which culminates in the Last Judgement. Interpreters have tended to view the first final battle, in which the two Beasts (the Sea Beast and Earth Beast or False Prophet) are killed, as a sort of forerunner for the definitive and more universal final battle in Rev. 20 during which Satan himself is finally and completely overcome.[3] Just as the earlier battles that have taken place in Revelation may be seen as little victories on the way to this final and definitive victory, so each event in this final sequence (Armageddon, Millennium, Armageddon 2, and Last Judgement) prepares the way for the next, with the ultimate climax arriving in the establishment of the New Jerusalem, considered in the next chapter. Thus within the interpretative context of Revelation, Armageddon, the Millennium, and the Last Judgement should be viewed as necessary precursors to the New Jerusalem, although, as with other concepts within the text, they have often become decontextualized in visual, literary, and more popular interpretations. This particular sequence of events can also be seen as a necessary journey from the specific judgement of the Beasts to the corporate judgement of the whole of humanity.

# Armageddon

No term from Revelation is more widely found in common usage, and arguably more misinterpreted, than Armageddon. In popular thought and culture, Armageddon is practically synonymous with the term Apocalypse itself, and the two often seem virtually interchangeable as a sort of short-hand for the end of the world, particularly if there is some idea of a nuclear disaster in the background. References in the popular media abound, from the humorous 'Dial 00000000 for Armageddon. US's top secret launch code was frighteningly simple' (*Daily Mail*, November 2013), to the biblical 'Is Syria the latest sign of Armageddon?' (*Daily Mail*, September 2013), a theme also taken up in *The Spectator* in January 2014. So the word Armageddon has become an all-purpose cliché, used almost as a knee-jerk reaction, to describe any environmental, nuclear, or financial disaster, real or imagined. Thus 'Prepare for Armageddon: banks told to prepare for Eurozone collapse' (*Sun*, December 2011); 'Global warming Armageddon: it may be more likely than you thought' (*Independent*, July 2013).[4] Many will also be familiar with the Bruce Willis vehicle *Armageddon* (the highest-grossing film of 1998, in which he plays an astronaut charged with destroying an asteroid making for Earth). Finally, there is even a yearly comic book convention in New Zealand known as the Armageddon Expo, though the notion of a yearly Armageddon is somewhat paradoxical.

The sense of Armageddon as being some final catastrophe is not entirely wrong, though we have to make the usual caveat. In Revelation Armageddon, the location of the decisive battle between good and evil, is a catastrophe only for Satan, the Beasts, and their followers. In Judaeo-Christian thought there was the conviction that evil cannot continue indefinitely, but will ultimately be defeated.[5] For Christians Armageddon is the glorious moment when history begins to be definitively transformed, and therefore worldly success and reputation meet their nemesis. We say 'begins' here because, as outlined above, the battle itself is only one of a number of stages on the way to the New Jerusalem.

The first surprising thing to note about Armageddon is that the word itself occurs only once in Revelation, at Rev. 16.16, which is earlier than one might have imagined for the final battle, given that there are twenty-two chapters in the text. It is described as 'the place that in Hebrew is called Harmagedon', the site where the demonic forces will gather for what will be a crucial battle on the way to their final defeat. However, the demonic forces do not in fact assemble straight away, as the following three chapters detail the rise and fall of the Whore of Babylon (see Chapter 7) and the subsequent Marriage Feast of the Lamb.[6]

As a real place Armageddon is usually identified with Megiddo, a town near a pass through the Carmel Mountains into the Jezreel Valley in southern Galilee in Israel (Plate 38). Historically this area had seen a number of actual defeats and victories for the Jewish people, including a disastrous defeat in 609 BCE at Megiddo itself, which paved the way for the Babylonian captivity, and so had all sorts of resonances, sweet and bitter, in their collective memory.[7] There is a slight problem with this standard identification, in that Har-Megiddon in Hebrew actually means 'Mountain of Megiddo', and Megiddo itself is not particularly high (only about seventy feet). It is probably not fruitful to fixate on trying to pinpoint the exact geographical spot that is being referred to in Rev. 16.16 (although this has been researched by biblical scholars).[8] Indeed, Boxall argues that in light of the fact that at other points in the text (such as Rev. 11, 14, and 18 where Jerusalem, Mount Zion, and Babylon are referred to) Revelation's geography is symbolic rather than literal, this reference too should be taken symbolically as an evocation of past and more recent battles involving the Jewish people.[9]

Thus the final battle is envisaged in Revelation as taking place in a historically and symbolically significant location, the literal coordinates of which are not important. Such theological caution has inevitably been lost on today's fundamentalist interpreters of Revelation, and associated self-styled 'prophecy scholars', who tend to interpret biblical texts literally. The physical site of Megiddo, as a place in northern Israel, plays an important part in their end times schema or timeline, particularly for the so-called Dispensationalists. This interpretative conviction has important political consequences, not least in their unerring support for the establishment and continuance of the State of Israel.[10] While such an idea may seem far-fetched, there is no denying that Megiddo has existed on the fault line of the Middle Eastern conflict throughout the twentieth century. Towards the end of the First World War, in September 1918, there was indeed a crucial battle of Megiddo, which ensured the end of Ottoman domination in the area. An image from an unlikely source reminds us of this fact. If you visit the refectory in Haileybury School in Hertfordshire, you will see a large portrait of 'Field-Marshall, Viscount Allenby of Megiddo and Felixtowe,

Conquerer of Syria, Liberator of the Holy Land' presiding over the horde of pupils assuaging their hunger. Whatever one thinks now of the 'liberation' of the Holy Land back in 1918, when Allenby was there as commander of the allied forces, there is surely something laughably incongruous in this coupling of Felixtowe and Armageddon.

The second surprising fact to note about the reference to Armageddon in Revelation is that Rev. 16.16 is actually describing the sixth of the sequence of Seven Bowls being poured on the earth by the seven angels. This is the third and final sequence of seven woes in Revelation, the first two being the sequences of Seals and Trumpets respectively. It comes immediately after the moment when foul spirits have been spewed from the mouths of the Dragon and the two Beasts, who reappear at this moment, having faded out at the end of Rev. 13 (see Chapter 6). In a recapitulation of earlier themes to do with deception and parody on the part of the Beasts, these frogs can be seen as a demonic parody of the double-edged sword that emerges from the mouth of Christ at Rev. 1.16.

Thus the reference to Armageddon as a gathering place for the followers of the Beasts is rather tacked on to the finale of the sequences of seven. As the followers of the Beasts gather at Armaggedon, the Lord is said to come quietly into their midst, 'like a thief'.[11] This is then immediately followed not by a battle, but by the pouring out of the seventh bowl, and the consequent series of natural disasters, lightning, thunder, earthquakes, destruction of islands and mountains, and huge hailstones that this initiates. The actual battle which is foreshadowed or set up at Rev. 16.16 does not begin until Rev. 19.11, when the Rider on the White Horse thunders down from Heaven and gathers his army around him. At Rev. 19.19 John sees the enemy army amassing: 'the beast and the kings of the earth with their armies gathered to make war against the rider on the horse and against his army'. Although the name Armageddon is not mentioned again, it is clear that this is the same 'gathering' of evil characters (note the 'kings of the earth' who are mentioned in both places) that was alluded to at Rev. 16.16. No gory details are given regarding the battle, save to tell us that the Sea and Earth Beasts were thrown into a lake of fire and sulphur and everyone who had supported them killed and eaten by birds. One thinks here of Hitchcock's 'avian apocalypse', his chilling adaptation of Daphne du Maurier's *The Birds* in which the townspeople begin to see the attacking birds as a sign of the apocalypse. Indeed, Federico Fellini called the film an apocalyptic poem.[12]

There then follows a period of millennial calm, with Satan bound for a thousand years in the abyss into which he is thrown by the angel. During this time the earth is ruled by Jesus and his army of martyrs who are raised from the dead for that purpose. This is a prefiguring of the New Jerusalem and, as mentioned above, is followed by the second final battle (Rev. 20.7–10). After the Millennium Satan is released from the abyss for three and a half years. He gathers his forces once more, here referred to by the terms Gog and Magog, shorthand for the eschatological enemies of God's people. Both the army and Satan himself are conclusively and, this time, permanently defeated. Satan is thrown into the lake of fire and sulphur where the Sea and Earth Beasts already languish in eternal torment (Rev. 20.10). Earth and Heaven then disappear whilst Christ reappears on a great white throne in preparation for the Last Judgement.

So what we have here are, on the face of it, two cosmic battles, the first at Armageddon, announced earlier, but taking place after the fall of Babylon, and the second after the Millennium, possibly also at the symbolic site of Armageddon. Interestingly only the pre-Millennial battle is described in any detail (and here the detail is given in connection with the battle preparations rather than the battle itself). The second battle, after the unchaining of Satan, is huge, but—Gog and Magog and the allusions to Ezekiel and the sands of the sea notwithstanding—it is described in a pretty peremptory way, as if to leave no doubt in the reader's mind as to its outcome. Satan has already been defeated once before the Millennium (and at various other occasions throughout the text, cf. the defeat of the Dragon/Satan by Michael and his angels in Rev. 12), and we can be confident that he will be again.

Maybe, as we have seen in other parts of Revelation, we should understand an apparently sequential narrative as actually describing the same event or state of affairs from different perspectives, or at different stages in its development. Or maybe we are to think of the battle(s) as something going on all the time. Christ too, according to Revelation, is there all the time as well. Sometimes he is hidden, like a thief, which would pick up on the beautiful description in Rev. 3.20 of the Lord knocking at the door, waiting (hoping?) for the believer to hear his voice. At other times the battle is more overt and public (such as when he appears as the Rider on the White Horse in Rev. 19). But even after an apparent victory at the first Armageddon, Satan will come again—and again. The Millennium will never be definitive until the end of time.

Before turning to some images of Armageddon, it is worth mentioning a passage from Aldous Huxley's early novel *Crome Yellow*, which makes an extended connection between Armageddon and the First World War. The Rev. Mr Bodiham, the gloomy rector of Crome, preaches a sermon just after the war. In the sermon the Great War is explicitly identified with Armageddon (Rev. 16.16), and the drying up of the Euphrates (Rev. 16.12) with the ending of the Ottoman empire. In the gathering which then ensues at Armageddon, the Dragon is initially seen as pagan Rome, as was traditional, but generalized to represent the spirit of Infidelity. The Sea Beast is identified with the papacy and the False Prophet or Earth Beast with the Jesuits with their False Morality. The Dragon or Infidelity is further identified with the 'higher biblical criticism' then emanating from Germany, while (perhaps surprisingly) Germany is seen as a Catholic country. So, in Mr Bodiham's metaphorical version of the war, two Catholic countries (Germany and Austria) are fighting six anti-papal states (France and Italy being anti-papal for the purpose). The three enemies, the Dragon, the Beast, and the False Prophet, have all emerged as the Ottoman power is coming to an end, and the final Armageddon initiated by the Great War is at hand. While the preacher is clearly content with what is happening, as it is in line with biblical prophecy, he reminds his listeners that millions of the unrighteous will end up as 'putrefying flesh' to be devoured by ravens and vultures.[13] All great fun, one might think. But what might have been seen as an outrageous parody of fanciful biblical prophecy by a mischievous author is, as Huxley tells us, actually an address given in 1916 by the Rev. E. H. Horne to a meeting of clergy, and included in his own book *The Significance of Air War*, which was reprinted in 1937. Maybe the Rev. Horne was just a bit ahead of his time, anticipating the flood of 'prophecy scholars' who followed him in the latter half of the twentieth century.

## Images of Armageddon

The earlier representations of Armageddon included below (such as *Beatus*, *Metz*, and *Gulbenkian*) visualize the battle with just a few symbolic figures, and they also tend to foreground the definitive defeat of the Beasts and Satan. Thus, for them, what was important was the outcome and not the detail of the battle. The battle begins to become important, as a real struggle worth depicting as such, only with the *Flemish Apocalypse*. By the time we get to typical twentieth-century Armageddons, inspired by mass war and aerial bombardments, the battle itself and its colossal destructiveness becomes the focus, and normally without any suggestion of a hopeful resolution, let alone wholesale redemption for the chosen.

## Medieval visualizations of Armageddon

The *St Sever Beatus Manuscript* of *c.*1076 provides a vibrant example of an early visualization of Armageddon (Plate 39). Readers will remember that the Beatus illustrated manuscripts were a series of vividly illustrated commentaries on Revelation and Daniel made between the tenth and twelfth centuries and based on the commentaries of the eighth-century Spanish monk Beatus of Liebana. This image is striking both in its simplicity and in its three-tier design. It depicts a conflation of what has been referred to as the first and final Armageddon (Rev. 19.11–21 and Rev. 20.7–10). On the upper tier the Lamb stands in judgement, in anticipation of the Last Judgement that will take place at Rev. 20.11–13. Interestingly, the death of the Earth Beast has been separated from those of the Sea Beast, Satan, and the Dragon. Thus in the middle tier of the image the Earth Beast is beheaded by an angel. In a detail that betrays the influence of popular medieval Antichrist legends, which sometimes identified the Earth Beast as well as the Sea Beast (both of Rev. 13) with Antichrist, he has been depicted here in human form (as Antichrist) rather than as the hybrid animal described in Rev. 13.11 (see Chapter 6 for a more detailed exposition of this). On the lower tier another angel beheads the Sea Beast, here depicted as a black leopard, while a serpentine Dragon and Satan himself, here depicted as a grotesque figure with both animal and human characteristics, await their fate. Again it is interesting to note that Satan and the Dragon have been depicted as separate entities. In interpretative terms this implies that the Dragon was merely a manifestation of Satan and not Satan himself. This uncluttered, carefully structured image, whilst depicting a moment of triumph for the Lamb, exudes an air of calm control and inevitability. Unlike some later, wilder images of Armageddon, the result of this final battle does not appear to be in any doubt.

The image we have chosen from the *Lambeth Apocalypse* dates from around 250 years later (Figure 8.2). In what became a fairly standard iconography, this image visualizes, with just a few figures, the battle at Armageddon between Christ and his army (although his army is not seen here) and the

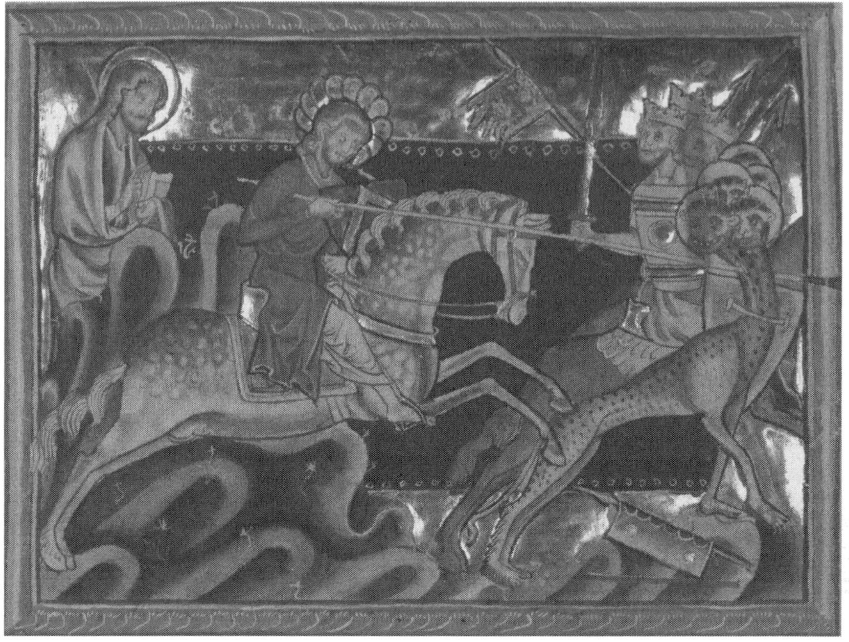

**Figure 8.2.** The *Lambeth Apocalypse*, *c.*1260, Christ and his Army versus the Army of the Beast (Rev. 19.11–21), London: Lambeth Palace Library. © Trustees of Lambeth Palace Library

army of the Beast. It captures the moment of the Beast's defeat (Rev. 19.20), as he is speared by Christ, here depicted as the Rider on the White Horse. Christ, wearing a crown adorned with multiple diadems, spears the Beast with such force that the spear protrudes through the frame of the picture (on the right-hand side). Although the Anglo-Norman family of Apocalypse manuscripts are known for their very literal illustrations of the text, this detail is surely a visual metaphor for the definitive nature of Christ's defeat of the Beast. In an interesting iconographic detail, one of the members of the Beast's army holds a flag bearing a frog design. This echoes the mention of the frogs emanating from the mouths of the Beasts and the Dragon at Rev. 16.13–16, which is also where the battle of Armageddon is first mentioned. This leaves the reader/viewer in no doubt that it is the battle of Armageddon (as opposed to any other battle) that is being depicted in this image. John, sometimes viewed as a stand in or cipher for the viewer themselves in these manuscript series, through whom they can re-experience John's visions, shelters behind a rock on the left-hand side of the image.

The next *Lambeth* image depicts a later moment in the Armageddon sequence, after Armageddon 2 (Rev. 20.10), when Satan, here depicted as the Dragon, is cast into the pit of fire (Hell) with the two Beasts (Plate 40). The *Lambeth* image, despite being visually striking, is cluttered and confusing and needs a certain amount of decoding. As was traditional in Anglo-Norman manuscript illustration at this time, Hell has been depicted as a Hellmouth. The distinguished French art historian Emile Mâle has argued that the Hellmouth iconography arose from an identification of the Leviathan monster in Job as an agent of Satan.[14] This identification, once established, led to Hell—described in Revelation only as a lake of fire and sulphur—being depicted from the Middle Ages onwards as an open-jawed Leviathan, a mythical sea monster devouring all those condemned to spend eternity in its realms. In this *Lambeth* image the two Beasts are only partially visible, having already been semi-devoured, while the Dragon/Satan teeters on the edge. Unlike the *Beatus* image where it is angels who are administering justice to the Beasts and Satan, here it is another demonic creature who pushes the Dragon into the Hellmouth with a stick. This may represent a visual attempt to distance those in the divine inner circle (God, Christ, and their angelic agents) from Hell itself.[15] Also visible are the screaming faces of those already within the Hellmouth, and a frog, a visual remnant of the erstwhile power of the Beasts and the Dragon. To the right of the Hellmouth hovers a butterfly, an interesting iconographic detail. Morgan has argued that to the medievals the butterfly may have represented the souls of those repentant sinners who were destined not for the Hellmouth but for purgatory.[16] Thus this butterfly represents the possibility of escape to the repentant reader/viewer.

*Gulbenkian* is in the same family as *Lambeth*, though slightly later. In the Introduction we have already alluded to an interesting aspect of its depiction of the final battles, namely that while the forces of Satan are armed with the full panoply of medieval weaponry, the forces of the elect fight not with weapons but with mitres and croziers, with prayer and the Eucharist (Figure 8.3). There are plenty of images of the church (and indeed of churches) being attacked by force, but in another *Gulbenkian* image (not pictured) Gog and Magog are destroyed by fire from Heaven and by heavenly hosts, and not by armies of fanatical Crusaders. The saints remain passive in their city, which seems to us to be a convincing representation of the New Testament injunction not to resist evil with force. This is all the more striking as it occurs in what is, on the face of it, one of the most militant

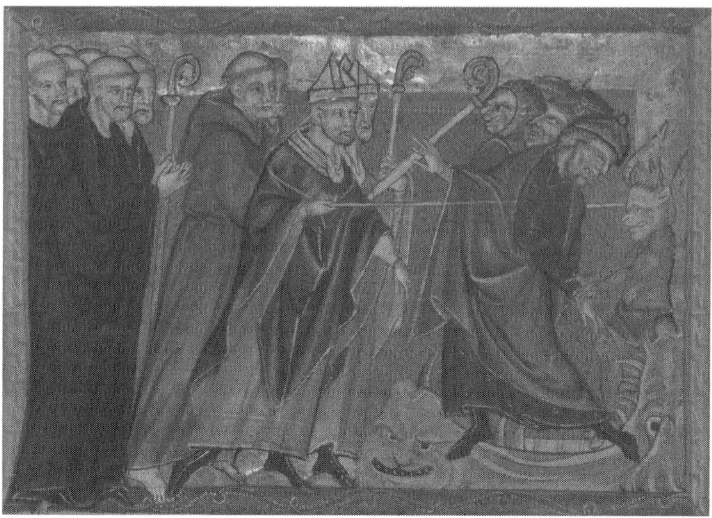

**Figure 8.3.** The *Gulbenkian Apocalypse*, c.1270, The Saints Attacked by the Armies of Gog and Magog (Rev. 20.8), Lisbon: Museo Calouste Gulbenkian. © Museo Calouste Gulbenkian

books of the Bible. Is there a correct way of reading this aspect of Revelation? Maybe there is not, but at the very least *Gulbenkian* suggests that even at its violent climax it is possible to read Revelation in a way which, from the perspective of the believer's behaviour at least, is consistent with the more pacific aspects of the Gospel. Indeed, given the power and might of the world, even as represented in Revelation, maybe what is implied here is that any other way of reading it would not only be disastrous, practically speaking, but it would also be a case of seduction by Antichrist, a diabolical misreading of Christ's real message.

A final medieval visualization of Armageddon comes from the *Flemish Apocalypse* (Figure 8.4). As has been alluded to in previous chapters, the *Flemish Apocalypse*, which can be viewed as a direct precursor to Dürer's seminal Apocalypse series of 1498, represents the beginning of a more condensed, synchronic way of visualizing Revelation. Thus in this image, the penultimate image in the series, we see several events from Rev. 19–21 pictured together. In the top left-hand corner the Marriage of the Lamb and Israel takes place (Rev. 19.4–10). Underneath, in the middle tier of the image, the battle between the Rider on the White Horse and the army of the Beasts is raging. In contrast to the Metz image where the battle was evoked using just three figures, in this image the battle scene is a much more crowded

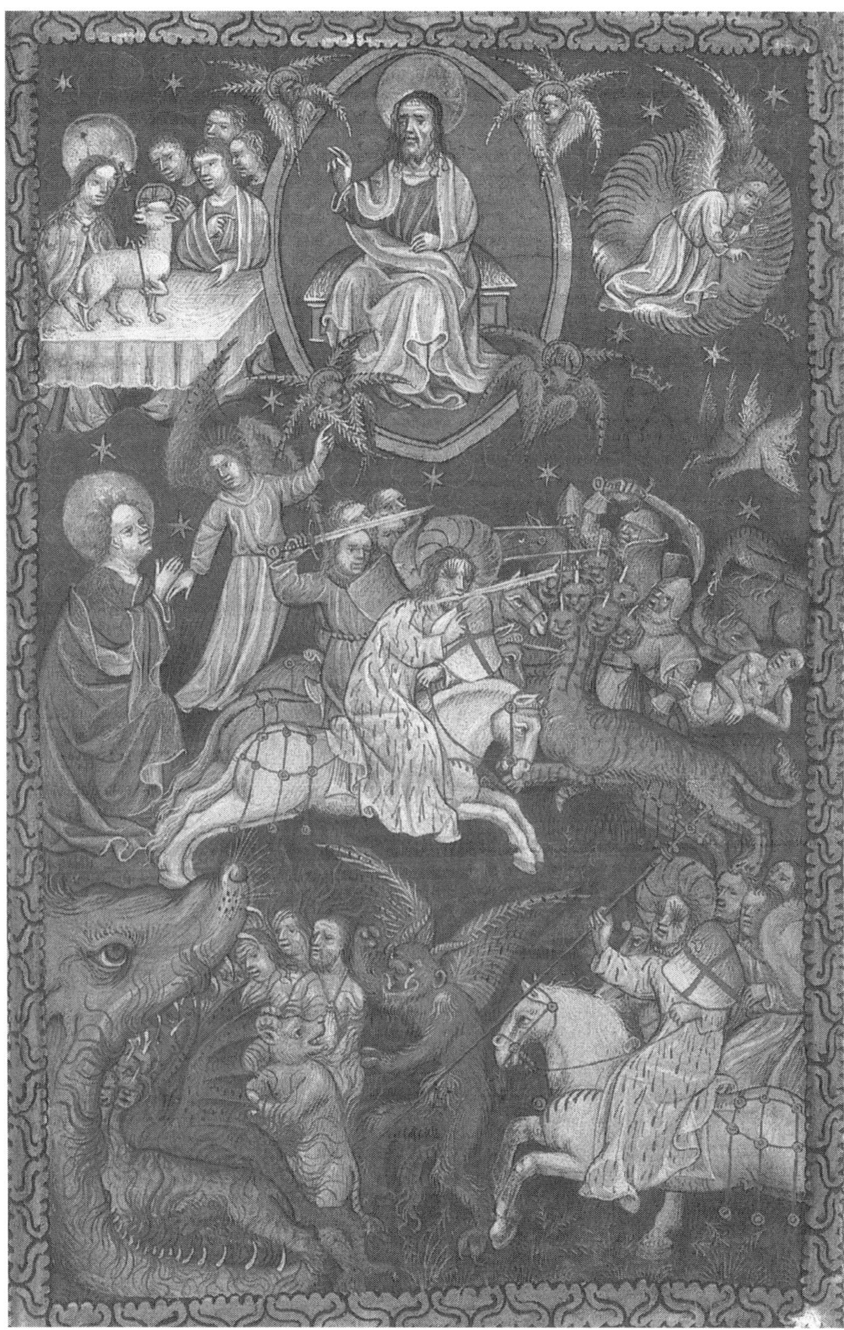

**Figure 8.4.** The *Flemish Apocalypse*, *c.* 1400, The Marriage of the Lamb, Armageddon, and the Last Judgement (Rev. 19–20), Paris: Bibliothèque Nationale. © BnF

one. Christ has been visualized in a very literal, slightly alarming fashion, in line with Rev. 19.12–13. Thus his eyes are emitting flames ('his eyes are like a flame of fire') and his white robe is flecked with blood ('he is clothed in a robe dipped in blood'). Even the birds of Rev. 19.21, who gorge on the flesh of the defeated army of the Beast, hover expectantly above the battle. Below this, the two Beasts, the Dragon, their followers, and Satan himself are pursued into a gaping Hellmouth by Christ and his army.

Although this image has been described rather dismissively by the art historian Van der Meer as a collection of 'variations of the standard types [of iconography connected with this scene]',[17] the composition is interesting. The way in which the events unfold in a zigzag trajectory from the top to the bottom of the image gives an appearance of coherence to this Armageddon sequence which it could be said to lack even in the textual source. Here the fact that there are two final battles seems to make sense. The first battle is presented as an obvious precursor to the final defeat of Satan, here depicted at the bottom of the image. The fact that this grotesque red figure is missing from the battle in the middle tier of the image makes it obvious that this is not the final Armageddon, as the great Satan is absent. Additionally the fact that the army of the Beast is pursued off to the right and then reappears (this time followed by Satan) in the lower tier running in the opposite direction creates the impression that the Beasts and their followers have been chased 'across the earth' by the army of Christ.

## Modern visualizations of Armageddon

Finally we turn to two images from the twentieth century that form a complete contrast to these medieval and late medieval evocations of Armageddon. The first, a brush and ink drawing by the Belgian artist Frans Masereel dating from 1944 entitled *Aeroplanes over Mankind* (Figure 8.5) has been included not on account of its faithfulness to the text of Revelation, it being an evocation of the apocalypse as a whole, but because it captures the global panic and suffering that is now associated with the word Armageddon. Masereel, a pacifist who lived in Paris, fled the city in 1940 following the German occupation. The experience of being part of this two million strong human exodus, all the while being pursued by German dive bombers, inspired Masereel to begin a series of drawings which became *Die Apokalypse unserer Zeit* (The Apocalypse of our Time).[18] *Aeroplanes over Mankind* in particular hints at the fact that for a postmodern reader or viewer, the Beasts

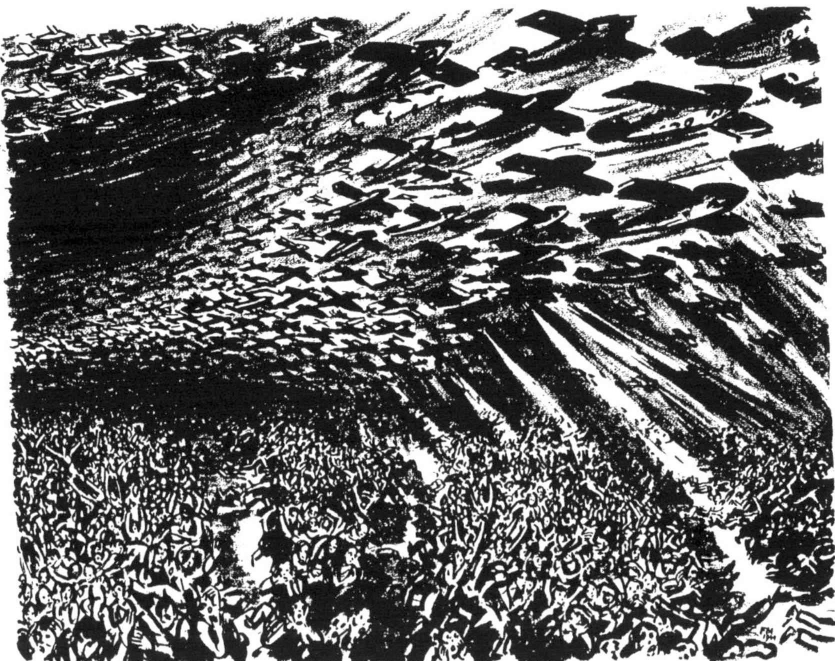

**Figure 8.5.** Frans Masereel, *Aeroplanes over Mankind* (*Flügzeuge über Menschheit*), 1944. © DACS 2014, Die Apokalyptische Reiter (1954), plate no. 5, Flügzeuge über die Menschheit

and the final battles are now more readily interpreted through the prism of modern warfare. It is nuclear weapons and fighter planes, as well as chemical weapons and even computer viruses, that scare us now and not the cavalries and hybrid animals of John's first-century imagination. To this end, in 2013–14 we became involved in a project called De/Coding the Apocalypse with modern artist Michael Takeo Magruder, artist in residence at King's College London. Its focus was to render the threat of the apocalypse in ways that will strike a chord with a twenty-first-century audience (rather than just repeating historical visualizations of the apocalypse which may not have the same impact now). He was particularly interested in the way that cutting-edge technology (ranging from computer games to drones to 3D printing to the ubiquitous Google search engine) has taken on apocalyptic significance and potential in the twenty-first-century imagination.

Finally and contrastingly, for many readers their first brush with Armageddon and certainly their first visual associations of the final battle(s) may have been supplied by scenes from C. S. Lewis' *Chronicles of Narnia*, his famous series of seven fantasy novels—the first published in 1950—about the adventures of various human children (the Pevensies and their cousins) in an alternative world known as Narnia. Pauline Baynes supplied the pen and ink drawings that are still used today. The final novel in the series is actually called *The Last Battle* and details the struggle between Aslan (a lion with Christlike qualities) and his followers and a false Aslan and his followers (cf. Rev. 13 and the False Prophet who was integrated into the Antichrist legend). There is a last climactic battle (Armageddon?) that is nearly lost but is turned around at the last minute by the forces of good. In an action that is reminiscent of the passing away of this world prior to the establishment of the New Jerusalem at the end of this novel, Aslan terminates the world. There are some very evocative accompanying images to the Last Battle, no doubt inspired in part by medieval and early modern visualizations of Armageddon (Plate 41).

However, in the spirit of Revelation, this is not the only 'last battle' to take place in the series. At the end of *The Lion, the Witch and the Wardrobe*, the first book published in the series, in what is presented as the definitive battle, Aslan's forces take on the forces of Jadis, the White Witch, and eventually manage to overpower her, leading to the coronation of the Pevensie children as the kings and queens of Narnia. This better-known battle has been visualized often, not only in Baynes' initial illustrations but also in the animated film of the book (1979, directed by Bill Melendez), the BBC TV series of 1988–90, and the Hollywood film version of 2005. For many people brought up from the 1980s onwards, seeing the film and VHS/DVD versions of the C. S. Lewis stories would have been their first experience of decisive, end of the world battles. These childhood images are difficult to shake off; the battle for the future of Narnia always comes into mind when thinking of Armageddon.


# The Millennium


We recently celebrated a millennium, an acknowledgement of the passing of two thousand years since the birth of Christ. The term millennium in this context refers quite simply to a unit of time (one thousand years). Within the context of Revelation, the Millennium refers to the one thousand-year reign of Christ prior to the final (final) battle and the Last Judgement, a sort of prefiguring of the New Jerusalem (see Rev. 20. 1–6). As we have seen, after (the first) Armageddon the Dragon, the ancient serpent, is thrown by an angel (often identified as Michael) into the bottomless pit, and locked in there for a thousand years. During this Millennium the followers of Jesus, 'who had been beheaded for their testimony' and who had not been marked by the sign of the Beast (Rev. 20.4), come to life again in what is called the first resurrection and, seated on thrones, judge and reign with Christ for the duration of this thousand-year reign.

As discussed in the Introduction, whether the Millennium is to be interpreted literally as a thousand-year reign that will take place on earth, whether it has begun or not, or whether it is to be interpreted symbolically (amillennialism) has been a matter for keen theological debate over the past two millennia, with accusations of heresy never far from the surface.[19] The Millennium is indeed problematic, if it is interpreted at all literally. For whatever the first audience of Revelation might have thought, from that time to this there has been no perfect rule on earth. Human work, even with the best of intentions, is always flawed, subject to mistakes, with unintended consequences. The very idea of the Millennium can, then, look like a dreadful temptation, in which utopian believers attempt to enforce a perfect rule on the elect (and on everyone else). If history has shown us anything it has shown us that utopian—millennial—political visions invariably lead to hells on earth. Indeed, it has become something of a cliché in historical commentary to see such bloodthirsty events as the French and Russian revolutions and the depredations of Mao and Pol Pot as secular attempts to realise millennial dreams in a secular way. Millennial—or, in Greek, chiliastic—thinking can be disastrously inflammatory, convincing those addicted to it that they can do what can never be done, and carrying with it the temptation to eliminate all those who stand in the way of the envisaged utopia.

In *The City of God,* written in the early fifth century CE, St Augustine established what has come to be seen as the orthodox Christian line on the Millennium, or at least the line taken by the established churches, both Catholic and Protestant. For Augustine, Christ's redemptive work (initiated by the resurrection) is already underway, and there is already a church of the elect, so in this sense the Millennium is happening now, but not in the sense that there is (or could be) a perfect regime here on Earth.[20] For Augustine the Millennium is taking place in the hearts of believers and those converted to Christianity. Satan is bound in a metaphorical sense—but only partially, and not completely. We only have to go to the start of John's vision, where he upbraids the seven churches of Asia (Rev. 2–3) for their laziness, idolatry, and lack of faith, to know that churches of the elect are not automatically perfect. Even if Satan is already chained, and will ultimately be defeated, his deceptions will continue to reach to the four corners of the earth, including the apparently saintly regions, as represented by the churches and the faithful. Even while he is chained, his deceptions leak out, all the more insidious because he seems to be safely beneath the surface, and his wiles appear as emanating from an Antichrist, often a bearer of a false peace. So for Augustine we are to imagine Christ coming like a thief. The Millennium (which Augustine sees in terms of the activity of the church of the saints here on earth) and the Satanic deceptions and struggles are all happening simultaneously, all going on all the time, rather than being implausibly sequential, with the otherwise mysterious thousand-year period of virtue and saintly rule between the two final battles.

In this interpretation, the unchaining of Satan and the three and a half years which follow are taken to refer to a period before the Last Judgement in which Satan's power is much more visible and terrifying. For Augustine the first resurrection of believers during the current millennial era is read as a spiritual resurrection, of the souls of the redeemed believers, 'the resurrection of souls here and now' through faith and baptism, as Augustine puts it, who are still, as it happens, subject to Satanic temptation. The material resurrection of their bodies, which Augustine refers to as the second resurrection, will come only after the 'great and last' judgement, in which both the saved and the wicked will be resurrected in both bodily and spiritual form.[21] The abyss into which Satan is thrown during the Millennium is interpreted by Augustine as the hearts of the wicked, who are untouched by the redemptive work of the church. Most importantly, the New Jerusalem, the new Heaven and new Earth which, as we will see, follow the Last Judgement, are not of or in this world at all, nor could they be. And, to underline Augustine's amillennial reading of Revelation, the whole spirit of his theology is to insist that as humans our task is not to exercise idle curiosity about the hidden workings of God's providence, or indeed its timing, but rather to concentrate in our own lives on pursuing the good and shunning the bad.

However, despite the efforts of Augustine to see the Millennium in a non-utopian, non-political, and non-materialistic way, over the years there have been many literalistic readings of the Millennium of Rev. 20.1–6, of which Hitler's Thousand-year Reich is only the most egregious. A number of medieval thinkers, most famously Joachim of Fiore, the radical Franciscan, rejected the Augustinian reading of the Millennium as referring to an embattled church in a problematic world and proposed that there would indeed be a period of millennial bliss on earth, an earthly paradise, so to speak.[22] We have already seen in the Introduction that both before and after Joachim the Middle Ages were peppered with popular or populist millennial movements, which were often deemed heretical, and often attacked the official clergy. The sixteenth century saw readings of the Millennium both in terms of the Protestant Reformation and in terms of the Spanish establishment of an idealized colonial rule in South America, governed by a Creole aristocracy. In the seventeenth century the Catholic Jacques-Bénigne Bossuet saw the Protestant reformers as Gog and Magog, while various radical Protestants saw both the English Civil War and the American colonies in millennial terms and some interpreted the driving out of the Catholic James II from Britain in 1688 as the binding of Satan.[23] And in the Middle Ages, the Saracens, the Turks, and Muslims more generally were often seen as Gog and Magog (Rev. 20.8), the diabolical figures released after the Millennium.

## Images of the Millennium

Perhaps unsurprisingly, given the difficulties involved in evoking a thousand-year rule of bliss, particularly if interpreted in the symbolic Augustinian way, most depictions of the Millennium tend to focus on the binding of Satan, and because of this somewhat restricted approach, this section will be brief. St Augustine saw both the binding of Satan and the Millennium itself as metaphorical characterizations of the time between Christ's redemptive sacrifice and the Last Judgement at the end of time. During this period some are saved and Satan's power is restricted, but there is no question of a literal 'reign of the saints' here on Earth before the Last Judgement.

The first two of the three images we have selected visualize this scene in contrasting ways. The third image, *The Mystic Nativity* by Botticelli, is a more metaphorical rendering of the Millennium, which needs unpicking, but which is both very beautiful and very profound once one gets to grips with it.

A fairly standard (in iconographical terms) but very striking medieval visualization of the binding of Satan is offered by the *Trinity Apocalypse* (Figure 8.6). Here we see two scenes from the 'binding' process. On the left

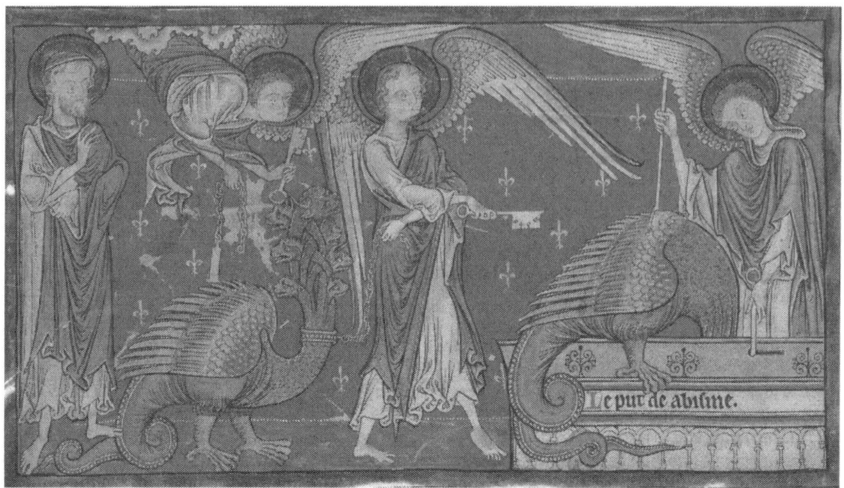


**Figure 8.6.** The *Trinity Apocalypse*, *c.*1260, Satan Bound and Led to the Pit (Rev. 20.1–3), Cambridge: Trinity College. © The Master and Fellows of Trinity College, Cambridge

Satan, here realized as the Dragon from Rev. 12, is led by two angels to his tomb-like pit. Whilst one must be wary of reading too much significance into vagaries of scale in pre-Renaissance images, the small size of the Dragon in this image is telling, particularly in comparison to his larger size when he was attacking the Woman Clothed with the Sun in folio 13r. There he was a magnificent red beast who took up at least a third of the image, whereas here he seems small and subdued, almost like a dog on a lead. In the text we are told that the angel 'seized' Satan but here he is presented as walking to his fate in defeat: no seizing necessary. Just as the tomb or pit into which the Dragon is being pushed (with spears) looks completely unassailable, so too the whole image is very controlled, something that is emphasized by the thick gold borders of the image frame. Evil has been successfully brought to heel and should no longer be viewed as a threat. The only intimation that this is not in fact the final end of Satan is the presence of his serpentine tail winding menacingly over the outside of the pit.

At the top of the following page and above an image of the final Armageddon, the millennial reign itself is rendered not metaphorically, as Augustine argued it should be, but in literal terms (Figure 8.7). Here four martyrs sit upon thrones on Heaven, symbolizing the first resurrection of those who have resisted the Beasts and continued Jesus' witness. To the right stand more martyrs. The throne itself resembles an altar. While faithful in

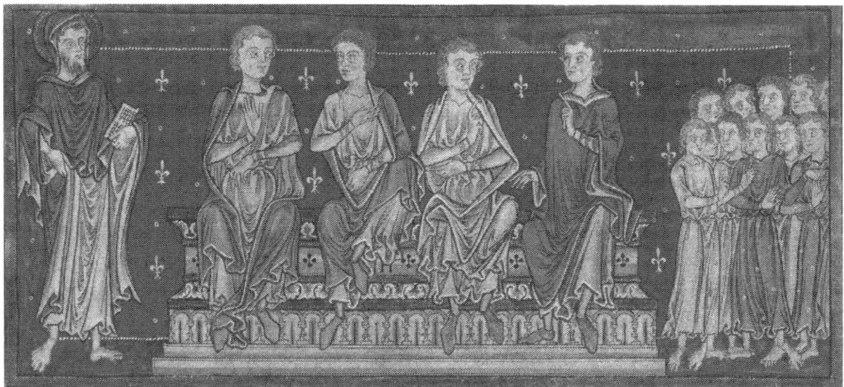

**Figure 8.7.** The *Trinity Apocalypse*, *c.*1260, The Millennium (Rev. 20.4–6), Cambridge: Trinity College. © The Master and Fellows of Trinity College, Cambridge

textual terms, the former image of the actual binding of Satan which facilitates the Millennium is much more evocative. Although Satan/the Dragon seems pacified and weak, the image of Satan being bound is more visually powerful than that of the anonymous martyrs taking up their place on the millennial throne.

While, as we will shortly see, Botticelli's visualization of the Millennium is truly metaphorical, esoteric even, Dürer too makes a break with the medieval tradition with his image of the binding of Satan/Millennium. It is the last in his series of fifteen woodcuts depicting the whole of the Apocalypse (Figure 8.8). Thus in the foreground an altogether more menacing, snarling Satan, rendered here as a hybrid monster, is forced into a hatch in the ground by a huge angel. The metallic lid of the hatch and the huge key carried by the angel give the viewer a sense of reassurance that Satan will not be able to escape his prison.

And what of the Millennium itself? Is this visualized via the peaceful landscape that we see depicted behind the binding scene? The short answer is that we do not know. Commentators are divided as to whether the scene being shown to a now old and wizened John (the visionary task has taken its toll?) is a millennial scene or whether it is the New Jerusalem itself. In favour of this being a millennial scene is the fact that hardly any of the features of the New Jerusalem (outlined in more detail in the next chapter) have been depicted here. Thus there are no precious stones (Rev. 21.19), no trees laden with fruit (Rev. 22.2–3) and no River of Life (Rev. 22.1).

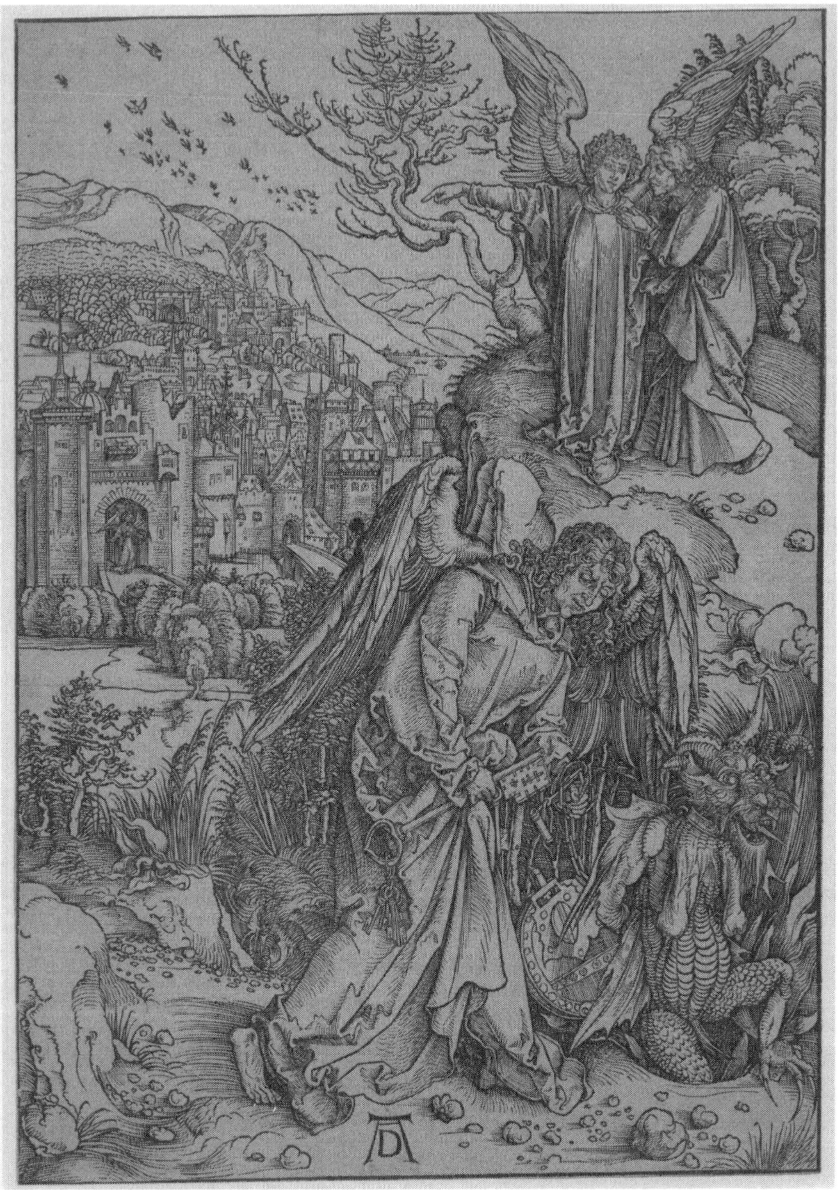

**Figure 8.8.** Albrecht Dürer, *Apocalypse* Series, *c.*1498, The Binding of Satan (Rev. 20), London: British Museum. © The Trustees of the British Museum

Additionally, the city that we can see is strangely reminiscent of Nuremberg. Was Dürer playing with the idea of the Millennium as an earthly reality (*pace* Augustine and in line with a more Joachite interpretation of Rev. 20.1–4)?

However, if we follow this interpretation then, somewhat bizarrely, Dürer's visualization of Revelation ends at Rev. 20.4–6. Thus others have argued that this image does indeed show the New Jerusalem in the background. In favour of this reading is the fact that there are three angels clearly visible in the three gates of the city, in accordance with Rev. 21.12. The fact that John's angelic guide is pointing down at the city may also indicate that it has just descended from Heaven, as predicted of the New Jerusalem in Rev. 21.2.[24] There is probably more merit in the first suggestion, as it seems to fit better with the young Dürer's world-view to leave the series open-ended. The fact that the viewer is presented with this visual challenge means that one is more likely to be drawn into the image and its complexities and not just focus on the binding of Satan, as was the case with most of the medieval images of the same passage.

Whilst very different in style, focus, and scope, both the *Trinity* images and the Dürer image are recognizably visualizations of the binding of Satan and/or the Millennium. Botticelli's *Mystic Nativity*, now housed in the National Gallery, is very different (Plate 42). Indeed, on first viewing it appears to be a Nativity scene based fairly closely on Luke 2.1–20. However, several strange details have led scholars and commentators over the ages to question this superficial interpretation. At the bottom of the image, below the Nativity scene, little imps and devils frolic or are being pushed down into some cracks in the rocks. Above them, men and angels embrace on the grass. Above the Nativity scene three angels sit on the roof of the shelter and above them, twelve angels hover under a golden opening in the sky. Above the image itself is an inscription in Greek which confirms that the work was made by Botticelli in 1500 and relates the image not to the Nativity but to the eleventh and twelfth chapters of Revelation (the measuring of the Temple and the Woman Clothed with the Sun), as well as to the current 'troubles of Italy'. These troubles refer in all likelihood to the French invasions of Italy in 1494–9 and to Cesare Borgia's ravaging of Italy in 1500–1.

Anyone vaguely familiar with Florentine history will also know that the 1490s saw the arrival of the 'apocalyptic' prophet Savonarola in Florence. Savonarola, best known for his 'bonfires of the vanities' (the burning of any materials deemed to be temptations to sin and which allegedly included works by Botticelli himself), preached about the need for radical moral reform in Florence and was extremely popular and influential until his execution in 1498 by the Florentine authorities. His sermons were preached against a backdrop of a new millennium of spirituality where 'the angels would come to live together with men'. Botticelli is widely believed to have been a *piagnone* or supporter of Savonarola and to have been deeply influenced by his millennial world-view. Piagnonism, although illegal after Savonarola's death in 1498, continued until well into the 1500s. Interpreting *The Mystic Nativity* in a way that makes sense of all its components and the history surrounding it is extremely difficult. Suffice it to say that it is possible, but not verifiable, that despite the inscription which links the painting to Rev. 11–12, this is in fact also a visual exploration of the type of millennium (Rev. 20) envisaged by Savonarola.[25]

The coming of the messianic kingdom and the final defeat of Satan that this foreshadows, as evoked in Rev. 12 and 20 in particular, is visualized by Botticelli not in a straightforward way as the figure of Satan being chained and stowed in his pit underground, as exemplified in the *Trinity* or Dürer image, but as a second Nativity, complete with elements of Florentine ritual that are based, for the most part, on the longed-for Savonarolan notion of the millennial union of mankind and angels that would precede the Last Judgement and the coming of the New Jerusalem. It is therefore a metaphorical rather than a mimetic or representational image. Satan has, for instance, been symbolized not as one hybrid creature, as was traditional, but by the seven little imps or devils at the bottom of the image. Their small size may point to Satan's lack of power during the Millennium. The focus, in contrast to both the *Trinity* and the Dürer image, is not on Satan himself but on Christ's royal rule (Rev. 20.4; see also Rev. 12.14) and the intermingling of the human and the divine that this was expected to engender.

While complex and difficult to grasp on first viewing, Botticelli's *Mystic Nativity* represents not only a unique visual interpretation of the Millennium as a second (Florentine) Nativity that leads to the ultimate defeat of Satan (and in doing so manages to fuse the contrasting theological interpretations of that event, the Augustinian and the more Joachite or political) but also gives tangible form to a very different way of picturing Revelation, not as a chronological narrative but as a complex of visual ideas and themes that can be brought together in one space in a painting of great beauty but also of great challenge to the viewer.

# The Last Judgement

As mentioned above, Revelation devotes three verses to the Last Judgement (Rev. 20.11–13). In what is effectively a second resurrection, all the dead who had not been taken up in the first resurrection then rise again and are divided into two groups before the 'great, white throne'. Those whose names have been recorded in the 'book of life' escape being thrown into the eternal lake of fire and proceed (we imagine) to the New Jerusalem. Those whose names are not found there are thrown into the lake of fire alongside Satan, the two Beasts, and 'Death and Hades' themselves. Thus this moment represents a victory over (and an end to) Death itself. Commentators stress two facets of this Last Judgement scene. First this represents the moment of corporate human judgement, in contrast to the scenes of individual judgement and destruction of the previous chapters (of the Whore of Babylon, the Beasts, and Satan).[26] The sense of a corporate judgement being meted out upon a faceless humanity is usually captured well in visualizations of this passage. Second (and crucially for understanding visualizations of the Last Judgement) there are parallels and overlaps with the Last Judgement described here and those in Matthew 3, 12–13, and 25 and John 5 as well as with the Jewish apocalypses Daniel (chapter 7) and 1 Enoch (chapter 1). There are also some parallels with the judgement passages in the Pauline Epistles of Romans 2 and 2 Corinthians 5. Most visualizations draw on a range of these texts. The Last Judgement is therefore the visual equivalent of a literary creation, such as Antichrist, which draws on references from a range of biblical texts and which then becomes embedded into popular consciousness in its final composite formation (see Chapter 6 for more on Antichrist). Thus, while Last Judgement images abound, it is very difficult to know if they are based directly on Revelation's Last Judgement or not. With this caveat in mind, we will refer now to just a few interesting examples, which can, as far as possible, be directly linked to Revelation.

# Images of the Last Judgement

What images of the Last Judgement can capture, which verbal narratives even in Revelation itself cannot, is the synchronicity of the corporate sentencing envisaged in Rev. 20.11–13—both the damned and the righteous being dealt with, rising up to Heaven and being driven down to Hell simultaneously. In addition, in many of the depictions of the whole canvas of the Last Judgement, there is often a greater fascination with the mechanics of damnation than with the bliss of the redeemed, which may reflect a human fascination with the darker things of life, or even, more cynically, with a desire of church and other authorities to control wayward and lawless behaviour. There is also a question of the extent to which in representations of the Last Judgement any hint is given of the mercifulness of God, tempering his justice, and of the possibility of a humanizing compassion and even intercession on our behalf. As we will see, this is an element present in many medieval representations of the Last Judgement, which here go beyond the fierce tone of Revelation at this point ('all were judged according to what they had done', Rev. 20.13).

Including even Michelangelo, whose great Last Judgement owes much more to Dante than to Revelation, many of the most well-known images of the Last Judgement from earlier times come from church frescos and sculpture. However, a very early example of Last Judgement iconography is a dramatic carving in ivory from the ninth century now housed in the Victoria and Albert Museum (Figure 8.9). The narrative is in different sections, but what it depicts can be seen as taking place simultaneously. God/Christ sits in judgement at the top of the relief surrounded by trumpeting angels (cf. Rev. 8–9) while suspended below them are the open graves of those being resurrected. The resurrected are being pushed down into tunnels on either the left or the right. Those on God's right are being welcomed into Heaven/ the New Jerusalem, while those on his left are being fed into the Hellmouth at the bottom of the image. The clear demarcation of the saved going to God's right-hand side and the damned to his left comes directly from Matthew 25.34–46. In most other respects this ninth-century ivory relief is quite a neat visual synthesis of Rev. 20.11–13, although crucially the 'book of life' is missing.

One of the best-known representations of the Last Judgement is the tympanum above the great west door of Amiens cathedral, dating from the thirteenth century (see Figure 8.1). Part of the point of a Last Judgement door at the entrance to a church or cathedral is to impress on the worshipper that in entering the church he or she is entering a foretaste of the New Jerusalem, and so must proceed through judgement. At Amiens, as is very common, the human narrative (as opposed to the divine) progresses upwards from the bottom to the top of the tympanum. Thus at the bottom of the

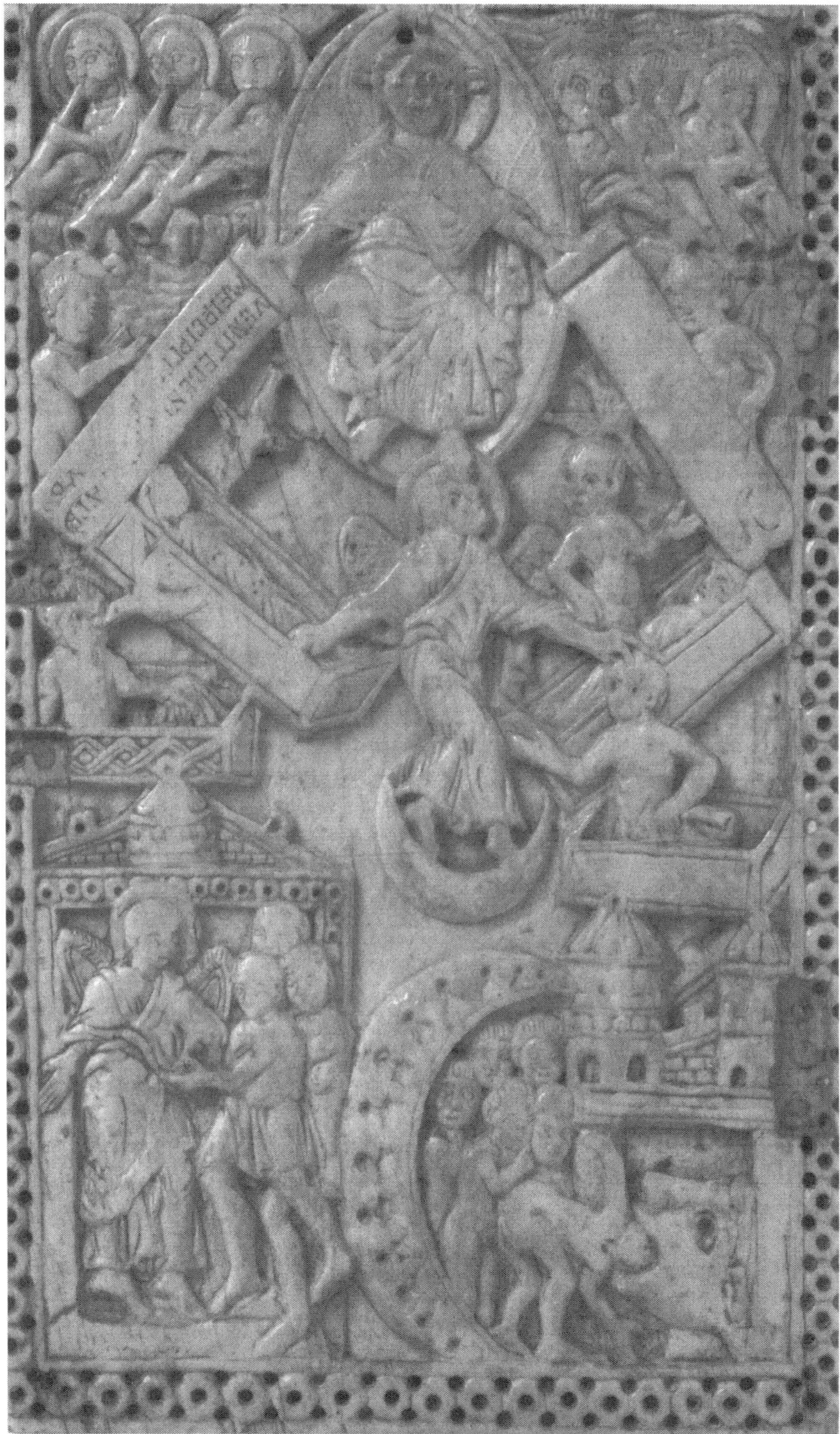

**Figure 8.9.** Last Judgement ivory relief, ninth century, London: Victoria and Albert Museum. © Victoria and Albert Museum, London

scene angels blow their trumpets and we can see the people coming up out of their graves and tombs. In the middle stands an angel (Michael) holding a pair of scales. In one scale there is the Lamb of God, while in the other the head of an unrepentant evildoer, which suggests strongly that salvation is an act of divine grace, that the virtues by which we might be saved are themselves outpourings of grace. On the level above this, the divided souls progress to Heaven on the left-hand side (to God's right) and to Hell on the right (God's left). The damned are naked, being pushed by devils into a gaping Hellmouth (the Leviathan mentioned in the Book of Job, rather than Revelation's lake of fire), while those going to Heaven are clothed with angels holding crowns above their heads. On the level above (the divine level), the figures are about one and a half times as big as on the levels below. This level is, of course, dominated by a majestic Christ, seated in judgement, but still and with hands raised. His hands show the wounds of the cross, signifying a mercy not explicit in the text of Revelation at this point, while angels accompanying him hold the instruments of the Passion (cross, lance, etc.). The raised hands are a reminder of the significance that the right- and left-hand sides play in the great judgement, as foretold in Matthew 25.33, though not mentioned in Revelation itself.

As in many medieval Last Judgments, on Christ's left and right kneel Mary and John the beloved disciple, pleading for those being judged—a humanizing element, and one emphasizing the divine mercy again, but as mediated through Mary. The mediating and intercessory role of the Virgin was central to medieval Christianity, and so this is what we see in most thirteenth-century cathedral representations of the Last Judgement. (We saw a variation of this motif in the *Ghent Altarpiece*, where God/Christ in majesty is flanked by a seated Mary, wearing a crown with twelve stars, calmly and demurely reading a book of hours, and a seated John, but in this case a bearded John the Baptist, also seated and gesturing towards Christ's divinity and majesty.)[27] It is, though, something not to be found in the sterner words of Revelation, or indeed elsewhere in the scriptures, which is yet another indication of the typically syncretic nature of representations of the Last Judgment both in the Middle Ages and later. The shape of the Amiens tympanum lends drama to the main image, as all around the semicircular levels of the outer tympanum fly angels bearing witness to the judgements.

Below the Last Judgement tympanum is a single column in the middle of the entry to the cathedral. On this column stands a sternly sublime image of Christ, known as Le Beau Dieu. In *The Bible of Amiens* Ruskin wrote that here every worshipper meets Christ at the Temple gate. Here is 'the pure, joyful, beautiful lesson of Christianity' that medieval men and women knew for three hundred years or more, Christ as 'incarnate Word—as the prefect friend—as the Prince of Peace on Earth—and as the Everlasting King in Heaven'. But this perfect friend, this Lamb, is also the God of the Last Judgement. 'He holds the Book of the Eternal Law in His left hand; with His right He blesses,—but he blesses on condition: "This do, and thou shalt live…this *be* and thou shalt live…This, if thou do *not*…thou shalt die."' So Ruskin's Christ blesses *some*, shows mercy to *some*, but on condition; for those who have not repented will not be blessed but condemned: this is dual message of Revelation itself, which has been encapsulated perfectly by the sculptor of Le Beau Dieu in his stone relief and by Ruskin in his words.[28]

*The Trinity Apocalypse*, with which readers are now familiar, also offers a magnificent example of a Last Judgement scene (Plate 43). This multi-tiered, oversized scene, itself unusual within the context of the manuscript as a whole, surely owes something to the—by now, standard—composition of the great monumental Last Judgements from cathedrals such as Amiens and Chartres, although some of the details are quite different. This reflects the fact that, in contrast to the monumental Last Judgements, which are based on an amalgamation of textual sources, as explained above, this Last Judgement is based only on the text of Revelation. Here the dead are pictured on the right-hand side of the upper tier as arising naked from the sea to be judged (see Rev. 20.13). The first two are depicted as holding books, which perhaps symbolize the 'book of life' (Rev. 20.12). Underneath them, still on the right-hand side, others arise from an earthly Hellmouth also to be judged (as opposed to Amiens, where they are being pushed into it).

The Hellmouth here is intended to symbolize 'Death and Hades giving up the dead that were in them' of Rev. 20.14, but in medieval terms it probably also symbolizes purgatory.[29] Those 'not found written in the book of life' are being dragged down by grotesque devils into Hell itself, while the clothed figures on the left-hand side of the middle tier, some of whom are attired as monks, represent the saved. Above them are three angels holding some of the instruments of the Passion, such as the cross, a spear, and a chalice. Christ himself, sitting in a large mandorla in the middle of the image, prominently displays his stigmata. Thus the redemption made possible by his sacrifice, for those on the left-hand side of the image, is clearly being emphasized; in addition a sense is given of divine mercy countering divine judgement. However, it is a curious, or perhaps an intended, feature of the image that it is the descent into Hell, and not the salvation of the saved, that receives the most striking visual emphasis. There are three more images in the *Trinity* series, all of which depict the New Jerusalem (see Plate 45 for a *Trinity* image of the New Jerusalem). These images, however, focus not so much on the salvation of those who are listed in the 'book of life' as on the architectural splendour of the New Jerusalem. Thus it could be argued that the *Trinity Apocalypse* lacks a moment of corporate salvation to balance out the scene of corporate damnation that is evoked with such vigour in this image of the Last Judgement.

We jump now some six hundred years forward to an image that does manage to synthesize the Last Judgement with the New Jerusalem, although arguably it is still the Last Judgement in its darkness and drama that ends up dominating the composition. John Martin (1789–1854) is well known for his large-scale scenes of biblical destruction. Canvases such as *The Fall of Ninevah* and *The Deluge* were amongst his earlier works. And in 1853 Martin completed three huge paintings, a triptych in fact, which sought to provide a visual synthesis of Revelation itself. The first image is actually entitled *The Last Judgement*, while the second is entitled *The Plains of Heaven* and deals with the New Jerusalem, and the third, *The Great Day of His Wrath*, deals in more detail with the destruction envisaged in Rev. 6 (the Seven Seals).[30] Compared to his brother, Jonathan, a self-styled apocalyptic prophet who set fire to York Minster and was incarcerated in Bedlam, John Martin's highly rhetorical apocalyptic imaginings are tame.[31] But they were very popular, in a way that his contemporary, William Blake's images of the Last Judgement, of which more below, were not. Indeed, this triptych of images was taken on tours of both England and America after Martin's death in 1854 and viewed by hundreds of thousands.

*The Last Judgement*, in keeping with the much earlier monumental images of this scene (such as at Amiens), is divided into two main tiers, an upper and a lower, and the left- and right-hand sides of the image are separated by an abyss (Figure 8.10). On the upper tier we see the New Jerusalem, although the way that it has been depicted is more reminiscent of the descriptions of Heaven given in Rev. 4–5 (the heavenly throne room) than of the magnificent city described in Rev. 21. Here God sits on a raised throne, flanked by rows of crowned elders. The scene is notable for its orderliness and the brilliant white of their attire. Below, on the left-hand side of the image (at God's right hand), is Mount Zion where the great and the good await their call to the New Jerusalem. Amongst those assembled

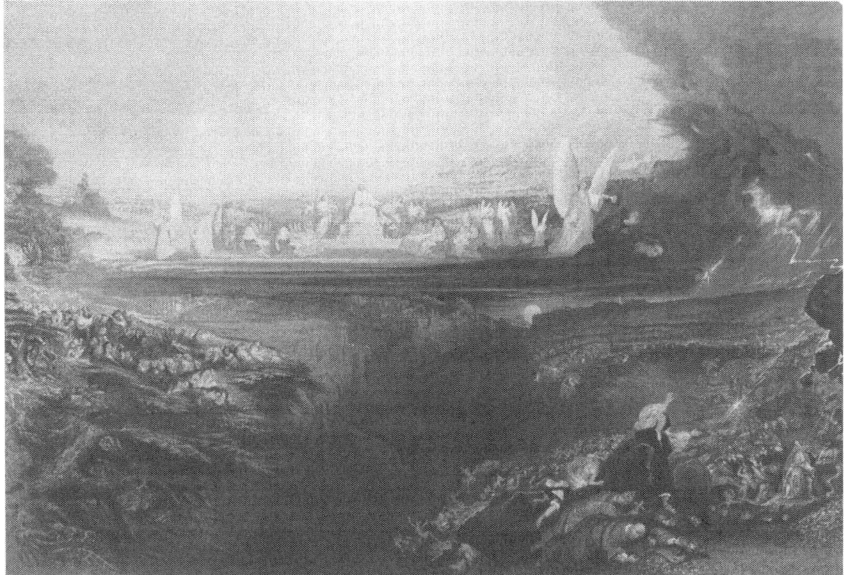

**Figure 8.10.** John Martin, *The Last Judgement* (engraving by Charles Mottram), 1853, London, Tate. © Bridgeman Art Library

there are thirty-four named individuals, including Thomas More, Wesley, Canute, Dante, Washington, Copernicus, Newton, Watt, Chaucer, Tasso, Corneille, Shakespeare, Michelangelo, Rubens, Dürer, and Wilkie.[32] On the right of the abyss, those whose names were not found in the 'book of life' and inhabitants of the city of Babylon are being gradually pulled down into the abyss. Most prominent at the front is the Whore of Babylon, recognizable by her scarlet robe and ostentatious jewellery and the cup of abominations which lies at her feet. Under her robes slides a bishop, possibly a Catholic, a reminder of the fallibility of the church, as well as the secular world.

Martin also takes the opportunity here to pillory the perceived chaos of the modern industrial world. In the middle distance (although this is very hard to see except when viewing the canvas up close) two trains career towards the abyss. The first train's carriages are marked 'London', 'Paris', etc, a reminder of Martin's more practical concerns about the need to 'purify' London (he wrote many pamphlets about the need for water and sewage reforms) as well as his more metaphorical concerns about the moral standing of these modern cities (modern Babylons). In the background of the image, the sun sets on this world of human folly, another reminder from

Martin of the transient nature of humanity in the face of the permanence of God's judgement and the New Jerusalem. Although not to everyone's taste, either then or now, there is no denying that this image, perhaps more than any of the others in this section, captures the corporate feel both of the Last Judgement and of the entry into the New Jerusalem, against a background of an Earth in its final throes.

William Blake's *The Vision of the Last Judgement* (1808), painted in his characteristic watercolour format, is some forty-five years earlier and quite different in feel (Figure 8.11). Set entirely within the heavenly/demonic realms, Michelangelo's influence on the image is well known, although Blake's Christ is more impassive and less threatening than Michelangelo's.[33] Blake's *Last Judgement* is also reminiscent in many ways of Botticelli's *Chart of Hell*, conceived as part of his series to accompany Dante's *Divine Comedy*.[34] Botticelli's drawing depicts Dante's circles of Hell as a sort of cross-section of ever-decreasing ellipses culminating in a circle which encloses the Devil at the centre of the Earth. In Blake's image, too, the Devil, recognizable from Blake's other images of Satan, such as *The Great Red Dragon and the Beast from the Sea*, is chained in a fiery cavern (in Blake's own words) at the centre of the earth (see Figure 6.7).[35] Indeed, the whole image has the feel of taking place underground, although it is unclear whether this was Blake's intention. Above the Devil's cavern, the Whore of Babylon also sits naked and chained, perhaps an allusion to Blake's less than straightforward relationship with this figure, who, like the Dragon, he seems unable to condemn as wholly evil, but perhaps regards more as a victim of an evil system. To the right of the image (to God's left) the damned are either pulled into or jump down to the fiery pit, while on the left-hand side others ascend from a pit at the bottom of the image, and also from graves further up the left-hand side, up towards the throne room. On both sides the descent and the ascent have been depicted with real force and movement, and seem to almost flow into each other via the heavenly throne room, almost to the extent that one wonders if this is intended to represent an eternal cycle of damnation and salvation.

Indeed, Rowland argues that, in line with John 5.24, the image represents the idea that eternity is always 'ready and available'.[36] Although there is not the sense of rigid separation between the divine realm and the earthly realm that we have seen in other images of the Last Judgement, there are no humans in the heavenly throne room, suggesting, in line with Blake's own theology, that the only path to God is through Christ. This image, although

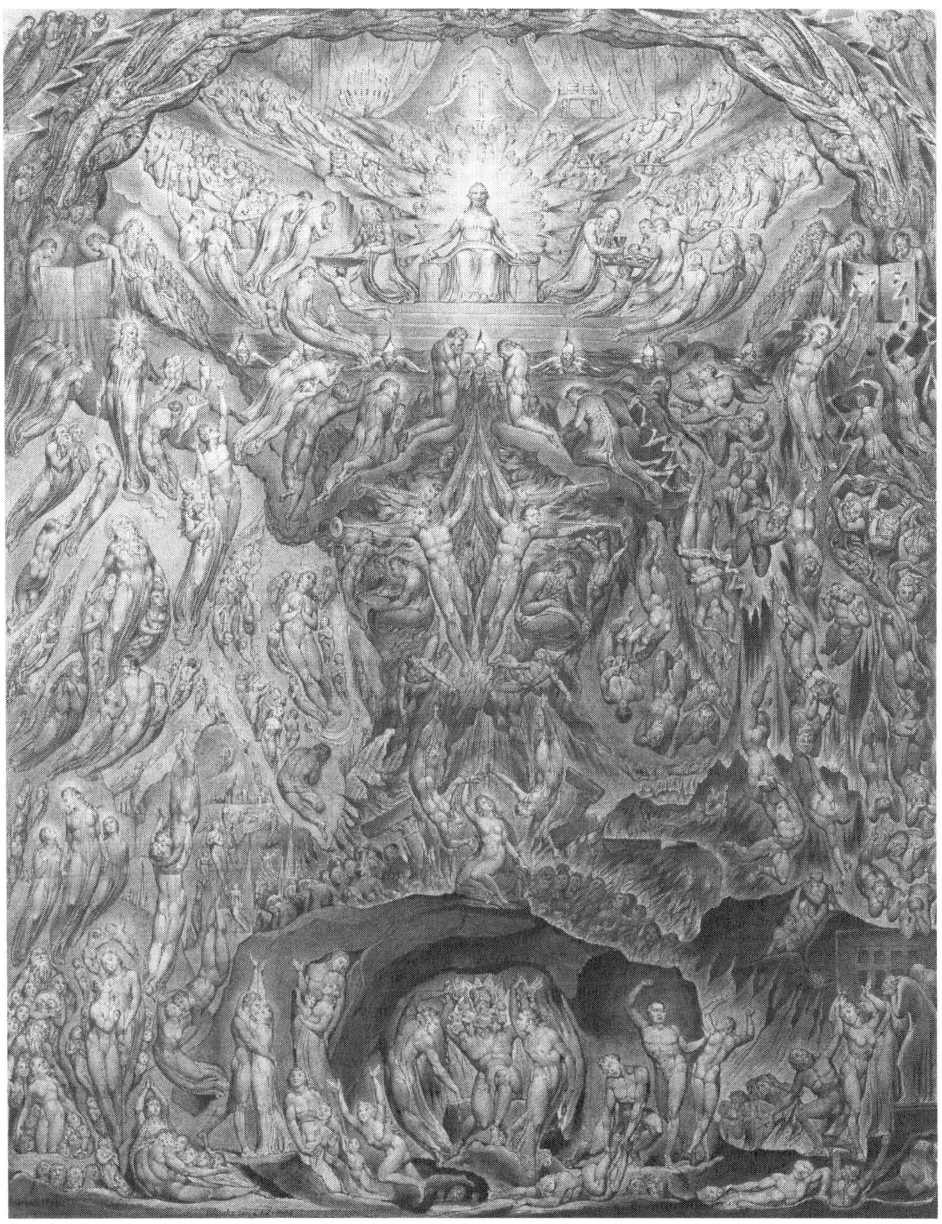

**Figure 8.11.** William Blake, *The Vision of the Last Judgment*, 1808, Sussex: Petworth House. © Bridgeman Art Library

faithful to Revelation in many ways—the enthroned Christ, for instance, is clearly holding a 'scroll of life' and is flanked by two angels holding 'books of life'—seems larger in scope than just a Last Judgement image. Indeed, it has been described as 'a summation of the history of the human spirit' and as an attempt to 'bring together all biblical prophecies of the redemption of man' (see for instance the figures of Adam and Eve just below the throne).[37]

For Blake, then, unlike the medievals—although perhaps similarly to Martin, albeit in a much less obvious way—the Last Judgement cannot simply be extricated or decontextualized from the New Jerusalem that follows it. Armageddon, the Millennium even, and the Last Judgement are all part of one synchronic whole. Once again this accords with Rowland's contention that, owing to the vaginal nature of the shapes formed by the trumpeting angels at the centre of the image, Blake was perhaps summoning the viewer to 'enter once more into the womb to embark on the path of judgement leading to new birth'.[38] The Last Judgement, far from being an end in itself, represented the potential for a new beginning.

This would seem a good place to draw this chapter to a close. Before doing so brief mention will be made of an image by German artist Max Beckmann from 1918 called, quite simply, *Resurrection* (Figure 8.12). This image was inspired by Beckmann's experiences as a soldier in the First World War, and has been related to Rev. 6.12–15 (the opening of the Sixth Seal, when the kings of the earth, the rich and the mighty, as well as every 'free man' shelter in the mountains to try to avoid the great earthquake). However, as it depicts a form of grotesque resurrection, replete with deformed bodies in contorted poses, from which Beckmann and his friends shelter in the lower right-hand corner of the image, it seems reasonable to equate this image also with the resurrection described in Rev. 20.11–13. Thus Beckmann and his friends are witnesses to a resurrection without God and therefore without hope.

Indeed, in a letter to a friend in 1919 Beckmann writes, 'My religion is arrogance toward God, spite for God . . . In my pictures I reproach God for everything he has done wrong.'[39] The effect is very striking. So conditioned are we by the many Last Judgement images that confront one every time one enters a church or an art gallery, that it is quite shocking to encounter an image entitled *Resurrection* over which a rather benign-looking God or at least some divine force does not preside. For Beckmann, the events of the First World War had definitively removed the possibility of the sort of divine resurrection and redemption set out in Rev. 20–2 and related texts. It is,

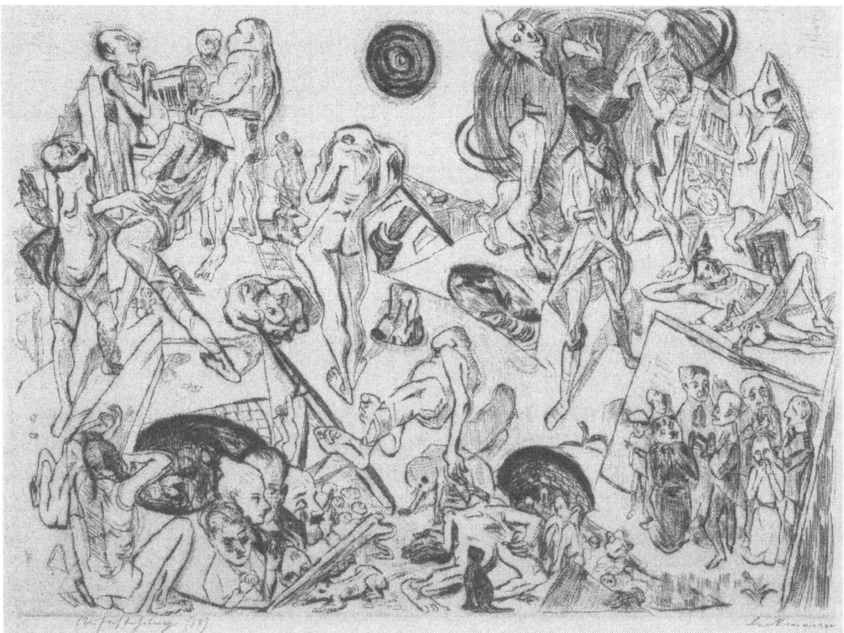

**Figure 8.12.** Max Beckmann, *Resurrection*, 1918, London: British Museum. © The Trustees of the British Museum

however, worth mentioning that Beckmann returned to Revelation as a source of inspiration during the Second World War, whilst in exile in Amsterdam from 1937 to 1947. Here he produced, among other works, an *Apocalypse* series, a set of twenty-seven coloured lithographs which depict the twenty-two chapters of the text (with additional illustrations). These lithographs are discussed in the final chapter of this book.

# Conclusion

We have journeyed in this chapter, via some magnificent images, from the battle of Armageddon, which takes place in two stages, to the Millennium, where the New Jerusalem is foreshadowed, to the moment of humankind's final judgement. In doing so we have moved from the specific, the deaths of the Beasts and finally of Satan himself, to the general, the Last Judgement as a corporate event. Whether one is religious or not, and so whether one sees these events in terms of reality or of myth and metaphor, one cannot fail to be moved by the efforts of the artists surveyed to try to visualize these momentous and all-encompassing events. Thus we have moved from the symbolic, the ninth-century ivory relief now housed in the Victoria and Albert Museum, which evokes the enormity of the Last Judgement via a few naïve figures, likewise the *Lambeth Apocalypse* with Armageddon, to Blake's fiendishly complex depiction of the Last Judgement, which comprises hundreds of fluid figures. What the visualizations of the Last Judgement that we have surveyed were able to bring to the task of interpretation is a powerful sense of synchronicity. In both of the main descriptions of the Last Judgement found in the New Testament (Rev. 20.11–15 and Matthew 25.31–46) the saving of the righteous and the condemnation of the damned are seemingly taking place at the same time but this is impossible to capture with any force in a prose text. In the images surveyed, however, particularly the Martin and the Blake, there is a clear sense that we are being given a snapshot of the eternal and simultaneous salvation and damnation evoked by the passage of biblical text, which in turn makes the viewer reflect again on the texts in question. At the other end of the spectrum entirely, we paused for a time over Botticelli's *Mystic Nativity*, a metaphorical depiction of the Millennium as a second Nativity, as opposed to a literal one thousand-year reign of the saints, a concept which has been shown to be a problematic one by theologians since Augustine. The plethora of ways in which these themes have continued to be visualized is testament not only to the enduring appeal of Revelation itself but also to the complexity and the magnetism of ideas surrounding final events, final battles, and final judgments or reckonings, both in former times and today.

It is notable that most, if not all, religions contain within them myths which rectify the injustices and imbalances of life. Immanuel Kant, that most rational and intellectually self-restricting of Enlightenment thinkers, found himself unable to conceptualize morality itself as rationally binding on us unless somewhere there was a balancing of the injustices of this life. So he invoked an afterlife in which the immoral wrongs and the moral goods of this life were rectified and rewarded appropriately. It cannot be said that since Kant's day philosophers have shown clearly and without begging numerous questions how morality can be seen as binding on each of us in the absence of some final judgement or reckoning. If we can get away (in this life) with doing wrong, what rationally is there to stop us? Even though we can all easily see the benefits (to us) of most people behaving morally, what reason is there against me or you doing wrong if we could get away with it, and if doing so did not disrupt a general adherence to morality?

The vividly metaphorical imaginings of the end times in Revelation are drawing on tendencies deep within our nature. Even if we reject its doctrine of a Last Judgement, questions remain for all of us as to the ultimate reasonableness of morality in a world where the wicked often thrive at the expense of the good, whether we are religious or not. And even if these philosophical ruminations do not strike a chord, it is surely worth remarking on the endless fascination many of us have with stories and films in which the evildoers are punished and the innocent are saved or at least revenged.

# 9

# The New Jerusalem

Then I saw a new heaven and a new earth, for the first heaven and the first earth had passed away, and the sea was no more. And I saw the holy city, the new Jerusalem, coming down out of heaven from God, prepared as a bride adorned for her husband…

Rev. 21.1–2

So opens the concluding episode of Revelation (which occupies chapters 21 and 22). The destruction and conflict of the preceding fourteen or so chapters (ever since the Four Horsemen were released in Rev. 6) is brought to a close and we are finally presented with a positive vision of the future. Earth is brought into alignment with the vision of the heavenly throne room that we saw in Rev. 4–5 and the seemingly impenetrable barrier that had existed between the two realms (the heavenly and the earthly) is dissolved for ever. Although the New Jerusalem is foreshadowed in the narrative pauses of Rev. 7 and 14–15, where we are given glimpses of gatherings of martyrs and those who have resisted the Beasts, all dressed in white and singing the praises of the Lamb, nothing can prepare us for the splendour and complexity of the New Jerusalem as revealed in John's final vision. Indeed, it should come as no surprise that the great Gothic cathedrals were themselves designed to reflect the splendour of the New Jerusalem (which is itself a reflection of the glory of God; see Rev. 21.11). Interestingly, these New Jerusalems were entered through a portal on which the Last Judgement was often represented. So worshippers would foreshadow physically in this life the journey that all of humanity will supposedly take at the end of the world. Similarly, hymns such as Parry's 'Jerusalem' (originally a poem by William Blake) turn on the concept of the New Jerusalem, a celestial city on earth.

# The meaning of the New Jerusalem

A particularly important aspect of the New Jerusalem in terms of its original context is the fact that Revelation was written only shortly after the wholesale and sadistic destruction by the Romans of the Old Jerusalem (in 70 CE), an event that would have been very much in the mind of the visionary and his audience. The Gospels included Jesus prophesying the destruction of Jerusalem and the demolition of the Temple, and clearly Revelation's announcing of a celestial Jerusalem—without a Temple, because God will be actually dwelling there—should be seen in this light. The new religion was not looking for another destructible city and temple, but for something altogether different, which marked a clear distinction between it and its Jewish antecedents. Four further aspects of the vision of the New Jerusalem have been rightly stressed by commentators. First, as in many other places in Revelation, there are parallels with passages from the Old Testament and particularly with Ezekiel, who is himself given a vision of a great city, an idealized Jerusalem, in Ezekiel 40–7. More general parallels are found in Isaiah—of Israel as a bride, and also of the return from exile (the Exodus motif).[1] In Revelation, though, it is not Israel who is returning from exile, but the whole of humanity. Thus the New Jerusalem may be viewed not only as the climax or culmination of Revelation but in some ways as the climax of human history (according to its author). Whether one accepts these claims or not, the New Jerusalem, as described, undoubtedly possesses a great universality. God is said to dwell there amongst his peoples (Rev. 21.3) and nations (21.24–6). The New Jerusalem's gates will be permanently open to all whose names have been recorded in the 'book of life', regardless of nationality or ethnicity. In this we are reminded of Paul's radical claim in Galatians that 'there is no longer Jew or Greek, there is no longer slave or free, there is no longer male and female; for all of you are one in Christ Jesus' (Gal. 3.28).

Second, and leading on from this, there is a certain amount of debate regarding the extent to which the New Jerusalem should be viewed as a completely new reality. To be sure, there is no possibility of a return to the former dimension, as we are told definitively in Rev. 21.1 that the 'first earth had passed away'. However, there are also significant lines of continuity with what has gone before. Thus the city itself has parallels with both the Woman Clothed with the Sun and the Bride who marries the Lamb in Rev. 19. In particular she is cast as the diametric opposite of that decadent yet ultimately doomed city of Babylon. Perhaps more tangible is the fact that (as we shall see below), the city is constructed using naturally occurring jewels and precious stones that we are still familiar with today (jasper, gold, glass, sapphire, emerald, etc.). Those who inhabit the New Jerusalem are still embodied human beings (they are called upon to drink from the water of life), and the beauty of the New Jerusalem is very much a material beauty, and described as such. Finally, there are many parallels, in Rev. 22 in particular, with the Garden of Eden. So while the New Jerusalem should be seen as having a different nature from anything on earth—apart from anything else, being incorruptible and untainted—it is still a physical realm. Thus in many ways this is a restoration of what should have been, rather than an alien reality, or as Boxall puts it, the New Jerusalem should be seen as a compensation for the failure of the first Jerusalem.[2] This is certainly reflected in the Greek word used for the 'new' in 'New Jerusalem' in Rev. 21.1 ($\kappa\grave{\alpha}\iota\nu os$), which has connotations of restoration and renovation. Perhaps then, in trying to understand the relationship between the first earth and the New Jerusalem, one should focus less on the total destruction of the former and more on the idea of radical recreation and renewal.[3]

Third, and this is something that presents a real challenge for artists, in Rev. 22 the vision of the New Jerusalem as a celestial city on earth gives way to a vision of a sort of second Garden of Eden through which flows a river (of the water of life) and which is adorned with fructifying trees of life.[4] How does this vision fit with the former and how are we meant to visualize it? It is telling that most artists have tended to focus on either the city or the garden, perhaps implying that they are different symbolic evocations of the same idea.

Lastly, and this is something that has perplexed and inspired commentators since the time of the earliest church, is the New Jerusalem entirely a future reality? Is it partially accessible in the present via the Christian life, as theologians from the time of the early church to the present day have argued, but ultimately a future event that will occur outside of time after the Last Judgement and the destruction of the 'first earth'?[5] Or can it in fact be realized through human endeavour and within the time of this world? As was the case with the Millennium, several groups throughout the ages have believed in their own ability to bring about the New Jerusalem on earth. Thus from Joachim of Fiore in the thirteenth century to the Munsterites in the sixteenth century to the Fifth Monarchists in seventeenth-century England to Jonathan Edwards in eighteenth-century America to Marxist philosopher Ernst Bloch in the twentieth century, there is a long tradition of those who have argued either that the New Jerusalem is already here or within touching distance.[6] Such wholesale attempts to realize the New Jerusalem within the confines of time and the 'first earth' have always been rejected by orthodox Christians and, on a straightforward reading of Revelation at least, represent a misinterpretation of the text. Rev. 21 quite clearly conveys the importance of definitive divine action in the realization of the New Jerusalem. In Rev. 21.5 the divine voice proclaims, 'See, *I* am making all things new.'

However, Rowland suggests that there is textual support in Rev. 21 for the idea, held by many Christians, that human agency can still play a part in *contributing* to the 'building of the kingdom', presumably in a metaphorical rather than a literal sense.[7] The fact that the city wall is built on twelve foundations named after the twelve Apostles (Rev. 21.14) suggests that human endeavour lies at the foundation of the city, as does, more obliquely, the references to building and craftsmanship as a whole. Ultimately, though, it seems, based on Rev. 21–2, that the New Jerusalem is more a result of 'eschatological miracle' than any human action. Indeed, as we are told in Rev. 21.1–2, it is something which descends from Heaven, after this Heaven and Earth have passed away. This is a fact that may frustrate and depress, or alternatively relieve, those living in contemporary times, where the scope of human agency, particularly in relation to technology, grows ever wider.

Turning now to the vision itself, John initially hears the voice of the Lord, proclaiming Himself as the Alpha and the Omega, the beginning and the end, who is about to make all things new, and who will make his home among mortals, wiping away every tear from their eyes and indeed banishing Death itself from those who are saved (Rev. 21.1–4). Interestingly, the fact that the sea has passed away with the first Heaven and Earth is highlighted (Rev. 21.1). While this is odd in practical terms (as so many details of the New Jerusalem are), it is symbolically crucial. Throughout Revelation the sea has been linked with threatening presences such as the Sea Beast (see Chapter 6) and the Whore of Babylon (Chapter 7), who both emerge from the sea, that primeval source of creation and destruction. This is the first intimation (of many) that the New Jerusalem is a very different city from Babylon.

If the content is startling, so too is the mode of delivery. This is the first time in Revelation that God himself has spoken directly to John. If the idea of God dwelling amongst mortals is too much to take (hitherto throughout the Bible, even to Abraham and Moses, God's actual presence has always been shielded and he remains a shadowy presence in the Gospels too), this is followed by a salutatory reminder that evildoers will not be allowed entry to the New Jerusalem to enjoy physical proximity to God, but rather will be banished to the eternally burning lake of sulphur of the Last Judgement (Rev. 21.8).

John is then shown the city, as it descends, by an angel, who proclaims the city the 'bride of the Lamb' (cf. Rev. 19). John witnesses all of this from a 'great, high mountain' (Rev. 21.10). So we, the reader, feel as if we are experiencing the New Jerusalem at the same time as John. There are similarities here with Ezekiel, who is also taken to a high mountain 'in visions of God' and shown a vision of an idealized Jerusalem Temple by an angel with a measuring rod (Ezek. 40.2ff.). The main difference in these two visions is the prominent position afforded to the Lamb/Christ in John's vision (Rev. 21.22) and the fact that John's New Jerusalem is open to all, not just to the Jewish people. Further, the New Jerusalem descending from Heaven underlines the idea that this is not something that can be built up by humans (and this surely counts against those throughout history who have believed that they could construct the New Jerusalem for their own times). In contrast to earthly cities, such as Babel, Babylon, Rome, London, New York, and Dubai, which are built from the ground up in a frenzy of toil and capitalist dreams, the heavenly city comes down from above, a gift from God at the time of his choosing. This idea has obvious resonances with the Tower of Babel narrative, where men tried to build a tower to climb up to Heaven (Genesis 11); and this allusion to Genesis paves the way for the Garden of Eden motifs that occur in Rev. 22.

With regard to the artistic history of this revelatory section, it is interesting to note that John's position on the mountain, observing the New Jerusalem as it descends from Heaven, is rarely adhered to. In fact Dürer's ambiguous image of the New Jerusalem/Millennium (discussed in Chapter 8) is one of the only examples of this (Figure 8.8). Here an aged John is depicted viewing the New Jerusalem (or millennial city?) with his accompanying angel from their vantage point at the top of a mountain.

The description of the New Jerusalem given in Rev. 21 has a complex yet crystalline architectural beauty, which has, of course, been picked up by artists through the ages in depictions that range from the comically literal to the impressively symbolic. Rowland emphasizes, against those who would seek 'paradise' in the countryside, that the New Jerusalem is very much a city, an urban environment and not some sort of rural idyll.[8] The description given by John of the city progresses from metaphors and similes about God's glory being like that of precious stones to some extremely precise details and measurements about the layout of the city. It has twelve gates, arranged in threes at each of the four compass points, protected by twelve angels, with the names of the twelve tribes of Israel inscribed on them (Rev. 21.12). This reference to the presence of the twelve tribes of Israel at the end of the world has no doubt contributed to perennial speculation about the remnants of the ten 'lost' tribes of Israel (i.e. those which disappeared from history after the collapse of the biblical northern kingdom in the eighth century BCE), as well as to the more general belief that the end times would see a regathering of the Jews in Jerusalem.[9] Within mainstream biblical interpretation, the twelve gates have usually been taken to refer to the twelve Apostles of the New Testament, and we might also think in this context of the twelve stars that make up the crown of the Woman Clothed with the Sun.

This perfect symmetry is continued in the description of the city itself as a perfect cube of gold (which John has to measure with his gold measuring rod, just as Ezekiel had to), built on foundations of precious stones. The measuring of the city throws up some interpretative problems. The cube itself is said to measure 12,000 stadia, which amounts to about 1,500 miles. The city is therefore on a vast scale: 1,500 miles wide, long, and high. However, the city wall, both literally and symbolically crucial in John's day, is only 144 cubits (approximately 216 feet)! This would render the city's wall comically tiny in relation to the city itself. Most commentators try to smooth this out by arguing that this measurement should be applied to the thickness of the wall and not the height, but perhaps this serves to re-emphasize the idea that the descriptions of the New Jerusalem are supposed to be more metaphorical than literal.[10] This idea is corroborated by the final detail that each of the twelve enormous gates are carved from a single pearl, again a metaphysical impossibility. What we, and the artists who have attempted to visualize the city, are confronted with therefore is an attempt to hint at the incredible, yet ultimately indescribable, grandeur of the New Jerusalem. Strangely, given the level of detail present in the architectural descriptions, the city ends up being mysterious and paradoxical in nature, both a gift and a curse for artists.

The city's mysterious nature is compounded by the fact that in Rev. 21.22–7 we are told that not only is there no Temple in the New Jerusalem, due to the fact that God and the Lamb, who the earthly Temple provided imperfect access to, live there, neither is there any need of the sun or the moon. Once again, God and the Lamb are believed to provide all necessary light. Then, rather abruptly, at the beginning of Rev. 22, in what some commentators have used as evidence of a second 'New Jerusalem source', we are told that through the public square of the city flows a river of the 'water of life, bright as crystal'. The river, which flows from God's throne and the tree of life, which grows next to the river and which produces twelve kinds of fruit (presumably one for every month), and healing leaves, presents another visual challenge.[11] For the tree of life is described in the singular form, but as being present on both sides of the river. Such a tree is impossible to visualize literally, and most depictions of this scene (see, for example, Blake's *River of Life*; Plate 44) tend to depict several fructifying trees to give the impression of abundance. Most commentators have argued that the 'tree of life' is presented in the singular form in order to mirror the 'tree of life' that existed in the Garden of Eden and from which Adam and Eve were forbidden to eat (see Genesis 2.9). In a final reversal of the Eden narrative, where Adam and Eve were shut out of the garden, it is implied in Rev. 22.2 ('the leaves of the tree were meant for the healing of the nations') that humanity, as well as being welcomed back into the garden/New Jerusalem, *can* now also eat from the 'tree of life'. The 'tree of life' of Genesis 2 carried with it the promise of the knowledge of good and evil. The New Jerusalem is not therefore intended as a place of blind faith but one of knowledge and understanding.

In some of the earlier episodes of Revelation, readers may have overlooked the way John is recounting in his visions events that lie in the future, and not things which have happened; here, though, the futurity of what is seen is made very evident, and in a way which ties the end of the text to its beginning. In Rev. 22.8 John reiterates that it is 'I John…the one who heard and saw these things' and at the conclusion of the angelic tour of the city, John attempts for a second time (cf. Rev. 19 at the conclusion of the Babylon vision) to worship the angel, but is rebuffed: 'I am a fellow-servant with you and your comrades the prophets…Worship God' (Rev. 22.9). Finally, in Rev. 22.10 John tells us that he is warned by Jesus himself that what he heard and saw in his vision is about to be realized soon: 'the time is near'. And this is the message which John is to deliver to the churches, as he himself told us in Rev. 1.

Even more emphatically there are dire warnings about the fate of anyone who presumes either to add to the prophecy of the book (plagues will be added to him), or to take away from the prophecy (he will have his share in the tree of life and the holy city taken from him). In a final direct address to the reader, Christ himself speaks once more as Alpha and Omega: 'I am coming soon; my reward is with me, to repay according to everyone's work' (Rev. 22.12).

To conclude, the New Jerusalem, the heavenly city, is presented, throughout Rev. 21 especially, as a city and a garden but also as the Bride of Christ, adorned in jewels and gold, ready for her celestial husband. She is thus the antithesis of Babylon (the earthly city) and of the Whore, and as such has been identified since the earliest commentators with the church and also associated with the Woman Clothed with the Sun/Mary, as the women who gave birth to the enemy of the Dragon (Rev. 12).[12] The problematic aspects, for feminist interpreters, of this identification and subsequent developments of this antithesis between the Whore and the Bride/New Jerusalem, were flagged up in Chapters 5 and 7, which discussed the Woman Clothed with the Sun and the Whore of Babylon. It is easy to see how commentators such as Tina Pippin have dismissed Revelation as irredeemably sexist.[13] Femininity is presented either as whorish, immoral, and dangerous, as in the case of the Whore of Babylon, or as passive and bridal, as something beautiful handed down from Heaven by God, as in the case of the Bride of Rev. 19 or the New Jerusalem of Rev.21. There is no middle ground. While this is hard to dispute, the modern reader can emphasize the urban and architectural aspects of the New Jerusalem over and above the feminine aspects. While the city (as described by John) is not workable in literal terms (given the dimensions and the materials used), John's descriptions synthesize wonder and reality into a powerful symbol that shares much of the form of life of this world but also inspires longing and intrigue in its readers and hearers. This is no doubt why it has proved so fertile a subject matter for the artists who have tried to express its beauty in 'this-worldly' visual media so as to appeal to the senses of human beings as we now exist, while at the same time capturing some of its otherworldly wonder.

## Visualizations of the New Jerusalem

While those who occupy a more radical Christian position and those who are not Christian at all may want to resist an orthodox interpretation of the New Jerusalem as the logical panacea to the devastation and harsh morality of the rest of the text, it is certainly important, in visual terms at least, to explore significant artworks associated with these final chapters of Revelation. If nothing else they represent a powerful and often neglected counter-balance to the better-known images of cosmic destruction that often pervade the mind when Revelation is mentioned. For the pre-moderns, the images of plagues and judgement were but a necessary precursor to the longed-for eternal New Jerusalem that would surely follow. And, whether one can accept such a concept philosophically or not, Rev. 21–2 provides the most complete images and symbols of what is commonly referred to as Heaven within the New Testament.

Having said all this, though, the New Jerusalem, by the very nature of the way it is described in Revelation, presents the visual artist with a number of tough challenges. In the first place, in Rev. 21 it is a city, made of very specific materials and with very detailed, if inconsistent, measurements. In Rev. 22, by contrast, in the preamble particularly, the place is much more like a second Eden, rather what we see in the Van Eycks' *Lamb of God* or even in the middle tier of Botticelli's *Mystic Nativity*. In the medieval treatments this problem was often addressed by depicting the New Jerusalem in three or more separate images, to capture different aspects. The results are often mixed, with the New Jerusalem characteristically depicted in the first instance as a somewhat ramshackle castle descending from the sky. The second image usually shows John measuring the New Jerusalem and the third traditionally focuses on the River of Life and the fructifying trees of Rev. 22. *Trinity* deviates from this schema slightly, following up its first image of the descent of the New Jerusalem with a second, almost bird's eye, image of the city that goes in for architectural precision, in order to present the magnificence if not the precise proportions of the city. Unusually the River of Life appears within this same image. The *Flemish Apocalypse* populates the city with people, in an attempt to capture Rev. 21.24, which tells us that the city is full of people. *Ghent* (the Van Eycks), Blake, and Martin all prioritize the Edenic aspects of the New Jerusalem over the urban, while Beckmann, like the *Flemish Apocalypse*, understands the new relationship between the human and the divine as the essence of the New Jerusalem.

Related to the theme (discussed above) of whether we should understand the New Jerusalem in spiritual more than in physical terms is the question of time. For looking at visualizations of the New Jerusalem also prompts one to ask the question of whether the celestial city exists outside time or inside it. And if it is inside time, is it of the nature of the present world, or does it represent a future we could only imagine? Without prejudging how a given visual representation answers the basic question, it is noteworthy that many of the medieval visualizations see it in terms of cities of their own day, as indeed does Dürer. The Edenic versions (*Ghent*, Blake, Martin) have a more timeless, even mystical quality that may seem to suggest timelessness.

Despite the somewhat comical aspects of some of the medieval visualizations of the New Jerusalem, particularly when they attempt to adhere to the words of the text, they are still important exegetically. For what they are all trying to do is to present to us the moment in which the barriers between the divine and the human are removed (by the descent of the heavenly city). And this sense is often powerfully evoked even in the literalistic versions of the medieval, with their emphasis on the human and architectural detail of the New Jerusalem. From the other side, the Edenic New Jerusalems, even in their idealizations of the theme, with their divinely infused landscapes, still retain a strong human presence and reality. We might then, in summing up the attempts to visualize the New Jerusalem, say that they all offer an insight into the essence of the climax of Revelation, the reconciling descent of the divine into the human and the sweeping up of the human into the divine. And in their honest, if faltering attempts to do this, they can often be more powerfully evocative of the idea than the biblical text itself, let alone commentaries on it. Similarly, the fact that there are certain conflicts and inconsistencies between the images and how they have visualized the climax of Revelation should not be seen as evidence of a certain weakness regarding the capacity of images to interpret a biblical text, but on the contrary, it should be regarded as a strength. For what we have, in the images collected here, is a collection of visualizations which reveal the differing interpretative biases and priorities of their artists and patrons in relation to the New Jerusalem. Viewing them may reveal new emphases to us, the viewer, and viewing them side by side may help to determine in our own minds which aspects of the New Jerusalem are the most important or essential. Just as we may consult a range of commentaries on a biblical text, so we should consult a range of contrasting visual interpretations in order to form our own judgements.

## The New Jerusalem as cathedral

Before we turn to some individual illustrations and paintings, it is worth underlining that for the medieval mind the most powerful physical images of the New Jerusalem are the great churches and cathedrals of the era, starting in the physical Jerusalem itself, with the Church of the Holy Sepulchre. This great and somewhat sprawling edifice was constructed in the twelfth century, after the Crusaders had taken Jerusalem in 1099. There already existed from the fourth century a comparatively small chapel where Christ's tomb was supposed to be, and there was also a chapel on the hill of Golgotha, and another basilica, somewhat ruined, where Helena, Constantine's mother, had found the true cross in 320. These three buildings, marking the spots of Christ's death and resurrection, were all united under one roof in the 1140s, in a huge and magnificently decorated building, which was consecrated in 1149. Given that what had happened in Jerusalem in 33 BCE was the means by which the New Jerusalem had been inaugurated, it was quite natural that the Church of the Holy Sepulchre should itself be thought of as the gate to the New Jerusalem, and a symbol of it, that in entering the church the pilgrim came as close as could be possible in this world to his or her heavenly home.

Not all medieval Christians could make the pilgrimage to Jerusalem, particularly after the successful Islamic reconquest of 1187. But in the shape of the great medieval cathedrals there were plenty of other images of the New Jerusalem to which the faithful could journey. Often, as has been mentioned, they would enter the sacred space through doors dominated by Christ presiding over the Last Judgement, and Mary too, as the mother of Christ and image of the church. Inside the church, the pilgrim would be transported not just by the soaring, uninterrupted height of the pillars and roof, but also by the sense of divine light filtered through the amazing coloured glass which filled so much of the wall area. In the glass he or she would typically see the whole of Salvation History, from the fall of Adam, through the Old Testament patriarchs and prophets, and on to the New, often, as at La Sainte Chapelle in Paris and at York Minister (both referred to in Chapter 7), culminating in a great representation in glass of the Revelation itself. Sermons of the period often made the analogy between the building and the spiritual reality explicit, pointing out for example that just as the mortar in the cathedral held the stones of the building together, so love between the faithful holds the church together. And when in Chaucer's *Canterbury Tales* the pilgrims at last see the cathedral of Canterbury rising in the distance before them, the Parson prays: 'And Iesu, for his grace, wit me sende/ To shewe yow the wey, in this viage,/ Of thilke parfit glorious pilgrimage/ That highte Jerusalem celestial.'—So, may this earthly pilgrimage show you pilgrims the way to the perfect pilgrimage (that through life itself), which culminates in entry to the heavenly Jerusalem.[14]

## Medieval visualizations

The *Trinity Apocalypse* devotes two of its relatively large, sumptuous, and uncluttered images to the New Jerusalem. The first depicts the city coming down from Heaven out of the clouds, whilst John is ordered to write down what he sees into his open book. The second image is perhaps more interesting, combining as it does architectural design with figurative representation (Plate 45). As mentioned above, for the most part the image is conceived from a sort of bird's eye perspective. It clearly depicts the twelve gates of the city, interspersed with walls adorned with multicoloured jewels. The walls of the city are arranged in a perfect square (as in Rev. 21.16) and have an air of architectural symmetry and precision in keeping with the text, although it must be added that there is no allusion made to the vast proportions given in Rev. 21.16. All of this is set against a gold background, supposed to evoke the fact that the New Jerusalem is made of 'pure gold'. Using this much gold leaf would have been expensive and so this image represents a fitting climax to the visual drama of the *Trinity* images.

John and the angel are depicted as almost crouching in worship at the bottom left-hand corner of the image on a grassy knoll, in a direct contravention of Rev. 21.10, which says that they are looking down on the city from a mountain. However, by arranging the composition with John and the angel at the bottom looking up at the New Jerusalem, the artist(s) have successfully emphasized the magnificence and grandeur of the city. In the centre of the city, on the golden streets, sit God and the Lamb in a mandorla. This slightly undercuts the idea that God and the Lamb mingle freely with humans in the New Jerusalem but the fact that the mandorla could not be abandoned even at this final stage shows the strength of this reverential iconographic convention. Next to them is a slightly tangled representation of the River (and trees) of Life. In fact, if one did not know the text fairly well, this would be hard to recognize. Below God and the river is the angel with the gold measuring rod, measuring the city with his head deeply bowed. Although this is not the final image in the *Trinity* series (there is one final image of John worshipping the angel, before Christ), this extremely distinctive image provides a serene yet impressive climax to *Trinity*'s visual narrative.

It is also an important example of how, even within the Anglo-Norman manuscript tradition, of which *Trinity* is a part, different artists/patrons chose to emphasize different aspects of the text. While more conventional iconographic schema such as those found in *Lambeth* and *Angers* (see below) emphasize the dissolution of the barriers between the human and the divine (which lie at the heart of Rev. 21–2), *Trinity* emphasizes the splendour of the New Jerusalem and its divine perfection.

The *Angers* images of the New Jerusalem are less impressive than the *Trinity* image in architectural terms, but interesting in interpretative terms nonetheless, particularly in relation to the development of John's role at this point in the narrative. Throughout the *Angers* images John has watched the action from his shelter at the side of the images. Here, therefore, when presented with the New Jerusalem, here depicted as a rather jumbled-looking medieval castle or small city, which represents the high point not only of the Christian story and of the cosmic future but also of John's own understanding of the visions he has received, John's left foot is poised to leave the shelter and his right hand points forward to the New Jerusalem (Plate 46). In the next image (see Figure 1.4) he is depicted as erroneously kneeling at the feet of the angel with the measuring rod. In the final (remaining) image of the *Angers* series (Plate 47), the New Jerusalem is depicted not as a city but as an Edenesque garden. The River of Life is seen flowing down from God's throne, which, as with the *Trinity* image, is still safely enclosed in a heavenly mandorla. Once again this slightly detracts from the idea of the New Jerusalem as a place where God and the Lamb mingle freely with mortals (Rev. 21.3) but even though this is clearly stated in the text, actually to visualize this may have been considered provocative or even blasphemous. One practically has to wait for Beckmann's twentieth-century image to see this scene visualized in a straightforward way. However, one can perhaps make a case for the idea of boundaries having been broken down being presented in a more subtle way. The presence of John's empty shelter at the left-hand side of the image draws attention to its redundancy. If one takes the shelter as a symbol of the barrier that has hitherto had to exist between God and humankind, between Heaven and Earth, the fact that it now stands empty and discarded while John himself stands almost level with God and the Lamb, linked to them by the River of Life—this may well be taken as visual confirmation that these other barriers have also been dissolved. Thus the superficially naïve images of the *Angers* tapestry can actually be seen to raise some complex theological issues. The sheer size of each tier of the images (around 2 m high) also serves to emphasize the visual drama and the mix of theological complexity and simplicity in the New Jerusalem.

The *Flemish Apocalypse* of *c.*1400 is the last medieval manuscript that we shall consider in this chapter. In an extraordinary oversight by the artist/designer of this manuscript, the New Jerusalem image comes far too early within the image sequence—between Rev. 16 (the Seven Bowls) and Rev. 17 (the Whore of Babylon), to be precise. But as Van der Meer argues, the primary focus of the *Flemish Apocalypse* was clearly not iconographical.[15] Leaving this novelty aside, the New Jerusalem image is interesting chiefly due to the way in which (as in many of the other *Flemish* images) a large chunk of the narrative has been synthesized and compressed into one legible image (Figure 9.1). Albrecht Dürer is often thought of as the first artist to compress the narrative of Revelation successfully in this way, but in fact the artist(s) behind the *Flemish Apocalypse* were well ahead of him.[16]

Once again, as with *Trinity* and *Angers*, God presides over the image from above, which, as before, somewhat contravenes the textual assertion that barriers between Heaven and Earth will be removed via the New Jerusalem. The Lamb is, however, clearly represented at the centre of the city. The Lamb itself is huge in scale (larger than the Apostles who stand at the twelve gates of the city). To God's right the angel with the gold measuring rod looms over the city from above (the attention to detail here is impressive: the angel is said in the text to be one of the seven angels who brought the Seven Bowls/Vials and so this angel is clearly carrying a vial). John meanwhile ascends a hill or mountain on the left of the image in order to have a better view of the city (see Rev. 21.10), although slightly paradoxically his eyes are not on the city but are turned upwards towards God.[17]

There are several unusual details in this image which are worthy of comment. First, in a detail not included in the text, the turrets at the four corners of the city are topped by the Four Living Creatures of the heavenly throne room of Rev. 4–5. This serves to emphasize visually the mingling of Heaven and Earth that is taking place via the New Jerusalem. Secondly, in the foreground of the image an emperor and three kings are exchanging gifts. This is an interpretation of Rev. 21.24 ('The nations will walk by its light, and the kings of the earth will bring their glory into it'). This detail serves to emphasize the 'human' side of the New Jerusalem and the fact that it will be peopled by real, embodied people doing recognizable things.

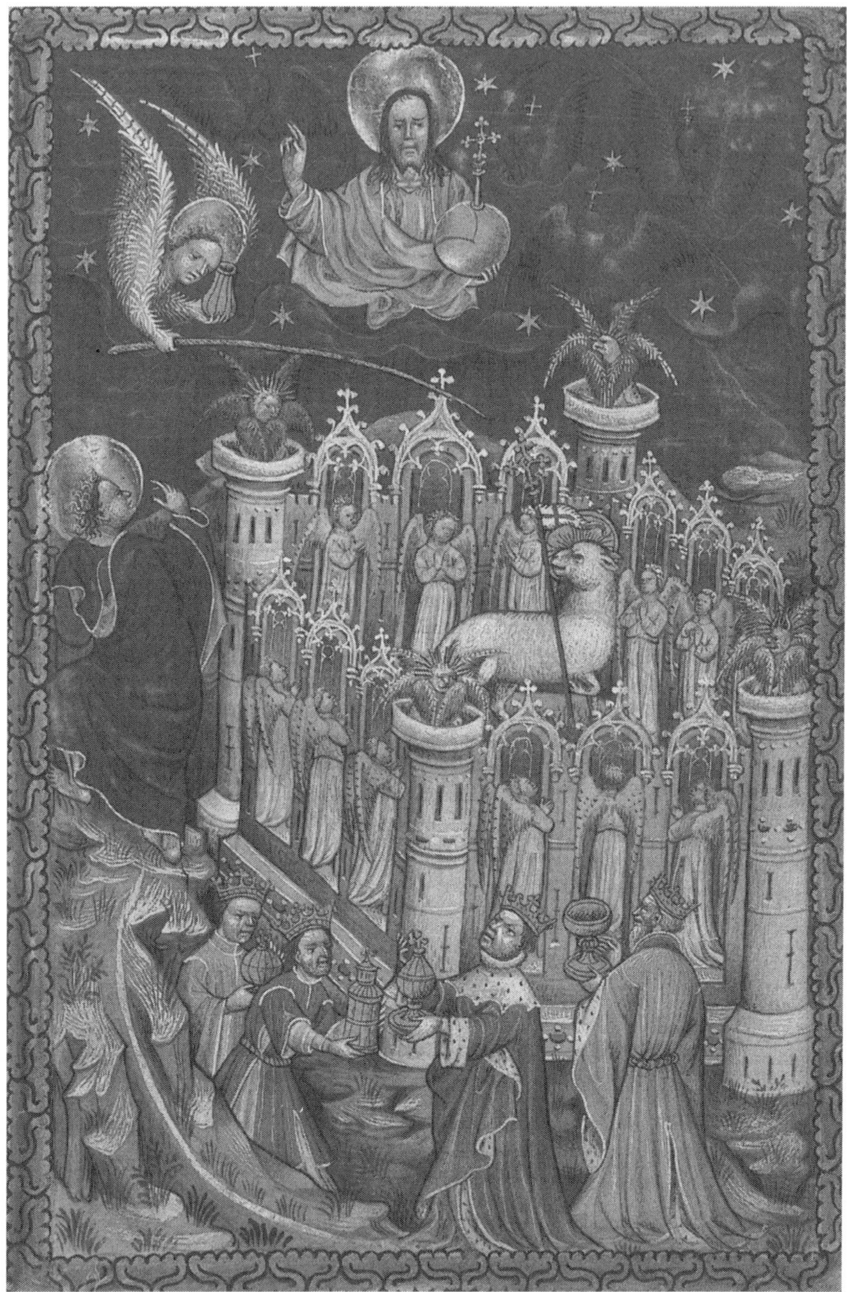

**Figure 9.1.** The *Flemish Apocalypse*, *c.*1400, John is shown the New Jerusalem (Rev. 21), Paris: Bibliothèque Nationale. © BnF

## Early modern visualizations of the New Jerusalem

Thus far we have looked at visualizations that have attempted to present both the urban and the horticultural aspects of the New Jerusalem, usually by depicting it first as a city and second in terms of a river or trees. In the central panel of the *Ghent Altarpiece* of *c.*1432, which was considered in Chapter 2 in relation to the Lamb of God motif, the paradisal, horticultural aspect of the New Jerusalem is forcefully foregrounded (see Figure 2.3). Although real buildings (in idealized form?) from the cities of Utrecht and Ghent can be seen in the background of the central panel, they remain very much on the periphery of the image. It is the garden itself that is the focus, and the water of life (Rev. 22.1–2), here conceived of as a fountain in the foreground of the image, provides one of the panel's focal points (along with the Lamb and the Holy Spirit/dove that also sit on the vertical axis). This helps to bring out the idea of the New Jerusalem as a second Eden, an interpretative emphasis that is reinforced by the fact that the altarpiece (which is comprised of twenty-four panels in total) is enclosed on either side by life-sized panels of Adam and Eve. These rather serene figures are themselves topped with grisaille scenes of Cain killing Abel, a reminder of the sin that stemmed from Adam and Eve's decisions in the Garden. (See Plate 1 for a reproduction of the whole altarpiece.)

However, even the casual viewer will note that there is more going on in the central panel than is described in Rev. 21–2. As flagged up in Chapter 2, this ambitious altarpiece is a visual synthesis of the Bible from Genesis to Revelation. More specifically it is a visualization of the concept of Salvation History, which Christians perceive as running through the Bible. Salvation History is, in short, the idea that everything that has happened within human history is part of God's ultimate plan for the salvation of the human race. This altarpiece thus focuses on what might be seen as the beginning (Genesis), middle (the Annunciation of Christ's birth as described in the Gospels), and end (Revelation) of this narrative. The outer panels are mainly devoted to the Annunciation, while the inner panels are arranged into a heavenly upper tier (featuring God/Christ, Mary, and John the Baptist) and an (idealized) earthly lower tier.[18] The aforementioned Adam and Eve stand at the edges of the upper tier, perhaps a sign of their ultimate redemption within this salvation schema. The central panel, which sits in the lower tier, brings together elements of Revelation 5, 7, 14, 21, and 22, the end of the Christian salvation narrative. Rev. 7 and 14, with their descriptions of gatherings of martyrs and of the 'saved' in idealized settings, prefigure the New Jerusalem, while Rev. 5

focuses on the Lamb/Christ whose existence will facilitate the bringing about of the New Jerusalem according to Christian doctrine.

Thus in the central panel four large groups of martyrs and saints process towards the Lamb from the four corners of the panel/Earth. These include female martyrs (in the top right-hand corner), confessor saints, Old Testament patriarchs and pious pagans, Apostles, and popes (those wearing red robes are martyrs). On the outer panels of the lower tier more groups of worshippers process towards the Lamb (these are divided into knights, judges, hermits, and pilgrims).

As lush and detailed as the foliage and greenery of the central panel is, therefore, it is, very unusually, the characters populating this New Jerusalem that capture both the eye and the imagination. The New Jerusalem is here being presented not foremost as a bejewelled and golden city beyond the realms of human imagination (although, in a nod to Rev. 21.19–21, there are jewels carefully scattered around the fountain), but rather as spiritual place with foundations based in the sacrifices and faith shown by its human inhabitants. By placing the (rather small and apparently insignificant) Lamb at the centre of two diagonal axes, the Van Eycks have managed to evoke a sense of movement towards him that conveys the sense that these human pilgrims will continue to arrive in the New Jerusalem indefinitely, the mythical garden presumably expanding to accommodate them. This is therefore not a static event, just as the altarpiece itself would not have remained static but would have been opened and closed in different formations on different feast days.[19]

Finally, and in keeping with the spirit of this interpretation, there is some evidence to suggest that this central panel is not a vision of the New Jerusalem as it will be, but merely a foreshadowing of the real thing. The top-heavy upper tier, which houses God/Christ, Mary, and John the Baptist, almost seems to be crushing the central and lower tier, leading one to question whether this isn't the real New Jerusalem descending from the sky (cf. Rev. 21.2), ready to replace forever the earthly vision of paradise evoked in the central panel. The sophistication inherent in such a visualization marks the Van Eyck altarpiece out as something quite unique within its late medieval/early modern context.


## Eighteenth- and nineteenth-century visualizations

We turn now from the fifteenth century to the nineteenth. That is not to say that there are not images of the New Jerusalem from the intervening years (of course there are), but in the interests of both economy and contrast, it is important to end this chapter with a survey of some images of the New Jerusalem that form a complete contrast with the medieval and early modern examples discussed thus far. From the intervening years clearly Dürer's visualization of the New Jerusalem is noteworthy but, as has been alluded to above, it is ambiguous in that one is unclear as to whether this is a vision of the Millennium or of the New Jerusalem (see Figure 8.8). What is interesting is the fact that, in contrast to his other images of the Apocalypse, where John appears as a young man, in this image he is stooped and haggard, as if worn out by the visionary journey and ready to shake off his mortal body.

William Blake's New Jerusalem (*c*.1805), or *River of Life*, to give it its proper name, is ambiguous for different reasons (see Plate 44). On the face of it, this could be interpreted as a fairly literal visualization of Rev. 22.1–2, which, as discussed above, speaks no longer of the details of the gilded city but of a River of Life flowing from God's throne through a street of the city and enclosed by the fructifying tree of life.[20] We may assume that the sun in the background, enclosed by angels, is 'God's throne', although the river is flowing towards it, rather than from it. Blake certainly saw the sun as a signifier of the divine.[21] The river itself, looking as if it is about to burst its banks, flows through a city adorned with classical buildings. Fructifying trees bend lavishly over the river, in a commonsense circumvention of the notion that one tree of life could straddle both sides of the river (see Rev. 22.2). The overall impression is one of space and light, which, as Rowland points out, contrasts with Blake's own London (Babylon), which was very dark and cramped.[22] What is difficult to pinpoint with any certainty is the identity of the figures in this watercolour. As Bindman suggests, the androgynous figure dressed in white and swimming with his back to us with two children in the middle of the river may be Jesus but this cannot be certain.[23] Similarly, the pointing angel swooping down over the river could be the angel sent by Jesus to the churches in Rev. 22.16. The other figures cannot be identified directly with any mentioned in Rev. 21–2 and it is unclear whether any are supposed to be identified with John. Particularly strange is the woman with the knife or bowl in the foreground of the image.

Two further points are worthy of note. First, in contrast to Blake's other visualizations of Revelation, there is no disparity in size between the angelic/ divine and 'human' figures. This surely signifies the overcoming of the barrier between the divine and earthly realms that the New Jerusalem itself represents. Humans, however, remain human and have not been transfigured into angelic beings in Blake's vision. The 'human' figures appear willowy compared to the muscular angel, the very image of bodily perfection, and on the left a female figure reaches for the fruit of the tree, presumably with the intention of eating it. There are also three children clearly visible, and although it is possible that they died as children and have therefore been received into the New Jerusalem as children, there is also, on the left-hand side, a mother nursing a very small baby. This raises the interesting question of whether people continue to procreate in the New Jerusalem or whether this baby too died as an infant (which would not of course have been uncommon in Blake's London). Whatever the intricacies of the details, it is clear that Blake imagined the New Jerusalem as a fully human experience and none the worse for it.

Blake's image can usefully be contrasted with John Martin's New Jerusalem canvas of 1851–3 entitled *The Plains of Heaven* (Plate 48). As mentioned in Chapter 8, Martin undertook a triptych of canvasses of Revelation, large in both scale and ambition. While the New Jerusalem/heavenly throne room hovers tantalizingly over his *Last Judgement* canvas, bathed in white light in order to form a contrast with the gloom and fiery reds below, in *The Plains of Heaven* it takes centre stage. The great and the good who were gathering on the left of the *Last Judgement* (as opposed to the damned who were being pulled into the ravine in the centre of the piece) and who included such luminaries as Dante, Luther, Shakespeare, Dürer, Newton, Galileo, and Washington, as well as some 'Holy and Virtuous Women' (Martin included a key diagram of the figures), have been transposed to the centre of the *Plains of Heaven*.[24] Here, attired in white and themselves resembling fluffy clouds, these luminaries assemble in the centre of the canvas but are perhaps intentionally dwarfed by the vast and paradisal landscape in which they have been placed. These sweeping plains, valleys, mountains, and clear waters, an idealized version of Martin's beloved Tyne Valley, are the antithesis of the industrial landscape that symbolized Hell in *The Last Judgement*.[25]

Feaver writes interestingly on how Martin synthesized several other 'heavenly' landscapes from earlier works (such as *The Celestial City* and his *Paradise Lost* illustrations) to create this 'ultimate' composition. Thus for Martin, like John, it seems that the New Jerusalem, envisaged here as the ultimate romantic English landscape, marks something of a career epitome. As evocative as this image is (and who wouldn't want to spend eternity here, in this English Xanadu?) it perhaps fails to capture some of the more important elements of the New Jerusalem. As stressed above, the communal, urban aspect of the New Jerusalem seems very important in the descriptions given in Rev. 21–2. Martin's vision is singularly rural, a paradisal wilderness into which the great and the good have been inserted and marooned. Similarly, unless nature is the personification of the divine, it is difficult to see how God can be viewed as walking among his people (Rev. 21.3) in this image. Indeed, the grandeur of the environment may seem, paradoxically, to imply the continued existence of a Creator god who, even at the moment of reconciliation, remains aloof from his people.

## Twentieth- and twenty-first-century visualizations

Such continued separation (between the human and the divine) is comprehensively overturned in Max Beckmann's remarkable visualization of Rev. 21.4 dating from some ninety years later (Figure 9.2). As discussed in Chapter 2, Beckmann had a troubled relationship with his Christian faith following his experiences in the First World War. Part of a series of coloured lithographs of the Apocalypse dating from 1943 (when he was living in exile in Amsterdam), a winged figure is depicted by Beckmann dressed in a golden robe wiping away the tears from a squat, human figure lying on a table (who may be intended to be Beckmann himself). Through a circular window, which resembles a port hole and which is decorated with the colours of the rainbow, lies what one presumes to be the new Heaven and the new Earth (Rev. 21.1), here represented just as the river (sea?) of life and not as a city. The fact that one has to gaze through the rainbow port hole to glimpse the New Jerusalem is fascinating and reminds one of Memling's Apocalypse altarpiece of 1474–9, which depicts the heavenly throne room as existing in a circular rainbow resembling an eyeball. It has been argued that this visualization implies that the heavenly throne room (described in Rev. 4.3 as being enclosed in a rainbow) is akin to the all-seeing divine eye.[26] Thus, in this image, if it is Memling who is being evoked here, the viewer, like John, is in the privileged position of seeing the future through the divine eye, as it were.

However, this theological intrigue plays second string to the central image, which would surely have resonated with viewers as somewhat strange, shocking even, in the 1940s. The concept of visualizing God/Christ himself wiping the tears from human eyes is not without artistic precedent

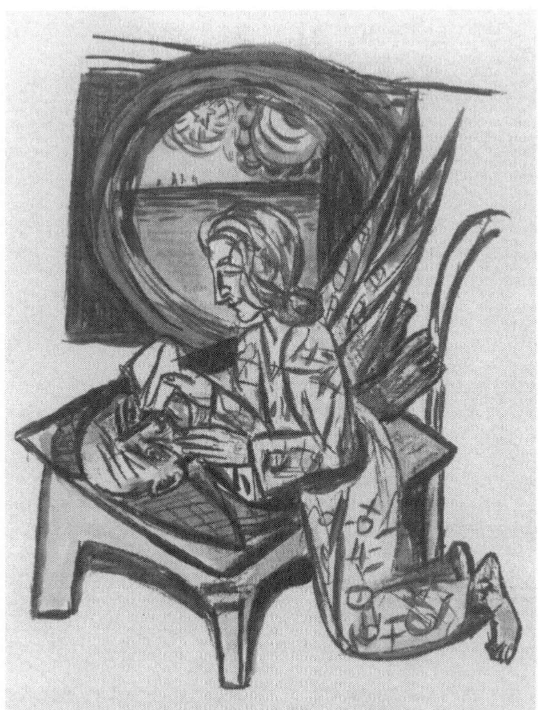

Figure 9.2. Max Beckmann, 'And God shall wipe away all tears' (Rev. 21. 4), 1943, from *The Apocalypse*, Washington, DC, National Gallery of Art. © Washington, National Gallery of Art, Bequest of Mrs Mathilde Q. Beckmann

but it is rare. Giovanni di Paolo's illustrated fifteenth-century antiphonal depicts 'God wiping away the tears of the faithful', for example.[27] However, this is such an intimate image, and the divine figure (perhaps God/Christ or perhaps an angel) so human (apart from the wings, of course), that one cannot help being affected by the image. This New Jerusalem is a place of consolation built on relationships and not monumental landscapes such as in Martin's *Plains of Heaven*.

It is nevertheless the monumental visions of the New Jerusalem that capture the public imagination. Thus contemporary British–Chinese artist Gordon Cheung's *Rivers of Bliss* of 2007, the last image of the New Jerusalem that we will consider, is immediately recognizable as an image of paradise (Plate 49). Heavily influenced by John Martin, this large canvas also explores the impact of new technology, in this case computer technology and capitalism, as the foundation of paradise.[28] As in Martin's *Last Judgement*, Cheung's

*Rivers of Bliss* (the River of Life of Rev. 22.1?) emerge at the forefront of the image while the towers of capitalism or of technology (we are not sure), evoked here by skyscraper montages of pages from the *Financial Times*, are consumed by fire in the background. A lone figure watches from a mountain top (a latterday John?) as the rivers of bliss are protected by a rainbow. As in Martin's *Plains of Heaven* this seems a lonely and windswept New Jerusalem and the fact that the rivers of bliss are also made out of datascapes of pages from the *Financial Times* markets pages would seem to indicate that the binary clarity found in Martin's work does not hold here. Cheung himself has said that a key theme in his work is the oscillation between utopia and dystopia perceived in reactions to technological advancement, and that is seemingly what we are confronted with here: a messy, ambiguous New Jerusalem for the twenty-first century, for a generation that cannot decide whether technology is the Lamb or the Beast.[29]

# Conclusion

In the preceding survey of a range of images of the New Jerusalem, several themes have emerged. The medieval images on the whole depict the New Jerusalem first as a city and then as a second Eden complete with the River of Life and the 'tree of life'. The New Jerusalem itself is normally unremarkable, owing in part to its unvisualizable quality, as described in the text, and also to the artistic limitations of the artists involved. However, what comes through in these images, and in *Angers* in particular, is John's emphatic reaction to seeing the New Jerusalem for the first time. He leaves the safety of his shelter and falls (misguidedly) at the angel's feet, secure in the knowledge that he has reached the climax of his visionary journey and knowledge, before finally ascending via the River of Life to the divine throne, a move that symbolizes the overcoming of the barriers between the human and the divine. As we move into the early modern era, John's importance overall and particularly in relation to the New Jerusalem diminishes. Thus in the *Ghent Altarpiece* (central panel) the focus is on the Lamb of God and the famous inhabitants of the New Jerusalem, never mind the fact that some of them may, with hindsight, actually be burning eternally in the lake of fire and sulphur!

The more modern evocations of the New Jerusalem discussed above have imagined it either as sweeping, even intimidating, landscapes (Martin and Cheung), as watery cities (Blake), or as a place founded primarily on intimate relationships (Beckmann). All of the last four have their merits and as visions of paradise will resonate differently with different viewers. All have, however, moved away from the medieval tendency to attempt to visualize all the different aspects of the New Jerusalem. To be sure they were working with different media to the episodic medieval book illustration style (not to mention a very different artistic mindset), but there is in these more recent works a tacit acceptance that the New Jerusalem cannot and perhaps should not be visualized literally as described in Revelation. John's language was but an evocation of the most splendid city available to his own first-century imagination, but, as discussed at length above, the details render it completely unworkable as an actual city without some serious textual manipulation. Thus the New Jerusalem of Revelation is John's metaphorical paradise, and not an earthly city at all. As such it provides a powerful impetus to artists seeking to evoke that wonderful-sounding city. In doing so the artist must bring his or her own rationality and imagination to the task. In grappling with the problems inherent in depicting something impossible in detail and which cannot by its nature be an earthly city or Eden, we have seen a number of different strategies. Nevertheless, through these differences of approach and emphasis, many of the artistic treatments powerfully evoke the key message of divine–human reconciliation.

# 10

# The Apocalypse in the Twentieth and Twenty-First Centuries

## A Survey of Different Approaches to Revelation in the Arts and Popular Culture

In a classic Simpsons episode on Bible stories, when faced with fiery Armageddon, we see Marge exclaiming, 'Oh No! It's the Apocalypse. Bart, are you wearing clean underwear?', Bart replying, 'Not any more', while Lisa exclaims, 'It's the rapture, and I never knew true love.' Homer meanwhile reflects, 'I never used those pizza coupons …'.[1] Since the series began in 1989, The Simpsons has cast its irreverent brand of humour over almost every area of contemporary American life. It is therefore revealing that in this episode the family is presented as being completely familiar with the concept of the apocalypse as well as with that of the Rapture (more on which below). Like those Americans interviewed by *Time Magazine* in 2002, 59 per cent of whom declared that they believed the events of Revelation would come true, for Homer, Marge, et al., the apocalypse is not an abstract, outmoded concept but a real possibility. Perhaps in response to such surveys, Leonard Sweet has argued that beliefs about the apocalypse are 'even more than baseball, America's favourite pastime'.[2] What exactly they, and others in the twentieth and twenty-first centuries, actually understand by the term is the subject of this final chapter.

## Revelation and the apocalypse in the secular West

As has become clear throughout this book, the term apocalypse did not have a universally agreed meaning prior to the twentieth century—far from it. However, up until the twentieth century, the word *was* closely linked with Revelation, which purports to 'unveil' (see the literal Greek translation of the word ἀποκάλυψις, meaning an 'unveiling' or 'revealing') the truth about the world to its audience. As we have seen throughout the preceding chapters, this book presents us with a dichotomy between those who 'follow the Beast' (Rev. 13) and love worldly things, and those who follow Christ. Despite the horrific visions of punishment (plagues, earthquakes, etc.) which Revelation is well known for, the text also offers a redemptive vision of the future in which a paradisal New Jerusalem is ultimately established (Rev. 21–2). Thus, although complex, this is in many ways intended to be a reassuring, and resolutely Christian, vision of the future.

In the twentieth century this redemptive, more positive aspect of the term apocalypse has largely fallen away. In the secular Western consciousness, which can be linked with the advent of Western modernity more generally, which began around the time of the American and French Revolutions, it has become synonymous with the 'end times' and with the dark catastrophes associated with those events.[3] These events are strictly covered by the term eschatology (literally, 'things concerning the end'). Thus, in the dominant Western cultural imagination, the terms apocalypse and eschatology have become conflated. Of course, the growth of secularization in Western Europe and some sections of America and of this secular understanding of the apocalypse and apocalyptic does not imply either that there are not still strong religious voices or that other understandings of apocalyptic do not still exist. As we shall see, certain sections of the evangelical community in America in particular have a developed and unique understanding of Revelation, which has found expression in, among other examples, the hugely popular series of books and films known as the *Left Behind* series.[4] American evangelicals (not of course a homogenous group but one with which millions self-identify) are also increasingly using secular media (e.g. film, radio, social media) to convey their views on Revelation and the end times (among other things), which enables some intersection, if not dialogue exactly, between the secular and the evangelical positions. What follows in the first part of this chapter is therefore an overview of the dominant secular understanding of Revelation and the apocalypse in our own times. Religious understandings of Revelation and the apocalypse, and the *Left Behind* series in particular, will be returned to below.

Seemingly lost for any other explanation, the front page of the *Daily Mail* on 12 September 2001 simply carried a photograph of the burning Twin

Towers with the word 'Apocalypse' superimposed over the top. In this media context, the word has strict connotations only of large-scale destruction and annihilation, as well perhaps as the ushering in of a darker age. The destruction of the Twin Towers is presented here as gratuitous and lacking in coherent reason, whereas, as we have seen, the destruction in Revelation is always viewed, from John's privileged position, as part of a wider plan. As we saw in Chapter 3 on the Four Horsemen of the Apocalypse, there is also a long history of themes from Revelation being taken out of context in order to be used in political satire. There, we looked at some political cartoons which made their political points via various visual representations of the well-known figures of the Four Horsemen. Their mere presence in a political cartoon has instant connotations of impending disaster, whether this is intended to be taken in a serious way, in the case of the *Express* cartoon satirizing the Nazis in 1943 (see Figure 3.10) or in a more flippant way in the case of the cartoons satirizing contemporary American life from the turn of the century (see Figure 3.1).

In recent times in particular, in light of the financial crisis that has gripped the world since 2008, as well as the increasing preoccupation with matters to do with the climate, apocalyptic references have quickened. Thus it is no surprise to find that a serious article on the US debt ceiling and credit limit that appeared in the *Guardian* in summer 2011 by Gary Younge began with a discussion of American apocalyptic beliefs, including the fact that President Obama himself had talked of 'averting Armageddon' with reference to the financial crisis.[5] As flagged up in Chapter 8, this is but one example of how terms lifted from Revelation have become a convenient journalistic shorthand for summing up the threat to the Earth posed by climate change, as well as for discussing the threat posed by nuclear weapons and their possession by states such as Iran and North Korea. The term Armageddon enjoys particularly frequent usage, so much so that in May 2010 the satirical online newspaper *The Onion* was able to run a video piece entitled 'Christian groups: Biblical Armageddon must be taught alongside global warming'.[6] By contrast, in 2013 the economist and green campaigner Andrew Simms published a book entitled *Cancel the Apocalypse: The New Path to Prosperity*, in which he argued that the whole British economy should be run with renewable energy.[7] Thus apocalyptic terms and references have journalistic currency at all ends of the political and religious spectrum.

And not only in dealing with weighty issues. *Guardian* columnist Marina Hyde has managed to work in references to the apocalypse into satirical pieces on figures as diverse as Mel Gibson, Ashton Kutcher, Joan Collins, and even the 2022 football world cup.[8] The piece on Kutcher refers interestingly not to any event described in Revelation but to the Mayan apocalypse, which was rumoured to take place in 2012, based on the fact that the ancient Mayan calendar ends in that year. Some of the popular references to the apocalypse that follow below involve a conflation of material in Revelation with Mayan predictions (cf. in particular the film *2012*). In 2011 Hyde's preoccupation with matters apocalyptic even earned her the title of 'fifth horsewoman of the apocalypse' in *Paper Monitor*, the BBC's trade publication.

Nor have other media, and particularly the blogosphere, the Twittersphere, social networking sites such as Facebook, and online petition sites like Avaaz, been blind to the enduring appeal of apocalyptic speculation in their quest to increase web traffic. Thus Facebook has many user-led pages devoted to apocalyptic themes, some serious and some tongue in cheek, such as, 'If Sarah Palin wins in 2012, it will be the end of the world!!!!!' or 'I Will Survive 2012'. More specific are pages such as 'The Four Horsemen of the Apocalypse in popular culture'. Similarly, the Twittersphere was set alight in 2011 by a Christian pastor and numerologist from America called Harold Camping who predicted, based on biblical evidence from Daniel 12.9 and Rev. 22.10 (as well as other passages from 1 Peter and Ephesians), that the Rapture would take place on 21 May 2011, followed by the first day of judgement for all those 'left behind', and that the world would end completely on 21 October 2011. As discussed in the Introduction to this book, the Rapture is an event anticipated by certain groups of American Christians, loosely based on 1 Thessalonians 4.16–17 ('For the Lord himself... with the sound of God's trumpet, will descend from Heaven and the dead in Christ will rise first'), in which the most faithful Christians will be taken up into Heaven prior to a period of judgement (known as the Tribulation) for all those 'left behind', which will then be followed by Armageddon, the Millennium, the second final battle, the Last Judgement, and the New Jerusalem.[9] This therefore interjects another event into the already complex sequence of events which constitutes the Christian understanding of the end of the world. Camping's predictions were backed by the Family Radio Worldwide, a Christian radio corporation which owns 150 radio stations in the United States and which Camping helped to set up in the 1960s. They spent $100 million on the information campaign for Camping's 2011 predictions. While some Christians took the predictions seriously, others on the Twittersphere were more circumspect, with this tweet from British physicist Brian Cox being typical: 'I think we should all pretend the #rapture is happening so that when Harold Camping gets left behind later today he'll be livid.'

This tweet, as well as being an example of dry, apocalyptic-based humour, refers to an important current within contemporary dialogue about the end of the world. While those without a particular religious faith may fear the notion of a conventional 'apocalypse' (such as a nuclear holocaust, for instance), evangelical and fundamentalist Christians (as well as Muslims) have a more complex relationship with the idea. While frightening on many levels, in another way they long for the apocalypse to come as it will usher in the New Jerusalem or paradisal age, in which the perceived wrongs of this world will be redressed. This position, itself a fundamental part of the evangelical imaginary, can lead to a rather strange relationship with the extreme violence depicted in Revelation itself and with which many have come to be familiar (e.g. the Four Horsemen of the Apocalypse and their woes of war, famine, pestilence, and death or the Beast of Rev. 13 who is permitted to wage war upon the earth for a set time), a theme that will be explored further below.

Returning now to the secular media, in February 2014 the online petition site Avaaz sent its followers an email entitled 'Internet Apocalypse' asking them to help to keep the internet 'democratic and free' (cf. 'net neutrality') by not allowing the US government and the EU to give faster content rights to the highest bidders (i.e. big corporations). Their use of the word 'apocalypse' in the subject line of the email gives their presentation of what might otherwise seem an issue of at most moderate importance an air of desperate urgency, with potential catastrophe in the wings.

Neither is this popular apocalyptic fervour limited to the print and online media. References also abound in popular music, film, theatre, art exhibitions, and even video games. Musical references are to be found mostly in the world of Heavy Metal, Black Metal, and Goth Rock. These genres of music tend to be anarchic in tone and have a fascination with violence and the extremities of human experience. Such music might be described as consisting of a 'roaring cacophony of mind bending dimensions', as Wikipedia has it. This fascination with evoking extreme experiences for the listener has clear similarities with both Revelation itself and with many of the artists who have attempted to evoke this text. Thus it is no surprise that the band Metallica have in their catalogue both a song called 'The Four Horsemen' (1983) and 'My Apocalypse' (2008). Another Heavy Metal group, set up as a tribute to Metallica, even called themselves 'Apocalyptica'. There is also a German Metal band called Die Apokalyptischen Reiter (The Apocalyptic Riders). The lyrics of these groups' songs reveal, however, only a tangential connection with Revelation itself. Metallica's 'My Apocalypse', for example, focuses on Hell and the end of the world but the connections go no deeper than that. It seems, then, that while a certain use of apocalyptic imagery, relating specifically to nihilism and Hell, has a strong presence in Heavy Metal and related genres, it is not directly related to Revelation itself. Rather, in this musical genre the term has taken on a new life and a darker but more generalized meaning.

More recently Revelation, and in particular the Four Horsemen, have inspired music by Muse, Coldplay, and even the rapper Canibus, among many others. The band Muse released an album called Black Holes and Revelations (2006). The album, which has a futuristic sound and is in part a political critique of global politics, has a distinctive album cover featuring the Four Horsemen sitting around a table on Mars. Their horses, depicted as plastic toy horses, have been placed on the table in front of them, supposedly representing how their respective afflictions (War, Famine, Pestilence, and Death) have far eclipsed the horses in size. Such imagery has connotations of a world out of control, which clearly has connections to Revelation if only in the vaguest of terms. It is difficult to tell whether the cover designer thought in this way, but the size of their afflictions points to a limited, fallible God who could not control what he had unleashed on the world. It thus represents a radical recasting of Revelation, in which God does not remain in control all the time.

Coldplay's Viva la Vida or Death and All His Friends (2008) is an album with a revolutionary theme whose title and last line 'I don't want to follow Death and all of his friends' represents an oblique reference to the Fourth Rider of Rev. 6.2–8, Death, who is followed by Hades, which could encompass the entire population of Hell, and had often been pictured in this way (see Figure 3.4, for example.) Finally Canibus, the Jamaican-American rapper, formed a group called The HRSMN in 2000 with three other rappers. In their songs each member of the group takes on the characteristics of the four different Horsemen. Thus many areas of popular music, from rock to rap, have drawn inspiration from the ancient figures of the Four Horsemen, even if their original meaning has been left behind or distorted.

Following Bergman's *The Seventh Seal* (1957), which centres around two lines from Revelation about a heavenly silence that follows the opening of the Seventh Seal in Rev. 8.1 and 8.6 (see section '*The Seventh Seal*' for more on this), and Francis Ford Coppola's re-visioning of Joseph Conrad's *Heart of Darkness*, *Apocalypse Now* (1979), both of which will be discussed below), the film world has continued to be preoccupied with vague concepts of apocalypticism. Many disaster movies centre around the idea that the world has a predetermined end point that will be preceded by untold disasters, ranging from floods, to ice ages, to catastrophic explosions, to alien invasions against which a group of brave heroes fight on against the odds. *Independence Day* is perhaps the most famous of these offerings, whilst more recently the block-buster *2012* (Roland Emmerich, 2009) can be seen as a response to the afore-mentioned Mayan apocalypse of 2012. Both these films centre around the idea of a righteous few either fighting against malign alien forces or freakish natural disasters in a post-apocalyptic landscape. (See also *28 Days Later* (2002), *28 Weeks Later* (2007), *The Day After Tomorrow* (2004), and *Children of Men* (2006) for confirmation that we are here dealing with a trend.) In this vague sense these films mirror one of the central themes of Revelation, that of a smaller group of the righteous martyrs being separated off from the unrepentant masses (not unlike the way some evangelical Christians think of those 'left behind' after the Rapture, as we will see). At the art house end of the spectrum, Lars von Trier's film *Melancholia* (2011) explores the concept of depression against the backdrop of an impending apocalypse in which the Earth will be destroyed by a rogue planet named Melancholia. In this film von Trier examines the different reactions of the main characters to their impending and certain deaths. The destruction of each main character is shown at the beginning of the film, in order to exorcise the sense of suspense associated with conventional disaster films and turn the focus on their contrasting responses. At the more light-hearted end of the spectrum are *Seeking a Friend for the End of the World* (2012) and *This is the End* (2013). Both these films centre on the notion of the Earth teetering on the edge of catastrophe, but instead of using this as a platform for the stereotypical hero or disaster movie conforming to Todorov's well-worn narrative structure of equilibrium–conflict–restoration, the apocalypse is used either as a catalyst for seeking more meaningful relationships or (in *This is the End*) as a vehicle for an exploration of post-apocalyptic behaviour via an ensemble of famous comedians (including Jay Baruchel and Seth Rogen) playing themselves.[10] The attention to certain details from Revelation in *This is the End* (such as the earthquake of Rev. 6 and the presence of winged demons, plus the fascination with the concept of the Rapture, Baruchel and Rogen both being raptured at the end) is the more striking considering that it was written and directed by two Jewish artists, Rogen himself and Evan Goldberg. By way of contrast, a purely comedic response to Revelation is found in the theatrical offering of a company called Barbershopera. In *Apocalypse No!*, which toured the UK in 2010–11, 'God summons four dastardly horsemen to unleash total destruction on the world, but unfortunately Beth turns up instead of Death', the Fourth Horseman in Revelation. The ensuing plot turns on the humour that this error engenders. All of these dramatizations, whether comedic or serious, rely on some basic cultural understanding of the apocalypse and its associated ideas and images. Most do envisage a post-apocalyptic reality but they are, on the whole, no more hopeful than the journalistic understandings of the apocalypse surveyed above. Like the journalistic examples, most of these cinematic and theatrical examples present the post-apocalyptic reality that emerges as unremittingly bleak and inferior to what has come before. Thus, while they may echo some of the main themes from Revelation in a general sense, they fail to engage with its essential core in any meaningful way (and neither was that their intention, of course). They may therefore be referred to as examples of decontextualized interpretations of Revelation.

Successful computer games, like Heavy Metal music, often rely on their ability to evoke a violent netherworld into which gamers can immerse themselves. Indeed, so great is the appeal of the end of the world that in October 2010 the *Guardian* actually published a list of the 'Ten greatest post-apocalyptic video games of all time'. As was the case with popular music, the most popular theme to be appropriated by the world of gaming is that of the Four Horsemen of the Apocalypse (see Chapter 3). They appear in one guise or another in no less than twenty-five current video games. In the game City of Heroes, for instance, the player must defeat the Four Riders, who are named as War, Famine, Pestilence, and Death respectively and who represent the most fearsome warriors of the Rikti race of aliens who the player is attempting to defeat overall. The 1998 Sony Playstation game, which was called Apocalypse, stars Bruce Willis as Trey Kincaid, who has to defeat the evil Reverend and his band of soldiers who include the Four Horsemen. In 2002 the gaming company 3DO announced plans for a mainstream game actually called The Four Horsemen of the Apocalypse, focused on a set of characters who had been 'left behind' after the Rapture. They would have to fight against characters from Revelation, such as the Four Horsemen of the Apocalypse (Rev. 6.2–8) and Abaddon, the angel from the bottomless pit (Rev. 9.11). It was originally destined to be released on PC, PS2, Gamecube, and Xbox, but by 2004 3DO had gone bankrupt and the game was never made. It nevertheless stands as testament to the ongoing appeal of some of Revelation's characters, an appeal which extended to a desire to see them utilized in an apparently unconnected setting and genre.

More recently, Gears of War (made for Xbox in 2006) features a Locust Horde who arrive on Emergence or 'E-Day' on the planet Sera and threaten to pull any human victims they can get their hands on to their death in their underground caverns. Gameplay focuses on the Delta Squad who are the only ones that can save the remaining human inhabitants of Sera. The link to the locust army and their leader Abaddon who emerge, like the Locust Horde of Gears of War, from the 'bottomless pit' in Rev. 9.1–11 seems unmistakable. As Rosen argues, Darksiders (also made for Xbox in 2010) has taken inspiration from Revelation in an even more focused way. In this game, originally subtitled The Wrath of War, the player takes control of War, the fourth Horseman of the Apocalypse, whose main weapon is a scythe (in line with conventional iconography of this figure).[11] War's role is to wrestle control of the Earth back from bad angels Abaddon and Azreal, who have brought about the apocalypse prematurely and allowed the forces of Hell to overtake the Earth. Although perhaps lacking in theological depth, it is certainly a strange fact that some of the most popular video games in existence have been inspired by and conform to the conventions of Christian apocalyptic. The fact that the same games are often cited following shootings by young people in the USA in particular is symptomatic of a moral panic that has failed to engage with the content of its polemical targets.

The millennium gave rise to two important London exhibitions on Revelation and its far-reaching artistic and cultural influence: The Apocalypse and the Shape of Things to Come at the British Museum and The Apocalypse: Beauty and Horror in Contemporary Art at the Royal Academy. More recently there were the Tate's successful Gothic Nightmares (2006) and John Martin: Apocalypse (2011–12). These exhibitions were all indebted to the continuing allure of the apocalypse as a concept. In 2013 the interactive theatre company thinkdreamspeak (in conjunction with the National Theatre) put on a production at Somerset House in London entitled In the Beginning Was the End, in which viewers were taken on a surreal walking tour of a post-apocalyptic world, very loosely based on Revelation, as well as on the mechatronic designs of Leonardo da Vinci. The piece sought to explore the complex relationship between technological advance and the flourishing of the human spirit and seemed to ultimately reject technology in favour of a lemon grove (an oblique reference to the fructifying trees of the New Jerusalem of Rev. 22, perhaps). Whether technological advancement was being interpreted as one of the signs of the Beast (see Rev. 13.17), or perhaps even as the false statue set up by the Earth Beast/False Prophet in Rev. 13.14, is unclear. What the piece did capture well is the profound sense of unease engendered by the concept of apocalypse. At points during the walking tour viewers confronted actors removing and then replacing all their clothes, perhaps a visual metaphor for the concept of unveiling contained within the Greek term ἀποκάλυψις. And does this in fact get to the heart of what apocalypse represents for us now? The stripping bare of all human pretension, wealth, and artifice in the face of something far greater—whether that be the divine or the natural disaster that will bring about the end of the world in its current incarnation?[12]

The above survey has provided a smorgasbord of more recent cultural references to Revelation and the concept of the apocalypse more generally. These phenomena are fascinating on an anthropological or sociological level. They demonstrate that although many of us no longer believe in the notion of a religious apocalypse, anxieties (and excitement even) surrounding some sort of apocalypse, heightened by reports of ecological disaster and terrorist threats, are deeply embedded in our cultural psyche. For those of us interested in the ongoing legacy of Revelation in the twentieth and twenty-first centuries, we might think of some of the examples so far mentioned as promiscuous appropriations of the term apocalypse, with only loose connections to Revelation itself. Nevertheless, there have been more thorough treatments throughout the twentieth and twenty-first centuries which do not use Revelation as a mere jumping-off point or merely pluck characters out of Revelation in a decontextualized way, but which actually seek to get to grips with both the essence and the particulars of the text of Revelation, and with what it might have to say to our modern age. The remainder of this chapter will explore a carefully chosen selection of these treatments. The survey is necessarily selective, as rather than simply listing examples we have decided to focus in more depth on a few, and in so doing hope to unearth for the reader some more or less hidden gems of modern apocalyptic interpretation.

# Revelation in the visual arts

Over the course of the preceding chapters we have already considered a number of twentieth- and twenty-first century visual artists who have been inspired by the specific themes and characters of Revelation. Here we will consider twentieth-century and contemporary artists who have used imagery from Revelation more generally in response to their own individual situations.

The first examples are drawn from a group of northern European artists, including Max Beckmann, Otto Dix (both of whom we have met in previous chapters), and Frans Masereel, who all endeavoured to make sense of the First World War via their art. In many ways these artists are the direct antecedents of those from the worlds of art, media, music, and popular culture discussed above who have appropriated the term apocalypse in the more secular sense. These three artists should be viewed not only against their First World War context, but also against the themes of secularism and individualism that had so influenced Western European artists and writers in the late nineteenth and early twentieth centuries, as well as in the light of Nietzschean rumours of imminent global catastrophes. The notion that mankind was moving inexorably towards a destructive apocalyptic eschatology had already been seriously canvassed before the war by intellectuals, many of whom initially welcomed the war in 1914, believing that Europe needed to be purged of decadent tendencies.

The First World War therefore acted as a fearsome corroboration of the apocalyptic pessimism that already existed. Thus Max Beckmann's *The Grenade* of 1915 reflects not only his horrific experiences as a medical orderly on the Western Front but also a sense of cosmic catastrophe (Figure 10.1). It is as if the figures are all being sucked towards the darkened sun, towards annihilation. The darkened sun is perhaps the eclipsed sun of Rev. 6.12 ('the sun became black as sackcloth and the full moon became like blood') but there is no intimation of the redemption to be found at the end of Revelation in this image. It is resolutely bleak. His *Resurrection* of 1918 (see Figure 8.2), when taken in combination with Beckmann's own comments on the work, compound this notion. In a letter to a friend Beckmann described this grotesque vision as a resurrection without God, a form of reproach to God for everything He had done wrong.[13]

However, as we saw in Chapter 9, in the 1940s Beckmann returned to Revelation as a source of inspiration, producing a series of coloured

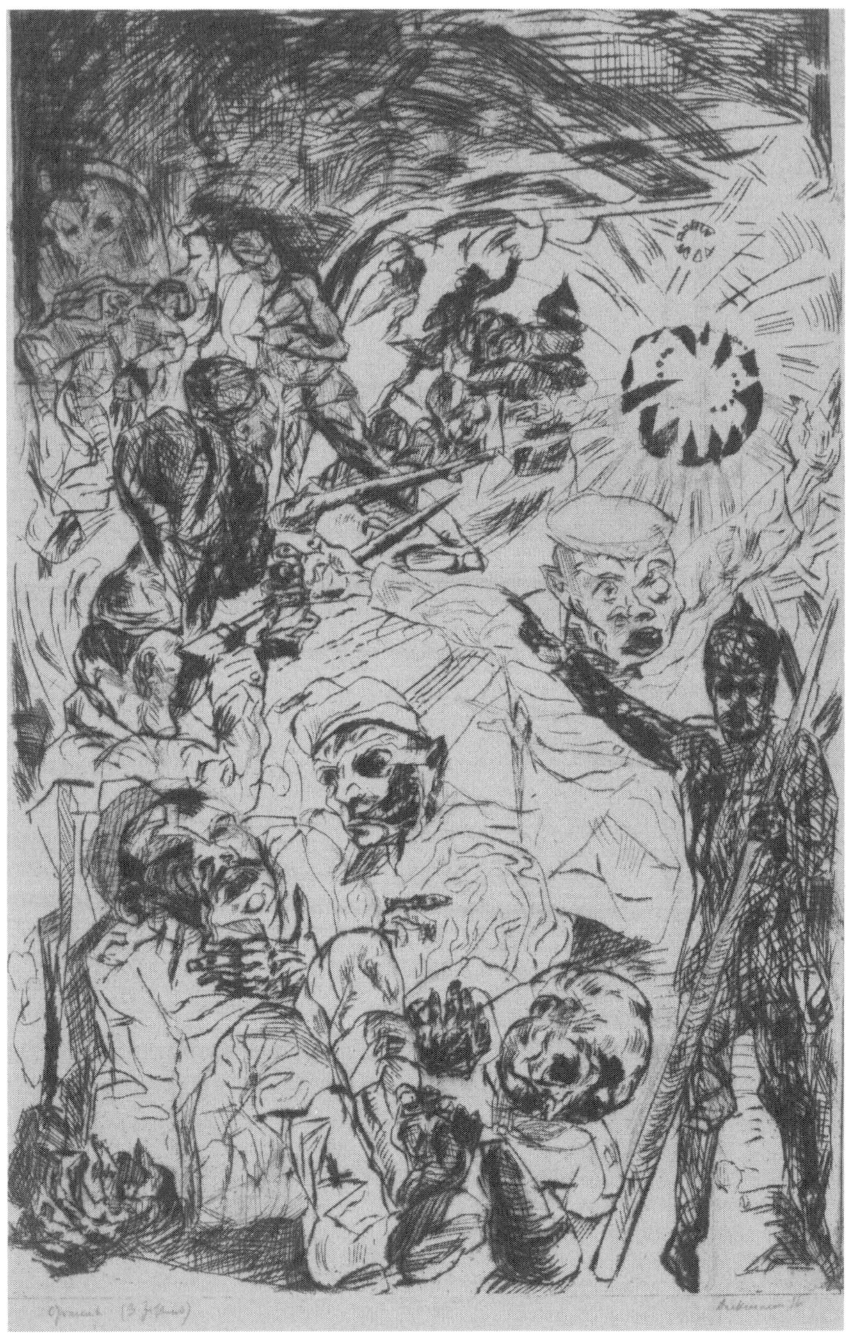

**Figure 10.1.** Max Beckmann, *The Grenade*, 1915, London: The British Museum. © The Trustees of the British Museum

lithographs of the book. In striking contrast to his earlier, angrier and more agnostic, works, here Beckmann clearly identifies on some level with Revelation's seer, John, inserting a self-portrait into the title page of the work. In this curious composition Beckmann appears in profile in between two headstones, onto which are carved the opening lines of John's Gospel (a nod to the erroneous yet long-held belief referred to in the Introduction that it was John the Evangelist, author of the Gospel and the Johannine Epistles, who also wrote Revelation).[14] By inserting himself thus, Beckmann was following self-consciously in the footsteps of Dürer, Duvet, and Blake, who had also identified with John. Beckmann's Four Horseman image depicts the riders galloping past his window at which a candle burns. This is a significant recasting of an iconic image, the Four Horsemen as glimpsed by a frightened onlooker through their bedroom window. As mentioned in Chapter 9, Beckmann depicts the New Jerusalem in very human terms, eschewing the magnificent city and the River of Life in favour of a moving depiction of Rev. 21.3–4 (God wiping tears from human eyes; see Figure 9.2). Carey argues that it is Beckmann himself who is having his eyes wiped by God/the angel in this image.[15] Thus, seen within the context of Beckmann's wider oeuvre, his First World War images need not perhaps be seen in a wholly nihilistic light, although for Beckmann this was clearly a time when God seemed absent from the world. It could very well be argued that this is also the case in some chapters of Revelation, such as Rev. 13 where the Sea Beast and the Earth Beast rampage over the earth, marking its citizens with the 'mark of the Beast' and coercing them into false worship, before divine control is re-established in Rev. 14 and beyond. Beckmann's Revelation-inspired images could therefore be seen as mirroring in some unconscious way the trajectory of the text's own narrative, a trajectory that also seems to have been picked up on by Ingmar Bergman in his film *The Seventh Seal* (1957), which is discussed below.

Otto Dix's *Dance of Death* of 1917 (from his *Der Krieg* series) depicts a circle of dead bodies hanging on barbed wire in no man's land in a horrible imitation of a dance (Figure 10.2). The ghostly scene is lit against a black background by what assumes is the light of a flare. The image plays with the medieval notion of the dance of death. This allegory (inspired by the admonitions in apocalyptic passages of the New Testament such as Mark 13 for people to be prepared for the end) was supposed to remind people of the fragility of earthly life. In Dix's etching, however, the dance of death is presented very much as the end of all life, any possibility of an afterlife

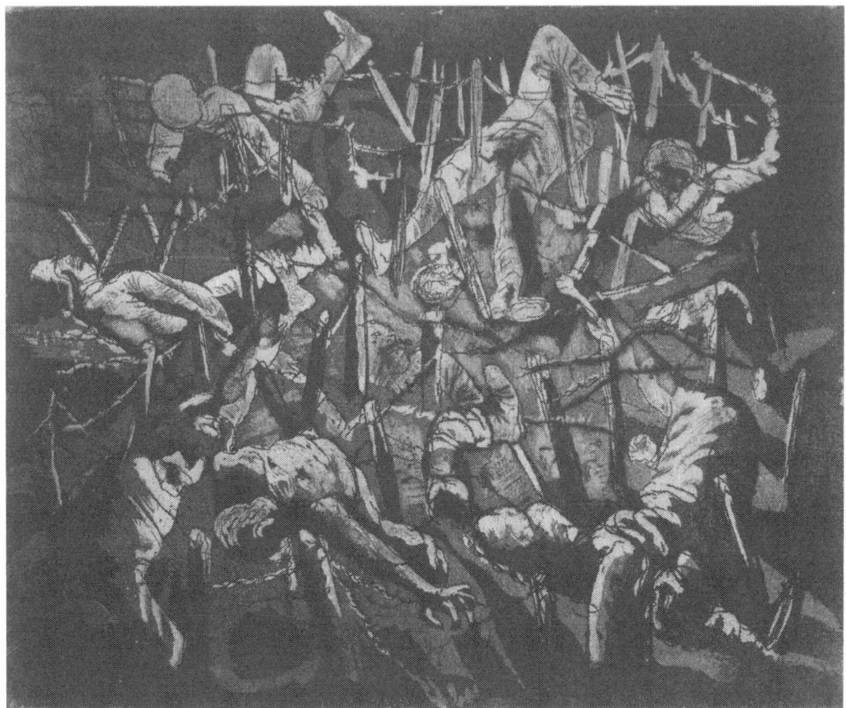

**Figure** 10.2.   Otto Dix, *Dance of Death*, 1917, London: British Museum. © The Trustees of the British Museum

seemingly impaled alongside the soldiers on the barbed wire, who themselves are silhouetted against the blackness of an eternity without God. This apocalyptic scene, whilst undoubtedly drawing on general themes from Revelation (and we know of Dix's interest in the text from his visual evocation of a contemporary Whore of Babylon in his *Visit to Madame Germaine at Méricourt*, see Figure 7.6), lacks any engagement with the more reassuring, redemptive elements of the text. It is interesting to note the pivotal role that the notion of the dance of death also plays in Bergman's aforementioned *Seventh Seal*. Early on in the film the Squire talks with a painter painting a dance of death onto the wall of a church. They discuss the purpose of such paintings (to scare people into maintaining a strong faith). At the very end of the film, the 'hero', Antonius Block, and the other characters (except for the two who are saved) are led by Death in a dance across the hills in order to symbolize their own deaths.

Finally, as we saw in Chapter 8, Belgian artist Frans Masereel's later *Flugzeuge über die Menschheit* evokes in a striking way the international-scale destruction of both world wars (see Figure 8.5). The busy magnitude of this brush and ink image, with a swarm of bombers and destroyed buildings stretching out as far as the eye can see, reminds the viewer of the Armageddon of Rev. 16.12–16 (and Rev. 20) but without any of the hope of the resolution found in Rev. 21–2. Instead, here mankind is simply presented as an eternal victim on an epic and uncompromising scale, an interesting transposition or updating of the themes of Rev. 16 and Rev. 20, using the images and mechanics associated with modern warfare.

Rather in contrast to these earlier twentieth-century artists, who visualized apocalyptic themes in a largely public, catastrophic sense, the English painter Cecil Collins saw his art as the external expression of the inner visionary experience of the artist. Collins' work focuses particularly on the figures of the Fool, the Woman, and the Angel, the last named usually seen in rather general terms as a mediator between us and the world of the divine, leading us into the spiritual. This Angel becomes the *Angel of the Apocalypse* of 1969, which we considered in Chapter 1 (see Plate 9). Equally visionary but more specifically anchored in the narrative of Revelation is a series of black and white pictograms by contemporary artist Kip Gresham, created for inclusion in the Epworth Commentary on Revelation by Christopher Rowland (1993). Gresham's image of the Whore of Babylon has already been discussed in Chapter 7 (see Figure 7.7). In Gresham's images the moments depicted from Revelation have a haunting, dreamlike quality. They are simple and do not always progress chronologically, thus capturing the essence of John's vision, which, as mentioned in the Introduction, darts around in a sometimes confusing manner. In this way Gresham intended his images, which he deems not as illustrations but as 'associated ideas', to be the opposite of Dürer's iconic *Apocalypse* series, which depicts the text of Revelation both chronologically and, for the most part, literally. Thus Gresham captures the spirit and not always the letter of the text.

Another contemporary artist who has drawn on apocalyptic themes extensively is Gordon Cheung, as mentioned in Chapters 3 and 9. His works, which often combine large, bleak, painted landscapes with cuttings from the financial pages of newspapers, evoke global collapse and the end times. Their style is a combination of sci-fi and the surreal, with bleak desert or mountainous landscapes back lit by huge suns, angular rocks, geometric buildings, and pools of liquids unknown in the natural world. Human figures are largely absent from the canvasses. Subjects and titles do have Revelatory reference, for example *The Four Horsemen of the Apocalypse* (see Plate 14), *Burning Lake*, and *Rivers of Bliss* (see Plate 49), and there are obvious and admitted borrowings from John Martin (particularly his Great Day of Wrath, from the *Last Judgement* triptych, 1843–53), but again this is more of an attempt to evoke what Cheung clearly feels is the very bleak spirit of Revelation rather than the textual or chronological detail. The resultant images, even *Rivers of Bliss*, which depicts the New Jerusalem, are eerie and once again (as was the case with the works of Beckmann and Bergman) seem to invite reflection on the absence of God in a desolate world. Certainly Cheung stands at the opposite end of the spectrum to the medieval artists who always made sure to conclude their Apocalypse cycles with comforting images of the New Jerusalem and an ecstatic John gazing into the face of Christ.

And, to round off this brief survey of recent and contemporary visual art, much the same could be said of the so-called *Manchester Apocalypse*, shown at the Incognito Gallery in Manchester in November 2011, and thought to be worth featuring on the BBC's website. In it the artist, James Chadderton, says that he is only interested in depicting the aftermath of the apocalypse (a 'human devoid wasteland', in his words), and not the thing itself. By means of impressive photographic montages what he depicts is ruins of buildings, bridges, buses, etc. in a totally depopulated Manchester. The image we have included here is from the more recent *Apocalypse V2* series (2014) and depicts a post-apocalyptic vision of London in which we see a collapsed London Bridge in the foreground and a wrecked Tower Bridge further down the Thames (Plate 50). Buildings on the right are clearly blown out and empty although the Shard itself seems strangely unaffected. As in the Manchester series, this image is completely and eerily devoid of human life. Chadderton lists a number of games he has been influenced by, such as Metro 2033 and S.T.A.L.K.E.R, and films such as the aforementioned *28 Days Later* and *The Road*, the latter based on Cormac McCarthy's novel in which a few survivors from some unnamed total disaster try to make their way across the wasteland which the USA had become, and fighting (to the death) with other survivors equally desperate for food and shelter.[16]

In line with what we saw earlier in our survey of popular culture, Cheung and Chadderton (and McCarthy) are firmly in the camp of those who use the word apocalyptic to refer in general terms to some definitive catastrophe, or to what is left after it. Unlike earlier visual artists they are less concerned with illustrating the rich visionary detail of Revelation itself, or with grappling with its theological meaning. Rather, they have lifted some of its major themes and used them as inspiration for their contemporary reflections around apocalyptic themes.

# Revelation in classical music

## Three apocalyptic oratorios

Strangely, perhaps, and the notable exception of Handel's *Messiah* apart, treatments of Revelation in classical music are not that common. The twentieth century, however, saw four major forays into the territory, of which three are oratorios. Two of these are played but rarely, and the other not at all. The one not played at all, the fictional oratorio written by the Faustian character Leverkühn in Thomas Mann's *Doctor Faustus*, like some of the visual artists we have been considering, takes Revelation in entirely cataclysmic terms, while Franz Schmidt's oratorio *Das Buch mit sieben Siegeln* (The Book with Seven Seals) emphasizes the redemptive and even the brazenly triumphalist aspects of the text. Vaughan Williams' *Sancta Civitas* may not be brazen, but it certainly a positive treatment, focusing on the fall of Babylon and New Jerusalem, though is interesting in that it laments rather than exults over the fall of Babylon.[17]

Vaughan Williams' *Sancta Civitas*, which was first performed in 1926, is unusual in two ways. First, for all its composer's roots in the English choral tradition, it is the only composition of his to be called an oratorio; and secondly it is a rare example of treating the fall of Babylon as tragic, as a matter for regret and mourning. The Sancta Civitas, the holy city, of the title is, naturally enough, the New Jerusalem, but the work is really a tale of two cities, based as it is on texts from Revelation 18–22, though not in chronological order. By means of solo baritone and choruses it tells of John's vision of the adoration and Marriage of the Lamb, of the gathering of forces to fight with the Faithful and True and the Rider on the White Horse, then of the fall of Babylon (all described in Rev. 19), and finally of the descent of the New Jerusalem as the Lamb's Bride (Rev. 21).

Vaughan Williams, while being an agnostic religiously speaking, had a strong sense of the immortality of the soul, or at least of a realm beyond sense and knowledge, and indeed he prefaced the score of *Sancta Civitas* with words to that effect from Plato's *Phaedo*. He also, in 1926, could hardly help being affected by the events of the First World War in which he had served both as a stretcher bearer and as an officer in the artillery. His experience of war may go some way to explaining why he treats the fall of Babylon as a matter for sorrow and weeping, rather than, as so often in earlier art, as an occasion for revengeful triumph and as a pretext for the representation of battle and bloodshed. So in *Sancta Civitas* we are presented with the passing away of a great worldly city and its replacement by a heavenly one, not of this world, but descending from another realm.

The music for the Lamb and for the New Jerusalem is by turns mysterious, grand, mystical, and, it seems, visionary, while that for Babylon is desolate, sorrowful, even bitter, suffused with regret, even though it had to pass. Was this regretfulness at this point due to Vaughan Williams' own recent experiences on the front line in the First World War? Even the destruction of an enemy is a destruction, cruel, bloody, and in the end so wasteful of so much, as the music intimates.

In the course of the work, whose pace is for the most part slow and measured, Vaughan Williams draws on powerful orchestral and choral forces, and on his own considerable power in marshalling large ensembles and in exploiting their expressive potential. Having said that, one of the most telling passages is that in which Babylon sinks beneath a solitary cor anglais, to be replaced by a solo violin, lyrical and rapt, to usher into our presence the city from above.

But *Sancta Civitas* is a vision, and Vaughan Williams, visionary by nature, saves what is perhaps his finest dramatic stroke till the end. As we approach the end of the work, the music grows to a great and glorious gathering of praise to the Lamb and to his Bride, brass, cymbals, full and melodious strings, and the huge choir all in a great fugal symphony. We might expect this climax to be the end of the work. But mysteriously it fades away, while to those of us who are left on Earth a solo tenor, heard here for the first time, promises the new covenant ('Surely I come quickly'), while the earthly chorus, those of us who are left, perhaps, murmurs, 'Even so, come Lord.'

The reason why Schmidt's Book with Seven Seals is rarely performed cannot be because it is musically weak. It is in fact one of the most powerful, dramatic, and original works in the twentieth century repertoire. In addition it has its own powerful characterization of John, who is the cornerstone of the work, narrating the events which unfold. Schmidt's John is not some old, monkish figure, but a young, vibrant, heroic tenor, in the mould of the Evangelist in the Bach *Passions*, but in far more positive mood. The Lord, who proclaims Himself Alpha and Omega, the beginning and the end, is a rock-like bass, presiding grandly upon a solemn brass chorale. The musical writing is spare and astringent, tonal to be sure, but neither lush nor romantic, with brass and wind predominating over string textures, and in many ways harking back to early baroque music from the seventeenth century. There are passages of lyrical tenderness when the Lamb appears and also for the Woman Clothed with the Sun. Other passages are of astonishing power, with a huge choir which wrestles with the woes unleashed by the Four Horsemen and by the seven angels, before exulting over the Lamb's ultimate triumph in a great ecstatic chorus, in which excited rising musical figures lead no less than eight times to solemn and triumphant hallelujahs beaten out over a fierce and spacious Magyar rhythm.

Schmidt's voice in this work contrives to be fiercely personal—it is neither that of his teacher Bruckner nor of his contemporary Schoenberg—yet he achieves a monumental impersonality wholly at one with his great theme. *The Book with Seven Seals* was composed between 1933 and 1937, at a time of personal turmoil for its composer and, of course, of world historical catastrophe, nowhere more so than in Schmidt's Vienna. Yet what shines through is Schmidt's own rocklike Catholic faith, as, in his own reordering of parts of the text, he moves through Revelation: the heavenly throne room, the Lamb, the opening of the Seven Seals, the Woman, and the Dragon, the casting down of Satan by Michael, the many woes visited on sinful mankind, until the Lamb's final victory and the ushering in of the new age. Although Schmidt in no sense underplays the horrors of war or the apocalyptic travails of humanity, he omits completely the Whore of Babylon and the fall of the Great City.

Is this significant? Schmidt was after all at the heart of what many would come to see as the Babylon or even the Rome of his day, the Third Reich. And worryingly for Schimdt's admirers, the first performance of *Das Buch* was given in Vienna, shortly after the Anschluss, to Nazi acclaim. Could it be that this believer in a greater Germany (as Schmidt was) saw the climax of his great work in Nazi terms? Schmidt's own character would belie any such suggestion (he had many Jewish friends, for example), as indeed does the work's impersonality and its faithfulness to the essential spirit of Revelation. In retrospect Schmidt's lacerating depictions of mothers and women weeping over the desolation and destruction unleashed by the Horsemen seem eerily prophetic of what the Nazis were about to visit on Europe, rather than any endorsement of their blood and steel militarism, nor would Schmidt's monumental depiction of the all-judging God of the

Bible have appealed to the essentially pagan and anti-Christian temperament of Hitler and the Nazis. We should not allow the occasion of the work, nor even its composer's desperately ill-judged final work honouring the Führer, to act as a critical strike against it. It is surely better to see *Das Buch* as a passionate, even if unconscious, protest against the time and circumstances in which it was written—but a protest in which hope is still to be found, as it is in Revelation itself.

If Schmidt is fundamentally orthodox in his understanding of Revelation, the same could not be said of our other apocalyptic oratorio, the one which will never be heard, Adrian Leverkühn's *Apocalypsis cum Figuris*. Thomas Mann's *Doctor Faustus* was his own response (in 1947) to the disasters which had befallen Germany and European civilization during the Nazi era. Adrian Leverkühn, the novel's hero, is a composer—an amalgam of Nietzsche and Schoenberg, as well as of the medieval doctor Faustus—who has sold his soul to the Devil. In return Leverkühn plumbs the secrets of music, developing for himself a new style, which dispenses with romanticism and even classicism, to go backwards towards a pre-baroque style and purity (a bit like Schmidt, perhaps), but—unlike Schmidt, and like Schoenberg—towards a new musical intellectualism.

In *Doctor Faustus* Leverkühn's story is being written by an old school friend of his against the apocalyptic events unfolding in Germany from 1943 to 1945, to which continual reference is made in Mann's text. Leverkühn himself is a tortured Nietzschean, who like Nietzsche lapses into a mental collapse for the last twelve years of his life, dying in 1940 before his friend writes about him. Mann is, of course, asking us to see the Germany of the Nazi period and the destruction of its cities and monuments in generally apocalyptic terms, but a more precise deployment of Revelation is the fact that Leverkühn's own *magnum opus*, composed in the early 1920s, after the horrors of the First World War, is actually entitled *Apocalypsis cum Figuris*, a conscious reference on Leverkühn's part to Dürer's aforementioned series of fifteen images of the same name, on which Leverkühn self-consciously draws in his oratorio (see Figures 1.2, 1.3, 2.1, 3.5, 4.5, 4.6, 5.5, 5.6, 6.1, 7.4, and 8.8 for examples from this series). The identification goes further: in introducing his work to the narrator, Leverkühn follows Dürer in picturing himself as John in his cauldron of oil, with the emperor Nero looking on, with Nuremberg in the background (Figure 10.3).[18] (The omniscient author is here mistaken: in both Dürer and the ancient legend it is Domitian who presides over John's boiling.) But there is no doubting here where

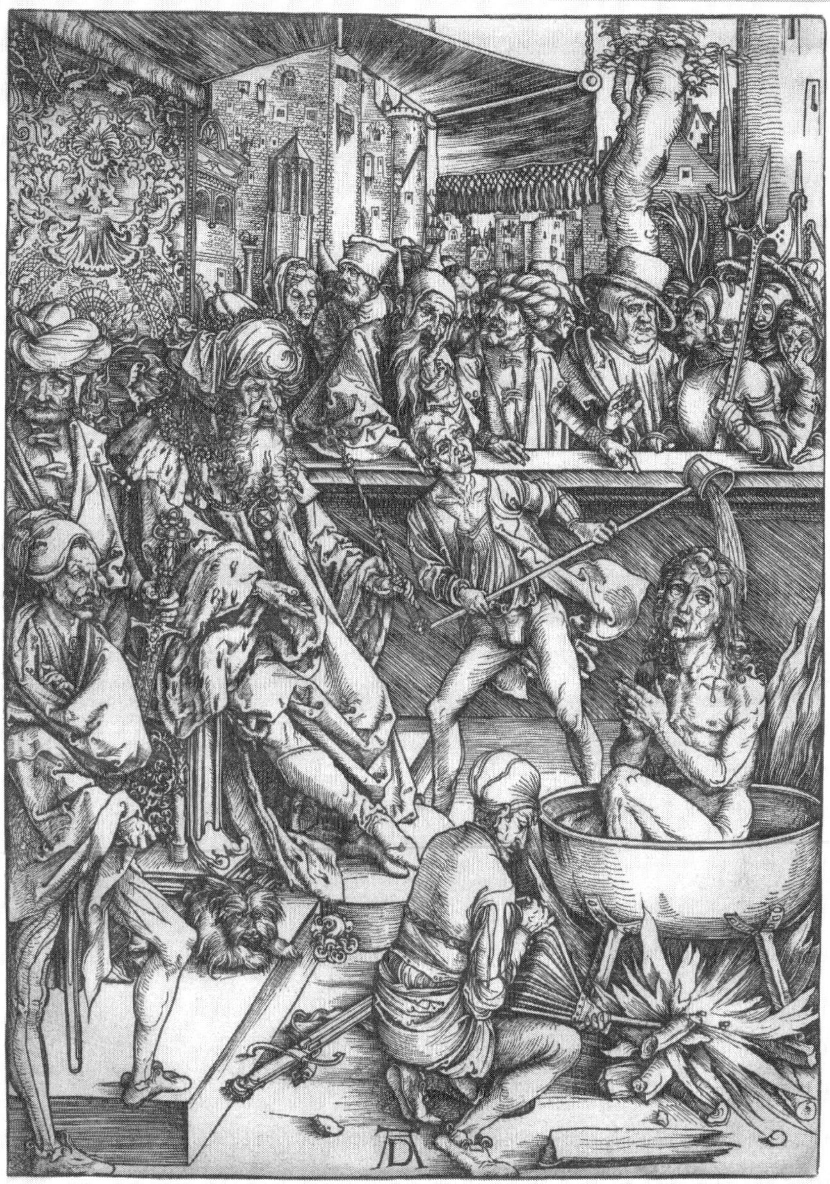

**Figure 10.3.** Albrecht Dürer, *Apocalypse* Series, *c.*1498, The Martyrdom of St John, London: British Museum. © The Trustees of the British Museum

Mann's sympathies lie, given the fact that, long after Dürer, Nuremberg had come to signify the literal and symbolic home of Nazism.

And, from what Mann tells us, Leverkühn's apocalyptic oratorio is unremittingly demonic.[19] The vocal music introducing many of the scenes is in the form of a speaking chorus, whisperings, antiphonal speech, humming, over gongs and tom toms, savage and fanatical. The Four Angels (Rev. 7) as they destroy a third of mankind are accompanied by terrifying glissandi and howling from the frightful, shrieking human voices as the Seventh Seal is opened. The Whore of Babylon (Rev. 17) starts as a graceful coloratura, but the music descends to a grotesque *vox humana*, and eventually into the Pit, where we find a parody of insipid wantonness: a melange of bourgeois drawing room music, Tchaikovsky, music hall, and jazz. Demonic laughter predominates, but is balanced by a heavenly children's chorus, a music of the spheres, icily clear, glassily transparent, we are told (cf. the heavenly throne room of Rev. 4, which is described as resting on a 'sea of glass'). Mann is insistent that all this apparent horror and cacophony ends up in music of the most sublime purity, and also that the spirit is represented in it by dissonance and the diabolic by firm tonality, a perverse paradox, if you like. But most paradoxical of all and most diabolic is that the children's music of the spheres turns out on examination to be in exact correspondence with the laughter of the angels in Hell. So Heaven is as sterile as Hell in this vision. This is clearly an apocalypse without redemption, in which the promise of redemption turns out to be the most cruel illusion.

So, three apocalyptic oratorios at the heart of the hell which was the European twentieth century, Schmidt's a firm invocation of what Revelation stands for, four-square in the European tradition of music and belief, Vaughan Williams' agnostic in a sense, but positive in its overall message. And the third a corruscating inversion of anything positive, born out of what seemed to Mann to be a European renunciation of everything his Europe meant. After considering these large-scale choral works, for our fourth piece of twentieth-century classical music we will now turn to one of the most unusual and distinctive musical works of the twentieth century.


## Olivier Messiaen, Quartet for the End of Time

Messiaen's *Quatuor pour la fin du temps* (Quartet for the End of Time) may well be its composer's most famous work, as much for the circumstances of its composition as for its intrinsic value.[20] Scored for the highly unusual combination of clarinet, violin, cello, and piano, it was composed while Messiaen and his three fellow performers (one of whom was actually Jewish) were prisoners of war in Stalag VIIIA in East Prussia. The first performance took place in Barrack 27 of the camp, with the help of an anti-Nazi guard (and a somewhat dilapidated piano), before 400 prisoners and some of the German officers in freezing conditions in January 1941.

Given this context and given its apocalyptic theme, the work is the more remarkable. For though it is explicitly based on the appearance of the mighty angel announcing the end of time in Rev. 10.6–7, it is entirely without either rancour or bitterness on the one hand or, on the other, the triumphalism of the oppressed celebrating the overturning of the world. The aspects of Revelation which so enthused Schmidt and which have offended others (see the discussion in section 'D. H. Lawrence, *Apocalypse*' below) are completely bypassed in the quartet, which if nothing else is testament to the many-sidedness and fecundity of the vision.

What Messiaen focuses on is the deeply stirring announcement by the angel that the mystery of God is about to be finished, and that, with what is in effect the end of the world, time will cease to exist, itself a profound, if not ecstatic, conception (Rev. 10.6–7: 'There should be time no longer . . . the mystery of God should be finished'—at least that is the way that Messiaen understands this somewhat problematic saying). One might ask how the ending of time and the onset of the timeless, the post-temporal, and the eternal can be conveyed in a medium such as music, whose very essence involves the beating and counting of time, and whose most acclaimed works quite clearly move logically and emotionally from beginning to end, through carefully measured stages and climaxes. That Messiaen comes near to succeeding is itself as impressive as it is mysterious. Unlike most works in the Western classical tradition, in this piece there is virtually no movement forward, or at least what movement there is leads us to stillness. In the two stillest of the work's eight movements the piano does in a sense beat time, but slowly, slowly, in a way to still time, as the cello and the violin, respectively, powerfully and gently unfold endless melodies reaching, in the words of the composer himself, a 'tender and supreme distance'. The clarinet meanwhile contributes its own plaintive note to the work, in meditating on the weariness of the temporal world (third movement) and elsewhere evoking birdsong and cosmic turbulence.

Stillness is at the beginning and the end, and also at the heart of a work which, rather than involving linear development, is, as one commentator has suggested, akin to a window through which the reality beyond time is glimpsed. In this window we do see, in the second movement, the mightiness of the angel of Rev. 10, his legs firmly planted on the sea and on the earth, represented by great and spacious piano chords at the beginning and end of the movement, but between these two we hear 'the impalpable harmonies of Heaven' (in Messiaen's words), in cascades of distant chimes and suggestions of plainchant. We also (in the sixth movement) hear something of the fury and icy intoxication of the six catastrophes which precede the end of time, while in the seventh movement there is a sense of the swords of fire, turbulent stars, and outpourings of blue-orange lava (the composer's description again) which might attend great cosmic beginnings and ends. But overall the timbre of the work is of stillness and of mystical ascent out of this world, into regions of crystalline purity and intensity, particularly in the last movement, which is one of two 'praises' of Jesus' eternity and immortality.

The Quartet for the End of Time is a work of a very Franciscan piety: no darkness, bitterness, or rage, but rather reconciliation, affirmation, ecstasy, and transcendence. There is a cosmic, even a worldly, aspect to it in its references to birdsong and other natural phenomena, suggesting the redemption and renewal of the whole world as well as that of the believing soul. However, in contrast to most depictions of the New Jerusalem, which emphasize its communal, collective aspect, Messiaen's is a distinctively individualistic take on Rev. 21–2.

# Revelation in popular music

## Gary Davis, Johnny Cash, Bob Dylan, and Leonard Cohen

A very different musical evocation of the New Jerusalem of Rev. 21 is given by the Reverend Gary Davis (1896–1972), an American blues and gospel singer, in his song 'Twelve Gates to the City' (1960).[21] Davis appeared on a billing with Pete Seeger, a prominent civil rights activist and folk singer (in 1958 and 1967) and also appeared in the iconic 1970 film *Black Roots* about the experiences of black musicians in America. Thus, while not strictly a civil rights activist himself, Davis was in strong contact with this movement and the theme of political struggle is a prominent one in his music.[22]

'Twelve Gates to the City' is striking for several reasons. First, the fact that Davis dwells solely on the ending of Revelation, on a passage pertaining to the all-encompassing nature of the New Jerusalem, is both significant and unusual. Davis' song is a musical evocation of the New Jerusalem as described in Rev. 21. He appears to have been particularly influenced by the following verses:

> It [the New Jerusalem] has a great, high wall with twelve gates, and at the gates twelve angels, and on the gates are inscribed the names of the twelve tribes of the Israelites; on the east three gates, on the north three gates, on the south three gates, and on the west three gates. And the wall of the city has twelve foundations, and on them are the twelve names of the twelve apostles of the Lamb. (Rev. 21.12–14)

Davis was inspired not by the eschatological aspect of apocalyptic, as so many other twentieth-century commentators have been, but by its redemptive, revelatory, even hopeful side. Indeed, Davis was praised for reflecting the 'humanistic core of Christianity' in his music.[23] Secondly, the repetition present in the song serves to evoke the reality of the heavenly city: the New Jerusalem is portrayed in this way as more real than Earth. He also dwells on the geographical detail of the city, the three gates in the east, the north, the south, and the west (Rev. 21.13), which once again serves to underline the tangibility of this magnificent city which is destined to descend to Earth from Heaven. This 'realism' is reinforced by the reference to the narrator's mother in the middle of the song, who he asks to be given a message to meet him in Galilee (itself a reference to Matt. 28.10). This indicates a tangible belief in the renewal of real human relationships in the New Jerusalem, as we also saw in Blake's *River of Life* (see Plate 44). This sense of optimism may initially seem a surprising response from a blind black musician who had been raised in South Carolina by a single mother in the first decade of the twentieth century, one of only two surviving children out of an original eight. His subsequent experiences as an itinerant musician and preacher, not least the fact that his father was shot by the High Sheriff of Birmingham, Alabama, must have brought him into contact with some of the darker aspects of humanity, but Davis' relationship with the concepts of the afterlife and judgement was anything but trite or banal.[24]

For him the song, whilst joyous, also had a clear connection with judgement. One fellow musician (Paul Oliver) reminisces that at a concert in 1965 someone requested 'Twelve Gates to the City'. Davis replied: 'That's a judgement number. If Gabriel called for you to go, you wouldn't be ready;

and I know I ain't.' And he refused to play the song.[25] Whilst in one sense part of the counter-cultural movement which swept across America in the 1960s, Davis had also been immersed in a fairly orthodox Christian imaginary (fairly common within the black church in the United States, which tends to be both socially and theologically conservative). He, like many who came before him within Western Christianity, understands Revelation as an ultimately hopeful text, culminating in the establishment of the 'beautiful city' of the New Jerusalem. And while 'Twelve Gates to the City' represents a positive twentieth-century response to one of the most important and positive sections of Revelation, Davis was clearly aware of the text's other, more judgemental currents.

These darker currents are very much to the fore in Johnny Cash's powerful late song 'When the Man Comes Around' (2002). Cash was a very successful singer and hell-raiser who became increasingly evangelical in middle age (from the mid-seventies onwards), even striking up and maintaining a strong friendship with well-known evangelical preacher Billy Graham.[26] Despite their many differences, Davis and Cash do have one thing in common: theirs is the music of ordinary people (gospel or folk, and country and western respectively), and, even more significant, they are both singing, without shame or embarrassment, as sincere Christian believers. If we wanted to understand the difference between middle- or working-class America and modern Europe, a good place to begin might be to attempt to understand this, or at least to appreciate its significance. This is not the place for a general disquisition on American country music, but, in contrast to many other types of pop music, its essence is moral in an old-fashioned sense (placing a high value on traditional family life and on personal integrity), Christian (embracing rather than mocking evangelical religion), and patriotic (unquestioningly committed to America and to the ideals of the founding fathers, and hence highly critical of politicians who betray those ideals).

This seems to us to be true even or perhaps especially where the theme of a particular song is a lament for a failure to live up to these ideals, and the mode of presentation is, to European eyes, brassy and vulgar. In short it is the music of the white working class in the USA, relayed by hundreds if not thousands of radio stations all across the country (if not to East Coast or Californian sophisticates). Johnny Cash was a cut above the average country and western production, musically and lyrically, but a song like 'When the Man Comes Around', released in 2002, a year before Cash's death in 2003, is unimaginable in any other context.

'When the Man Comes Around' is based on a dream Cash had, which also included allusions to the Book of Job. It is framed by two extracts from Rev. 6, enunciated by Cash at the beginning and end of the song in decidedly sepulchral tones, with John seeing first the white horse (Rev. 6.2) and then the pale horse with 'his name that sat on him was Death, and Hell followed with him' (Rev. 6.8).[27] The music in between the readings is spare, with the vocal line clear and dominant, underlined at crucial moments by a resounding bass guitar. The words are by Cash, although replete with biblical resonance and reference, the result, according to him, of seven years' reflection on his original dream as well as on biblical texts.[28]

Their gist is that the Man (Christ) is coming to judge us all. Multitudes march to God's big kettledrum (as in the Van Eycks' image of the Holy Lamb of God); some are born and some are dying, it's Alpha and Omega's kingdom come, in which (echoing Rev. 22.11) the unjust will be unjust still, the filthy, filthy still, and the righteous, righteous still. Above all, 'till Armageddon, no shalom, no shalam': only with the coming of the Man will there be any end to the travails and torments of this life. If Cash emphasizes tribulation and the severity of the judgement to come, in true Revelatory mode there is salvation for the faithful. In that sense 'When the Man Comes Around' is similar in import to that of Hal Lindsey, to whom we will turn shortly, though in both its music and its language it has a far more genuinely prophetic feel, deriving perhaps from Cash's own troubled life and his identification both with the downtrodden and with the Christian message. Unlike Lindsey, however, Cash also expressed uncertainty about how well it was possible to truly understand a text like Revelation, thus revealing a more complex, troubled, and less simplistic relationship with the text than is traditional for evangelical Dispensationalists. The origins of the song (in a dream) on which he then reflected alongside passages from Revelation and other biblical texts also forms a strange parallel with the writing process that John of Patmos may have undertaken. John, in many of the artistic representations we have looked at, was certainly on a journey from vision to its expression, and in the vision from incomprehension to understanding.

Both Bob Dylan and Leonard Cohen, among many other popular musicians, have also dwelt on apocalyptic or, more precisely, end time themes. One of Dylan's constant refrains from the very beginning has been divine retribution on the evildoers, as in the early 'Hard Rain'. This seam became more pronounced when Dylan also underwent a conversion to evangelical Christianity, with songs like 'No Shelter from the Sun' and 'When He Returns'.

Leonard Cohen's most notable foray into this territory is his doom-laden and dirge-like 'The Future': 'The blizzard of the world has crossed the threshold/ And it overturned the order of the soul/ When they said REPENT, REPENT, I wonder what they meant…'.[29] It may well be that Dylan and Cohen actually mean what they say, and are not just using apocalyptic imagery for effect, or simply to express a generalized *Weltschmertz* or weariness and disgust with the world, which is the impression given by many other pop music incursions into the territory. Nevertheless, neither Dylan nor Cohen appear to engage with the substance and detail of Revelation in the way of Johnny Cash, and to that extent their offerings are less interesting from our point of view, symptomatic of the way the text has in our times become a generalized metaphor for crisis and decline.

# Revelation and the moving image

When we turn to look at cinema, we find examples of both approaches to Revelation, the more theologically engaged and the more secular. We will look at one example from each category, each of which is in its own right a landmark in the history of the cinema.

## *The Seventh Seal*

Ingmar Bergman's *The Seventh Seal*, which dates from 1957, is now one of the most famous films of the twentieth century. When he made the film, however, Bergman was by no means an internationally acclaimed director and it was made quickly and cheaply (for approximately $150,000) in thirty-five days.[30] *The Seventh Seal* presupposes an understanding of historical and theological issues that, despite its subsequent popular success, indicates that the film was aimed at an elite or intellectual audience.[31] The complex imaginary from which the film arose can be linked very closely with Bergman's own background and philosophy, which has been well documented.

Bergman, a Swede born in 1918, was a lapsed Lutheran who had fled his oppressive family context (his father was an overbearing Lutheran chaplain) aged eighteen. In his book on the film, Melvyn Bragg comments particularly on the fact that silence was used as a cruel punishment within the Bergman household.[32] The divine silence of Rev. 8.1–2 (following the opening of the Seven Seals of Rev. 6, we are told that there is silence in

Heaven for half an hour) is usually viewed as a positive moment in the text by biblical commentators. In *The Seventh Seal*, however, this quotation, which opens and closes the film, is more like a punishment with a particular resonance.

Despite his own religious scepticism, Bergman wrote an introduction to the script of the film (which he also wrote as well as directed) in which he bemoans loss of faith on both a general level and also in terms of the extent to which this has affected the relationship between artists and their art.[33] Whereas formerly artists sought to glorify God with their creations, in Bergman's opinion the artist's individualism had become almost holy.[34] With *The Seventh Seal* Bergman harked back to the reconstruction of Chartres Cathedral in the twelfth and thirteenth centuries and the crafts-men who played a part in that, a role which he himself seemed to want to emulate via the making of his film: 'Regardless of whether I am a Christian or not, I would play my part in the collective building of the cathedral.'[35]

As mentioned above, the film opens and closes with the same quotation from Revelation: 'And when he [the Lamb] had opened the Seventh Seal, there was silence in heaven about the space of half an hour' (Rev. 8.1). The divine silence occurs at the end of the seven disasters brought to Earth by the Four Horsemen. It thus marks an ending in one sense, and there is a moment of calm in Heaven and on Earth at this point, but more disasters are to follow. Boxall argues that we should interpret this silence as either an appropriate response to the divine or as 'the lull before the storm, the silence out of which the creative and re-creative Word of God emerges'.[36] Whatever the exact sense of the verse, Boxall and most other biblical com-mentators agree that this is a rare positive moment within Revelation, prior to the New Jerusalem of Rev. 21–2 (perhaps to be set alongside Rev. 7.14 and 21–2, which also focus on positive manifestations of divine worship). We might therefore expect that the events of the film, which supposedly takes place within this apocalyptic half hour, to be calm and perhaps even positive.

But what Bergman does not quote in the film is that in Revelation this silence is followed by fire being cast on the earth by an angel, followed by thunder, lightning, and earthquakes. Most of what happens in the film is also very grisly, with violence, plague, and starvation already stalking the land. Like a visualization of some of the medieval movements described by Norman Cohn, there are processions of flagellants singing the *Dies Irae* in anticipation of the end of the world, and the burning of a teenage witch.

There is an evil apostate priest, who dies in terror, and sinister villagers. Given its mood, it is far more plausible to see the silence which Bergman is referring to as something quite different from Revelation's half hour of calm, and rather more attuned to Bergman's characteristic aesthetic: the silence Bergman gives us is the desolate silence of a God who is absent, experienced as silent and absent by those on Earth who are already subject to the scourges of Revelation. Antonius Block, the main protagonist of the film, a Crusader knight, is himself tortured by the absence of any sign of God. The film opens with him returning to his country, which is riven by the Black Death, after fighting in the Crusades. He is stalked throughout the film by the figure of Death, which only he can see. Block engages in a desperate game of chess with Death in an effort to postpone his own death. Block is accompanied along his travels by his optimistic squire, Jöns, and forms a sort of friendship with some actors named Jof and Mia and their baby (who are reminiscent of the Holy Family, Jos and Mia perhaps representing Joseph and Mary).

'Death' might well be the Fourth Horseman of the Apocalypse, and, in Johannine mode, Block is indeed a visionary. Like John of Patmos, he is the only character who actually sees Death; the other characters think that he is playing chess by himself. In what is perhaps an attempt to cement this interpretation, the opening scene on the beach features an eagle (the symbol of John the Evangelist, with whom John of Patmos was confused in medieval times) circling the sea near Block.[37] Interestingly, though, Block is not the only visionary. Another character, the actor-juggler Jof, is constantly having visions, which his childlike wife Mia only half believes in. He is also, like John, nearly burnt alive by his enemies. Even more strikingly, one of his visions is of the Virgin Mary with the child—portrayed in the film very much like the Woman Clothed with the Sun of Rev. 12.

Despite these moments of light, for the most part the film is unremittingly bleak. For Block and his companions it ends after a night of apocalyptic storms, interspersed with a period of eerie stillness, maybe itself a direct reference to the half-hour silence of Rev. 8.1. We then see the film's most famous image: a grisly dance in silhouette on a still, dark hillside just before dawn as Death takes his victims away. A still from this moment in the film is shown in bold silhouette on the French version of the publicity poster for the film (Plate 51). Because of the way this image has become so embedded in the mind, many are surprised to learn that this is not actually the end of the film, which sees Jos and Mia and their infant son in the bright morning of a new day, having escaped the fate of the others. Are Jof and Mia Joseph and Mary, and their child the redeemer? Is Bergman hinting at a New Jerusalem for the saved, perhaps, for those (like Jos) in touch with the vision of the seer of Patmos?

It is hard not to read *The Seventh Seal* in this way if one sees it in the context of Revelation—and so to see the film as giving at least a nod in the direction of an orthodox interpretation in which the faithful are indeed written into the 'book of life' (Rev. 21.12). However, this ostensibly happy ending is so out of character with the rest of the film as to make thought of a New Jerusalem here seem naïve in the extreme. Bergman, we are told, was obsessed not just with loss of faith but also with the devastation of nuclear war, for which his tale of medieval apocalypticism (flagellants, dances of death, and the like) stands as an allegory. Even more pertinent, though, is the suggestion that Bergman and his film are taking the silence of God in Rev. 8.1 to be God's absence on earth, and hence presenting an agonizing existential conundrum for the would-be believer.

For if there is no God in the traditional sense, then there can be no New Jerusalem at the end of the suffering that John of Patmos saw and which we still see all around us today. However, Kalin argues that the divine is present in *The Seventh Seal* in other subtler ways, such as in the 'joy and love of Jof and Mia's family, the sharing of wild strawberries, the knight's meaningful deed'.[38] Perhaps, then, Bergman is attempting in this film to subvert the quest for the traditional Judeo-Christian God (in whose existence he almost certainly did not believe), represented in the film by Block's efforts to find God, in favour of a more nuanced appreciation of the existence of the divine in human relationships and interactions. This would be a markedly twentieth-century reading of Revelation, but, if we think of Dürer's image of the heavenly throne room of Rev. 4 and 5 in which the Nurembergers have no inkling of what is going on in the Heaven above them (and indeed are entirely unable to access the secrets being revealed to John), it is not entirely without precedent (see Figure 2.1).[39]

## *Apocalypse Now*

The sense that the idea of a grand redemption or restoration or reunion with God is in fact a misleading myth is brought to the fore once again in Coppola's *Apocalypse Now* of 1979 (based on Conrad's *Heart of Darkness*). Here the personal crisis of Captain Benjamin Willard (Martin Sheen) is interwoven with the story of Colonel Kurtz (Marlon Brando), a renegade colonel turned cult leader and cannibal, against the backdrop of the Vietnam War. Towards the end of the film Kurtz (who is eventually murdered by Willard, who has been sent by the US army to assassinate him) recites some lines from T. S. Eliot's *Hollow Men* of 1925: 'This is the way the world ends/ This is the way the world ends/ This is the way the world ends/ Not with a bang but with a whimper.' Once again, even if we can see Willard as a sort of latter-day John experiencing an apocalyptic vision, any sense of the pre-twentieth century redemptive understanding of the 'apocalypse' of the film's title is swept away on a tide of underwhelming nihilism; the film's invocation of apocalypse is of the generalized type characteristic of recent appropriations of that theme.[40] Apart, perhaps, from *The Seventh Seal*, the main exception to this general rule are the *Left Behind* films, based on the books of that name, which, in luridly dispensationalist manner, attach Revelation's apocalyptic message to the near future of the world as it is today. We will look at this phenomenon in the next section, which considers some approaches to Revelation in modern literature.

## Revelation in literature

In turning to twentieth-century literature, having already considered one major contribution to the apocalyptic corpus (Thomas Mann's *Dr Faustus*), we will now consider some very different approaches to Revelation. First we will look at D. H. Lawrence's powerful but highly personal take on Revelation, after which we will consider the much more literal treatments in popular American prophetic and evangelical writing, both fictional and non-fictional. Finally, we will look at two treatments of Revelation in a more recent literary genre, that of the graphic Bible.

### D. H. Lawrence, *Apocalypse*

If, in the main, twentieth-century treatments of Revelation either take an orthodox Christian reading of the text, emphasizing its triumphal aspects, or see it simply as a metaphor for universal catastrophe, D. H. Lawrence's *Apocalypse*—his last work, published posthumously in 1931—emphatically does neither.[41] Lawrence was, of course, deeply hostile to Christianity, which he saw as moralistic, life-denying, and (following Nietzsche) the revenge of the weak on the strong. He also, he tells us, had come to find Revelation deeply unattractive in the unnaturalness of its imagery and, even more, in the fact that, in its vivid descriptions of the toppling of worldly grandeur and of the punishment of the sinful, it may actually have had more influence than the Gospels and the Epistles, at least among uneducated people. Clearly Lawrence would have been far less surprised than most contemporary commentators by the success of the *Left Behind* series, a hugely popular series of American novels based on Revelation (which we consider below).

Despite his negative feelings about it, Lawrence knew Revelation in great detail. He was also clearly stirred by much of its imagery, what he calls its mythology, which in *Apocalypse* he analyses closely, drawing both on biblical scholarship and on the study of comparative religion. His underlying thesis is that Revelation is not one but two or even more books, composed over a long period of time, centuries even.[42] It is based on ancient religious myths and mysteries—about the sun and the moon, about new births individual and collective, about the Great Mother as creator and destroyer, about ages waxing and waning, about the creative necessity of strife, about dragons as forces of life and death, of twins as sources of fecundity and limit; but on to this mythology have been grafted both Jewish and, to a greater extent, Christian themes.

Lawrence is far more positive about the first half of Revelation than about the later chapters. He sees the initial appearance of God in the heavenly throne room (Rev. 4) as having nothing humble about it, but as symbolizing what he calls the Kosmokrator—the creator of the cosmos—while beneath the Lamb of Rev. 5 Lawrence sees the Lion of Judah as dominant, a lion in lamb's fleece, so to speak, 'as if' slain, but actually slaying millions of 'inimical kinds'.[43] This reverses the conventional understanding of this passage, whereby John expects to see the Lion of Judah next to God in the throne room and instead sees the slaughtered Lamb (see Chapter 2). This has traditionally been seen as an embodiment of the Christian message (that true greatness is found in humility and obedience) that Lawrence so despised.

Lawrence himself saw the world and all of us as bound up in a throbbing unity of life and creativity. He calls this vision religious but essentially godless, godless because it is gods which have tended to introduce divisions between us and the cosmos, and, even worse, to impose restrictive and impossible commandments on their followers. It is precisely this negative godliness which Lawrence sees as dominant in the second part of Revelation, which depicts the sacrilegious destruction of the whole cosmos by an avenging divinity. This is, of course, welcomed by Christian believers, as their resentful revenge on the powers of the world—Babylon, Rome, or whatever.

Nor is Lawrence a fan of the New Jerusalem. In his Introduction to Frederick Carter's *The Dragon* he writes: 'Of all the stale buns, the New Jerusalem is one of the stalest... only invented for the aunties of this world.'[44] It is full of impudent and revengeful saved people, insisting on wiping out the whole universe, but also, in true 'bourgeois' spirit, containing flowers that never fade.[45] And to add final insult to injury, Lawrence sees in the atheistical revolutionary Lenin the same resentful, egalitarian, and soul-destroying impulses as he finds in the Christian saints.[46]

Lawrence's very negative conclusion is that Revelation shows us the true nature of Christianity as vengeful and petty-minded, as maniacally anti-life; but it also, in its very resistance to life, it shows us what the human heart secretly yearns for, and what the apocalypse would destroy: 'the sun and the stars, and all kings and all rulers, all scarlet and purple and cinnamon, all harlots... passionate love and the proper unison of men... and the very marvel of being alive in the flesh', all as part of 'the living incarnate cosmos'.[47] Lawrence is surely right to see in Revelation different levels and different strands, and his *Apocalypse* demonstrates once again the power and adaptability of the visions it contains. And for all the idiosyncracy, if not perversity, of its interpretations, Lawrence's *Apocalypse* is valuable in suggesting the archetypical nature of many of the symbols and images of Revelation, and their parallels in other religions and cosmologies. Nor, obviously, is he wholly negative about Revelation, extolling as he does the kosmodynamical (as he might have put it) elements underlying what he sees as the Christian veneer.


## Hal Lindsey, the *Left Behind* series, and graphic Bibles

In the *Guardian Magazine* in September 2011 the novelist Audrey Niffenegger wrote that her 'biggest disappointment' was, 'The Rapture—I was hoping that it would take away all the folks who wanted to be taken away, leaving room for the rest of us to get on with things.' This is an ironic comment from a writer unsympathetic to fundamentalist Christianity, but it is indicative of how complex, and to an extent polarized, attitudes to Revelation and the end times have become in recent times, particularly in the USA. As Lawrence lamented in the 1920s, in certain circles Revelation has great popular appeal. Its capacity for popular appeal has coincided with the rise of 'prophecy culture' and evangelical Dispensationalism, in the USA in particular, over the last fifty to one hundred years (although the roots of the movement date back to John Darby, 1800–82, and his belief in a Scriptural prophetic calendar, which drew heavily on Revelation).[48] This phenomenon and the relationship of evangelical Dispensationalism to Revelation was outlined in the Introduction (section 'Revelation and the end times'). Dispensationalists believe, in short, that history is divided into seven dispensations or ages. We are currently living in the sixth age (the age of the church) which will be followed by the Rapture, the Tribulation period, the Millennium (the seventh age), after which the New Jerusalem will be established. Revelation is one of the key texts drawn upon by Dispensationalists in the formulation of this timeline (alongside Isaiah, Ezekiel, Daniel, 1 Thessalonians, to name but a few). By the 1970s around eight million Americans were committed to Dispensationalism, and today this number is estimated to be at around twenty-five to thirty million.[49] One of the fundamental tenets of the movement, which should of course not be viewed as a wholly homogenous one with homogenous beliefs, is a belief in their 'marginality', their status at the fringes of popular American society, which they so despise. Indeed, it is now almost a truism to state that although the literature associated with the movement claims to be about the future, it is, in fact, very much about the present, in that underneath the predictions regarding the end times is a 'faith-based and conservative critique of American modernity', its politics, particularly its foreign policy, its embrace of cutting-edge technology (although this is beginning to change as the utility of social media in promulgating the evangelical message becomes clearer), and its quest for 'spirituality'.[50] However, even discounting the fact that a number of American politicians, including ex-president Reagan himself, seem to identify with aspects of the Dispensationalist position, both non-fiction and fiction books (and films) by evangelical Dispensationalist authors have, in recent times, begun to enjoy more mainstream popularity, even making it onto American bestseller lists.[51] Thus claims to marginality and outsider status are starting to look more questionable.

A preacher and author who was in part responsible for the proliferation of evangelical Dispensationalist ideas regarding the end times into the American mainstream was Hal Lindsey. Following the success of his speaking tours of the USA in the 1960s as part of the 'Campus Crusade for Christ', Lindsey capitalized on what he saw as a renewed interest among Americans in the future and wrote *The Late Great Planet Earth* in 1970.[52] The book, in which Lindsey maps his understanding of 'biblical prophecy' onto contemporary world events, went on to be the number one non-fiction bestseller of the decade, selling more than thirty million copies worldwide overall (according to some estimates). In 1979 a documentary-like film version of the book featuring Lindsey and narrated by Orson Welles was released by Pacific International Enterprises.[53] In a bizarre twist that confirms the existence of a theological and a practical alliance between the Dispensationalists and Israelis (see below), Israel's UN ambassador, Chaim Herzog, even gave an interview for the documentary.[54]

Lindsey deplored the fact that Americans were turning to astrology and even to politicians for advice about the future when, in his eyes, the most reliable prophecy about future events can be found in the Bible. Focusing particularly on Zechariah, Daniel, and Ezekiel from the Hebrew Bible and on Revelation from the New Testament, Lindsey makes a series of predictions about the near future. In particular, he locates himself and Christians like him at a pivotal point in the eschatological schema of the world. The Rapture, Tribulation (a period of unrest following the Rapture of the most faithful), Armageddon, and the start of the Millennium are all perceived as near.

In terms of his methods Lindsey is a 'biblical literalist' in that, in contrast to most biblical scholars, he believes that different parts of the Bible, deriving from very different times and places, can be selected at random and woven into a sort of über-prophecy. The rationale behind this approach is that every part of the Bible is seen as the Word of God and so there is no conflict involved in piecing various different sections together. Based on the combination of this biblical evidence and the historical events occurring around him, Lindsey argued that the creation of the Jewish state in 1948 and the return of Jews to Israel, which also prompted hopes that the Temple would be rebuilt, had been a significant turning point in Christian history. This is because the Jewish return to Palestine is the fulfilment of certain predictions made in Zechariah and Daniel in particular, as well as in the writings of Paul and Revelation. This is seen as a positive event, which will prepare the way for the establishment of the millennial Christian Kingdom of God within around twenty years from when he wrote in 1970, Lindsey argued.[55] However, in line with the prophets (see Daniel 9.27, for example) this new kingdom will be preceded by certain world conflicts, in particular an attack on Israel by Russia and certain Arab and African powers, and the establishment of a new Rome or Babylon in Europe. He argues that this new Rome will take the guise of a 'ten nation European confederacy' (the European Economic Community at the time Lindsey was writing) headed up by Antichrist, who himself is described using terminology from Rev. 12 and 13 (see, for example, the ten horns of the Sea Beast in Rev. 13.1).

The Antichrist described by Lindsey, who must come to earth before the end times, will be a political leader, more evil even than Mao, Stalin, or Hitler, and will be identifiable from the fact that he will experience a head wound that will be miraculously healed (Rev. 13.3). In addition to the terrifying political rule of Antichrist, Lindsey also argues (on the basis of Rev. 17), that Antichrist will introduce a 'one-world religion' as represented by the Whore of Babylon in Rev. 17, who can be seen to represent religious 'harlotry' as well as sexual immorality. (This reveals the fear that fundamentalist Christians have of ecumenism, and also draws on their sense that the USA is collapsing internally through drugs, crime, false religions, and sexual immorality.) The book climaxes with an evocation of World War Three or Armageddon, which Lindsey believes will literally be fought in the Valley of Megiddo in Israel, involving not just Russia and the Arabs but an 'incredible Oriental (i.e. Chinese) army of 200 million soldiers', as well as representatives of the USA, Western Europe, and the rest of the world.[56] For Lindsey, Armageddon is both a symbol of the end and also the literal site of the battle which will herald the setting up of the millennial kingdom, a thousand years of God's kingdom on earth (which he treats pretty summarily), before the final battle (with the decisive defeat of Satan's forces), the Last Judgement, and eternity. Needless to say, and in line with Lawrence's bitter scorn, there is plenty of swift and righteous destruction of the ungodly both around Armageddon and at the Last Judgement a thousand years later, about which Lindsey is remarkably untroubled both humanly and theologically.

Lawrence's scorn would doubtless have been magnified by the fact that the faithful believers are not themselves to undergo the seven years of tribulation, let alone Armageddon. They will be raptured into Heaven, smugly to observe what is going on below, and it is notable that the Rapture forms something of a hiatus in Lindsey's sensationalized account of mankind's accelerating rush to doom. (Not surprisingly, perhaps, apocalyptic Christianity gained in popularity in the nineteenth century when its prophets began to stress the Rapture of the elect; the struggles of Armageddon would not be for them!) It is also notable that none of the characters involved in Lindsey's prophecies seems to have any ability to deflect the inexorable course of history: one wonders what would happen if they all read *The Late Great Planet Earth* and took steps to avoid its prophecies.

Despite Lindsey's confident, 'prophetic' writing style, and despite his conviction that Armageddon and the rest would happen and develop 'in the near future', most of his predictions have not come true, at least not so far; nor is the world now as he described it then, a fact which does not seem to have prevented millions of new copies of *The Late Great Planet Earth* being sold even since 1990, the end of the decade to which most of his predictions pertained.[57] While many readers may find his ideas nothing short of preposterous, his book, and especially the parts that focus on Revelation, are testament to the enduring potency of the images, characters, and themes contained therein. And Lindsey's breathless prose betrays a conviction that he is experiencing John's (and Ezekiel's and Daniel's) visions afresh and with as much enthusiasm and assurance as the original seers themselves. Once again the 'author' has succumbed to the desire to self-identify with the Johannine visionary, although in this case to a lesser artistic effect than Dürer, Beckmann, and the rest.

No doubt a successor to Lindsey could weave a similar but different tale around the world as it is in the second decade of the twenty-first century (as opposed to 1970), though that would, needless to say, discredit Lindsey himself. Nevertheless Lindsey represents the Dan Brownish edge of a somewhat bizarre phenomenon which has accompanied the decline and collapse of the Ottoman empire ever since the nineteenth century, namely a fundamentalist reading of biblical prophecy in which the return of the Jews to Palestine and the rebuilding of the Temple and the conversion of at least some of the Jews to Christianity will herald Armageddon and the Millennium. And obviously a fascination with Revelation has played its part here, and so—by a big jump—contributed to support for the State of Israel among the Christian right in the USA.[58]

The *Left Behind* phenomenon began life as a series of books written by two evangelical Christian authors, Jerry Jenkins and Tim LaHaye. The series, published by Christian publishers Tyndale House, has sold nearly sixty-five million copies since the publication of the first book in 1995 and is now a multi-million-dollar international franchise, which includes films, graphic novels, children's novels, and computer games. Although initially slow to attract mainstream attention, the seventh novel in the series was published in 2000 (*The Indwelling*) and went straight to the top of the *New York Times* bestseller list, a remarkable achievement for a 'Christian' novel.[59] The Barna research group found that one quarter of the American population is aware of the *Left Behind* books and 9 per cent had read at least one. While the majority of this audience was drawn from conservative Christians, they estimated that around three million 'non-born-again' Americans had read at least one of the books.[60] Thus it is no exaggeration to refer to the *Left Behind* series and its related media as a phenomenon, the like of which has not been seen since Hal Lindsey's prophecy fiction of the 1970s. The main difference between the two is that while Lindsey's speciality is alarmist non-fiction prose, the *Left Behind* novels are a fictional exploration of the end times from an evangelical Dispensationalist perspective. The books are futurist in tone, referring to events leading up to the seventh and final dispensation, whilst simultaneously revealing the evangelical concerns of the present.[61] What they have in common with Lindsey is what one might call their readability factor. They cleverly combine the Dispensationalist take on Revelation with the racy writing style of a Tom Clancy or Stephen King novel. As one reviewer has written, 'The plotting is brisk and the characterizations Manichean. People disappear and things blow up.'[62] More damning is a review from *The Times* in which the series is described as 'the oddest literary phenomenon in the English speaking world' and as 'Nostradamus written by Jeffrey Archer'.[63]

LaHaye (b. 1926), a pastor, is the founder of an organization called the Christian Coalition, and has spent much of his life caught up in resistance against what he calls 'secular humanism'. He has written on subjects as diverse as marriage guidance and social issues, but particularly on Dispensationalism and eschatology.[64] In the early 1990s he teamed up with children's author Jerry Jenkins and they began to produce the *Left Behind* books, which now number sixteen in total and include four volumes of prequel, which were published after the first eleven novels and before the final instalment in the series, *Kingdom Come: The Final Victory* (2007). The first novel (*Left Behind: A Novel of the Earth's Last Days*, 1995) is set in the aftermath of the Rapture, when all the 'good' evangelical Christians and all unborn and prepubescent children will be taken up to Heaven.[65] Those 'left behind' at this point will suffer many disasters and attacks at the hands of Antichrist but also have the chance to repent and turn to Christ prior to his second return and judgement.[66] The series, which also draws heavily on prophecies found in

Revelation, Daniel, Isaiah, and Ezekiel, traces the fate of a group of Americans who have been left behind after the Rapture but who repent, become born-again Christians, and form a Tribulation Force to help save the lost and fight Antichrist, who has appeared on earth in the form of the secretary-general of the UN.

As with other Rapture films and books the Antichrist figure (called Nicolae Carpathia; see Plate 32) is the key character on which the plot necessarily turns (as it is his ultimate defeat which will usher in the Seventh Dispensation or, to use the language of Revelation, the New Jerusalem). He is a perfect reflection of evangelical/Dispensationalist fears about the modern world, such as the spread of internationalism, an increasingly powerful federal Europe, and the subsequent desirability of United States isolationism.[67] He is a charismatic Romanian whose bloodline can be traced back to the Roman emperors (clearly a link to Revelation's original context as a protest text, written at the height of the Roman empire around 90 CE), who takes over the UN and establishes a replacement body known as the Global Community, of which he is the head. Just like the Beasts of Revelation 13, who have commonly been identified with Antichrist in popular interpretation since the medieval era, Carpathia uses deception and false promises of global unity to secure his position. In an echo of Rev. 13.12, which speaks of the Sea Beast surviving a fatal head wound, he even survives an assassination attempt by an Israeli (see *Assassins*, the sixth book in the series). Although dead for three days, with Satan's help Nicolae Carparthia rises again (in a Satanic parody of Christ's resurrection) and amasses a huge army ready for the fight against Christ's army at Armageddon (in *The Indwelling* and *The Mark*). His virtuous opponents, meanwhile, are for the most part North American and born again with all-American names such as Buck Williams and Chloe Steele. In *Kingdom Come*, the final book of the series, which deals with the Millennium, the believers who have not been raptured live for 1,000 years, though there are unsaved people too, who die when they have reached one hundred. By the end of the Millennium the unsaved are numbering billions, and they turn on the righteous in Jersualem (where the Temple has been rebuilt). Jesus then appears, and the whole army of the unrighteous is destroyed by fire. The Last Judgement occurs, Satan, the Beast (Nicolae Carpathia), and all the damned are cast into the lake of fire, and the New Jerusalem descends.

Thus the series follows the chronology and plot of Revelation fairly closely, going through the stages of the rule of the Beast (Rev. 13), Armageddon (Rev. 16, 20), and finally the establishment of the New Jerusalem (Rev. 21) chronologically, as set out in the text. It can at times feel as if Revelation is being presented as a sort of timeline of events that will happen before the end of the world. This is what is known as a radically futurist reading of the text, although, as alluded to above, there are many clues to present evangelical Dispensationalist concerns running through the novels and films. Thus the authors embellish the concept of the apocalypse or end times by adding in details such as the Rapture, which are not found in Revelation itself but are very much part of their own cultural milieu as Dispensationalists. At the same time they remain true to the dominant themes found within the biblical text, such as the plausibility of the revelation of heavenly secrets via human agents and the final redemption that is symbolized by the New Jerusalem. The *Left Behind* series and the related films and media products are thus a very interesting case study for anyone interested in contemporary interpretations of Revelation that challenge the dominant (secular) Western cultural understanding of the text and its related terminology, which tends to be more metaphorical and/or decontextualized. It is a very engaged interpretation of Revelation that reflects the Dispensationalist agenda through fictional media. Walliss argues, in relation to the *Left Behind* films (although his conclusions can be applied to the novels as well), that they can be seen as operating on two levels. On one level they operate almost as teaching aids for the Dispensationalist community, the end goal of such teaching being repentance and conversion to the born-again faith. However, they also provide an opportunity 'whereby a contemporary form of evangelical identity may be articulated and redefined through the language and imagery provided by a premillennial reading of apocalyptic texts'.[68] Thus the *Left Behind* films and other so-called Rapture films represent a mapping out of the evangelical identity through the lens of Revelation and other associated prophecy texts.

Not that the series has escaped criticism from within its own community. Evangelical critics have taken issue with the prophetic teachings present in some of the books. For example, one character (Chang Wong) receives the mark of the Beast (cf. Rev. 13), yet is later accepted into Heaven, an event that explicitly conflicts with material found in Revelation, which states clearly that anyone who receives the mark of the Beast will be thrown into Hell for eternity (Rev. 14.9). Similarly, others have struggled with the changes that LaHaye and Jenkins have made to the Dispensationalist tradition. For example, they include much higher numbers than would normally be deemed realistic in the initial Rapture (interfering with the strongly held conviction that many evangelical Dispensationalists feel that they are a much maligned minority amidst a hostile mainstream American society). Following on from this, they also include all unborn and prepubescent children in the Rapture (whereas formerly this had been restricted to children of evangelical believers).[69] Furthermore, they also include the pope (John XXIV) and a congregation of Catholics in the Rapture. This ecumenical gesture is undermined by the fact that John XXIV's replacement is aligned with Nicolae Carpathia, the Antichrist figure, but nevertheless the initial gesture contrasts strongly with the usual (polemical) evangelical attitude towards Roman Catholicism. Whether this was motivated by ecumenism or capitalism is hard to know: Tyndale House estimates that 11 per cent of the series' readers are Catholics.[70] Finally, many have also taken issue both with the glorification of violence that is found in the novels as well as feeling uncomfortable with the attribution of the Rapture and the terrible tribulations that follow it to a benevolent God. The computer game connected with the series, *Left Behind: Eternal Forces*, has also been criticized for introducing unacceptable degrees of violence into a religious context, as well as for relying on negative racial stereotypes.

Whatever one thinks of the *Left Behind* franchise, however (Europe is the only continent on which it has enjoyed little success), there is no doubting its resilience. Aware of their counter-cultural status, the three films of the books were produced and distributed through Christian media companies. The first film, to the annoyance of the original authors, went straight to DVD but ended up outselling every other title in the United States during the first week of its release.[71] If the books owe not a little to pulp fiction blockbusters, the original films draw on the tired clichés of the standard disaster movie, as we saw earlier in this chapter, in which small groups of heroes and villains battle their way through cataclysmic events. In this case, of course, the cataclysms are those familiar to readers of Revelation and associated prophecy literature, both scriptural and present-day evangelical. But the acting is wooden (not surprising, given the scripts), the plots clunk, and the seams are everywhere evident. The first film, *Left Behind, the Movie*, contains three scenes of Rapture, or rather of the result of Rapture. Because the raptured ascend naked (which we do not see), we are given the unintentionally humorous sight of distraught people screaming at piles of abandoned clothes left on aircraft seats, in cars, and in beds. The religiously enlightened are continually nudged in a biblical direction: the UN will move to 'New Babylon'; Solomon's Temple will be rebuilt in Jerusalem; and we see the main characters finding a video, made by the reassuring Afro-

American 'Pastor Billings', foretelling the Rapture three years (!) before it happened (and he himself disappeared). Decontextualized biblical references are trotted out on cue, in case we have missed them: 1 Thessalonians (the Rapture), Ezekiel 38 (attack on Israel from the north), Daniel 7 (Rapture marks the start of the reign of Antichrist), 2 Thessalonians (Antichrist sits in the Temple of God), Daniel 9 (peace in the Middle East). After this onslaught of 'prophecy', the film's hero, who is not yet a believer, but is about to become one, utters the deathless line, 'This stuff is compelling!' A mainstream remake of the first film, starring Nicholas Cage and seemingly with higher production values, was released in October 2014 to critical dismay.

The *Left Behind* movement can thus be seen as a hugely successful, significant, independent, perhaps self-sufficient even, offshoot of the evangelical movement, and one that importantly has primarily drawn its inspiration from Revelation. Far from diminishing, in this sphere at least the influence of this 2,000-year-old text is stronger than ever. D. H. Lawrence must be spinning in his grave!

Finally it is worth briefly mentioning two more mainstream contemporary literary responses to Revelation. They are the Action Bible (2010) and the Manga Bible (2007), which can be seen as representatives of a wider tradition of what might be termed graphic interpretations of the Bible. Graphic interpretations of the Bible, which gained some critical credibility with cult graphic artist Robert Crumb's publication of his graphic novel *The Illustrated Book of Genesis* (2009), have become increasingly popular in recent times and represent an accessible way not only of bringing the Bible to children and to those who are functionally illiterate, but also of encapsulating or bringing together what might be termed the main messages of this text in a visual format.

Both the Action Bible and the Manga Bible (Figure 10.4) deal with Revelation fairly briefly. Not surprisingly, given their visual appeal, both Bibles focus on the dramatic events of Revelation, with the Four Horsemen charging along, trailing destruction in their wake (Rev. 6.2–8), the final battle between the Dragon and Christ's army, the burning pit of sulphur bubbling menacingly in the background (Rev. 19–20), and both have an evocation of the New Jerusalem (Rev. 21, although neither is visually very successful, the New Jerusalem being notoriously hard to depict visualize). These Bibles thus represent a new take on Revelation for the twenty-first century: Revelation recast for the new millennium in the style of the graphic novel or manga comic, a genre that is renowned elsewhere for its depictions of

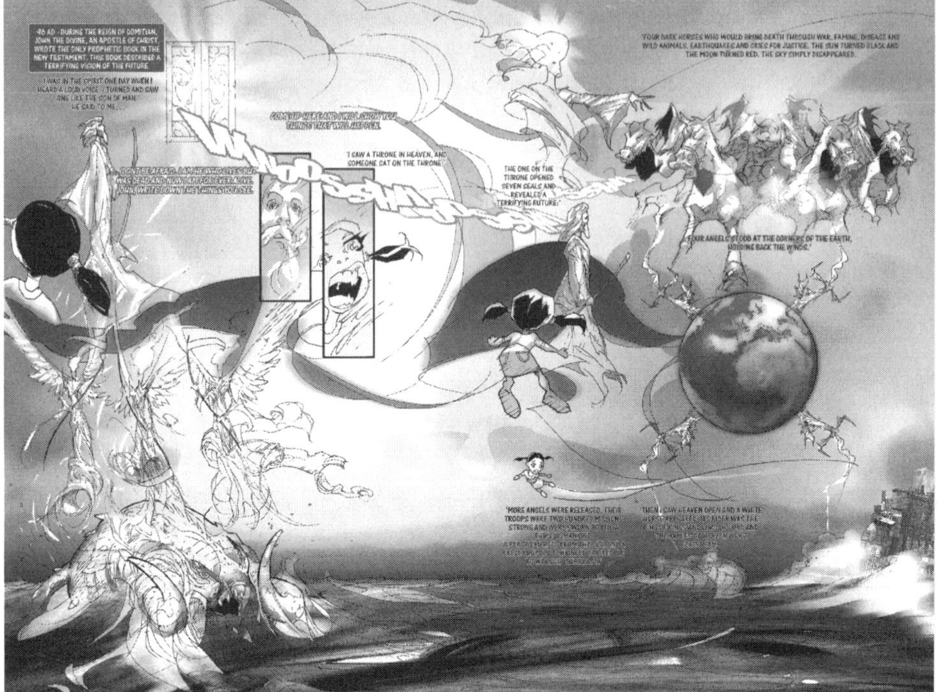


**Figure 10.4.** Detail from the Manga Bible, 2007. Reproduced by kind permission of Siku

violence and pornography. The Action and Manga Bible images are dramatic and striking in their own way even though the text accompanying them in both Bibles is theologically conservative. It either consists of direct quotations from the text of Revelation or quite literal précis of the text. In contrast to what we shortly see in the case of Latin America, the opportunity for a more radical juxtaposition of text and image has not been taken up by these graphic artists. This is doubtless because of their own predilections, but perhaps also reflects the hopes of their publishers for the Bibles to appeal to the more conservative end of the market in the UK and the USA.[72]

## Revelation in African and Latin American cultures

We will end this chapter by looking briefly at how Revelation has been viewed more recently by communities from cultures other than the Western European and North American models that we have focused on thus far.

Some interesting interpretations have arisen in both Africa (Ethiopia and South Africa) and Latin America.

Surprisingly, perhaps, the 'African' Christian tradition of the last century or so (if one can even speak with confidence of *a* tradition, there being many different variations stretching across this vast continent) has largely neglected Revelation as a text. The newer, Pentecostal forms of Christianity in particular, while tending to prioritize biblical texts that emphasize restoration (such as Isaiah), reject millenarianism and thus along with it millennial texts such as Revelation and Daniel. However, there are two notable counter-examples from Africa which are worth mentioning, though one is from much earlier than the twentieth century.

The first is an interesting tradition from Ethiopia, which centres on an Amharic commentary on Revelation dating back to the years following the first century CE. The Amharic commentary material (on all biblical books) is used by the Ethiopian Orthodox Church to this day. It is passed down through generations of priests orally, but interestingly the text of the commentary on Revelation has been printed and is also very extensive. This gives it a position of importance in the Ethiopian Orthodox tradition despite the fact that, as is the case with other African churches, Revelation is the least frequently read text in Ethiopian Orthodox services. The aspects of Revelation that are focused on in Ethiopian theology are the eschatological perspective (Rev. 21–2), its teaching about the False Messiah (Rev. 13), and the Last Judgement (Rev. 20). In the commentary itself there are special excursuses dedicated to, among other things, the resurrection and judgement (Rev. 20.11–15) and the New Jerusalem (Rev. 21). The author of the commentary rejects any historical or 'presentist' reading of the text, preferring to see Rev. 1–3 as having occurred within John's lifetime (which he compares with times of Christian persecution under Islam) and the remainder of Revelation as being set to take place in the future.[73]

Ethiopia also has a very rich and distinctive heritage of church painting, dating from the earliest days of Christianity, though most extant examples are actually from rather later. Notable references to Revelation are to be found in the churches at Narga Sellase, Koraro, Lalibela, and Tigray. The focus in these images (as it was in very early Western Christian and Byzantine church art) is primarily on the Twenty-four Elders and the Tetramorph (the Four Living Creatures). The dome of the rock-hewn church of Abuna Gabre Mikael at Koraro, for example, has been painted with a striking image of twelve of the Twenty-four Elders, giving the impression that the heavenly realm of Rev. 4–5 is suspended above the worshipper (Plate 52). The result-ant effect is actually quite unnerving, giving the viewer the impression that the Twenty-four Elders are staring down at them, observing their every move. Another Ethiopian visual tradition which has its origins in Revelation is the prevalence of striking images of St Michael killing the Dragon (cf. Rev. 12).[74]

Much more recently in South Africa, as already mentioned in the Introduction and Chapter 7, Allan Boesak, a minister from the Dutch Reformed Church in South Africa and a vocal opponent of the apartheid regime, wrote a very influential commentary on Revelation in 1987, after a period of imprisonment during which, like John of Patmos, he claims to have been the recipient of an angelic visitation.[75] His commentary views Revelation as an example of 'underground protest literature' from which those suffering under the apartheid regime could draw comfort and inspi-ration. Taking a 'contemporary historical understanding of the text', he views Revelation as prophetic but not in a fixed or rigid sense: 'What was true in the time of John is proven to be true over and over again in the history of the church.' Thus Boesak, like some of the other commentators and artists we have looked at in this book, sees no inconsistency in linking his own situation in the 1980s to those described in the ancient text. He sees the South African state as a clear embodiment of the 'beast from the sea' of Rev. 13, a state which had the opportunity to be a 'servant of God' but ended up, through acts of extreme racism, exploitation, oppression, and inhumanity, in a parody of that role. The second beast of Rev. 13.13–15 (and here he also finds parallels with Nazi Germany) he sees embodied in the South African Dutch Reformed Church, which provided theological jus-tification for the acts of the 'first beast'. This interpretation brings out the deceitful aspects of the 'second beast' highlighted in Rev. 13.13–15.[76] In a later chapter he addresses the Whore of Babylon, another metaphor for the apartheid regime, saying, 'Your fate shall be the fate of Babylon, which is called Egypt, which is called Rome, which is called Pretoria.'[77] Although Boesak's political integrity was challenged by accusations of embezzlement in the post-apartheid era, his commentary remains a powerful reminder of Revelation's continued capacity to speak to those suffering from injustice and oppression.

This brings us finally to Latin America where Revelation has been used, along with other key biblical texts, in a directly political manner, similar in its way to Boesak, though without the dangerously self-defeating literalism of the prophetic of evangelical writers like Hal Lindsey and the *Left Behind* authors. It is in Latin and South America that we see the greatest enthusiasm for this brand of what its advocates would think of as 'theology as praxis'. Known as liberation theology, it originated in the 1960s and took off in earnest in the 1970s and 1980s, particularly in places where there have been active revolutionary movements outside the church. Liberation theology calls for a re-examination of the Christian tradition from the perspective of the politically and economically oppressed. Carlos Mesters, for example, a Carmelite priest and biblical scholar, used his experience of interpreting the Bible with the poor via grass-roots 'Bible circles' to develop an approach to biblical study which eschews any taint of elite, sterile, or scientific activity in favour of one in which ordinary people bring their own experiences to the Bible. The poor and oppressed are encouraged to read the stories they find there through the prism of their own lives, and then to go on to act in the light of what they have discovered.[78]

By reflecting on the Bible 'from below' as it were, and often within a varied, oral context, biblical interpretation can be both 'liberated' from the shackles of conventionally academic ways of doing theology, and 'liberating' for the practitioners, who like the readers of Boesak's commentary find immediate and renewed relevance in biblical stories. Boesak, like the liberation theologians of South America, believes that the Holy Spirit works through local and grass-roots communities in accordance with the rallying cry found in Rev. 2.7: 'Let anyone who has an ear listen to what the Spirit is saying to the churches.' While the Gospel parables and the prophetic texts of the Old Testament are important for liberation exegesis, Revelation has established itself as the preferred book of the base Christian communities, as these local groups of poor believers are known.

Revelation and other prophetic texts are seen as encapsulating both the memory of the struggles of the poor and calls to present political action, with liberation theology inspiring social criticism and subversion of the existing order, by means of image and symbol rather than by systematic argument. Revelation is particularly valued for the way it unmasks reality, in showing the toppling of the Beasts and the Whore of Babylon; through its imaginative power it leads the believer to reject the current, dominant ways of interpreting the social order, the new Rome in this case encompassing both the capitalist and authoritarian regimes of South and Latin America of today, and the earlier destruction of indigenous peoples and ways of life by the Spanish conquistadores of the sixteenth century. The approach is not, though, spiritual and unworldly; the reality of this world is vigorously embraced, but so as radically to recast that reality.

While for the liberationists in this present time of oppression the Lamb continues to be slain and the Beasts to rule, Revelation presages a New Jerusalem in the here and now, one to be achieved by politico-evangelical action. The prophecy the new grass-roots churches are enjoined to practice in Rev. 11 is one of no compromise with the current order, but rather to institute a new order, via the base Christian communities, for whom the meaning of a biblical text is in the application it has in their lives and actions (particularly actions), rather than in some timeless, once and for all meaning. In the words of Pablo Richard, a liberationist theologian, 'the eschatological is not the end of history, but rather what puts an end to the Beasts and Satan and all their followers, who have controlled the world'. And Richard emphasizes that the eschatology of Revelation is realized in the present time, in the process of working towards the construction of a utopian political order by the revolutionary activity of the base communities, the building of what he calls the reign of God in history.[79]

The liberation understanding of Revelation is one in which the book is illustrated not primarily in pictures or music or words, but rather in the lives and actions of the downtrodden, which partly explains why there are few actual images from this theological source. But only partly; given the dangers involved in their activity, many of the liberation communities found it safer not to keep records or document their activities visually or in writing, which helped to compound the sense that what really counts is what the people do rather than what they write or paint or draw. There has, moreover, been a tense relationship between liberation theologians and the official Catholic Church, due to their political radicalism and what is perceived officially as their tendency to concentrate on the material at the expense of the spiritual.

However, there have been visual responses to Revelation from within the movement. As discussed in Chapter 5, Alma Lopez, a Mexican-born Chicana artist, has re-envisaged the Woman Clothed with the Sun as a young Mexican illegal immigrant. Another particularly striking image is from Yolanda Lopez's *Virgen de Guadelupe* series. Yolanda Lopez is also a Mexican-American artist who seeks to challenge the portrayal of Mexican women in the media through her work. Her *Woman Clothed with the Sun* is itself an updating of the famous Virgin of Guadeloupe, one of the most revered icons in Latin America. This is supposed to be the imprint which the Virgin Mary, envisioned as the Woman Clothed with the Sun, left on the cloak of the peasant who, in 1531, had just had the vision. The icon, which is housed in the Basilica of Our Lady of Guadeloupe in Mexico City, depicts the young Virgin standing on a crescent moon (cf. Rev. 12.1), enclosed in a golden mandorla (representing the sun) and wearing a dark-blue cloak decorated with gold stars.

Lopez's series of three Guadalupe paintings (1978) replaces the conventional figure of the Virgin with contemporary Mexican women. The first is the artist herself as an exuberant running Virgin, apparently breaking free of the chains of oppression of her people. The third is of an elderly woman, Victoria Franco, calmly and stoically waiting for death, according to the artist herself empowered in that she is no longer struggling with life and sexuality. The second of the paintings is of Lopez's own mother, Margaret F. Stewart, depicted at her sewing machine, bespectacled, unadorned, and far from glamourous or glamourized (Plate 53). But she is a strong working woman who is making her own destiny in the form of the Virgin/Woman Clothed with the Sun's traditional gold-starred cloak that she is sewing, and she also bears other attributes of the original Virgin of Guadalupe, including the roses scattered during the vision.[80] This and the others in the series can very much be seen in terms of the church working from below (although significantly, when Pope John Paul II reiterated the Catholic Church's critical line on liberation theology, he chose to do it at the foot of the original icon of Our Lady of Guadeloupe).

Liberation theology is not without its critics, of course. Among other things, its insistence on the religious primacy of political activity over anything more spiritual or transcendent, and above all on an economic-cum-political fundamentalism in which a simplistic quasi-Marxist analysis of the state is utilized, have been called into question. Against this the liberationists point to passages in the Gospels, such as Matt. 25.31–45, in which Christ's followers are also commanded to see the incarnate Christ in those who are poor and vulnerable here on earth, and will be condemned if they not.

Whatever we decide about the liberationists' precise use of Revelation, as in that of Lindsey and his followers, we see once again the extraordinary ability of the book to inspire and to structure people's understanding of their situation. For those of us brought up in modern secular cultures, any such biblical literalism may seem to belong to a different age altogether. But, as our survey of Revelation in the twentieth and twenty-first centuries shows, it certainly does not. And even where biblical literalism and Christian belief more generally have gone out of fashion, in popular culture at least the potency of the notion of apocalypse and of its related cast of characters seems, if anything, only to have grown.

# Revelation
## Artistic Reception and Relevance

In the Introduction to this book we set out two main aims. First, we sought to demonstrate, via our visual and artistic examples, that non-academic interpretations from the reception history of Revelation can provide those who engage with them with important insights into that complex text. They may even provide a healthy challenge to some of the presuppositions that may have been formed from reading academic commentaries on Revelation. Second, it was our contention that if interested parties could be encouraged to look behind the decontextualized and usually negative impression that they may have formed of Revelation and apocalypticism in general, they would discover many themes and questions of relevance. It was for this reason that the book has been organized around nine themes from Revelation, which most people would have heard of, but possibly without having a full understanding. In what follows we will draw the findings of this book together around the two main aims of the book, namely visual exegesis and contemporary relevance.

## Visual exegesis

Whilst there are many commentaries that elucidate the theological complexity of Revelation in far deeper and more scholarly ways than ours, it is our hope that we have demonstrated that the visionary and contrasting aspects of this fascinating text are often brought out most forcefully and most successfully through artistic, musical, and literary interpretations of the text. In one sense Revelation is a special case in that it is the only 'visionary' text in the New Testament. Its visionary nature, frequent references to 'seeing', and highly symbolic language lend themselves, we have argued, very naturally to visualization and other non-academic artistic forms of interpretation. It is through these sorts of interpretation that the viewer/hearer/reader gains a sense of the experiences that might have inspired John to set his visions or imaginings to paper, as well as bringing to those visions a sense of immediacy and synchronicity that is hard to conceptualize either from reading Revelation or a commentary on it. Alongside the visionary illumination that artistic interpretations can bring to Revelation are many other exegetical insights. This section on visual exegesis is an attempt to bring together and analyse some of the main trends in the visual interpretations or, to use a theological term, exegesis, of Revelation that we have discussed in this book.

In our survey of visual treatments of Revelation over the ages, we have seen a big distinction between the episodic approach of the medieval and a more synchronic, condensed style in subsequent times. While there are, of course, important differences between the medieval Apocalypses we have looked at, they all attempt literalistic and detailed coverages of the text (sometimes devoting as many as eighty-five images to the task). The level of detail can be extensive: *Trinity* devotes no less than six images to the Woman Clothed with the Sun, while *Angers* has seven for the Beast sequence of Rev. 13. In the fifteenth century, with the *Flemish Apocalypse* and the altarpieces of the Van Eycks and Memling, we get a more concentrated, condensed approach and, partly for economic reasons, this trend continues with the woodcuts of Dürer and Cranach. By the time of Velázquez, and subsequently, often single images stand for the meaning of the whole text.

This more condensed approach has advantages. The power that the image has to bring different aspects of a text together (known as synchronicity) allows artists the interpretative freedom to bring together elements of the text that interest them or their patron, or that they feel should be juxtaposed with each other, and this seems to us a particularly apt way of interpreting a visionary text, such as Revelation, which may not find its fullest expression in textual (diachronic) format.

To take the three sequences of seven as an example (Rev. 6, 8–9, and 16), we have seen how (according to most interpreters) these may in fact, with some caveats, be a recapitulation of the same event (rather than three separate, discrete sequences) and that they may also be interpreted as occurring simultaneously. This is very difficult to conceptualize in writing (either in the text of Revelation itself or in a commentary passage). However, these ideas are forcefully brought out in a visual interpretation such as Dürer's condensed image of the Seven Trumpets (see Figure 4.6) in which all the trumpets appear to be unleashed at the same time. He does not depict the Seven Bowls at all, a seeming endorsement of the notion that they are a mere recapitulation of the same event, already expressed in the Seven Seals and Trumpets. Similarly, many of the later images of the fourth Horseman (see Haynes/Mortimer, Figure 3.7; Gillray, Figure 3.8; Blake, Figure 3.9) offer an interpretation whereby the Horseman comes to epitomize all of the sequences of seven. While the viewer may not be ultimately persuaded by such an interpretation, such images nevertheless offer a forceful expression of such an alternative viewpoint.

The more condensed approach of later visualizations also has the advantage that incidents that may not really be separate or which are best seen in conjunction can be so captured, as can the whirling confusion of the whole text (and this a possibility which musical interpretation can also exploit by running together contrasting themes and melodies). Hans Memling's *Apocalypse Panel* is an excellent example of this approach (Plate 3). And in Velázquez's *St John the Evangelist on the Island of Patmos* (Plate 24) we get a masterly combination of both John as visionary and, in the tiny image of his vision of the Woman being chased by the Dragon, of a condensed version of the whole sense of Revelation.

On the other hand the medieval images, which painstakingly illustrate every seal, trumpet, and bowl, and indeed everything else in the text, can bring out nuances and balances which may well be left out of more concentrated visualizations, which can, by contrast, seem reductive. The medieval approach is particularly strong in giving full weight to the balancing of Armageddon and the other woes with the New Jerusalem, and the Horsemen with the Lamb—aspects of Revelation which are, of course, characteristically overlooked in more recent interpretations of Revelation and apocalyptic themes more generally. The medieval manuscript visualizations and works that they inspired, such as *Angers*, also provide the viewer with a sense that they are following John through his visions, as he sees what he sees (as readers will remember, John appears in a minimum of around two-thirds of all the images in the Anglo-Norman Apocalypse iconography). This is experienced particularly powerfully when walking through the huge *Angers* tapestries. Sometimes in the manuscript versions John is depicted as standing or sitting outside the vision, which can give the viewer the sense that he or she is in a similar relation to the experienced vision as

John was or is when he had or has it. We are thus fully engaged in what is set before us. This not only helps the viewer to internalize the narrative, and is a reminder that the visions had to pass through the visionary, but also encourages the viewer to step into John's shoes, as it were, and enter the world of the text (something that may have come more easily to the medieval reader/viewer than the contemporary one).[1]

The more modern literary examples we have considered, whilst diverse in content and relying on a diachronic format, have often tended to take particular sections from Revelation and either expand upon them and apply them to their own time (as in the case of Lindsey, LaHaye, and Jenkins) or to take themes and integrate them into their own thought or line of argumentation (Lawrence, Boesak, and the liberationists). In both cases Revelation has served as inspiration, or as a jumping off point, for new literary ventures, however we may evaluate their ultimate worth. Likewise, as in the past hundred years or so Revelation has been attacked from feminist standpoints, artists such as Yolanda Lopez, Alma Lopez, and Kip Gresham have attempted to redress the balance by presenting what they see as more positive representations of the Woman Clothed with the Sun and the Whore of Babylon.

Throughout the book it has therefore become evident that artists, musicians, and authors working in different time periods have focused on or emphasized differing aspects of Revelation. Thus in some of the earlier, medieval examples we saw the more triumphalist aspects of Revelation being brought out in all manner of nationalist and feudalistic interpretations (although this was often tempered by some sort of emphasis on the humble nature of the Lamb), whereas as we moved through the Reformation and beyond, Revelation began to be used as a platform for political and ecclesial critique, something that it has continued to provide right up until the present moment, although a far more contemporary take on Revelation has been the purely negative apocalypses we see in so much twentieth- and twenty-first-century art and popular culture. We hope, though, that by showing Revelation and its artistic interpretations through the ages we will have helped to demonstrate which interpretations are merely of their time, using Revelation as a peg on which to hang their own convictions, and which can contribute to a fuller and more rounded interpretation of the text. Thus we would claim that one of the strengths of our approach is the way it has allowed us to recalibrate and rebalance impressions of Revelation, so that amidst the battles the centrality of the Lamb is acknowledged, and Armageddon offset by the New Jerusalem. And, as stressed in Chapter 9 on the New Jerusalem, it is only by looking in depth at many visual interpretations, side by side (just as one would do with biblical commentaries) and in conjunction with textual interpretations, that one can come to an informed opinion regarding Revelation and its essential themes and nuances.

## An impossible book?

In this final section, we will briefly summarize the main trends in interpretations of Revelation as a whole that have emerged throughout the book. This will enable us to elucidate the other main contention of the book, that Revelation still has a real contemporary significance, even in the twenty-first century and whether we are believers or not. We will take textual and visual interpretations alongside one another, as to impose a rigid distinction upon them would be at odds with how they themselves have evolved, the one informing the other, over the past two millennia. It is only in more recent times that more formal biblical criticism has been privileged over other types of interpretations as holding the definitive key to understanding biblical texts. We will also connect interpretations from different moments in history.

In doing this we will consider some of those who have seen Revelation as a guide for the present, both as a call to arms or political action and in more guarded polemical terms. But in giving due attention to those interpretations (of which there are many) which emphasize the destructive side of Revelation, we will emphasize that in the medieval and early modern visualizations this was always balanced by a glimpse of the New Jerusalem. Finally, in contrast to the warrior-like and polemical readings of Revelation, we will offer an analysis of Revelation, based on its own reception history, as a legitimation of passive resistance and sacrifice, and a rejection of what one might refer to as 'earthly values'.

Looking back over Revelation and the images that it has inspired, what we see is a fantastic kaleidoscope of images and visions, many of which remain indelibly imprinted on the mind, even if we cannot grasp their full meaning, and even as their literal sense puzzles us, as it has puzzled so many over the centuries. We are left with an image of the visionary, John of Patmos, trance-like on his rock, as Memling or Velázquez imagine him. The Angels, the Lamb, the Four Horsemen, the Woman Clothed with the Sun, the Dragon and the Two Beasts, Babylon and its Whore, the hosts gathered at Armageddon, the Last Judgement, the New Jerusalem, and the River of Life; these and so many other images born of John's subconscious or impressed on him from without pass through his mind, merge into each other, and await their articulation in the book called Revelation.

Encoded in Revelation's powerful language, they then continue their psychic existence, coming to haunt and obsess other minds and brains, and also to inspire myriads of artists, seers, and other visionaries over the centuries, as we have seen. In some cases the images they have inspired have overtaken the original literary descriptions. Thus the Four Horsemen have become synonymous with Dürer's iconic woodcut image (see Figure 3.5) and the Lamb of God with the monumental Van Eyck altarpiece (see Plate 1), while the Antichrist (that hybrid medieval invention drawing upon the Beasts of Rev. 13, among other sources) has been immortalized in Signorelli's Orvieto Cathedral fresco (see Plate 30).

However, beneath the shifting phantasmagoria and behind the mythical figures conjured by John, whoever he might actually have been, and before him by Daniel and Ezra, by Enoch, Ezekiel, and the two Isaiahs, and by all the other seers of apocalyptic visions and beneath the myriad examples of art, music, and literature inspired by these visions, it is possible to discern a message, or rather messages. It is these which have worked their way into the brains and then the actions of so many since 90 CE, or whenever John was on Patmos, and continue to do so even today.

There are those who have read and imagined Revelation as a book for this world and for now, or if not for now, for some real time, a time in the near future of this world. For them, as perhaps for John himself, at least some of the figures in the visions stand for people or institutions in time, in their time or our time. So Babylon is Rome, or the papacy, or the EU. This polemical strand of 'decoding' interpretation was most memorably captured by Cranach the Elder in his simple yet devastatingly effective image of the Whore of Babylon wearing the papal triple tiara (see Figure 7.5). Once one has seen this image, it is difficult to shake the association. Others have seen the same character or symbol of the Whore of Babylon in more general terms as the power of the Islamic 'other' (see Blake's image of the Whore of Babylon for a subtle parody of this Orientalist strand of interpretation, Plate 36). The medievals were sometimes prepared to see those who fought against the Satanic trinity (perhaps themselves embodied by contemporary enemies such as the English invaders, as in the *Angers Apocalypse Tapestry*) as divinely inspired Crusaders blessed by popes and destined for the New

Jerusalem. Even today there are those, ranging from extremist Islamic preachers to Christian sects, who directly identify the United States government with Revelation's Satan and/or Antichrist.

Alongside and sometimes part of what we might call these 'presentist' or decoding readings and visualizations, there are and have been those who have interpreted the Millennium and the New Jerusalem as referring to realities and regimes achievable on earth through human endeavour, and probably soon (no doubt responding to the urgency of Revelation itself, it is always soon from the point of view of the visionaries, whether they are some of John's first readers suffering under the Roman empire, medieval peasants in revolt, or present-day end time preachers). These readings of Revelation emphasize not only its temporal urgency, but even more its messianic aspects and its judgemental divisiveness. Allusions to this idea discussed in this book range from Dürer's ambiguous visualization of the Millennium/New Jerusalem (see Figure 8.8), a possible challenge to the viewer to bring about or at the very least imagine the Millennium and the New Jerusalem for themselves (and see also the open-ended nature of the Memling *Apocalypse Panel* and the *Master Bertram Altarpiece*, which stop well short of the end of Revelation; Plates 3 and 28), to those more recent theologies of evangelical Dispensationalism (at one end of the spectrum) and liberation theology (at the other). Although both would no doubt ultimately stress the omnipotence of God, the Dispensationalists believe that they can play a decisive role in the end (the Armageddon, Millennium, Last Judgement, New Jerusalem matrix) by helping to protect Israel and by evangelizing, and in the end times by fighting against the forces of what they consider evil; while the liberationists argue that the base Christian communities must work together to 'speak truth to power' and establish a new order, a New Jerusalem for the poor and oppressed. This may or may not involve retribution and revolution.

It cannot be denied that destructive, divisive, and violent impulses are present in Revelation and that it promotes a very black and white philosophy in which good triumphs definitively over evil, categories that may or may not be predetermined (see Rev. 13.8), but which are very difficult to move between. Indeed, many of the most dramatic and powerful images that we have looked at reflect these violent impulses and divisions. The following come especially to mind: the fiery destruction of the Whore of Babylon in the twelfth-century *Hortus Deliciarum* (see Plate 33); the victims of Dürer's Four Horsemen being trampled indiscriminately underfoot (see Figure 3.5); Danby and Martin's monumental tableaux of the global destruction caused by the opening of the Sixth Seal and by the Last Judgement respectively (see Figures 4.4 and 8.10), the Martin image being all the more poignant for its clear representation of the contrasting fates of the saved and the damned; and on that theme, the desperate and terrified struggle of those cast into Hell in the medieval manuscripts (see Plates 23 and 43). Looked at like this, Revelation is very much in the tradition of Judaic messianism, yearning for the militaristic Lion of Judah, and, more broadly, in the spirit of revolutionary politics wherever that is found, and wherever human beings have dreamed of earthly millennia and fought holy (or not so holy) wars in their violent pursuit.

But earthly millennia are not possible. Human works are inevitably flawed, whatever the merits of their motivation or the benignity of their creators. Whether we are Christian or not, it is hard to deny that history is littered with visions of Heavens on Earth leading to Hells on Earth. Many of the later works that we have looked at capture this sense of ambiguity over blind adherence to and/or identification with the more divisive, uncompromising elements of Revelation. Masereel's *Aeroplanes over Mankind* canvas perfectly captures the senseless and epic scale of the destruction wrought by modern warfare, a sort of visual apocalypse for our times that calls into question any sort of literal adherence to a text such as Revelation (see Figure 8.5).

Read as a recipe for present political action, Revelation is therefore an impossible book, as the orthodox Augustinian interpretation would insist. So is Revelation not a book for now at all, in no way for this Earth? Is it a book only for the end of time, for when time is no more, for a new Heaven and a new Earth, when the old Earth and time itself will have passed away? And if it is for the end of time, it must also be for existence in another dimension, and not only in a temporal (or spatial) sense. Can it not speak to us at all in the here and now? To leave things there would surely be too quick, and it is our fervent hope that this book has sought to reveal a greater depth and complexity to Revelation. While the text's black and white philosophy may be best avoided as a blueprint for a call to direct action (although even this may have its place for the severely economically and politically oppressed), neither should it be dismissed merely as an esoteric meditation on a future reality.

At the start of Rev. 5, when it is asked who is worthy to open the book with the Seven Seals, one of the elders cries out that the Lion of the tribe of Judah has conquered, and is therefore worthy (Rev. 5.5). There are indeed remnants of Judaic messianism and the Lion of Judah tradition in Revelation, as we have seen. The Anglo-Norman Apocalypses pick up on these, with their images of Christ as a dashing medieval knight, spearing and scattering enemies (see Figure 8.4). But what actually enters the throne room in Rev. 5 not a messianic warrior riding high with sword aloft, making his enemies his footstool, but the Lamb standing 'as if slaughtered', just as the *Angers Apocalypse* image and the *Ghent Altarpiece* show us (see Figures 2.5 and 2.3 respectively). In the *Angers* image, the Lamb is not just 'as if' slaughtered, but has blood pouring from his neck and with holes in his feet, all of which remind the viewer of his sacrificial crucifixion. Similarly, in *Trinity* Christ and his forces often appear in a realm above their enemies, ethereally calm, rather than flailing around, and in *Gulbenkian* the followers of Christ—bishops, knights, clergy, and laity—fight not with weapons and armour, but with masses, prayers, penance, and episcopal blessings (see Figure 8.3). Both in Revelation itself and in the associated images, passive resistance is often emphasized over and above armed struggle.

The enemies of the Lamb, meanwhile—Satan, the Beasts, Babylon, and its Whore—are consistently shown as those who to earthly eyes will inevitably seem 'the establishment'—as deceptive and cunning. Thus the fight between good and evil explored in Revelation, if it is to be framed in those terms, does have a complexity that might initially pass the reader, hearer, or viewer by. It melds a metaphorical consideration of the paradox of Christianity (the incarnate Messiah is crucified as a criminal and resurrected to save mankind) with a sustained exploration of the deceptive nature of evil, again via a series of colourful visions. As Signorelli so memorably illustrates in his Antichrist fresco, it is the defining feature of the Antichrist that he is imbued with faux-Christian wisdom and teaching (see Plate 30). Similarly, Blake's Beasts are often pictured with angelic features, forcing the viewer to re-evaluate their own moral processes (see Plate 31 and Figure 6.7).

What we need to recognize at this point, therefore, is that Revelation is not either purely about this world or purely about the next. It is about the next, when this Earth and Heaven and the former things will have passed away (Rev. 21.1–4), and when (if we interpret him in this way) the mighty angel of Rev. 10.6 tells us that time itself will be no more. But what it tells us about the next is highly relevant to our conduct in this, and of course (if we are believers) for our interpretation of the earthly role of the Christian church, as, of course, Augustine insisted. We must not forget—what often tends to be overlooked—that it begins with John writing to the seven churches, chiding them for their failings, above all for their failing to understand and implement the message of the Lamb (see Figure 0.2). So while Revelation is not proposing a new earthly order to replace the old ones, it *is* proposing a moral transformation in which human beings come to worship the suffering Lamb who has voluntarily undergone sacrifice. And in so far as security and safety in the world depend on violence and force, however these are disguised and made gentle, its message of willing victimhood is profoundly counter-cultural. In that sense it is divisive and judgemental: it is commanding its readers, in the light of John's visions of the last things, not to act and judge as the world judges and acts. Here we are reminded of another Blake image, that of the Lamb tucked almost imperceptibly under God's throne (see Plate 12), possibly missed by many viewers, a visual exemplification of the suffering Lamb of Revelation and of Christianity more generally. When taken in conjunction with Blake's *Last Judgement*, however, we are reminded that although the Lamb may be overlooked by those too preoccupied with 'worldly' things, he is ultimately (in Blake's schema) the only route to salvation/the New Jerusalem (see Figure 8.11).

If we see Revelation in what are genuinely revolutionary terms, in *morally* revolutionary terms, and not in terms of some apocalyptic and political agenda, then this could still be a book for our time, with a real wisdom beneath the tantalizing and ever-fascinating images. Its very impossibility, if read over-literally as applying politically to this world, if read more sensitively, switches the focus onto what it tells us about moral transformation and about the next world. For believers, Revelation will inspire a hope for another form of existence altogether in which all worship the Lamb and are given the grace to emulate the ethic of acceptance and compassion. And believers are assured by the narrative of Revelation that the way of the Lamb is the way to ultimate triumph. Revelation is thus showing Christian believers that they must exile themselves from every earthly country (in the words of Simone Weil), and in doing so open themselves to a greater reality. Of course, this message is present in the Gospels, but Revelation gives a vivid, visionary representation to that message that brings it fiercely alive.

But for non-Christians too Revelation is a challenge. Is there any truth in the implied critique of the values and forces of the world? Does the truth of the implied critique rest on what might seem to be the compensatory reward in the New Jerusalem, when the Lamb is revealed as God? Does morality depend on something like a Last Judgement? How do we account for our primeval desire that justice will not only prevail, but will be revealed too? Do we see value as existing in the world beyond human choices, as Revelation's angels might suggest? How far do the Beasts, and even the Antichrist, reveal the true nature of worldly power? Are hopes for a Millennium and a New Jerusalem in this life dangerous illusions? How do we live in the face of the ever-present woes unleashed by the Four Horsemen? How should we address fears of apocalyptic catastrophes? These are the questions and concerns Revelation raises, and their significance and importance explain the durability of its images.

At the very least, the vividness and drama of Revelation's vision and the underlying critique of the way the world is should force us to reflect on the nature of power and of value, and even more on the illusory and mendacious forms these realities so often take (see, for example, the Beckmann image of the resurrection without God, Figure 8.12). And having reflected, we may then be encouraged, in our own lives at least, to temper them with the virtue of the Lamb, even without the visions of ultimate triumph that John affords those who believe.

# *Notes*



1. Following Kovacs and Rowland 2004 and many other Revelation scholars, throughout this book we acknowledge that the titles Revelation, the Apocalypse, and the Book of Revelation have been used interchangeably by interpreters through the ages. When we refer to the text in question, we will use the term Revelation.
2. Lincoln 1999: 6.
3. *Rainbow: A Magazine of Christian Literature, with Special Reference to the Revealed Future of the World*, 1866.
4. Ridley 2014: 2.
5. Lawrence 1995: 144.
6. Boesak 1987: 116.
7. For further literature on biblical reception history see Luz 1994, Kovacs and Rowland 2004, and Sawyer 2006.
8. Boxall 2006: 5–7.
9. See Rowland 1993.
10. During the course of this introduction we will give a brief overview of Revelation itself, and through the book we will from time to time refer to other examples of apocalyptic literature in both Jewish and Christian traditions. However, our emphasis throughout is on the visual interpretation of Revelation, rather than providing an exhaustive analysis of Revelation itself, or of apocalyptic literature more generally.
11. See Michelangelo's *Pietà* in St Peter's Basilica in Rome, and, even more, the later one in the Museo dell'Opera del Duomo in Florence.
12. Particularly by Marsilio Ficino and the group of Florentine intellectuals and artists active in the circle of Lorenzo di Medici (Lorenzo the Magnificent) in the latter half of the fifteenth century. Botticelli was the greatest of these, and, as we will see, one of his major works (*The Mystic Nativity*) is an attempt to capture the sense of Revelation 12 and/or 20. See Chapter 8.
13. Lessing 1984: 78–97.
14. Luz 1994: 19.

15. We should point out that the word 'apocalypse', though now inextricably linked with connotations of some cosmic ultimate destruction, is actually simply Greek for 'revelation' or 'unveiling'. On secularization and modernity see Meland 1966.
16. Lawrence 1995: 70–89.
17. Luther 1958–86, 35: 399.
18. See Chapter 10 for further discussion of Boesak. See also Boesak 1987: 15–39.
19. For more detailed commentaries, see Boxall 2006, Rowland 1993, Kovacs and Rowland 2004, Aune 1997–9, Yarbro Collins 1984.
20. See the end of this introduction for details of the main works of art featured throughout this book, of which the *Angers Apocalypse Tapestry* is one.
21. See Chapter 6 for a fuller exploration of the figure of the Antichrist in art and literature.
22. See Muir Wright 1995: 4–8.
23. See Aune 1997–9, Bauckham 1993, Brook and Gwyther 1999, Rowland 1993, and Schüssler Fiorenza 1993 for an array of differing interpretations of Revelation, its mode of compilation, and emphases.
24. See O'Hear 2011: 243–53 for a longer explanation of the nature of visionary experience.
25. Boxall 2006: 2.
26. See Schüssler-Fiorenza 1993: 29, 51 and O'Hear 2011: 199–254 for more on this debate. See Boxall 2006: 304–5 for an explanation of the walls.
27. For more detail on apocalypticism in the Middle Ages and beyond see Potesta 2003: 299–322 and Barnes 2003: 323–53, both in McGinn, Collins, and Stein (eds) 2003.
28. Rowland 1982: 193–267 in particular.
29. See Daley 2003: 232–3 on Lactantius' special brand of apocalypticism.
30. Kermode 1967.
31. It should also be pointed out that a holy war Messiah was not the only theme in the Hebrew Old Testament. At the time of the Assyrian conquest, in the eighth century BCE, the prophet Isaiah looked forward to the child named Emmanuel, who would be the prince of peace, but who would rule over all nations. Swords would be beaten into ploughshares and spears into pruning hooks; they would learn war no more, the wolf would dwell with the lamb and the leopard with the kid. So the pacific elements of Christianity were not without Old Testament precedent; that part of the Gospels and indeed of Revelation did not come from nowhere.
32. Jerome, *Commentarium in Isaiam* 18, prologue (CC 83A 40–1); *Commentarium in Danielem* (CC 75A 848). Cited in Emmerson and McGinn 1992: 18–19, 51.
33. See further the information on Hal Lindsey and the *Left Behind* series in Chapter 10. See also Boyer 1992 and Frykholm 2004 on this phenomenon.
34. See McGinn 1985 and Daniel 1992: 72–88 for more on Joachim of Fiore.
35. Daniel 1992: 86–7.

36. Lerner 1992: 66–8.

37. Cohn 1993.

38. See further Arjomand 2003: 380–413 and particularly 380 on Islamic apocalypticism, and also Akhtar 2008: 32. See also Amanat 2003: 582–606 on apocalypticism in modern Islam.

39. For more on historical apocalyptic movements across the ages see Boyer 1992, Carey 1999, Kovacs and Rowland 2004, Himmelfarb 2010, Lisboa 2011. On Waco, see Himmelfarb 2010: 148–51. An informed fictional treatment can be found in the concluding section of John Updike's *In the Beauty of the Lilies* (Updike 1996).

40. See Walliss 2010: 93–5 for a helpful and short summary of Dispensationalism. See Boyer 1992: 80–112 on the development of Dispensationalist thinking.

41. See the *US News and World Report* (1994), cited in Wojcik 1997: 8.

42. See Walliss 2010: 105–9.

43. Price and Price 2011: xvi and 9–16; <http://www.pewforum.org/2006/08/24/many-americans-uneasy-with-mix-of-religion-and-politics/#2>.

44. Lessing 1984: 108.

45. See further O'Hear 2011: 87–104 on Memling's *St John Altarpiece*.

46. See O'Hear 2011: 92, 102–4.

47. See Carey (ed.) 1999: 47 and Van der Meer 1978: 93–102 on the *Trier Apocalypse*.

48. There may well have been more but these are the extant ones. See Mentré 1996 for more on the illuminated *Beatus* manuscripts.

49. See Morgan 1990 on the *Lambeth Apocalypse*; McKitterick 2005 on the *Trinity Apocalypse*; and O'Hear 2011: 11–42 on both.

50. See Muel 1986 and 1996 on the *Angers Apocalypse Tapestry*.

51. See Van der Meer 1978: 203–36 on the *Flemish Apocalypse*.

52. See O'Hear 2011: 69–104 on the *Ghent Altarpiece* and the *St John Altarpiece*.

53. See O'Hear 2011: 135–97 on Dürer and Cranach's Apocalypse cycles. See also Price 2003 on Dürer and Scribner 1981 on Cranach and his polemical images.

54. See O'Hear 2011: 184–8.

55. Rowland 2010: 224–31.

56. Carey (ed.) 1999: 313.

## 1. THE ANGEL OF THE APOCALYPSE: JOHN'S JOURNEY AND HIS ANGELIC GUIDES

1. Boxall 2006: 270, 314.

2. On the role of angels in apocalyptic literature, see Himmelfarb 2010, especially chs 2, 5, and 6.

3. O'Hear 2011: 63–4.

4. See O'Hear 2011: 29–34.

5. On the Bosch painting, see Bosing 2012: 81–2 and 89.

6. Mâle 1961: 364.

7. Camille 1992: 283–9.
8. Rowland 1982: 428–9.
9. Koerner 1993: 220; O'Hear 2011: 163–6; Van der Meer 1978: 296, 298, 306.
10. O'Hear, N. 2011: 243–53.
11. Schüssler-Fiorenza 1993: 27.
12. Rowe 2008.
13. See Genesis 4.8 and Judith 13.6–10. Adam and Eve weeping over Abel is not actually mentioned in Scripture, while the Book of Judith is regarded by some as apocryphal.

## 2. THE LAMB

1. In Christian iconography, the infant Christ with a lamb is a premonition of Christ's sacrificial death (as, for example, in Leonardo's *Virgin and Child with St Anne*).
2. See Bauckham 1993: 23–65.
3. See Bauckham 1993: 31.
4. Boxall 2006: 98–9.
5. See Girard: 1977 and 1986.
6. See Bauckham 1993: 64.
7. See Plate 1 for a reproduction of the full altarpiece.
8. Thomas Bradwardine (*c.*1290–1349, *De causa Dei contra Pelagium*, commenting on Romans 9.16), and see Chapter 6, section 'Interpreting the Beasts'.
9. Kinney 1992: 207.
10. Rowland 2010: 145.
11. On Schmidt, see Corfield 1989. The literature on Bach and Handel is voluminous; on the B Minor Mass and *Messiah* respectively, see Butt 1991 and Burrows 1991.

## 3. THE FOUR HORSEMEN

1. Boxall 2006: 109–12 and Rowland 1993: 81–8.
2. Boxall 2006: 107–8.
3. See, for example, 'The Knight and the Landsknecht' of 1497.
4. On Cranach's relation to Dürer, see O'Hear 2011: 175–8.
5. See O'Hear 2011: 193.
6. See Carey (ed.) 1999: 208–28; 247, 250, 253.
7. Myrone 2006: 187.
8. See Wright 2009: 87.
9. See the DVD *Discussions with Richard Dawkins: The Four Horsemen*, 2008.
10. Dawkins 1986: ch. 11; see also Dennett 1995: 365.

## 4. THE SEVEN SEALS: ANGELIC DESTRUCTION

1. See Table 0.1 for an outline of the content of the three sequences of seven.
2. See Boxall 2006: 103–5; Kovacs and Rowland 2004: 78 for more on this point.
3. Boxall 2006: 113–14.
4. Rev. 6.12–17: 'When he opened the sixth seal, I looked, and there came a great earthquake; the sun became black as sackcloth, the full moon became like blood, and the stars of the sky fell to the earth as the fig tree drops its winter fruit when shaken by a gale. The sky vanished like a scroll rolling itself up, and every mountain and island was removed from its place. Then the kings of the earth and the magnates and the generals and the rich and the powerful, and everyone, slave and free, hid in the caves and among the rocks of the mountains, calling to the mountains and rocks, "Fall on us and hide us from the face of the one seated on the throne and from the wrath of the Lamb; for the great day of their wrath has come, and who is able to stand?"'
5. See O'Hear 2011: 37–8.
6. The *Annunciation* is now in the Central Hospital, Madrid; and the *Baptism* is in St John the Baptist Church, Toledo, Spain.
7. Cossio 1908: 355–7; Mann 1986: 111–46.
8. See Carey (ed.): 1999: 289. The sublime in this context refers to terrifying scenes artistically represented, so as to give a thrill of pleasure to the viewer.
9. See Chapter 10 for more on these.
10. Boxall 2006: 128–9; Kovacs and Rowland 2004: 106–8.
11. See McKitterick 2005 for detailed discussion of the *Trinity Apocalypse.*
12. See McKitterick (ed.) 2005: 52.

## 5. THE WOMAN CLOTHED WITH THE SUN

1. Boadt 1984: 114–18.
2. Yarbro Collins 1993: 20–33.
3. Boxall 2006: 174–7.
4. Boxall 2006: 180.
5. Kovacs and Rowland 2004: 134–5.
6. John Milton, *Paradise Lost*, 5.661–6.
7. The great twelfth-century monastic reformer Bernard of Clairvaux called Mary the Conqueror of Dragons. In Milton's own time Rubens depicted a full-blown *Blessed Virgin Mary as the Woman of the Apocalypse* dramatically crushing the serpent under her foot, aided by Michael and various other angels, as she rises up to Heaven with the child. (See his *Blessed Virgin Mary as the Woman of the Apocalypse*, Getty Museum, Los Angeles, sketch for an altarpiece in a cathedral in Germany, 1623–4.)
8. Boxall 2006: 178–9; Kovacs and Rowland 2004: 135–7.

9. And also by Joachim of Fiore, who saw one of the Dragon's heads as Nero (and others, all referring to persecutions of the church, include Herod, Mohammed, and Saladin; cf. Kovacs and Rowland 2004: 141).

10. Van der Meer 1978: 103.

11. Williamson 2004: 29.

12. See Carr 2006: 134.

13. See Barocci, *The Immaculate Conception*, 1574–5, Galleria Nazionale delle Marche, Urbino, Italy.

14. Williamson 2004: 29–30.

15. See Carey (ed.) 1999: 274–5, 298.

16. See Pippin 1992 and Jack 2001, for example.

17. Cady Stanton 1985: 183.

18. Pippin 1992: 100–5.

19. Yarbro Collins 1993.

## 6. THE SATANIC TRINITY

1. Boxall 2006: 197–9; Kovacs and Rowland 2004: 148.

2. Kovacs and Rowland 2004: 148.

3. See Walliss 2010: 99–102, 108–9. See also Boyer 1992: 254–90 on interpretations of the Beasts and the number 666 in modern American prophecy culture.

4. See Rowland 1993: 133–41.

5. Boxall 2006: 187–8.

6. There are complications with the correct reading of the Greek in this verse which has implications for how the verse should be understood. Should the phrase 'since the foundation of the world' be taken with the verb 'inscribed' or with the 'Lamb, which has been slaughtered'? In other words, is it the names of the faithful who have been predetermined or Christ's sacrifice? For more on this see Boxall 2006: 191, and Chapter 2, section 'The Lamb in Revelation'.

7. They didn't; Bonhoeffer himself endured, right up to his execution in 1944. See Bonhoeffer 1965.

8. 'Of the eternal election, by which God has predestined some to salvation, and others to destruction'—the title of Bk 3, Ch. 21 of Calvin's *Institutes of the Christian Religion*, first published in 1536.

9. A table summarizing the numerical values of the Greek alphabet can be found here: <http://en.wikipedia.org/wiki/Greek_numerals>.

10. See Boxall 2006: 197–9.

11. See further Muir Wright 1995 on the medieval understanding of Antichrist.

12. Scribner 1981: 150–7.

13. Boxall 2006: 231–2.

14. *Magnolia*, 1999.

15. See Kauffmann 1968: 1–2.

16. See Kauffmann 1968: 40.

17. See O'Hear 2011: ch. 5, especially 171–5.

18. See further Reiss 1995 on the frescos.

19. Cf. Rev. 13.15, the Earth Beast 'was allowed to give breath to the image of the beast, so that the image of the beast could speak …'.

20. O'Hear 2011: 143.

21. Carey (ed.) 1999: 221.

22. Carey (ed.) 1999: 256.

23. This theme is further exploited in books such as those by Dennis Wheatley and horror films such as *The Devil Rides Out* (novel published 1934, film adaptation released 1968).

24. See <http://www.sodahead.com/fun/barack-obama-the-antichrist/question-3178925/?link=ibaf&q=shepard%2Bfairey%2Bobama%2Bantichrist&imgurl= images.sodahead.com%2Fpolls%2F003178925%2F4246663039_ Barack20Obama_The20Antichrist_xlarge.jpeg> for a weblink to the doctored poster, which we were not able to reproduce for legal reasons.

## 7. THE WHORE OF BABYLON

1. See <http://www.theparisreview.org/interviews/3379/the-art-of-poetry-no-24-peter-levi>.

2. Within the Old Testament, harlotry was an allegation often levelled at Israel and Jerusalem in particular and had connotations of false religion, of turning against Yahweh (see Isa. 1.21; Jer. 14.27; Ezek. 16.15ff. and 23.1–4). See further Boxall 2006: 238–51 and Kovacs and Rowland 2004: 177–8.

3. See also Bauckham 1993: 17–18 and 35–6.

4. See Rowland 2002: 78–113.

5. Kovacs and Rowland 2004: 178.

6. See Chapter 10 for more on liberation theology and Revelation.

7. Boesak 1987: 116.

8. Pippin 1992: 57–68. See also Jack 2001.

9. Boxall 2001: 68.

10. For a more detailed survey of the Whore of Babylon in medieval art, see O'Hear 2009.

11. See Kovacs and Rowland 2004: 188: Rev. 17–18 'suggests the complexity of oppression. Babylon is deceived and culpable but ultimately at the mercy of the Beast.'

12. Wright 1996: 194.

13. See Graham 1947 on the 'y' motif in *Angers*. See also O'Hear 2009.

14. See further Said 2003.

15. For more detail on the York Minster Great East Window, see French 1995.

16. See further Zika 1994 on 'Riding Women' and morality in the Renaissance period.

17. See Morgan 1990: 235.

18. For more on the Sainte Chapelle rose window see Leniaud and Perrot 2007: 121–99.

19. See Brook and Gwyther, 1999: especially ch. 6.

20. See O'Hear 2009: 320–4.
21. See Bialostocki 1986: 282–9 for a review of the arguments.
22. See Boxall 2001: 65–7.
23. Rowland 2010: 226.
24. See Carey (ed.) 1999: 305–7.
25. See Lindsey 1970: 122–5.

## 8. ARMAGEDDON, THE MILLENNIUM, AND THE LAST JUDGEMENT

1. Interestingly in the illustrated manuscripts and earlier cycles the later chapters were somewhat neglected, apart from the New Jerusalem. Were they found to be too repetitive?
2. See Kovacs and Rowland 2004: 214–19 for a summary of Revelation's Last Judgement in art, literature, and song.
3. See Boxall 2006: 286–7.
4. <http://www.independent.co.uk/environment/climate-change/globalwarming-armageddon-it-may-be-more-likely-than-you-thought-8736249.html>.
5. Boxall 2006: 231.
6. This may give weight to the idea, alluded to in the introductory chapter, that Revelation is intended to be read not as a linear narrative, where later events follow earlier ones in a logical fashion, but rather as a series of expositions of the same themes, centring round the battle between good and evil.
7. See Boxall 2006: 223. One notable victory against the Canaanites at Megiddo is described in Judges 5.19.
8. See Day 1994.
9. Boxall 2006: 232–3.
10. See further on this, Chapter 10.
11. See Matt. 24.42–4; 1 Thess. 5.2; and Luke 12.39–48 for other references to Jesus returning like 'a thief in the night'.
12. See Stafford on Turner Classic Movies: <http://www.tcm.com/tcmdb/title/30594/The-Birds/articles.html>.
13. Huxley 1973: 43–50.
14. Mâle 1961: 379–80.
15. This is a marked contrast with Plate 34, where the Whore of Babylon is gleefully speared into the pit of Hell by two winged angels.
16. Morgan 1990: 56.
17. Carey (ed.) 1999: 310.
18. See Kovacs and Rowland 2004: 200–13 on contrasting historical interpretations of the Millennium.
19. Augustine 1984: Book 20.
20. Augustine 1984: Book 20, ch. 6.
21. Kovacs and Rowland 2004: 209–10.
22. Kovacs and Rowland 2004: 211–13.

23. O'Hear 2011: 169.
24. An attempt to survey the many different interpretations of this painting and to offer some new insights is made in O'Hear 2011: ch. 4; see also Hatfield 1995.
25. Boxall 2006: 288–9.
26. See Mâle 1961: 370–4, where he also points out that this humanizing tendency was something new to Christianity in the twelfth and thirteenth centuries, possibly rooted in popular piety rather than in earlier theology or even the sterner pre-Gothic forms of Christian art. Devotion to the intercessory role of the Virgin became central to the art of the time, as reflected in the great Gothic cathedrals, even as here playing a central role in the representation of the Last Judgement itself.
27. Ruskin 1908: 134–5.
28. McKitterick 2005: 94. Purgatory was a doctrine which gained prominence in the Middle Ages, along with the mediating role of Mary, a way of moderating the finality of the judgement.
29. <https://www.tate.org.uk/art/artworks/martin-the-last-judgement-t01927/text-summary>.
30. Carey (ed.) 1999: 223–8.
31. A contemporary remarked on the somewhat disproportionate number of painters in this select group. See Myrone 2011: 174.
32. Rowland 2010: 228.
33. See Hein-Th. Schulze Altcappenberg 2000: 39 for a reproduction of Botticelli's 'Chart of Hell'.
34. See Carey (ed.) 1999: 258–9.
35. Rowland 2010: 229.
36. Carey (ed.) 1999: 258.
37. Rowland 2010: 229.
38. Carey (ed.) 1999: 303.
39. Idem.

## 9. THE NEW JERUSALEM

1. See Boxall 2006: 292–315 and Rowland 1993: 153–9. See Isaiah 54 (Israel as Bride) and Isaiah 40–55 (Exodus motif generally).
2. Boxall 2006: 299.
3. This would at least get rid of the philosophical difficulty of envisaging a new earth, complete with its heavenly city and embodied inhabitants, existing in no time at all and presumably changelessly.
4. Note the inherent difficulties for artists depicting this part of the New Jerusalem due to the fact that the tree is said to be on either side of the River of Life (Rev. 22.2).
5. Augustine 1984: Book 20, especially ch. 17.
6. Rowland 2010: 226–31. Indeed in nineteenth-century England, Michael Brothers, a self-proclaimed prophet with a following, actually had plans drawn

up for his New Jerusalem by the engineer Wilson Lowry along the lines of a town-planning grid (Carey (ed.) 1999: 245).

7. Rowland 1993: 155.

8. Rowland 1993: 158.

9. Entine 2007: 133.

10. See Boxall 2006: 304–5 on the measurements of the city's parameter wall.

11. See Boxall 2006: 310.

12. See, for example, Augustine 1984: Book 18, ch. 16: 'The City of God, that is to say, God's Church'. But note that Augustine includes more than those formally baptized in the heavenly city, such as many Jews and others before the time of Christ, and also good, but unbaptized people from the time of Christ onwards. Conversely, not all members of the church on earth will be saved.

13. Pippin 1992.

14. Chaucer, Prologue to the Parson's Tale, lines 48–51. See <http://www.gutenberg.org/files/22120/22120-h/22120-h.htm#parsonpro>.

15. Van der Meer 1978: 232.

16. See O'Hear 2011: 150 on whether Dürer used the *Flemish Apocalypse* as an inspiration for his own *Apocalypse* series.

17. This could be an indication of the fact that the New Jerusalem as pictured is the vision he is seeing in his head. See Memling's Apocalypse Panel of 1474–9.

18. See O'Hear 2011: 73–6 for a fuller exposition of the altarpiece.

19. See Brand Philips 1971 on this.

20. Blake is also indebted to Ezekiel 47 for the inspiration of this image. Ezekiel is led through a freshwater river surrounded by fructifying trees as part of his vision of the idealized Jerusalem Temple.

21. See Rowland 2010: 227.

22. Rowland 2010: 227.

23. Carey (ed.) 1999: 257.

24. Feaver 1975: 188–204.

25. Feaver 1975: 198.

26. O'Hear 2011: 94–100.

27. Carey (ed.) 1999: 60.

28. See Myrone (ed.) 2011: 56–9 on Cheung and other contemporary artists influenced by Martin.

29. <http://www.gordoncheung.com/index.html>.

## 10. THE APOCALYPSE IN THE TWENTIETH AND TWENTY-FIRST CENTURIES: A SURVEY OF DIFFERENT APPROACHES TO REVELATION IN THE ARTS AND POPULAR CULTURE

1. Extract from *The Simpsons*, Episode 18, Series 10.

2. Sweet, quoted in Wojcik 1997: 6.

3. See Taylor 2004: 92–100 on the advent of Western modernity and the fragmentation of cultural identities or 'imaginaries' that this entailed.

4. See Oswalt 2003 on the strength of the Christian voice in contemporary America and Boyer 1992 for a history of evangelical interpretations of Revelation.

5. Younge 2011.

6. <http://www.theonion.com/video/christian-groups-biblical-armageddon-must-be-taugh,17491/>.

7. Simms 2013.

8. Hyde, 'Lost in Showbiz' columns in *The Guardian*, 5.6.2009; 10.2.2011; 29.9.2011, and 4.10.2013.

9. See Walliss 2010: 93–5 for a helpful and short summary of Dispensationalism. See Boyer 1992: 80–112 on the development of pre-Millennial thought.

10. Todorov 1969.

11. Rosen, 2013.

12. <http://www.nationaltheatre.org.uk/shows/in-the-beginning-was-the-end-dreamthinkspeak-at-somerset-house>.

13. Carey (ed.) 1999: 303.

14. Carey (ed.) 1999: 312–13.

15. Carey 1999: 313.

16. McCarthy 2006. See also <http://www.bbc.co.uk/news/uk-england-manchester-16054633>.

17. On Vaughan Williams, see Kennedy 1992: 213–16; on Schmidt, see Corfield 1989, and also 'Roderick Dunnett talks to Austrian conductor Franz Welser-Möst about Franz Schmidt's "Book with Seven Seals"', 2000: <http://www.mvdaily.com/articles/2000/08/bombshl1.htm.> There is an excellent recording of Sancta Civitas conducted by David Hill (on Naxos 8572424), and several recordings are available of the Schmidt, including one by Welser-Möst (EMI Gemini 5857822).

18. Mann 1968: 341.

19. Mann 1968: 358–65.

20. On Messiaen's quartet, see Rischin 2006; the liner notes for the excellent EMI 'Great Recording of the Century' version of the piece (EMI Classics 2 12688 2) are also helpful.

21. See for a recording of the song: <http://www.youtube.com/watch?v=uR7tvPeiYJE>.

22. Tilling (ed.) 2010: 5–20.

23. Tilling (ed.) 2010: 102.

24. Tilling (ed.): 2010: 5–6.

25. Tilling (ed.): 2010: 95.

26. Lyons 2009: 97–105.

27. Lyons 2009: 106–7. See <http://www.youtube.com/watch?v=k9IfHDi-2EA> for a recording.

28. Lyons 2009: 107.
29. See <http://www.youtube.com/watch?v=D97OxHZzBeQ> for a recording.
30. Bragg 1993: 26.
31. Monaco 2000: 311–12.
32. Bragg 1993: 45.
33. Quoted in Bragg 1993: 9–10.
34. Bragg 1993: 9–10.
35. Bragg 1993: 9–10.
36. Boxall 2006: 128–9.
37. Wright 2009: 87.
38. Kalin 2003: 60–1.
39. See further O'Hear 2011: 161–3 on this Dürer image.
40. See Conrad 1998. On the film itself, see Cowie 2001. Eliot's 'Hollow Men' is in Eliot 1969: 81.
41. Lawrence 1995. Interestingly, in view of what is being said in this chapter about the secularization of apocalyptic themes in recent times, although Lawrence's book is suffused with references to the specifically biblical imagery of Revelation, the cover of this Penguin edition is a painting by Meidner of a completely generalized destruction of a modern city.
42. On this, Lawrence has *some* academic support, from Aune 1997–9. See especially Aune 1997: cxviii–cxxxiv.
43. Lawrence 1995: 99–100.
44. Lawrence 1995: 47.
45. Lawrence 1995: 143–4.
46. Lawrence 1995: 71.
47. Lawrence 1995: 149.
48. Gribben 2009: 4–11.
49. Gribben 2009: 10.
50. Gribben 2009: 3.
51. Gribben 2009: 10.
52. Lindsey 1970.
53. See Wojcik 1997: fig. 5.
54. Boyer 1992: 204.
55. See Lindsey 1970: 53–4, where he argues that 'within forty years, or so, of 1948, all these things could take place'. 1948 is the year the State of Israel was founded: 'all these things' is a reference to Matt. 24.34 when Christ foretells his return. The Tribulation, the time between the Rapture and Armageddon, is taken to be seven years, following a characteristically imaginative reading of Rev. 11.2–3.
56. Lindsey 1970: 162.
57. Lindsey 1970: 181.
58. See Boyer 1992: 187–8; 192–3; 203–8.
59. Gribben 2009: 129.

60. Forbes 2004: 8–9. Perhaps this is not so surprising when one discovers that 44 per cent of American Christians believe in the Rapture (see Wojcik 1997: 8 and 42).

61. See Wright 2009: 82.

62. Goldberg 2002.

63. Morrison 2002: 2–3.

64. Gribben 2009: 136–7.

65. See Gribben 2009: 137–8 on evangelical disagreements about exactly who will be raptured.

66. See Boyer 1992: 254–60 and Wojcik 1997: 41–2 for more on contemporary American beliefs surrounding the Rapture.

67. See Walliss 2010: 98–105 and Wright 2009: 82.

68. Walliss 2010: 108.

69. Gribben 2009: 137–8.

70. Gribben 2009: 138–9.

71. Gribben 2009: 130.

72. See Zordan, forthcoming.

73. See Cowley 1983: 74.

74. See Friedlander and Friedlander 2007, and Friedlander, Friedlander, and Pankhurst 2014.

75. See Boesak 1987: 9.

76. Boesak 1987: 93–107.

77. Boesak 1987: 116.

78. See Rowland (ed.) 2007, especially the editor's introduction, pp. 3–16.

79. Richard 1995: 172–3.

80. See Devalos 2008: 89–95.


### REVELATION: ARTISTIC RECEPTION AND RELEVANCE

1. For more on the role of John and the reader/viewer experience in relation to the Anglo-Norman Apocalypses, see O'Hear 2011: 31–4 and 40–2.

# *Glossary*

**Alpha and Omega:** Title used to describe God and Christ in Rev. 1.8 and 22.13. The title refers to the first and last letters of the Greek alphabet (the language in which Revelation was written) and so encompasses the eternal nature of God.

**Annunciation:** The moment when the Angel Gabriel announced to the Virgin Mary that she would bear the Son of God.

**Antichrist:** Mythical figure that became popular from around the tenth century onwards. He is literally the anti-Christ, a demonic parody of Christ that many thought would appear at the end of time and would perform anti-miracles before being 'raised' from the dead after three days. The figure, who is directly referred to only in 1 and 2 John of the New Testament, was fleshed out with other biblical material from 2 Thessalonians and Revelation. The Sea Beast of Rev. 13 (see also Rev. 11) was commonly associated with Antichrist from the Middle Ages onwards on account of his being worshipped by those persuaded by the false prophecies of the Earth Beast. But the Antichrist also has some of the properties of the Earth Beast, such as miracle working, with whom he is sometimes identified as well. The first (white) Horseman is also on occasion seen as a parody of the rider, faithful and true of Rev. 19.11, and so also as the Antichrist.

**Apocalypse:** The final book of the New Testament. From the Greek word ἀποκάλυψις, meaning unveiling or revealing. The term apocalypse with a small 'a' is usually used to refer to a vision of the (often cataclysmic) events at the end of time.

**Apocalyptic:** in colloquial terms, 'apocalyptic' means anything relating to the apocalypse or the end of the world. The term is also used to describe Jewish and Christian literature (such as Daniel, 1 Enoch, 4 Ezra, Revelation) that purports to reveal heavenly secrets passed to an earthly recipient by a heavenly intermediary. These secrets do, in general, also relate to the end of the world. In more recent times, certain secular works have also been described as belonging to the apocalyptic genre.

**Armageddon:** In colloquial terms, Armageddon has come to stand for the final battle that will mark the end of the world. The word only appears once in the New Testament, at Revelation 16.16 (before the battle against the Beasts and the Whore), and is thought to refer to Mount Megiddo in northern Israel, the location of various ancient battles. Some evangelical Christians, such as Hal Lindsey, believe that Armageddon (Megiddo) will be the literal location for the battle between good and evil that will end human history. In a strict reading of Revelation, Armageddon is the first of the final battles, before the Millennium, but the term is used more colloquially to refer to any apparently decisive end-time catastrophe.

**Beast:**  See Earth Beast, Sea Beast.

**Day of Judgement:**  see Last Judgement.

**Diadem:**  A type of royal crown made up of many layers or bands. The Rider on the White Horse (Christ) is said to be wearing a diadem in Rev. 19.12, as is the Dragon in Rev. 12. The diadem later became associated especially with Eastern monarchs.

**Domitian:**  Roman emperor, AD 81–96.

**Dragon:**  Diabolical red creature who appears in Rev. 12 who has seven heads and ten horns. Thought to be a manifestation of Satan, the Dragon attempts to kill the Woman Clothed with the Sun and her child, themselves a loose symbolization of Mary or Israel and Christ. The woman and child are saved and the Dragon is defeated by the angel Michael after a battle in Heaven. This chapter forms the basis for the legend of St George and the Dragon.

**Earth Beast:**  The second Beast to appear in Rev. 13, a sort of follower of the Sea Beast. This Beast is characterized by its deceptive nature and anti-miracles (such as causing fire to fall from the sky) and, as a false prophet, induces mankind to worship the Sea Beast.

**Eschatology:**  Literally means concerning the end (eschaton). A narrower term than apocalypse and apocalyptic, which can have wider implications than just the end of the world (see Apocalypse).

**Eucharist:**  Christian sacramental rite, commemorating Christ's Last Supper and Crucifixion.

**Ezekiel:**  Old Testament prophetic book based on the seven visions of the exiled prophet Ezekiel (*c.*593–571 BCE). Ezekiel's influence can be felt throughout Revelation. The throne room vision of Rev. 4–5 in particular can be seen to have been influenced by Ezekiel 1, in which he has a vision of God's throne-chariot or *Merkavah*.

**Four Horsemen:**  probably the best-known figures from Revelation. The Four Horsemen enter the text at Rev. 6.2 and are not mentioned again after Rev. 6.8. They represent the first tranche of disasters unleashed upon the world, namely war, famine, pestilence, and plague.

**Four Living Creatures:**  These creatures, derived from one of Ezekiel's visions, are said to surround God's throne in Rev. 4–5. They resemble a lion, an ox, a person, and an eagle and are also covered in eyes and have six wings each. In Christian art they have come to be associated with the authors of the Gospels (Matthew, Mark, Luke, and John). Depictions of the Four Living Creatures are often referred to as a Tetramorph.

**Hades:**  Greek term for the underworld, ruled over by Pluto.

**Heavenly throne room:** Place where God and the Lamb reside surrounded by the Four Living Creatures and the Twenty-four Elders in Heaven (see Rev. 4–5). The heavenly throne room is eternal and immutable.

**Illuminated manuscript:** Manuscript, usually from the Middle Ages and usually of a sacred text, richly decorated with paintings and other designs.

**John of Patmos:** The author of Revelation and thus a self-professed recipient of heavenly visions. Not much is known about him except what Revelation itself tells us. In Rev. 1.9 we are told that he has been exiled to Patmos 'because of the word of God and the testimony of Jesus', which basically means for his preaching and/or missionary work. During the Middle Ages, as was the case with all the significant early Christian figures, John's life was fleshed out in the apocryphal *Acts of John*. Despite being a common tradition, the author of Revelation was almost certainly not the author of the fourth Gospel.

**John's Gospel:** The fourth Gospel, traditionally attributed to John the beloved disciple, notable for its introduction of Greek philosophical themes. Its author is not to be confused with John of Patmos, author of Revelation.

**Lamb of God (Agnus Dei):** The term by which John the Baptist identified Christ at his baptism; Christ as sacrificial victim. In Revelation Christ is referred to simply as the Lamb.

**Last Judgement:** The moment at the end of time when all will be definitively judged and separated into the saved and the damned. Most famously found in Matthew's Gospel (Matt. 25.31–6), but there is also a version of the Last Judgement in Rev. 20.11–15.

**Millennium:** The period of a thousand years, ruled over by Christ, between the first and final defeats of Satan. This is described in Rev. 20.1–3. There has been a great deal of debate, almost since Revelation was written, as to whether this thousand-year period should be interpreted literally or metaphorically. The orthodox interpretation, as espoused by Augustine, is a metaphorical one.

**Nero:** Roman emperor, AD 54–68.

**New Jerusalem:** Celestial city which will descend from Heaven after the final defeat of Satan in Rev. 21–2. The New Jerusalem represents a completely new reality.

**Patmos:** Greek island, the abode to which John had been exiled, and where he wrote the Book of Revelation.

**Paul:** Apostle and author of letters (epistles), which are the earliest Christian documents and the first expositions of Christian theology.

**Rapture:** The sudden removal of faithful Christians to Heaven prior to the tribulations that will take place on earth during the end times or apocalypse. Based loosely on 1 Thess. 4.17, the Rapture is a non-orthodox expectation held only by certain Christians, usually American evangelicals.

**Revelation:** The final book of the New Testament. The title literally means 'making un-secret' or unveiling. See also Apocalypse.

**Rider on the White Horse:** The leader of the army against Satan and his forces in Rev. 19. This figure is usually identified with Christ.

**Satan:** The enemy of God and Christ in the apocalyptic struggles, the fallen angel Lucifer who reigns in Hell. Only referred to three times in Revelation (Rev. 12.9 and Rev. 20.2, 7) but evoked frequently via symbolic figures such as the Beasts (Rev. 13), the Dragon (Rev. 12), and the Whore of Babylon (Rev. 17–18). Satan is definitively defeated in Rev. 20.14.

**Sea Beast:** The first Beast to appear in Rev. 13, often referred to as the Sea Beast on account of the fact that it emerges from the sea. Like the Dragon of Rev. 12, from whom it derives its power, the Sea Beast has ten horns and seven heads but its body is a hybrid of a leopard, a bear, and a lion. In many ways this beast is presented as the most powerful beast in Revelation; it appears again in Rev. 17. Worshipped as a result of the false prophecies of the Earth Beast, and in medieval tradition often identified with the Antichrist.

**Seven Asian churches:** The seven churches to which Revelation is addressed, mostly located in modern-day Turkey. The seven churches are named in Rev. 2–3 as Ephesus, Smyrna, Pergamum, Thyatira, Sardis, and Philadelphia. They are chastised by John for their apathy and immorality.

**Seven Seals/sequences of seven:** Often referred to out of context in colloquial English, the Seven Seals are the first cycle of seven woes unleashed in punishment upon an unrepentant world in Rev. 6.2–17. These are followed by another cycle of seven woes (the Seven Trumpets) in Rev. 8–9 and a final cycle (the Seven Bowls) in Rev. 16.

**Synoptic Gospels:** the Gospels of Mark, Matthew, and Luke. They are linked by a wide range of shared source material. John's Gospel is normally viewed as a different type of Gospel, both in terms of its depiction of Jesus and its more theological style.

**Twenty-four Elders:** Like the Four Living Creatures (see above), the Twenty-four Elders remain seated around the throne of God at all times (Rev. 4), engaged in constant worship of him and the Lamb.

**Two Witnesses:** Two rather mysterious figures who appear in Rev. 11 and who seem to represent the prophetic ministry of the church. John has a vision of them prophesying, being killed by a Beast and then rising again after three and a half days in a sort of imitation of Christ's resurrection.

**Whore of Babylon:** A frightening female figure from Rev. 17 who represents the perceived immorality but also the allure of the Roman way of life. She is depicted as riding on the seven-headed Sea Beast. Interestingly she is destroyed not by angels or the army of Christ, but by the Beast himself, a sign of the Satanic system turning in on itself but also perhaps a sign of the apparently timeless fear of the powerful female.

**Woman Clothed with the Sun:** The symbolic counterpart to the Whore of Babylon, the Woman Clothed with the Sun of Rev. 12 is attacked by the Dragon but ultimately both she and her child are rescued by divine agents.

# *Suggestions for Further Reading*

Bauckham, R. 1993: The Theology of the Book of Revelation. Cambridge: Cambridge University Press. A serious yet accessible analysis of the main theological themes in Revelation. It has an interesting few pages at the end on the relevance of Revelation for today.

Boxall, I. 2006: The Revelation of St. John. London: Continuum. A detailed yet clear commentary on Revelation with an excellent introduction that would serve as a great starting point for readers new to the text.

Emmerson, R. and McGinn, B. (eds) 1992: The Apocalypse in the Middle Ages. New York: Cornell University Press. A superb collection of articles on the different ways that Revelation was interpreted in the Middle Ages. The articles range from theological interpretations to art to wider culture.

Kovacs, J. J. and Rowland, C. 2004: Revelation. Oxford: Blackwell. Part of the Blackwell Bible Commentary series, which provides chapter by chapter analysis of the reception history of key biblical texts. This book also has a very useful introduction, which provides not only a concise overview of the reception history of Revelation but also attempts to categorize the diverse types of interpretation that have arisen from this multi-layered text.

McGinn, B., Collins, J., and Stein, S. (eds), 2003: The Continuum History of Apocalypticism. New York, London: Continuum. This is a more manageable condensation of the three-volume *Encyclopaedia of Apocalypticism* published in 1998. This single volume contains many useful articles on the origins of apocalypticism, the development of apocalypticism in the Middle Ages, and finally on apocalypticism in the modern age. In this last section there are articles on modern Jewish and Islamic apocalypticism as well as the continuing development of Christian apocalyptic themes and movements.

O'Hear, N. 2011: Contrasting Images of the Book of Revelation in Late Medieval and Early Modern Art: A Case Study in Visual Exegesis. A more in-depth look at some of the artistic examples discussed in this book (the *Lambeth Apocalypse*, the *Angers Apocalypse Tapestry*, the Van Eycks' Altarpiece, Memling's Apocalypse Panel, Botticelli's *Mystic Nativity*, and Dürer and Cranach's apocalyptic woodcuts) with a focus on the type of theological interpretation of Revelation offered in each.

Rowland, C. 1993: Revelation. London: Epworth Press. A concise and extremely useful commentary on Revelation, which takes a thematic approach to the text and includes an extended introduction that introduces the reader to some of the more complex ethical, political, and visionary dimensions to Revelation.

## OVERVIEWS OF ART AND CULTURE INSPIRED BY REVELATION

**Carey, F. (ed.) 1999: The Book of Revelation and the Shape of Things to Come. London: British Museum Press.** Beautifully produced catalogue of the exhibition of the same title. It is divided into chronological sections and provides a very comprehensive, although not exhaustive, overview of the art inspired by Revelation from the early Middle Ages to the present day.

**Van der Meer, F. 1978: Book of Revelation: Visions from the Book of Revelation in Western Art. London: Thames and Hudson.** Although now somewhat dated, in this coffee table book, in contrast to the Carey book (above), Van der Meer selects key visual interpretations of Revelation, such as the *Angers Apocalypse Tapestry*, the *Flemish Apocalypse*, and Memling and Dürer's Apocalypse-inspired artworks, and gives them in-depth treatments. Although it does not go beyond the sixteenth century, it remains an important introductory work.

## MORE RECENT PUBLICATIONS ON THE RECEPTION HISTORY OF REVELATION AND APOCALYPTIC MORE WIDELY

**Himmelfarb, M. 2010: The Apocalypse: A Brief History. Oxford: Wiley-Blackwell.** A study of apocalypses, plural, rather than the Book of Revelation. Focuses mainly on Jewish apocalyptic writing from the third century BCE onwards. While comparatively brief on Revelation, it is interesting in providing the ideological and symbolic context in which Revelation was written.

**Lisboa, M. M. 2011: The End of the World: Apocalypse and its Aftermath in Western Culture. Cambridge: Open Book Publishers.** A work of cultural study, broadly conceived. Apocalypses of all sorts and in all media, mainly from fairly recent times, are considered. Few have direct connection with Revelation, though it is pointed out that characteristically apocalyptic scenarios envisage radical change rather than complete endings.

**Pagels, E. 2011: Revelations: Visions, Prophecy and Politics in the Book of Revelation. New York and London: Penguin Books.** Sees Revelation very much in a Jewish context, stressing its messianic reversal of the current (Roman) world order—which it has in common with other Jewish apocalyptic writing of its time—and goes on to show how its original sense altered as Christianity became established and the end time did not arrive. But underplays Revelation's Christian and Christological significance.

# Bibliography

Action Bible 2010: Colorado Springs, CO: David C. Cook.

Akhtar, S. 2008: *The Quran and the Secular Mind: A Philosophy of Islam*, Abingdon: Routledge.

Amanat, A. 2003: 'The Resurgence of Apocalyptic in Modern Islam' in McGinn, B., Collins, J., and Stein, S. (eds), *The Continuum History of Apocalypticism*. New York and London: Continuum, 607–27.

Arjomand, S. 2003: 'Islamic Apocalypticism in the Classical Period' in McGinn, B., Collins, J., and Stein, S. (eds), *The Continuum History of Apocalypticism*. New York and London: Continuum, 380–413.

Augustine 1984: *City of God*, tr. J. O'Meara. London: Penguin Books.

Aune, D. 1997–9: *World Biblical Commentary: Revelation*, 3 vols. Dallas: Word, and Nashville: Thomas Nelson.

Barnes, R. 2003: 'Images of Hope and Despair: Western Apocalypticism ca 1500–1800' in McGinn, B., Collins, J., and Stein, S. (eds), *The Continuum History of Apocalypticism*. New York and London: Continuum, 323–53.

Bauckham, R. 1993: *The Theology of the Book of Revelation*. Cambridge: Cambridge University Press.

Bialostocki, J. 1986: *Durer and his Critics. Saecula Spiritalia 7*. Baden-Baden: Valentin Koerner.

Boadt, L. 1984: *Reading the Old Testament: An Introduction*. New York: Paulist Press.

Boesak, A. 1987: *Comfort and Protest: The Apocalypse from a South African Perspective*. Westminster, Louisville, KY: John Knox Press.

Bonhoeffer, D. 1965: *No Rusty Sword: Letters, Lectures and Notes, 1928–1936*. London: Collins.

Bosing, W. 2012: *Hieronymus Bosch c 1460–1516: Between Heaven and Hell*. Koln: Taschen.

Boxall, I. 2001: 'The Many Faces of Babylon the Great: *Wirkungsgeschichte* and the Interpretation of Revelation 17' in Moyise, S. (ed.), *Studies in the Book of Revelation*. Edinburgh and New York: T. and T. Clark, 51–68.

Boxall, I. 2006: *The Revelation of St John*. Peabody, MA: Hendrickson Publishers.

Boyer, P. 1992: *When Time Shall Be No More: Prophecy Belief in Modern American Culture*. Cambridge, MA: Harvard University Press.

Bradwardine, T. 1974: *De causa Dei et de virtute causarum ad suos Mertonenses*, ed. Henry Savile (London, 1618). Frankfurt: Minerva.

Bragg, M. 1993: *The Seventh Seal*. London: British Film Institute.

Brand Philip, L. 1971: *The Ghent Altarpiece and the Art of Jan Van Eyck*. Princeton: Princeton University Press.

Brook, W. and Gwyther, A. 1999: *Unveiling Empire: Reading Revelation Then and Now*. New York: Orbis.

Burrows, D. 1991: *Handel: Messiah*. Cambridge: Cambridge University Press.

Butt, J. 1991: *Bach: B Minor Mass*. Cambridge: Cambridge University Press.

Cady Stanton, E. 1985: *The Woman's Bible: The Original Feminist Attack on the Bible*. Edinburgh: Polygon Books.

Calvin, J. 2009: *Institutes of the Christian Religion* (1541 edition). Grand Rapids, MI: Wm Eerdman Publishing.

Camille, M. 1992: 'Visionary Perceptions and Images of the Apocalypse in the Later Middle Ages', in Emmerson, R. and McGinn, B. (eds), *The Apocalypse in the Middle Ages*. Ithaca and London: Cornell University Press, 276–89.

Carey, F. (ed.) 1999: *The Apocalypse and the Shape of Things to Come*. London: British Museum Press.

Carr, D. 2006: *Velázquez*. London: National Gallery Company.

Cohn, N. 1993 [1957]: *The Pursuit of the Millennium: Revolutionary Millenarians and Mystical Anarchists of the Middle Ages*. London: Pimlico.

Conrad, J. 1998: *Heart of Darkness and Other Stories*. Ware: Wordsworth Editions.

Corfield, T. B. 1989: *Franz Schmidt (1874–1939): A Discussion of his Style with Particular Reference to the Four Symphonies and 'Das Buch mit sieben Siegeln'*. New York: Garland Publishing.

Cossio, M. B. 1908: *El Greco*. Madrid: Victoriano Suarez.

Cowie, P. 2001: *The Apocalypse Now Book*. New York: Da Capo Press.

Cowley, R. W. 1983: *The Traditional Interpretation of the Apocalypse of St John in the Ethiopian Orthodox*. Cambridge: Cambridge University Press.

Daley, B. 2003: 'Apocalypticism in Early Christian Theology' in McGinn, B., Collins, J., and Stein, S. (eds), *The Continuum History of Apocalypticism*. New York and London: Continuum, 221–53.

Daniel, E. 1992: 'Joachim of Fiore: Patterns of History in the Apocalypse' in Emmerson, R. and McGinn, B. (eds), *The Apocalypse in the Middle Ages*. Ithaca and London: Cornell University Press, 72–88.

Davalos, K. 2008: *Yolanda M. Lopez*. Los Angeles: UCLA Chicano Studies Research Center Press.

Dawkins, R. 1986: *The Selfish Gene*. Harlow: Longmans.

Day, M. 1994: 'The Origin of Armageddon: Revelation 16:16 as an Interpretation of Zechariah 12:11', in Porter, S., Joyce, P., and Orton, S. (eds), *Crossing the Boundaries: Essays in Biblical Interpretation in Honour of Michael D. Goulder*. Leiden: Brill, 315–26.

Dennett, D. 1995: *Darwins's Dangerous Idea*. London: Allen Lane.

Eliot, T. S. 1969: *The Complete Plays and Poems of T. S. Eliot*. London: Faber and Faber.

Emmerson, R. and McGinn, B. (eds) 1992: *The Apocalypse in the Middle Ages*. New York: Cornell University Press.

Entine, J. 2007: *Abraham's Children: Race, Identity and the DNA of the Chosen People.* New York: Grand Central Publishing.

Feaver, W. 1975: *The Art of John Martin.* Oxford: Clarendon Press.

Forbes, B. 2004: 'How Popular are the Left Behind Books…and Why?' in Forbes, B. and Kilde, J. (eds), *Rapture, Revelation and the End Times: Exploring the Left Behind Series.* New York: Palgrave Macmillan, 5–32.

French, T. 1995: *York Minster: The Great East Window.* Oxford: Oxford University Press, for the British Academy.

Friedlander, M.-J. and Friedlander, B. 2007: *Ethiopia's Hidden Treasures: A Guide to the Paintings of the Remote Churches of Ethiopia.* Addis Ababa: Shama Plc.

Friedlander, M.-J., Friedlander, B., and Pankhurst, R. 2014: *Hidden Treasures of Ethiopia: A Guide to the Remote Churches of an Ancient Land.* London: I. B. Tauris.

Frykholm, A. 2004: *Rapture Culture: Left Behind in Evangelical America.* Oxford: Oxford University Press.

Girard, R. 1977: *Violence and the Sacred.* Baltimore: Johns Hopkins University Press.

Girard, R. 1986: *The Scapegoat.* Baltimore: Johns Hopkins University Press.

Goldberg, M. 2002: 'Fundamentally Unsound'. *Salon.com*, 29 July. <http://salon.com/2002/07/29/left%20behind/>.

Graham, R. 1947: 'The Apocalypse Tapestries from Angers', *Burlington Magazine*, 89, 227.

Gribben, C. 2009: *Writing the Rapture: Prophecy Fiction in Evangelical America.* Oxford and New York: Oxford University Press.

Hatfield, R. 1995: 'Botticelli's *Mystic Nativity*, Savonarola and the Millennium,' *Journal of the Warburg and Courtauld Institutes*, 58, 89–114.

Himmelfarb, M. 2010: *The Apocalypse: A Brief History.* Hoboken, NJ: Wiley-Blackwell.

Howard-Brook, W. and Gwyther, A. 1999: *Unveiling Empire: Reading Revelation Then and Now.* Maryknoll, NY: Orbis Books.

Huxley, A. 1973: *Crome Yellow* (1921). Penguin Books: London.

Jack, A. 2001: 'Out of the Wilderness: Feminist Perspectives on the Book of Revelation' in Moyise, S. (ed.): *Studies in the Book of Revelation.* Edinburgh and New York: T. and T. Clark, 149–62.

Joynes, C. and Rowland, C. 2009: *From the Margins 2: Women of the New Testament and Their Afterlives.* Sheffield: Sheffield Phoenix Press.

Kalin, J. 2003: *The Films of Ingmar Bergman.* Cambridge: Cambridge University Press.

Kauffmann, C. M. 1968: *An Altarpiece of the Book of Revelation from Master Bertram's Workshop in Hamburg.* London: HMSO, Victoria and Albert Museum, Museum Monograph no. 25.

Kennedy. M. 1992: *The Works of Ralph Vaughan Williams.* Oxford: The Clarendon Press.

Kermode, F. 1967: *The Sense of an Ending: Studies in the Theory of Fiction.* New York: Oxford University Press.

Kinney, D. 1992: 'The Apocalypse in Early Christian Monumental Decoration' in Emmerson, R. and McGinn, B. (eds), *The Apocalypse in the Middle Ages.* Ithaca and London: Cornell University Press, 200–16.

Koerner, J. 1993: *The Moment of Self-Portraiture in German Renaissance Art*. Chicago: Chicago University Press.

Kovacs, J. and Rowland, C. 2004: *Revelation: the Apocalypse of Jesus Christ*. Oxford: Blackwell Publishing.

La Haye, T. and Jenkins, J. B. 1995–2007: *Left Behind: A Novel of the Earth's Last Days*. 16 vols. Wheaton, IL: Tyndale House Publishers, Inc.

Lawrence, D. H. 1995: *Apocalypse* (1931). London: Penguin Books.

Leniaud, J.-M. and Perrot, F. 2007: *The Sainte Chapelle*. Paris: Editions du Patrimoine, Centre de Monuments Nationaux.

Lerner, R. 1992: 'The Medieval Return to the Thousand-Year Sabbath' in Emmerson, R. and McGinn, B. (eds), *The Apocalypse in the Middle Ages*. Ithaca and London: Cornell University Press, 51–71.

Lessing, G. E. 1984 [1766]: *Laocoon*, tr. E. A. McCormick. Baltimore: Johns Hopkins University Press.

Lincoln, F. 1999: *Alpha and Omega: Visions of the Millennium*. London: Frances Lincoln Limited.

Lindsey, H. 1970: *The Late Great Planet Earth*. Grand Rapids, MI: Zondervan.

Lisboa, M. M. 2011: *The End of the World: Apocalypse and its Aftermath in Western Culture*. Cambridge: Open Books Publishers.

Luther, M. 1958–86: *Luther's Works*, American edition, 55 vols. St Louis and Philadelphia: Concordia and Fortress Press.

Luz, U. 1994: *Matthew in History: Interpretation, History and Effects*. Minneapolis: Augsburg Fortress.

Lyons, W. 2009: 'The Apocalypse According to Jonny Cash: Examining the "Effect" of the Book of Revelation on a Contemporary Apocalyptic Writer' in Lyons, W. and Økland, J., *The Way The World Ends? The Apocalypse of John in Culture and Ideology*. Sheffield: Sheffield Phoenix Press, 95–122.

McCarthy, C. 2006: *The Road*. London: Picador.

McGinn, B. 1985: *The Calabrian Abbot: Joachim of Fiore in the History of Western Thought*. New York: Macmillan Publishing Company.

McGinn, B., Collins, J., and Stein, S. (eds) 2003: *The Continuum History of Apocalypticism*. New York and London: Continuum.

McKitterick, D. (ed.) 2005: *The Trinity Apocalypse*. London: The British Library.

Mâle, E. 1961: *The Gothic Image: Religious Art in France of the Thirteenth Century*. London: Collins (a translation of the 1910 edition of *L'Art religieux du XIIIe siècle en France*, originally published in 1899).

Manga Bible 2007: London: Hodder and Stoughton.

Mann, R. G. 1986: *El Greco and his Patrons: Three Major Projects*. Cambridge: Cambridge University Press.

Mann, T. 1968: *Doctor Faustus*, tr. H. T. Lowe-Porter. London: Penguin Books.

Meland, B. 1966: *The Secularisation of Modern Cultures*. New York: Oxford University Press.

Mentre, M. 1996: *Illuminated Manuscripts of Medieval Spain*. London: Thames and Hudson.

Monaco, J. 2000: *How to Read a Film*. Oxford: Oxford University Press.

Morgan, N. 1990: *The Lambeth Book of Revelation, Manuscript 209 in Lambeth Palace Library: A Critical Study*. London: Harvey Miller Publishers.

Morrison, R. 2002: 'Armageddon Ahead, Please Fasten Your Bible Belt'. *The Times*, T2, 20 September, pp. 2–3.

Muel, F. 1986 (ed.): *La Tenture de l'Apocalypse d'Angers*, Cahiers de l'Inventaire 4, Pays de Loire: Association pour le Développement de l'Inventaire Général des Monuments et des Richesses Antiques en Region des Pays de Loire, 19–30, 53–282, and 290–8.

Muel, F. 1996: *The Tapestry of the Book of Revelation at Angers, Front and Back*. Pays de Loire: Images du Patrimonie.

Muir Wright, R. 1995: *Art and Antichrist in Medieval Europe*. Manchester and New York: Manchester University Press.

Myrone, M. (ed.) 2006: *Gothic Nightmares: Fuseli, Blake and the Romantic Imagination*. London: Tate Publishing.

Myrone, M. 2011: *John Martin: Apocalypse*. London: Tate.

O'Hear, N. 2009: 'Images of Babylon: A Visual History of the Whore in Late Medieval and Early Modern Art' in Joynes, C. and Rowland, C., *From the Margins 2: Women of the New Testament and Their Afterlives*. Sheffield: Sheffield Phoenix Press, 311–33.

O'Hear, N. 2011: *Contrasting Images of the Book of Revelation in Late Medieval and Early Modern Art*. Oxford: Oxford University Press.

Oswalt, C. 2003: *Secular Steeples: Popular Culture and the Religious Imagination*. Peabody, MA: Trinity Press International.

Pagells, E. 2012: *Revelations: Visions, Prophecy and Politics in the Book of Revelation*. New York: Viking.

Pippin, T. 1992: *Death and Desire: The Rhetoric of Gender in the Book of Revelation of John*. Westminster, Louisville, KY: John Knox Press.

Potesta, G. 2003: 'Radical Apocalyptic Movements in the Late Middle Ages' in McGinn, B., Collins, J., and Stein, S. (eds), *The Continuum History of Apocalypticism*. New York and London: Continuum, 299–322.

Price, D. 2003: *Albrecht Durer's Renaissance: Humanism, Reformation and the Art of Faith*. Michigan: University of Michigan Press.

Price, S. and Price, M. 2011: *The Road to Apocalypse: The Extraordinary Journey of Lewis Way*. London: Notting Hill Editions Ltd.

Reiss, J. 1995: *The Renaissance Antichrist: Luca Signorelli's Orvieto Frescoes*. Princeton: Princeton University Press.

Richard, P. 1995: *Apocalypse: A People's Commentary on the Book of Revelation*. Eugene, OR: Wipf and Stock Publishers.

Ridley, M. 2014: 'The world's gone to Hell—but, trust me, it's getting much better', *The Times*, T2, 12 August, 2–4.

Rischin, R. 2006: *For the End of Time: The Story of the Messiaen Quartet*. Ithaca, NY: Cornell University Press.

Rosen, A. 2013: 'Playing the Apocalypse: Video Games and Religion', 16 October. <http://rationalist.org.uk/articles/4382/playing-the-apocalypse-video-games-and-religion>.

Rowe, N. (ed.) 2008: *In Celebration of Cecil Collins: Visionary Artist and Educator.* London: Tate.

Rowland, C. 1982: *The Open Heaven.* London: SPCK.

Rowland, C. 1993: *Revelation.* London: Epworth Press.

Rowland, C. 2002: *The Open Heaven: A Study of Apocalyptic in Judaism and Early Christianity.* Eugene, OR: Wipf and Stock Publishers.

Rowland, C. (ed.) 2007: *The Cambridge Companion to Liberation Theology*, 2nd edition. Cambridge: Cambridge University Press.

Rowland, C. 2010: *Blake and the Bible.* New Haven and London: Yale University Press.

Ruskin, J. 1908: *The Bible of Amiens*, in *The Works of John Ruskin*, ed. E. T. Cook and Alexander Wedderburn, vol. 33. London: George Allen, pp. 21–187.

Said, E. 2003: *Orientalism.* London: Penguin Books.

Sawyer, J. F. 2006: *The Blackwell Companion to Bible and Culture.* Oxford: Blackwell.

Schulze Altcappenburg, H.-T. 2000: *Sandro Botticelli: The Drawings for Dante's Divine Comedy.* London: Royal Academy of Arts.

Schussler-Fiorenza, E. 1993: *Revelation: Vision of a Just World.* Edinburgh: T. and T. Clark.

Scribner, R. 1981: *For the Sake of Simple Folk: Popular Propaganda for the German Reformation.* Cambridge: Cambridge University Press.

Siku and Akinsu 2007: *The Manga Bible.* London: Hodder and Stoughton.

Simms, A. 2013: *Cancel the Apocalypse.* London: Little Brown.

Taylor, C. 2004: *Modern Social Imaginaries.* Durham, NC: Duke University Press.

Tilling, R. 2010: '*Oh, What a Beautiful City*': A Tribute to the Reverend Gary Davis *(1896–1972)*. Pacific, MO: Mel Bay Publications, Inc.

Todorov, T. 1969: *Grammaire du Décameron.* The Hague: Mouton.

Updike, J. 1996: *In the Beauty of the Lilies.* London: Hamish Hamilton.

Van der Meer, F. 1978: *Book of Revelation: Visions from the Book of Revelation in Western Art.* London: Thames and Hudson.

Walliss, J. 2010: 'Calling the End Times: The Contours of Contemporary Rapture Films' in Walliss, J. and Quinby, L. (eds), *Reel Revelations: Apocalypse and Film.* Sheffield: Sheffield Phoenix Press, 91–111.

Wheatley, D. 2007: *The Devil Rides Out.* Ware: Wordsworth Editions.

Williamson, B. 2004: 'Altarpieces, Liturgy and Devotion', *Speculum* 79, 341–406.

Wojcik, J. 1997. *The End of the World as We Knew It: Faith, Fallibilism and Apocalypse in America.* New York: New York University Press.

Wright, M. 2009: 'Every Eye Shall See Him: Revelation and Film' in Lyons, J. and Økland, J. (eds), *The Way the World Ends? The Apocalypse of John in Culture and Ideology.* Sheffield: Sheffield Phoenix Press, 76–94.

Wright, R. M. 1996: *Art and Anti-Christ in Medieval Europe.* Manchester: Manchester University Press.

Yarbro Collins, A. 1984: *Crisis and Catharsis: The Power of the Apocalypse*. Philadelphia: Westminster.

Yarbro Collins, A. 1993: 'Feminine Symbolism in the Book of Revelation', *Biblical Interpretation* 1.1, 20–33.

Younge, Gary 2011: 'As the US nears the brink, the budget row is exposing Republican madness', *Guardian Weekly*, 17 July. <http://www.theguardian.com/ commentisfree/2011/jul/17/us-default-debt-ceiling-obama-congress>.

Zika, C. 1994: 'Durer's Witch, Riding Women and Moral Order' in Eichberger, D. and Zika, C. (eds), *Dürer and his Culture*. Cambridge: Cambridge University Press, 118–40.

Zordan, D. Forthcoming: 'Robert Crumb's *The Book of Genesis*: Representing Biblical Imaginary in Comics' in D. Pezzoli-Olgiati (ed.), *Religion in Cultural Imaginary. Explorations in Visual and Material Practices*. Baden-Baden: Nomos and Zurich: Pano.

Abaddon (Rev. 9.11) 103, 131, 243
Abraham 17, 53, 216
*Action Bible* 277
Adam 23, 34, 49, 57, 64, 113, 171, 208,
    216, 218, 222, 227, 298
Adso, Bishop:
    *Life and Times of Antichrist* 137, 146
*Agnus Dei* 57, 67, 311
Alexander Commentary, the 145
alpha and omega, the 57, 58, 67, 219, 252,
    261, 309
Amiens Cathedral 176, 177, 200, 202,
    203, 204
amillennialism 191, 192
angels 119–20, 122, 160, 180–1, 194–5,
    297–9, 302, 312
    angel in the sun (Rev. 19.17) 47
    angel of the heavenly throne-room
        (Rev. 4–5) 43, 53, 55–6
    announcing the end of time 256–9
    of the Apocalypse 38–51
    avenging (Rev. 9) 12, 200
    beheading the Beasts 183, 185
    Blake and 171, 229, 230
    and the Four Horsemen 71, 76, 81, 253
    guides/messengers 7, 31, 38, 39, 156–7,
        197, 216, 218, 223, 229, 233, 280
    and the Last Judgement 202–3
    mighty angel (Rev. 10) 8, 39, 43, 44,
        45, 46, 47, 49, 122, 257, 29
    in the New Jerusalem 49–50, 197–8,
        217, 223–5, 229, 230
    and the Seven Seals 93–110
    warrior 47–9
*Angers Apocalypse Tapestry* 10, 33, 43, 44,
    49, 50, 61, 64, 76, 78, 90, 102, 129,
    141–4, 153, 159, 161, 162, 164, 224–5,
    233, 282, 285–6, 289, 292, 296–7, 301,
    313–14

Anglo Norman Manuscripts 22, 32–4,
    39, 61, 75, 96, 98, 103, 119, 140, 158,
    164–5, 184–5, 224, 286, 292, 307
Annunciation, the 64, 99, 116, 227,
    299, 309
Antichrist, the 26, 31, 33, 101, 137–9, 141,
    186, 192, 199, 289, 290, 294, 296,
    300, 312
    and the Beasts 13–14, 132, 139, 141,
        145–8, 153, 154, 183, 309
    defeat by Christ/Mahdi 19, 24
    Dutch Reformed Church as 6
    and the False Prophet 190
    first Horseman as 74, 76, 137
    in *Left Behind* 139, 152, 153, 273–4,
        276–7
    Lindsey and 271
    Napoleon as 25
    Obama as 139, 152–3, 301
    Roman papacy as 6, 138, 146
    Signorelli and 139, 146, 147, 153,
        289, 292
anti-Semitism 33, 97–8
apartheid 2, 6, 132, 280
*Apocalypse No!* 242
*Apocalypse Now* 96, 108, 241, 265
apocalyptic literature 38, 53, 66, 73, 112,
    156, 295, 297
Apollo 111
Apostles 115, 215, 217, 225, 228, 259
Armageddon 3, 6, 13, 14–15, 25, 31,
    138, 177, 178–82, 286–7, 289–90,
    309–10
    images of 182–90, 194, 208, 210
    medieval visualizations 183–8
    twentieth and twenty-first
        centuries 188–90, 235, 237–8, 249,
        261, 270–2, 274, 306
    *see also* final battles (Rev. 19–21)

Augustine, St 3, 157, 194, 197, 210,
    293, 311
  *City of God* 21, 191–2, 193, 304
Avaaz 238–9
Azreal 243

Babylon (the city) 138, 166, 172, 179, 181,
    205, 271, 276, 289
  the 'establishment' as 292
  German authorities as 171–2
  London as 36, 229
  and the New Jerusalem 213–14, 216,
    219, 251–3
  Pretoria as 280
  Rome as 2, 13, 156–7
Bach, Johann Sebastian 4
  *Agnus Dei* 67, 68, 69
  *Mass in B minor* 61, 67, 298
  *Passions* 67, 252
*Bamberg Apocalypse* 116–19
baptism 41, 68, 99, 192, 299, 311
Barbershopera 242
Barocci, Federico 122, 125, 127, 300
Baruchel, Jay 241–2
base Christian Communities 281–2, 290
Bauckham, Richard 53, 296, 298,
    301, 313
Beast from the Abyss (Rev. 11)
    148–9, 168
Beasts, the, *see* Earth Beast (Rev. 13); Sea
    Beast
*Beatus* manuscripts 32–3, 117–19, 182–3,
    185, 297
Beau Dieu, Le 202–3
Beckmann, Max 37, 220, 224, 234, 245–7,
    250, 272, 294
  *Apocalypse* series 209, 231–2, 245–7
  'and God shall wipe away all
    tears' 231–2
  *The Grenade* 245, 246
  *Resurrection* 208–9, 245
beloved disciple, the 2, 27, 202, 311
Berengaudus Commentary 33–4,
    98, 141
Bergman, Ingmar 5, 24, 93, 102, 241, 247,
    248, 250, 262–5
Bernard of Clairvaux 299
Bindman, David 150, 229
bird motif 49, 83, 180, 188

*Bird, The* 180
bishop motif 22, 27, 81, 106, 145–6, 160,
    205, 292
Blake, William 18, 25, 36–7, 39, 90, 130,
    150–1, 159, 173, 212, 220, 221, 247,
    286, 293, 304
  *Death on a Pale Horse* 85–7
  *The Four and Twenty Elders* 66, 69
  *The Great Red Dragon and the Beast
    from the Sea*, Blake 50–1, 206
  *The Great Red Dragon and the
    Woman Clothed with the Sun:
    the Devil is Come Down* 115,
    126–7
  *The Number of the Beast is 666* 139,
    150–1, 292
  *River of Life* 36, 218, 229–30, 234, 259
  *The Vision of the Last Judgement* 204,
    206–8, 210, 293
  *The Whore of Babylon* 159, 164, 170–1,
    173, 289
Block, Antonius 248, 264–5
Boesak, Allan 2, 6–7, 157, 280–1,
    287, 296
Bondol, Jean de 33, 76
Bonhoeffer, Dietrich 136, 300
book of life (Rev. 20) 136, 199, 200,
    203–5, 213, 265
Bosch, Hieronymus:
  *St John the Evangelist on Patmos* 40–1,
    43, 297
Botticelli, Sandro:
  *Chart of Hell* 206, 303
  *The Mystic Nativity* 193, 195, 197,
    197–8, 210, 220, 295, 313
Boxall, Ian 18, 111, 158, 179, 214, 263,
    296, 299–301, 304, 313
Bradwardine, Thomas 60, 298
Bragg, Melvyn 262
Bride, the (Rev. 19) 129, 158, 175, 212–13,
    216, 219, 251–2, 303
Brookes, Peter 89
Brothers, Michael 303–4
Bruckner, Anton 253
Buffy the Vampire Slayer 1, 5
butterfly motif 127, 185

Cady Stanton, Elizabeth 129
Calvin, John 136, 300

Camping, Harold 238–9
Canibus 240
Carpathia, Nicholae 139, 153, 274, 276
Carter, Frederick 268
Cash, Johnny 5, 258, 260–2
Chadderton, James:
    *Apocalypse V2* 250
    *Manchester Apocalypse* 250
Chartres Cathedral 59, 64, 203, 263
Chaucer, Geoffrey 205
    *Canterbury Tales* 222–3
Cheung, Gordon 249–51, 304
    *Burning Lake* 250, 268
    *Four Horsemen of the Apocalypse* 90–1,
      249–50, 304
    *Rives of Bliss* 232–3, 234, 250
Christ, *see* Jesus Christ
Church of the Holy Sepulchre 222
climate change 19, 237
Cohen, Leonard 258, 261–2
Cohn, Norman 23–4, 27, 263
Coldplay 240
Collins, Cecil 39, 46, 238, 249
    *Angel of the Apocalypse* 46, 249
computer games 70, 189, 242–3,
    272, 276
conquest through suffering 57
Conrad, Joseph:
    *Heart of Darkness* 241, 265
Coppola, Francis 108, 241, 265
Cox, Brian 239
Cranach the Elder, Lucas 90, 95, 166
    Apocalypse woodcuts 36, 81–2,
      139, 148–50, 159, 166, 168–9, 285,
      289, 313
    *Passional Christi und Antichristi* 137–8
Crowley, Aleister 152, 154
crown motif 202, 204
    Christ 184
    First Horseman 71, 73, 74, 76, 85
    Sea Beast 131, 133, 146
    Twenty-Four Elders 41, 66
    Whore of Babylon 159
    Woman Clothed with the Sun 115,
      121–2, 217
    *see also* diadem
crucifixion 11, 21, 25, 56, 60, 102,
    292, 310
crusader imagery 164, 185, 264, 289

Crusades 22, 264
cup of abominations (Rev. 17.6) 155–6,
    158, 160, 162–3, 171, 173, 205

da Vinci, Leonardo 244, 298
*Daily Mail, The* 178, 236
Danby, Francis 96, 100–1, 291
Daniel, Book of 17, 19, 25–6, 38, 133, 148,
    176, 183, 199, 238, 269–70, 272, 274,
    277, 279, 289, 309
Dante 200, 205, 230
    *Divine Comedy* 168, 206
    *Purgatorio* 139, 168–70
Darby, John 269
Davis, Gary:
    *Twelve Gates to the City* 258–60
Dawkins, Richard 91–2
*Day After Tomorrow, The* 241
de Quincy, Eleanor 160
Death 1, 9, 12, 73, 75–6, 81, 84–7, 91–2,
    96, 199, 203, 215, 240, 242, 247–8,
    261, 264
Dennett, Daniel 91–2
diadem 74, 133, 184, 310
Dispensationalism 22, 25–7, 179, 261,
    266, 269, 270, 273–5, 290, 297
Dix, Otto 159, 171–2, 245
    *Dance of Death* 247–8, 264–5
    *Der Krieg* series 171, 247
    *Visit to Madame Germaine at*
      *Mericourt* 172, 248
Domitian (Emperor) 12, 254, 310
double-edged sword, the (Rev. 1.16) 180
Dragon, the 277, 279
    and the Two Beasts (Rev. 13) 9, 29, 31,
      35, 36, 47–8, 78, 109, 131–54, 180–5,
      188, 191, 206
    and the Woman Clothed in the Sun
      (Rev. 12) 9, 13, 36, 47–8, 78, 83,
      109, 111–30, 194–5, 219, 253, 280,
      286, 288
dreams 8, 11, 15, 23, 35, 249, 261, 291
Dürer, Albrecht: *Apocalypse* series 34,
    35–6, 39, 44–5, 46, 47, 48, 53, 54, 61,
    65–6, 75, 79–81, 83, 89, 90, 91, 95–6,
    100, 102, 225, 130, 167, 186, 196, 247,
    249, 254–6, 265, 272, 285, 314
    The Binding of Satan 195–7, 198
    The Four Horsemen 289, 290–1

Dürer, Albrecht (*cont.*)
  New Jerusalem/Millenium 216, 221,
    229, 290
  The Seven Trumpets 104–8, 286
  Two Beasts 134, 135, 140, 145–6, 148
  The Whore of Babylon 159, 164,
    165–8, 173, 175
  The Woman Clothed with the
    Sun 115, 122–4, 125, 129
Dutch Reformed Church 6, 280
Duvet, Jean 125, 247
Dvořák, Max 168
Dylan, Bob 258, 261–2

eagle motif 55, 62, 71, 73, 103, 106, 112,
  120, 127, 264, 310
Earth Beast (Rev. 13) 9, 13–14, 131–4,
  136–42, 144–8, 150–1, 168, 177,
  180–3, 244, 247, 301, 309–10, 312
Earthquake (Rev. 6.12–17) 11–12, 97–8,
  208, 242, 299
Eastwood, Clint 91
eclipse motif 11–12, 94, 97, 103, 245
Eden, Garden of 65, 214, 216, 218, 220–1,
  224, 227, 233–4
*Edward Young's Night Thoughts* 170
El Greco 96, 104
  *Saint John the Evangelist Witnessing*
    *the Mysteries of the Apocalypse*
    98–100
Elijah 98–9, 141
Eliot, T. S.:
  *Hollow Men* 266, 306
Emmanuel 296
1 Enoch 53, 56, 176, 199, 309
eschatology 24, 70, 236, 245, 273,
  282, 310
Ethiopian Orthodoxy 279–80
EU, the 132, 152, 239, 271, 274, 289
eucharist, the 34, 59, 64–5, 155, 158, 162,
  185, 310
Euphrates 12, 95, 103, 106, 182
evangelicalism 152, 239, 241, 281–2
  American 132, 236, 260–1, 266, 272–7,
    310, 311
  Dispensationalist 22, 25–6, 269, 290
Eve 34, 49, 64, 111, 113–14, 208, 218,
  227, 290
exegesis 281, 284–5, 313
Exodus 94, 111, 144, 213, 303

Ezekiel, Book of 8, 17, 44, 66, 181, 213,
  216, 217, 269, 270, 274, 277, 289,
  304, 310
4 Ezra 17, 19, 56, 94, 309

Fairey, Shepard 152
False Prophet, *see* Earth Beast (Rev. 13)
Family Radio Worldwide 238
feminist criticism 287, 115, 129–30,
  158–9, 173–5, 219
Ficino, Marsilio 295
final battles (Rev. 19–21) 3, 13–14, 20, 25,
  31, 47, 94, 109, 138, 177–8, 181, 183,
  188–90, 192, 210, 238, 271, 277,
  309–10
*Financial Times, The* 233
First World War 37, 171, 179, 182, 208,
  231, 245, 247, 251–2, 254
*Flemish Apocalypse* 34, 41–2, 44, 108, 139,
  145–6, 162–3, 171, 182, 186–7, 220,
  225–6, 285, 297, 304, 314
fountain motif 65, 125, 227–8
Four Horsemen of the Apocalypse (Rev.
  6.2–8) 50, 61, 70–92, 134, 288
  Dürer and Cranach 35, 66, 79–82, 106,
    108, 289, 291
  eighteenth and nineteenth
    centuries 83–7
  medieval images 29, 75–9
  in Revelation 3, 7, 11, 31, 70–4, 93–5,
    131, 212, 294, 310
  twentieth and twenty-first centuries 1,
    87–9, 237–40, 242–3, 247, 249, 253,
    263, 277
  in visual imagery 75–89
Four Living Creatures (Rev. 4) 41, 52,
  55–6, 62, 71, 73, 75–6, 225, 279,
  310–12
Franciscans 27, 139, 141, 145, 147, 157,
  192, 258
French Revolution 24, 83, 236
frog motif 109, 142–4, 164, 171,
  180, 184–5
fructifying trees (Rev. 21) 214, 218, 220,
  229, 244, 304
fundamentalism 26, 139, 152, 173, 179,
  268, 271–2, 283

Gabriel, angel 38, 116, 259, 309
Galatians, Epistle to the 213

Gears of War 243
Genesis, Book of 20, 34, 52, 64, 111, 164, 216, 218, 227, 277
*Ghent Altarpiece* 22, 34, 59, 64–5, 144, 164, 202, 220–1, 227, 233, 292, 297
Gillray, James 87, 286
   *Presages of the Millennium* 83–5
Giovanni di Paolo, Giovanni 232
Girard, René 57–8
Gog and Magog (Rev. 20) 181, 185–6, 193
gold motif
   New Jerusalem 217, 223, 225, 228
   Twenty-four Elders 41
   Whore of Babylon 155, 156, 159, 160, 164, 173
   Woman Clothed in the Sun 120, 121, 219, 283
Gospel of John 2, 52–3, 137, 176, 199, 206, 247, 310–12
Gospel of Mark 94, 247, 310, 312
Gospel of Matthew 21, 176, 199–200, 202, 210, 310–12
Graham, Billy 260
Great Mother 267
Gresham, Kip:
   *The Whore of Babylon* 159, 173–4, 249, 287
grisaille 40–1, 227
*Gulbenkian Apocalypse* 22, 27, 32–3, 98–9, 116, 141–2, 145, 182, 185–6, 292

Haacke, Hans:
   *Gift Horse* 91
Hades 73, 75, 78, 81, 83, 86, 91, 96, 199, 203, 240, 310
Haileybury School 179
Handel, George Frederic:
   *The Messiah* 61, 67–8, 251
Haynes, Joseph:
   *Death on a Pale Horse* 75, 83–4, 90, 286
Heaven 17, 24–5, 94, 112, 238, 258
   half hour of silence in (Rev. 8) 9, 12, 93, 101–2, 241, 262–5
   war in (Rev. 12) 13, 63, 68, 119, 122, 132, 310
   *see also* New Jerusalem (Rev. 21–2)
heavenly throne room (Rev. 4–5) 9, 10, 29, 35, 41, 43, 52–5, 57, 59, 71, 76, 78–9, 102, 122, 204, 206, 212, 225, 230, 231, 253, 256, 265, 267, 311

Heidegger, Martin 51
Hell 185, 206, 240, 256
Hellmouth 78, 185, 188, 200, 202, 203
Herzog, Chaim 270
Hitchcock, Alfred 180
Hitler, Adolf 27, 37, 132, 254, 271
Holy Spirit, the 22, 114, 125, 227, 281
Hondius, Hendrick:
   *Papist Pyramid* 148
horns motif 152–3
   Dragon 112, 150, 310
   Earth Beast 136, 137, 139, 141, 145, 146, 147
   Lamb 52, 56
   Sea Beast 131, 133, 139, 150, 155, 160, 271, 312
*Hortus Deliciarum* 158–60, 173, 175, 290
Huxley, Aldous:
   *Chrome Yellow* 182
hybridity 189, 195
   Sea Beast 131, 146, 150, 183, 312
Hyde, Marina 237–8

Immaculate Conception 114, 125, 300
*In the Beginning Was the End* 243
*Independence Day* 100, 241
Isaiah, Book of 25, 213, 269, 274, 279, 289, 296, 303
Islam 19, 222, 239, 279, 289
   apocalypticism 24, 297, 313
   association with the Beasts 118, 132, 145
   fundamentalist 152, 290
Israel 19, 59, 69, 111–12, 114, 156, 186, 213, 217, 259, 301
Israel, State of 22, 26, 109, 179, 270–1, 272, 306

Jehovah's Witnesses 155
Jenkins, Jerry 152, 272–3, 275, 287
Jerome, St 1–2, 21, 296
Jesus Christ 3, 4, 6, 8, 9, 18, 29, 34, 38, 40, 41, 49, 50, 95, 97–8, 131, 141, 142, 147–8, 180, 236, 270, 273, 283
   at Armageddon 183–6, 188
   defeat of the Antichrist 19, 24, 137
   and the False Prophet 136–7
   and the first Horseman 74, 76, 78, 90, 112

Jesus Christ (*cont.*)
   as the Lamb 11, 20, 27, 52–3, 56–61,
     65, 68, 71, 138, 216, 228, 292,
     298, 300
   and the Last Judgement 200, 202–3,
     206, 208, 222, 261, 274
   Millennial rule 14, 19, 181, 190–3, 198
   and the New Jerusalem 29, 213, 215,
     218, 219, 229, 231–2, 250
   as the Rider on the White Horse
     47–9, 68, 87, 184
   second coming 25, 26
   and the Woman Clothed with the
     Sun 113, 114, 115, 119, 122
jewel motif 53, 81, 155, 160, 205, 214, 219,
   223, 228
Jewish tradition 18–19, 51, 56, 96
   apocalyptic literature 17, 38, 53, 73–4,
     94, 199, 309, 313, 314
   messianism 19, 52, 56
Jews 22, 179, 216, 217, 253, 257, 304
   Antichrist as 137, 147
   return to the Holy Land 25–6,
     270, 272
   Roman persecution 16
Jezebel 129, 158, 164
Joachim of Fiore 22–3, 192–3, 214,
   296, 300
Job, Book of 133, 136, 185, 202, 261
1 & 2 John 13, 137, 309
John of Patmos 1–3, 5–11, 13, 15–20, 29,
   31, 33, 35, 38–53, 55–9, 66, 71, 76, 81,
   97–8, 100, 102–4, 106, 108–9, 111–12,
   115, 122, 125, 131–3, 136–8, 140, 145,
   147, 155–7, 160–3, 165–6, 172–3, 175,
   180, 184, 189, 191, 195, 197, 212,
   215–20, 223–6, 229, 230–1, 233–4,
   237, 247, 249–52, 254–5, 261, 264–7,
   272, 279–80, 285–90, 293–4, 311–12
John of Rupescissa 23
John Paul II 283
John the Baptist 29, 34–5, 52–3, 65, 68,
   99, 202, 227–8, 299, 311
John the Evangelist 2, 125, 144, 247,
   252, 264
Judaism 17, 18, 19, 22, 24, 25, 26, 38, 51–53,
   56, 73–4, 94, 96, 97–9, 137, 147, 179,
   199, 213, 216–17, 242, 253, 257, 267,
   270, 272, 295, 304, 309, 313, 314

Kermode, Frank 19
*Koberger Bible* 35, 95
Kovacs, Judith 132, 142, 157
Kutcher, Ashton 238

Lactantius 19, 21–3, 296
LaHaye, Tim 152, 272–3, 275, 287
lake of fire and sulphur (Rev. 19–21) 17,
   91, 113, 138, 180–1, 185, 199, 202,
   216, 233, 274
Lamb (of God) 52–69, 298
   in Revelation 7, 9, 11, 20–1, 27, 29, 31,
     43, 44, 52–60, 71, 73, 79,·101, 112,
     129, 136–7, 138, 179, 202, 203, 212,
     213, 216, 217–18, 259, 267, 282,
     292–4, 299, 300, 311, 312
   later visualizations 36, 65–6, 92, 151,
     289, 293
   medieval visualizations 34, 61–5, 76,
     102, 162, 183, 186–7, 223–5, 227–8,
     233, 261, 263, 286, 287, 292
   modern interpretations 261, 263
   in music 67–8, 251–3
   in visual imagery 61–6
*Lambeth Apocalypse* 32–3, 40, 49, 76–7, 98,
   116, 159–61, 164, 184–5, 210, 224,
   297, 313
Laodicean Church 10, 16, 93
last days 2, 22, 24, 273
Last Judgement (Rev. 20) 46
   imagery 27, 65, 147, 177, 187, 199–209,
     214, 222, 230, 232, 238, 250, 271, 274,
     279, 289–91
   in Revelation 7, 14–15, 24, 25, 31, 59,
     137, 147, 190–1, 192, 193, 198, 199,
     216, 294, 302, 202, 310, 311
Lawrence, D. H. 277, 287
   *Apocalypse* 1–2, 5–6, 7, 257, 266–9,
     271, 306
*Left Behind* Series 26, 139, 152–3, 236,
   266, 268, 272–7, 281, 296
*Left Behind, The Movie* 276
Lessing, Gotthold Ephraim 4, 28
Leverkühn, Adrian 251, 254, 256
Leviathan 133, 185, 202
Lewis, C. S.:
   *Chronicles of Narnia* 189–90
   *The Last Battle* 190
   *The Lion, the Witch and the Wardrobe* 190

liberation theology 7, 74, 157, 281–3, 287, 290
Lindsey, Hal 26, 152, 173, 261, 269–70, 273, 281, 283, 287, 306, 310
   *The Late Great Planet Earth* 270–2
Lion of Judah (Rev. 5) 43, 146, 267, 291–2
locust army, the (Rev. 9) 12, 18, 94, 96, 103, 108, 131, 243
London 36, 88, 205, 216, 229, 230, 250
Lopez, Alma 127–8, 130, 282, 287
Lopez, Yolanda 287
   *Virgen de Guadelupe* series 283
   *Woman Clothed with the Sun* 282–3
Louis of Anjou 33, 64, 76
Luther, Martin 4, 6, 23, 27, 36, 81–2, 138, 148–9, 155, 168–70, 230, 262
Luz, Ulrich 5

MacMillan, James:
   *Woman of the Apocalypse* 130
Madonna (Ciccone) 155
Magruder, Michael Takeo
   De/Coding the Apocalypse 189
Mâle, Emile 185, 303
mandorla 203, 223–4, 283
*Manga Bible* 277–8
Mann, Thomas:
   *Doctor Faustus* 251, 254–6, 266
Marriage of the Lamb (Rev. 19) 29, 69, 179, 186–7, 251
Martin, John (1789–1854) 96, 204–6, 208, 210, 220–1, 233, 243
   *The Deluge* 204
   *The Fall of Nineveh* 204
   *The Great Day of His Wrath*, John Martin 204
   *The Last Judgement* 204–6, 230, 232, 250, 291
   *The Plains of Heaven* 204, 230–1
martyr motif 12, 96–7, 99–101, 194–5, 227–8
Masereel, Frans 245
   *Flugzeuge über die Menschheit (Aeroplanes over Mankind)* 188–9, 248–9, 291
*Master Bertram Apocalypse Altarpiece* 115, 139, 144–5, 290
Mayan Apocalypse 238, 241

McCarthy, Cormac:
   *The Road* 16, 250
measuring rod (Rev. 11 and 21) 216–17, 223–5
Medici, Lorenzo di 295
Megiddo 179, 271, 302, 309–10
Meidner, Ludwig 306
*Melancholia* 241
Memling, Hans 95, 100
   *Apocalypse Panel* 29–30, 40, 78–9, 90, 231, 286, 290, 304, 313, 314
   *Mystic Marriage of St Catherine* 29, 35
   *St John Altarpiece* 29, 34–5, 121–2, 144, 231, 285, 288
*Merkavah* vision 310
Messiaen, Olivier 102
   *Quartet for the End of Time* 39, 47, 256–8, 305
Messiah 19, 24, 56, 113, 279, 292, 296
Mesters, Carlos 281
Metallica 239–40
*Metz Apocalypse Manuscript* 182, 186
Michael, angel 9, 13, 47, 112–13, 119, 122, 129, 132, 181, 191, 202, 253, 280, 299, 310
Michelangelo 4, 205, 295
   *The Last Judgement* 176, 200, 206
Middle East, the 156, 164, 179, 277
millennial thought 19–27, 191–5, 197–8, 209–11, 214–16, 238, 270–2, 279, 290–4, 305
Millennium, the (Rev. 20) 7, 19, 21–3, 27, 214, 216, 272, 294, 310
   images of 193–8, 209, 229, 243, 269–70, 274, 277, 290, 311
   in Revelation 9, 14, 31, 113, 190–3, 238
Milton, John:
   *Paradise Lost* 113–14, 230, 299
mirror motif 158, 160–1
misogyny 7, 158–9, 174–5
mitre motif 27, 81, 146, 185
Mohammed 132, 139, 144–5
monk motif 139–40, 145, 148, 168, 203, 252
Morgan, Nigel 185, 297
Mortimer, John Hamilton 75, 83–4, 286
Mount Zion 138, 179, 204
Muse 240
Muslims 22, 145, 193

myriad horsemen (Rev. 9.16–19) 104,
    106, 108
mythology 6, 51, 112, 153, 267

Nativity, the 197–8, 210
Nazism 87–8, 136, 171, 237, 253–4,
    256–7, 280
Nero (Emperor) 12, 114, 131, 133–4, 254,
    300, 311
New Jerusalem (Rev. 21–2) 15, 17–18,
    20–2, 26, 27, 29, 31, 38, 46, 58–9,
    95, 101, 109, 156, 181, 192, 195,
    204, 212–34, 236, 238, 286–94, ·
    303–4, 311
  angels in 49–50
  as cathedral 221–3
  early modern visualizations 34, 35,
    65–8, 197–200, 227–8
  eighteenth and nineteenth centuries
    25, 49, 206, 208–9, 228–31
  meaning of 1, 6–9, 11, 213–19
  medieval visualizations 165, 177–8,
    223–6
  twentieth and twenty-first
    centuries 190, 231–3, 239, 244, 247,
    250, 251–2, 258–60, 263, 265, 268–9,
    274–5, 277, 279, 282
  visualizations of 219–33
Nietzsche, Friedrich 245, 254, 266
Niffeneger, Audrey 268
non-believers 25, 51, 136
nuclear war 16, 19, 22, 178, 189, 237,
    239, 265
Nuremberg 35, 47, 122, 197, 254, 256, 265

Obama, Barack 132, 139, 152–3, 237
Olivi, Peter 23
one who is seated on the throne, the
    (Rev. 4) 10–11, 35, 53, 58, 68, 142,
    267, 293, 299, 311–12
Onion, The 237
Orientalism 164, 170
Orvieto Cathedral 146, 289

Paisley, Ian 155
Pale Rider 91
Palestine 22, 26, 270, 272
papacy 22, 81, 139, 148, 289
  and the Antichrist 6

and the Sea Beast 182
and the Whore of Babylon 155–6, 157,
    159, 168–70
Paper Monitor 238
Passion, the 27, 34, 67, 202–3, 252
1 Peter 238
piagnone 198
pilgrimage 222–3, 228
Pippin, Tina 158, 219
Pitt, William 83
Plato:
  Phaedo 251
precious stones (Rev. 17 & 21) 156, 195,
    214, 217
Pretoria 2, 280
prophecy scholarship 26, 74, 179, 182,
    268–77
prophetic mission (John of Patmos) 8–9,
    14, 17, 38–40, 44, 52, 137, 261, 266,
    280–1, 310, 312
Purgatory 185, 203, 303

Quodvultdeus 114
Quran, the 24, 145

Rainbow Magazine 1, 5
rainbow motif 10, 29, 35, 39, 44, 53, 66,
    120, 231, 233
Raphael:
  Michael and the Dragon 122
Rapture 25–6, 112, 235, 238–9, 241–3,
    268–77, 306–7, 311
Reagan, Ronald 132, 269
recapitulative readings 4, 11, 14, 27, 75,
    94–5, 108, 180, 285–6
Redon, Odillon 127
  A Woman Clothed with the Sun
    127, 128
Reformation 6, 65, 79, 81, 99, 146, 148, 155,
    157, 165–6, 168, 170, 193, 198, 287
resurrection 9, 112, 164, 191–2, 194,
    199, 208
Richard, Pablo 282
Rider on the White Horse (Rev. 19) 20,
    50, 60, 68, 87, 137, 168, 180–1, 184,
    186, 251, 310, 312
River of Life (Rev. 22.1) 36, 195, 214, 218,
    220, 223–4, 227, 229, 231–3, 247, 250,
    259, 289, 303–4

Roberg, Robert 159, 172–3, 175
  *Babylon the Great is Fallen* 172–3
  *The Whore of Babylon Riding on a Beast
    with Seven Heads* 173
Rogen, Seth 241–2
Roman Empire 3, 6, 11–12, 16–17,
    19, 56, 58, 93, 134, 145, 165,
    274, 290
  and the Beasts 131, 132, 133, 137
  Satan as 13
Romans, Epistle to the 3, 199, 298
Rome 2, 13, 36, 62, 170, 271, 280,
    281, 289
  and the Dragon 182
  Whore of Babylon as 13, 156–7, 159,
    166, 168, 171, 172
Rowland, Chris 132, 142, 157, 171, 206,
    208, 215–16, 229, 249, 295–7,
    299–304, 307, 313
Rubens, Peter Paul 130, 205, 299
Ruskin, John:
  *The Bible of Amiens* 202–3

*Sainte Chapelle Apocalypse Rose Window*
    164–5, 171, 222, 301
Salvation History 22, 65, 68, 116,
    222, 227
Satan/the Devil 3, 13, 25, 9, 119, 122,
    148, 152, 165, 209, 253, 274, 282, 290,
    292, 312
  binding (Rev. 20.1–3) 21, 36, 181,
    191–2, 193–8, 206
  defeat of (Rev. 19–20) 9, 14, 20, 47,
    94, 112, 114, 177, 181, 182, 188, 198,
    271, 311
  identification with the Dragon 47,
    112, 113, 132, 183, 185, 310
  release 14, 181, 192
Satanic Trinity 31, 112–13, 130–54, 289
Savonarola, Girolamo 197–8
sceptre motif 140–1, 145
Schmidt, Franz 102
  *Das Buch mit Sieben Siegeln* 67–8, 102,
    251–4, 256–7, 298, 305
Schoenberg, Arnold 253–4
Schussler-Fiorenza, Elisabeth 46, 296
scroll motif 8–9, 11, 39, 43–4, 52,
    55–7, 62, 65, 71, 73, 86, 140–1,
    208, 299

Sea Beast 9, 13–14, 29, 35, 113,
    122, 131–154, 160, 170, 172,
    177, 182–3, 215, 247, 271, 274,
    309–10, 312
Second World War 209
Seeger, Pete 258
*Seeking a Friend for the End of the
    World* 241–2
Seven Asian Churches 8–13, 16, 40–1, 52,
    55, 58, 93, 192, 218, 312
Seven Bowls 9, 11–12, 39, 47, 93–5,
    108–9, 171, 180, 225, 286, 312
  depictions of 108–9
  sequence of events 12
Seven Candlesticks, vision of
    (Rev. 1) 165
Seven Seals 9, 11, 31, 39, 43, 93–102, 180,
    253, 262, 286, 292, 299, 312
  depictions of 96–102, 204
  Lamb and 52, 62, 65, 66, 67, 71
  sequence of events 12
  *see also Seventh Seal, The*
Seven Trumpets 9, 11–12, 24, 39, 43, 66,
    93–5, 112, 171, 180, 286, 312
  depictions of 102–8
  sequence of events 12
Seven-headed Beast, *see* Sea Beast
*Seventh Seal, The* 5, 24, 93, 102, 241,
    247–8, 250, 262–5
Sibylline Oracles 24
sickle motif 134, 146
Signorelli, Luca
  *The Sermon and Deeds of Antichrist* 139,
    146–8, 152, 153, 289, 292
Siku 278
666 131, 133, 134, 150, 152, 300
skeleton motif 29, 76, 78, 83, 87, 174
snake motif 148, 158, 164–5, 171
Son of Man 8, 18, 41, 50, 53, 138
South Africa 2, 6, 157, 279–80
St Bavo's Cathedral, Ghent 34, 59
St Paul 16–17, 52–3, 74, 199, 213,
    270, 311
*St Sever Apocalypse Manuscript* 32, 183
star motif 12, 119, 202, 258, 268, 283
  falling from the sky 97, 98, 299
  Woman Clothed with the Sun 112,
    115, 122, 125, 217
Wormwood 12, 103, 106

sun/moon motif 39, 44, 205, 229,
        267, 268
    'angel in the sun' 47–9
    angel with a face like the sun 39,
        44, 49
    darkened/eclipsed 11, 12, 97–8, 103,
        106, 245, 299
    Woman Clothed with the Sun 112,
        116, 122, 125, 127, 129, 283
*Sunday Express, The* 87–8
*Sunday Times, The* 88–9
Sweet, Leonard 235
sword motif 8, 49, 72–3, 76, 79, 85, 138,
        180, 292
synchronic visualisations 4, 28, 35, 44,
        78–9, 95–6, 106, 108, 132, 141, 171,
        186, 199, 208, 210, 285

Tavener, John 1–2, 6, 27, 29
Temple at Jerusalem 24, 197, 203, 216–17,
        270, 272, 274, 276–7, 304
    destruction of 3, 12, 16, 19, 213
Tertullian 159
theocentric theology 53
1 Thessalonians 25, 238, 269, 277
2 Thessalonians 31, 137, 148, 277, 309
Thinkdreamspeak 243
throne, *see* heavenly throne room
        (Rev. 4–5)
topology of Revelation 8, 9
Tower of Babel (Genesis 11) 20, 216
tree of life (Rev. 22) 218–19, 229, 233
Tribulation 25–6, 238, 261, 269–71,
        274, 306
*Trier Apocalypse* 32, 62, 70, 72, 74–6, 78,
        90, 297
*Trinity Apocalypse* 32–3, 55, 61–3, 69,
        95–8, 100, 102–4, 106, 115–16,
        119–21, 139–40, 193–5, 197–8,
        203–4, 220, 223–5, 285, 292,
        297, 299
Turner, Joseph 39, 49, 51, 96
    *Angel Standing in the Sun* 49
Twelve Tribes of Israel 112, 217
twenty-four elders (Rev. 4–5)
        11, 41, 43, 55–6, 62, 66, 279–80,
        311–12
*2012* 100, 238, 241

two witnesses (Rev. 11) 14, 46, 131, 141,
        147–8, 312
Tyconius 21, 114

United Nations 153, 270, 274, 276
Updike, John:
    *In the Beauty of Liles* 297

Van der Meer, F. 116, 188, 225,
        297–8, 314
Van Eyck, Hubert and John 261
    *Adoration of the Lamb* 64, 69
    *Ghent Altarpiece* 22, 34, 59, 64–5, 144,
        164, 202, 220–1, 227–8, 233, 285, 289,
        292, 297, 313
Vaughan Williams, Ralph 256
    *Sancta Civitas* 251–2, 305
Velázquez, Diego 40, 122
    *The Immaculate Conception* 115, 125–6,
        129–30
    *St John the Evangelist on the Island of
        Patmos* 115, 125–6, 285–6, 288
Victorinus 94, 159
Virgin of Guadeloupe 128, 282–3
Virgin, the/Mary 33, 34, 65, 144, 202,
        222, 227, 228, 299, 303
    and the Woman Clothed with Sun 13,
        68, 111, 113–16, 120–2, 125, 127–9,
        219, 264–5, 282–3, 310
visual exegesis 284–7, 313

Walliss, J. 275, 297, 305
Weil, Simone 293
West Portal Last Judgement scene,
        Amiens Cathedral 176–7, 200,
        202–4
West, Benjamin 150
Whore of Babylon (Rev. 17) 3, 6, 7, 9, 13,
        31, 38, 59, 109, 113, 116, 148, 155–75,
        138, 155–175, 179, 205, 215, 271,
        301–2, 312
    as antithesis of the Bride/New
        Jerusalem 219
    Blake 36, 170–1, 206, 289
    interpreting 156–8
    medieval interpretations 159–65
    Renaissance and Reformation
        visualizations 139, 165–70, 289

and the Sea Beast 113, 138, 148
twentieth and twenty-first century
171–4, 248, 249, 256, 280, 287
in visual imagery 158–74
Woman clothed with the sun (Rev. 12)
24, 111–30, 197, 264, 299–300
Blake 36, 126–7, 150
fourteenth and fifteenth century 40,
78, 121–4
imagery 115–29
medieval visualizations 116–21,
194, 285
Redon 127

in Revelation 7, 9, 13, 31, 47, 110,
111–15, 132, 158, 175, 213, 217, 219,
264, 288, 310, 312
Schmidt 68, 253
twentieth century 127–9, 282–3, 287
Velázquez 125
Wormwood (Rev. 8.10–11) 12, 103, 106

York Minster East Window 159, 164, 171,
222, 301
Younge, Gary 237

Zechariah, Book of 270

The manufacturer's authorised representative in the EU for product
safety is Oxford University Press España S.A. of El Parque Empresarial
San Fernando de Henares, Avenida de Castilla, 2 - 28830 Madrid
(www.oup.es/en or product.safety@oup.com). OUP España S.A. also acts
as importer into Spain of products made by the manufacturer.
Printed and bound by CPI Group (UK) Ltd, Croydon, CR0 4YY

13/05/2026

02109668-0003